D1126672

Encounters with Aging

Encounters with Aging

Mythologies of Menopause in Japan and North America

MARGARET LOCK

University of California Press

BERKELEY   LOS ANGELES   LONDON

The costs of publishing this book have been defrayed in part by the 1992 Hiromi Arisawa Memorial Award from the Books on Japan Fund with respect to *Labor and Imperial Democracy in Prewar Japan*, published by the University of California Press. The Fund is financed by The Japan Foundation from generous donations contributed by Japanese individuals and companies.

University of California Press
Berkeley and Los Angeles, California

University of California Press, Ltd.
London, England

Library of Congress Cataloging-in-Publication Data

Lock, Margaret M.
    Encounters with aging : mythologies of menopause in Japan and North America / Margaret Lock.
        p.   cm.
    Includes bibliographical references and index.
    ISBN 0-520-08221-4 (alk. paper)
    1. Middle aged women—Japan. 2. Middle aged women—North America.
    3. Menopause—Japan. 4. Menopause—North America.   I. Title.
HQ1059.5.J3L63   1993
305.24'4—dc20   93-21379
                                                                          CIP

Printed in the United States of America
9 8 7 6 5 4 3 2 1

For Ishii-*san* and the women
of the Life Education Institute

Contents

Illustrations

Acknowledgments

Ruth Benedict wrote many years ago that people in Japan are expected to keep careful account of all that they receive, not merely objects, but gifts of all sorts including care and consideration, time, and even life itself, in order that they may eventually reciprocate wherever possible. Repayment of kindness is sometimes very difficult; not all debts can be fully reciprocated, and such I feel is the case with the numerous gifts of knowledge, time, and assistance I received from people who in one way or another contributed to this book.

Above all thanks are due to Patricia Kaufert; her generosity, support, and insight have been boundless. I realized at the outset that, contrary to my inclinations, I would have to use not only the usual ethnographic methods of anthropology but also quantitative methods in order to deploy the argument that I put forward in this book. Pat shared with me the fruits of her long experience in conducting survey research into middle age in Manitoba; she warned of pitfalls and, together with Penny Gilbert (unsurpassed in the management of large data sets), guided me through the mechanics of collection and management of survey materials as we juggled back and forth between two continents using Japanese, English, and computerese. Both Pat and Penny are much better at numbers than I am, but we share nevertheless a sensitivity to the hazards and limitations of survey research, especially outside Western settings; there was tacit agreement from the outset that the numbers would at most be supportive data for the ethnographic findings. I owe a debt of gratitude to Sonja McKinlay as well for making available the results of the Massachusetts survey. Sonja has worked closely with Pat and me for nearly ten years, bridging the chasm between her expertise in biostatistics and the "softer" social sciences. We have spent a good deal of time, assisted in recent years by the invaluable contributions of Nancy Avis and Kirstin Vass, in making our data as comparable as possible, the results of which appear in various journals as well as in this book.

I can never fully repay Christina Honde. Our relationship goes back nearly twenty-five years to when she was the teaching assistant for one of the first courses I took in Japanese at the University of California, Berkeley. Chris is a remarkable teacher, with a gift for giving floundering beginners self-confidence; she also became a dear friend and, more recently, the best research assistant that anyone could hope to have. When I went to Japan in 1983 to commence this research Chris had been living in the Kansai area for fifteen years. She had ingenuity and energy available and used them to orchestrate the massive job of coding the survey data. She also carried out about a third of the interviews with Japanese women in their homes, a task that involved, among other things, several memorable trips resulting in great gastronomic experiences and the creation of lasting friendships in Nagano, Shiga, Shimane, and Ehime prefectures. Throughout the ensuing years Chris has continued to make an important contribution in both research assistance and insights. Thanks go also to Ishii-san and her friends, whose dedication and thoroughness as coders have become legendary in Canada. Hirai Tomoko also carried out several interviews and provided excellent assistance with library searches and translation of technical materials, for which many thanks. On my return for an extended stay in Japan in 1990, Kamata Masue painstakingly filled in the gaps in statistics, references, and citations. Her expertise in classical Japanese was a boon, and her thoughtful interjections as I worked the book into its final shape are much appreciated.

I am indebted to Drs. Matsushima Shōsui and Inui Shunen for starting off the necessary train of introductions to make contact with women working on farms and in factories. Without their support and the expert assistance of Yokoyama Takako, extensive interviewing could not have taken place. Dr. Eguchi Shigeyuki, a psychiatrist with a keen interest in medical anthropology, sought me out for an exchange of ideas and then paved the way for interviews in Shiga prefecture; his support was and is invaluable. Mori Hiroshi of the *Kyōtō shinbun* kindly accompanied me to several of the Kyoto factories and took two of the photographs that appear in this book.

Above all I can never repay the numerous women who freely gave of their time to fill out questionnaires and especially those who volunteered to discuss at length the intimate details of their lives with a stranger. Their hospitality, cooperation, and patience produced the narratives that have become the heart of this book. I can only hope that eventually, indirectly, their kindness will be repaid. I owe an enormous debt of gratitude to the numerous doctors who made time in their unbelievably busy days to discuss their ideas without reservation. They, like the women who were interviewed, remain anonymous, but with several of them I have formed lasting bonds that I value enormously.

Over nearly twenty years of going back and forth to Japan—even though it is my fate, together with all foreigners, to remain in some ways eternally an "outsider"—I have nevertheless come to feel that Kyoto is my second home. This sense of belonging is sharpened by the periodic renewal of friendships on most return journeys. Among those who have profoundly shaped my understanding of Japan and its people are Yasui Hiromichi (his insights written on paper napkins from coffee houses and restaurants over half of Japan are now carefully filed away), Nakagawa Yonezō, Yoneyama Toshinao, Minami Hiroko, Sakai Shizu, Ikegami Naoki, Kinoshita Yasuhito, and Hayase Machiko.

The Social Sciences Research Council of Canada provided funding for the entire project, including a joint grant with Patricia Kaufert to assist with analysis of the survey research. I am grateful for their support. My colleagues in Social Studies of Medicine at McGill, Don Bates, Allan Young, George Weisz, Faith Wallis, and Alberto Cambrosio, are always there, argumentative, humorous, and supportive—they brook no sloppy thinking and spark some of the best thoughts. Claudine Houston shielded me when it was most needed from the onslaught of administrative duties, leaving some clear space for an occasional moment of tranquil reflection.

My husband, Richard, is as ever the person to whom I am the most indebted. He and I have been together on the Japan adventure since 1964, and his store of recollections, experiences, and insights inevitably contribute to my understanding of things. Most of the photographs in the book were taken by him, and he took time out to read the entire manuscript in addition to providing unflagging support and making those endless sacrifices and adjustments that are inevitably part of a dual career household.

Prologue   Scientific Discourse and Aging Women

The most creative force in the world is the menopausal woman with zest.
>   (Attributed to Margaret Mead)

Woman's capacity for reproduction normally lasts as long as menstruation is regular. With the cessation of the function, she ends her service to the species.
>   (Helene Deutsch, *The Psychology of Women*, 1945)

"The dangerous age" is marked by certain organic disturbances, but what lends them importance is their symbolic significance. . . . When the first hints come of that fated and irreversible process . . . [a woman] feels the fatal touch of death itself.
>   (Simone de Beauvoir, *The Second Sex*, 1952)

Far more extensive than the hard sense of loss suffered during menopause . . . is the depression about aging.
>   (Susan Sontag, *Saturday Review of Society*, 1972)

There is no typical menopause, there are as many menopauses as women.
>   (Iris Murdoch, *The Good Apprentice*, 1985)

Some women can escape *kōnenki* [menopause] altogether.
(Factory worker, Kyoto, 1984)

I've been having *kōnenki* for over seven years. Everyone said it would come early and that there would be lots of problems because I had a really difficult time with childbirth.
(Farmer, Nagano prefecture, 1984)

Kōnenki means that the body loses its balance for a while.
(Housewife, Kobe, 1984)

I was so busy with all the things that were happening in my life that I didn't really notice *kōnenki* at all.
(Interior designer, Tokyo, 1986)

It's important to approach *kōnenki* with the right attitude, I don't expect any problems, it depends upon how you let yourself feel about it.
(Nurse, Tokyo, 1986)

I should observe, that though this climacteric disease is
sometimes equally remarkable in women as in men, yet
most certainly I have not noticed it so frequently, nor so
well characterized in females.

(Henry Halford, "On the Climacteric Disease," 1813)

A woman is often unhinged at the change of life.

(Edward Tilt, *The Change of Life*, 1870)

The typical menopause [is] a colorless, uneventful
experience.

(Andrew Currier, *The Menopause*, 1897)

The unpalatable truth must be faced that all
postmenopausal women are castrates.
(Robert A. Wilson and Thelma A. Wilson, "The Fate of the
Nontreated Postmenopausal Woman," 1963)

Menopause indicates the final menstrual period and occurs
during the climacteric. Present estimations date this at
about 51 years.

(W. H. Utian and D. Serr,
"The Climacteric Syndrome," 1976)

Presbyopia is a normal aging process, but none will deny
the need for spectacles. To do nothing other than offer
sympathy and assurance that menopause will pass is
tantamount to benign neglect.

(R. B. Greenblatt and A.-Z. Teran, "Advice to postmenopausal women," 1987)

Menopause, the cessation of menses caused by ovarian
failure, can be considered an endocrinopathy.

(I. H. Thorneycroft, *American Journal of Obstetrics and
Gynecology*, 1989)

Functional disturbances of the autonomic nervous system
are the principal symptoms of *kōnenki*, but added to these
are metabolic and psychological-nervous disturbances.

(Okamura Yasushi, *Kōnenki Shōgai*, 1977)

Kōnenki [menopause] is a difficult time today, because
Japanese people are not used to nuclear families. In
extended families women didn't have any problems at this
stage of the life cycle.

(Internist, Kyoto, 1982)

Menopausal syndrome is a sort of "luxury disease." . . .
Women with lots of free time on their hands are the ones
who say it's so bad. . . . Women who go out a lot, who have
lots of hobbies and friends don't have so many symptoms.

(Gynecologist, Osaka, 1983)

Kōnenki is not very important, after all it's not life
threatening, and it's not a big problem for most women.

(Gynecologist, Tokyo, 1984)

Why do Western women make such a fuss about
menopause?

(Asked by a Japanese gynecologist
at a Florida conference, 1985)

The relation between what we see and what we know is
never settled.

(John Berger, *Ways of Seeing*, 1972)

Why should menopause, an ostensibly private experience that is painless
and presents no obvious threat to life, command so much attention? Can
the apparent confusion in the preceding quotations be explained away because the authors are not actually referring to the same thing? Is menopause merely the end of menstruation, or is it part of something larger—
middle age, perhaps? Is it a clearly bounded event or a gradual process? Is
it limited to the female of the species? Can menopause really be a "disease"
or an "endocrinopathy," as certain gynecologists suggest? Is it something
that can be entirely avoided, as the Japanese factory worker cited above
states?

In trying to bring a common language to this tower of Babel, we may
be tempted to offer a definition at the outset, to make clear just what
menopause is in order to develop a discussion of it. But menopause is not
a "fact," and hence it cannot be neatly packaged or contained in a single
precise term that transcends time and space, history and culture. On the
contrary, it is a concept with boundaries and meanings that shift depending
upon the viewpoint and interests of speaker and listener. Such variation
interests me, most particularly the way in which, even as we strive to
produce clarity on a few points, we descend deeper and deeper into an
abyss of contradictions.

Given its elusiveness, perhaps menopause is not a useful term at all.
But despite its fuzziness, it contains some meaning about which surely
everyone can agree, namely that it has something to do with becoming
older. We are no doubt correct in thinking that human females everywhere
have a finite number of reproductive years and, if they live long enough,
all reach that stage of the life cycle marked by an absence: the end of
menstruation. In North America and Europe we usually assume today that
this end is what is meant by menopause, but such was not always the case,
nor is it necessarily so in other cultures, with significant consequences for
what is said and done about this stage of the life cycle.

In contemporary scientific language the end of menstruation is described as the result of changes in the exceedingly complex relation between certain chemical signals and several organs of the body.[1] Is this
perhaps, the real menopause, an event stripped of all extraneous baggage,

its complexity skillfully explicated by scientists in terms of biological language? But whose menopause is this, and what relation does it have to subjective experience and narratives about the end of menstruation and growing older? It seems likely that on most occasions when the word menopause is used, people have something different in their minds than mere physiological and biochemical transformations, and clearly one source of confusion about the term lies here. But we cannot resolve the muddle simply by specifying the difference between an objective, scientific approach to menopause and the subjective experience of individual women. We have to take a step further back to ask first of all just what we mean by both "objectivity" and "subjectivity" and to consider how these fundamental concepts are constituted in specific historical and cultural contexts.

When I started this study, the bulk of the literature to date was based on clinical and, to a lesser extent, epidemiological research confined largely to Western populations (Kaufert 1988). Moreover, firsthand accounts by women themselves were, and remain, very scarce. My original intention, therefore, was to carry out the first large-scale study that would juxtapose the results of survey research carried out among a nonclinical sample of Japanese women with narratives from individuals and with professional and popular accounts about this portion of the life cycle.[2] These differing viewpoints, while they provide several lenses for seeing the aging female body in Japan, are nevertheless historically and culturally contingent and, as products of the same locality, have much in common. Thus each set of findings, taken both separately and together, provides a comprehensive picture of middle age in Japan today.

While carrying out the research, and in particular on my return to Montreal and after presenting the findings to several different types of audiences, I determined to carry the results of this project beyond a simple interpretation of the Japanese materials that left a comparison with North America largely implicit. During the time it has taken me to produce this book, menopause has been transformed into a much publicized and politicized event in North America. It was recently characterized in *Newsweek* as "the women's health topic of the 90s," and perhaps in anticipation of this, medical literature is now supplemented by a good number of exceedingly popular explorations including those written by Germaine Greer (1991) and the polemic by Gail Sheehy (1992). It takes only a cursory glance over the medical literature to realize that, with a few notable exceptions, the subject of concern is not the end of menstruation but the sheer number of women, baby boomers, soon to become old, and hence a burden to society.

The Japanese are equally concerned with their aging population but, in addition to health, give much attention to social matters, in particular to the part that middle-aged women are expected to take in care for the elderly. Thus, concern about the "graying" of society has resulted in the politicization of female midlife in Japan and in North America, but it has taken a remarkably different course, with important consequences for the approach to the end of menstruation. By making an explicit comparison between medical and political accounts of female middle age in Japan and in North America, my intention is to challenge views taken as self-evident and universal about menopause and, further, to question the responsibilities assigned to middle-aged women by their respective societies.

An approach that simply dwells on the biology and politics of menopause, however, assumes that women's aging is essentially a passive process, subject only to the wear and tear of nature and manipulation by those with expertise and power; such an approach overshadows crucial issues of how women experience aging and actually live out this part of their lives. This book, in contrast, makes extensive use of narrative accounts from middle-aged Japanese women. Not only do they illuminate a segment of Japanese life about which little has been published; they form a basis for questioning some of the statements about middle age and menopause asserted by scientific authority in both Japan and the West, accounts used to buttress political arguments about middle-aged women and their function in society.

Many readers doubtless agree that subjective interpretations of menopause in Japan and North America are culturally produced and therefore differ, with certain social consequences. I want to push the argument further and show how physical changes at the end of menstruation—as well as their subjective interpretation and representation—are sufficiently different to have far-reaching social and even political consequences. The quantitative part of the project is comparable with survey research already conducted in Manitoba and Massachusetts (Avis and McKinlay 1991; Kaufert 1980, 1982a, 1984, 1988; Kaufert and Syrotuik 1981; Kaufert et al. 1987, 1988, 1992; McKinlay et al. 1985, 1987a, b). Results of this part of the study provide evidence to question the assumption that endocrinological changes associated with female midlife are universal facts on which culture weaves its tapestry. The comparative examination of current discourse about the end of menstruation, both professional and popular, reinforces the study's results.

Although scientific knowledge saturates discourse about the life cycle in Japan as it does in North America, a comparison of these two areas reveals that culture also permeates popular and scientific discourse as well. This comes as no great surprise, to anthropologists at least; but in addition to tacit beliefs about the aging female body and its function in society that shape these respective discourses, what I shall term "local biologies" also play a part. Without question similar endocrinological changes are implicated in both cases, yet these changes are sufficiently unlike so as to substantially influence subjective experience. Thus, differing accounts about biological aging are not simply the result of culturally shaped interpretations of a universal physical experience but the products, in Japan and North America alike, of an ongoing dialectic between biology and culture in which both are contingent.

Discussion in this book will range, therefore, across individual narratives about aging and the subjective experience of middle age, to the minutiae of symptoms reported at the end of menstruation in Japan, to medical discourse about female midlife and the politics of aging in Japan and North America, in the past and today. Although this account sets out to examine the phenomenon of menopause from several different vantage points, it concerns above all the lived experiences of middle-aged Japanese women and their relation to the social and political order in which they find themselves in late modern Japan; from this vantage point we can look again at the way female middle age is completely subsumed by the end of menstruation and its supposed consequences—the dominant vision in North America today.

Compartmentalizing the Aging Body

A characteristic feature of modernity (in North America and in Japan), most particularly from the beginning of this century onward, is the way in which the experience and portrayal of reality is fragmented (Frisby 1986). Nietzsche stated that *"modern society* is not 'society,' not a 'body,' but a sick conglomerate of components" (Nietzsche 1980, 13:238; original emphasis). One result of this fragmentation has been the generation of knowledge within ever increasingly differentiated disciplines and subdisciplines, so that there exist today, for example, several powerful competing discourses about the aging body, most of which regard their methods as scientific.

All scientific approaches to the body, regardless of their disciplinary base, start from the assumption that the thing or event under study can most accurately be represented through an objective approach in which measurement and classification into categories of inclusion and exclusion are central. By far the most powerful and widely disseminated approaches to female aging and menopause are based on research in the basic sciences and epidemiology, together with their application in clinical medicine. But, although both claim objectivity, they are often fundamentally contradictory: the terrain of basic scientists is virtually restricted to an analysis of bodily structure, process, and products; and these findings are assumed to have universal application. Epidemiologists, in contrast, work with populations; they traverse body boundaries and use the language of mathematics to range through time and space; their findings produce probabilities. As we will see, the knowledge sets that basic scientists and epidemiologists create about female aging are not easily reconcilable with one another, nor do they necessarily coincide with subjective experience. It is in clinical practice that this confusion becomes most evident.

To complicate the picture further, psychiatry, grounded in a theory of the unconscious, psychology, which makes use of probability theory and various reductionistic theories of mind and behavior, and certain subdisciplines of sociology and anthropology, both of which draw heavily at times on probability theory, all contribute additional fragments to the scientific story of aging. Despite the fact that "objectivity" is common to all of these approaches, the body is nevertheless carved up and interpreted differently by them.

Our current understanding of the process of growing older is, therefore, grounded in several sets of knowledge that do not intersect consistently to produce a neat or comprehensive picture. Sometimes there is interdisciplinary struggle over the signifying process itself, in that the units used for analysis—how the body is classified, framed, measured, or segmented in order to explain it—generate debate and argument. As Haraway comments, "struggles over what will count as rational accounts of the world, are struggles over *how* to see" (1988, 587). More usually, knowledge produced in one discipline is virtually ignored in the others, which together selectively plunder, ignore, or actively dismiss subjective accounts as invalid. This situation becomes infinitely more complex in geographical settings where the Western scientific tradition has been imported and grafted onto local knowledge, scientific and popular as well.

More than thirty years ago Jean-Paul Sartre pointed out the difficulties that arise when we try to contextualize scientific knowledge in the conscious world of individual human activity:

> If after grasping "my" consciousness in its absolute interiority and by a series of reflective acts, I then seek to unite it with a certain living object composed of a nervous system, a brain, glands, digestive, respiratory, and circulatory organs . . . then I am going to en-

counter insurmountable difficulties. But these difficulties all stem from the fact that I try to unite my consciousness not with my body but with the body of others. . . . In fact the body which I have just described is not my body such as it is for me.

(Sartre 1956, 401)

What people experience and report in connection with their bodies is not in essence the same kind of information produced through observation, measurement, and abstraction. Arbitrary decisions must be made in connection with the creation of scientific standards, scales, and other techniques of measurement. Criteria for inclusion and exclusion have to be set, which in the case of the body are often simultaneously moral decisions about what is normal and abnormal. Sartre highlights an important point that in our eagerness for accuracy, replication, and control we tend to minimize or ignore to our peril: if we are to talk about human beings, and not simply about physiology and biochemistry, then we must resort to other forms of description and analysis. The subjective "me" cannot be replaced by the universal "body," molded and packaged out of the objective language of biology. Nor can it be replaced by the bodies produced as probabilities.

But here we encounter other difficulties. Scarry, for example, vividly describes what she terms the "resistance of pain to language" (1985, 5). She points out that we become aware (largely through socialization into a particular culture, I take it) of the interiority of ourselves by moving out beyond the boundaries of our own bodies into the external, communal world. We can understand our own interiority only to the extent that we have the ability to articulate its existence by resorting to shared visual and verbal representations of it. Scarry limits her discussion to pain, but I would extend her argument to the vast majority of physical activity in the body, almost all of which has no external shared referent—no object onto which it can be projected and made communal. Since no sensation is associated with most somatic activity, everyday language does not exist to describe it. Our bodies carry on silently, surreptitiously, unnoticed by ourselves. Even when we become aware of bodily sensation, we can make it fully conscious only through culturally shared idioms of expression. This process is selective; many sensations go essentially unrecognized and are, therefore, unspeakable.

This lack of language has been, of course, a perennial stimulus for medicine to develop technologies in order to "see" into the body, to speak "on behalf of" those who are in distress (Scarry 1985, 6). The task has become one of getting around the poorly articulated, unreliable narration of the patient: to extract the objective, fragmented essence of what is thought to have gone wrong inside the body, displace "the human subject from his [sic] place in society" (Young 1980, 133) and then, ideally (although this is often neglected), give some words to the patient with which to interpret subjective sensations. But the materialist, abstract language of modern medicine does little for the imagination. Harry Berger points out that through speech, writing, and printed publications, what becomes constituted as truth about the body is progressively extended outward, abstracted from it (Berger 1983). Scientific concepts do not offer means for human beings to share their sentience and give little assistance to women as they try to communicate any distress they may have at midlife to family, friends, nurses, and doctors.

Over the past two hundred years, with the development of modern science ever in search of better predictions and more control through various technologies, subjective knowledge about the body has been transformed from valuable information into something that is deliberately avoided or judiciously contained in most modern medical practice (Figlio 1977; Sullivan 1986; Lock and Lella 1986). Part of my concern is to recuperate the voices of individual women. However, although I draw extensively on the narratives created by women and examine their relation to scientific discourse about middle age current in Japan, I do not see the exercise as a simple effort to establish some sort of a rapprochement between the limitations of subjectivity and objectivity, for reasons that will be made clear shortly.

Before I embark on an explication about middle age in Japan, and as a prelude for comparison with this less familiar scene, I offer readers a quick look at the assumptions, internal debates, and fissures in current conceptualizations about menopause and midlife in North America. In the second part of the book I return again to North America and to nineteenth-century Europe, to the "discovery" of menopause and the subsequent development of various lively, sometimes acrimonious, competing discourses as to what exactly is its significance for women and for medical professionals. My hope is that by moving back and forth through space and time I will defamiliarize that which is taken as self-evident about female middle age, in North America and also in Japan.

Aging Women as Anomalies

Systematic interest in a scientific approach to the process of aging began at the end of the last century. The excitement of the time created by the publication of the *Origin of Species* stimulated research, not only into transformation and change in the natural world at large, but also into biological change throughout the life span of individual organisms, including humans. Initially, as a result of interest focusing largely on growth and development, questions were posed as to the nature of life itself, and what factor or factors stimulate maturation. Not until early in this century was senescence given serious consideration, and as late as 1959 it was still acknowledged that "youth has been the traditionally preferred period of life to study, where research on aging may provoke uneasy feelings, rationalized by regarding it as an unsuitable subject for objective examination" (Birren 1959, 3). Nevertheless, largely because of demographic changes leading to a greater proportion of people aged fifty and older in the population, new questions were eventually asked that focused, in contrast to earlier ones, on the nature of physical decline and death.

Recently, as a result of developments in molecular biology and genetics, a little of the earlier fragmentation characteristic of research into the life cycle has been reversed. Acknowledgment of aging as an ongoing genetically programmed process that starts early in the life cycle, as opposed to something that commences relatively late in life, has forced some reconsideration of the biases inherent in research questions that are limited to a particular segment of the life cycle. It is now recognized, for example, that ovarian changes that eventually result in the end of menstruation commence during fetal life, and menopause can, therefore, be understood as one aspect of a larger process that starts before birth, continues until well into middle age, and has repercussions for old age.

Among mammals the aging process involves a constellation of changes affecting virtually every physiological function and organ system, changes that happen at a remarkably consistent rate and that are species specific. The rate of this so-called deterioration can be calibrated and is known as the "maximum life span potential" for any given species (Weiss 1981, 28). Since the origin of *homo sapiens* about one hundred thousand years ago, this maximum span is generally thought to be virtually unchanged: present estimates vary and place it between ninety and one hundred fifteen years (Calkins 1981; Kirkwood 1992; Weiss 1981).[3] Thus, for approximately the past hundred thousand years people could in theory live to a ripe old age, although evidence shows that in fact very few of them did so.

Since the possibility of life beyond the end of the female reproductive years is not a recent phenomenon, another question can be asked: is postreproductive life in women an evolved pattern that has been actively selected for over thousands of years (Lancaster and King 1985; Mayer 1982)?[4] Alternatively, does the ever-increasing percentage of elderly people in historical times indicate that culture alone is at work (since historical time is too short for biological involvement)?[5] Or could both culture (over the short term) and biology (over the long term) be at work? These questions remain unanswered, but analysis of data from the middle of the last century shows that most of the change in life expectancy since that time can be attributed to a decrease in infant mortality, and to a lesser decrease in that of adolescents and young adults, changes that are believed to result largely from improved nutrition (McKeown 1976; U.S. Bureau of the Census 1973, table 13). Lowered mortality during childbirth has also contributed to an increased female life expectancy. In Scotland, for example, women's life expectancy at birth increased from forty-four to seventy-four years between 1871 and 1977. For fifty-year-olds, however, remaining life expectancy rose only seven years—from twenty-one to twenty-eight years—indicating clearly that changes in demography have been overwhelmingly caused by increased survival of children rather than to lower mortality in old age (Gosden 1985, 5). In Japan life expectancy at birth increased from forty-four to nearly eighty-two years between 1891 and 1989, but for fifty-year-old women, remaining life expectancy changed from twenty-one to thirty-three years (Kōseishō 1991). If for the past hundred years a woman in Europe or Japan lived through infancy and young adulthood and did not succumb during childbirth, she had a very good chance of living to age seventy or more, provided, that is, she was neither ruthlessly exploited nor living in abject poverty.

Nevertheless, among the many articles and books published about menopause today, for the general public and for professionals, the majority usually say something to the effect that "At the turn of the century, a woman could expect to live to the age of forty-seven or -eight" (Sheehy 1991, 227). The implication of such a statement is that women rarely lived past what is now middle age until at least the beginning of this century, and hence that the survival of females over the age of fifty is a recent phenomenon—an assertion that a moment's reflection must surely prove to be absurd. More people than formerly do indeed achieve their full life span potential today, and an increasing number of women live not only to reach menopause but for a further twenty-five years or more beyond it, but this does not mean that older women were until recently anomalies or oddities. Nevertheless, the myth that women (men never appear in these arguments) dropped dead in their late forties is pervasive.

An extrapolation is very frequently made from this latter argument, even in biological textbooks, to the effect that women are not well suited physically to life beyond menopause—that their very existence, as Gosden suggests, is "unnatural," an "artifact" of our "recent mastery of the environment" (Gosden 1985, 2).

It is not simply their biological age that makes women "unnatural," however; according to Gail Sheehy, "human females today are monkeying with evolution" (Sheehy 1992, 30) because they alone, among the higher primates, live beyond the end of their reproductive years. This sentiment is also echoed in the biological and medical literature:

> The cessation of menstruation, or the menopause, in the human female is . . . a relatively unique [sic] phenomenon in the animal kingdom. With increasing longevity modern woman differs from her forebears as well as from other species in that she can look forward to 20 or 30 years . . . , after the menopause.
>
> (Dewhurst 1981, 592)

An ideological position is taken in these arguments, in which it is asserted that something abnormal and inherently contrary to nature's purpose has happened over the past one hundred years. The thinly disguised assumption in this viewpoint is that reproduction of the species is what female life is all about, and that the situation we now find ourselves in, of having a large number of women of postreproductive age living in "advanced" societies, is not only an anomaly but a costly superfluity. Despite the fact that a greater number of aging men is also very apparent in these same societies, this number seems to pose no problem.

Received wisdom has it, of course, that men have the "natural" potential to reproduce successfully until the day they die. It has been shown, however, that aging affects the reproductive capacities of men: testicular body volume decreases with age and leads to decelerating spermatogenesis, decreasing sperm mobility, and an increased production of defective sperm; impotence also increases with age (Asso 1983; Baker et al. 1976; Vermeulen et al. 1982). However, research of this kind tends to be ignored and, to the best of my knowledge, no argument has appeared to the effect that men become biologically inefficient and hence superfluous during the second half of their life cycle. Very occasionally in the decrepitude stakes the tables are turned: it was recently reported that the portion of the brain known as the corpus callosum becomes progressively smaller in men between the ages of twenty-five and seventy, whereas in women it appears not to change in size (Witelson 1991, 211–12). Surely, in our rational society, there could be no more convincing evidence for having outlived one's purpose in life than a shrinking brain!

A more positive argument could be made about old age for women and men as well. Given that the maximum life span potential for humans, as we understand it at present, is about one hundred years, is it not more appropriate to consider this a "normal" state that everyone has the potential to attain, very often in good health (see also Alington-MacKinnon and Troll 1981)? The questions that would then naturally follow are, why do fewer men than women live to old age? and what protective factors do women have that men naturally lack?

Middle-Aged Woman as Pathology

The 2 million primordial follicles that are present at birth are lost from the ovary either by ovulation or by *follicular atresia,* which is the physiologic degeneration of the oocyte and its surrounding stroma. Atresia begins as early as the fifth month of fetal life and continues throughout the menstrual years.

(London and Hammond 1986, 906)

When one turns to the largest body of scientific literature on middle-aged women, that produced by the medical profession, arguments in which the older woman is thought of as an artifact or an anomaly are very much in evidence. Many physicians start out their articles with a rhetorical flourish: "In the U.S. today, one-third of all women are over 50 years of age" (Utian 1990, xi); "More than 40 million American women are menopausal; another 3.5 million will be reaching the climacteric age each year for the next 12 years. These women will have a life expectancy of more than 30 years after menopause" (Sarrel 1988, 2S); "It is estimated that every day in North America 3,500 new women [*sic*] experience menopause and that by the end of this century 49 million women will be postmenopausal. . . . Complaints referable to menopausal symptoms have been estimated to initiate approximately one million visits to physicians annually in Canada" (Reid 1988, 25); and in a journal for family physicians: "An unwelcome consequence of increased longevity, osteoporosis eventually develops in almost all untreated Caucasian women who reach their 80th year. The direct cost of osteoporotic fractures is estimated to be $7 to $10 billion each year in the United States alone, and the population of postmenopausal women is continually increasing" (Lufkin et al. 1989, 205).

In addition to drawing attention to the "surplus" of older women, the bulk of the literature produced by physicians over the past thirty years on menopause and its consequences has shown a morbid interest in pathology, a fixation on decrepitude: "A progressive physical deterioration of climacteric women is scientifically established. Its course is subtle and often difficult to diagnose, especially in the early stages. . . .It is now widely recognized that ovarian deficiency is the cause of these manifestations" (Jern 1973, xiii). The end of menstruation is most usually described as the result of "failing ovaries" (Haspels and van Keep 1979, 59; Willson et al. 1975, 638) or the "inevitable demise" of the "follicular unit" (London and Hammond 1986, 906), which, it is said, no longer secretes the hormone estrogen, sometimes characterized as the "essence" of the female. Since this process starts in fetal life, females are, if one follows this line of argument, on the path to decay even before they are born.

"Ovarian failure" was first described at the end of the last century (Oudshoorn 1990), a characterization that was later refined, after ovarian secretions were "discovered" in the laboratory, as a "lack" of the hormone estrogen (Frank 1941, 856). By the 1960s menopause had been designated as a "deficiency disease," although some physicians disputed this characterization (Kase 1974), and more recently it has been termed an "endocrinopathy" (Thorneycroft 1989, 1306). A few writers (particularly of medical textbooks) are careful to caution their readers that menopause is a "natural" process, but the majority of researchers today simply describe an ovarian failure leading to a "hormonal imbalance," which in turn is said to be responsible for characteristic symptoms, described by many as a "menopausal syndrome" (Greene 1984, 6; van Keep et al. 1976) and by others as a deficiency disease comparable to diabetes (Koninchx 1984; Shorr 1940).

Among these symptoms, the one that is thought to be the sine qua non of menopause is the hot flash, and here too dramatic statements are characteristic of the literature: "hot flashes occur in 85% of perimenopausal women" (Notelovitz 1989, 8); "The hot flash or flush is the most common symptom compelling menopausal women to seek medical attention. Approximately three-quarters of women will experience flashes at the menopause" (Judd et al. 1981, 268).

A more modulated approach was taken by a group formed by the World Health Organization (WHO) to produce a comprehensive report on menopause (1981), and in a few publications one or two physicians are careful to contextualize their statements: "The climacteric is sometimes, but not necessarily always, associated with symptomatology. When this occurs it may be termed the 'climacteric syndrome' " (Utian 1980). Occasionally, clear counterarguments to a pathological approach have come from within the medical profession (Jones and Jones 1981, 799), and most current gynecological textbooks, although they use terms such as "failure," "regression," and "deficiency" in connection with the ovary, nevertheless make a sharp distinction between a "normal" menopause, and one that is the result of surgery, or in some other way aberrant. However, the dominant argument in the literature, particularly in medical journals (as opposed to textbooks), is disease oriented, and hence one in which intervention on the part of physicians and their "management" of menopause is called for. Treatment usually recommended today is one of several kinds of hormone replacement therapy, and some physicians actively campaign among their colleagues for its use:

> Clinicians abound who believe the menopause is a physiological event, a normal aging process, therefore estrogen replacement therapy (ERT) is meddlesome and unnecessary. Presbyopia is a normal aging process, but none will deny the need for spectacles. To do nothing other than offer sympathy and assurance that the menopause will pass is tantamount to benign neglect.
> (Greenblatt and Teran 1987, 39)

Professional literature on menopause has rapidly multiplied and become infinitely more complex over the past fifteen years, largely for two reasons. The first is the increasing interest shown in this subject by several medical specialities; the second is related to the current debate over the use of hormone replacement therapy. It has been postulated since classical times that ovarian secretions produce a profound effect on many parts of the female body, and, although explanations have changed over the years as to just how this effect occurs, such an understanding remains central in contemporary medical thinking. The current language describes "target" organs and tissues, which include the pelvic organs (the vulva, vagina, and uterus), breasts, skin, and bones, and notes their negative response to "ovarian failure." The heart and the cardiovascular system are also implicated by the literature, but indirectly, and so too are mental states. In particular as a result of the involvement of bones and the cardiovascular system, interest in the possible pathological effects of lowered estrogen levels on older women has spread beyond gynecology to other disciplines, most notably orthopedics, cardiology, and geriatrics (Kaufert 1990a).

Because the medical interests and clinical approaches of these various disciplines by no means always coincide, the conducting and the reporting of research often involve different assumptions. Thus the current scientific literature is not easy to interpret or to reconcile as a systematic body of information. What is more, concern over failing ovaries and dropping estrogen levels is no longer confined to the treatment of hot flashes during and immediately after menopause (never of great interest to the medical profession). It now extends throughout the latter part of the life cycle, and to the projected number of elderly women who will, researchers assert, incur health-care expenses from broken bones and ailing hearts.

There is also a heated and unresolved argument about the use of hormone replacement therapy, its reported therapeutic action and possible side effects, especially cancer, and the partisan involvement of certain drug companies in the promotion of its use. This means that "estrogen failure" and "the postmenopausal woman" have become popular topics in the medical world. One striking piece of evidence for this was the publication in 1990 of well over two hundred articles that dealt with hormone replacement therapy. Menopause and its spin-off are currently big business; estrogen sales alone in 1990 were estimated at $460 million in the United States (Office of Technology Assessment 1992).

Creating a Language of Menopause

The medical approach to middle age has attempted to make itself more scientifically oriented and systematic in recent years, and clarification of definitions, for example, has been central to this endeavor. By 1976 general agreement occurred among specialists that "a phase in the aging process of women marking the transition from the reproductive stage of life to the nonreproductive stage" should be designated as the climacteric (Utian and Serr 1976, 1). This was then distinguished from the menopause, an event indicated by the final menstrual period, which occurs "during the climacteric" (Utian and Serr 1976, 1). Menopause, when using this definition, can be established only in retrospect, after the fact. In epidemiological research further subdivisions are usually made into pre-, peri-, and postmenopausal segments of time, based on the presence or absence, regularity or otherwise, of menstrual cycles in individual women. For most everyday clinical encounters, this classification is sufficiently accurate, and clinicians are usually comfortable with thinking of middle-aged patients either simply as menopausal, or else as pre-, peri-, or postmenopausal women. But creation of divisions such as these is simply an heuristic device (Kaufert 1988, 339), and placement of a woman in a division usually depends on subjective reporting about presence or absence of menstruation. Since menstruation has an annoying habit of starting and stopping for a number of reasons aside from menopause—including pregnancy, pathology, or stress—its presence or absence can by no means be taken as an accurate measure of the fact of menopause. Moreover, no straightforward correspondence exists between the final menstrual cycle and changes in body chemistry; and the dichotomous and trichotomous divisions serve in fact to conceal a "considerable degree of biological heterogeneity" (Hutton et al. 1978; Kaufert 1988, 340).

Basic scientists and an increasing number of physicians cannot be satisfied with subjective reporting. They further subdivide the Menopausal Woman into objective cellular changes (particularly of the endometrium and ovary), endocrine levels, bone density measures, calcium and lipid levels. They compare these measures with profiles of younger "healthier" women and generally describe a decline or an increase from what they take to be "normal," that is, the bodies of women of reproductive age. Using this kind of approach, they treat menopause as if it were a fact, a universal event, the result of essentially the same "unnatural" decline in hormone levels that in turn produces pathologically inclined cellular and tissue changes in females everywhere. But, as Greer points out, "What we are really doing is denying the process [of aging] . . . and pushing the woman off the rung of the ladder of life that she has arrived at, to a lower one" (1991, 200).

In the interests of scientific objectivity, therefore, the Menopausal Woman has steadily fragmented over time from an individual who is simply aging, to one who is undergoing the end of menstruation, to a body in which numerous molecular changes are taking place. Paradoxically, while segmented the Menopausal Woman remains essentialized, a universal figure who smells faintly of old age, decrepitude, and death.

Hormone Replacement Therapy: Russian Roulette

Estrogen replacement therapy enhances a woman's feeling of well-being and reduces the morbidity, mortality, and health care costs associated with osteoporosis and atherosclerotic heart disease.

(Notelovitz 1989, 15)

Until the mid-1970s estrogen replacement therapy was usually prescribed to counter specific symptoms associated with menopause, notably the hot flash. At that time, in the United States, estrogen was among the top five most frequently prescribed drugs, but between 1975 and 1980 its use sharply declined owing to the publication of several studies that linked it to an increased risk for endometrial cancer. They produced a protracted debate in the medical literature (Kaufert and McKinlay 1985) and a widely accepted recommendation for the addition of a second hormone, progesterone, to the medication in order to counter the toxic effects of estrogen.

From the early 1980s campaigns for the use of hormone replacement therapy (HRT; combined estrogen and progesterone) escalated dramatically, not merely to counter hot flashes, but as a "prophylactic," a preventive medication against osteoporosis and coronary heart disease. WHO defines the disease osteoporosis as a state in which the "bone mass/volume ratio" is lower by a designated amount than that of "healthy *young* adults of the appropriate sex" (WHO Scientific Group 1981, 42; emphasis added). The chemistry of women of reproductive age is once again, as in the case of estrogen levels, taken as the standard measure for what is normal and healthy, and the aging body is designated as abnormal: "If the bone mass/volume ratio is below the young normal range, but within the normal range for the age and sex of the subject, the term 'simple osteoporosis' should be used" (WHO Scientific Group 1981, 42). A label of "accelerated osteoporosis" is recommended for those women who fall outside the range of what is considered normally abnormal. It is now widely accepted, on the basis of research done almost exclusively in North America and northern Europe, that certain women (white, slender, smokers, lacking exercise or else exercising excessively) are at a greater risk for osteoporosis (accelerated) than are other women, ergo, they in particular should be strongly encouraged to use hormone replacement therapy. Whereas some physicians recommend selective use for high-risk women, others argue for virtually universal use; some suggest use for five years' duration, others for ten, and others lifelong use (Reid 1988). But there is also a major debate over the possibility of being at greater risk for breast disease with the use of hormone replacement therapy, especially for those women with "preexisting benign breast disease" (WHO Scientific Group 1981, 76). Some recent research has shown that women who use combined progesterone and estrogen are at greater risk for contracting breast cancer (Bergkvist et al. 1989; Hunt et al. 1987; Jick et al. 1980), but an earlier study reached the opposite conclusion, namely that progesterone protects against cancer (Gambrell et al. 1983). Physicians, therefore, cannot rest assured that they are necessarily making the best choice when recommending hormone replacement therapy for their patients, although many assume that the results of some research are more reliable than others and make their judgments accordingly.

The parallel heated argument over estrogen and heart disease turns on whether the imbibing of estrogen increases the risk of heart disease (Wilson et al. 1985) or, on the contrary, protects against it (Nachtigall and Nachtigall 1990; Ross et al. 1981; Bush et al. 1987; Criqui et al. 1988). This picture too is further complicated by the addition in recent years of progesterone to the therapeutic regimen, a change that many believe alters the picture significantly. The use of hormone replacement therapy is also thought by many to increase the risk for gallbladder disease (Honoré 1980), while others believe that no such association can be shown (Nachtigall et al. 1979).

There is no consensus as to how to interpret these results, which in any case are based largely on noncompatible data sets. Nevertheless, out of this maze of contradictory assertions and predictions, assured statements are made about the Menopausal Woman and what will happen to her if she accepts or rejects replacement therapy. This tenuous situation has apparently been recognized by the United States National Institute of Health (NIH) since it plans a ten-year, $500-million epidemiological study involving more than one hundred forty thousand women past menopause and including for the first time extensive clinical trials to measure the effectiveness of hormone replacement therapy against chronic disease. This proposed study has already been severely criticized before it is even under way, evidence, perhaps, as to just how sensitive this topic has recently become (Palca 1991).

Knowledge for Everywoman

Not surprisingly, the debate about menopause and its possible long-term effects has been taken up in the popular press. Essays that appear in pamphlets, newsletters, magazines for women, self-help guides, manuals, books, and so on have followed the maze of medical arguments that are then usually reproduced in plain language. The thrust of most of this literature is to try to counter what is thought of as an overwhelmingly pathological orientation common to physicians. Menopause is described as "a time for positive change" (Fairlie et al. 1987), a time for "reassessing and rebuilding" (*Homemaker's Magazine* 1979). One of the most widely cited books starts out by proclaiming that it is "revolutionary" in that its purpose is to overturn the fears associated with menopause and aging (Reitz 1977). Nevertheless, ambivalence lingers in some of this literature and shows up in titles such as *Surviving the Change* (Israel et al. 1980).

Some of the assumptions made in the basic scientific and medical literature, most notably that the existence of older women is a recent phenomenon, also appear in articles written for the general public: "At the turn of the century, when the average life expectancy of women was about 55, menopause coincided with a woman's final years" (Gerson and Byrne-Hunter 1988). Moreover, the pamphlets and books that I have read (with the notable exceptions of Cobb 1992 and Fairlie et al. 1987) are not usually significantly different from the medical literature. Although their emphasis is on what is normal rather than pathological (in a few articles, for example, authors insist on the use of the word "signs" rather than the "symptoms" of menopause [Fairlie et al. 1987, 12; Siegal et al. 1987, 117]), the subject matter still focuses on physical changes associated with middle and later life (Greenwood 1984). A paragraph or two may describe "role changes," "the empty nest," or "changing expectations about older women," but beyond this, the literature rarely puts menopause into a larger context and gives short shrift to the subjective experience of individuals. Furthermore, in spite of a few nods by one or two of the articles to possible class or ethnic variation, essentially the same drive exists as in the medical literature: to produce a tidy, rounded discourse, a "how to live through it" manual about biological changes in the Menopausal Woman.

There is, however, one striking difference between scientific writing and that created for general consumption. In contrast to scientific writing today, most of which remains deliberately aloof from any obviously moralizing stance, books and articles written for women are not so cautious in their approach. They often emphasize, for example, that because "our" society (North America, northern Europe) places great store in youthfulness, aging is fraught with difficulties, most particularly for women who have been socialized to think of youth as beauty and of the female role as reproduction. Here emotional instability, depression, and "feeling blue" make their entry. This topic has almost disappeared from mainstream medical literature on menopause over the past seven or eight years—jostled aside by the interest in osteoporosis, heart disease, and other "serious" illnesses of aging; overshadowed by considerable doubt as to the authenticity of depression as a bona fide symptom directly associated with the dropping estrogen levels central to the contemporary medical definition of menopause.

Facing Death: The Crisis of Midlife

"The dangerous age" is marked by certain organic disturbances, but what lends them importance is their symbolic significance. . . . Long before the eventual mutilation, woman is haunted by the horror of growing old. . . . To hold her husband and to assure herself of his protection, and to keep most of her jobs, it is necessary for her to be attractive, to please; she is allowed no hold on the world except through the mediation of some man. . . . When the first hints come of that fated and irreversible process which is to destroy the whole edifice built up during puberty, she feels the fatal touch of death itself.

(de Beauvoir 1953, 542)

"Middle age" is the part of the life cycle that was discovered most recently. Until the 1970s research focused almost exclusively on childhood, adolescence, and, belatedly, the elderly. Middle age, in contrast, remained largely unexamined, a time of "no change" and inherently dull. There were one or two well-known exceptions, of course, most notably Erikson's gender-blind theory of the eight stages of psychosocial development, a Freudian-inspired crisis model in which the basic building blocks laid down in childhood culminate in the production of a mature autonomous man, provided, that is, he successfully negotiates the universal developmental tasks (Erikson 1965). Although Erikson did not postulate a midlife crisis, the notion of developmental crises as normal experience dominated life-cycle research until very recently, most particularly in connection with midlife: "Somewhere about the age of 40, he [? she] often begins to realize that life is half over for him. When a person looks equally backward and forward, he is aware of middle age. . . .Deterioration is the basis of mid-life. . . .Physical deterioration takes us to death" (Rayner 1979, 169).

What is known as "normative crisis model" research has employed male subjects and focused overwhelmingly on career development (Levinson 1977, 1984; Vaillant 1977). Aside from some general asides to aging, this kind of research proceeds largely as though biological change produces no major effect, and as though women do not exist. In contrast, research on women has developed its theories from ideological positions with respect to female biology, in particular to the menstrual cycle. Perennial unresolved arguments revolve around the relative contribution to female aging of what are deemed biologically determined hormonal changes on the one hand, and of numerous social and cultural variables on the other.

Many gynecologists when writing about menopause today deliberately confine their attention to biological changes associated with menopause and turn their backs on anything other than "hard" data (but perhaps observe this distinction with less rigor in actual clinical practice). As a result, at present, physicians often subscribe to the belief that the only "true" symptoms of menopause are the so-called vasomotor ones, that is, the hot flash and sudden sweats, said to be the direct result of estrogen withdrawal, which is also held responsible for "senile" changes in the reproductive organs (Campbell 1976; Utian 1980). This means, then, that aside from the complex changes that develop later in the target organs, all other less easily circumscribed signs and symptoms—including depression, irritability, insomnia, headaches, anxiety, and loss of ability to concentrate, often traditionally lumped together as part of the menopausal experience— are now ruled out as invalid, tossed out disdainfully by many physicians who dismiss them as unscientific. In line with this kind of argument, a considerable amount of research now attempts to separate out symptoms induced by "psychosocial factors" from those "best predicted solely by menopausal status," often specifically to assist physicians in their care of patients (Hunter et al. 1986).

In contrast to gynecologists, psychiatrists, many of whom subscribe wholeheartedly to the crisis model of human development, tend to cling to the idea that the more psychological and psychosomatic symptoms are authentic, even if not "truly" menopausal:

> The ingredients of the female's midlife problems are well known: the empty nest, the struggle over career, the unhappy and sometimes adulterous husband, the illness and death of parents, the disappointments of past and present, and the fear of the future. The empty nest is certainly a real phenomenon and may be exacerbated by the onset of menopause with which it may be coincident. . . .It is infinitely more acceptable to attribute depression to menopause than it is to acknowledge that the loss of one's children is the major cause of the dysphoria.
>
> (Fink 1980, 114)

This writer agrees that menopause does not cause depression but emphasizes instead that "real losses and a decrease in self-esteem" at this stage of the life cycle are implicated.

For the purposes of such arguments, both those of the gynecologists and of the psychiatrists, the Menopausal Woman must be split, not into smaller and smaller biological segments as the basic scientists would prefer, but in twain, by the familiar mind-body dichotomy basic to so much Western thought. Gynecologists (those of them who are interested in treating middle-aged women) take the menopausal body and "manage" its chemistry, while they hold the woman and her feelings at bay, whereas psychiatrists and psychologists take the crisis-ridden psyche, beleaguered by past losses and future fears, and tinker with it, all the while ignoring the biological process of aging. Recently, in an effort to overcome this dichotomy, certain interested clinicians have begun to promote menopause clinics and consultation centers where physicians and psychologists work side by side to provide a "complete" service for the menopausal woman. However, in an age of considerable economic incentive for medical care innovations (in the United States at least), their motives may not be entirely ones of concern for the well-being of middle-aged women.

There is yet more to this complex story, because over the years and from several directions have come reactions to the pathological, crisis-oriented approaches of the clinical world. Several social scientists and social epidemiologists have conducted survey research that encourages a re-evaluation of the assumptions embedded in much of the medically oriented research (Avis and McKinlay 1991; Holte and Mikkelsen 1991; Kaufert 1990a; Kaufert et al. 1987; McKinlay et al. 1992). Feminist scholarship, although not internally free of disputes, has also opened up the way for some radically new interpretations of the body that have profound consequences for our understanding of middle age (Birke 1986; Harding 1986; Hubbard 1990). But the dominant way of thinking about menopause, in North America at least, remains heavily influenced by the medical world.

Objectivity, Subjectivity, and Ideology

Assumptions and contradictions are, perhaps unavoidably, incorporated into descriptions and analyses of a complex phenomenon such as menopause, leading to a blurring of fact and value. These assumptions guide the reconstruction of the middle-aged female body; as we have seen, it is then framed, fragmented, and compartmentalized accordingly—split along disciplinary lines (Kaufert 1990). But the various scientific disciplines do not simply create categories in different ways. There is, in addition, variation within disciplines, and variation in the way the same discipline represents the body in different cultural settings. Tacit culturally informed meanings about the end of menstruation are implicated in each case. Like so many bodily processes, menopause, because it cannot be neatly dissected and either reduced to chemical change or contained in the cross-tabulations of statistics, is what is known in anthropology as an "empty sign," open to many interpretations that are never arbitrary. These interpretations are the product of culturally produced knowledge that in turn influences both popular and scientific discourse.

Japanese ideas about midlife and menopause—those of women, of the public at large, and of health-care professionals—are notably different from those in North America, at least as those ideas appear in the current literature. Competing discourses exist in Japan too, but they are grounded in sets of assumptions that lead to remarkably different attitudes about female middle age; so far, neither the pathological nor the crisis-oriented approach to menopause is dominant, although this situation may change in the future. There exists in Japan, therefore, a local corpus of scientific knowledge about the end of menstruation that sits in somewhat uneasy alliance with international scientific discourse. I will discuss these anomalies, not in order to subsume the Japanese perspective into the dominant

North American medical perspective but rather to show how both are products of local histories and cultures.

But we must go yet further. A study that is limited to a discussion of the representations of menopause is only half the exercise. We are dealing with a segment of the life cycle that has only recently come to the full attention of various professional and politically motivated groups whose members often believe that they have a right to authorize what should be done concerning middle-aged and older women. It is necessary to move beyond contested descriptions about what exactly menopause is and who is said to be at risk for a difficult menopause and its consequences. We need also to ask what motivated the production of the discourse in the first place and, further, on what grounds is it then legitimated and reproduced over time.

An approach such as this entails a discussion of the relation between representation and social action: how do people in North America and Japan—women, feminists, gynecologists, psychiatrists, epidemiologists, social scientists—understand menopause and middle age, and what do they think should be done, if anything, for and with women in their forties and fifties? What implications do these beliefs and actions have for the lives and subjective experience of individual women? Conversely, what influence does the experience of middle age and menopause have, if any, on popular and professional knowledge about the subject? Above all, why has menopause become an issue at this particular moment? In summary, what is the relationship among the subjective experience of midlife, the occurrence of the end of menstruation, and the various objective bodies of knowledge and their application to this part of the life cycle?

It will be apparent by now that I do not accept the view that scientific knowledge is privileged and exempt from cultural analysis or that other forms of bodily representation can simply be dismissed as arbitrary or capricious. Having said this, I do not propose to reduce all forms of knowledge about the body to the same order. Scientific research, dependent on measurement, produces fragmented abstract information, both statistical and physiochemical, from which we can begin to build a picture about certain regular changes associated with this part of the life cycle. In contrast, we cannot measure subjective experiences but must narrate them. This kind of information, usually neglected by biological and social scientists alike, allows us to enter vicariously into the life world of individuals. Narratives of subjectivity do not permit broad generalizations and abstractions but encourage instead a contextualization of specific pieces of the puzzle and provide a very important constraint on the way in which we obtain and interpret biological and statistical information. However, because the experience of subjectivity, and the language that describes it, is a cultural product, personal narratives are inevitably circumscribed in specific ways; as Scarry and others suggest, the narratives emphasize certain features while leaving others unrecognized or unspoken.

Although my position with respect to current scientific discourse about menopause is on the whole critical, I by no means dismiss a scientific approach in toto and use survey research in this study with two purposes in mind: to make comparisons with similar data bases created in Japan and North America; to juxtapose the quantitative results obtained in Japan with personal narratives given by Japanese women, and also with textual materials and verbal reports produced by Japanese researchers in connection with menopause.

Survey methods must be used with extreme caution in cross-cultural settings; it cannot be assumed that scales and questionnaires developed in one cultural context will have universal applicability. If we start with the assumption that culture is more than just the icing on the cake and cannot, therefore, simply be controlled for and factored out of sight, then a questionnaire that is culturally contextualized becomes necessary. This means that the point of departure must be cultural categories that will be the guiding framework in survey research, both for creating questions and for interpreting answers. Throughout the collection and analysis of data, it is necessary to move back and forth between ethnographic materials and survey data—from narratives to numbers, contextualization to abstraction, and back again to context.

If, for example, a researcher takes the Blatt Menopausal Index, the symptom list most widely used in quantitative research in connection with menopause, and simply translates and administers it in Japan or elsewhere, the researcher is making the assumption that the symptoms in this list have universality. But no one has ever tried to generate a symptom list from the subjective reporting and observations of women in cultures elsewhere than in the West. In order to counter this deficiency, I based the questionnaire used in the present study on extensive knowledge of the Japanese situation accrued over the previous fifteen years of research into health-related issues (Lock 1980a, 1982, 1984, 1988a). One of the first difficulties I encountered was that Japanese has no one simple and unequivocal word to describe a hot flash, the symptom assumed by virtually all researchers and many women in the West to be ubiquitously associated with menopause. I examine this apparent anomaly in detail later on but mention it here as an example of the dangers inherent in assuming that cross-cultural variation can be safely ignored (see also Kaufert et al. 1987; Kleinman 1986; and Manson et al. 1985 with respect to research into depression). Sensitivity to the influence of culture on survey research has important implications for drawing comparisons from questionnaires administered in different local settings, or even those given to different populations within one culture. We should not assume, even with carefully designed studies, that the results are directly equivalent; they cannot be neatly equated one with another, since all results are at best approximations from which comparisons, when they are made, must be interpreted in context.

In the present study I use quantitative methods not only to compare results but also in order to expose contradictions between subjective experience and ideology, that is, between the individual narratives about midlife and menopause and the current ideologies common to the various discourses and practices relevant to this stage of the life cycle. Two sets of contradictions are involved, the first being discrepancies between the actual experiences of individual women during menopause (whatever corner of the globe they live in) and professional discourse about the universal Menopausal Woman. A second set of contradictions exists, between what women assume the menopausal experience to be like and their reported subjective experience of what actually happened—in other words, there is a disjunction between individual experience and the culturally infused expectations or received wisdom (myths) that women hold about menopause before they reach that stage of the life cycle (Barthes 1957; Kaufert 1982b).

Despite these contradictions, there are certain themes in the narratives of women and professional researchers in any given culture that occur frequently and that reflect both culturally constructed assumptions and often repeated contradictions about the aging female. When we juxtapose such narratives and expectations with actual behavior in connection with menopause, we understand how individuals come to embody and accept ideological knowledge as natural and inevitable, even when at times it contradicts their own experience. We see, too, how people consciously accept, resist, or even reject the ideology outright.

In creating this argument, I take it, following Young, that ideological knowledge refers to the "facts and meanings which have entered into the consciousness of a particular person and now affect that individual's choice of socially significant action" (Young 1983, 204). Production of ideological knowledge, moreover, is intrinsically linked to practical activities, social relations, and the functioning of institutions. Ideology infuses subjectivity: many ideological practices shape ordinary everyday events based on tacit

knowledge or unexamined assumptions that pervade our speech and behavior in social groups. Young points out that "in industrial societies the
most powerful ideological practices are ones which claim that their facts
are non-ideological because they are scientific" (Young 1983, 209). Despite
evidence to the contrary, our usual assumption today is that science accurately reproduces the "real" world "out there," while ideology represents particular social interests; but, Young argues, although science le-
gitimizes its position by claiming to be nonideological, in reality
knowledge that is assumed to be factual is frequently shot through with
value judgments. Nevertheless, the language of science is so persuasive
that these assumptions are rarely questioned; on the contrary, once scientific data about the body are accepted as accurate, they are taken as exact
replications of nature, easily legitimated, and therefore not contested. Figlio points out that the very endeavor of science is an activity "dedicated
to the naturalization of both experience and ideology and to the expression
of that achievement in language" (Figlio 1976, 19). He understands science
as having a "double nature": its abstract, theoretical, and observational
elements and its persuasive impressions that communicate these elements
to others and that convey an unexamined ideology.

In order to expose the way scientific discourse about menopause seamlessly incorporates ideological knowledge, it is necessary to examine not
only narratives that focus directly on menopause but also the cultural
construction of sex and gender, the representation of nature (including the
position of individuals and society with respect to it), and the conceptualization of time and its relation to the creation of knowledge about the
life span of women. These culturally produced ideas about gender, nature,
and time influence the production of expert knowledge about women's
bodies. Reformulated and refashioned as a result of scientific research, this
knowledge in turn reinfuses cultural knowledge in an ongoing mutually
reinforcing feedback loop. Since scientific research into menopause fails to
incorporate the subjective experience of ordinary women into its analysis,
the discourse becomes a diffusion of ideas between, on the one hand, clinically oriented scientific research (much of it not applicable to the vast
majority of ordinary women) and, on the other hand, ideological assumptions and superstitions about the nature of women and aging (with little
or no foundation in empirical reality). The feedback loop between popular
and scientific knowledge creates a self-perpetuating rhetoric, a myth that
posits a bleak time of individual suffering and distress leading to an inevitable decline in health, a myth that persists largely in ignorance of and
abstraction from the lives of middle-aged women.

The aging female body, a potent and malleable signifier, provides not only a locus for medical practice, however, but a synedoche for women's position in society. Conflated in the debate about aging women and the health or otherwise of their bodies is an argument about "what women are for" (Kaufert and Lock 1991), and to what extent they should be granted freedom to shape their own lives independently of the needs of society. In order to see how effective this myth is, it is essential to talk with individual women, intrude into their family lives, follow them into the clinic, and observe them in various social settings. It is only at these sites of action where we can disengage to some extent myth from reality and tease apart the inevitable mixture of individual subjectivity with culturally constructed ideological knowledge.

Comparison with the Japanese experience encourages us to ask certain questions in connection with our understanding about menopause and the Menopausal Woman. They center on the recent emergence in North America of concern over menopause. Does the interest in the number of women on the verge of what is termed a "menopause boom" relate not so much to middle-aged women themselves but to the large numbers of old women who will shortly be so evident and who are frightening to contemplate? Is this a fear of approaching death, lurking behind the barrage of technology designed to thwart illness and even aging itself? Is death itself culturally constructed?

Because, thanks to contraception, women now take charge of their own reproductive lives, and hence misogynist arguments that a woman's sole function is to reproduce no longer make sense, perhaps more subtle ways must be found to keep them in their "proper" place. Or possibly the issue of menopause emerges as the result of the expansion of scientific knowledge, or of profiteering on the part of certain drug companies and self-interest on the part of certain physicians. Perhaps the woman's movement and feminism have alerted the general public to menopause as a problem, and middle-aged women, having assumed more control over their bodies, now demand more information about menopause. Or the concern with menopause may come from a combination of some or all of the above.

At a more abstract level why do we slip, apparently so comfortably, into mind-body splits when discussing the human body? They may reflect a dichotomy that is such a "natural" and powerful heuristic device that we use it despite its shortcomings. Why do we tend to dismiss subjective experience as invalid: does science hold such sway over us that we are no longer comfortable with the "capriciousness" of subjectivity? Perhaps we simply wish to fill in the book of aging according to numbers. In the insistent modern search for order and control over our lives, we seem to be willing to glean our understanding of aging from scientific information alone, however rough and ready, rather than allow local knowledge, individual narratives, and poetry to contribute equally to our encounter with aging.

1

JAPAN: MATURITY AND $\overline{KONENKI}$

1 The Turn of Life—
Unstable Meanings

Kōnenki: the turn [change] of life; the critical age;
the menopause.

       (*Kenkyūsha's New Japanese-English Dictionary*)

In Osaka in 1984 the organizer of a public lecture about menopause started out the session by asking the entirely female audience, "What do you think of when you hear the word *kōnenki*?"

"The end of one's prime as a woman."

"I think of things like migraines."

"The beginning of one's second life, when you can start to do what you like."

"My mother is in the middle of *kōnenki* and complains a lot of shoulder stiffness [*katakori*], so that's what I think of."

"My mother had several very trying years suffering from rheumatism and she had a bad time with her autonomic nervous system too, so I feel quite frightened about what the future holds in store for me."

"I think right away of *kōnenki shōgai* [menopausal disorders], but I don't know if they're psychological or physical, or both mixed up together. When I look at my mother, who's just reached that age group, I notice that she's becoming more timid. She worries about little things that don't matter and complains of insomnia and other things going wrong with her body. I came here today to hear about the physical changes, but I also want to learn about how to deal with *kōnenki* by approaching it with the right attitude."

"I'm already past that stage in life, but I never had any problems—I just laughed it off when people said I was having *kōnenki*, and I was fifty-five before I knew it, and now I'm having a great time."

"I'm forty-five and right in the middle of *kōnenki*, and I think of it as mother's time of rebellion [*hahaoya no hankōki*]." A ripple of laughter

3

mixed with murmurs of agreement ran through the audience at this juncture.

No mention of the symptoms most usually associated with menopause in North America: hot flashes, drenched sheets from night sweats, or even menstrual changes—but perhaps one doesn't talk about these things in public in Japan, even at a small informal meeting of women? These comments did not sound particularly unusual to Christina Honde and me, however; on the contrary, they had a remarkably familiar ring to them. The two of us had visited a total of 105 households in several different regions of Japan for over 150 hours in all, while women between forty-five and fifty-five years old had recounted their experiences, beliefs, and concerns about *kōnenki*.[1] During the course of our conversations we asked everyone to explain the term to us and soon recognized that we would find no easy consensus about its meaning. On the contrary, it was surprisingly indeterminate, usually clustered with several other equally amorphous concepts that varied and nuanced the way women interpret *kōnenki* as both an idea and as experience. *Kōnenki* and terms such as the autonomic nervous system (apparently familiar, yet in this context paradoxically strange to Western ears), were not neatly packaged and separated out in the narratives of the women but spilled over into one another to form loose, relatively unstable associations.

I edit and frame the narratives, artificially separating out the concepts for the sake of clarity in this preliminary discussion. This strategy goes against my natural inclination as an anthropologist, which is to start with a broad sweep of the canvas—to situate the term *kōnenki* in a cultural context in order to understand it. But because in the West we tend to reduce the experience of female midlife to physical changes associated with the Menopausal Woman, I temporarily pare the Japanese narratives to relatively isolated units that focus on the body in middle age. This first set of comments does not, in the end, completely violate the Japanese understanding of *kōnenki*, because the concept includes sensitivity to biological change. Yet before we come close to the usual Japanese understanding of the term, we must recontextualize the subjective experience of *kōnenki*, and the physical signs and symptoms associated with it. Some of the same comments will reappear in later chapters as part of the longer narratives of which they originally formed a part. This strategy highlights from the outset important differences between the concepts and lived experiences of individuals as they go through the transitions of *kōnenki* and menopause, respectively, and the reader will soon see that, despite the dictionary definition cited above, they are not one and the same thing.

Aging and Kōnenki

Ito-*san*,[2] born in Korea of Japanese parents, lives in Kyoto in a Buddhist temple that she manages while her husband, the head priest, spends most of his time as a taxi driver. She says of *kōnenki*:

"It's something no one can avoid, but it's nothing to be afraid of or worry about—one should just accept it naturally. It's not simply the end of your periods, though. Things like high blood pressure, becoming farsighted, and going gray are all included. It isn't really that one's value as a woman is decreasing, it's just part of the aging process. I have high blood pressure now, which I never had when I was young, and I think it's part of *kōnenki*."

"How old are you?"

"Let me see . . . Forty-six, nearly forty-seven."

"You said a lot of women become irritable at *kōnenki*? Do you think this will happen to you?"

"Well, maybe, but given my personality, I think I'll get over it easily."

Matsuda-*san* lives in an isolated forestry village in central Japan where she works long hours in a tiny factory outlet making car upholstery with twelve other women, in addition to growing her own rice and vegetables and tending the family trees at the weekends. Unlike most of the women we interviewed who appeared to our eyes younger than their age, Matsuda-*san* looks a little older than her forty-nine years but gives the impression of boundless energy. "I almost never sit down, I'm always on the move," she says, so her comments come as a surprise:

"I'm in *kōnenki*, that's for sure. I get tired easily these days, and I have headaches and my periods are over—or irregular, anyway—I don't think I've had one for about a year. Anyway, I get really tired."

"When did you start to get tired?"

"Last year. I can't stick at things the way I used to. I get something like my sewing almost finished, and then I'll just let it go. Before, I'd have stayed up all night to finish it. It's because of my age . . . I hate it—I'm not young anymore. When I was young I used to try to take care of my complexion at night, but nowadays I'm so tired I don't even feel like washing properly, I just lie in the bath and soak . . . I'm just getting old."

"Were you expecting something like this to happen?"

"Yes. I used to go and work in the rice fields with *obāsan* [mother-in-law] and she always told me, 'Things are fine for women while they have their periods, but once *kōnenki* starts, then you feel irritable and get weaker and can't do anything properly any more. You young people are lucky.'"

Transplanting rice seedlings. This backbreaking work, usually carried out by women, is now mostly automated, but small plots and awkward corners must still be planted by hand.

"Does *kōnenki* have some relation to when a woman stops menstruating?"

"Yes, I think so. While menstruation is regular her body is fine, but when it stops, various problems start to happen. For a lot of people their eyes get worse, and the first thing I noticed was losing dexterity, so I can't tie knots in thread easily or do up buttons smoothly any more."

"When do you think *kōnenki* starts?"

"About forty-five I think. *Obāsan* told me that a few years before they stop menstruating most women start to get irritable, then five or six years after their last period, things settle down again. I'm forty-five now, so I have about another ten years to go I suppose."

Kōnenki apparently means something more encompassing than the end of menstruation for these two women, part of a general aging process in which graying hair, changing eyesight, and an aching and tired body appear to have more significance than does the end of the menstrual cycle. Some women believe that one can avoid *kōnenki* altogether, indicating that, in their minds at least, the end of menstruation is for all intents and purposes not involved. Kawamura-*san* lives in a fishing village on the island of Shikoku where, about twenty years ago, she was the first woman to get a driving license. She leaves the house at six o'clock in the morning six days a week and goes to the fish market together with her husband where she buys fish, which she then spends the rest of the daylight hours selling from the back of her truck:

"I think maybe I won't have *kōnenki*. I'm forty-nine, so if I were to have it, it would start right about now. Some people don't have *kōnenki*, you know. It depends on how you let yourself feel about it [*kimochi no mochiyō*]; it's just like morning sickness, which I never had."

"Do you think it has anything to do with the end of menstruation [*seiri no owari*]?"

"Well, I wonder if that's about when it starts? . . I don't really know."

"Do you think there are specific disorders associated with *kōnenki*?"

"No one really understands it, I think, but maybe *kōnenki shōgai* [menopausal disorders] is something like a 'neurosis,' an illness caused by being nervous, perhaps. Like today, for example, I rushed around selling fifty kilograms of fish in just a couple of hours; then my hands started to shake—I'm wondering if that isn't *kōnenki*? When I was young, even if I was rushed, I didn't have that happen to me; but now when I'm in a hurry, I can't even hold the calculator properly because my hands shake. This must be *kōnenki*—getting older [*toshi no are*]."

Tanabe-*san*, who works on an assembly line in a cake factory, puts it this way:

"Some women start having problems when *kōnenki* begins, but others never really have *kōnenki*. My co-workers all talk about it, some of them have headaches and shoulder stiffness—the symptoms differ depending on the person, and so does the time when it starts and stops. I still get my periods every month, which is a nuisance since I'm fifty-one already, but I suppose I'll feel I'm in even more trouble when they stop!"

Forty-nine-year-old Yamada-*san*, a housewife who sews designer dresses in her home now that her children are grown, makes it clear that *kōnenki* is part of aging but nevertheless believes it is avoidable:

"It's a time when a woman's body is changing, when it's just on the verge of starting to get old—it usually starts about fifty, I think."

"Can men have it too?"

"I don't know . . . Yes, I suppose men go through *kōnenki*. With women, their periods start to get irregular, but actually I think men are particularly vulnerable and are likely to get sick in their fifties more often than women. I'm still menstruating regularly so I hope I can get by without noticing it when it's my turn."

"So the first sign of *kōnenki* in women is irregular periods?"

"I think so. Umm . . . Well I wonder if it's related to menstruation or not?"

"Which lasts longer, do you think?"

"Well, I don't really know. I suppose it depends on the person. My friends talk about their bodies . . . The hormones get unbalanced and they get irritable. One of my friends is getting shots from her gynecologist. But there're some people who stop menstruating without any sign of *kōnenki*. I know an older woman who goes swimming every day and plays mahjongg—judging from her, you can reach the end of menstruation without having *kōnenki*."

Many of the women who state that *kōnenki* can be avoided entirely apparently have uppermost in their minds unpleasant symptoms that they associate with this stage of the life cycle but that they believe not everybody necessarily experiences. In contrast, women who dwell less on specific symptoms and focus instead on the more general signs of aging assume that everybody goes through *kōnenki*. Urushima-*san*, married to a taxi driver who does the night shift, spends her afternoons giving her sister a hand in a bar that she owns. She focuses her explanation on the end of reproduction:

"It's the first step into old age. I feel sad when I hear the word—it's awful to think of not functioning as a woman any more [*geneki no josei de naku naru*]."

"When do you think it starts?"

"About fifty-two or fifty-three, although my doctor said it's forty-two or forty-three, and according to him it's getting earlier these days."

"So it starts soon after menstruation has finished?"

"Well, I think so, but it seems my doctor doesn't think the same way!"

Eguchi-*san*, a full-time housewife and mother, paints a broader sweep than Urushima-*san*:

"I think *kōnenki* starts around thirty-five and goes on until about sixty. I think of it as part of *rōka genshō* [the phenomenon of aging] . . . Don't Western women think this way?"

"Most North American women would say it's a short time, I think, right around when they stop menstruating."

"My sister is fourteen years older than me, and to hear her talk you'd think she's been in *kōnenki* all along, and she's turning sixty now."

"Do you think there's any connection between *kōnenki* and the end of menstruation?"

"No, I don't really. The time when your periods stop is related to when they first start, you know, and also to one's *taishitsu* [physical constitution]. I don't think you can necessarily say *kōnenki* is over when your periods stop . . . There really isn't much of a relation between the two."

Other women express similar sentiments but for different reasons. Some think, for example, that one can pass through *kōnenki* entirely and still be menstruating:

"I'm through *kōnenki*—it wasn't too bad."

"But you're still menstruating, aren't you?"

"Yes, but *kōnenki* is a hormone imbalance, and the body can adjust before a woman stops menstruating."

A few women make a very tight connection between the end of menstruation and *kōnenki* and state that they are in essence the same thing. For these women the meaning of *kōnenki* comes closest to the usual meaning given today in North America to the term menopause. Other women, like Honda-*san*, a full-time housewife, while agreeing that *kōnenki* and the end of menstruation are intimately connected, conclude nevertheless that they cover a different time span. Honda-*san* said during the interview that she was in the midst of *kōnenki*.

"*Kōnenki* is when your periods stop, and when your sacred function as a woman, the bearing of children, is over . . . After that you're just an ordinary person. I'm almost forty-nine, and for a while I couldn't decide whether I was in the midst of *kōnenki* or not. I was having so much physical trouble that I thought I was, but I also thought I still had a long way to go. But then I started skipping periods, so I must be in the midst of it."

"So you think *kōnenki* and the end of menstruation are identical?"

"No. I think the body takes time to adjust after one's periods stop, so it's usual to have some [physical] trouble [*chōshi ga warui*] for a while. *Kōnenki* extends before and after the end of menstruation. It starts when you're about forty-two and finishes at about fifty-five or so. *Heikei* [the end of menstruation] takes a year or so, not so long as *kōnenki*."

"You said you're having a lot of symptoms right now. What are they?"

"Mostly dizziness and headaches. I heard from a friend that hormones might help, so I asked my doctor about it, but he said he would only prescribe them if the symptoms got really bad. He suggested that I just learn to live with it."

A primary-school teacher, fifty-four years of age, stated that she "failed" at getting through *kōnenki*.

"*Kōnenki* is a turning point in one's life [*toshi no kawarime*], and everyone probably goes through it. I associate it with a loss of energy, needing spectacles, and getting what we call in Japanese 'fifty-year-old shoulders.' "

"Does it happen to men too?"

"Well, women seem to have more problems, although men have trouble too, but for them it's usually from overwork. For women it's linked to the end of menstruation, but you start to feel it much earlier than that. From about forty-two or forty-three on, you find you tire more easily, you start to feel your age. Somehow you don't feel as healthy as usual. Actually, I guess I really failed at getting through *kōnenki*. I was so tired that I had to take sick leave from work. After fifty, things usually settle down again though."

Many women stress that *kōnenki* is a turning point, a milestone (*kugiri*) or an important change, and often the idea of a descent from the peak of one's physical well-being is implied: "It's the peak of life, just before you start getting old." One woman who farms in northern Honshu stated that the worst part about *kōnenki* was that people stopped calling her *obasan* (middle-aged woman) and started to call her *obāsan* (old lady; grandmother; this term also indicates one's mother-in-law and occasionally one's mother).

Clearly, if accuracy is what we want, we should not translate *kōnenki* as "menopause" because the English term has come to be synonymous with the end of menstruation in the minds of the vast majority of people over the course of the last forty or fifty years in North America. *Kōnenki*, by contrast, sounds a little more like the now rather archaic "the change," or "change of life," terms still used in isolated parts of the English-speaking world such as Newfoundland (Davis 1986). What is most striking about the Japanese descriptions is the lack of agreement about the meaning of *kōnenki*. Almost everyone states that it has something to do with aging, but beyond that, there is little consensus as to what the term conveys.

Even in its timing and the relation of *kōnenki* to the end of menstruation, there is dispute. Some people believe it is a long gradual change from the midthirties to about sixty, while others state that it starts about forty or forty-five and goes on to fifty-five, and still others that it coincides with the end of menstruation and therefore lasts for only a span of one or two years at most. Those who opt for a longer transition usually think of the external markers of aging, among which they give the end of menstruation little or no importance. Less frequently, women focus on internal hormonal changes that they view as taking place gradually over several years. Some women believe that the end of menstruation depends on the time of its onset in adolescence and see both events as physiological milestones. But even these women usually give *kōnenki* a meaning that is much broader than simple physiological change.

While some believe that a woman can be menstruating after *kōnenki* is over, others state that after menstruation *kōnenki* is yet to come. Still others assert that it can be avoided altogether—by which they apparently mean that not everyone has troubles or disorders at this time in the life cycle. In contrast, some women think of *kōnenki* as a difficult time for just about everyone in terms of physical symptoms, an unavoidable episode, after which full health returns. Others visualize it more as a turning point, so that *kōnenki* signals the beginning of old age and the inevitable approach of declining physical powers and eventual death. Several women stated emphatically that they have no knowledge about *kōnenki*, and that they don't really know what it is.

We might surmise that educational level or occupation account for some of the differences in responses, but such is not the case. A few rural residents, urban blue-collar workers, housewives, and professional women subscribe to a close link between *kōnenki* and the end of menstruation, but the majority of women from all walks of life would either equivocate on this point or actually dispute it.

Signs and Symptoms of Kōnenki

In common with the women who attended the public lecture in Osaka described above, most women when asked to describe the signs and symptoms associated with *kōnenki* report aches and pains of various kinds or else mention rather vague general complaints. Ogawa-*san* manages a farm in Nagano prefecture where she was born and grew up. Her comments about her friends and neighbors are very typical.

"I hear from other people that their heads felt so heavy that they couldn't get up. They didn't exactly have pain but just generally felt bad and didn't feel like working. Luckily I didn't have anything like that."

A woman of forty-seven, who works in a Kyoto factory where she makes underwear, comments about symptoms:

"It depends on the person. In my case my eyesight became weak and when I visited a doctor for my backache, he told me it was because of *kōnenki*. Some people tell me they have headaches and get irritable and that they become extremely nervous and sensitive. It depends a lot on one's physical constitution."

A rather well-to-do housewife of fifty-one focuses on changes associated with aging:

"All of a sudden I found I had lots of gray hair and my eyes became farsighted—that was when I started *kōnenki*. My eyes started to feel tired and painful in the evenings too. The optometrist explained to me that eyes start to get hard and lose their elasticity with age, and so they tire more easily. After hearing that I thought, Oh! All my muscles must be losing their elasticity just like my eyes. I have high blood pressure too, and when

I went to see my doctor about it last year he said I was just beginning *kōnenki*. Some women get irritable, but it doesn't seem to affect me that way."

A forty-seven-year-old housewife who is still menstruating says that she had a very brief *kōnenki*:

"I had this prickling feeling, like ants crawling over my skin. My husband said, 'Oh, that must be *kōnenki shōgai*.' He'd read about it in some book. It didn't last long, although this one remains [Hosokawa-*san* pointed to her checkmark beside the question about 'lack of sexual desire']. My husband says it's because I'm too busy during the day—I'm not so sure about that though ... "

Many women talk about a temporary physical unbalance:

"I think *kōnenki* means that the natural physical balance the body usually has is lost. The symptoms are headaches, tiredness, and irritation."

Rather few people described symptoms that sound more familiar to Western ears. Midori-*san*, who has spend all her adult life in Ponto-cho, Kyoto, where she is a geisha, was one of them. At fifty-four she still has many working years in front of her:

"I'd heard that in *kōnenki* you feel suddenly hot and then cold, but that never happened to me. They told me that it happens at the age your periods stop. I was all prepared for it, but nothing happened."

"Where did you hear this?"

"Well, I live in a society of women, of course, and so you get to know what happens to everyone else. When you hear about someone saying that they're sweating a lot, then for sure someone else will say, 'that's *kōnenki*.' "

"Did you hear about people becoming irritable or anything else like that?"

"No, not really, but I was quite worried. In the end, though, nothing happened."

"Do you worry about getting older?"

"No, I'm not worried. My periods stopped and I was relieved that it was so easy. Now that's over I think of myself as a little older, but it doesn't bother me much. It all depends on how you let yourself feel [*ki no mochiyō*]. It doesn't affect my work as long as I take care of my appearance properly and keep up with things. I read a lot and watch television and listen to what other people are talking about. I have to keep in touch— especially with what young people are saying—then I can talk with the customers."

Yamanaka-*san*, now forty-nine, recently quit her job with a bookbinding company. She talks about feeling suddenly hot at times but does not give this symptom more significance than the others that she mentions:

"I'm in *kōnenki* now. I often have stiff shoulders—especially when I knit or sew and I sometimes suddenly feel hot [*katto atsukunaru*]."

"When does this happen?"

"When I'm in a crowd my face becomes hot suddenly, and it feels as though it turns red."

"Do you perspire as well?"

"No, it only lasts a few seconds—less than a minute."

"Do you have any other symptoms?"

"I get a headache every two or three days, and I get irritated then and take it out on my children. But I don't have any problems that really affect my daily life. I'd heard that *kōnenki* is awful and people get really serious symptoms like dizziness or unsteady feet. My headaches must be *kōnenki* I suppose, but I don't say anything, especially not at home. If I complained to my husband he would just tell me to shut up; I can't expect any sympathy from him so I manage by myself."

Hattori-*san* runs a farm while her husband works in a nearby town in an insurance company. She says, "The most noticeable thing was that I would suddenly get hot—I'd seen older women have that problem—but then it happened to me, and I thought, Oh, so this is *kōnenki*. It's gone now, it just lasted for about six months or a year. It happened every day, three times or so."

"Did you feel embarrassed?"

"No, I just thought it was because of my age."

"Did you go and talk to anyone about it?"

"No, I didn't go to the doctor."

"Did you take any medicine?"

"No."

"Did you have any other symptoms?"

"My head throbbed, really badly sometimes—that was very unpleasant, but it's better now. I suppose it was something to do with the hormone imbalance, it's just aging really, isn't it?"

A total of 12 out of the 105 women interviewed reported symptoms that resembled hot flashes, but the descriptions were often rather vague, and the experience took on very little significance. Some women had heard other people talking about hot flashes, but an equal number had never heard of this symptom at all. Not one woman we talked to complained of major sleep disturbance, or of waking up with drenched sheets in the middle of the night. When talking about *kōnenki* they usually emphasized various aches and pains and feelings of lassitude, dizziness, irritability, and

Working on the assembly line in a cake factory.

so on, rather than what North Americans think of as the classical symptoms of menopause.

If we dissect the accounts to separate out myth and hearsay from what individual women recall as their actual lived experience, a rather large chasm appears. A good number of women say something to the effect that they heard that "Some women's heads are so heavy they cannot get out of bed," or "*Obāsan* said that after *kōnenki* you get weak and can't do anything." And more often than not they go on to state, "but luckily I haven't had anything like that." Or they talk about changing eyesight, graying hair, aching joints, and other symptoms of aging that many men of the same age also experience. By far the majority of people gave the impression that, although there is plenty of gossip and banter about *kōnenki*, much of it negative, in general it is not a subject that generates a great deal of anxiety or concern; even so, as an augury for the future, as a sign of an aging and weakening physical body, it is not particularly welcome.

Among the women who were interviewed in their homes, the one person who confessed to a difficult time was fifty-two-year-old Tabata-*san* who lives with her husband and his father, together with her son and his wife, in a modernized farmhouse in Nagano prefecture.[3] She spends her days tending the rice paddies and row upon row of chrysanthemums that she sells commercially, and she also works for several hours in the middle of the day making tiny electrical circuits for a nearby factory.

"I've been having *kōnenki* for over seven years. Everyone said it would come early and that there would be lots of problems because I had a really difficult time with childbirth and got sick afterward. I worry about my health, but the doctor just laughs and won't listen to me. I have a heavy feeling around my throat and I feel as if I can't breathe, but the doctor can't find anything wrong with me. It feels like something is stuck there. I've had the problem for five or six years and I'm worried that I have cancer, but the doctor thinks I'm silly. I sweat around my face, even in winter, and when I wipe it off I feel cold. I get the same hot, sweaty feeling at night too. The doctor said that hormone shots would help prevent this, but that it's not good to have them unless it's absolutely necessary. He gave me some medicine, but I don't take it. I keep telling myself that I'm not really hot and that way I can control it. People say my face gets red when I feel hot and then, when I think how embarrassing it is to be sweating in front of other people, it gets worse. I don't care about the family, but it's embarrassing outside."

"Do you have any other symptoms?"

"Oh yes. I get headaches and shoulder stiffness. But the doctor doesn't listen to me when I talk about these problems. My husband's sister started having *kōnenki* about three years ago. She doesn't have my kind of physical problems at all, but she's started to think that people are talking about her and she gets weird feelings about people she never worried about before."

"How old were you when *kōnenki* began?"

"I was about forty-six. We had a big problem in our family then, and I was worrying all the time. I started getting *kōnenki* symptoms then with the big shock that I got."

"How awful for you. What happened?"

"I can't tell you about it, but it made me go mentally crazy, and my hormone balance was all upset.

"I think of myself as a nervous type, you know, because I always worry about people getting cancer. Also I worry that I can't manage to stretch the household money until payday, and then I panic. I'm very tidy about the house too. My daughter tells me that I worry about the tidiness too much, and she thinks that my daughter-in-law who lives with us will start disliking me. I never used to care about this kind of thing when I was young, but since I married into this household I've become very conscious about things like tidiness. It's partly due to my husband and my mother-in-law (although she's dead now). I'm still scared of my husband—he gets mad just when last week's newspaper is hanging around. He's got me into the habit of feeling nervous, I think. I'm not really like this—it wasn't built into me from the start. It seems like even my basic physical nature [*taishitsu*] has changed over the years since I've been married."

"Do you think some of your problems, like suddenly feeling hot, have anything to do with the end of menstruation?"

"I stopped menstruating last year. I wonder . . . What do you think?"

"Well . . . I think some people would think so, and I'm inclined to agree with them, about suddenly feeling hot at least."

Tabata-*san*, in contrast to the other women who were interviewed, is noticeably distressed by the symptoms she experiences, but she is reluctant to explain her physical discomfort solely in terms of physiological changes associated with the end of menstruation. Long before the interview (I feel sure), she created a narrative to account for her discomfort, composed of several plausible causes ranging from her husband's intransigence, to the bad shock she received that drove her temporarily "crazy," to her own personality. She distills, condenses, and telegraphs this narrative into the polysemic term *kōnenki*, which represents for her not simply aging and physical discomfort but distress of many kinds. Tabata-*san* was eager to tell her story to me and started out with the emphatic announcement that she had been having *kōnenki* for seven years. Unlike the majority of women we talked to, who dismiss *kōnenki* as hardly worth talking about or else interpret it simply as an inevitable sign of aging that may entail uncomfortable but temporary symptoms, Tabata-*san* loads this concept with an array of meanings and almost flaunts her troubles. In contrast to most women in the study, she freely admits that she is not happy and openly acknowledges that the anxiety she experiences is disabling; but she can find no way out, no responsive ear or helpful council. Her doctor laughs at her when she seeks to account for a large portion of her distress as caused by *kōnenki*, and her social problems remain undiscussed and un-resolved. She is afraid of her husband; her own mother (to whom she might have turned) is dead, as is her autocratic mother-in-law. Her sister-in-law has her own troubles, and her daughter simply chides her. She is embarrassed to talk to her friends about the secret "family" problem that caused her so much distress and so remains isolated.

Tabata-*san* was expecting a bad time at *kōnenki* long before she reached this stage partly, she says, because she had a difficult time with childbirth. Both the end of menstruation and *kōnenki* are closely associated by many women with other concepts, one of which, *chi no michi*, posits a rather close relation between difficulties at earlier stages of the reproductive cycle and a distressful *kōnenki*. When we consider the end of menstruation and *kōnenki* with *chi no michi*, the puzzle becomes yet more complex.

Chi no michi *(path of blood) and* Kōnenki

The end of menstruation has long been recognized in traditional Sino-Japanese medicine as the seventh stage in a woman's life when a quality known as *tenki*, intimately associated with the female reproductive cycle, goes into decline. One of the results of an abrupt decline in *tenki* can be the collection of "stale blood" in the body, associated with numerous non-specific symptoms, including dizziness, palpitations, headaches, chilliness, stiff shoulders, and a dry mouth. The phenomenon often lasts for a few years (Yasui and Hirauma 1991, 370) and is one part of a more embracing concept widely used in Japan until well into this century and commonly called the "path of blood."

The concept of the path of blood appeared as early as the tenth century in Japanese medical literature, and a priest writing in 1362 stated that *chi no michi* is related to the thirty-six symptoms that appear only in women (Murōga 1984). Its use was not limited to the medical world, however, and the path of blood crops up regularly in literary works from the fifteenth century onward. A 1986 movie entitled *Yari no Gonza Kasane Katabira* based on a classical *bunraku* drama by Chikamatsu Monzaemon makes much of this concept. In it the travails of an Edo-period love affair between a samurai and an "older" woman suffering from *chi no michi*–related distress are recounted in laborious detail.

Today the term *path of blood* is decidedly old-fashioned, and use of the concept of stale blood is virtually confined to those hundred or so physicians specializing in herbal medicine who posit a close relation between it and the symptoms of *kōnenki* (Fujihira 1982). The majority of women who were interviewed had heard about *chi no michi*, but most were rather vague on the subject. A Kobe woman says, for example,

"I guess it's some kind of women's disease, although I suppose it's something to do with menstruation, and so it's not really a disease—I don't really know. Old people used to talk about it with childbirth—they said you had to rest thoroughly so as to avoid *chi no michi*, but I don't know exactly what they were talking about."

A good number of women had heard about *chi no michi* from their mothers:

"My mother used to use the word *chi no michi*, and I suppose she was talking about what we call *kōnenki shōgai*. People used to say herbal medicine worked well for it."

The clearest answers were given by women living in remote rural areas.

"They say if you overdo it after childbirth, then you could have trouble for many years after that. That's all part of the 'path of blood.' You should take it easy for seventy-five days after birth. You shouldn't even read the newspapers or sew."

"Do you think it has anything to do with *kōnenki*?"

"Yes, I do, to a certain extent. If you overdo it the effects will show up after you get older and you may well get *kōnenki* disorders."

Another woman makes an explicit connection between *chi no michi* and what appeared to be hot flashes.

"I've heard about *chi no michi*. They say you get hot suddenly, or that your blood goes up to your head [*nobose*], but I've never had anything like that."

In her 1984 study of an isolated village in northern Honshu, Nancy Rosenberger found that all the women she interviewed believed in *chi no michi*, and that middle-aged women regularly used the term to discuss physical problems at the end of menstruation. One woman she talked to referred to the idea of stale blood: in the old days "it wasn't like now when the nurses massage your uterus to get the blood out. After the baby was born, blood sometimes got left in there and got rotten like. It stays in there and causes problems later on in the menopausal years" (Rosenberger 1987, 164). Many women link the hardships of prewar days, extended families, and *chi no michi*, as does one woman who works in a textile factory in Kyoto.

"My mother and her friends used to say that if you got up and worked soon after childbirth, you'd have *chi no michi* when you got older. But of course, people used to have their babies at home, and if you had a mean mother-in-law, then she probably wouldn't let you rest but made you get up and start sewing clothes and so on right away."

Watanabe-*san*, who lives in a forestry village in Shiga prefecture, said she had wanted to be careful after childbirth, but that was impossible:

"I didn't get better after my son was born. I had to stay in bed for a hundred days, more than the usual seventy-five days of rest. Three days after he was born, I got a call saying that my mother had collapsed and was dying and that I should come right away, but I couldn't move. I couldn't even walk, and the blood rushed right to my head. So I felt terrible and I got really sick after that. When I went to see the doctor years later he said it was *chi no michi*."

"The doctor said that?"

"Yes, he asked me if I'd had any emotional trouble right after childbirth, and I told him about the shock of my mother's death. It took about five years to get over it. I had all kinds of medical tests and they told me that my liver was bad and that I had sugar in my urine."

"Do you think *chi no michi* has anything to do with *kōnenki*?"

"No, I don't."

A few women think of *chi no michi* as more of an emotional than a physical problem.

"*Chi no michi* is a kind of hysteria, I think—with headaches, and irritability. In fact, I told my friends I might have it when I had a bad spell a few years ago."

Clearly *chi no michi*, like *kōnenki*, is a polysemic term to which a rather wide range of meanings can be attached. In the minds of some people these two concepts have an intimate connection, and frequently the old-fashioned term *chi no michi* is thought of as essentially the same thing as *kōnenki* disorders, the more modern concept that apparently superseded it. Books written for the general public by physicians often account for *chi no michi* this way (Matsumura et al. 1981, 56). Other people accept the idea of *chi no michi* as a broad concept that can be applied to the entire female reproductive cycle, and they usually assume that a difficult childbirth signals trouble at the end of the reproductive years. They visualize this trouble as stale blood remaining in the body from wear and tear during a stressed confinement or birth, later illnesses that affected the reproductive system, or an abrupt end to menstruation. In contrast, some women who believe in *chi no michi* make no connection between it and *kōnenki*. To the majority of people *chi no michi* is a physical phenomenon; to others it is primarily psychological.

Since most women, except those who live in rather remote rural areas, associate it with their mothers rather than themselves, we might be tempted to think that *chi no michi* will be relegated shortly to the category of superstition, but to date it remains as an entry in contemporary Japanese dictionaries: "*Chi no michi*: A general term for the special illnesses of women. At the time of birth, menstruation, *kōnenki*, and so on, irregularities in the blood circulation lead to various symptoms including headaches, dizziness, sudden feelings of heat, and an unstable nervous system. An illness of the blood [*chi no yamai*]" (Gendai Yōgo no Kisochishiki 1988).

The Autonomic Nervous System and Kōnenki

While talking about *kōnenki* many women made reference in their explanations to the autonomic nervous system—an allusion that lends to the discussion a tone of scientific authority (see also Rosenberger 1992). A housewife who lives in the Nagano countryside stated, when asked, that references to people having trouble with their autonomic nervous systems are everywhere: in newspapers, on television, from friends, and so on. Kitayama-*san*, a Kyoto factory worker, suffers from *jiritsu shinkei shitchōshō* (an imbalance of the autonomic nervous system).

"What's it like?"

"I get very upset and nervous, sometimes so badly that I can't read. Often people get this kind of upset at *kōnenki*, but in my case it's just an emotional thing—nothing to do with *kōnenki*. I went to see an internist about it because I was so nervous and I was having stomach trouble too."

A Kobe housewife who is an accomplished dyer comments on her many friends who received a diagnosis of imbalance of the autonomic nervous system.

"I don't know what it is exactly, but they seem to have a lot of vague symptoms, palpitations, dizziness, and other minor complaints. They always seem to have something wrong with them, and I'm tired of listening to them so I don't pay much attention. Quite a lot of them talk about losing their appetites."

"Is it connected in any way to *kōnenki*?"

"Oh yes, for some people it's more or less the same thing I think, but for others it seems to be quite different."

Everyone is in agreement that imbalance of the autonomic nervous system is a technical medical term, in tone nothing like the anachronistic *chi no michi* and also unlike *kōnenki*, used simply to describe part of the life cycle. Men and women can suffer from this problem, but women are thought to be much more susceptible. Reasons given for female vulnerability vary, but many people pointed out that hormonal changes influence the autonomic nervous system, and hence women are particularly at risk at the onset of adolescence, at each menstrual cycle, and at menopause. Physicians who specialize in herbal medicine believe that stale blood (*oketsu*) can have a negative effect on the functioning of the autonomic nervous system. A further reason commonly given is that women are "by nature" more nervous than men; an explicit link is made between an imbalance of the autonomic nervous system and "mental" problems. Oda-*san*, who works in a factory that makes underwear, talks about her experience.

"I once had it [*jiritsu shinkei shitchōshō*]—when I had a thyroid problem. I got very impatient and irritated. It seems to be a state that is just one step before madness. The doctor gave me a tranquilizer and then my *ki*[4] settled down gradually. It lasted about a month."

"So it doesn't have anything to do with *kōnenki?*"

"Well, I'm still menstruating, but I've heard that serious problems happen at *kōnenki*. I'm haunted by this thought, and maybe because I'm a bit physically unstable it might be bad."

Adachi-*san* works in an internist's office as a receptionist, and she reports that many patients come to see the doctor with problems related to their autonomic nervous system. Unlike Oda-*san* she does not link them closely to *kōnenki*.

"I've never had it myself. Some people say their hair starts to fall out, and some are very irritable and others just seem to feel bad. I don't think it has much to do with *kōnenki*."

Another forty-six-year-old woman who works in an electrical appliance factory stated that both she and her friend have regularly experienced dizziness and nausea for over five years. Her doctor diagnosed a problem of the autonomic nervous system but assured her, when she asked, that it was nothing to do with *kōnenki*. Eguchi-*san*, who works in a cake factory, states that she too was given a diagnosis of *jiritsu shinkei shitchōshō*.

"It was something like a serious depression. It happened right after we moved to Osaka. I couldn't stay quiet, I kept jumping up and down all day. It took me more than a year to get over it. I was aware that something was wrong, but I just couldn't control it, and I knew it was connected with our living conditions. Anyway, I went back to my old home to see the family doctor near my parents' house, and he was very understanding and gave me some medicine."

It gradually emerged from our talks with Japanese women that for many the concepts of *kōnenki*, *chi no michi*, and *jiritsu shinkei shitchōshō* are not clearly separable entities. Other people make a sharp distinction between one or more of them, and the majority no longer really believe in *chi no michi*. Perhaps a discussion of all these apparently rather obscure ideas is an unnecessary semantic exercise, since surely, if we specified ahead of time that we wanted to talk about the end of menstruation, all this confusion could be swept aside?

It is possible, of course, to ask about the end of menstruation, for which the word *heikei* (the end, or shutting off of the menses) is used in scientifically oriented texts. This term is probably closest to the current meaning of menopause in English, but it is a technical term that many women do not readily understand, and they sometimes have to see the written Japanese characters before they fully appreciate what is meant.[5] Women, when they talk among themselves, and patients and doctors use *kōnenki* and not *heikei* when conversing; several doctors stated that they explicitly avoid the use of *heikei* with patients because it is too "hard" and technical a term.

Alternatively, we could simply talk in everyday language about the end of menstruation (*seiri no owari*). If women are encouraged to explain further, they will usually elaborate in scientific terms how the menstrual cycle works, or else they will say they don't have much education and can't explain these things or, alternatively, exclaim: "I was hoping you'd explain that to me!" If the interviewer persists and asks, for example, what symptoms if any are associated with the end of menstruation, the conversation quickly slides into an exchange about *kōnenki*. In other words, we are forced to talk about *kōnenki* and its linked concepts, because physical changes or difficulties that occur at this time are attributed by most women to larger, more encompassing events, internal and external to the body, not simply to observable changes in the menstrual cycle or to declining estrogen levels. Many women have a good scientific grasp of the menstrual cycle and are well versed in simple endocrinology. When talking about the end of menstruation, however, the majority take a broad approach to what it represents, which often encompasses ten or more years, and they move easily back and forth between social meanings associated with midlife changes, personal experience, and physical changes over this time.

Limiting a conversation about *kōnenki* to the end of menstruation (even a conversation with the typical physician) is, therefore, an entirely artificial exercise in Japan and imposes an alien framework around the exchange that soon brings it to an awkward halt. If, in the interests of an accurate conversation, we reject the use of the term *kōnenki* because of its lack of precision, there is no language left with which to talk about the experience of *kōnenki* or the social meanings attributed to it.[6] It would be like asking women to explain how it felt to give birth to a baby, while insisting that they confine their language to the intensity of the contractions, the number of centimeters of dilation, and the pain. Although the English term menopause has systematically been stripped of meaning in most quarters, save that of the end of menstruation, *kōnenki*, in contrast, remains as a rich, condensed, and polysemic concept around which people can weave narratives about aging in which mind and body, self and other, past and future, can be reflected on and partially reconciled.

The Medical World and Kōnenki

We might expect that Japanese doctors when discussing menopause, in their professional writing at least, would summarily dismiss the word *kōnenki* from their vocabulary, and confine themselves to the use of a more precise term. Until very recently, such has not been the case at all. In discussing this part of the life cycle, both informally and in writing, the majority of physicians, although they have an image of declining estrogen production in their minds, tend not to isolate this knowledge or focus their narratives on one particular hormone but rather emphasize a complex of interdependent changes. Dr. Shimada, a Tokyo gynecologist, explains.

"The English word 'menopause' should be translated as *heikei* since this means the end of menstruation. *Kōnenki* is a much larger event, it's the time when the physical symptoms that mark this part of the life cycle appear."

"Do all women get physical symptoms?"

"I think most women have *kōnenki shōkōgun* [menopausal syndrome], but they don't usually come to the doctor. When the estrogen levels drop, the hypothalamus becomes very active and this is near the center of the autonomic nervous system. So this center is stimulated, which results in many nonspecific symptoms of various kinds."

"Can symptoms like shoulder stiffness [*katakori*] be part of this syndrome?"

"Yes, this could certainly be one of the symptoms, but of course, this is not the only reason for shoulder stiffness."

"What about emotional states? Would they also be involved?"

"Certainly. A woman could quite easily become psychologically unstable at this time."

"Is it a more difficult age emotionally than say twenty or thirty?"

"Yes, I think so. There's a lot of individual variation, but generally speaking it's quite a difficult time."

The majority of physicians who were interviewed incorporated the concept of the autonomic nervous system into their explanations in order to account for menopausal symptoms. An Osaka gynecologist put it this way:

"Headaches, ringing in the ears, shoulder stiffness, and sudden heat are all related to the autonomic nervous system."

"These are all symptoms of *kōnenki*?"

"Yes, they're all related. You see, the mechanism is that when estrogen and progesterone are not secreted normally by the ovaries this has an effect on the vasomotor nerves and the general circulation is impaired. I believe that troubles with the autonomic nervous system, including all the *kōnenki* symptoms, are related to poor circulation. When I prescribe medication to improve the hormone cycle, my understanding is that it also indirectly helps blood circulation. I often give peripheral circulation boosters at the same time, and sometimes minor tranquilizers, depending on the woman's condition."

Not all doctors would agree with this statement entirely, but its gist resembles the type of explanation that dominated discourse in Japanese medical journals until recently. For example, a gynecologist's talk at a meeting of the Japanese Medical Association started out: "It is common knowledge that an imbalance of the autonomic nervous system often occurs in connection with the changes in ovarian function that happen at *kōnenki*" (Ikeda 1979, 1405).

When asked about the symptoms of *kōnenki*, the majority of physicians produce a long list that includes shoulder stiffness, headaches, a heavy head, palpitations, feelings of heat combined with feelings of cold (*hien-obose*), lack of concentration, ringing in the ears, tiredness, dizziness, insomnia, irritability, and depression (Mori 1978, 249). In scientific articles these lists are subdivided and grouped in various ways in order to assist in the selection of appropriate treatments. It is striking how close the descriptions given by women and physicians are, despite the technical language that, naturally, pervades the medical literature.

Over the past fifteen years or so, general discussions about *kōnenki* have appeared regularly in the mass media. Described here as in the professional medical literature, *kōnenki* is said to last for about ten years from the midforties to the midfifties, and a large number of symptoms are associated with this stage of the life cycle. Books designed for the intelligent layperson usually have a scientific air about them and resort to a very liberal sprinkling of medical jargon:

> Functional disturbances of the autonomic nervous system are the
> principal symptoms of *kōnenki* but added to these are metabolic
> and psychological/nervous disturbances [*seishin shinkeishō*] that
> lead to a variety of symptoms. . . .
> The psychological/nervous symptoms include headaches, heavy
> head, dizziness, ringing in the ears, insomnia, lethargy, irritability
> . . . farsightedness, memory problems and melancholy. Circulatory
> disturbances include sudden feelings of heat, palpitations, feelings
> of cold, sweating and changes in the pulse. Disturbances of the ki-
> netic system include shoulder stiffness, lumbago, back pains, joint
> pains, and tiredness.
>
> (Okamura 1977, 40–41)

A few physicians, especially in recent years, give more significance to the hot flash than did earlier writers in professional and in popular literature. When asked by a newspaper reporter in 1987 about the symptoms of *kōnenki*, Dr. Honda, a Tokyo-based gynecologist, responded:

The most frequent symptom is *nobose* [a rush of blood to the head], even when there is no reason to blush, the face suddenly gets hot and there is sweating. . . . It cools down after a very little while but then starts all over again. This has nothing to do with the outside temperature, or whether one is in or out of doors. It happens many times a day. . . .

Is this caused by lack of harmony in the autonomic nervous system?

Yes, and then many things go wrong with the functioning of various organs. The next most usual symptoms . . . include dizziness, nausea, ringing in the ears, palpitations, and a choking or stifling feeling.

(Asahi shinbun 1987a)

Since almost all Japanese doctors read English-language publications with great regularity, in addition to numerous Japanese journals, the disparity between their explanations and dominant Western medical thinking is striking, a disparity that is now beginning to be aired among interested physicians. In one recent popular magazine article, for example, where medical professionals took a thorough look at *kōnenki* and compared it with menopause, an edition of two hundred thousand copies sold out in the space of a few days (*Shufu no tomo* 1991). A brief historical excursion is necessary in order to unravel some of the reasons for the discrepancies that exist between Japanese and North American medical thinking about female midlife.

The Invention of Kōnenki

Although a sensitivity to the human life cycle has long been a part of Japanese consciousness, middle age, the prime of life (*sōnen*), was until well into this century a relatively undifferentiated time span that commenced with marriage and lasted until ritual entry, at sixty, into old age. An age-grade system and associated rituals traditionally marked the passage of groups of people through successive stages of the life cycle (Segawa 1947; Norbeck 1953) but, as in many other societies, most of these rituals occurred during the first twenty years of life. Individual biological aging, although recognized, was in general subordinated to a communally based concern with social maturation, and the timing of events in the two cycles, the biological and the social, did not necessarily correspond very closely.

Although physical aging was not marked by the community at large, family celebrations were in order when a young woman reached menarche. At the other end of reproductive life, however, the end of menstruation was not socially recognized in Japan (as it appears was probably the case in virtually all other societies), leaving the event essentially unmarked. We noted in the prologue that when the average life span is less than fifty—as was the case in Japan until the middle of this century—it is often assumed very few women lived beyond the end of their reproductive years, and for this reason no attention was paid to the end of menstruation. However, a study done in the village of Yokouchi, in what used to be the province of Shinano in central Japan, examined the population registers all village headmen were required to keep and showed that the fifty-six women born between 1751 and 1775 who reached sixty years of age could expect to live sixteen years beyond that age (Cornell 1991). Having survived infancy, and later the dangers associated with childbirth, a woman might live well past *kōnenki* into old age; a lack of ritual concern about this part of the life cycle cannot simply be accounted for by an absence of older women.[7] Nevertheless, the end of menstruation was probably unnoticed except by each individual, who no doubt wondered what distress *chi no michi* might bring to her.

In addition to ritual celebrations of social maturation, the Japanese also paid attention to *yakudoshi* (years of calamity or dangerous years), when people were thought to be at great risk for illness or misfortune. The idea of *yakudoshi* is still widely acknowledged in Japan today (Lewis 1986), and while only a very few of the women in the present study observe the required precautions against misfortune, all were well aware of the "calamitous years" and just about everyone pointed out that the most dangerous age for men is forty-two and for women thirty-three.

At the Meiji Restoration of 1868, with the official opening of Japan to the outside world after two hundred fifty long years of self-imposed isolation, the Japanese deliberately set about creating a modern nation state. When they sent emissaries to Europe and America to observe the process of modernization elsewhere, they discovered much that was reasonably compatible with their own ideas about the life cycle. In Europe, although the word *climacteric* is now more or less confined to medical usage in connection with female midlife, it was originally used in daily conversation to describe the dangers associated with the many critical transitions conceptualized throughout the life cycle, regardless of age or gender—thus climacteric originally corresponded quite closely with *yakudoshi*. Despite this compatibility, contact with Europe appears to have stimulated the need to create a new term, *kōnenki*, which made its first appearance in the late nineteenth century when medical scholars translating texts from German into Japanese apparently were not satisfied with the folk term the "dangerous years" as the medical version for the climacteric. Nishimura believes that *kōnenki*, when it was first invented, was originally used, like climacteric, for male or female transitions throughout the life cycle and not simply those of middle age (1981).

Beyond the bounds of the medical world, *kōnenki* first appeared in print in 1909 in a novel by Oguri Fūyo entitled *The Spring of Youth* (*Seishun*); its protagonist laments the loss of his sexual vigor after three years in prison and likens his state to the "agony of women who, entering *kōnenki* in their forties or fifties, lose their femininity" (Oguri 1971, 3:505). The Chinese ideogram selected for the *kō* of *kōnenki* means renewal and regeneration, while *nen* means year or years, and *ki* means a season—a period or stage. As with so many other Chinese ideograms, the meaning is condensed and various possible interpretations exist. For example, in addition to renewal, *kō* refers to the time from sunset to sunrise and can also convey the idea of "deep into the night." Hence, as Rosenberger points out (Rosenberger 1987, 167), *kōnenki* could be translated as the "darkening years"—and this appears to be the meaning Oguri wished to convey, since he likened *kōnenki* to autumn nights, to corpselike weakness, to bleakness, and to loneliness. In contrast, the image of the sun has long been associated with menstruation in Japan, and *sekihan*, the red bean rice cakes traditionally used to celebrate the onset of menstruation, are likened to the sun.

At the end of the last century Germany became the model for the new Japanese medical system, in part because government representatives stated explicitly that Germany and Japan shared institutional and political interests (Powell and Anesaki 1990, 27). The conceptual approaches of the two medical systems also had much in common. Japanese medical knowledge (originally adapted from China) placed emphasis on the interaction among the various parts of the body. The meridians and points used for acupuncture, and the concept of *ki* (which translates very loosely as energy),[8] along with other fundamental ideas, provide the framework for an integrated approach to the body. Restoration of a homeostatic balance is the basis for all therapeutic interventions in this system.

Japanese doctors of the late nineteenth century found their thinking compatible with the newly formulated European medical concept, eagerly touted in Germany, of the "autonomic nervous system," that visualized various body systems as intimately related. The concept had been in the air for at least one hundred years but caused a stir throughout the Western medical world when it acquired this name in 1898 (Sheehan 1936); contemporary Japanese physicians, a good number of whom lived and studied in Germany, incorporated it with ease into their professional discourse

(Suzuki 1982). When the idea of the endocrine system was formulated and explicated in the 1920s, close links were postulated between the autonomic nervous system and the endocrine system (Sheehan 1936, 1110); the effects of these links are still apparent in contemporary Japanese descriptions of *kōnenki*.

A compatible approach to the human body was not all that made Japanese physicians feel at home in Europe. Until the end of the nineteenth century European doctors used a concept of "plethora" or "stale blood" to explain symptoms such as headaches, dizziness, palpitations, and the so-called hot blooms (later renamed hot flushes or flashes) associated with the climacteric (Tilt 1870; Barnes 1873; see also chapter 11). Japanese beliefs about the path of blood and stale blood must have allowed Japanese doctors to understand nineteenth-century European accounts of menopausal problems and also encouraged the belief that their knowledge, since it was so similar to that of European doctors, was an accurate scientific representation of female physiology. Indeed, it seems as if Japanese physicians had little, if anything, to learn from nineteenth-century Europe about the end of menstruation, with the notable exception perhaps of the emphasis given to hot blooms, which no doubt incited some curiosity.

In Europe, although the word climacteric has its roots in antiquity, the term menopause was not created until the middle of the nineteenth century by a doctor in France, Gardanne. Its origin was closely associated with the emergence of the gynecological profession, and it was specifically designated as the end of menstruation. During the latter part of the nineteenth century the meaning of climacteric was gradually pared down and refined within medical circles to represent only the female midlife transition, believed to last several years and to be accompanied by a variety of characteristic symptoms. Menopause was understood as just one part of this larger process.

A Japanese medical dictionary published in 1909, no doubt reflecting these changes, translated the German term *Klimacterium* as *gekkei heishi ki* (meaning the time during which menstruation stops) and the word menopause simply as *gekkei heishi* (the end of menstruation, a term related to the now current shorter *heikei*). Early medical discussions of *gekkei heishi* were limited to obvious pathologies, and *kōnenki* appears to have been understood as a natural event, of medical interest but largely outside the purview of the new field of gynecology. Not until the discovery of the endocrine system in the 1920s and, in the 1930s the development of a simple hormone replacement therapy, did a few Japanese gynecologists start to take an interest in the "normal" transition of *kōnenki*, but even these developments did not interest many. Nevertheless, from the 1920s onward the narrowly conceived, pathologically oriented terms fell out of use, and gynecologists adopted in their place the concepts of *kōnenki shōgai* (disorders) and *kōnenki shōkōgun* (syndrome), terms they could comfortably apply to nearly all types of discomfort experienced by middle-aged women, and ones they could use freely in conversations with patients.

Japanese gynecologists remained heavily under the influence of German medicine until the end of World War II. Yamada, for example, writing about menopause in 1927, cited only German references. At the top of his list of general symptoms of *kōnenki shōgai* appeared mood changes, memory loss, and becoming easily anxious or upset, to which he added the most common symptom, loss of temper, which happens to "90 percent of all women" (1927, 1097). He also pointed out that women are at high risk for cancer between the ages of forty and forty-five and linked this to age-related changes in "physical constitution." Other symptoms that he listed include dizziness, perspiration, ringing in the ears, headaches, and hot flashes, for which he invented a cumbersome word to gloss the German term—*sōkōekishakunekkan* (this particular neologism apparently never caught on with other physicians). He also included increased blood pressure, nausea, diarrhea, severe constipation, shortness of breath, spasmodic palpitations, frequent urination and pain on urination, perceptual disorders, and backache. All these symptoms he associated with changes in "ovarian function" and also with the autonomic nervous system.[9]

For women having a major problem with uterine bleeding Yamada recommended surgery or radiation therapy of the ovaries or the spleen. He also ascribed to the German literature's suggestion that irradiation of the thyroid gland was sometimes necessary since reduced ovarian function was believed to cause an increase in thyroid activity. He recommended hormone therapy and therapeutic baths but concluded that the selection of treatment depended on each individual case. This theme of a close association between changes in ovarian function, the autonomic nervous system, and a bevy of nonspecific symptoms remains central to gynecological literature in Japan right up to the present time and is also, as we have seen, the thrust of professional writing for the general public.

Dr. Mori Ichirō, who works in Kyushu, has spent the greater part of his career doing research on *kōnenki*. He thinks that neither its definition nor its symptoms coincide with the current Western concept of menopause. He distributed questionnaires among his patients several times over the past ten years and consistently found that shoulder stiffness, backache, headaches, fatigue, forgetfulness, a "heavy" head, constipation, eye problems, dizziness, and low blood pressure are the most frequently reported symptoms. Dr. Mori notes that perspiration and *hoteri* (hot flashes) occur to some extent in the two years immediately after the end of menstruation, but he emphasizes that they are apparently less frequent than in the "West" and cause few problems for most Japanese women (Mori 1978). He also points out that his observations and those of other Japanese doctors are compatible with what is common knowledge in Japan. He believes that "environmental differences" account for variation in symptom reporting and that Japanese patients can be taught to overcome most of their symptoms without resort to medication. In common with other gynecologists he recommends the use of *jiritsu kunren* (discipline or training of the autonomic nervous system, through meditative exercises).

Why are there discrepancies between Japanese descriptions of *kōnenki* and those that predominate in contemporary North America and Europe? Perhaps Japanese women and their doctors misread or misrepresent their bodies or simply lack the precision that has slowly emerged in North America over the past decade about the menopausal transition. Or, alternatively, are we perhaps misreading our bodies? I have been asked by more than one Japanese doctor, for example, why Western women make such a "fuss" about hot flashes. These remarks have a jingoistic ring to them because they have their source in the common belief, held mostly by people over fifty, that Western women cannot endure pain and suffering as can Japanese women. But, aside from lurking discrimination, confusion may nevertheless exist in the minds of Japanese physicians about the Menopausal Woman. What they read in international medical journals, observe in their own clinical experience, and find in their culturally constructed understanding of *kōnenki* do not mesh very well at all. Could it be that the menopausal body, and perhaps the Menopausal Woman as well, is not after all universal? Survey research proves to be a useful device for exploring this possibility.

2 Probabilities and *Kōnenki*

Enumerating the Signs and Symptoms of Kōnenki

The results of a cross-sectional survey questionnaire that I gave in 1984 to 1,738 Japanese women let us go beyond the accounts of *kōnenki* by women and health-care professionals recounted in the previous chapter. I received a total of 1,316 usable replies from women: the majority of them were factory workers, women who work on or manage farms, or housewives (many of whom have part-time work); all were between forty-five and fifty-five years old inclusively.[1] In contrast to most research on menopause the sample is not a clinical one and does not include women who had undergone gynecological surgery (of the uterus and/or ovaries) or who had stopped menstruating as a result of radio- or chemotherapy. My purpose was to find out about *kōnenki* as a "normal" experience.

I base my collection of symptom data on a method developed by Kaufert and Syrotuik (1981) and used in both Manitoba and Massachusetts (Kaufert 1984; McKinlay et al. 1987a; Avis and McKinlay 1990).[2] The survey tries, as these two studies did, to minimize the impact of preconceived notions about menopause on symptom reporting. A long list of questions about general health and reproductive history begins the survey, and explicit inquiries about *kōnenki* occur only when women are already halfway through their responses. In addition, those symptoms associated closely with menopause (in the West) form part of a longer list of general symptoms. Since the list must include the many nonspecific complaints, such as shoulder stiffness, dizziness, a heavy head, ringing in the ears, that are usually associated with *kōnenki*, it differs considerably from the original list and has fifty-seven items, in contrast to the original English version with twenty-two.

We experienced one difficulty over translation of the term *hot flash*. The Japanese language makes particularly fine distinctions among various bodily states, much more than English does, but, surprisingly, has no single word that unequivocally represents a hot flash. One term, *nobose*, usually translates as a "rush of blood to the head" or a "hot fit" and applies to vertigo or dizziness. But it is both an everyday and a medical term and can also describe a person who is "hotheaded," easily excited, or infatuated with someone. A second term, *hoteri*, can simply translate as feeling hot or flushed and most often expresses the East Asian propensity for becoming flushed when drinking alcohol. Both these terms specifically convey the idea of feelings of heat in the face and head. When women spontaneously talk about hot flashes they usually refer in a very general way to feelings of getting warm or hot (*atsuku naru*), but they use an everyday expression that can refer to the temperature of anything, animate or inanimate. A few women also refer to *kyū na nekkan* (a sudden feeling of heat). In the questionnaire we include all the terms, *nobose*, *hoteri*, and *kyū na nekkan*, together to gloss the meaning of a hot flash because we decided that "feelings of getting warm" (*atsuku naru*) were so vague that they could lead to considerable confusion. It is my impression that, over the years since the questionnaire was administered, the term *nobose* has become the most usual one in both popular and medical literature.

A researcher must recognize the problem of accurate recall when respondents are asked to remember events that happened longer than two weeks before they answer a questionnaire. Accordingly, as with the earlier Canadian and American studies, the survey asks the Japanese respondents to check which symptoms they had experienced in the previous two weeks. The overall frequency of responses to the Japanese symptom list is low.[3] The two symptoms usually associated with *kōnenki* in daily conversation are, not surprisingly, reported most frequently: shoulder stiffness (52 percent) and headaches (28 percent). Other symptoms are cited in a descending order of frequency as follows: lumbago, constipation, chilliness, irritability, insomnia, aches and pains in the joints, frequent colds, numbness, sore throat. Loss of memory and hot flashes are reported equally by only one hundred women (9.5 percent), followed closely by ringing in the ears, depression (8 percent), heavy feeling in the head, dizziness, and eventually, well down the list, at item thirty-five, night sweats by only 3.2 percent (Table 1).

When we compare a core symptom list of sixteen items, we note that Japanese responses are lower, often considerably so, than those in North America in every case but two, where they are about the same (Table 2).

Table 1. Percentage of Women Reporting Symptoms in the Previous
Two Weeks.

$(N = 1,141)$

Symptom		Fre-	Percent-
Japanese	English	quency	age
katakori	Shoulder stiffness	590	51.7
zutsū	Headache	316	27.7
yōtsū	Lumbago	256	22.4
benpi	Constipation	241	21.1
hieshō	Chilliness	186	16.3
iraira	Irritability	136	11.9
fumin	Insomnia	130	11.4
kansetsutsū	Aches and pains in the joints	124	10.9
kaze o yoku hiku	Frequent colds	119	10.4
shibirekan	Numbness	112	9.8
nodo no itami	Sore throat	109	9.6
kiokuryoku gentai	Loss of memory	108	9.5
kyū na nekkan (nobose, hoteri)	Hot flash	108	9.5
miminari	Ringing in the ears	97	8.5
ki ga meiru	Depression	90	7.9
zu chō kan	Heavy feeling in the head	87	7.6
memai	Dizziness	82	7.2
henzutsū	Migraine	77	6.7
mukatsuki	Nausea or upset stomach	70	6.1
shūchūryoku gentai	Difficulty in concentrating	70	6.1
sutoresu	Stress	62	5.4
shinkei no shinchō	Nervous tension	58	5.1
dōki	Palpitations	56	4.9
kintsū	Muscle pains	55	4.8
mukumi	Edema	52	4.6
seiyoku fushin	Lack of sexual desire	50	4.4
shokuyoku fushin	Loss of appetite	50	4.4
seki ga tsuzuku	Persistent cough	49	4.3
kyū na hakkan	Sudden perspiration	48	4.2
te ashi ga piripiri itamu	Tingling in the extremities	47	4.1
kentaikan	Exhaustion	45	3.9

Note: Cases of surgical menopause are not included.

Table 1. *Continued*

Symptom		Fre-	Percent-
Japanese	*English*	quency	age
yūutsu	Melancholy	44	3.9
ka fuku tzū	Abdominal pain	44	3.7
geri	Diarrhea	42	3.6
ne ase	Night sweats	41	3.2
handan ryoku gentai	Loss of judgment	36	2.9
ikigire	Shortness of breath	33	2.8
datsuryokukan	Loss of energy	32	2.7
zakotsutzū	Pain in the ischium	31	2.4
nyūbō no itami	Breast pain	27	2.4
yakan no honyō	Frequent night urination	27	1.9
sekitsuitzū	Pain in the spine	22	1.9
kyū na hiekan	Cold flash	20	1.8
zannyōkan	Feeling of residual urine	20	1.8
shita bara no kayumi	Abdominal itching	19	1.7
koshi ke	Leukorrhea	18	1.6
appakukan	Feeling of oppression	17	1.5
gyakujōkan	Rush of blood to the head	11	1.0
kyōfukan	Fear	11	1.0
shinkeishitsu ga hidoku naru	Increased nervousness	8	0.7
senkōkan	Coruscation	8	0.7
hainyōtzū	Pain on urination	6	0.5
chikaku kabin	Hyperesthesia	6	0.5
chikaku donma	Hypoesthesia	4	0.3
fusei shikyū shūkketsu	Uterine bleeding	4	0.3
gisōkan	Formication	2	0.2
daeki bunpitsu zōka	Increased salivation	2	0.2

Of particular interest is that among women in the Manitoba and Massachusetts samples, 31 percent and 35 percent respectively reported having experienced a hot flash in the past two weeks, and 20 percent and 11 percent reported night sweats—very much higher than the Japanese responses.

In order to examine the relation of menstrual status to the reporting of hot flashes, we divided respondents into pre-, peri-, and postmenopausal categories. In all three surveys women who stated that they were still

Table 2. Rates of Reporting Core Symptoms in Previous Two Weeks, by Study

Symptom	Percentage			Chi-square (2df)
	Japan	Manitoba	Massachusetts	
Diarrhea or constipation	24.5	12.8	21.4	62.8*
Persistent cough	4.2	5.2	10.1	68.4*
Upset stomach	6.3	12.9	16.1	85.1*
Shortness of breath	3.1	8.2	15.6	177.6*
Sore throat	10.5	9.1	10.7	2.9
Backache (lumbago; pain in the spine)	24.2	26.8	29.6	17.7*
Headache	27.5	33.8	37.2	45.2*
Aches or stiffness (aches and pains in the joints)	14.5	31.4	38.6	279.1*
Dizzy spells (dizziness)	7.1	12.3	11.1	21.4*
Tiredness (lack of energy; exhaustion)	6.0	39.8	38.1	503.3*
Irritability	11.5	17.1	29.9	246.6*
Feeling blue or depressed (depression; melancholy)	10.3	23.4	35.9	365.1*
Trouble sleeping (insomnia)	11.7	30.4	30.6	189.8*
Hot flashes or flushes and/or sudden perspiration	12.3	31.0	34.8	246.6*
Cold sweats and/or night sweats	3.8	19.8	11.4	158.2*

Note: In order to create a core symptom list across the studies, we collapsed several of the Japanese categories from Table 12.

menstruating regularly were classed as premenopausal; the perimenopausal group included women whose menstrual cycle had become irregular during the previous year or who had menstruated in the past twelve but not the previous three months. Women who had not menstruated for twelve months or more were considered to be postmenopausal. As we would expect, the incidence of hot flashes is associated with menstrual status in the three samples, but their relative frequency, as already noted, is very low in Japan. Similarly, the incidence of night sweats is very low and not significantly related to menstrual status (Table 3).

Table 3. Reports of Vasomotor Symptoms, by Menopausal Status

Menopausal Status	Japan[a]	Manitoba[b]	Massachusetts[b]
	Hot Flashes		
Premenopause	6.4	13.8	17.9
Perimenopause	13.5	39.7	38.1
Postmenopause	15.2	41.5	43.9
Total (100%)	1,104	1,039	5,505
	$x^2 = 15.77$	$x^2 = 84.17$	$x^2 = 269.510$
	Night Sweats		
Premenopause	4.1	10.6	5.5
Perimenopause	4.0	27.6	11.7
Postmenopause	3.0	22.2	11.3
Total (100%)	1,104	1,039	5,484
	$x^2 = 0.772$	$x^2 = 33.71$	$x^2 = 31.335$

Note: Massachusetts N differs because of missing data. Cases of surgical menopause have been removed.

[a] $p = 0.00$ and 0.68
[b] $p = 0.00$

Fewer than 20 percent of Japanese women responded that at some time in the past (there were no time constraints on this question) they experienced at least one hot flash, whereas 65 percent of Canadian women said that they had.[4] When peri- and postmenopausal, but not premenopausal, women were asked if they had ever experienced a hot flash, 25 percent of the Japanese women answered that they had, in contrast to approximately 75 percent of both the Canadian and American women respectively; the results would indicate that many fewer Japanese than North American women can expect to experience a hot flash during their middle years.

The present results agree with those of Dr. Mori discussed in the previous chapter: among those women who had ceased to menstruate within the previous year, nearly 18 percent of the sample had experienced a hot flash in the previous two weeks. This number drops off to 13 percent among those who had stopped menstruating between one and two years earlier, and still further to 8 percent among those who had not menstruated for three years. Among Japanese women, hot flashes seem to be rather tightly clustered around the end of menstruation.

In terms of severity, only 3 percent of Japanese women reported experiencing hot flashes almost daily in the previous two weeks, whereas among the Canadian and American women 15 percent and 18 percent respectively reported a daily occurrence.[5] It seems that with respect to both incidence and severity, North American women suffer considerably more from hot flashes than Japanese women do. Of the 108 Japanese women who were having hot flashes, 75 percent reported that they experienced only a little discomfort or were undisturbed by them; nearly 90 percent said that they were only a little or not at all upset emotionally by the experience, leaving fewer than 10 percent who were clearly troubled; over 90 percent stated that they were not embarrassed, or only a little, when flashes occurred. This last result was somewhat of a surprise to me since many Japanese women, in particular urban residents, seem to be quite self-conscious about the image they project in public.

Because Japanese culture encourages concern about an aching body, shoulder stiffness, headaches, and backaches, perhaps many women simply ignore hot flashes entirely and hence do not report them. I think this possibility highly unlikely, however; people in Japan are in general very sensitive to small physical changes of all kinds in their bodies and use an exquisitely nuanced vocabulary to express these changes (a vocabulary that closely resembles the language of the traditional Japanese medical system, Lock 1980a).[6] The absence of a specific word for hot flash, therefore, seems highly significant.

Deliberate underreporting because of embarrassment or reserve is also unlikely, I think; since the actual experience of a hot flash rarely produces embarrassment, retrospective reporting in a confidential questionnaire would not seem to pose a problem. Moreover, anyone well acquainted with Japan becomes aware sooner or later that people usually discuss physical attributes and changes in their bodies frankly and openly, particularly with others of the same gender, and may, if anything, cause embarrassment to an outsider rather than local listeners. Confusion over terminology of the hot flash could lead to underreporting, but when discussing this possibility in the interviews I noticed that some women reported barely perceptible and highly transitory changes. Given a well-developed Japanese consciousness about changes in internal body states and the fact that, on the whole, informants were trying to be cooperative when filling out the questionnaire, there may be some overreporting.[7]

In light of these results, to claim unequivocally that the hot flash is the most usual symptom of menopause, and that between 75 and 80 percent or more of all women will experience it, is clearly inappropriate. Yet this claim shows up often in the Western medical literature, as we have seen. The Japanese data indicate that, although hot flashes are certainly experienced by some women, the overall incidence is 25 percent or lower; this figure includes those women who had just one or two. The question immediately arises as to whether these findings result from cultural or biological differences or both. I am convinced that both contribute, and that we must entertain the possibility of biological variation in the endocrine system within and between populations. We might account for such variation as differences in nutrition, or in genetic makeup, or in some combination of the two. A recent letter to the *Lancet* reports preliminary comparative research into a typical Japanese diet, which includes soybean and many soy products such as tofu and miso, making it rich in phytoestrogens. The researchers, commenting on the findings of the survey research I conducted, conclude that a diet that contains natural estrogens could make a significant difference in the incidence of hot flashes (Adlercreutz et al. 1992, 1233). This difference in turn will influence shared cultural expectations, subjective reporting, and interpretations of *kōnenki*.[8] Certain interested parties, after reading these results, have already latched onto soybean as the answer to all menopausal problems (*Vegetarian Times* 1993). It has been shown that the level of circulating hormones in the bloodstream is not directly related to the incidence of hot flashes (Hutton 1978); a reductionistic explanation dependent on dietary intake is not satisfactory. My position is that we should investigate the soybean story more thoroughly, as just one possible component in a complex biological puzzle profoundly shaped by cultural expectations and beliefs.

There are other examples of biological variation among populations, one common to the majority of the world's peoples being the difficulty of digesting milk in the absence of the enzyme lactase (Harrison 1975); another, shared by the majority of East Asians and native populations of the Americas, concerns alcohol metabolism (it usually manifests as a flushing of the face after alcohol consumption, owing to the lack of the enzyme aldehyde dehydrogenase); a third is variation among populations in reactions to medication, particularly antidepressants (Lin et al. 1986; Yamashita and Asano 1979). I suspect that numerous other differences will be found, if and when we grow more willing to acknowledge the possibility of their existence. At present the very idea of systematically investigating biological difference leaves us vulnerable to accusations of racism, since such investigation is usually assumed to involve value judgments about human behavior and capabilities; hence the possibility of a balanced dialogue on the subject is not easily entertained.

Nevertheless, I believe these findings allow us to postulate not only that cultural beliefs influence the construction, experience, and interpretation of aging and other biological processes but that biological difference—sometimes obvious, at other times very subtle—molds and contains the subjective experience of individuals and the creation of cultural interpretations. A dialectic of this kind between culture and biology implies that we must contextualize interpretations about the body not only as products of local histories, knowledge, and politics but also as local biologies. I suggest, therefore, that we cannot assume the universality of either the menopausal body or the Menopausal Woman.

Kōnenki *and the Aching Body*

In order to ascertain if Japanese women judge themselves to be in *kōnenki* based on their menstrual status, we asked them to assign themselves to one of four categories in the questionnaire: no sign, beginning, middle, or end of *kōnenki*. This subjective assessment overlaps somewhat, but by no means entirely, with an objective epidemiological judgment based strictly on menstrual status (Figure 1). Among women in the sample classified as not yet menopausal (because they were still menstruating regularly), only 50 percent of the respondents replied that they had no sign of *kōnenki*. At the other end of the spectrum, among women classified as postmenopausal (that is, those who had not menstruated for more than a year), 24 percent regarded themselves as not having yet started, 12 percent as being at the beginning, and another 30 percent as in the middle of *kōnenki* (Table 4

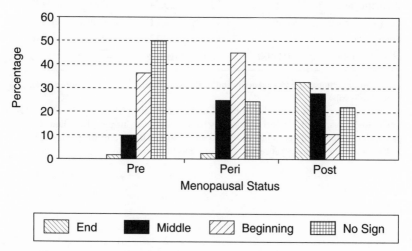

Figure 1. Japan: *Kōnenki* Status of Women

Table 4. Cross-Tabulation of *Kōnenki* or Menopausal Status,
by Study

Menopausal Status	End %	Middle %	Beginning %	No Sign %	Total Number (100%)
Japan: Self-defined Kōnenki Status					
Surgical menopause[a]	15.5	26.4	20.9	37.3	110
Premenopause	0.6	11.4	37.3	50.6	332
Perimenopause	2.1	26.4	46.5	24.9	329
Postmenopause	34.3	29.8	12.0	23.9	376
$x^2 = 348.7$	$p = 0.00$		Missing cases = 169		
Manitoba: Self-defined Menopausal Status					
Surgical menopause[a]	27.7	39.4	16.1	16.5	249
Premenopause	0.3	15.2	37.5	46.5	389
Perimenopause	7.1	38.4	47.8	6.0	268
Postmenopause	59.8	31.0	4.7	3.6	358
$x^2 = 713.3$	$p = 0.00$		Missing cases = 46		
Massachusetts: Self-defined Menopausal Status[b]					
Surgical menopause[a]	41.18	23.53	17.65	10.29	68
Premenopause	0.00	7.54	29.74	58.66	491
Perimenopause	5.56	21.32	46.11	9.16	1,529
Postmenopause	44.58	18.75	9.17	0.83	240
$x^2 = 1195.865$	$p = 0.0000$		Missing cases = 7		

[a]Surgical menopause assessed according to the Korpilampi definition (Kaufert et al. 1986, 1285–86).

[b]The data are taken from follow-ups 1–3 of the longitudinal Massachusetts study. Age range: 46–57 years. The Massachusetts study has an additional category, Near End of Menopause, that includes 7.35 percent for surgical menopause, 4.07 percent for premenopause, 17.85 percent for perimenopause, and 26.67 percent for postmenopause.

and Figure 1). These results confirm the ideas expressed by many women in narrative form, that they tend to ignore or minimize the importance of their menstrual pattern when assessing whether or not they are in *kōnenki.*

Moreover, Japanese women's responses about the relation of *kōnenki* to menstruation do not correspond to answers given by Canadian or American women about menopause and menstruation. The statements made by North American women show that on the whole they consider, as objective scientific observers do, menstrual irregularity and cessation to be the significant marker of menopause, an event sometimes but by no means always accompanied by hot flashes, which they interpret as another significant sign of menopause (Table 4 and Figures 2 and 3).

When we compare Japanese women who define themselves as being in the middle of *kōnenki* with the rest of the Japanese sample by the number of symptoms that they report, they consistently report more. Those women who state that they are all through with *kōnenki* have fewer symptoms, and those who have no sign of *kōnenki* report the smallest number of symptoms. These findings suggest that the presence of symptoms such as shoulder stiffness, headache, and chilliness encourage Japanese women to think of themselves as being in *kōnenki*, regardless of whether they are menstruating regularly or not. Whereas in Japan menstrual status has no effect on the number of symptoms reported, in Manitoba and Massachusetts (setting aside cases of surgical menopause), women in perimenopause

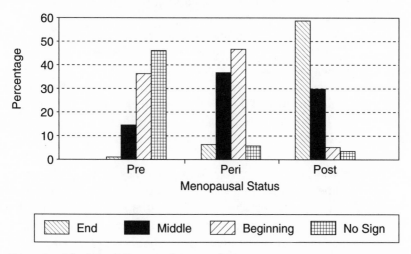

Figure 2. Manitoba: Menopausal Status of Women

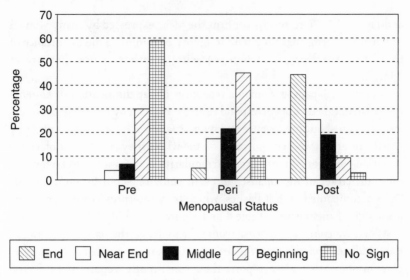

End   ☐ Near End   ■ Middle   ▨ Beginning   ▦ No Sign

Figure 3.   Massachusetts: Menopausal Status of Women

report the most symptoms (Table 5), reinforcing the argument that the symptoms associated with *kōnenki* are not the same as those of menopause and that the concepts are not one and the same thing.

Of those few Japanese women who report experiencing hot flashes, most classify themselves as being in the middle of *kōnenki*; but among those who report having experienced a hot flash at some time, 12 percent state that they have no sign of *kōnenki*, indicating that for them at least the hot flash seems to be an insignificant symptom.

Not all the symptoms on the questionnaire relate to *kōnenki*: frequent colds and a sore throat for example, which were reported quite often, do not. But all the other frequently reported symptoms could derive from a disturbance in the autonomic system and therefore rank as bona fide symptoms of *kōnenki*. In terms of their own culture, then, Japanese women are reading their bodies "correctly," and their judgment corresponds closely to the objective assessment of Japanese doctors implicating changes in the autonomic nervous system.

The complexity of the narratives given by Japanese women only rarely results, as some might be tempted to believe, from minds unschooled in human biology. What they reveal, on the contrary, is women's unwillingness to reduce the meaning of the end of menstruation to endocrine changes alone. Even when the interviewer probed them for detail about the biological specifics of *kōnenki*, most narratives, although their content varies somewhat, resemble that given by Teraoka-*san*, who at forty-nine

Table 5. Reports of Five or More Core Symptoms, by
Menopausal Status

Menopausal Status	Japan	Manitoba	Massachusetts
Surgical menopause	9.9	29.1	41.4
Perimenopause	8.3	34.2	34.6
Premenopause	9.9	17.6	22.5
Postmenopause	10.4	27.4	32.1

Note: Core symptoms are diarrhea or constipation, persistent cough, nausea, shortness of breath, sore throat, backache, headache, aches and pains or stiffness in the joints, dizzy spells, tiredness, irritability, feeling blue or depressed, trouble sleeping, hot flashes or flushes and/or sudden perspiration, cold sweats and/or night sweats.

manages by herself a flourishing Nagano farm. Teraoka-*san* thinks she has been in *kōnenki* for four or five years.

"I learned about *kōnenki* from a lecture that the public health nurse gave to our women's group. She gave a very up-to-the-minute talk with slides and so on, and so she didn't say anything about *chi no michi*, but I often heard about that when I was young. I suppose it has something to do with women's diseases, but I don't really know what it means . . . My mother mentioned it often but I don't hear about it anymore. I think *kōnenki* starts about forty-five, and I suppose it's the modern *chi no michi*. Ever since I was around forty years old, whenever I had anything wrong I started to suspect it might be because I was in *kōnenki*; my hips started to hurt and I had lumbago, so I thought that was it, but the nurse said it's not likely to happen until forty-five. I can't concentrate like I used to, and that's definitely *kōnenki*. When I talk about it with my friends they all complain of headaches and lumbago and so on."

"Do you still have your periods?"

"Oh yes, but I think I'm getting to the point where they're going to end. I'll be glad about that. I don't think about my body too much. I think people who fuss and worry about their bodies get *jiritsu shinkei shitchōshō* [disturbances of the autonomic nervous system], and then they're likely to have a difficult *kōnenki*. It all depends on one's attitude really."

"When do you think you'll be through with *kōnenki*?"

"Somewhere between fifty-six and fifty-eight, I suppose."

"Do you think the headaches and lumbago that your friends have will go away then?"

"Yes, I think the body gets adjusted and finds a new balance, and so probably headaches won't happen so often. Lumbago—well, maybe that's different—maybe that's just plain getting old, like poor concentration, and gray hair, and so on."

Like Teraoka-*san*, by far the majority of Japanese women make it clear that for them *kōnenki* represents, above all, an inevitable part of the aging process. They focus on the signs of aging of which the end of menstruation is but one. *Kōnenki* is an entirely natural event that may produce some temporary discomfort, but one that is of little concern to many women. Only 4 percent of the sample responded that *kōnenki* is of great importance and 33 percent of some importance, whereas 63 percent stated that it is an event of "little" or "no importance."[9]

Several Japanese women state explicitly that *kōnenki* is the beginning of old age (*rōka genshō*) and, although having little significance as such, can be a potent sign for the future. Some women report, for example, mixed feelings of regret and nostalgia, both for their departed youth and for what the future may bring, most particularly in terms of ill health. At the same time they often express relief about the end of menstruation and unwanted pregnancies.[10] Because *kōnenki* is thought of as a process and not an event (the concept, it will be recalled, has the idea of a time span built into it), its occurrence encourages reflection about the life cycle as a continuous process and reinforces a sense of continuity between past, present, and future.

Although *kōnenki* represents physical aging for most women, other familiar meanings attach to it. For example, several women in telling their narratives emphasized sadness, as the nineteenth-century novelist Oguri Fūyo suggested was the case, because their reproductive years were over, and described *kōnenki* as the end of one's "functioning" or "prime" as a woman. One woman reported that her husband had teased her that she was not a "real" woman any longer. But when asked in the questionnaire if they worried about not being able to bear any more children, fewer than 2 percent responded in the affirmative; only 30 percent expressed unhappiness at the thought of their children leaving home (some women continue to live in an extended family, with a married child).[11] A few women stated that they were concerned that from now on they would be at risk for being called "granny" or "mother-in-law" rather than "wife" or "mother" in daily life, and in the survey just over 40 percent admitted to being "a little" worried about loss of attractiveness.[12] But even when they thought about loss of reproductive capacity and sexual attractiveness, they usually still emphasized what the future might have in store for an older woman, most notably in declining health and strength, rather than long nostalgically for the past. For example, over 80 percent of women when answering the questionnaire expressed concern about the possibility of illness in the future but appeared relatively unconcerned about their own death, although more than 60 percent of them worried about the death of family members.[13]

For most Japanese women, therefore, *kōnenki* signals the beginning of an inevitable physical decline accompanied by a rising concern about future illness that raises the possibility of becoming a burden on other people, something many women worry about a good deal.[14] It also acts as a reminder of the likelihood that in the near future they will have to nurse other family members, particularly elderly parents-in-law with whom they live. And yet *kōnenki* does not have close symbolic associations in the minds of most women with either loss of reproductive capacity or the specter of death.

Sometimes, as Tabata-*san*'s narrative in the previous chapter showed, *kōnenki* becomes an extra burden in an already troubled life. But even in cases such as these women rarely think of it as causing social or psychological troubles. On the contrary, unresolved social problems drain the individual of her natural willpower and energy to surmount any expectable duress that *kōnenki* may produce.

Despite the negative myths about *kōnenki*, most women suffer no disabling symptoms and apparently feel no deep sense of loss at this time of life. When encouraged to create their own stories about middle age and aging, as opposed to answers for an interviewer's questions, relatively few Japanese women give much weight to either the end of menstruation or *kōnenki*. Instead, they choose to focus much more on human relationships, and the way in which in middle age a woman turns from being concerned primarily with children and their care to enjoy a brief spell of relative freedom ("mother's time of rebellion"), before she becomes fully occupied with the care of aged people for a good number of years. It is changes in gendered activities, the social rather than the physical consequences of aging, that are usually uppermost in women's minds when discussing middle age. *Kōnenki* is peripheral to most discourse, although it acts as a portent of things to come.

Making *kōnenki* the point of departure for a discussion about midlife is, therefore, a rather awkward imposition in Japan. This is particularly so because from birth to death people think of the body primarily as a social rather than a biological entity: individuals do not treat their own bodies as their personal possessions but as parts of the family into which they were born. In order to place these descriptions of *kōnenki* into perspective I turn next to the life stories of individual women, where we soon see that topics other than *kōnenki* have preference in narratives about middle age.

3 Resignation, Resistance, Satisfaction—Narratives of Maturity

As a landscape in the far distance
is how human life appears
and in autumn wind
upon the extended fields
a black locomotive goes.

(Saitō Fumi)

Ishida Atsuko, a divorced housewife of fifty-three who works part-time in a company designing interior decors, was the individual who first alerted me to the fact that by focusing on *kōnenki* I was forcing middle-aged women into an inappropriate pigeonhole.

"Why do you want to study *kōnenki*?" Atsuko asked. "It's not a big deal at all. Japanese women have a lot of problems, but *kōnenki* is really low on the list."

We were sitting in the cramped but sunny living room of her high-rise apartment outside Osaka where I had been her guest for a few weeks. I replied that over the last fifteen years or so in North America menopause had been a topic of considerable concern, and that I believed it was so in part because of the women's movement and also because of a climate of rather aggressive medicalization.

"Well, meetings and books about *kōnenki* are springing up all over the place here too, but I think that's mostly because doctors are trying to make money out of a few nervous types. After all, Japanese women live the longest in the world, so most of us must be pretty healthy.[1] What we still have to deal with, though, is the remains of the feudal system. You know, the fact that women are pushed out of company work when they have children—that we are still number two behind the men, despite changes in the law. These things are much more important than a few aches and pains."

Having already completed the survey research and conducted many interviews on *kōnenki*, I was feeling particularly receptive to Atsuko-*san's* chiding. What I now wanted to know was why articles about *kōnenki* were starting to spring up everywhere, when clearly the majority of women were in agreement with Atsuko and did not find it a particularly trying time. Was menopause indeed, as Atsuko suggested, simply an entrepreneurial creation of the medical world? Or were the Japanese media with their sensitive antennae picking up on the rising interest in menopause in the West? Or alternatively, was something else involved, a change of consciousness on the part of women, perhaps, about which even Atsuko was not aware? Atsuko agreed with me that if I collected life histories from several women, then I would begin to get a little more perspective on the problem, and she consented to be the first storyteller.[2]

Dutiful Daughter-in-Law

"I really didn't notice when I went through *kōnenki* at all because things were so difficult here at home at the time. I suppose, thinking about it, it must have happened about three years ago.

"I don't think my husband and I ever had a very good marriage, but when my mother-in-law moved in things started to get worse. She was widowed, and because my husband is the oldest son, she decided that she wanted to come here and live with us; my daughter was living here too then, in this small apartment. *Obāsan* had the front room where you're sleeping now. As you know, I teach the tea ceremony to students here at home; that front room has the special tatami mat that can be taken up easily so the teakettle can be heated up in there. It wasn't easy after *obāsan* came because there was always tension about having to ask her to stay out of her room for a few hours once a week while I met the students. My husband and I slept in the room next to hers, with just the sliding doors separating us from her—that was very difficult too. My daughter was in the little single room at the back where I sleep now."

"It must have been very crowded for you all."

"When she first came it wasn't so bad, although she was quite bossy and tried to make me do everything her way. I changed a lot of my habits about cooking and so on just to keep the peace. But she went out a lot and was involved with various social activities. Then, all of a sudden it seemed, she started to decline quite rapidly, and about three years after she'd been living with us I noticed she was becoming forgetful and doing strange things like hiding food in the closets. Then she had a mild stroke and she was in hospital for a good number of months. After she came out, things were never the same again. She was taking medication, but she had become really senile, and she was incontinent too. I did all the nursing myself, and of course, the worst part was changing the diapers. She was bedridden and wouldn't do anything for herself."

"Did your husband help at all?"

"No! You know what Japanese men are like. It was my job, naturally, to look after *obāsan* and he barely talked to her even when he was here. Toward the end she would call him in when he came home at nights and tell him I was trying to poison her by giving her rotten food. All he did was to tell me to try harder to be nicer to her. I really didn't go out much for about eleven years except to do the shopping. I always had to be here looking after her."

"Couldn't you get any outside help? No social services or anything?"

"Well, the doctor came twice a week, and he was always very kind, but of course there was nothing to be done. He said if things got really bad, I could ask to have a volunteer come round sometimes, but I didn't feel comfortable about that, and *obāsan* wouldn't tolerate the idea for an instant. In fact, we tried a volunteer one time and *obāsan* was so awful to her I didn't dare ask anyone in again. When my daughter got older she was very helpful though, and sometimes, after she came home from school, I could go out for a while."

"How did you endure it?"

"You know, Japanese women still think they're supposed to endure everything and put everyone else first. I decided I'd see the job through until she died. Fortunately it happened almost at the same time as my daughter left home and entered college. I wasn't angry with *obāsan*—she was pitiful—but I decided I couldn't live with my husband any longer. I asked him to leave. I own this apartment so I just drove him out. He'd been having an affair for some time anyway, so I just said he had to go. It was then that I started to look back over my early life and felt some regrets. Not that it could have been any other way, I suppose . . . Well, maybe it *could* have been different. My mother died when I was thirteen, and I had four young brothers. My father decided to take me out of school and make me into a kind of maid at home. I had to do all the housework for all those men. I think he probably could have afforded a caretaker quite easily, but he didn't want to ask a stranger into the house."

"Didn't he ever marry again?"

"No. So what I really regret now is not having had a proper education. All my brothers went to university, but I didn't even go to high school."

"That must have been really hard on you when you had to find a job after your separation."

"Well, not too bad considering, because I'd done a lot of reading all those years I was looking after *obāsan*, and I'd started to get interested in interior design as well, so my mind wasn't dead. Anyway, for most ordinary jobs they expect to have to train you more or less from scratch, so they weren't too hesitant, even though I'm getting a bit long in the tooth. I have an exam next week, and I'm rather nervous about that."

"So you didn't have to look around a long time to find a job?"

"No, not really, because I don't want to work full-time. I can manage if I work two or three days a week. They weren't looking for a young, full-time woman, but for someone older like me so they don't have to pay any benefits. It works out well because I go to study two mornings a week, I work two and a half days a week, and I still have time to teach the tea classes on Saturday afternoons."

"Do you feel happy in your new life?"

"So far it's fine—I'm fairly healthy, and I don't mind commuting too much. I've made some friends at work, but I'm a bit lonely sometimes, especially because my daughter lives in Tokyo now."

"Do you see your brothers and their families?"

"Not very often, about once a year."

Kōnenki does not loom large in this narrative, and Atsuko is far more concerned about the recent changes in her family life than she is about the biological changes of aging. Like many other divorced women of her age, she has no interest in getting married again and, although she looks after herself carefully, she spends very little time or money on cosmetics and clothes (unlike many other urban women today). She is not representative of middle-aged Japanese women in one other way, in that divorce is still rather unusual in Japan—the national divorce rate in 1988 was 1.26 per 100,000 people (Nihon Fujindantai Rengōkai 1989). In the present survey, 88 percent were married, 3 percent single, 4 percent widowed, and 3 percent divorced or separated.[3] But divorce is on the increase in Japan, particularly among middle-aged women, who often wait until their children complete their education or marry and who then take whatever money they managed to salt away and depart. These women, as of 1986, are entitled to half of their husbands' pensions should they divorce after thirty or more years of marriage. Until that year they were unlikely to receive financial support, even if they sought it through a court order, and, since most of those who want a divorce spent their adult lives as housewives (*sengyō shufu*), they are rarely well equipped to manage in the world at large. Households headed by divorced mothers have an average income that is about 40 percent of that of households headed by men (*Mainichi Daily News* 1985a).

Madoka Yoriko has become rather well known in Japan as the author of a best-selling book, *The Housewife Syndrome* (*Shufu shōkōgun* 1982).

She also runs a divorce counseling service that goes by the unlikely name of Smiling Divorce Consultations (*Niko niko rikon kōza*). From her many years of experience with divorce in Japan she is keenly sensitive to the way in which most women, even today, try to suppress their own feelings and stay in a marriage even if they are extremely unhappy. When I talked to her in 1984 she said that one obvious change these days is that some older women have decided that they will opt for insecurity and relative poverty rather than continue in an unhappy marriage once their task of raising the children is finished. National statistics support the impression Madoka-*san* received from running the counseling service, since the proportion of women aged forty-five and over who are divorcing has been increasing steadily for the past thirty years (Kōseisho 1986).

In other respects Atsuko is typical of many Japanese women in their early fifties: when they were children, their education was considered relatively unimportant and was frequently sacrificed to the needs of other family members (see also Lebra 1984a; Plath 1980). In many narratives a theme of regret clearly emerges about the way in which choices made by their parents when the women were very young imposed major limitations on what they can realistically expect to do in middle age. A large number of women were trained, however, in one or more of the traditional Japanese art forms, most often flower arranging, the tea ceremony, or calligraphy, in preparation for marriage. Many of them by middle age hold high rank in these arts and are respected teachers, but the majority teach only two or three students in their own homes. For women whose husbands want them not to work, or for women who do not want to try to overcome the many obstacles involved in getting back into the work force after raising children, to teach the traditional arts can be a rewarding compromise. In fact, for many it is no compromise at all but a highly creative use of time.

Taking care, or waiting to take care, of fragile or sick elderly relatives is a theme that recurs again and again in these narratives. As a typical Japanese woman of her age, Atsuko-*san* assumed without question that it was her duty to look after her mother-in-law. She stated that it was hard work, which she often resented, but she took pride in "seeing the job through" and only then put her plans for divorce into action. It is commonly believed in Japan that younger generations of women may be unwilling to continue such dedication. For example, marrying off the eldest son is exceptionally difficult because so few contemporary brides want to live with their parents-in-law and above all run the risk of eventually having to look after an aged and infirm mother-in-law. In rural areas the prospect of marrying an eldest son, running a farm, and living with the in-laws is so unappetizing to most young women that families must accept foreign brides from South and Southeast Asia and South America.

At first glance mothers-in-law, traditional arts, and educational levels seem unrelated to *kōnenki*, but these themes are repeatedly woven into the rhetoric about middle age. The themes appear in popular and professional literature and in the narratives of individual women with varying life-styles. But if an interviewer rigorously directs conversation to a narrow focus on biological changes, symptoms, and mood swings, then these crucial social themes never surface; they are censored at the outset.

Factory Work in the Forest

Matsuda-*san* has lived all her life in a tiny forestry village in Shiga prefecture—a beautiful village, with a mountain river cascading through the middle of it, replete with traditional-style large wooden houses with plots of land around them where carefully tended vegetables and flowers of all kinds grow in abundance. Although compared with urban houses the buildings are rather generous in size, outdoors in the village itself a visitor always has the sense of being in a narrow space because the mountains, densely planted with pine trees, rise up steeply around the village from the narrow valley where the river and the house-lined road wind their way out, toward Lake Biwa. A few thatched roofs remain in the village, but tiles or surprisingly elegant painted metal sheeting will replace them when next they need redoing. The most obtrusive change is the presence of four or five very small factory outlets where village women work as part-time employees. Most of the factories are converted houses or storage places where ten or twelve women sit side by side at small industrial machines busily sewing car upholstery, bedding materials, or room dividers.

Matsuda-*san* is fifty years old and lives with her husband in a rather dilapidated house. Her only son is married and lives nearby in a newer elegant house, very spacious by Japanese standards. As she talks, she betrays a tension between her usual extroverted easygoing style and the constraint she feels at talking with a foreign professor, who sometimes loses her way in the local dialect. As do many of the other women living in rural areas, Matsuda-*san* starts by emphasizing the narrowness of her life, and with it the idea that she is not adequately educated.

> "I've never been anywhere, and I don't know anything. I'd like to visit some other parts of Japan ... I hate the city, but I'd like to go and see the mountains around Kyoto [about three hours away by car]. My father was a charcoal maker and he grew rice as well. Even today we grow all our own food; we have rice paddies, and

vegetable fields, and we grow tea too. I even make my own miso. I'm always on the run, because I work in a little factory in our village as well as taking care of the fields and the trees."

"What do you do in the factory?"

"We make pleated curtains out of vinyl leather for dividing up rooms—I sit and sew at the machine all day—most of the women in the village work at sewing now."

"Do you like your work?"

"Yes, but it's the same thing over and over. I'd like to try doing some other kind of work because I get bored. Really what I'd like to do is operate a big machine of some kind all by myself."

"It sounds as though you have a really busy life."

"Well yes, it's because I have to take care of the trees as well, I almost never stop working. Actually, I don't like to let up, and so even during our rest periods at the factory I go off and collect wild vegetables. Then on Saturdays, Sundays, and holidays I have to go up into the mountain to look after the trees."

"What has to be done to the trees?"

"The small ones have to be taken care of, you have to see they don't get knocked over with the snow and so on and weed around them. It's hard work, especially in the winter. Sometimes my husband comes too, but usually I go by myself."

"Tell me about your daily life: how do you fit everything into your day?"

"I get up about 5:00 A.M.—not very early really—put on the rice cooker, do the laundry and the house cleaning, and take the dog for a walk. I work at the factory from 8:00 A.M. until 4:30 P.M., and then when I finish I do the shopping and pick up some fish. Then I go home and change and go off to the fields. I come home about 6:30 and make dinner. My husband works in an office in a small town about thirty minutes away. He almost always does overtime and gets home about 8:00 in the evening. In the evenings I often read, we have a library in the village . . . I do flower arrangement sometimes and a little calligraphy. I'm still in the village group for housewives. I'm supposed to leave that when I'm fifty-five, but when I'm sixty I can join the old people's group.

"I go to bed about 11:30, I guess I have about five or six hours of sleep a night. Sometimes I forget to write in my diary, when there are too many things to do.

"I'm in *kōnenki*, that's for sure. I get tired easily these days, and I have headaches and my periods are over—or irregular, anyway—I don't think I've had one for about a year. Anyway, I get really tired."

"When did you start to get tired?"

"Last year. I can't stick at things the way I used to. I'll get something like my sewing almost finished, and then I'll just let it go. Before, I'd have stayed up all night to finish it. It's because of my age . . . I hate it—I'm not young anymore. When I was young I used to try to take care of my complexion at night, but nowadays I'm so tired I don't even feel like washing properly, I just lie in the bath and soak . . . I'm just getting old."

"Were you expecting something like this to happen?"

"Yes. I used to go and work in the rice fields with *obāsan* and she always told me, 'Things are fine for women while they have their periods, but after a while *kōnenki* starts, then you feel irritable and get weaker and can't do anything properly anymore. You young people are lucky.' "

"Does *kōnenki* have some relation to when a woman stops menstruating?"

"Yes, I think so. While menstruation is regular her body is fine, but when it stops, various problems start to happen. For a lot of people their eyes get worse, and the first thing I noticed was losing dexterity, so I can't tie knots in thread easily or do up buttons smoothly anymore."

"At what age do you think *kōnenki* starts?"

"It starts about forty-five, I think—*obāsan* told me that a few years before they stop menstruating most women start to get irritable, then five or six years after their last period, things settle down again. I'm forty-five now so I have about another five years to go, I suppose.

"My husband says I'm not as spry as I used to be, but he's no comfort. He was an only child and he thinks about himself all the time. The people round here think he's selfish and tell him to give me a hand, but he doesn't change. *Obāsan* was a wonderful person though. I was really sad when she died. She cared about me more than my own mother, and she really helped me when I had to go to hospital with a heart problem, not like my husband who wouldn't even buy me some oranges or get me an ice bag when I was in bed."

"Did you ever think about changing your life?"

"I never thought about divorce because my own family was so strict. My mother always said, 'When a woman marries she has many troubles; if she is thrown out of the front door, she must go right around and come in again though the back door; if she's thrown out of the back door, then she must come in at the front.' So I was always prepared to stand up to anything. My mother would never even listen to my complaints, and when two of my brothers were killed in accidents I felt very lonely. I've had so many troubles I think of writing them all down in a novel. I took care of the whole family at home from when I was in third grade, because my mother had to go to the mountains with my father to make charcoal."

"It sounds as though your life was really hard when you were young."

"Yes, it's been tough, but it was nothing like as hard as my mother's. She really suffered for us. Thanks to her raising us strictly I can stand anything."

"Right now do you have any worries?"

"I worry most about my health . . . I hope that neither my husband nor I get sick. Aside from that, things are fine really. My son is married now and I asked him to stay in the village for at least ten years even though they wanted to go to Tokyo. He agreed. They come over for meals all the time, and my daughter-in-law works in the fields with me sometimes because she doesn't have any other work to do. In our village we've never had the custom of the newly married couple living with their parents. We've always had plenty of land to build a new house when it's needed, so they live separately for at least five years and then move in when the old people are too frail to manage by themselves anymore. I don't expect my daughter-in-law will take care of me though, she'll be in Tokyo by then. That's why I pray at the local shrine that I'll die quickly if I get sick."

In nearly all Japanese narratives about daily life, talk about work and being busy are central, and in the minds of most women *kōnenki* and work are intimately related, as Matsuda-*san*'s narrative indicates. The remarkable blend she portrays in her own life—the hard repetitive work of both farming and factory, but also the keeping of a diary, the dreams of writing a book, and, until lately at least, the concern about her complexion—are by no means unusual. A good number of women who live a hard-working rural life show a keen interest in "culture" and in becoming cultured. Matsuda-*san*'s description of her working day is probably not exaggerated very much at all. Many women possess a keen sense of competition and pride they exhibit by getting up early and starting out the day's work while everyone else is still sleeping. Very few would admit to the possibility of staying in bed while their husbands made their own breakfasts, and I suspect this could happen only rarely in the Japanese countryside. In the cities it is probably more common but even then usually only among younger people.

There is a glimpse in Matsuda-*san*'s story of the community life still active in rural areas, and of the age-graded groups in which most people take part. By participating in these groups women cooperate and help one another, share their life experiences, and are at the same time exposed to a lifelong education including the latest ideas on health, preventive medicine, and good nutrition. When Christina Honde and I stayed in this Shiga hamlet, most of the women gathered together one evening in the tiny village hall to engage in a question-and-answer session about *kōnenki*. We learned that whereas many of the younger women assumed that *kōnenki* might well be a tough time, almost all the older women were in agreement that it was nothing much to worry about, and none of them admitted to having had much difficulty.

Answering their numerous questions at this meeting was for me a very tricky exercise. The women were eager to hear what the foreign professor had to say about aging and menopause in the "West," but I knew that if I talked freely about differences in symptom reporting there was a danger of reinforcing a common Japanese belief, namely that "the Japanese" are fundamentally different from other "races," an assumption that I did my best to counter but with little success, I fear.

Matsuda-*san* pointed out three other important themes in her narrative. First, that not all relationships between mother-in-law and daughter-in-law are fraught with difficulty, despite popular belief to the contrary, and that not all Japanese mothers necessarily dote on their sons; some even side with their daughters-in-law against them, especially if they think the son is lazy or inconsiderate (as was apparently the case in this instance). Matsuda-*san* also expressed gratitude toward her own mother for the strict upbringing she received that now allows her, she believes, to overcome any kind of hardship. This theme is central in *kōnenki* rhetoric. Women who are at present middle-aged usually believe that their lives are not as hard as those of their mothers, but neither are they as "soft" as those of the next generation.[4] Most take pride in leading a disciplined and controlled life and rather rarely resent younger people's newfound freedoms, which they regard as opulent and self-indulgent.

Last, Matsuda-*san* is concerned about her health together with the question of who will look after her when she is old. Like many middle-aged and older people in Japan, she is explicit about her hope that she will die quickly and not have a lingering illness. Whereas Atsuko's story revealed the burden of the elderly on middle-aged people, Matsuda-*san* is already thinking ahead with some trepidation to twenty or thirty years in the future and is expressing a widely felt concern about who will take care

Weaving kimono silk, Nishijin, Kyoto.

of the future elderly when extended families are no longer usual. Comments to the effect that "in the next eight or nine years, Japanese aged fourteen and younger will be outnumbered by those sixty-five and older" appear regularly in newspapers (*Mainichi shinbun* 1990b), contributing to the national anxiety about the aging population. Once again, the aching body at *kōnenki* fades into the background while other more pressing social problems come to the fore.

An Independent Architect

Miyata-*san* is a forty-eight-year-old architect whose son is at university in Hokkaido. She lives in Tokyo with her husband, a daughter who is in the last year of high school, and her mother-in-law. She was somewhat reluctant for me to come to her house because, she said, *obāsan* might interrupt the conversation, so I met her in a rather noisy coffee shop. Like most middle-aged Japanese women Miyata-*san* is very well groomed, but not ostentatiously so. She is a warm and friendly person who, like many of the other storytellers, wanted to hear my life story in exchange for hers.

"My husband is trained in architecture and engineering and his speciality is calculating strengths of pillars and beams. These days he has his own office with about ten employees."

"What do you do?"

"I work in interior design. I went to a woman's university where they have a special department called Housing. I was employed in an architect's office for three years after graduation but I quit when I had my first child, and I did a little part-time work at home after that until my second child was through elementary school. I was about forty then, and I went back to work in a design company for two years. I left there when *obāsan* came to live with us, and now I work out of my home. I'm my own boss now. In the company I was the only woman and sometimes the men expected me to wait on them: make cups of tea and so on. My chances of promotion were really poor, but I had a kind of security there that I can't have working for myself. I get anxious being on my own all the time and not having any colleagues to support me, it means more responsibility, and there's no one to discuss my ideas with. I have deadlines too, but people know that they can't always be met, it's really the isolation that bothers me the most."

"How about family life?"

"*Obāsan* has been living with us for six years, and there was a fair amount of friction before we got to the point where I could be left alone to work freely in the house. My husband and I are good friends, and we talk about things, but he doesn't help with his mother. He had lived away from her for about thirty years when she moved in. It's a little strange, as if they're not really parent and child. They hardly talk. In fact, she doesn't talk much to anybody. I think she's getting a little senile and she has trouble with neuralgia—that's to be expected I guess—she's seventy-nine. I suppose we'll live together until she dies . . . It's depressing when I think about the years ahead, but I'm planning to ask my husband's sisters to help. They don't live nearby, but I'll ask them to come and help out when I'm really busy, or maybe I'll put her in a hospital. I certainly don't intend to stop working. So far, she can still take care of herself and I just cook for her along with the rest of the family."

"Does your husband help around the house at all?"

"Once in a while my husband cooks on Sunday—it's his hobby."

"How do you feel about your life? Do you think, for example, that your work is as important as your husband's?"

"I'm basically satisfied, and I certainly think of my work as being as valuable as his, but I can't do as much as he can. If I did, the household would go to pot. But I think Japanese women have made a lot of progress lately. My friends and I talk about this quite a bit. Of course I don't have time for any sports or hobbies—my job is what I live for, but I go out with my husband quite often and I can do the housework very quickly."

"What about *kōnenki?*"

"I don't know what *kōnenki* is, really. People usually seem to think it's something more than the end of menstruation. My periods stopped when I was forty-five, but I wasn't worried . . . I didn't have any problems at all. I don't go to a gynecologist, and I never take any medicine. In fact I've only been to a doctor about three times since I was married. The last time I went, when I was about forty-three, he said I was entering *kōnenki*, but I didn't pay any attention. Other women seem to get headaches, a heavy head, ringing in the ears, and I hear they sleep a lot. I think it's probably full-time housewives who get this, but it must also depend on their temperament and the kind of environment they live in. Being a full-time housewife must be really boring . . . Most of my friends work . . . about half of them have poor marriages and two of them are divorced, but I don't think that has much to do with the fact they work. My sister never got married at all and she's happy, I think."

"Do you have any special worries?"

"I worry a bit about the future, mostly about the health of my mother-in-law, but on the whole life is good."

Miyata-*san* is very typical of the modern Japanese woman who is determined to be a professional while she runs a household. Very few women of her age have an advanced education, and she is among only 5 percent in the present survey who obtained a university education or its equivalent. This story offers a strong contrast to the contemporary situation: as of 1989 more women than men (37 percent as opposed to 35 percent) embark on advanced education, and more than 81 percent of women who graduated from college recently found work (the same number as for male graduates) (*Mainichi shinbun* 1990a). However, despite the passing of an Equal Opportunity Law, discrimination in the work force is still rampant, and women have a very slim chance of moving up the ladder to success as men do (Saso 1990).

The social pressures to stop working when a woman has a child continue to be enormous in Japan, and to go on working after the birth of her son would have meant Miyata-*san* was a very exceptional individual. Her career is like that of many women I met who opt not to push their way back into the mainstream working world after their children are settled in school. Instead, because of a keenly felt gender prejudice, they decide to try and "go it alone," most usually by setting up an independent company or enterprise often close to their own home. Only thus is it possible to maneuver back and forth between the various domestic roles assigned to women in modern Japan and the career to which many of them are dedicated (see also Lebra 1984a).

Miyata-*san*'s case is typical in that, even in a dual-career household, she is expected to take full responsibility for the children and do almost all the domestic work. She assumes that this is "natural" and apparently feels only mild resentment that she expresses elliptically in her reference to her husband's "hobby" of cooking. Like every other woman with whom I talked she believes that the problems associated with aging parents-in-law are chiefly her responsibility. It could be that, if she asks her husband's sisters to help with *obāsan*, one or more of them may, even though the individual is their own mother, strongly suggest that Miyata-*san* give up her work to fulfill her duty as a daughter-in-law. This situation, family tension on the subject of an ailing parent, is extremely common, and so obviously *obāsan*'s health is of the utmost concern in Miyata-*san*'s mind, making *kōnenki* insignificant by comparison.

In her narrative, Miyata-*san* alludes spontaneously to what she thinks of as the vacuous lives of "full-time housewives" (*sengyō shufu*). She expresses a sentiment common to many informants, that it is women with no work, living an apparently boring life, who are likely to have trouble with *kōnenki* but hastily modifies this blanket statement to point out that inborn physical disposition (*taishitsu*) and temperament (*seikaku*) are also implicated, as are the physical surroundings in which individuals live.

A Floor Cleaner

Ikeda-*san* comes from a fishing village of about two hundred households in Kochi prefecture. She is strongly built and speaks her mind in a manner uncharacteristically forthright for a Japanese woman. Asked about her life thus far, she started out by talking nostalgically about the past as we sat together in a bleak side room of a Kyoto hospital where she is employed as a floor cleaner.

"My family were fishermen and I lived with my mother, father, grandfather, and two older brothers. Being the youngest and a girl meant that my father was very fond of me . . . but because he was away for about half of every year sometimes he seemed like a stranger. Both my mother and father were very good to us. My mother came from a poor family, and she was determined we'd have a better time than she had. When I was little we loved to go swimming, especially when there was a typhoon coming and the waves were really big. We used to tramp around in the muddy rice fields too after the harvest, catching dragonflies—I used to go everywhere my brothers went. And we went diving using face masks to collect shellfish—someone from the next village would buy them from us, and then we'd take the money and use it to buy 'slush' [iced drinks].

"I'm fifty-two now, so I was in the third or fourth grade when the war ended."

"Were you short of food then?"

"Yes, we had problems with food . . . we used to grow sweet potatoes and barley in the steep terraced fields on the mountain, and we mixed them with a little rice. We all helped in the fields, the children and the old people too, everyone.

"I went to school until the end of junior high. My brothers all passed the national exams to become qualified seamen . . . They encouraged me, and so did my mother, to go on to high school but I liked playing better than studying . . . We all knew I'd be marrying soon so I went to a sewing school instead of high school. By the time I was in my thirties I really regretted this, and I wish I'd followed my mother's advice.

"My father didn't want to let me get married, he tried to hang on to me, but finally I was married at twenty-six to a village boy after his family came and spoke to mine . . . unfortunately he drank a lot and he used to beat me. We're separated now. I thought it would be good, starting out a new life after I got married. My husband's father died when he was three, and his mother had a hard time bringing up the family, so I thought, he knows how to suffer, and so he'll make a good husband. But it wasn't that way at all. He always became violent—not right from the beginning, but after we moved to Osaka. Finally my son suggested that I shake his father up a bit, and that I should try leaving home, so I'm living with my son now. He's twenty-five and not married yet."

"How long did you live with your husband?"

"We left Kochi soon after we got married, and we've been in Osaka for twenty-six years. I made a lot of friends through the company where my husband made cardboard boxes. Our company houses were like an extended family—you could run next door and borrow soy sauce and at New Year all the couples would get together at one house and drink and sing. It was really fun."

"Did you ever work?"

"No, I was always a full-time housewife. I never worked in an office or anything. Even now I'd rather be one, but because I'm separated, I have to earn a living. [Ikeda-*san* has, in fact, worked all her married life in her husband's company—for as many as six hours a day at times—but she always thought of this work simply as an extension of her husband's job and counted herself as a full-time housewife because she was not fully self-supporting until a year ago when she left her husband.]

"We started having problems about a year after we got married, though my husband wasn't violent until later when he became a sort of weekend alcoholic. He used to hit my son too, and my son says he doesn't have any respect for his father now. I don't know if there was something I did wrong . . . I think he didn't like being head of a family. He was the youngest of seven children and he liked to *amae* [be dependent on others]. He would get violent over little things, like an argument over which was the best baseball team. I didn't tell anyone for a long time, but finally I told his brothers and they tried to talk to him, but it didn't do any good."

"It must have been a difficult decision to separate from your husband."

"Yes, I've never had to look after myself before. But this job isn't hard, and the people here are easygoing, they joke around with me. I'm not sure about my status though, but I get health insurance and a pension, so I guess it's a full-time job. I don't understand these things—all that was always taken care of by my husband's company. If I was still young I'd find out all about it but now I feel I'm a bit behind other people. It doesn't seem I'm going to get any benefits from my husband's company, and I don't have anything saved up to retire on . . . it's a little bit late to be realizing that."

"What about your health?"

"I had my uterus and ovaries out when I was thirty-two. I used to get bad headaches after that, and I had shots from the hospital every month for ten years . . . I get a bit of shoulder stiffness now, but I think it's just my age. I'm pretty strong on the whole.

"I'm worried about what will happen when my son gets married. He says he'll take care of me, but I can't lean on him for everything [*onbu ni dakko to iu wake ni wa ikanai*]. I think I'll go back to Kochi then, I have lots of relatives there. But I'll cross that bridge when I come to it. Since I can work, it's better to spend my time keeping busy rather than go back to my husband. I phone my old friends at the company housing, and I have cousins in Osaka, so I'm not really lonely.

"As you can see, I'm just dumb—there isn't a single clever place in my brain, but I always like to be lively and have fun. What I regret now is not getting divorced much earlier. It would have been better for my son."

People in Japan who were young when the war ended recall very vividly the suffering that their families went through. Most middle-aged people remember being short of food, and the standard description of those times is of "pulling up the grass by the wayside and eating it." When asked to reminisce about the past, almost all individuals think of hardship, not so much their own, but that of their parents' generation. An implicit comparison in such statements about character-building hardship juxtaposes postwar people, having grown up in ever increasing luxury and ease and thus ill-suited to stick at or endure anything, to their grandparents. Today's fifty-year-olds live suspended between tradition and modernity, schooled in tradition but fated to live in modern and postmodern Japan. They had their share of hardship, but only as children; their parents bore the brunt of wartime misery. Nostalgia for the past, the "golden" days of hardship, is never far beneath the surface in the narratives of many middle-aged women, most particularly those, like Ikeda-*san*, whose present lives are not considered successful.

In her story Ikeda-*san* reveals the extent to which many married Japanese women depend on their spouses for financial security, health care, pensions, and similar matters. Like many women, Ikeda-*san* lived her married life with little thought for social security, assuming, quite rightly, that she was covered reasonably adequately by her husband's company. But her life deviated from the natural course of events. Her separation meant that she had no rights as far as her husband and his company were concerned. Her vagueness about her present position will come as no surprise to readers who are familiar with Japan: when joining an institution or company, workers may know little about working conditions and benefits, particularly for menial jobs. An employee may receive nothing in writing before the job begins, as was the case for Ikeda-*san*, who did not know what her pay would be until she received her first paycheck in her bank account. A rather widespread unspoken assumption remains that the employer will be benevolent, that employees should feel grateful to be given jobs and accept that they will be adequately taken care of. Ikeda-*san*, because she works in a hospital, receives health care and medication free. But she may not receive any other benefits at all from her place of employment, in which case if she wants some recompense for her later years she should pay into the national scheme now. Although anxious, she does not deal effectively with the situation.

Ikeda-*san* did not experience a usual *kōnenki* because of the surgery she underwent. She has no interest at all in talking about *kōnenki* and what it might mean to her but emphasizes instead her current physical strength and then abruptly cuts off that part of our conversation to return to the more pressing problems on her mind to do with her work, potential dependence on her son, and approaching old age. In the survey sample, fewer than 12 percent have had gynecological surgery, and Ikeda-*san*, therefore, is among a small minority of Japanese women.[5]

A Bar Owner

Hayase-*san* was born near Nagasaki, six years before the atomic bomb was dropped. Elegant in appearance and very animated, she sat and chatted with me in the bar that she owns in the wealthy Akasakamitsuke district of Tokyo. I had exchanged banter with Hayase-*san* a good number of times already, perched on a stool in her bar across the counter from where she orchestrates the evening's eating, drinking, and therapeutic chitchat for her largely (but not exclusively) male customers. She readily agreed to tell me her life story and suggested that I come to the bar one afternoon about lunchtime, after she had done the day's ordering and shopping for the numerous delicacies that would be available for the evening customers. She said that she and I could sit down and talk, and at the same time her chef could consult with her about anything if he needed to as he prepared for the five o'clock opening. We were interrupted several times during our conversation by phone calls and deliveries, and by a friend of Hayase-*san*, but not by the chef. Hayase-*san* comes from a background entirely different from Ikeda-*san's*, from merchant rather than peasant ancestry, and her family was quite well-off. Yet like Ikeda-*san* she recalls her early life with mixed feelings of nostalgia and sadness.

> "My clearest childhood memories are connected with eating. I remember things from about the age of five onward. We didn't actually experience the bomb, but I would say I have more unhappy than happy memories about that time. My family made *wagashi* [Japanese confectionery], so there was always lots of food around. I lived with my grandparents, my parents, my brother, and some servants. At table we all had our assigned places and no one was allowed to start eating until *ojīsan* [grandfather] started. We were

trained not to make any noise while eating, and we had to go to bed at 7 P.M. without fail.

"I'm sure that my life as a mother, if I'd had children, would have been completely different from that of my own mother. My mother was very stoic. She believed until the day she died that endurance was a virtue. We had people of three different eras living in our household, Meiji [1867–1912], Taishō [1912–26], and Shōwa [1926–89]. Meiji women were supposed to keep quiet and walk three steps behind their husbands, although when they voiced their opinions they did it clearly. Endurance was supposed to equal strength, that's what my mother taught me. In her day Taishō women [unlike the Meiji women before them] didn't even voice their own opinions, and my father certainly expected it to be that way. But he involved himself with the children and discussed with my mother what she should say when she went to talk to the teacher.

"My mother had a well-defined place in the family; there was a sharp distinction between her role and my father's and, because it was an extended family, clear rules of politeness toward my grandparents. We never saw my parents argue, not once."

"What about the bomb, did that have a big effect on your childhood?"

"Some of my father's relatives were killed, but it was in school that I really came face to face with it, because there were survivor children there, and it was quite a shock. I knew that I shouldn't discriminate against them, but I was squeamish about the way they looked and was afraid that I would catch something if I touched them. I felt repelled by them, and when they stayed home from school with radiation fever we had to visit them, but I was always afraid I'd catch something. We also had mixed-blood children in our school from the American base nearby so it was really difficult for us all to get along.

"I liked the sports though, and swimming in the ocean, but my memories of school aren't too good. We moved to Tokyo when I started high school, right after my grandparents died, and became a nuclear family for the first time. My mother had a little more time, she didn't have to help manage the business anymore, and I started to feel a little warmer toward her. Like the rest of her generation, she always felt it wasn't good to acquire things too easily; she didn't like throwing anything away, and she always insisted we use made-over things out of bits and pieces she'd saved.

"I didn't like school because I was different. I had a Kyushu accent and everyone laughed at me when I talked. They teased me too because of the homemade pencil cases and so on that my mother made me use. I stayed away from school for a time, I actually lost my voice and couldn't speak. But my teacher came and visited me, and he was determined to get me back to school. I had no appetite and had fevers, but he got me into the sports club and that really helped. I had my first period at that time too, and it was a bit of a shock even though we had all talked about it in junior high. I felt embarrassed to walk in front of my father and brother for a while and I wouldn't let my mother do the traditional *oiwai* [family celebration with red bean soup] because I didn't want her to tell them."

"Had your mother explained all about menstruation to you?"

"No, nothing at all. But we learned a little at school. When it started she said I wasn't to worry, that even if my stomach hurt it wasn't a bad thing, it was just the poisons coming out little by little and nothing to be afraid of. She told me years later she'd been worried about me because it was so late starting, and she'd talked it over with my father and wondered whether she should take me to the doctor, but he told her not to worry, that some girls start later than others."

"You were a geisha for a while, right?"

"Yes, I became a geisha after graduating from high school. My mother was very unhappy about the idea, but I'd taken Japanese dance lessons since I was six years old and I loved it. My mother wanted me to get married, of course, but my father thought I should be free to do what I wanted. The geisha world is really rigorous . . . it was nothing like amateur dance lessons. Geisha are professionals and it takes twenty years to become fully qualified in dance. For the first time I appreciated my mother's strictness, it gave me the strength to deal with the training.

"We all had lessons together, but we trainees had to get there really early and then watch the others after we were through. Some of the older ones had days when they weren't so good. I know now, of course, that was probably *kōnenki*—as you get older the screws start to come loose![6] I was a geisha for seven years, and I'm still close with four friends from that time."

"Why did you stop that kind of work?"

"Well, I suppose I wanted to see more of the world. I went abroad for two years to South America, that was a terrific experience, and my life really opened up for a while. Actually I followed a lover there. I liked it because people were friendly and relaxed, but I missed the seasons in Japan."

"Can you speak Spanish?"

"*Un poco*! Then I ran a snack bar for someone else for a long time, and then, two years ago, I finally bought this little place. It's really hard work, and I don't know if I'm going to make it financially. I spend the days organizing the menus and buying and ordering the food, then the bar opens at 5:00 P.M. and closes finally at 1:00 A.M. I'm on my feet all the time, and after that I have to clean up before I can go home. The next morning I have to telephone the best customers and thank them for coming to the bar the previous evening. I usually only get about five or six hours of sleep. It's six days a week, and on Sunday I spend the time getting my kimono[s] back into shape. I may cut the time I'm open down to five days, it's really exhausting at present."

"Do you like the work?"

"I get tired of listening to other people's troubles. That's what my job is really all about you know, but it gets exhausting. Men come and tell me their problems, they pour out their souls to me, and then when they feel better they go home to their families. Japanese husbands and wives live completely separate lives, as you know, and they don't understand each other at all. I have to stay bright and sympathetic all the time, and I also have to be on top of the news. Some customers like to talk over work-related things, and also politics and the state of the world, so I must keep up with things. Most of the time, though, I'm simply like a Pierrette, a jester [*dōkesha*], it's all banter and surface talk. Sometimes I go home and I think to myself I never want to talk to anyone again . . . life feels so strange sometimes. I don't know who is me and who is Pierrette, and on days like that I don't want to do anything. It's really quite a lonely life.

"The most important thing is to remember everyone's name and workplace properly. If I get people confused with one another that doesn't look good at all."

"If you had your life over, would you choose this work again?"

"Probably not, not now. What I'd really like to do is go abroad and work. I don't regret not getting married though, and I wouldn't want to change that."

"What will happen to you as you get older? How long can you do this work?"

"I'll be all right until I'm sixty or so, I think. But it's worrying, I'm frightened of getting old."

"I suppose it's important to keep your looks in your job?"

"Well, of course it's important to keep up *appearances*, but it's perfectly all right to be an older person. It's failing health I worry about most—that's the most important thing. I worry about being lonely too, but I'm planning to live together with my girlfriends when I retire . . . we have it all figured out, and we're saving up for it."

"Do you think *kōnenki* will make any difference to you?"

"No. I'm not expecting any problems, I'm much too disciplined for that. I had one ovary out when I was thirty because it had adhered to the intestines, so my periods have always been rather irregular anyway. But I do worry about losing my memory. In my work it's so important to be able to put a name to every single customer. If one starts to look a little older that's only natural after all, and one can still be a good shoulder to cry on—but not being able to remember people's names—that's terrible."

Hayase-*san*, although she is not explicit about this, must have been well aware when she opted for a life as a professional dancer and a geisha that she was at the same time rejecting the possibility of an ordinary marriage (although some geisha do ultimately get married). Until very recently in Japan, marriage was considered natural and inevitable for all women. Exceptions were those who were forced by poverty or who were selected because of particular talent to go into the entertainment world, those who opted for a career, most often as a schoolteacher or a nurse, and a very few who became Buddhist nuns.

Hayase-*san* gives us a glimpse of the strict discipline that was characteristic in the families of former samurai and wealthy merchants. Autocratic husbands are still described today as Meiji men, and Hayase-*san* paints a vivid picture of the subservient position of women and children usual in such families until the outbreak of World War II. But, like so many other women, in retrospect she is grateful for the discipline and believes that because of it she was able to make a successful career as a geisha and now as a bar owner (indeed a very demanding occupation). She also points out that the same discipline will enable her to overcome any physical difficulties she may experience at *kōnenki*, and she shares this attitude with very many other middle-aged women.

Because she is not married, old age will present a particularly difficult time for Hayase-*san* since society designates no one for her to lean on. For her, in contrast to many married women, the building of intimate bonds beyond those usually expected in friendship is crucial. Fortunately for her, Hayase-*san* has apparently accomplished this.

Frugal Farmer

Hattori-*san*, age fifty-four, lives with her mother, her husband, and her three sons, ages twenty-eight, twenty-four, and twenty. The eldest son is a garage mechanic, the second works in an office and is studying for examinations to become a builder, and the youngest is studying English literature at a university in Tokyo. Hattori-*san* has lived her whole life in the same village in Nagano and has spent the past twenty-four years in the house where I interviewed her. The farmhouse is typical of the older architecture of the area: a single-story dwelling of about six rooms. Visitors remove their shoes and step up into a small reception area that leads into the first of two or three tatami-matted rooms lined up parallel to the road and linked by sliding screen panels. The outer walls of each of these rooms consist of sets of sliding wooden and paper panels (*fusuma*), which when opened reveal a narrow corridor that runs the entire length of the house and has on its outer side sliding doors as well as solid wooden storm shutters, usually open by day. Partly sheltering from passersby the interior of the house and the narrow garden ablaze with azaleas is a hedge. It was springtime just before rice-planting season when I visited the Hattori family, and still not warm enough to have the *fusuma* open. We sat on cushions placed round a low central table, and I was served homemade pickles, sweet bean cakes, and green tea.

Hattori-*san* is the eldest daughter in her family and has no brothers and so, when it was time for her marriage, her parents arranged for her future husband to be adopted into the household, an arrangement many Japanese people believe results in an excessively strong woman and a weak dissembling husband. But Hattori-*san*, diminutive, slightly gray-haired, and with a quiet deferential manner, does not appear especially assertive or demanding. Her mother, well under five feet tall, somewhat bent, but very alert, came into the room soon after my arrival to look over the foreigner but left again shortly after introductions. I remarked on her spry deportment.

"My mother is eighty-four but fortunately she's still very healthy. I haven't been going to the rice fields much this year because I haven't been well, and so my mother has done it all. She's got some bean fields too, and she's always at work making pickles and so on, most of which she gives to other people—you know, they say that using your hands keeps you from going senile. There was a time when she was working too hard and she had dizzy spells. I tried to make her ease up, but that made her feel as though she didn't belong, as though she had no use anymore, so now she does what she feels like."

"Does your husband work the fields too or is his work in town?"

"In the early days my husband farmed our land and my mother and I helped; my father died when I was six, you see. But my husband always had a job in town as well. We had silkworms too, which were usually my job to look after. The boys all helped too, once they were old enough. But we don't plant all the land these days, it just stands unused.

"My husband has been in and out of the hospital for the past two years with a problem the doctors don't understand. He has high fevers and his whole body aches. One theory is that it's some kind of viral infection. It's been a real worry. He took time off work. Now he's back again, but he doesn't farm anymore. My eldest son tries to do all the heavy work before he goes off to work in the mornings and on Sundays, and my mother and I usually do all the rest of it. Another big trouble is that I've had kidney trouble for about fifteen years. I was told that one kidney is only half functioning. I get really tired, but for a long time I tried to keep up with everything and go to various social activities as well. I thought that if I just kept on going normally then I wouldn't get depressed but a few years ago, at one of my checkups, the nurse told me that if I have to go on dialysis I won't be able to do anything at all, and she said I should rest more and not go out to my clubs and so on in the evenings. So I stopped all my activities. This year it seems to be worse and I can't even work in the fields." Hattori-*san* looks unhappy as she talks. She goes back over the history of her illness with no prompting on my part and explains that in retrospect she thinks she should have gone into hospital when the illness first started and rested properly, but she believed at the time that she couldn't leave the children.

"I promised the doctor that if he let me stay at home I'd rest, but of course I could see the work waiting to be done—I couldn't just leave it. My husband was busy in town and the fields needed to be planted. Even though the doctors told me not to go into the water for the first rice planting,[7] my mother couldn't do it all by herself and so I *had* to do it.

"I'd always thought my husband and I would go off and do a little traveling once the children were grown up, but now that we're both sick it doesn't look as though it's going to work out that way. Anyway, I'm trying to do the best I can. I went away for a couple of days last year, but my husband decided he couldn't go because of his health."

"What was it like for a child growing up here?"

"Well, I was sent away to my grandparents' during the war. My uncles were both off fighting and so I was supposed to help on their land. I didn't like that and kept asking to go back to my mother, but everyone said I had to stay. Finally, toward the end of the war, one of my uncles was sent back from New Guinea with malaria and I was sent home again.

"I did quite well in school and the vice-principal suggested that I could go on to train to become a teacher. I really wanted to do this, but in those days there was a saying: Never marry a teacher

or a nurse—women in those professions were never liked because
everyone thought they were too logical and pushy. So my mother
was set against it, and so were my uncles. In the end they let me
work in an office. That was all right, I liked it quite well, and we
certainly needed the money.

"My mother was always worried because everyone assumed
that children raised by a widow would have lots of troubles. So she
was very strict with us, my younger sister and me. She used to
slap us and pinch us for no reason at all. When I got older I
wanted to run away—she was always too concerned with what
other people would think, and she never respected us as people."

"So did you raise your own children differently?"

"With my first child I was almost like my mother. I feel sorry
for him now when I think about that. I finally realized after reading books and hearing talks that I was ruining my children [ko-
domo o dame ni suru], and I changed completely and decided to
help them develop their good points."

"How did you meet your husband?"

"I'd seen him once when he came to the farming co-op where
I was working. I'd already met someone else I really liked, but he
went off to Tokyo. He said he didn't want to be adopted into anyone else's family, and so even though he liked me he took off. He
said I could come to Tokyo too, and I thought about that, but I
was the eldest daughter and I couldn't just go off and leave my
mother. After that I said to myself I'd never get married, but of
course the older people—my mother and her brothers wouldn't
stand for that. They finally forced me into a formal meeting with
my future husband. He seemed all right so I agreed, but my
mother didn't really like him because he was quite a drinker
(though he's stopped now because of his health). It was really my
uncles who set everything up."

"Did things work out all right in the end?"

"I wouldn't say that. He was teishu kanpaku [bossy around
the house]. I asked if I could go out to work in an office in a town
fifteen minutes away, but he said that would make him look like
less of a man and complained I was a bad housewife if I couldn't
manage on his salary."

"Do you think it was especially hard because he was adopted
into your family?"

"Oh yes, I always had to mediate between him and my mother,
and I didn't have anywhere to take my complaints. If you get married into someone else's household it may be hard with a tough
mother-in-law, but at least you can usually go back to your own
mother and pour your troubles out to her. But I could never do that."

"How old were you when you got married?"

"I was twenty-three, about like everyone else. The best time in my life was the few years before that. I was really happy then. I was in labor for a week with my first child. The midwife was really worried and called in someone from the hospital but they said the heartbeat was strong so they let the midwife do the delivery. When he was born the baby had the cord wrapped three times around him: around the neck, body, and legs, and that was why it took so long, he hadn't dropped down at all. He'd also swallowed some fluid so it was touch and go for a while.

"With the other pregnancies I worked very hard right up until the last minute. My mother kept urging me on, saying, 'This baby had better be born on time or we're going to lose this year's silkworm crop.' She needed me back on my feet to help her because it was the busy season, so I kept on working as hard as I could, and the baby was right on time."

"It sounds as though you've had a hard life, especially because you've been unwell for a long time."

"Yes, my health problems really worry me, the kidney trouble is the worst thing that's happened. But of course, there're a lot of people worse off than me. It's not good to wish for more than one has [ue o mitara ikenai]. Before the war we all grew up with nothing so we were very careful with our things. I don't think young people today could stand the kind of lives we had."

"Do you expect to live with your eldest son after he's married?"

"To tell the truth, I do. He's twenty-eight already and there's no one left in the village who arranges marriages these days. We keep telling him to go out and find someone he likes, but he wants us to do it for him. He says he never meets any girls at work. We have to get something done about it soon . . . oh dear! I hope we can find a good, gentle wife for him and that we can all get along well."

"Apart from the kidney problem how is your general health nowadays?"

"I have shoulder stiffness and back pains from working in the fields—it's been like that ever since I was young. I do TV exercises and some yoga that I learned from TV. Also I get acupuncture treatments sometimes and massage [shiatsu] too. It helps quite a bit."

"Tell me what you think about kōnenki."

"I'm all through now, I think. It's something like a 'time of misfortune' [yaku] in that the body changes in various ways that can be quite upsetting. Once you stop menstruating of course it's simpler, but it makes you realize you're getting older and that feels a bit sad. The most noticeable thing was that I'd suddenly feel hot—I had seen older women have that problem—but it also happened to me, and I thought, Oh, so *this* is *kōnenki*. It's gone now, it just lasted for about six months or a year. It started about seven years ago, just around the time I was hospitalized to check my kidneys."

"Did it happen every day?"

"Yes, it happened every day, three times or so."

"Did you feel embarrassed?"

"No, I just thought it was because of my age."

"Did you go and talk to anyone about it?"

"No, I didn't go to the doctor."

"Did you take any medicine?"

"No."

"Did you discuss it with your friends?"

"No, not really. But one or two of them did mention the same kind of thing."

"Did you have any other symptoms?"

"My head throbbed and it was so bad I had to squat down sometimes. It throbbed in time with my pulse—that was really unpleasant. It's mostly better now. I suppose it's something to do with the hormone imbalance."

"Do people round here talk about *chi no michi* at all?"

"Old people used to talk about it a lot, and there's some medicine that's supposed to help. I don't really know what it is and no one seems to talk about it these days.

"I think it's important to have a hobby, especially as you get older, otherwise it's easy to get depressed about illnesses and so on. I used to go to traditional dance lessons three times a month, I thought that would help me get better, but I also worried I'd let the others down when we did performances. Anyway, after the doctors and nurses told me to stop, I dried my tears and gave up dancing. But now I do folk songs with another group of women. It's great fun. I've always liked singing, and when I was younger I used to go off in a corner of the field by myself and sing at the top of my voice. That drove all the gloomy feelings away! I tried to get my children to like music too. I used to sing to them a lot, and I bought quite a few children's records and so on. But I'd like to dance again too. It would be wonderful if my husband could get well enough so that we could go to the social dances in the village occasionally."

Ill health, both her husband's and her own, dominates Hattori-*san*'s narrative, but uppermost in her mind is the question of whom her son will marry and the hope that the couple will agree to come and live together with the Hattoris. Her son is apparently content to have an arranged marriage, but the search for a suitable bride may well prove very difficult. Thus far no foreign wives have been brought into the village where Hattori-*san* lives, but the pattern may have to change in the near future. This problem seems to outweigh any concerns Hattori-*san* may have about looking after her mother when she grows infirm. That the old lady is a healthy eighty-four is of course a good omen, but because the person she must care for is her mother and not her mother-in-law, Hattori-*san* may have less concern about the next stage in her life.

Single Mother by Default

Kuriyama-*san*, forty-six, lives in a large apartment complex north of Tokyo with her three children, a daughter of seventeen and twin boys of fourteen. A common friend had introduced me to her, and so we were not well acquainted, although I had heard a lot about her from my friend, who feels rather sorry for her. We sat in her tiny living room over an afternoon cup of tea where Kuriyama-*san* seemed somewhat withdrawn but nevertheless talked very willingly, although her friend had hinted darkly that I probably would not get the "whole" story out of her. To this day I do not know if I did so.

> "I'm a housewife and have been ever since I got married. My husband works for a trading company . . . he's been living in Peking for the past two years."
>
> "What was your childhood like?"
>
> "I grew up in the countryside outside Tokyo right after the war when there wasn't enough food . . . I had pneumonia and maybe TB, and I had to stay home from school for a long time, but when I got to junior high school things were better. We had more good food by that time. My father was wounded in the war . . . they sent him home to convalesce but he died in 1946.
>
> "I have two sisters and my mother raised us by herself . . . I think she had a very hard time—she was a midwife—she couldn't really earn enough money because people were too poor to pay her, but we got by somehow . . . We all respected my mother for her hard work and for the way she helped people in the middle of the night. We children took it in turns to fix dinner and clean the house."
>
> "Did your mother like her work?"
>
> "Yes, I think so. She's seventy-three now and she's still working, not on her own, of course, but helping out. I go to see her

Conversation with mother-in-law.

once a week. I hardly remember my father, he died when I was three or so.

"After high school I went to work in the trading company where my husband still works. I wanted to go on to higher education but my family couldn't afford it. When I went to work I really set out to find a good husband and always planned to stop work once I got married, although my mother didn't really agree with this, she thought that was being frivolous. She had thought a lot about the position of women, and she always said that in the future Japanese women would all take jobs as a matter of course.

"I worked for about eight years before I got married, I was commuting three hours or so each day. I had one or two other *omiai* [formal meetings with prospective husbands], but since I was my husband's assistant at work we already knew each other pretty well and we liked each other. I was twenty-six when I got married and had my first child at twenty-seven."

"Do you feel now, looking back, that you found a good husband?"

A slight pause, and then Kuriyama-*san* continues: "My husband has always had a lot of business trips—he's always lived away from home for many months at a time. He was sent to stay in China several times before it really opened up, then as a family we all lived in China from '81 to '84. A year after we came back to Japan, he was sent back there again and he's been there for two years . . . He comes home twice a year, at New Year's and during the summer for about two weeks.

"I think my children are closer to him while he's over there than when he's home—they talk to him on the phone and write to him. Sometimes I feel lonely not having anyone to consult with or talk to, but the children sort of take care of me now, and I've grown used to this kind of life."

"Do you worry about your marriage because your husband is away so much of the time?"

"I don't worry that he's going to find someone else—is that what you mean? If it was a developed country that might be a problem, but China isn't like that, and even if there are some pretty women there I don't think there's much chance of that happening."

"How does your life differ from your mother's?"

"Well, I'm dependent on my husband, I wouldn't have a life if he didn't have a good job. My mother did everything by herself so her way of thinking is very strong and independent. When anything comes up, I always have to depend on my husband so it's very different."

"Do you want to go back to work soon? The children will soon be grown up, won't they?"

"I won't go back to work even when the children are older . . . My husband's company doesn't like wives to work, they think it gives a bad image to the company, as though they're not paying their employees enough and so the wives have to go out to make money."

"Are you sorry about that?"

"Not really . . . "

"What do you do with your time?"

"I do quilting and so on, that keeps me occupied in the evenings." After a considerable pause Kuriyama-*san* adds, somewhat defensively I think, "I enjoy it very much."

"Do you have any worries about the future?"

"I won't have to look after *obāsan*, even though my husband is the eldest son. Because he's in China, she's gone to her younger son in Osaka—so I won't have to deal with that. What I do worry about is my health. I seem to be a bit anemic and I get tired easily so I'm having some examinations, but I'm not taking any medication yet. I don't think I'm near *kōnenki*, but I don't really know anything about that. Also, I worry about when I'm really old. I'll have to depend on my children, but I wonder if they'll take care of me, of course it all depends on who they marry. I'm afraid I might end up in an old people's home, and that doesn't bear thinking about . . ." A long pause. "I wish I'd studied more when I was young, I might have been a different person."

Aside from the presence of the third child, the Kuriyama family is the prototypical Japanese family of today: salaried husband, full-time (professional) housewife, and two children. Long absences on the part of the husband in connection with business are typical in this modern ménage that becomes, in essence, a single-parent family to which the distant father occasionally returns for visits. Kuriyama-*san*'s life is what the architect Miyata-*san* and many other working women in Japan would describe as boring, but perhaps with a touch of wistfulness at times. Not all those in Kuriyama-*san*'s position fill their days with quilting after all; others go to cultural centers, where they can learn anything from Italian to preparing *nouvelle cuisine*, or go to concerts and exhibitions, play tennis or golf, and, when the children enter university, depart in droves to visit every corner of the globe.

In Kuriyama-*san*'s narrative the theme emerges once again of a hard-working and dedicated mother to whom the daughter does not measure up. And, as so often happens, the tie between Kuriyama-*san* and her mother has remained strong throughout her entire life. Once again, regrets about education dominate. Many women such as Kuriyama-*san*, although they rushed eagerly into a safe middle-class marriage as young women, come to believe in middle age that perhaps they might have done something different, if only they had received the education. Now that her husband has an executive position, Kuriyama-*san* finds—and this is no surprise to her, of course—that she cannot work because her husband's company would not approve of it. All she can hope to do is some sort of part-time activity such as "volunteer" work (for example, looking after the mentally ill or the elderly, for which she would probably receive a little money, despite the designation of volunteer), organize some local activities in her town that must be totally unrelated to politics (since the company will probably disapprove), or work part-time at some small-scale entrepreneurial activity. Alternatively, she can fill her time up with hobbies. Yet Kuriyama-*san* is lucky because she could well be fully occupied looking after her mother-in-law; fortunately for her, she has a cooperative sister-in-law in Osaka.

Kuriyama-*san* states that the major problem in her life at the moment is the education of the children. The twins will soon take high school entrance examinations and before long their sister has university entrance examinations. Kuriyama-*san* believes, as do most other full-time housewives, that she must take a very active part to ensure that her children prepare themselves properly. She adds, somewhat abashed, that this is not such a big problem really; but this concern completely overshadows any anxieties she might have about *kōnenki*—about which she does not bother in the least.

Life histories are "representations of lives, not lives as actually lived" (Bruner 1984, 7). In giving these accounts the narrators focus on certain incidents, reconstructing events from their memories and imaginations that irrevocably shaped their lives. Implicit in their narratives are allusions to a culturally shaped moral order, and in telling their stories the women let us glimpse how they understand themselves not only as middle-aged women but also as part of modern Japanese society. Obviously my presence affects their accounts, not only in the occasional deliberate foregrounding of *kōnenki* but also in a foreign interviewer's effect on the flow of the story. Nevertheless, as will become clear in the following chapters, these narratives, at once cultural constructions and individual stories, give us a critical perspective on the expectations about middle-aged women dominant in Japanese society.

In creating accounts of their lives none of the women offer more than a passing aside to the end of menstruation or appear particularly worried about *kōnenki* and its alleged difficulties. Middle age and maturity contain much more than this, and many women insist that they would not let such a minor event upset them. I noted that one of the women who attended the public lecture described earlier states that she wants to learn how to approach *kōnenki* "with the right attitude." Several women we interviewed stress, in common with those who spoke with Nancy Rosenberger (1987), that, with the right attitude, it should be quite easy to overcome (*norikoeru*) any difficulties one might encounter with *kōnenki*. So which individuals in Japan are we to consider "at risk" (as the epidemiologists put it)? And why does a stereotype of a difficult time exist if it adversely affects so few women? Obviously all are more or less equally susceptible to the general wear and tear of aging, but perhaps some are particularly vulnerable to the headaches, stiff shoulders, irritability, and the occasional hot flashes associated with *kōnenki shōgai*. What is wrong with their attitude—in what way do they lack moral fiber?

4 The Pathology of Modernity

Someday, when I am older, will I be able to get rid of this
impulse, this wanting to be a "good wife," without feeling
lost? . . . I'd certainly like to be a woman whose sense of
purpose comes from within.

(Uno Chiyo, *A Genius of Imitation*)

Children of the Dark Valley

In the women's narratives *kōnenki* is just one small part of the individual
life cycle, which in turn is partly a product of the larger social order. The
women who are in their fifties today, those in the cohort between forty-
five and fifty-five at the time of my research, not only experience the
physiological changes of this portion of the life cycle but also embody a
social conflict that is keenly felt in contemporary Japan: the passage from
tradition to modernity and postmodernity.

Today's fifty- to sixty-year-olds were children during the depression
and the early years of World War II, a time sometimes described as the
"dark valley" (*kurai tanima*), particularly when contrasted to the more
happy-go-lucky days of the Taishō era in the first years of the twentieth
century, and to the economic miracle of the postwar years. They are known
as the generation old enough to have suffered but young enough not to
have been implicated in responsibility for the war, a generation of individuals educated in the values of prewar Japan who lived their adult lives
in the postwar years of massive social change.

Monitoring the pulse of the nation today are censuses—conducted by
the government, newspapers, sociologists, and numerous commercial organizations, ad nauseam and on every conceivable subject ranging from
whether people worry about earthquakes to whom they want to have care
for them when they grow old and senile. Age almost invariably occurs as
a dependent variable in these surveys, and respondents are usually divided
into ten-year age groups: twenties, thirties, forties, and so on. At other
times a much broader division segregates prewar and postwar generations,
with finer distinctions of imperial reigns into which individuals were born

(Hayase-*san*, the bar owner, describes her family this way). The results of these surveys then often produce a discourse about shared beliefs, behavioral styles, and aspirations common to generational cohorts. Very old people, those in their eighties and over, belong to the Meiji era (1868–1912) and the transformation of Japan into a modern industrial state (a process begun well before the Meiji era). The following reign, the Taishō era (1912–26), is thought of as a time of prosperity, one that middle-aged Japanese often regard somewhat wistfully, especially in contrast to what was to follow.

The long Shōwa era (1926–88) is divided into prewar, wartime, and several postwar generations of approximately ten-year spans. People born in the early years of the Shōwa reign are known as the *shōwa hitoketa* (literally, those born during the first decade of Shōwa); they are usually characterized as extremely hard workers who have contributed selflessly to the postwar building of the new Japan. Most women in the present survey sample of over thirteen hundred fall into this category, that is, all those who were born between 1928 and 1934 inclusively, while the remainder, born between 1935 and 1939, fall into the second Shōwa generation believed to be much better at coping with the complexities of a technological world than are their immediate seniors.

Differences in the amount of formal education that women in the present study received correspond more or less to the first and second generation Shōwa division. Most women had more than eight years of education, but, of the 107 people who had eight years or fewer, all but 4 of them were born in 1934 or earlier. Of these 107 women, only three received almost no education at all, and another 16 completed only the compulsory prewar education of six years' primary school. The remainder finished two more years of schooling, known before the war as upper primary school.

There is no doubt that the first generation of Shōwa women, several of whom worked during their adolescence in weapons factories or at other occupations related to the war effort, had a disrupted and curtailed education. Nevertheless, despite the intrusion of the war, among more than thirteen hundred women from a variety of backgrounds, only 10 percent of the sample received primary school education or less, while 45 percent completed junior high school, another 31 percent finished high school, 9 percent obtained a junior college degree or diploma, and a scant 5 percent finished university education or its equivalent.

The younger women in the sample completed a few more years of formal education, probably because their schooling was less severely disrupted by the war (Figure 4). Yet this small difference in actual classroom years may be somewhat deceptive if we consider educational content. As Lebra points out (1984), prewar education was sex segregated, and girls' schools devoted most of their time to domestic skills, training in good manners, deportment, and so on. Not until after the war was education standardized throughout the school system for all children. Hence, the older women in the sample may well not have received much academic training, even though they spent a reasonable amount of time in school.

Another characteristic of contemporary Japanese life makes it extremely difficult to classify the abilities, behavior, and knowledge of both men and women according to the number of years of formal education they received. In most communities in Japan today, urban and rural, much knowledge is disseminated through group meetings, talks, lectures, bulletins, pamphlets, and local journals in addition to that available in well-stocked libraries, local and national newspapers, weekly and monthly magazines, and, of course, television. Education is highly valued, particularly among middle-aged and older people, and in this almost universally literate population, most people think it appropriate to continue educating themselves until the end of their life—hence, they often counter deficiencies in their formal education. Many older people with little formal training thus gain a basic knowledge in a range of subjects, including very often a good grounding in human anatomy, physiology, and preventive medicine.

Not surprisingly, although people talk as if a clear line could, in effect, be drawn between people born before or in 1934 and those born later, this turns out to be an arbitrary division designed to capture in numbers and words the essence of a group of people who are thought to share certain characteristics. There is little evidence that people can be so neatly packaged by birth during specific ten-year segments of the Shōwa reign (or that in fact many Japanese believe in this division). Some of the women in the present sample, including a good number of those born after 1934, seem to have some of the proverbial characteristics of the *shōwa hitoketa*. Conversely, many exhibit none of these features, whether they were born in early Shōwa or a few years later. But most Japanese do accept the rhetoric about the *shōwa hitoketa*, which is important to the present discussion, because this rhetoric contributes to the beliefs about those at risk for a difficult *kōnenki* and those likely to sail through or ride over it with few problems.

Several of the characteristics said to typify people born in the early Shōwa years apply equally to men and women. In the first place the sixty-year-olds of today are often described as "not quite normal" (Plath 1975,

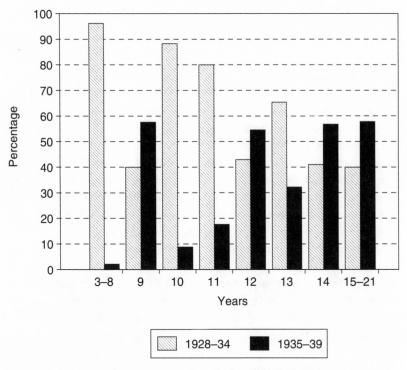

Figure 4. Education of Japanese Women ($N = 1,271$)

56). Their adolescence was severely disrupted by the war that robbed them of the relative freedom and lack of responsibility traditionally associated with youth; hence the early Shōwa generation went "gray" without ever having been "green" (youthful) (56). The *shōwa hitoketa* are known above all as workaholics (in a nation where the work ethic is perhaps the central value). They have experienced incredible hardship that not only they but many others believe to be important in the formation of a strong, balanced, and mature adult. They are frugal and not given to excesses, inept with members of the opposite sex (as compared to following generations), and less well educated. Plath summarizes the effect of the war on the education of the *shōwa hitoketa*:

> In most schools English was not taught, and there was a national campaign to extirpate the several hundred words of the "enemy language" that by then were part of everyday speech. . . . Sports and games were forbidden for the duration; by late in the war few balls or implements were available anyway. Secondary courses were accelerated or canceled, and students mobilized for work in

war material factories. In short the only thing the *hitoketa* were trained to do was to work hard.

(Plath 1975, 57–58)

Postwar Japan has transformed all this into a glittering success story. In the regular surveys conducted since the 1960s on the quality of life, educational levels, health, the work environment, and many similar topics, all are recognized as having improved. Only one exception repeatedly crops up: the state of the family is often said to be in decline. This exception brings women into sharp focus as the recognized "pillar" (*hashira*) of the family. Those women who are younger than the *hitoketa* are often described, in contrast to them, as lacking in social commitment, and as being overly interested in their own personal needs and wants (Kelly 1991). Comments on younger women frequently reflect nostalgia for the feminine qualities characteristic of early Shōwa women. One pediatrician who wrote a best-selling book, *Bogenbyō* (Illnesses caused by mother), claimed, for example, that whereas formerly Japanese women were good at child rearing, in the past twenty years they have become very poor at it. Industrialization has, he stated, distorted the "natural child-rearing instinct" into something that satisfies the mother's "narcissistic ego" (Kyūtoku 1979, 4).

Received wisdom about the women of early Shōwa, in contrast to younger people, is that they tended to preserve traditional values, particularly with respect to the household and work. The design of survey research often inadvertently supports such tacit beliefs. A summary discussion based on the results of a study by the Hakuhodo Institute of Life and Living (Japan's second biggest advertising agency) states, for example, that "older housewives" (that is, women aged forty-five through fifty-five) often do not feel comfortable with the social changes of postwar Japan:

Political rights for women, [the respondents] agreed, were necessary. However, they still believe that wives should listen to their husbands and try to support their husbands in any way possible.

Their married lives are characterized as adhering closely to traditional values: when their husbands returned home, sometimes around midnight, they made sure that the bath water was hot enough for their husbands to drain away the stresses and strains of the work day. They took out the kimono their husbands would wear while sipping hot sake and eating dinner.

They understood their husbands might not want to talk. "If I worked as hard as my husband did at his place of work, I wouldn't want to talk much," they thought. "In fact, I wouldn't want to be bothered much at all."

They did not bother their husbands with household affairs or
the problems they faced each day in raising children. Those were
their responsibilities as housewives and mothers. They fully realized that those were the qualities their husbands wanted.
(Hakuhodo Institute of Life and Living 1984, 111)

The subservient but nurturing characteristics of the older Japanese housewife, so apparent in this discussion, color the image from which the public
debate about *kōnenki* takes off. The debate in turn is just one small part
of a much larger and more pervasive recurring argument about how the
transformation of Japan from traditional to modern society affects the lives
and values of ordinary people.

From "Borrowed Womb" to "Good Wife and Wise Mother"

Contemporary Japanese feminists usually trace the origins of the inferior
position women have officially occupied through much of Japanese history
to concepts of pollution derived from Shinto, and, of even more significance, to early Buddhist doctrine about female inferiority (Uchino 1983).
The concept of *danson johi*, the "natural" subjugation of women, although
eventually legitimated by Confucianism, may have come to Japan with
Buddhism by way of India (Hirano 1984). In postwar years the middle-
class housewife became the representative of typical modern Japanese
women whose place in the home is by no means completely liberated from
danson johi but is tempered with a more recently created, benign-sounding
concept of "homebodies" (*kateiseikatsusha*). This latter image came into
vogue at the end of the last century during the Meiji era and reflects
European ideas current at the time.

Japanese society was, and remains, relatively homogeneous but has nevertheless been highly sensitive to rank, particularly before the Meiji Restoration of 1869. Until this era family structure had been reasonably flexible (except in the samurai class) and exhibited considerable regional
variation. Women's rights were limited under the feudal system that began
in the twelfth century; nevertheless, they could inherit property in certain
circumstances. Marriage and courtship customs were not strictly controlled, and, although women were expected to marry, they might even
(especially if they were peasants) choose their own marriage partners (Miyashita 1982). Despite this relative freedom menstruation and childbirth
symbolically marked women as ritually polluting, and they were segregated each month into menstrual huts[1] (Segawa 1947).

The official image of a woman was of a "borrowed womb," an *ie no
dōgu* (a household tool) or *karimono* (literally, a borrowed thing)—in

other words, a vehicle for the production of offspring to continue the paternal line. But in spite of this language, reproduction and the raising of children were not the sole determinants of a woman's maturation. The highly valued economic contribution of a young woman to the family was often sufficient to guarantee her security, even if she did not produce a child (Uno 1991; Walthall 1991). In a childless household the adoption of both males and females, often as adults, sometimes as married couples, was universally accepted as a means of providing heirs. Not only the male successor, the formal inheritor of the property, but his wife also had a recognized permanent position in the household; her name would join the roster of household ancestors (Backnik 1983).

It was among samurai families that repression of women was most apparent, as is evident from the best-known eighteenth-century treatise on the subject of women, *Onna Daigaku* (Greater learning for women):

> The five bad habits of a woman are being disobedient, bearing a grudge, being abusive, envious, and stupid. Of every ten women, seven or eight have these failings. They are the reason why women are inferior to men. Women should practice self-reflection to get rid of these habits. Being stupid is the principal cause of the five bad habits. Woman has the quality of *in* [yin in the classical Chinese yin-yang dualism]. . . .*In* is of the nature of the night and is dark. Hence, because compared to man, she is foolish, she does not understand her obvious duties. Nor does she bear in mind the chidings which she is given. Nor realize what brings misfortune onto her husband and children. . . .Because she is stupid, a woman must submit to her husband and behave modestly.
>
> (Kaibara Ekken [ca. 1714])

Books such as *Onna Daigaku*, grounded in Confucian morals, and written for families of rank, made almost no mention of women as mothers but instead directed attention toward the creation of appropriately servile and obedient daughters-in-law. They emphasized the teaching of etiquette and good manners, and the four virtues of *toku, gen, ryo,* and *kō* (morals, speech, looks, and work). "Morals" meant, in essence, chastity, while "speech" referred to the use of humble and polite female forms of language, "looks" to modesty and ladylike behavior, and the "virtue of work" meant the industrious performance of household enterprises such as silk weaving and paper making in addition to domestic activities (Kakehi 1985). Some Confucian scholars encouraged the teaching of reading and writing to women, but largely to improve their value as potential daughters-in-law.

The oldest extant book on child care in Japanese was written in 1695; it consists almost entirely of prohibitions and threats to induce unquestioning obedience and submission on the part of young mothers. The Confucian edict held that it was natural for women to obey: first their fathers, then after marriage their husbands, and finally in old age their sons. Moreover, it set up opposition between women of different generations, since the older woman was in charge of the training and discipline necessary to allow the younger woman to take over responsibility for the management of the extended household affairs. It was here, in the discipline for life in an extended household, that the foundations for the proverbial hostility between mother-in-law and daughter-in-law lay. Under this regime women could never become the official guardians of their own children. During the Tokugawa period (1603–1867) Confucian ideas supported the treatment of women as property: they had no independent legal rights, concubinage was actively encouraged, and women could be put to death for adultery or any suspicion of it (Sievers 1983, 4–6). This repressive attitude, combined with earlier Buddhist notions of the inferiority of women, ensured that in many samurai and socially aspiring merchant families women endured a miserable life.

With the opening up of Japan to outsiders after the Meiji Restoration of 1868, one of the driving forces for change was a desire to show the country's civilized standards. Although many government leaders were apparently comfortable with the continuation of their "geisha society" (Takamure 1977, 490), they acquiesced to the Western perception that the status of women was an important measure of any society's progress toward civilization. Debate about women's status became a national occupation in Japan, symbolized by the slogan of *onna mo hito nari*: women are people too. Predictably, reactions by those in power were mixed: on the one hand there was support for the public education of women and on the other hand for concubines who were given the same rights as wives; married women were no longer required to blacken their teeth with lacquer or shave their eyebrows (formerly the custom among samurai and some merchant families) yet were forbidden to cut their hair short, a fashion that smacked of rampant progressivism.

One or two influential statesmen believed that the low status of women contributed to Japan's "backwardness" and made family reform into a key issue. Although Fukuzawa Yukichi, Mori Arinori, and a few others pushed for equality between husbands and wives, they limited their arguments to changes in family relationships because their revolutionary ideals did not extend to the notion that Japanese women were ready to take their place in society at large (Sievers 1983, 22). Nevertheless, these statesmen agreed that improved education for women was necessary to allow them to contribute actively to the modernization of the family and in particular, for the first time, to the education of their children.

At the end of the nineteenth century in Japan, as in many European countries, female nurturance rather than mere fertility came to be valued. The inborn nature of woman, it was argued, is the way biology best "equips" her to nurture others (Nakamura 1976); such arguments referred to her position below man on the recently created ladder of social evolution (Herbert Spencer was widely read in Japan).[2] Until this time the "will of heaven" had legitimized the second-class status of women (Matsumoto 1988, 182), but the Meiji era's newly discovered scientific concept of a mothering "instinct" (*bosei honno*) now became available to justify their status.

In keeping with a biologically informed understanding of motherhood, a Japanese woman was encouraged, as her European counterpart had been counseled a quarter of a century earlier, to nurture her children and to become their guardian and educator during the formative years—yet only within the domestic sphere. Hence, education of females was recognized as important to equip them to carry out their life's mission successfully. Women were urged, therefore, to be conversant with morals, religion, etiquette, and with the newly emerging field of domestic science. Those women in the present study who were born in the late 1920s and early 1930s were the last ones to undergo the vestiges of this kind of schooling.

Nakamura Masanao, a Meiji statesman and Christian convert who had traveled extensively in the West, was a key figure in the popularization of the contemporary European appellation of the "affectionate wife, wise mother." The epithet, created by the poet Robert Burns, was translated as *ryōsai kenbo* (good wife, wise mother) and Meiji literature is replete with descriptions of how a woman might best deport herself in order to become both good and wise (Kameda 1984). Meiji women slowly received a degree of informal autonomy within the household, largely in order to fulfill their newly granted duties as guardians and educators of their children (Hirano 1984). They were to be at once modest, courageous, frugal, literate, hardworking, and economically productive—this last to such an extent that the rhetoric of the day has been described as a "cult of productivity," in contrast to the North American and European "cult of domesticity" (Nolte and Hastings 1991, 154). The shift, with its emphasis on productivity inside the home and the appropriate raising of children, overturned the premodern differentiation of women by class and for the first time addressed them as a whole, as women and as Japanese (Nolte and Hastings 1991).

Some reformers of the time, men and women alike, worked extremely hard for greater political and legal rights for women. Women were still expected to be servile (*hikutsu*), they claimed; talk of freedom and equality in fact referred only to men. If Japan was to attain "civilization and enlightenment" (*bunmeikaika*), then, they asserted, women must be given more independence (Mitsuda 1985, 110). However, aside from a brief ray of hope for major reform right after the Meiji Restoration, the official status of Japanese women remained largely unchanged until after the Second World War (Sievers 1983).

One preoccupation of the early Meiji period was the consolidation of centralized bureaucratic control over the nation as a whole, and with it the production of a modern citizenry. The Meiji Civil Code, enacted in 1898, imposed throughout Japan the family system of the samurai class. Among this privileged class during the feudal period the *ie* (household) had become established as a distinct economic unit (Cornell 1990). Etymologically, the term *ie* signifies the hearth; in practice it includes the idea of both the house and its residents—a property-owning corporate group. The *ie* emphasizes vertical ties between the ancestors, living members of the household, and the generations to follow. In theory, at least, the *ie* does not extend laterally to any extent, and a single married couple with their children live under one roof with the husband's parents, from whom they would eventually inherit the property. The Meiji Civil Code required everyone to be registered as part of an *ie*, and restricted inheritance of the property to the eldest son. Unless deemed mentally incompetent, the eldest son acted as the representative of his family to the state when his father retired; he assumed complete responsibility for its stewardship and for the well-being, behavior, and marriages of other family members. If the family had no sons, then the eldest daughter was married to a suitable candidate who was formally adopted into the *ie* and made responsible for its future. All children, with the exception of the one designated as heir, were expected to leave the *ie* on marriage and either start up a branch family or, in the case of daughters, become formally incorporated into another *ie* through marriage.

Under this new code the rights of women became more confined and restricted, disappointing those who had hoped that the overthrow of feudalism would bring some improvement to their position. The new code effectively denied women independent legal standing, relegating them to the same position as deformed and mentally retarded individuals (Sievers 1983, 111). They no longer had any say in their own marriage arrangements and could be divorced on almost any grounds, but most particularly if they did not produce a male heir (a childless woman was described as a "stone woman"). Confucian tenets of filial piety and unquestioning loyalty were the order of the day, and the primary obligation of all family members was to serve and preserve the *ie*, endowed with spiritual qualities, manifest most obviously in the presence of a Buddhist altar in the household, complete with memorial tablets to the ancestors.

The economic function of the *ie* was always crucial but, most particularly because the ancestors were present, the household was also a repository of moral order (Smith 1974, 151). When raising their children, parents made use of the presence of the ancestors to legitimize their authority beyond mere parental rights into a sacred mission. This custom was indirectly reinforced by the Meiji rulers who faced the problem that every nation-state must tackle at its inception, namely, how to make good citizens out of peasants whose native loyalties are to local communities and to regions. Their answer to this problem was to create a concept of the state-as-family (*kazoku kokka*) and to fuse the ethos of the continuity of the sacred line of Japanese emperors from time immemorial with the idea of the continuity of the patrilineal household. Thus each *ie* became a microcosm of the nation, the all-embracing macrocosmic family unit of which the emperor was the parent figure. As the state became the custodian of every aspect of society and culture, the household became, in effect, a public place subject to surveillance, where "private feelings should be forgotten" (from *The Meiji Greater Learning for Women*, cited in Nolte and Hastings 1991, 156).

Not everyone fully conformed to this authoritarian regime, of course. Nevertheless the ideology associated with the *ie* spread throughout Japan, identifying individuals and their needs with the household, the most fundamental of social units, and subordinating them to it. Under these circumstances the position of women remained severely constrained. Sievers comments, "*Danson johi*, that attitude of contempt for women that Meiji feminists had struggled against for three decades, was now reemphasized, with official approval. . . . Women once more were to be 'borrowed wombs.' The difference was that they were now expected to provide sons, not only for the family, but for the Empire" (Sievers 1983, 111).

In line with this ideology, women were educated for patriotism, since it was believed that love of one's country is best learned from that "natural teacher," the mother (Mitsuda 1985, 119). At the same time abortion was officially abolished in order to increase rural population, and women were encouraged to have large families. Although it was recognized that many women had to labor in the fields, they were nevertheless strongly encouraged to take very seriously their duties as mothers and to devote time to the household and education of their children in addition to doing piecework for money at home (117). In the name of the "improvement of the race" (*jinshukairyō*), attention was turned for the first time to maternal health. Thus, by the turn of the century, the "good wife and wise mother" had become central to a reactionary ideology that was bent on modernizing the Japanese nation under the banner of nationalism. Children were explicitly regarded as offspring of the state who must be molded into patriotic citizens. The raising of children, which continued to take priority over actual reproduction, was described as a "heaven-sent vocation" (*tenshoku*), in which training in "love of country" and physical strength were regarded as the most important qualities (Naruse 1894, cited by Mitsuda). Although being a good housewife was also recognized as valuable, this aspect of a woman's work was thought of as relatively private, whereas nurturance of children was considered to possess more importance since it was for the public good (127).

In contrast to the situation in feudal times, therefore, in turn-of-the-century Japan active maternalism (*bosei*), rather than servile obedience, became associated with ideal womanhood; some scholars interpret this shift as leading women toward the situation of thirty years later when they became known as *gunkoku no haha*: mothers of militarism. The inculcation of correct female behavior took place largely in the school system. Smith, drawing on the extensive field notes Ella Wiswell took in a remote Kyushu village in the 1930s, shows the effectiveness of this education in reducing the incidence of divorce, premarital sexual activity, and pregnancy, activities repressed less severely before this century (Smith 1983).

In summing up the situation of women at the turn of the century, Uno points out that they benefited from the formal education that was now required for girls (by 1910 over 97 percent were receiving at least six years of compulsory education [Nolte and Hastings 1991]) but that at the same time they were barred from politics and from universities and stripped of most property rights. It was at this juncture in Japanese history that a clear separation of home from workplace was evident for the first time, including a marked division of gender roles in terms of daily activities (Uno 1991, 41). Here lies the origin of the occupation that became known after the war as "professional housewife."

These changes in the status of women throughout the Meiji, Taishō, and early Shōwa periods have been summarized retrospectively by Japanese feminists as *boseiron*. This "treatise on motherhood" promoted equality between men and women in the domestic sphere in some measure while it opposed the participation of women in society at large, but it made one major exception, for blue-collar labor. Industrialization took off in Meiji Japan: textile and other light industries flourished largely with the conscription of young women, mostly from rural areas, who worked in appalling conditions for low wages until they were married off. Other women worked in the Kyushu mines, and still others helped to build roads. By 1890 women had become the backbone of the modernizing Japanese economy. Female workers outnumbered males in light industry, particularly in textiles, where a work force that was in some places as high as 90 percent female "produced 40 percent of the gross national product and 60 percent of the foreign exchange during the late nineteenth century" (Nolte and Hastings 1991, 1). Hence large numbers of women had the experience of working outside the home for a few years, even in the heyday of the homebody, but, as Smith points out, "with the rarest exceptions none ever had a career" (Smith 1987, 9).

During the early part of the century a growing feminist consciousness emerged, but most changes came from within the confines of the state-dominated political order (Garon 1993). Women who worked, particularly in white-collar jobs, were regarded with suspicion and officially encouraged to take the task of running a household seriously, to make it into a rational economic endeavor (Nagy 1991). In 1922 women achieved the right to take part in political activities, although they could not vote until 1947; an increasing number of women in the labor force joined unions. Women's newfound rights were eclipsed by preparations for war, as good wives and wise mothers were mobilized to produce male offspring for the army and later to work in factories for the war effort.

A conscious effort toward community solidarity during the 1930s focused on poorly integrated urban areas and their newly arrived migrants from rural areas (Smith 1983); it drew explicitly on a nostalgic and idealized view of village life with the *ie* as its spiritual center and the woman as the pillar of the *ie*: this sentiment was to surface again in the aftermath of defeat in war.

To a large extent, the state of women in prewar Japan indicates that the shades of Kaibara Ekken and like-minded eighteenth-century thinkers lingered on, as Smith sums up:

> Prewar Japan was a highly androcentric society in which women lived out their lives at a disadvantage that was not merely legally defined. Marriage meant being separated from their natal families and going into another with the chief requirement that they bear

children. Work meant short-term employment in dead-end jobs. Security, which lay in conforming to the ideal of good wife and wise mother, was to be found only in the domestic realm. Divorce rates were very high, and those who failed to achieve domestic security were likely to meet a very grim fate indeed. Underlying all this is the prevailing sentiment held by those who constructed and operated the political, economic, and social systems. In their view the good and virtuous woman . . . was nonetheless a limited being. Women were thought to be less intelligent than men, more emotional and so less rational, less reliable, vindictive, potentially dangerous if not rigorously disciplined, and worst of all, silly. It is a major irony of that system that the rearing of the men who made it was largely entrusted to women and that the harsh discipline thought so necessary in the training of a young wife was administered almost exclusively by her mother-in-law.

(Smith 1987, 9–10)

The specter of this premodern mother is still evident in Japan today. One of her latest incarnations hovers over a Kyushu school for girls that claims for its governance the spirit of *ryōsai kenbo* and that puts forth as its explicit educational goal the production of "wise mothers [*kenbo*] who will be household managers" [*Mainichi shinbun* 1983a]. The comments of many women interviewed in the present study also reveal the survival of an ideal of female subservience. When asked if men and women are basically the same in potential ability, a housewife who lives in Nagano put it this way:

"Oh, no! They are basically different. In personality, for instance, men are much more broad-minded and tolerant. Women tend to gossip and criticize others behind their backs; men never do that. If they have something to say, then they say it directly. I like men's personality better."

"Any other kinds of differences?"

"Men are healthier, and even when they are sick they don't brood over it."

"Do you think that women are inferior to men then?"

"No, I don't think that, just different. Men are smarter. Nowadays women are doing many things, but you know, in Japan they have always said that the worst man is equal to the best woman (my mother used to tell me this all the time), and if I compare myself to my husband, I can see what they mean."

Another housewife living in Kobe stated:

"I think there are inborn differences between men and women. Women seem to be lacking in the skills needed to get on in society. Career women, even those who work as hard as can be, always turn to the home when they run into problems on the job."

"So do you think that a woman should not work?"

"No, that's fine, but she must like to cook too. And of course she should be good at responding to other people's needs and wishes, or else she couldn't be comfortable with herself. I would want a daughter of mine to first have feminine things as a base and then find some job that would build on that."

A Nagano woman who grows chrysanthemums for sale throughout Japan was emphatic about inborn gender differences.

"I once heard a lecture in which the speaker said there's absolutely no difference in ability between men and women. I remember thinking at the time, That's not possible. Of course, housewives are always busy with little tasks, that's a woman's role. Still, when you put a man and a woman up together, I don't see how you can say there is no difference. It's not just physical strength either, women are just weaker in every way."

Another woman from Nagano who farms rice and vegetables illustrated her answer with the following story:

"Yes, I think women are inferior to men in some ways—well, maybe I don't really think that so much. Recently it was our family's turn to take part in a committee to do with local elections and since my husband wasn't well, I went instead. At first I was doubtful if I could do anything much, as a woman among mostly men. The group was supposed to go out and visit potential candidates, and I thought the women should just stay behind at the committee room and watch over the gas heaters to see they didn't go out or anything, but they said everyone should go. So then I tried to think what we as women could do and decided we could be useful in helping convince the potential candidate's wife. Afterward the committee chairman seemed very appreciative and admitted he'd had reservations about having women on the committee, but he said he'd changed his mind now. I hadn't been expecting anything like that and it made me really happy."

A worker in a small firm that makes Japanese dolls stated that she is not against women working but qualified her comments:

"Work is very hard for a woman. She mustn't use the fact that she is working as an excuse not to do her housework or not to look after the children properly. It's important that a woman keep up her duties at home first of all."

Of course, these women are rehearsing for the listener's benefit a set of values they may well not believe in very deeply or act on in their own daily lives. But, at the level of ideology at least, the majority of women hold an opinion more or less in agreement with that of the dollmaker. Most said something to this effect: Basically men are suited to be outside in society and women are suited to working in the house. The usual term for wife in Japanese (*okusan*), which literally means "the person inside" or "in the back," reinforces this attitude. Moreover, a good number expect their own daughters to adhere to this ideology and had deliberately raised them with this expectation in mind. A psychological counselor, married to a university teacher and the mother of three young women in their twenties, said:

"Nowadays girls don't do anything except study, and most of them have never even chopped a single cucumber. I don't think the motherly instinct just comes out naturally in women—it has to be cultivated. So I always taught my girls about feminine qualities and I encouraged them to create a warm atmosphere around other people. And I also taught them how to do things around the house properly. Even so my eldest daughter is still not feminine enough and she's never going to find a husband unless she changes her ways."

"How will you feel about your daughters working after they've had children?"

"Oh, that's the natural thing from now on in Japan. I'm ready to give up my work and become a full-time grandmother in order to take care of the children. That will be just fine with me."

A forty-five-year-old Nagano farmer deliberately raised her two girls differently from her son:

"I want my girls to have the same chance for university education as their brother. But most of my neighbors don't agree with me, and they hint that we'll be wasting our money. I must say that I'm worried about delaying their marriages if they go to university, but I've made up my mind, and if they want to go, then that's what they'll do."

"Did you raise them differently from their brother?"

"Yes, I've always trained them in housework and I taught them both how to sew. I think that a mother has to be able to make her own children's aprons and skirts by herself. During school holidays I sent the girls every day for a month to a sewing instructor for three or four years. And I've taught them how to knit too. I didn't exactly teach them good manners, but they learned that in school and I always made them sit up straight and talk with a gentle voice at home."

"What about your son?"

"I wanted him to help around the house too but somehow, with an older sister around, it didn't work out that way."

Making up a granddaughter for presentation at a shrine on her third birthday.

"How will you feel about your daughters working after they've had children?"

"I think the system is at fault at present. At the moment a woman can only take two months or so for maternity leave and I think that's much too short. We need to have a system in which a mother stays with her child until it's three years old, and then she can go back to her old job. I don't think that leaving a newborn baby at a nursery is right at all, not for nine or ten hours a day. If *obāsan* is at home and provides the child care then that's fine, but so often that's not the way things are these days. I feel really sorry for those city babies."

In contrast to most women who, judging from their responses, do not appear to think that any kind of radical restructuring of gender roles is in order, some were outspokenly in opposition to the present situation. A Nagano woman who works together with her husband as a pharmacist was emphatic about how things could be changed for the better:

"Japanese women have always been treated as inferior socially, but nowadays there are any number of women who are able to do the same work as men. Since that's the case, the ideal society would be one where the men share the housework. If men and women are equal outside the home, but inside the woman has to shoulder all the housework, she can't do her best at her job. For this to happen, men have to understand the woman's position, but that's impossible with older men. However, I think it will be different for our children; they've been educated differently—boys have to do some cleaning up and so on. I always tell my son: 'In this household, you just think it's natural for me to be doing all the housework, but you can't be like that when you have a wife.' Older men have been told since the time they were babies that men don't belong in the kitchen, so they're completely resistant to change."

Clearly there have always been women and men who resisted the norm of female subservience, but the evidence suggests overwhelmingly that service to the *ie* and its preservation did indeed guide the lives of many prewar Japanese women and that the legacy of this ideology is by no means laid to rest. In the world "outside," the majority of women in their forties and fifties apparently remain submissive, and it is customary even today for many of them to ask permission from their husbands before undertaking activities beyond the confines of the house (Higuchi 1985, 55).

These *shōwa hitoketa* are assumed to be, however, the last generation of homebodies who unobtrusively, frugally, and efficiently run a household in which their husbands play the central role. They are the only remaining cohort of women the great majority of whom received explicit instruction in how to be a "good wife and wise mother" under the forbidding tutelage of their mothers-in-law with whom they lived. Some believe that for the Japanese family the consequences of relinquishing this tradition will be dire and are already beginning to manifest themselves.

From Good Wife and Wise Mother to Professional Housewife

Unlike most of the developing societies of today, Japan was in a position to orchestrate its own transition to modernity, and to accept only those foreign values and commodities it deemed useful while rejecting those it considered threatening to traditional order. This relatively gradual transformation starting before the middle of the last century came to an abrupt halt at the end of the Second World War in defeat and the ensuing economic and spiritual crisis. After an initial period of numbed shock, the next twenty years or so appeared to bring Japanese society wholeheartedly into the Western sphere, including acceptance of the nuclear family as the natural primary unit for modern times. Arguments about individual rights and freedom, although by no means new, also occupied more time and energy than in prewar days, since traditional group-oriented values were thought to be responsible for the nationalistic regime that brought crushing defeat and crippling poverty to Japan. It is proverbial wisdom that after the war women, "like nylon stockings," became much stronger. The new Civil Code of 1947 franchised women and made them legally independent for the first time (although even today a considerable gap remains between the intent of the code and its implementation). The *ie* was abolished and, with the promotion of sexual equality, individuals were free to choose their marriage partners and establish their own households should they so choose.

During the postwar years the role of the Meiji homebody—now become the "professional" or "full-time" housewife (*sengyō shufu*)—was extended and refined (the autonomy associated with this position now commonly allows women to describe their husbands as an extra, troublesome child around the household, where they live together with their two children [1.53 according to the latest statistics]). The behavior and discipline (*shitsuke*) expected of women of today draw on an assorted mixture of values gleaned from rules laid down in feudal times for the wives of samurai, often glossed as *onna rashisa* (womanly behavior). The Confucian ideals encouraged discipline in women, not for military service, but for unquestioning submission and obedience to those they perceived as their superiors. The *shōwa hitoketa*, like their predecessors in Meiji times, were taught as children to believe that patience, diligence, endurance, eventemperedness, compliance, and gentleness all contribute to womanliness. Moral training in these virtues led to an internalization of the right attitude and behavioral style, outwardly manifested in many ways, but most obviously in physical comportment and language usage (Lebra 1984, 46). One extreme example of such behavior today is that of elegantly uniformed, white-gloved young women, using exquisitely polite language, who greet customers at select department stores in a high-pitched "refined" voice and bow them into elevators or wipe the already spotless rail of an escalator ready for their ascent to higher floors.

Use of feminine language (inevitably associated with submissiveness and gentleness) still goes virtually unquestioned by anyone over thirty (Ide 1982) with the exception only of a few outspoken feminists. This is not to suggest that women who farm or those who are in the labor force make frequent use of this language, but they, like housewives, do not seriously question the reasons for its existence. Modesty, reticence, and a soft voice are considered important, and covering with one's hand the unsightly opened mouth created by a smile is still common. Courteous greetings, good posture, a neat appearance, good manners, elegance in the handling of things, an orderly house, and established life-style routines are all connected with womanly behavior (Lebra 1984, 42). Many books are published to teach mothers how to discipline their girls correctly in these skills (Hamao 1987). Most of the women in the present study were

Young girls are disciplined from an early age in graceful deportment and behavior.

explicitly taught *shitsuke*, first of all as young children by their mothers, then in school, and again as young adults when they took classes that prepared them for marriage. Some women, even in their fifties, stated that their husbands still admonish them for not conducting themselves in a sufficiently "womanly" way.

A Kobe housewife of fifty-four commented on womanly behavior:

"Women have delicacy and gentleness. You know, they've talked about *onna rashisa* since the old days in Japan, and I think it's best to live in accord with that. Of course there are some women who are special, who can work the same as men, but even they are best at doing things like nursery-school teaching and nursing.

"Young girls have lost their *onna rashisa*, they have no consideration for others; equality and freedom are being misinterpreted. They drink and smoke and if you criticize them they say, 'It's my body, I can do what I like.' But a woman's most important job is bearing children, so her body is not her own; it's meant for leaving descendants."

This housewife, in common with many others we spoke to, prides herself on getting up at 5:30 each day in order to prepare breakfast and nutritious boxed lunches for the family, and she retires to bed at midnight once she has finished clearing up after everyone else. She claims that she never openly expresses an opinion contrary to that of her husband, but she admits that she goes ahead and acts on her own initiative in many matters of which her husband is unaware. Reinforcing these traditional values today are the mass media, where images of "foolish" and "green" young women who will, it is hoped, eventually become "wise" mothers, are the norm:

> Young, cute, smiling and apparently mute girl-women are on every genre of [television] program at any hour of the day or night. Why does this phenomenon exist? Television personalities reflect the ideals and values of any given society, and the women that appear on television are therefore only "ideal" women. . . .In Japan women, in order to fit the definition of the ideal woman, must not only be youthful and pretty, but they should also be sweetly silent.
>
> According to Tomoyo Nonaka, a newscaster, . . . "People think of women as flowers and if there were no women on TV it would be a bit bizarre. So they think, OK, let's put a nice flower on the table."
>
> These televised blossoms not only represent idealized women but they also act out the ideal role between women and men. The reason that these women are not outspoken is that they must be properly deferential toward men.
>
> (Itasaka 1984)

While some women such as Itasaka-*san* take an active stand against what they perceive to be rampant sexism, the majority of middle-aged women seem to be comfortable with their position in society. When asked to compare Japanese and Western women, a fifty-five-year-old woman from a Nagano farming family responded in the following way:

"I think that Japanese women don't fall short of Western women in any way. They hold back [*hikaeru*] just a bit, and I think that's more attractive—with apologies to you, professor [!]. For instance, take Nancy Reagan and Crown Princess Michiko [now the empress]: Nancy gets off the plane first, while Princess Michiko hangs back. I think the latter is more pleasing to see. Japanese women can go out into the world boldly these days and 'fly'—they can hold their own with anyone—but somehow they're more modest [*hikaeme*], and I think that's a Japanese woman's most beautiful point. I think even for active women, there is a basic female appearance that doesn't change. Doi-*san* [the former leader of the Socialist party], for instance, is quite impressive, but at the same time she is somehow *onnarashii* [feminine]. I often think Western women appear to be in a higher position than men and are somehow arrogant.

"Young Japanese women are changing, I guess, but even they have a basic femininity, and they treat their husbands with respect—well, maybe that's not the right expression, perhaps that's going too far, but anyway, even though they're more outspoken today, somehow their attitude is different from Western women."

Another Nagano farming woman living in a neighboring village is of a rather different opinion:

"I think it's terrible that discrimination against women in the workplace still goes on. But now that Doi Takako has become head of the Socialist party, I suppose women will do better, but there's still a long way to go before Japan produces someone as imposing as Thatcher. I think men are changing a little, though, but people still keep using expressions like 'because she's a woman . . . ,' and 'that's typical women's behavior' . . . and so on all the time; they should stop doing that."

Womanly behavior is not encouraged simply to produce elegant "flowers," despite the cynicism of some activists. Married women cultivate femininity as an integral part of the work ethic. It is a discipline expressly designed to produce submission of self for the task of nurturance, to create the pillar of the household, a stable, controlled but calm center on which other family members may depend for their well-being. As a young bride a woman was, until recently, schooled by *obāsan* in the traditions of the household she married into. In many parts of the country *obāsan's* retirement was the occasion when the rice paddle was formally handed over to the younger woman (*shamoji watashi*) as a signal of her expanding powers in the household, and at about fifty she would finally come into her own and receive a daughter-in-law whom she could train. At that time she would no longer do menial household tasks but instead take on a range of demanding responsibilities, including conducting religious rituals and managing the family business and finances of the extended family. While her husband and son acted as breadwinners, therefore, a middle-aged woman played a crucial managerial role (Lebra 1984, 135); in an extended family, middle age for both men and women was sometimes called *hatar-*

aki zakari (the full bloom of one's working life). In prewar days, at about the time she went through *kōnenki*, a woman achieved the greatest possible power and responsibility available to her, and maturity was in all probability a time of considerable pleasure. Most particularly, as a grandmother, a woman usually took over many aspects of child care, more than for her own children—care that often included close, relaxed physical contact while bathing with and sleeping beside grandchildren, customs still widely practiced today.

Plath points out that middle age is a "time of encounter between the life history and the life cycle: we become caught up as never before in the life events of others" (1975, 54). In an extended family this interconnection is salient, the more so because in Japan the individual process of aging has usually gone unmarked throughout the middle years of life; a woman was conscious of her aging more in terms of her relationships to other people than as a result of her changing biology. Individual events such as birthdays, and even the end of menstruation implying the closure of reproduction, had little significance. Of more importance were the special days such as when a woman took over responsibility from her mother-in-law and became the senior female in the house; when her son married and brought back a bride to join the household; or when her daughter married and left the household. Only then could a woman truly think of herself as *ichi nin mae* (a mature adult). Hence, the life course of an individual was plotted primarily in terms of the activities of those around her, and only secondarily in terms of individual aging. Not that individual age and aging were entirely forgotten, but they were overshadowed by changes in family relationships.

Leisured Illness

Shōwa hitoketa women are now poised like Janus, contemplating both tradition and modernity. When they muse on the past they can recall the comfort and duties of the extended family, of submersion of self in the household, of life lived above all for the sake of future generations. When they consider their present condition and the future, many of them face thirty years or more of life with a single obvious role to fill: nursemaid to husband and aged in-laws. Their spouses, also products of the extended family system, do not expect or know how to look after themselves or offer companionship for their wives; both partners were raised in the expectation of finding their strongest bonds of companionship with people of the same sex.

Whereas a middle-aged woman had a crucially important managerial role to play in the *ie* of prewar Japan, in a nuclear family her position is anomalous. Ambiguities of contemporary female midlife layer one on another: society values hard work, perseverance, and self-discipline; but running a small modern household for a husband absent most of the time requires few of these virtues. The media still laud middle-aged women as the pillar of the family, as women who devote themselves fully to the care of others. But critics often comment that these same women are bored and lonely, most particularly because they do not know how to work outside the house and in any case frequently encounter a good deal of resistance from husbands and others when they try. Many critics acknowledge that these women are the victims of modernization, that the nuclearization of the family has forced them into a structurally redundant position, but others apparently envy an imagined new freedom from the drudgery of the household into a life of luxury. From some quarters comes the suggestion that middle-aged women today are in *onna tengoku* (women's heaven), where they live a life of fun and leisure while their menfolk are worked so hard that some of them are worked literally to death (*Mainichi Daily News* 1990).

While the rhetoric about the luxury and the loneliness of many housewives has more than a grain of truth, it glosses over (deliberately?) the complexity of both working and living arrangements in pre- and postwar Japan to portray middle-aged women en masse as living a life of ease. The image of the postwar middle-class family is one composed of a salaried husband, a full-time professional housewife, and two studious children, but, although close to 90 percent of Japanese people regularly identify themselves in national surveys as middle-class, nevertheless most adult women in this category either work full time (although the work may be labeled part-time) or at least for several hours a day.

In the present study, 58 percent of the women living in what is recognized as the solidly middle-class environment of Kobe described themselves as something other than *sengyō shufu* (full-time housewives). In contrast, nearly 25 percent of the women living outside an urban middle-class environment described themselves as housewives and had no obvious employment. In all, only 20 percent of the sample described themselves as housewives—thus they are by no means representative of middle-aged Japanese women and we cannot simply distinguish between working women and urban professional housewives. Nevertheless, in most publications, and particularly in the media, the professional housewife is the one who comes to mind as Mrs. Average, and she is the one labeled as particularly at risk for *kōnenki* disorders. An Osaka gynecologist, when asked if he thought that all women experience trouble at *kōnenki*, answered:

"Not necessarily. Women who are busy, who don't have much leisure, don't have many complaints. *Kōnenki shōgai* is a sort of 'luxury disease' [*zeitakubyō*], it's 'high-class.' Women with lots of free time on their hands are the ones who say it's so bad."

A Tokyo internist, reflecting on the image he has of his middle-aged patients, said:

"These women have no *ikigai* [purpose in life]. They have free time but can't think of anything to do, so they get a psychosomatic reaction; they can't complain openly so they use *organ language* [said in English]. They find there is no reward today for all their sacrifice and suppression, and they're lonely. Working women have fewer symptoms and in any case don't notice them. Housewives can't control and master their symptoms as they used to."

And a physician practicing in Yokohama stated:

"They say women have become stronger, but I think they may have a mistaken idea about strength. Women must be gentle [*yasashii*] and must be able to comfort and take care of others. Taking care of people doesn't mean that one is weak. Nowadays women seem to feel they must really push themselves when they are in *kōnenki*, and instead of just living through it by looking after their health properly, they come for help from us doctors."

A physician who specializes in the practice of traditional herbal medicine focused on family dynamics in addition to individual shortcomings:

"Being in a nuclear family affects women very much. There is no one to teach life's wisdom to the children and everything falls onto the shoulders of the housewife. She often becomes neurotic, obsessed with trying to create a good child. Her husband doesn't talk to her. Also women have changed, they used to *gaman* [persevere, endure], but they've lost all that since women's lib. They have low self-control now."

One or two doctors commented on the attitudes of husbands:

"The husbands of women with *kōnenki* problems are often interested only in their work, and they may have trouble with sex, either because they're using all their energies in their work, or because they've lost interest in their wives: 'She's getting to be a dumpy middle-aged woman—no good any more.' In these homes the housewife may be just like a maid."

Several physicians pointed out that "lower-class" women who work, and others who live in extended families and do rural work, have few problems with *kōnenki* because they are (the doctors suggested) "too busy" to notice any minor physical ailments that might occur at this time. A physician who practices in the countryside in Shiga prefecture claims that he sees fewer women with problems related to *kōnenki* than was formerly the case:

"Lately I haven't had many women complaining about *kōnenki*, they haven't been coming with headaches and *darui* [lassitude] and so on. That's because nowadays all the fifty-year-olds are working. Because they have paid employment it helps them psychologically, and they feel they're contributing to the family income."

"But surely in the countryside women have always worked?"

"Yes, but around here they just went to the mountains two or three days a week for a few hours to take care of the trees, they had more free time then. Now they all work regular hours in the factory outlets and I think they feel more responsible. They don't come complaining about little things any more."

These excerpts from physicians' narratives reveal the extent to which a moral discourse accompanies the physical symptoms of *kōnenki*. But physicians are not the only ones who think this way. Many women have accepted the rhetoric at face value and see it as relevant to their own lives. A Kobe housewife stated:

"My mother had seven children, and the way it was in those days, she had no freedom, in fact she had no self [*jibun ga nai*]; she was always suppressing herself and not letting anything show on the surface. I can't do that, I'm a spoiled type and I had trouble at *kōnenki*. Women who work or have hard lives don't suffer."

Another Kobe housewife sought help from her doctor:

"My family doctor told me to take up another hobby when I went to see him about the headaches I kept having. He said it was *kōnenki* and that I needed to do something with my time. I'm tired of flower arranging and tea ceremony—that's for young girls who have to catch a husband. I tried doing watercolors for a time . . . My life has no purpose. My sole job is to look after my husband, but he's never at home and in any case we just avoid talking to each other. I've thought about going out to work, but I can't do anything, and anyway it doesn't look right if a professor's wife works."

Other women spontaneously gave information about how best to avoid problems at *kōnenki* or, in some cases, how to avoid *kōnenki* altogether. A Nagano woman who farms commented:

"I think if a woman keeps herself occupied every day and intellectually active, then she might be able to avoid *kōnenki*. It's a disease of housewives who are financially secure and have a lot of spare time and nothing much to worry about. I think they could avoid it by keeping their eyes open to the outside world and do some volunteer work such as becoming home helpers or helping with people who're mentally ill—by contributing to society instead of being so selfish. Around here we always encourage each other, and someone who might have a difficult *kōnenki* is usually asked to become the leader of our local women's group to keep her mentally active."

A woman who works in a textile factory responded:

"I've heard from one or two housewives that they have severe headaches—so much so that they can't keep their heads up. I told them it's because they have so much free time. I think they should get out and do some work, even if their husbands complain about it."

A factory worker who bottles beer all day feels much the same way:

"I'm glad I have a job. I hear some housewives can't even go shopping when they reach *kōnenki*. If you have something to do, even a hobby, then it helps. Even if you're just a housewife you should find something to do. Those women actually have mental problems as well as headaches and dizziness. They seem to get really irritable."

Nemoto-*san* is a "part-time" office worker who works eight or nine hours a day during the week and three out of every four Saturday mornings in addition to doing all the housework and taking care of her husband and twenty-year-old daughter who is being trained as a hairdresser. She says:

"I'm in *kōnenki* right now, I keep getting chilly and I feel tired. My husband says it's because I'm so lazy, and that if I don't pull myself together I'm not going to be able to move before too long. That sounds awful doesn't it? But, you know, that's his way of showing some sympathy."

Belief in the supposed vulnerability of the leisured housewife to menopausal symptoms is ubiquitous in Japan today, even though this housewife, like other fifty-year-olds, is part of the *shōwa hitoketa* generation. A physician writing about *kōnenki* in a series of popular books on medical matters quoted a correspondence he conducted with a potential patient:

> I am fifty years old and married. My three sons are grown up and either working or in college, and they all live their own lives. I have nothing to do each day but housework, and my husband and I seldom talk to each other. He says he's busy at work; he comes home late every night and goes out to play golf on his few days off.
>
> The only people I talk to are neighbors, and then only about everyday matters. I have no hobbies and I don't really know what I'm living for.
>
> Sometimes I feel anxious about my old age, and sometimes I think I can't stand the idea of just getting old this way. I vacillate

between times when my mind is just blank [*bonyari*], and times when I am anxious and upset. Do you have any advice for me?

First of all, you should be thankful for the fact that you have three sons, all of whom are already grown up, and that in addition your husband is still alive. There are some old couples who have only one child, and that one seriously handicapped, and they tell me they wake up in the night worrying about what will happen when they get old. There are also women who lost their husbands when they were young and are going out to work every day to support their children.

Since you are fifty years old, you are one of those who lived through the Second World War and the terrible years immediately afterward. Don't lose the spirit that helped you get through that time. Cheer up! You are only fifty; you have many years ahead of you. Try to find yourself a hobby, preferably one that will contribute in some small way to society.

In your case troubles at menopause are because of the way you are approaching it [*kokoro no mochikata*], I think.

(Okamura 1977, 112)

Apparently the impact of modernization on the moral and social lives of some of the *hitoketa*—namely, those who now appear to live a life of ease—has made them unable to practice the discipline they need to deal with the discomforts of *kōnenki*. In this myth we glimpse distinctions among the early Shōwa women: the hard-working rural resident, whom people associate with the running of a traditional household (*ie*), is in their minds when they laud the virtues and discipline of older women. In contrast, they conjure up a new middle-class housewife in a modern "nuclearized" household chock-full of appliances as the person who is vulnerable to menopausal distress. She is the one with too much time on her hands, who is selfish, and succumbs to this new "luxury syndrome," a condition inevitably associated with *onna tengoku* (women's heaven). This kind of person is not behaving like a real *shōwa hitoketa*, regardless of her date of birth.

Perhaps the existence of this myth explains why Atsuko-*san* and others like her who lead a middle-class urban apartment life insisted when speaking to me that *kōnenki* is not a big problem for Japanese women. I do not believe, however, that these women are deliberately covering up or living with a false consciousness that results in a blanket denial of symptoms simply because of negative moral value attached to them. For one thing, as we see in the following chapters, luxury, ease, and heaven are not words that spring to mind to describe the lives of the majority of Japanese women, whether fully employed or otherwise. And most women do not think of themselves as having an easy time. But beyond this, the majority of middle-aged women are both articulate and realistic about their position in society (remarkably so, to my mind at least). Their lives are not like those of Japanese men, nor do most of them aspire to literal equality since that means taking on the extraordinarily demanding and confined life of a working man (Iwao 1991). Very few women depend on their husbands for emotional intimacy and can thus develop a mature independence inside marriage, yet many are sensitive about their dependence on husbands for economic support and for this reason particularly regret their lack of education.

Japanese women conduct their lives and reflect on them with these and other constraints in mind. At the same time most take pride and satisfaction in accomplishing what they believe is worthwhile and within reach. The rhetoric of the selfish housewife simply does not make sense to the majority of women in terms of their own lives and thus probably does not constrain discussion about the subjective experience of *kōnenki*. Nevertheless, this myth produces a powerful impact on the way women think about the lives of other women, not so much women they know but Japanese women in the abstract. The rhetoric thus becomes a yardstick against which women measure and from which they dissociate themselves but also produces a stereotyped specter of the archetypal disciplined Japanese woman fallen from grace, a specter that helps to keep Japanese women divided among themselves and insensitive to the reality of one another's lives.

5 Faltering Discipline and the Ailing Family

The Fragile Family

An ark drifting along on a rough sea is an apt metaphor for the contemporary Japanese family.

(Higuchi Keiko 1980, 93)

Recent proposals for a new national holiday, Family Day, form part of the debate in Japan over the "health" of the country. Supporters of the proposal claim that the country's spiritual health is poor despite its economic soundness (Mochida 1980). Conservative social critics link the malaise to changes in the family system and most notably to a decline in the number of traditional households. They often explicitly contrast the strength of the *ie* to the fragility of the postwar nuclear family, home of the professional housewife, her husband, and children.

Although the *ie* was officially abolished at the end of the war, as Nakane and others point out, it is a "form of group consciousness" that survives (with much of the nationalism removed) as the structural basis for many contemporary Japanese institutions and organizations (Nakane 1983, 260; Murakami et al. 1979). It is this traditional household that people have in mind as the lost ideal when they talk about the spiritual malaise of the modern family.

The nuclear household exists, in contrast to the *ie*, as an urban residence, separated both in fact and in spirit from the seat of the ancestors. A nuclear household has undergone what is sometimes called "privatization" (Morioka 1983, 130) because it is no longer subject to either state or community surveillance as was the prewar household. Some social commentators consider the modern family, unlike the traditional one, to be a

107

brittle "pathological" system in which sexual equality, liberalization of parent-child relations, and egalitarian inheritance laws have disrupted the traditional forms of control, leading to an epidemic of social anomie (Eto 1979; Mochida 1980). Other analysts vehemently disagree with this position. Yuzawa, for example, a psychologist at the Tokyo Family Court, uses statistics to support his argument that no "pathological evolution of the family" has taken place in recent years (Yuzawa 1977; 1980, 77). He states that the mass media, by giving undue coverage to deviancy and divorce, have convinced the Japanese public that the family is an "ailing" system. He believes the reverse to be true: "The family has thrown off the shackles of the traditional . . . system, freed itself from poverty, and eliminated inhuman relationships" (Yuzawa 1980, 85). Higuchi Keiko, a well known social commentator, does not have such a rosy view. While she supports Yuzawa's position, she believes that too great a burden is being placed on the modern family and that critics should examine the goals of society at large (Higuchi 1980, 90).

The basic ingredients in the discussion of the modern Japanese family and its members are, nearly everyone agrees, limitations of space in the Japanese archipelago, urbanization and other demographic changes, postwar reform, loss of contact with nature, and an increasing acceptance of the Western value of individualism. Discussants sort and group this potpourri in various ways to create competing discourses about the family, some positive about the current situation but many, and most particularly in official documents, critical. Human relationships in urban areas are increasingly described as "thin," a state "symbolized by the phenomenon of elderly people dying alone and unnoticed" (Imazu et al. 1979, 43). Excess emphasis on the achievement of personal desires rather than self-sacrifice for the state or family is also noted as a problem (Monbushō 1983); the "social underpinnings" of the family are said to be weak, permitting the isolation of family members, and the "natural" order of the traditional community and the extended family is said to be destroyed (Imazu et al. 1979, 47; Kokumin Seikatsu Hakusho 1983).

This deterioration leads in turn, it is claimed, to more cases of suicide and to a "sharply increased . . . incidence of neurotic disorders and affective psychoses, as well as that of senile psychotic conditions" (Munakata 1986, 166). The absence of the father because of demands of work also produces social problems including an "undue" strengthening of the mother-child bond so that the mother is inclined to overprotect and dote on her child (Kitahara 1989, 64). A letter to the editor of the *Mainichi* newspaper in November 1983 suggested the reasons for juvenile delinquency and crime:

people once lived in extended families where someone was always watching the children, but not now. In the nuclear family, communication has diminished, children have their own rooms, and so parents do not know what their children are doing, and parents just give their children money and aren't really interested in them (*Mainichi shinbun* 1983a). A psychiatrist writing in the same newspaper the day before (and probably triggering the letter) stated that the trend toward giving children private rooms was "merely copying the outward forms of Western individualism while sticking to traditional overly close (*beta-beta shita*) human relationships, leading to anxiety states in children when they find themselves alone in their own private rooms" (*Mainichi shinbun* 1983b).

Conservative social critics also lament the way in which the younger generations, through lack of close contact with their grandparents, no longer know how to act properly in household religious rituals, at weddings, funerals, and other formal gatherings. A series of videotapes on the correct way to conduct various rituals are now available as substitutes for the elders, a phenomenon that the film director Itami Jūzō parodied in his film *Sōshiki* (Funeral). In response to this rampant social malaise, the government suggested that it is important to "regain a consciousness of the special character of the family and its role and to create a family system and a system of human relationships suitable for our country" (Kokumin Seikatsu Hakusho 1983, 258).

Resort to metaphorical images of sickness and pathology to describe the state of the nation or family relationships in times of rapid social change is not new. Such images were widespread at the turn of the century for example, most particularly to characterize migration from rural to urban environments. The well-known folklorist Yanagita Kunio referred to the transformation of farmers into townsmen as *shakai no yamai* (an illness of society) and deplored the way in which their descendants would become vagabonds (Yanagita 1912, 46–48). People interested in "getting ahead" at that time were said to be infected with "enterprise fever," "business fever," and "get-rich-quick-market fever" (Gluck 1985, 161). Similar metaphors occur today, although, in keeping with changes in diagnostic fashion, people no longer suffer from social "fevers" but from "syndromes" and "neuroses."

Diseases of Civilization: Bunmeibyō

The plethora of syndromes and neuroses said to be of recent origin and thought to abound in the urban centers of modern Japan are a delight for the news-hungry world of the mass media. Described as "diseases of modernization" (*gendaibyō*), or sometimes "diseases of civilization" (*bunmeibyō*) (Kyūtoku 1979, 19)—that is, of the postwar (un)civilization and loss of traditional values—these syndromes flourish in an environment that contrasts with "healthier" prewar times. This modern blight is ascribed in part to influences from the West, particularly the value placed on individualism and self-centered aspirations, but also to high-tech urban culture coupled with economic prosperity resulting in an excess of material comforts. In short, the blight stems from everything that the *shōwa hitoketa* and the generations who preceded them did not have.

People identified as at risk are usually members of the new middle class who live in urban nuclear families. Men, women, and children are all vulnerable to these diseases that, like their Meiji era forerunners, have arresting names: "apartment neurosis," "moving day depression," "child-rearing neurosis," "kitchen syndrome," "menopausal syndrome," "school refusal syndrome," "adolescent frustration syndrome," "video generation lethargy," "salaryman depression," "maladjustment to the job syndrome," "death from overwork," "fear of going to work," and so on. Accounting for these disorders is a moralistic rhetoric that postulates a close relation between health and well-being, physical as well as mental, and individual behavior. It often implicates rapid postwar changes, of both values and the structure of social relations, in the transformations of individual behavioral styles that undermine good health. But the problems it highlights and diagnoses as sicknesses are behavioral, disruptive of social relations at work, school, and home. Associated physical symptoms and individual suffering take second place, at least in public discourse. The middle-aged woman from a nuclear family who is vulnerable to the luxury-induced disease of menopausal symptoms is not, therefore, alone—other members of her family are equally at risk for various disagreeable problems.

The Absent Father

The shadow of Japanese fathers has become thin.
(Monbushō 1983, 26)

It is usual today for businessmen to be transferred at the whim of their employers to other parts of Japan or abroad for extended periods, often for several years or more, as was the case for Kuriyama-*san*'s husband. This phenomenon is on the increase, and many believe that should an employee refuse to comply he will not achieve promotion in the usual way (*Japan Times* 1984a). If the children are small a man's family may also join him, especially for a post abroad, but later in his career several factors mitigate against this. First, the company very rarely pays for the removal of a family or provides accommodation for them. Second, older children cannot be moved easily from one school to another. Most children study hard and many families struggle financially to have their children accepted into a specific high school to smooth their progress from there into a good university and hence to a rewarding career. Having attained temporary security in the highly competitive battle for educational success, the parents and usually the children are loath to relinquish this achievement. Furthermore, since formal education ends at junior high school, a high school has no obligation to accept transferred pupils, and refusals are not unusual. Moreover, new students are not always welcomed by their peers and may, as Hayase-*san* pointed out in her narrative, have to go through extensive hazing; bullying in schools is a major concern in Japan today. Finally, selling and buying houses in Japan is an extreme financial hazard, and renting houses (as opposed to tiny apartments) is not easy.

The result is that when salaried husbands with families are transferred on business for long stretches of time, they often live a single life, usually in dormitory accommodations, and return home two or three times a month, usually for fewer than forty-eight hours. Their families meantime become single-parent households. In 1984 a well-publicized case brought to public attention the suffering that these enforced absences may cause. A desperate wife left a suicide note for her husband, stating, "A woman has nothing good to live for. If you want to live just as a man, if you want to live with your job and not with me, then you should live alone. You don't need a family." She murdered her three children aged eleven, ten, and nine and then tried but failed to take her own life (*Mainichi shinbun* 1984a).

Particularly since that incident the family with an absent father serves as a central theme in the rhetoric about the modern Japanese family, often epitomized by the phrase *otōsan no kage wa usui* (father's shadow is thin), implying that father is no longer able to discipline his family:

> Are the fathers of Japan the men they ought to be? The government seems to be having doubts.
>
> In a new guide for parents of three-year-olds, authorized by the Health and Welfare Ministry . . . fathers are urged to take a more independent role in the upbringing of their children to demonstrate their masculinity and to teach them to be brave and strongminded.
>
> The new guide apparently stems from anxiety about recent social changes within the Japanese family structure that have made

father only a fleeting figure, if not nonexistent, and where not father but mother "knows best."

An overdominance [sic] of the mother in the child's upbringing, experts fear, is leading to the "feminization" of Japan, since many children are growing up without sufficient masculine influence to provide the balance they need.

(*Mainichi shinbun* 1985a)

Other articles feature the working life of Japanese men: a cross-cultural survey reveals that, comparatively speaking, Japanese are "worker bees" and that many put work before home. Training on the job produces "company-centered people" (*Mainichi shinbun* 1983d), particularly when employers can require all-night training sessions (1983e). Stress at work is thought to be severe because of the lifetime employment and seniority systems that advance the most devoted workers up the ladder to executive positions. According to one psychiatrist, "sober, diligent, but mediocre managers" who possess a "weak character and have few hobbies, [who] do not drink with colleagues after hours or play mah-jongg or golf at weekends" are particularly vulnerable to physical ailments (*Japan Times* 1984b). When surveyed, 73 percent of male workers reported that they suffered from "nervous tension" (1983f). Stress-related ailments include vomiting, heart attacks, loss of appetite, rheumatism, impotence, insomnia, and depression. The leading cause of these ailments is cited as overwork (1985b). Among middle-aged men inability to adapt to computer technology is cited as another major cause of stress (1985c). Several syndromes and neuroses particular to salaried workers are associated with stress; they include "fear of going to work," "fear of returning home from work," and "salaryman depression."

The suicide rate is reported as high, particularly among men in their late forties and fifties who are in positions of responsibility, and illness is most often given as the reason for suicide. The salaryman more than anyone else in Japan today is regularly subjected to excessive demands, and in an effort to combat it, a few companies are trying to force employees to take all of their allotted vacation (*Mainichi shinbun* 1991a). In several recently reported cases men dropped dead on the job from what was diagnosed as "death from overwork" (*karōshi*) and family members sued, often successfully, for compensation (Karōshi Bengodan Zenkoku Renraku Kaigihen 1990). A recent poll revealed that among salaried men who have worked for fifteen years or more, 40 percent fear that they are on the path to an early death from overwork (*Mainichi shinbun* 1991b). People believed to be at greatest risk are those who regularly put in one hundred hours or more of overtime a month (1984b).

The Japanese salaryman is frequently depicted today in comics and on television as a sad figure, fit only for ridicule. Disciplined by his employers to the life of a worker bee, stereotyped as *sodai gomi* (gross garbage) around the home, and labeled incompetent as both father and husband largely because of his enforced absence from his family, this shadow of controlled samurai-style masculinity and model for future generations has certainly worn a little thin.

The Resistant Child

It is said that juvenile delinquency arises when there is no human
kindness put into a mother's cooking. . . . A mother should season
rice balls by hand, only then is her care properly expressed. Packaged
rice balls that are bought at the market are not adequate. . . . It is important that mothers get up early in the morning for the children's
sake in order to make them a meal.

(Commentary by an educator, *Mainichi shinbun* 1984b)

The rigors and competition associated with the Japanese school system are common knowledge today, but the continuing national debate about what has been described as the "desolation" of modern education is less well known. The media and government reports reflect growing concern over accelerated rates of delinquency, bullying, violence, vandalism, school ab-senteeism, and apathy. Although statistics are unreliable, they support the claim that these problems are on the increase even though the absolute numbers of children involved are much smaller than those that would lead to concern in North America (Lock 1986, 1988b). While some commentary on these problems focuses on excess in the demands and rigors of the Japanese school system, most of the government-sponsored documents and essays written by conservative social critics and some medical profes-sionals ascribe the problems to loss of traditional values and urban life-styles leading to weakened family relationships and center their criticism on the poverty of child-rearing methods in the modern Japanese family.

Lack of contact with nature, and especially with the passing seasons, often figures as a crucial problem. One critic claims, for example, that urban children cannot associate their changing moods with the changing seasons and thus experience a sense of alienation; brought up away from a traditional community, they are "not good at playing in groups" (Hirata 1980, 36). The nuclear family is also a target. Mothers living in nuclear families are lonely and lack confidence in their ability to raise a child by themselves. They enter into a "symbiotic relationship" with their off-spring that becomes the source of neuroses (Hirata 1980, 42; Monbushō

1983; Suzuki 1983). Several writers accuse mothers of having lost their "natural" child-rearing instincts (Hirata 1980; Kyūtoku 1979). Other writers believe that many mothers have become selfish and unable to care sufficiently for their children. Specialists describe their personality types as anxious, worried, turned inward, unsociable, infantile, immature, unmotherly, overly methodical, unexpressive, dependent, and so on (Takuma and Inamura 1980). A psychiatrist of about fifty-five, herself a mother, told me that Japanese mothers had an easy time growing up surrounded by material abundance in the postwar years and consequently tend to treat their children "like pets" (Lock 1986, 104).

Absent fathers contribute to this breakdown: they do not project a "father image" (Monbushō 1983). The head of the section of the Japanese National Institute for Mental Health for research into family pathology states that a "hopeless" (*dame*) father stands "in the shadow" of every mother accused of causing illness in her children (*Mainichi shinbun* 1983g). Others characterize the personality types of fathers who are likely to produce "difficult" adolescents as lacking in confidence, poor at making decisions, turned inward, unsociable, verbose, and dependent (Takuma and Inamura 1980). Parents such as these, stereotyped linchpins of the nuclear family, produce deficient children, antisocial and nervous. A school administrator with whom I talked claims that children today have "expensive tastes," many dislikes about food, and are unable to "stick at anything." He says that they do not play in groups but live, instead, an isolated life looking at television and reading comics. Maeda-*san* believes that these children are poor at expressing themselves, which he attributes to the presence at home of an overprotective and bossy mother and the absence of a strong father figure. He also thinks that the usual image of a warm and harmonious Japanese family is a myth, and that these days people are "turned outward," thinking about themselves rather than caring about other family members (Lock 1986, 90). Another child psychiatrist states that the "root cause" of problem children lies with mothers who have no purpose in life except their children. Mothers such as these, Dr. Yokoyama says, cannot allow their children to develop independence; on the contrary, they tend to lean on their adolescent children for support, particularly because their husbands are rarely at home (Lock 1986, 91).

Japanese physicians claim that in postwar years the incidence of psychosomatic complaints in children, including asthma, ulcers, and heart disease (Ikemi et al. 1980), has risen dramatically, along with "poor brain functioning" and a general weakening of the body, including a tendency for bones to break easily (Masaki 1979; Hirata 1980, 37). An oversensitiv-

Most married women shop every day in order to prepare family meals.

ity in social situations is also described. The causes of these illnesses, in common with the behavioral problems of school refusal and bullying, are said to lie in urbanization, in changing family relationships, and especially in the behavior of mothers.

As one response to the perceived pathology of youth, the government promotes the teaching of moral education throughout the school system; despite opposition, recent directives on education call for the instruction of students in both "love of country" (*aikokushin*) and more knowledge about the role of the emperor in state functions. Another response has been to medicalize the problem: in numerous magazine articles, books, television, and radio programs medical experts inform the public on the proper conduct of family life (Lock 1991). Regardless of such measures, newspaper articles regularly intone something to the effect that "bullying is on the increase again and over half of the schoolchildren in Tokyo polled said they hate going to school" (*Mainichi shinbun* 1990c; *Nihon keizai shinbun* 1990).

The Selfish Housewife

Next time I want to be born a woman. Nowadays everyone wants to be born as a woman.

(Male consultant to a Tokyo Well Aging Club,
cited in N. Matsumoto 1988, 42)

The media occasionally portray a middle-class housewife's daily life as *san shoku hiru ne tsuki*, implying an easy permanent job with three meals and a nap thrown in. The shared myth is that housewives today are selfish and idle, unsurpassed consumers with endless time to fill in who just play around, living a life of ease and luxury unknown in Japanese society until today. In addition, they often lack a real identity, have "no self," and are deficient in the willpower and endurance characteristic of all the generations of Japanese women who preceded them. Alternatively, they may become excessively fastidious, withdrawn, and nervous, too concerned with tidiness and order. In both instances a middle-class housewife departs from the balanced and correctly controlled life of the good wife and wise mother and, whether selfish and empty-headed or withdrawn and neurotic, creates a poor family environment and produces ailing and deviant children. Like the other members of her family, the housewife is susceptible to disease, including apartment neurosis, child-rearing neurosis, and the "kitchen syndrome" (in which she experiences a variety of severe somatic symptoms the moment she enters the kitchen to prepare the evening meal [Katsura 1983]). Once she becomes middle-aged, *kōnenki shōkōgun* is her most likely disorder.

The story of the pathological family does not end here, because two crucial members of the *ie*, the parents-in-law, have been eased out of the nuclear family. Perhaps the most troubling problem on the horizon for the planners of Japan are the elderly, lonely and abandoned by the nuclear family as so much garbage (*kuzu*). Plans and projections for care of the elderly occupy the officials who scrutinize the lives of the *shōwa hitoketa* and the generations of women who will follow them to become middle-aged in their turn. Will the good wives of urban middle-class Japan continue to fulfill that important function assigned to them by custom: care of the elderly? Or will they abandon the discipline of childhood and early married years and opt instead for *onna tengoku*, a women's heaven replete with endless trips to exotic countries, a surfeit of money to spend on luxury items, and no assigned role in life other than preparation of the occasional meal for a husband? Such willful and selfish women, anomalies in a society that reveres hard work and dedication to family harmony, are clearly in people's minds when they describe *kōnenki* disorders as a "luxury disease."

Welfare Service for the Silver Agers

The foundation of welfare for the aged is believed to be in the home.

(Nisen Nen no Nihon 1982, 143)

The Ōhira government characterized the 1980s as the "age of culture," a time when the "freedom" and "abundance" produced by unprecedented economic prosperity were to be tempered by restoration of warm human relationships in the family, the workplace, and local regions (Ōhira Sōri no Seisaku Kenkyūkai Hōkokusho 1980). Driving this call for a return of "warmth" in the family appears to be an accelerating disquiet as the "aging" society and its nonproductive and dependent population rapidly proliferate.

In contrast to prewar days, an eighty-year life span (*jinsei hachijūnen*), rather than one of fifty years, is recognized as the average Japanese life (Hosoya 1987; Yamane 1979). Plath points out that this newly received "gift of mass longevity" is in some ways disquieting (Plath 1980, 1). While most individuals presumably look forward to a ripe old age, for planners, politicians, and bureaucrats an image of 16 percent or more of the population over sixty-five signals the approach of disaster. The graying of Japan is particularly disturbing because demographic changes that took eighty-five years in Sweden, one hundred thirty years in France, and seventy years in the United States have taken just twenty-five years in Japan (Kinoshita 1993). Some official estimates calculate that if present trends continue (that is, if fertility remains low and mortality continues to decline), by the year 2025 people of sixty-five and over will make up a remarkable 23.4 percent of the population. Among the elderly, more than 53 percent will be over seventy-five years old (Nisen Nen no Nihon 1982; Ogawa 1988; Kōseishō Jinkō Mondai Kenkyūsho 1987). Japanese life expectancy is the longest in the world, over seventy-six years for men and eighty-two for women, and already more than three thousand people are over one hundred years old (*Mainichi shinbun* 1990d).

The most dramatic demographic changes are projected for the first quarter of the next century, when the postwar baby boomers reach old age. As they join the elderly, the economy will probably be declining as the labor force rapidly ages and all expenditures for the elderly mount (Nisen Nen no Nihon 1982, 101; Ogawa 1988). Ogawa Naohiro estimates that by the year 2020 almost 55 percent of medical expenditures will relate to the elderly, that actual costs will increase tenfold, and that almost all this money will come, if the health insurance system remains unmodified, from national, prefectural, and municipal government sources—that is, it will come largely from the pockets of the declining younger population of taxpayers.

Ogawa goes on to point out that, again, if present trends continue, more than two and one-quarter million Japanese will be suffering from senile dementia by 2025, of whom just over two-thirds will be women, and more than two million people will be bedridden, of whom slightly fewer than two-thirds will be women. Ogawa voices a major government concern when he questions where the "manpower" will come from to take care of this decrepit population (Ogawa 1988, 274), known euphemistically as the silver generation (Plath 1988). Construction of facilities for the elderly, much of it government sponsored, is going on in most parts of the country, but it is far from adequate to deal with the projected future needs and in any case occurs with a good deal of foot-dragging on the part of local and national officials. Even so, Article 25 of the constitution proclaims that "in all spheres of life, the State shall use its endeavors for the promotion and extension of social welfare and security, and of public health."

Significantly, government documents on the graying of Japan usually point out that it is preferable for care of the elderly to take place in their homes and that the family should be the primary care giver (Nisen Nen no Nihon 1982, 121; Kōsei Hakusho 1989). Policymakers are clearly concerned by increasing public expectations that the government will assume a larger role in care of the aging population and have made several recent policy changes to try to reverse this trend. The elderly are no longer fully covered by the national health-care system but must shoulder some of the expense themselves, including part of the cost of hospitalization; at the same time, the government actively encourages all individuals to take responsibility for preservation of their own health (Kōsei Hakusho 1989).

Since the 1970s, when the aging society attracted the attention of policy makers, succeeding conservative governments in Japan have commented on the dangers of what they term the "English disease," with reference to the pre-Thatcher social welfare system of the United Kingdom, which they consider excessive. The ruling Liberal Democratic party set out to create, instead, what has come to be known as the Japanese Welfare Society, which assigns some responsibility to individuals and their families for care and financing of their needs. Hence, the long-term outlook committee of the Economic Planning Agency of the Suzuki government states:

> The home is extremely important to the aged for a secure life of retirement, their health and welfare. In an attempt to form a social environment ideal for future living, it will be necessary to correctly position the home in society . . . the role of people caring for the aged at home will become more important. . . . Also, it will be necessary to promote a land policy aimed at pressing for three family generations to live in the same place or for family members to live within easy reach.
>
> (Nisen Nen no Nihon 1982, 123)

Not even the most conservative policy makers resort to the term *ie* to describe the new-style extended family. Instead, the "new residence system" (*atarashii jūtaku shisutemu*) goes under the tag of "living together in three-generation households" (*san sedai dōkyo*). Income tax credits and loans are to be made available to allow the remodeling of homes so that elderly parents can join the household (Kōsei Hakusho 1989), and the latest devices to help with care of the elderly are to be installed in such houses (Ōhira Sōri no Seisaku Kenkyūkai Hōkokusho 1980).

A paragraph or two on the way in which middle-aged and older women should conduct their lives figure in the Ōhira government report on the proposed "enrichment" of the Japanese family. After pointing out the importance of hobbies, sports, cultural activities, and further education for women's psychological and physical welfare, the document states that women should take a positive attitude toward work, and that they should use their newfound freedom from family demands to take up suitable part-time employment or volunteer work (Ōhira Sōri no Seisaku Kenkyūkai Hōkokusho 1980). Perhaps in response to official encouragement of this kind, some women chose to go back to school in middle age to obtain nursing degrees (although occasionally husbands and other family members objected) and eagerly took the required entrance examinations in order to return to school. It was reported that these women, called "Nightingale mamas" and "angels in white," rarely missed a class and that they wanted to seek out something to add more meaning to their lives, although they hastily added, when asked, that being a housewife was already a rewarding life-style. All the women apparently claimed that their studies made them feel young again (*Mainichi shinbun* 1983h). Nursing and related care-giving activities are exactly the kind of interim work that the government would like women to perform so that when their parents-in-

Taking mother-in-law for an outing.

law become infirm, they will be ready to have the latest medical equipment installed in their homes and easily convert themselves into dutiful daughters-in-law.

In recent years it has become accepted policy, as far as possible, not to place the elderly for any length of time in hospitals or even nursing homes, although more of these institutions are gradually becoming available. Local governments administer most care of the elderly under a policy of cooperation between government and families so that, if at all possible, old people stay at home in the bosom of their families.[1] Funds have been set aside, in the Gold Plan for care of the elderly, to train home helpers, public health nurses, and nurses who do home visits, whose task is to assist middle-aged and older women caring for their spouses or parents-in-law. It is stressed that "the quality of life" of the elderly will be best enhanced if they remain at home (Kōsei Hakusho 1989).

Through such policy the government hoped, of course, to avoid raising taxes to foot the bill for social services, although five years ago, after massive public opposition, it introduced a small consumer tax on goods and services, most of the tax in theory to be set aside for implementing plans for care of the elderly. Despite the government's apparent acknowledgment of some responsibility for care of the elderly, financing of all aspects of the Gold Plan falls seriously short of the projected implementation of home care and intermediate facilities.

Several surveys have revealed that people of childbearing age assume that they will not depend on their children for care when they grow old; nevertheless the majority of Japanese people at present aged sixty and over prefer to be looked after by their children. In one five-country study, 58 percent of older Japanese stated that they would like to live with their children while only 3 percent of older Americans responded positively (Sōmu cho Tōkei Kyoku 1987). Should they become physically ill, 95 percent of Japanese aged sixty and over would like family members to take care of them and designated as preferred care givers almost exclusively wives, daughters-in-law, or daughters. Policy makers (many of whom are aged sixty or more) are drawing on the image of the *ie* and a well-entrenched consciousness among older people that, after a life of hard work, they can expect to depend on their offspring for care. The government reminds the public in its official handouts of what the elders—the *shōwa hitoketa* and their seniors—have done in the way of nation building:

> The people who will retire from their active careers and join in the formation of the aged group toward the twenty-first century will be those who have lived in turbulent periods, supported the era of high economic growth in Japan and helped establish the country's present economic affluence. It is the duty of the succeeding generation to assist these people in building an affluent society in which they can live well.
>
> (Nisen Nen no Nihon 1982, 116)

This document goes on to state that the Japanese sense of value of the home is fundamentally closer to that of Asia than it is to Europe and America, and that "it is possible to expect the home to act as a vital force" and function positively in supporting society in its care of the elderly (117).

Although Confucianism formally endorses filial piety and respect for the elders, a tradition honored in theory in Respect for Elders Day (a national holiday created in 1966), ambivalence about the elderly exists in numerous tales and legends from ancient times to present-day novels and films about the trials and tribulations of coping with old people (Ariyoshi 1972; Tahara 1980; Niwa 1947). Some of these tales refer to a mountain called *obāsuteyama* (the mountain for disposing of Granny), where the elderly (and perhaps especially women) might be abandoned and left to starve in times of food shortages. Imamura Shōhei's film *Ballad of Narayama* dramatized the family conflict that the plight of elderly parents created in feudal Japan, and a number of Japanese mountains still retain this name. That they were actually used for geronticide seems unlikely but does not preclude the possibility that such wishes existed "in the hearts and minds" of family members (Cornell 1991).

A shortage of food is rare today (although many elderly, even in prosperous Japan, live at or below the poverty level [Lock 1984]), but the conflict between filial piety and the interests of younger members of the family has become, if anything, even more acute in contemporary times. Not only are there more dependent elderly who live longer, but urban life is more complex and houses are small. Mixed feelings of duty and guilt, portrayed graphically in contemporary Japanese film (Ehrlich 1992), are very evident among middle-aged people; rather than place their aged relatives in a nursing home, which is often explicitly characterized as the modern *obāsuteyama*, many couples choose to adapt their own life-style so that they are joined by or, alternatively, join or rejoin their elderly parents (most usually those of the husband) in the family house. For the younger couple, one distinct advantage of such arrangements is inheriting the home—an arrangement that, given Japanese land prices, appeals to many people and more than compensates for burdens the elderly may impose. Because Japan is a highly mobile society, such arrangements do not always work out smoothly, however; many elderly parents today join the urban household of their children or take up residence nearby.

One other facet of traditional society acts in favor of the government in its effort to avoid "excessive" expenditures in care of the elderly. A Japanese home is a private place. Elderly individuals and those who care for them, as Atsuko-*san's* narrative indicated, are often exceedingly uncomfortable at the thought of having home helpers or nurses enter their houses and so choose to deal with the problem unaided. This attitude arises partly because it is "natural" that an extended family should take care of itself and not lean on others, and because embarrassment arises at having a stranger come into the house in any role other than that of an invited guest.

Fatigue from Nursing: The Latest Disease of Civilization

Until recently, the leading cause of death in Japan was cerebrovascular disease, and a large number of infirm elderly are people who have suffered from strokes and are therefore rather severely disabled. More than six hundred thousand people aged sixty-five and over are bedridden, and the majority of these people remain at home. In commenting on the large numbers of bedridden elderly, Kiefer (1987) notes the shortage of rehabilitation facilities in Japan. He points out, as do a good number of other researchers, that to be dependent on others is culturally "available" (particularly for the very young and the old); hence, in contrast to North America, in Japan there is indirect encouragement for individuals, once they become infirm, to stay dependent (see also Campbell 1984). The combination of a high incidence of stroke, a disease that renders people particularly helpless, and the cultural reinforcement for dependence as natural and highly acceptable, means that the care of in-laws may occupy many women from about the age of fifty or fifty-five: women make up 93 percent of those who look after senile or bedridden elderly individuals in Japan, and by far the majority of these women are wives, daughters-in-law, or daughters.

The original word for nursing in Japanese (mitori) incorporates the idea of caring for someone until death. If either partner of an elderly couple dies, then the survivor (usually mother-in-law) will most probably join the younger woman's household for the remainder of her life (assuming that she is not already in residence) and can expect to receive full care from her daughter-in-law. Should the daughter-in-law's husband later become dependent, she is expected to care for him and, once widowed herself, to lean in turn on her daughter-in-law. Hosoya Tsugiko, who works in a halfway house for the elderly in Tokyo, is very concerned about the burden that care of the elderly puts on middle-aged women. She describes Japan's current welfare system as a "private" one, based on the family, and points out that halfway houses and other interim-care facilities are too few in number (Hosoya 1987, 162). Recent studies show that care at home for the elderly with chronic diseases takes up on average four to five hours a day and that in addition a family incurs considerable expenses (Satō et al. 1988).

A recent study by the Ministry of Labor showed that out of nearly five hundred people who were nursing the elderly in their Tokyo homes over 81 percent were women whose average age was fifty-six years. More than 60 percent of these women had been looking after their relatives for three years or more, and over 16 percent of them had been doing so for over ten years (*Tōkyō shinbun* 1990). Another study included one ninety-year-old woman who was singlehandedly taking care of her bedridden husband; over 57 percent of the care givers were daughters-in-law or daughters, and many of these women were seventy years old (Serizawa 1989). Lebra notes that some of the most disruptive quarrels among relatives in Japanese families are to do with the question of who will take care of ailing parents. The situation becomes particularly acute if the wife of the eldest son for one reason or another cannot or will not fulfill what everyone regards as her "natural" duty (Lebra 1984, 254–55). But, as the length of time devoted to care giving grows longer and longer, and the care givers themselves reach old age, the burden becomes intolerable. Even the most devoted daughters-in-law or wives presumably do not relish the idea of nursing bedridden, incontinent, and often senile elderly for thirty or more years, with little or no relief; and, for all their well-meaning efforts, the quality of care at home may be inferior to that of professional help (Kobayashi and Reich 1993).

A white paper on women points out the inadequacies of professional and even volunteer assistance for those who nurse elderly relatives (Nihon Fujindantai Rengōkai 1989). The number of home helpers (untrained volunteers who receive a small financial reward for their services), a total of 27,105 in 1989, is inadequate (to augment this number the government now supports the training of female immigrant labor for home care). A half-day's help per week is the maximum time that most people receive, and they must pay for it. Short stays in nursing homes and other facilities are limited to seven days, and extensions are possible only under highly extenuating circumstances. In 1989 the total number of beds in the entire country for short stays was 2,374; more than 40,000 families requested this service, but the complicated procedures and questioning they were expected to go through on behalf of their elderly relatives overwhelmed many of these applicants. The government has written a great deal about Day Service Centers, but as yet fewer than 1,000 of these centers exist (although 10,000 more are promised by the year 2000). The white paper on women also reminds us, the government changed its policy on payments for hospital services, so that there is now little financial incentive, as was formerly the case, for hospitals to offer care for old people. Since there are few nursing homes and intermediate-care facilities are obviously insufficient, the elderly have only their families to turn to or return to (Nihon Fujindantai Rengōkai 1989; Kinoshita 1993) because, justifiably, first priority for institutional care goes to old people with no close relatives.

Given these circumstances we can understand an estimate that one in three women has to give up paid work in order to nurse her relatives

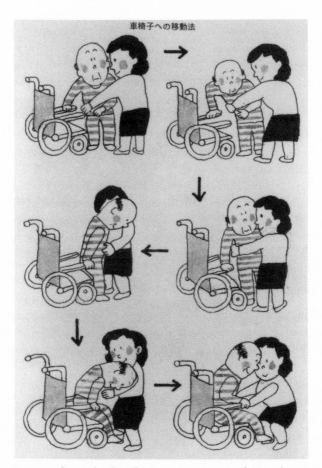

車椅子への移動法

Diagram from a book on home nursing care explaining how
to maneuver someone into a wheelchair. Reproduced with
permission from Gōdō Shuppan Kabushiki Kaisha.

(*Tōkyō shinbun* 1990), indicating that in addition to a physical and psychological burden is economic hardship. When middle-aged respondents nursing their relatives replied to a survey on health problems that allowed multiple answers, only 15 percent of them noted difficulties with *kōnenki*, whereas 53 percent complained of lumbago (perhaps from lifting immobile people), 44 percent suffered from lack of sleep, and 37 percent cited "nervousness" as a major problem (cited in Serizawa 1989, 43).

Recently the government acknowledged the existence of yet another disease of civilization, "fatigue from home care and nursing" (*kaigo tsukare*), and suggested that women diagnosed with this illness should be considered eligible for home help and respite care (*Asahi shinbun* 1991);

earlier, the well-known social critic Higuchi Keiko suggested that if a new national holiday is created it should be Welfare Service Day rather than Family Day (Higuchi 1980, 82). At present the government is considering the creation of a holiday to be called Nursing Day, not to honor over-worked and underpaid hospital nurses—whose work is bitterly described as *kitsui, kiken,* and *kitanai* (grueling, dangerous, and dirty)—but to rec-ognize home helpers, public health nurses, and nurses who do home visits; these are the future linchpins of the new welfare service directed at the home (*zaitaku fukushi*).

Among the many conversations I had with Japanese women about mid-life, one of the most moving was with Inagaki-*san*, a married woman who farms in Nagano, mother of a young woman of twenty-one and a boy of fourteen. She underwent major breast surgery for cancer two and one-half years ago.

Sacrificial Daughter-in-Law

"My husband is employed in a company—an electrical company. Until I had my operation *ojīchan*[2] [father-in-law] and I did all the farming, but now my husband has to help, although he's never done any real farming before."

"How big is your farm?"

"It's medium-sized, less than one *chō* [about two acres]."

"What do you grow?"

"Rice, and enough vegetables for the family and friends. We don't sell the vegetables. What we get from selling the rice is only just enough to buy fertilizer for the next year. We actually live on my husband's income."

"You must be very busy."

"Yes, there're always weeds to be pulled up somewhere, and you have to plant everything at the right time of course. We use machinery for the first plowing these days, but I do the rest, the hoeing and transplanting by hand."

"Do your children help?"

"No, they're no help at all. My daughter hates farming."

"Do you hope your son will take over from you later on?"

"Well, yes, but that's not very realistic. Young people are going to choose their own lives from now on. I think what we're really doing now is just taking care of the property until we die, it's been in the family for about a hundred years. Even so, it doesn't really seem necessary."

"But do you take pride in your work?"

"Well, that's a hard question. It's just that I am the *yome* [daughter-in-law] in this family, and if we sold the land people would criticize us; I just take care of it because we have it, but we don't make anything out of it."

"Do you have relatives nearby who can give you a helping hand sometimes?"

"Yes, thank goodness. Actually my husband is the second son in his family, but his older brother was adopted into his wife's family because they had no sons, so we have the farm and are taking care of my husband's parents. About a year ago my mother-in-law became bedridden. She's eighty-six, and she needs a bedpan. My father-in-law is also eighty-six and he has several health problems, but he is still quite active and he helps take care of *obāsan*; she's had to have special soft food for the past three and a half years."

"Does anyone come from the local hospital to help you?"

"No, the only help we get is from our relatives. They don't have enough nurses in the hospital; the only thing they've done is to come to give her shots. When she got worse, the doctor said we should put her in hospital, but she says she'd rather die than go there [*shinu hodo iya*]. Anyway, if she went into hospital, I'd have to take care of her there, and then the family would have trouble with meals."

"Tell me about your daily routine, would you?"

"Well, I get up at 6:30 A.M. in summer, and around 7:00 A.M. in winter. Actually, I get up at 6:00 A.M. to turn on the rice cooker and then I go back to bed for a while! Then we have breakfast. Fortunately my husband doesn't need a boxed lunch, but my son does, so I make that first thing. I do the laundry every other day, while I'm getting breakfast ready. I have to serve breakfast four times, first to my son, then my husband, next *ojīchan*, and finally he and I feed *obāsan* together.

"After breakfast I work in the fields until lunchtime. I eat lunch with *ojīsan* and then I spend some time with *obāsan*, I usually bathe her in the afternoon because there's no time in the evenings. I do the bedpan nearly all the time but sometimes *ojīsan* does it, although he doesn't really like to, but if I'm in the fields then he has to. Of course I can't go out much at all, except just to work in the fields. But *obāsan* isn't senile or anything so it's not too bad.

"At night I have to feed my son first again, because he's always hungry, then *ojīchan* and *obāsan*, and finally my husband and I eat together. It means a lot of time in the kitchen. I have two books checked out of the library now, but I'll never find time to read them."

"Do the children help?"

"My daughter is away most of the time these days but when she's here she helps sometimes, if she feels like it. My son's job is to put things away in the refrigerator at night, after we've finished eating."

"What kind of education did you have?"

"I finished high school. I came from a farm family, so I'd done this kind of work even when I was a girl."

"Does your husband help around the house?"

"He didn't do anything before my operation but he does a lot now. I was in hospital for a month and he and *ojīchan* managed OK, feeding my son and so on—I was surprised at how well they did!"

"Would you mind telling me a little more about the operation?"

"Well, I discovered I had a problem in August two summers ago. I was sleeping in a T-shirt, and I happened to brush my hand against my breast and all of sudden I felt a lump about the size of a soybean. I'd heard some lectures about breast cancer, and so right away I went to the hospital. They did a special test, and the doctor cut a little piece out. He said he thought it looked all right, but ten days later I got a call telling me to come to the surgical department right away. At first they said it wasn't really cancer but that it would be best to operate anyway. My daughter was with me, and she looked as though she'd had a concussion and went terribly pale when they talked to us, so I knew right away what was up."

"Japanese doctors don't usually tell people they have cancer, do they?"

"I think they do with breast cancer, because they can't really disguise it. But with stomach cancer they tell you it's an ulcer."

"You were in hospital for a month?"

"Yes, but I didn't have any radiation treatment. They put *obāsan* in hospital too because there was no one to take care of her properly at home, but she was sent home the same day as I was."

"How did you feel when you went home?"

"I didn't feel at all well, and I had to take some black medicine that didn't agree with me. I got an infection all around my mouth. When I told the doctor about it he scolded me. He said only one person in a hundred has that kind of reaction, but finally they changed the medicine. Now I'm pretty well, though I can't raise my arm very far. But I can carry heavy things again."

"Do you still go for examinations?"

"Yes, once a week. And I'm still taking medicine—they say I'll have to take it for six or seven years. I worry that it will reoccur, but because I'm afraid, I don't ask the doctor anything, and he never offers any information. If I think about it too much, I won't have the energy to go on living."

"Your experience must have affected the whole family."

"Yes, I feel very apologetic [*moshiwake nai*] to my husband. Cancer is a very frightening thing, and it would be hard for him if I died, especially while there are still the old folks to look after."

"Has your daily life changed?"

"Since I had the operation I haven't felt like having 'that' [sex] at all. I always liked it a lot, but I've lost that feeling. Actually, my husband never wanted it much after he was forty; I was the one who was interested. He comes home at 8 o'clock, and he's really tired every night.

"I've never showed him where I had the operation. At first I used to hang a towel over the mirror when I took a bath. Now I'm used to it, but when my husband comes in to wash my back, I always cover up with a towel. He says, 'What's wrong with showing it to me?' But I tell him he can see it when I'm dead. If he sees how ugly it is he won't be able to forget it, I know. I don't intend to let anyone see it while I'm still alive.

"You know, I've done some reading about cancer recently, and I found out that women with strong personalities are more prone to cancer—that's why so many foreign women get it. I may seem to be weak, but actually I'm strong; that's the reason I got it. Also, hormones have something to do with it, and once, when I was having some unusual bleeding, the doctor gave me some hormone shots; that was another cause, I think."

"What about *kōnenki*?"

"I stopped menstruating seven months after the operation. I'm forty-nine now so it was early, but I barely noticed the difference with all the other things in my life."

"How would you compare your life with your mother's?"

"Oh, mine is much easier. My mother married a man who was the second of eight children, and she always had to worry about his siblings' feelings. She told me she used to think about running away, but she decided if she went back to her parents' home it would cause her mother too much worry, so she just stuck it out. Working in the rice fields was tough for her too, and she had seven children, one after another. She had to put the baby down to sleep beside the rice paddy, and she said one time she found one of her babies covered with ants. We don't have to go through that kind of thing anymore—things are easier now."

"Are your own parents still alive?"

"My father is eighty-one and my mother is seventy-nine, but I can't see them very often although they don't live far away because I can't leave *obāsan*. Anyway that's life, one has to 'stick things out'—there are a lot of people less fortunate than me."

Obviously, contrary to official urgings that women take up hobbies, more education, volunteer services, and so on, individuals such as Inagaki-*san* are in no position to create their own lives apart from family obligations except by disrupting what is considered normal behavior and aspirations. Although she has put the family's well-being above her own health, she nevertheless feels apologetic about letting the family down; despite some dents and scratches, the good wife, wise mother, and dutiful daughter-in-law survives. In Higuchi Keiko's words, "Hidden behind the superficial glamour . . . the prewar family system lives grimly on" (1985, 53).

Of course, Higuchi-*san* and other outspoken Japanese women have not sat quietly on the sidelines while the government pushes them deeper into servitude. Among other things, they have organized a series of annual symposia by women on the aging society, in which dominant themes have been "to live and die in a society that supports independence in old age" and to create "as soon as possible a situation where old people can live satisfactorily on their own" (*Asahi shinbun* 1990a). Aspirations such as these call for nothing short of a complete revamping of both the pension system and all social support systems for the elderly—in which so far the government shows little interest.

A recent incident, involving a man of forty-two who nursed his prematurely senile wife of fifty-nine until he found a place for her in an institution, whereupon he divorced her, brought forth a flurry of responses from feminists. While many commentators showed sympathy for the man, they went on to state that if the incident had involved a demented husband with a younger wife, she would have been expected to deal with the burden of nursing him by herself at home. Although the case is a very unusual one, feminists have taken the opportunity of the publicity to demand consideration for the rights of people who nurse the elderly, in addition to the rights of the elderly themselves. In other words, they ask for radical modification in the Japanese-style welfare society to allow recognition of the "hidden assets" (*fukumi shisan*) that it draws on, namely free nursing services carried out almost exclusively by women in their homes, and the transfer of most of the burden to society at large. Nursing the elderly at home, feminists claim, should not be based on the "sacrifice and devotion of families" (*Mainichi shinbun* 1990e).

Turning to the elderly themselves, the 1989 white paper on women released by the Japanese Coalition of Women's Groups points out that four times as many elderly women as men live alone, a total of 1,286,000. Over 70 percent of people in old-age homes with special nursing care are women, 93 percent of people in ordinary homes for the elderly are women, and over 93 percent of bedridden people being nursed at home by younger female family members are women. Of those elderly who have Alzheimer's disease, 80 percent are women. Clearly, this paper concludes, the aging society is a woman's problem, and with poor social welfare policies the burden of care for the elderly simply drops into the laps of younger women (Nihon Fujindantai Rengōkai 1989).

As with so many other problems of national import in Japan, in grass-roots activism we observe the first signs of change. In 1985 eight housewives and several social workers living in Takamatsu city on the island of Shikoku formed a group to provide nursing care for needy elderly and their families. Since that time the size of the group has risen to four hundred sixty members, most of whom are full-time housewives, but it also includes twenty men. Volunteers, after instruction in treating bedsores, bathing the elderly, and so on, do simple nursing, prepare meals, shop, and chauffeur senile and bedridden old people. There is a small fee, but instead of receiving money most of the volunteers prefer to chalk up points that will ensure similar services for them once they become old (*Mainichi shinbun* 1991c). The movement has spread to Osaka and Tokyo and will shortly become a nationwide network. Although grass-roots activity such as this puts no direct pressure on the government, nevertheless it both solves individual problems and fans public and media consciousness into a ground swell that may eventually produce political change, particularly at the level of local government. However, one acquaintance who is a schoolteacher observed with a note of bitterness that only those who are not fully employed can hope to take part in such activities.

In Seven Hundred Years, Only Four Hundred Japanese

The graying of society does not come entirely, of course, from the numerous old people. The birthrate also contributes. The former minister of finance Hashimoto Ryūtaro suggests that the trend for Japanese women to obtain higher education is responsible for the "nation's sagging birthrate" (*Mainichi shinbun* 1990g). A government white paper recently reported that the 1989 birthrate hit an all-time low of 1.57 children per woman, a big drop from the 1988 rate of 1.66. It also advanced the date at which senior citizens would outnumber children from the previous estimate of the year 2004. At a news conference officials stressed the government's concern at the low birthrate because the welfare burden of Japan's aging society will be difficult to manage. When asked if the government intended to return to the prewar policy of encouraging women "to give birth and multiply" for the sake of the nation, the officials replied: "It isn't such an easy matter to get Japanese women to bear children" (1990g).

A national meeting for women in the Liberal Democratic party was told that if women do not bear 2.1–2.2 children "for us," then the population will decrease, "disrupting the pension system for retirees" (1990f). This recent statistic on the birthrate has been dubbed the "1.57 crisis" (the estimate has recently been revised to 1.32), and feminists and other commentators are very concerned because it threatens to invoke the specter of the government's involvement in family matters, especially childbearing, as occurred before the war. Unidentified experts apparently estimate that if the current Japanese birthrate remains unchanged, in another seven hundred years' time only four hundred Japanese will remain. Although some of the women at the conference were highly amused by this inanity, one delegate commented that she thinks every married couple should have at least four children because, she claims, larger families are essential for children to learn how to deal with traditional relations between superiors and inferiors.

The drop in birthrate reflects in part a smaller number of infants born to married women, a trend that more than one analyst links to the high price of land and inordinate cost of housing (*Mainichi shinbun* 1990h). It also relates to a dramatic increase in the number of single people in Japan. In 1985, 61 percent of men and 31 percent of women in their late twenties were not married. More recently, in Setagaya-ku, one of the wealthier sections of Tokyo, 68 percent of women between the ages of twenty-five and thirty were unmarried (*Asahi Evening News* 1991). Over 80 percent of both men and women between eighteen and thirty-four responded in a poll that there are "advantages to being single" (Arioka 1991). The government is worried about these trends; perhaps soon there will be not only proportionately fewer young to old people but also more elderly who never married and who therefore have no spouse or child to lean on in old age (Figure 5). Yet what the government fails to remind people is that the incidence of stroke is declining because of carefully implemented public health measures involving changes in dietary practices. If this trend continues, then the numbers of decrepit and bedridden elderly may not be nearly as high as projected. Furthermore, although young people are not rushing into marriage, so far they usually merely postpone rather than abandon the institution.

Public gatherings of all kinds organized by local governments, women's groups, and similar organizations again and again take up the theme of the aging society (*kōrei shakai*) and the state of the modern Japanese fam-

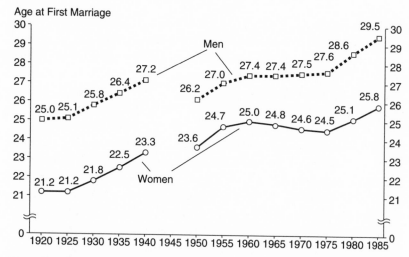

Figure 5.   Average Age at First Marriage
Source: Compiled from Ministry of Health and Welfare Statistics, Tokyo.

ily replete with its strengths and weaknesses. Participants in many of these meetings roundly criticize the government's proposals, but beyond a slow but steady expansion of public and private facilities for care of the elderly, little has changed. Even though a few of the women I talked to, especially if they lived in the country, hoped that perhaps they would be able to live with their sons in their old age, most women reluctantly accept the probability that an alternative will not be found. Although the majority consider that they are obligated to nurse their in-laws and their husbands in the years to come, they are resigned to the idea that by the time their turn comes the extended family's tradition of caring for the elders will be almost extinct.

Some women have started to discuss alternatives. Hayase-*san*, the bar owner, although still in her forties, stated that she will live with three friends of long standing, probably outside Tokyo, where she now lives and works. A Nagano farmer insisted that by the time she is old, children will not expect to look after their elders. She has talked quite a bit with her friends about the future, and they have decided that since so many of the younger people are leaving, the best hope for the future is for the old women who are left behind (themselves, that is) to band together and move into one of their homes (which will probably remain unsold because of the present taxation system). "We all think that some kind of co-op would be better than a senior citizens' home," this woman stated vehemently. "Although there are some round here, none of us want to end up in that kind of place." The *shōwa hitoketa* are indeed a "sandwich generation" as Plath suggests, caught between a life of hard work and dedication to others characteristic of prewar Japanese but facing a future in which they must exert their independence in order to survive.

During the interviews, when the discussion turned to changing family relationships and the aging society, most women participated actively. Indeed, at this juncture they usually took charge of the conversation. Many people were also reasonably animated over discussions about their general health, particularly if they had experienced episodes of difficult illness. But, aside from those very few women whose lives had been seriously disrupted by *kōnenki* symptoms, or the one or two who associated *kōnenki* with an unhappy life, most were not so interested in this part of the interview and volunteered much less information. The majority of women, although they had given some thought to *kōnenki*, were primarily interested in family vicissitudes and work; concern about *kōnenki* was usually confined to the fact that it signals the approach of old age and thus inevitably impinges on family matters.

6 Illusion of Indolence—
Ideology and Partial Truths

You must discard the word Fancy altogether. You have
nothing to do with it . . . You must use . . . combinations
and modifications . . . of mathematical figures which are
susceptible of proof and demonstration. This is the new
discovery. This is fact. This is taste.
> (Mr. Gradgrind, in Dickens, *Hard Times*)

The Tyranny of Numbers

The pathological nuclear family sketched in the previous chapter does not
resemble the lived experience of most Japanese people. Like all plausible
rhetoric, however, it contains elements of reality: there are many men
who rarely see their families, thousands of children who refuse for a while
to go to school, old people and housewives who are isolated and lonely.
Diagnoses of mental illness are more common today than in earlier decades
(although diagnosis tells us nothing about changes in prevalence). Yet a
small conceptual leap is enough to link these problems to a loss of traditional values and a concomitant increase in the consumer-driven way of
life common among modern urban nuclear families.

Discussion about the fragility of the nuclear family is one facet of the
larger internal cultural debate as to what Japan and its people represent in
the modern world. Debates such as these are an intrinsic part of the experience of modernity, and hence similar discussions are taking place in
most corners of the world today. Because the Japanese culture is infused
with a tradition of reflection and introspection, the participants have cast
their rhetoric into a genre known as *nihonjinron*: essays on being Japanese.
Recent governments, including various prime ministers intent on leading
the country in an appropriate direction, have been active and very visible
participants in the debate (Pyle 1987).

At the core of *nihonjinron* is a concept of racial homogeneity, which
focuses on unity of language and culture. It marks off the line between
insiders and outsiders and takes for granted notions of separateness,
uniqueness, and certain irreducible "essences" that make one Japanese.
This type of rhetoric is not limited to Japan, of course, and is not of recent

135

origin (it reaches back at least to the early eighteenth century [Kawamura 1980]), but the specific definition of unity, the "invention of tradition" (Hobsbawm and Ranger 1983), expresses topical themes that currently cause anxiety throughout Japanese society. Almost seven hundred monographs over the past thirty years belong to this genre, and if we add journal articles, the total must be many thousands of publications (Befu 1983).

The outpouring of *nihonjinron* represents a state of social and political unrest that has been designated as one of "moral panic," when self-appointed public critics air their views about the supposed breakdown of morality and the collapse of social control in the media, courtrooms, and popular literature (Cohen 1972, 28). Contemporary observers believe that the recent rapid so-called internationalization of Japan, and Japan's desire to impress on the world that it is something other than a mere "economic animal," has precipitated this current crisis of national identity. Paradoxically, the international exposure has provoked in some circles a reassertion of uniqueness and a marked increase in national self-esteem statistically charted and documented in the "survey of national character," carried out until recently every five years (Hayashi et al. 1975).

Well-known people from all walks of life contribute to *nihonjinron*. The specific subject matter varies but a large portion is directed at the family, perhaps because until relatively recently the family was modeled explicitly after the state and has experienced only just over forty years of liberation from direct government surveillance. Articles with titles such as "The Breakdown of Motherhood Is Wrecking Our Children" or "Analyzing Trends in Family Pathology" are commonplace. This literature tends to focus on traditional human relationships, particularly within the family, which it describes as disappearing at a rapid rate, to the detriment of society. And it frequently makes comparisons, latent or explicit, between the group-oriented moral foundation of traditional Japan and the amoral individualism believed to typify Western societies. It also contrasts traditional society with urbanized modern Japan—almost by definition overly Westernized (Moeran 1984). Its assertions about the contemporary pathological family often cite statistics such as the number of elderly living alone today, the falling national fertility rate, or the emergence of diseases of modernity (*gendaibyō*), in order to embed the rhetoric in a factual matrix.

Contemporary Japan is a number cruncher's paradise: the dissemination of national survey results and commentary is an integral part of the apparatus that promotes the postwar moral and behavioral order. Statistics, assumed to reflect an existing reality, serve to standardize national life along certain clear trajectories; they are the principal tool for the creation of order through the production of means and medians to define the behavior of individuals as appropriate or otherwise. Any well stocked library in Japan, for example, has compilations often extending to more than one volume per issue of the results of over thirty extensive national surveys conducted at regular periodic intervals, in addition to the results of endless smaller surveys.

Ian Hacking claims that the notion of probability is "the philosophical success story of the first half of the twentieth century" (1990, 4). He believes that we now live with an "imperialism" of probabilities that began to be calculated from the middle of the last century in the West (and a little later in Japan) when measurement and a "fundamentally quantitative feel for nature" first emerged (5). As social phenomena were enumerated, tabulated, and made public, the way was opened up for what Hacking terms the "making of people":

> The avalanche of numbers, the erosion of determinism, and the invention of normalcy are embedded in the grander topics of the Industrial Revolution. The acquisition of numbers by the populace, and the professional lust for precision in measurement, were driven by familiar themes of manufacturing, mining, trade, health, railways, war, empire. Similarly, the idea of a norm became codified in these domains.
>
> (Hacking 1990, 5)

Hacking considers that statistical information was developed explicitly for the purposes of social control; its categories of inclusion and exclusion into various classes and groupings demand the "normalization" of individuals and social units such as the family. The "boxification" of people (Kaufert 1990b) is an ostensibly neutral exercise, but policy decisions, therapeutic choices, incarceration, and so on inevitably reflect the results of survey research (see also Foucault 1979; Hewitt 1991).

A large number of people in Japan retain a healthy skepticism about statistics but must contend with a barrage of numerical information, including dire predictions for the future, that leaps from the pages of the newspaper every day:

> An overwhelming 98 percent of housewives in the large cities of Japan are dissatisfied or anxious about rising prices, old age, and environmental destruction, according to the twentieth annual survey by the Better Living Information Center [*Kokumin seikatsu sentā*].
>
> (*Mainichi shinbun* 1990i)

A total of 21,346 persons took their own lives in 1990. . . . This was 1,000 fewer suicides than the year before but still nearly double the figure for people killed in traffic accidents during 1990. . . . Managerial-level workers constituted the only occupation group to witness an increase in suicides. A total of 355 corporate managers took their own lives in 1990. This was 20 more than in 1989 for a 6.3 percent increase. . . . However, the majority of suicides, 12,802, were committed not by managers but by unemployed persons.

(*Mainichi shinbun* 1991d)

The lifetime birthrate could plummet to 1.32 children per woman in 1996, much lower than the record low of 1.57 children per woman recorded in 1989, according to a government institute projection. . . . As a result of the rapidly aging population, the proportion of elderly people will surpass that of children under fifteen in 1997, according to the institute.

(*Mainichi shinbun* 1991e)

"Marriage wanted more than work," was the reply of 92.6 percent of office ladies working for Kanebo [a cosmetics company]. Only 17.3 percent believe that they do work that is equal in worth to men.

(*Asahi shinbun* 1991b)

One out of every two young children in Japan has his or her own television set, and one in three has his own telephone, according to government research on the degree of mechanization of Japan's children. . . . The white paper reveals that the trend toward Japanese children remaining indoors and becoming obsessed with playing TV computer games with a small number of playmates has grown stronger. . . . At the same time, traditional games and amusements are dying out, according to the surveys. The report stated that 73.2 percent of children said that they had never picked flowers, 56.2 percent said that they had never collected insects, and 30.4 percent said that they had never jumped from a high place. . . . About 90 percent said that they cannot show their deepest feelings or that they meet with people only superficially.

(*Mainichi shinbun* 1991f)

An often repeated commentary on the frailty of the modern Japanese family, laced with statistics such as the above, voiced and penned by social critics and people in positions of authority, takes on a life of its own that is extremely hard to deny—even when a minimum of research shows that the statistics are misleading, as they so often are, particularly when decontextualized.

Despite erroneous statements, government documents and media commentaries are very persuasive, in part because of their stark simplicity and clear conclusions. Government documents have a much wider circulation in Japan than elsewhere; of course they do not make the best-seller lists but, because Japan is the information society par excellence, have endless exposure through discussion and interpretation in the media. Selected persons known collectively as social critics (hyōronka) and usually billed as "intellectuals" appear regularly on a variety of TV programs and in the press, where they discuss and offer up opinions on topical items. These "cultural intermediaries" (Bourdieu 1984) provide a streamlined version of the well established Japanese occupation of reflecting on the state of society and human relationships. Largely by means of hyōronka, various discourses—and in particular the dominant conservative ideology of the government, replete with ideas about uniqueness—disseminate throughout Japan.

Dissident viewpoints appear increasingly often today in roundtable and panel discussions on television and in print, but the viewpoints of women are still badly underrepresented, particularly by television (in newspapers they fare a lot better). Not surprisingly, feminists and other progressive critics also resort to statistics to establish their points; they often refer to exactly the same survey results from the endless government white papers that the conservative establishment draws on but interpret the numbers in quite a different way. Armed with the latest statistics, the government and conservative social critics deplore the alienation and pathology that they see everywhere. They cite as cause a documented increase in nuclear families, which they link to excessive individualism and loss of traditional values, and as an antidote promote nostalgia for the past (Kelly 1986). Feminists, in contrast, reach the opposite conclusion: the present social order is oppressive, there is still too much of the past in the present, and dramatic forward-looking changes are in order (Matsumura 1985).

Obviously, statistics have their uses (a position that Hacking clearly supports), and I make use of them liberally in this book. But if a survey poses questions that are ideologically predetermined, and if the results of such a survey generate decontextualized generalizations about the entire nation, generational cohorts, schoolchildren, housewives, salarymen, and so on, then the product is rhetorical mumbo jumbo—a cloud of unexamined platitudes that consistently obliterates the flexibility, contradictions, ambiguities, compromises, improvisations, hardships, and joys that inevitably exist in family life. I propose to combine numbers with narrative in order to refute some of the received wisdom about Japanese family life today, in particular about the situation of middle-aged women, and about individuals who are said to be at risk for distress at *kōnenki*.

In Search of the Typical Nuclear Family

Kubota-*san* is forty-eight years old and lives with her husband and two children aged twenty-three and nineteen. She grew up in a household of eight persons with her parents, her grandmother, an older brother and sister, and a younger brother and sister. She states that the older children were spoiled because they were raised by *obāsan* while their mother was out all day working as a nurse. The mother gave up full-time nursing when Kubota-*san* was small but continued working as a midwife while she raised her middle daughter. Kubota-*san* says that of the five children she received the strictest training, not only in *shitsuke* (behavior and discipline) but also with schoolwork because her mother was waiting to tutor her every day when she arrived home from school. By the time the two younger children were old enough to be tutored, Kubota-*san* says that her mother was getting too old to do it; however, at eighty her mother still attends classes for adults on various topical subjects run by the city of Kyoto. Kubota-*san* married an eldest son and lived, as expected, with her husband's parents for the first ten years of her married life. She helped her mother-in-law look after her father-in-law until he died and then moved with her husband to a smart new residential area, where they bought a six-room, two-storied house (reasonably large by Japanese standards). Her mother-in-law has lived on her own in the old family house for the past thirteen years, close by several of her other six children. She will join the Kubotas in their house in the next year or two, and the quarters will be quite crowded then unless their daughter gets married and moves out, but there is no sign of this so far. Kubota-*san* tentatively discussed the possibility of starting proceedings for an arranged marriage, an idea her daughter rather firmly rejected. Kubota-*san* has worked for the past thirteen years in a cake factory in order to pay back the loan on their house. She prefers extended to nuclear families and, although her household is classified at present in the government census as nuclear, has spent most of her life in an extended family situation.

Sonoda-*san* lives in a rather prosperous part of Kobe in a modern well-furnished house with her husband and her son, who is in junior high school. Immediately visible to the guest who sits down in the living room is a large and elaborate Buddhist altar in the next room, standing with its doors open and with large photographs of deceased *ojīsan* and *obāsan* hanging above it. Sonoda-*san* has lived in Kobe her whole life. She grew up in a large household with her grandparents, her parents, six brothers and sisters, and two servants. She married a second son right after her graduation from a junior college, and they lived by themselves for a few years until they built the house in which they now live. At that time her mother-in-law came to join their household because her eldest son, with whom she had been living, was moved to Tokyo by his company. In all, Sonoda-*san* spent twenty-one years of her life living with *obāsan*, who became an invalid about five years after she joined the household. Sonoda-*san* says that at times the relationship was difficult and strained, but that her son benefited enormously in that he understands and respects old people. She has never had a job but regrets this now, although she says that it would have been very difficult to do any work outside the house while her mother-in-law was an invalid. She recently persuaded her husband that it is socially acceptable for her to try to find a part-time job. This household is also classified as nuclear and will in all probability remain this way, but all three of the current family members have spent most of their lives in an extended family situation.

Kajimoto-*san* lives in a first-floor four-room apartment in a Kobe suburb with her father-in-law, her husband, and her youngest son, who is eighteen. She explained that she is very stressed, has high blood pressure, headaches, and irritability, all of which she attributes to the trouble she is having with her eldest son, now twenty-one. Her husband is a high-school teacher; even so, her son failed the college entrance examinations three times—largely, his mother claims, because he just doesn't care to study hard. The family recently bought him a one-room apartment nearby for two reasons: in order to improve the "mental state" of his mother, and also to allow *ojīsan*, whose wife died the previous year, to move in with the younger Kajimotos. "We had to find space for *ojīchan* somehow because he was all alone, so having my son move out solved the problem."

Kajimoto-*san* explained that the conditions her husband set when her son moved out were that he would come over on his motorcycle each morning for breakfast and, after studying during the day at cram school, return each evening for dinner with the family, and then go to his apartment to sleep. For a while Kajimoto-*san* went over to her son's apartment most days to clean up for him but now just goes over sometimes "because she enjoys it." Her son changes his clothes at his parents' house and so his mother does all his laundry. She says that her son seems to be enjoying his independence [!].

Kajimoto-*san* has also been doing laundry and meals for her brother-in-law, who was posted by his company to Kobe and for eleven years lived alone next door during the workweek; on the weekend he usually goes back to his family in Tokyo. Recently his daughter joined him while she goes to junior college in Kobe, and Kajimoto-*san* helps look after her too. Although this family is an extended one, it is listed at present as a nuclear family but at the next census will officially become a three-generation household for a few years until the younger son gets married and leaves home.

Kajimoto-*san* has never been employed and says she never had any desire to have a job; she feels somewhat isolated now that she is older because most of her friends are busy with work as well as complex and demanding households. In the future though, she will have to spend a good deal of time caring for *ojīsan*, a task she is prepared to take on reasonably cheerfully as an inevitable part of her duties as a housewife.

Out of the 105 women who were interviewed in their homes, only one person has lived all her life thus far in a nuclear family, which cannot be taken, therefore, as very representative of the modern Japanese condition to date (see also Long 1987). This cyclical change in family structure dates from before the Meiji Restoration (Koyama 1961), although the pattern may well change in the near future.

Peering through the Platitudes

Certain figures are often cited to illustrate the weakening of extended family ties in contemporary life: the estimate, for example, that 41 percent of eldest sons set up independent households when they marry (Nihonjin no Kekkon to Shussan 1988). Another frequently cited number is the percentage of noninstitutionalized elderly living with their children, which fell from 77 percent to fewer than 65 percent between 1970 and 1985 (Japan Statistical Bureau 1986). Hence proportionately more elderly live with a spouse or alone than was formerly the case. Figures on mean household size give supporting evidence for what is termed the "nuclearization" of the Japanese family: whereas in the 1920s mean household size was 5 persons, it is at present only 3.74 (Jetro Nippon 1989).

These changes are assumed to be largely postwar phenomena, but careful analyses of the figures show that the number of nuclear families has increased little in recent years, going from 54 percent in the 1920s to 55 percent in the 1960s, and increasing only by a further 5 percent over the past thirty years (Ogawa 1988). Throughout the 1980s the number has remained at approximately 62 percent (Nihon Fujindantai Rengōkai 1989). Despite this stability, the proportion of extended families has dropped,[1] because of the dramatic rise of single-person households in the postwar years, from 6 percent in the 1920s to 17.5 percent in the late 1980s: this change accounts in large part for the drop in average household size (Table 6).

Isolated statistics freeze relationships in time and do not (as is clear from the living conditions of the families cited above) convey the somewhat transitory character of most modern Japanese families. Moreover, the very notions and definitions of nuclear and extended families are open to interpretation, as the figures on the extended family indicate. With respect to middle-aged women, among the important variables that only careful perusal of the records brings to light are the following: households listed as "nuclear" very frequently refer not only to those of husband and wife living together, or those of parents and unmarried children, but also to households composed a middle-aged couple and their parents (of which there are many). The stereotype of the nuclear family is one without elders, but in fact many so-called nuclear families include one or more elderly persons whose son is listed as the household head and whose wife is taking care of her in-laws. Alternatively, many old couples live next door or very close to their married children; some families buy two or more apartments in an apartment complex in order to be close to their old people. This trend is on the increase, particularly in urban areas (Nihonjin no Kekkon to Shussan 1988). Statistics do not reveal complex adjustments such as these, often made deliberately to accommodate the elderly. Furthermore, because the working arrangements of many Japanese men require them to be away much more than they are at home, a good number of nuclear families are for all intents and purposes single-parent households, but this pattern too rarely shows up in survey research.

There are, clearly, changes in family structure from prewar days; more people spend a good portion of their life cycle living separately from their parents. Many young people, for example, live in single-person households, often in company dormitories; Yuzawa claims that this change largely accounts for the increase in single-person households (1977). In addition more married people set themselves up in independent households and so move out of the parental home, usually into tiny apartments. Turning to the latter part of the life cycle, people in their fifties, sixties, and even seventies often choose to live independently (provided they remain healthy). Changes such as these account for the nuclearization of the family; yet the majority of old people still move in with or close to their children for the final years of their lives. A recent survey shows that among those who are between seventy-five and seventy-nine years of age, 64 percent live with their children, and that among those over eighty years of age this number rises to over 74 percent (Kōseishō 1991).

Table 6. Distribution of Ordinary Households by Family Type (1955–85)
(percentage)

Year	Three-Generation Families	Nuclear Families				Households with Other Relatives	Households of Nonrelatives	One-Person Households
		Married Couple	Married Couple with Child(ren)	Father and Child(ren)	Mother and Child(ren)			
1955	96.1	6.8	43.1	1.6	8.1	36.5	0.5	3.4
1960	94.9	8.3	43.4	1.3	7.3	34.7	0.4	4.7
1965	91.8	9.9	45.4	1.0	6.3	29.2	0.4	7.8
1970	88.9	11.0	46.1	0.9	5.5	25.4	0.4	10.8
1975	86.2	12.4	45.7	0.8	5.0	22.3	0.2	13.5
1980	84.0	13.1	44.2	0.9	5.1	20.7	0.2	15.8
1985	82.3	14.3	41.6	1.0	5.6	19.8	0.2	17.5

Source: Adapted from Historical Statistics of Japan 1987, 169

In the present study, just over 63 percent of the families are nuclear (that is, they consist of two generations living together). The majority of the women, 54 percent, live in typical nuclear families with their husbands and children or else with their husbands alone. Another 5 percent are single mothers with children, and the remaining 4 percent live (usually together with their husbands) with their parents or parents-in-law but have no children in the household (Table 7).

Twenty-nine percent of the women live in an extended family; in all, just over 23 percent have three generations under one roof (higher than the national average because of the disproportionately large number of rural respondents in the present study). When we combine three-generation families with nuclear families that consist of middle-aged people living with elderly relatives, we find that over 27 percent of the sample live with one or both of their parents-in-law or, less often, their own parents or other elderly relatives. More than 10 percent of the women in this study are fully occupied nursing elderly relatives. But we must remember that by no means all of the women have living parents (the Second World War and a much higher prewar incidence of infectious disease account for many early deaths of parents: nearly 50 percent of fathers and fathers-in-law, and 36 percent of mothers and mothers-in-law had died) and that these women whose parents have died usually live in nuclear families. When we consider all the above figures and take note, in addition, of the large number of elderly who live close to their offspring and have extensive contact with them, we may infer that they are not left in isolation by their families. Moreover, since the parents of fifty-year-old women are usually not among the infirm, the number of elderly living with the women in this study has no doubt increased in the intervening years.

Families in Flux

Abe-*san* lives in Nagano prefecture on a small farm. The house she lives in, like many farmhouses in that part of Japan, has been entirely rebuilt and enlarged in a tasteful semitraditional style. At fifty Abe-*san* looks young—not a wrinkle to be seen. Her air of calm confidence hides some resentments about extended family life that created a few ripples in an otherwise relaxed exchange about her daily life:

"I get up at 6 o'clock in winter (5:30 in summer) and make breakfast and clean the house. After breakfast I do the laundry, every three days in winter, and every day in summer [Japanese washing machines are small, usually semiautomatic, and extremely inconvenient]. I watch a little TV in the morning until 8:30 to catch up on the news, and then I read the

Table 7. Women's Relationship to Other Members of Household
(percentage)

By Self	4.2
With	
Husband Only	14.3
Children Only	5.2
Husband and Children	39.5
Parent Only	.4
Parent and Husband	.6
Parent and Children	.4
Parent, Husband, and Children	.8
Parent-in-law and Husband	2.7
Parent-in-law only	.5
Parent-in-law, Husband, and Children	10.3
Parent-in-law and Children	1.0
Parent-in-law and Other Relatives	.1
Parent-in-law, Husband, and Other Relatives	1.3
Parent-in-law, Children, and Other Relatives	.5
Parent-in-law, Husband, Children, and Other Relatives	5.5
Other Relative	.2
Other Relative and Husband	2.0
Other Relative and Children	.5
Other Relative, Husband, and Children	3.7
Other Relative and Parent	.9
Other Relative, Husband, and Parent	.4
Other Relative, Parent, and Children	.5
Other Relative, Parent, Husband, and Children	.9
Unknown	3.6

Note: $N = 1,313$

newspapers and often a book until noon. After lunch I do anything I feel like in winter. In the summer [April to October] it's different, of course. I go right out into the fields after breakfast, pop back at 10:00 A.M. to do the laundry. Take a break after lunch, maybe even a nap, and go out into the fields again until the evening. We grow rice and recently soybeans too . . . they don't require much care. The local co-op plants the beans for us with our neighbor's machine so I mostly just have to weed, check the water levels, and keep an eye on things these days. When I was young I did all the planting by hand."

"Were you helping your husband then?"

"No, he's always worked in a company so I farmed alone. He's retired now and he hangs around all the time. But he's bored so he helps in the fields a little."

"Does your son help at all?"

"No, he's twenty-nine now, so he's not a child and I can't demand that he do things. I do all his laundry and so on. And my husband won't do any housework. Even if I'm busy he expects me to stay by him in case he needs anything. He'd starve to death if I wasn't around."

"Do you have any activities outside the house and farm?"

"I belong to a culture circle. We do calligraphy, and I go once a week for two hours. I've been doing it for four years now, ever since *obāsan* died. I didn't have time when she was alive. You know, I lived with her for twenty-eight years. She was bedridden for her last two months; before that she could sometimes do things for herself, but I had to help her dress. I had two sets of *futon* for her, so one was always hanging out, because there were quite a lot of accidents. It was just like having a baby in the house. She could eat by herself, but I had to carry her on my back to take her outdoors. It was like that for two years until she died. She was eighty-eight."

"What was it like when you were both younger?"

"At first I didn't know anything so it was very hard. That's natural, it takes a long time to master the customs of a particular house. It took me about nine or ten years. After that it was easy. *Obāsan* was very smart and she was a hard taskmaster, but she was never unreasonable. Because she was so strict I learned things really well. My husband pretended not to notice any conflict between us. He always said that my troubles were nothing compared to what he had as a soldier. At first I was never confident enough to say what I thought about anything, but after about ten years I got some confidence and began to speak up a bit. Once *obāsan* started to be nicer to me I started to feel that I wanted to take good care of her when she got older."

"What will it be like with your daughter-in-law?"

"I don't expect to be as strict as mine was. I think you have to talk things over with the *yome* [daughters-in-law] of today. I don't think they can stand up to the kinds of disciplining I had. It's a different generation, and they haven't been educated the same way."

"What do you think are the pluses and minuses of nuclear families and extended families?"

"Well, my ideal used to be a full-time housewife in a nuclear family. But there are advantages to the extended family, although there are difficulties too. When my son was little, *obāsan* looked after him while I worked in the fields. But, on the other hand, she took too much care of him. I regret that now, because he's turned out spoiled. That's what happens when an old person raises a young child. When I tried to control him a little *obāsan* would say, 'Don't be so hard on him.' He should have had some discipline but she disciplined *me* and not her grandchild. She didn't become bedridden until after he was an adult, before that she was so active that she never made him do anything. *Obāsan* always got up with me and we did all the housework in the morning, so there was nothing for him to do. Until about fifteen years ago they used to shut the school when we were busiest in the fields and he helped me out a lot. That was fun, we did the harvesting together when he was younger. But all that stopped when he got older."

"What will happen in the future? Will your son take over from you?"

"I think eventually he'll start to feel a sense of responsibility and work on the farm. By that time it will all be mechanized and all one will have to do is a bit of farm work in the mornings and evenings, the co-op will come and do all the rest. When that happens everyone can farm and have another job as well. The young ones will still have to learn from us older folk though. I suppose my son's wife will help too."

"So will you live with your son and his wife later on?"

"Well, he hasn't found a wife yet. I always assumed that we would arrange a marriage for him but he isn't interested. He's going to find his own wife, but he's twenty-nine already and doesn't seem to have met anyone. I'd like to live with him if they agree, but of course, no one can rely on these things any more. An extended family has its problems, but these days, now that it's not so strict, I think it's the best way to live."

Abe-*san* reveals some of the ambivalences that many people in their middle age today feel, including lingering resentment about the treatment they themselves received at the hands of their mothers-in-law. Nevertheless, they often indicate a desire to live together with their offspring on the unspoken understanding that one doesn't treat daughters-in-law too harshly; particularly since they are not as tough as they used to be, having experienced neither the hardships nor the disciplinary training of older women.

Most women have given some thought to the advantages and disadvantages of nuclear and extended families, and, although many have resigned themselves to living apart from their children, the majority in this age group tip the scales in favor of an extended family or, alternatively, households in close proximity. They usually justify these arrangements on the grounds that they offer the best kind of family for children to grow up in. Although there is nostalgia about the extended family and its positive influence on children, an interviewer need not probe very deeply to uncover stories that reveal the extent to which the lives of many women have been dominated until the recent past by their "elders and betters."

When discussing her relationship with her mother-in-law, another woman had tears in her eyes:

"It was horrible. I couldn't go back to my parents' house at all. I couldn't even go and take a bath without *her* permission and I couldn't get my hair permed unless she told me to, or buy my own clothes. Neither my in-laws nor my husband gave me any money to buy clothes. I remember mending old socks again and again."

"How long did that go on?"

"About fifteen years or so, then I began to receive my husband's salary directly and I took care of the household budget. It was easier after that. *Obāsan* died last year—we'd lived together for twenty-eight years—and *ojīsan* is still in good health. He's no trouble, he does most of his own things so far."

It was most often in connection with reproduction that the extended family exerted its greatest pressure. Tanigawa-*san*, born into a farming family, runs a small farm singlehandedly, does piecework for an electronic company on the side, and takes part in a group where they recite Chinese-style poems for relaxation. She lives with her husband who is an office worker in a nearby small town. During the early part of their marriage the family was moved several times by his company. Eventually, at her husband's request Tanigawa-*san*, together with her two young children, returned to the family farm to help her in-laws run it. Her husband stayed in Tokyo where he lived with his sister's family while he continued his office work. For most of their married lives the Tanigawas have only been together for one or two weekends every month. In his late fifties Tanigawa-*san* was diagnosed as having high blood pressure, and so he retired from his Tokyo job and came back to live in the countryside where he soon found work at a reduced salary in a company that makes relatively few demands on him. Both the Tanigawa children, a twenty-one-year-old boy and a nineteen-year-old girl, are students at universities in Tokyo. Tanigawa-*san* admits that she misses them but says that she is getting used to it.

"I think my mother suffered a lot of hardship—she was born in the Meiji era. During the winter women had to weave cotton cloth for the entire family, and they sewed all the kimonos, as well as doing all the farm work and so on. My life has been easy compared with my mother's. But I also had a very bad time. My first child, a daughter, lived to be only six years old. The labor took about thirty hours and the baby had a kind of neurological paralysis when it was born. She could never eat properly, and it was impossible to communicate with her at all.

"As you know, it's the custom for a wife to go back to her own parents' house to have her child. But in my case, because my husband wasn't in the house and my parents-in-law would have been alone, my mother-in-law persuaded me to stay and have the baby here. So a midwife was called who wasn't very competent. I think she was partly to blame for what happened. If I'd been with my husband in Tokyo, or even with my own parents, I think I would have gone to a hospital. I'm sorry now that I wasn't strong enough to ignore all the pressure to stay here, I really regret that, and feel that if I'd been stronger in my own mind, somehow the baby would have been born healthy."

Most of the reminiscences about the extended family dwell on the way in which women who are now middle-aged endured, how they silently bore an oppressive, virtually unquestioned ideology of subservience. The majority of women then had no possibility of resistance, no realistic alternative but to acquiesce to their lot. In contrast women today, even in the countryside, can air their feelings in various shelters and community houses. One such house in Nagano was established explicitly to develop the "independence of women." Tsuchihira-*san* founded and runs the center as a free service for local women, and states that in most cases after ventilating their feelings, her clients go back to their husbands' families, even though they left determined never to return. Middle-aged women living in rural areas still cannot usually see their way clear to any alternative other than family life—separation and divorce are largely urban phenomena—but at the community house they can share their troubles with other women, and most of them have enough independence to build warm and vital friendships there on which they come to depend, especially for help in getting through the bad patches in their lives.

Tsuchihira-*san* points out that not only *yome* (daughters-in-law) but also *shūtome* (mothers-in-law) suffer at times in extended families. This is particularly true for the older woman today, who may find that because she no longer succeeds to a position of power in midlife, an extended family, while it can benefit a young married couple and their children, may not offer much pleasure or comfort for grandmothers. Middle-aged women are increasingly finding that in addition to spending a good portion of their life taking care of their in-laws, they are being called on by their daughters or even their daughters-in-law to mind the grandchildren. In the traditional family, care of grandchildren while their mothers worked in the fields was, of course, one of the crucial tasks of grandmothers who, at the same time, educated the youngest generation in various aspects of local culture, discipline, moral behavior, and so on. Today, however, some grandmothers find themselves in an awkward position, one closer to exploitation than respect.

Shiba-*san*, now fifty-two, worked for nearly thirty years in the farm co-op in the village where she lives, keeping the account books. She resigned from this job two years ago to take care of both her parents-in-law with whom she lived. Until she became ill Shiba-*san*'s mother-in-law had done all the housework and cooking while Shiba-*san* worked a full day at the co-op, and her husband worked their land in addition to doing a part-time office job in the nearby town. Two months after she resigned from her job her mother-in-law died, but Shiba-*san* cannot take up employment outside her home again because her father-in-law is not able to take care of himself.

Her son, married to a nurse and with two small children aged two years and eight months, intimated that now Shiba-*san* was at home all day she probably felt rather lonely and suggested that perhaps his family should move into the "big house." Shiba-*san*'s husband encouraged his son with this idea, with the result that as of six months before the interview the family had been living with four generations under one roof.

"What's your day like?"

"Well, I get up at 6:30 and make breakfast for everyone. My daughter-in-law helps sometimes, but because she's a nurse she often works at nights so I pretty much do everything. After everyone leaves for work I do the cleaning and the washing. The washing has increased enormously with all these people in the house. My daughter-in-law does some of the children's things, but I help with the diapers and so on."

"How does it feel to be a housewife after working full-time most of your life?"

"Well, the best part about working was getting out of the house each day. I really enjoyed it, and I had a lot of friends. I was doing some counseling too, and I particularly liked that. Now as a hobby I manage to do Japanese classical dancing once a week. It's good exercise and I feel really fit afterward. But, unfortunately, I can't do any practice at home because my father-in-law is here and it would disturb him."

"Do you find it constraining to live in an extended family? What was it like when you were first married?"

"When I came here my mother-in-law was only about forty-six years old. She was a very independent woman and at first it was hard. I was working in the co-op already, but I had to start looking after this huge family as well—my parents-in-law, my husband, and his four brothers.

"It's never been my intention that my daughter-in-law should experience the same kind of hardships I had. My husband knows it's a bit hard on me at present but he says that if we are to keep the peace in this family, then everything depends on me. So I must stay quiet and try to fit in with the young people's needs. On Sundays, when my daughter-in-law is at home, in order to let her sleep in, I try to stay in bed as long as possible although I really want to get up. In the past, if a mother-in-law got up earlier than her daughter-in-law and fixed breakfast then the daughter-in-law wouldn't be able to swallow the food from shame. But now young people don't take things that way any more."

"Will you live together for a long time?"

"Well, we have some land. We could build a house on one of the rice fields, but . . . "

"How do you feel about taking care of the grandchildren?"

"They go to a day care center for a few hours each day so that helps." Here Shiba-*san* paused, clearly wondering whether she should go on. She looked down, sighed, and then continued in one long rush:

"My daughter-in-law has a good steady job, and she may be an exception, but in general I think that a mother should stay at home for a while and raise her own children, otherwise everyone suffers. Of course, if my daughter-in-law stopped her work as a nurse she would probably never find a decent job again. I think the children are much too small to go into day care all day, and anyway there are no facilities around here for full-time care. So it's very hard on me, but I'm still young and so I'm helping her. Sometimes I feel upset, I don't really agree with how things are working out, but I keep that to myself . . . "

"Do you find it hard to do that?"

"Yes, but I was trained to suppress my feelings, and I've had plenty of practice living with *obāsan* for so long. When I get older I will be able to say what I want . . . but not yet."

Shiba-*san* assumes that when she is old and infirm, her daughter-in-law will probably not give up her work in order to look after her. When pushed she admits that she feels caught between the generations, since she expects little recompense for a life devoted to the care of others (see also Lebra 1984, 266). In common with virtually all women of her age, Shiba-*san* believes that raising children is a woman's vocation. Men are usually characterized as helpless and passive onlookers at home; one epithet to describe newly retired men is "wet fallen leaves" (*nurete ochiba*), implying that they are difficult to clear out of the way, clinging to their wives for their every need, and no longer fulfilling a useful function. Another recent appellation is *kyōfu no washi zoku*—the "take-me-with-you gang," which describes husbands who tag along on their wives' outings thus spoiling the female camaraderie. Shiba-*san* has no expectations that her husband can ease her present burden, and she does not call on either him or her son to give even the minimum of assistance with the children.

Shiba-*san* does not mention this, but her family may well have suffered some economic hardships when she had to give up her job to nurse her mother-in-law, despite the fact that they own their house and the land it stands on. The household shows no signs of affluence but is on the contrary somewhat run down compared to a good number of tastefully modernized Nagano farmhouses. In addition to being the pillar of the family the majority of middle-aged women must work to contribute to the basic family income.

Working behind the Scenes

Women today constitute nearly 40 percent of all employed workers in Japan, and it is estimated at present that 58 percent aged between fifteen and sixty-four are active in the labor force (Nihon Fujindantai Rengōkai 1989). This figure is probably on the low side, however, because a large number of women are part of the "hidden economy," whereby they work but do not register the fact in order to avoid taxation. In the 1960s the majority of working women in Japan were young and unmarried (56 percent), but the situation has steadily changed since that time so that in 1982 over 68 percent of the female work force were married. However, only 27 percent of women remain at work after the birth of their first child. In the United States about 70 percent of women continue to work outside the home from their early twenties until their midforties, but most Japanese women take eight years or more off to raise their two children to at least primary school age. In 1987, for example, whereas 65 percent of women aged thirty-five to fifty-five were employed, only 54 percent of twenty-five- to thirty-five-year-olds worked outside the home (Japan Statistical Yearbook 1988).

When they return to jobs after raising their children, the majority end up in low-paid, unskilled work that is classified as part-time. Part-time work is officially defined as fewer than thirty-five hours of work per week, but in reality at least half of the women in such positions work between six and eight hours a day; the majority are not covered by health insurance, social security, or unemployment compensation, and most have no right to a paid vacation (Higuchi and Sakamoto 1976; Saso 1990). Among older women in Japan 15 percent continue to work after the age of sixty-five (Japan Statistical Bureau 1988), whereas in the United States only 7 percent do so.

Japanese women are sometimes accused of working simply for pin money, but given the current cost of living, the price of land, and the expenses of higher education, no sensible person can take such an accusation seriously. Moreover, a large number today are single, widowed, separated, or divorced (nearly 12 percent in the present sample). The reality is that most women work because they have to, at a wage considerably lower than what men receive for the same work, and under conditions of insecurity (despite the existence of an equal employment law). It is now generally recognized that part of Japan's economic success can be attributed to a system of subcontracting so that in times of recession major companies are relatively unaffected (Japan External Trade Organization 1978). It is largely middle-aged women, those like Matsuda-*san* in the village in Shiga prefecture, who work on the periphery of a subcontractor's network, and are hired and fired in boom and bust cycles so that the mainstream economy may prosper.

If they are willing to take part-time menial jobs, middle-aged women today have little trouble finding them. There is a shortage of unskilled labor in Japan owing to strict immigration laws, and, although this situation is changing, middle-aged women are preferred for many factory tasks since they are reliable hard workers who make no excessive demands on employers and are reasonably content to work for low pay with no benefits. In return, there is flexibility on the part of at least some employers so that women can fit urgent family matters into their day if necessary; some may be able to arrange for several months of unpaid leave, for example, in order to take care of sick relatives. Others have to give up work entirely at short notice because of nursing duties, but since a replacement can usually be found with little trouble employers are rarely inconvenienced. Most women find themselves out of economic necessity, therefore, with a double load of labor, paid employment together with household duties, and often face exploitation in both arenas.

To describe the working life of women in the present survey proved to be an even more difficult exercise than to assign them a family type. For example, women who take part in a family business—a farm, a store, or a company—often report that they do not work if they consider that their prime job is to raise children, even when they actually spend many hours

Sewing draperies in a factory outlet in the country.

a day occupied with the family business. Since they usually receive no direct payment for their work, these women do not consider themselves employed. Furthermore, middle-class women are sometimes embarrassed to admit that they work, and occasionally they will not report it. A further complication arises because the term part-time is so imprecise. A good number of the questions in the survey were allotted to type of employment and housework, and the number of hours of time devoted to each in order to try and tease apart some of these discrepancies.

In the present sample, 76 percent of the women replied that they work for pay (higher than the national average of 65 percent for forty-five- to fifty-five-year-olds [Japan Statistical Yearbook 1990], indicating that some women probably reported "unofficial" work), and over 95 percent of these women stated that they are primarily responsible for care of the family at the same time that they hold down a job. Of these women, 30 percent reported that they work at home in a family business, piecework, or free-lance work; another 26 percent classified their employment as part-time, although they work a full day in blue-collar jobs (but many are periodically laid off); 32 percent reported that they work outside the home and classified themselves as full-time employees, usually in factories, or in "pink-collar" or professional jobs. Some of these women run their own independent businesses, which range from selling fish to selling dolls to running a travel agency. A further 1.5 percent are mostly part of the entertainment world.

Family business	16.5 percent
Piecework at home	9.6 percent
Freelance work at home	4.0 percent
Part-time work outside home	26.3 percent
Full-time work	32.1 percent
Other work	1.5 percent
Missing cases	9.9 percent

The single most important reason for working, stated by 56 percent of the women, is that an income is essential for a reasonable standard of living. Over 80 percent of women reported that their work is interesting, 78 percent were satisfied with their present work situation, and 64 percent preferred being employed over being a housewife.

Only 21 percent of the women described themselves as full-time housewives,[2] but of these women, 67.5 percent were employed at some time in the past and a few others were actively looking for work. Nevertheless, virtually all of those women who were currently without outside employment described themselves as devoted to housework and family care and thought of themselves at present as full-time housewives.

We noted above that among the more than thirteen hundred women who were surveyed 54 percent live at present in a typical nuclear family with either their husbands alone or husbands and children. These women appear to be possible candidates for the label of selfish housewife until we consider how employment affects this percentage. Among nuclear family residents, over 33 percent are employed, indicating that we cannot make hasty associations between nuclear family life-styles and "unoccupied" middle-aged women. What is more, as was indicated earlier, 58 percent of women living in the solidly middle-class environment of the Kobe suburbs described themselves as something other than full-time housewives, and 25 percent of the women who live outside urban areas described themselves as full-time housewives. The typical middle-class urban nuclear household with its archetypal selfish housewife becomes more and more elusive, and we can by no means type the professional full-time housewife as the representative of modern Japanese women. Similarly, the typical traditional rural extended household with its archetypal devoted *shōwa hitoketa* is equally hard to pin down in reality.

"Extended" Nuclear Family

Hosokawa-*san* lives in a small apartment in a Kobe suburb. Her husband is in the manufacturing industry, and they live together with their eldest son of twenty-four who is soon to be married to a young woman he met at college. The younger son is in his last year of college. Although the college is within commuting distance, the Hosokawas decided to have their son board away from home. Hosokawa-*san* states that this is because she likes to lead a "regular" life, which means that she does not like being awakened at all hours by her sons since she has to take care of her eighty-four-year-old mother-in-law, who lives nearby with her rather severely handicapped daughter.

"Before we moved here, we were *tenkinzoku* [always being transferred by her husband's company], but it wasn't too hard on me because I belong to a nationwide group for housewives, so wherever I go I can quickly find friends who think the same way I do."

"Could you tell me about your daily life?"

"Yes, as a matter of fact my group is just now keeping a record of the way we spend our time, so I can tell you precisely. I get up at 6:20 A.M. and do morning exercises with the radio. Then we have breakfast and I send my husband off at 8:00 A.M. Fortunately he doesn't need a boxed lunch. I usually do the washing every day even if it's a small load and then I go on "patrol" [to mother-in-law's house]. I come back by 9:00 A.M. and finish up the housework and sometimes look at the newspaper and then from about 9:30 onward I usually sew unless I have a meeting. After lunch I go back to *obāsan's* place and help them with the shopping and the heavy laundry and also I help *obāsan* have a bath three times a week. Then I do our shopping and other errands and come home about 4:30 P.M. to start dinner. When that's under way, I go on patrol again. My husband usually returns about 6:30 or 7:00 P.M. and we eat right after he gets home and chat for an hour or so. Then I wash the dishes while he watches TV. At 9:00 P.M. we watch the news and chat, or I work on the household budget and then go to bed at 10:30 P.M."

"You're licensed as a nurse, right?"

"Yes, I worked for a while, but that job didn't suit me. Anyway, my husband felt that a woman's place was in the home [*onna wa katei ni hairu mon da*]. But I think my training was a plus for me and it helped me to be a good housewife."

"Why did you train as a nurse?"

"Well, my father died when I was rather young, and I wanted to get out into the world and not just stay at home. I could live in the hospital dormitory while I trained; that seemed to be the only way I could study and support myself. But I only worked for two or three years; I stopped as soon as I got engaged. I'm glad I had the training, but I'm a pretty emotional type and I don't really have the cool head you need to be a good nurse."

"Did you ever think of trying some other kind of job?"

"Well, I did think I'd like to get out in society and work, but I didn't really have any idea of what kind of jobs were available. I didn't care about earning money; I'm not good at that. Still, I actually work at the club I belong to—it's like volunteer work really. We're concerned about things like nutrition and family budgeting and the problems of the elderly. I meet a lot of people this way and it enriches my life. People look at me and comment on the way I always seem busy and happy. I think it's boring to just stay at home like a frog in a well."

"Do you think of child rearing as work?"

"Definitely. Very important work."

"You said that you've had trouble with your eyes."

"Yes, I have glaucoma. I've heard that people who are easily upset, nervous types are very susceptible. I don't really think of myself like this, but I do sometimes have trouble controlling myself. Anyway, the acute kind of glaucoma can come on overnight after a big shock or something like that, but mine is the chronic kind. I think it started when I had the responsibility of sewing a wedding kimono out of very expensive fabric. I don't like to have heavy responsibilities very much, and I have to avoid psychological stress so that the glaucoma won't get any worse. It's under control now."

"You also said that you've had some unusual sensations lately."

"Yes, when I answered your questionnaire I had this prickling feeling like ants crawling over my skin. My husband said, 'Oh, that must be *kōnenki shōgai*.' He'd read about it in some book. It didn't last long though, although this one remains [Hosokawa-*san* pointed to her check-mark beside the question about 'lack of sexual desire']. My husband says it's because I'm too busy during the day—I'm not so sure about that though . . . Anyway, I guess those ants might have been the start of *kō-nenki shōgai*, but I got over them right away."

"What do you think about *kōnenki*?"

"I think it's not too good to have too much free time. If you just sit around and think, it's no good. My husband said I was getting touchy and joked that it must be my *kōnenki* starting. I'm lucky though because he took it so lightly."

"What do you think of as the ideal family?"

"One like mine. I think living with parents is better than a nuclear family, well actually, preferably in separate houses on the same property.

I think if a man works very hard at his job that means he's concerned about his family. It's a question of sincerity. Women seem to be lacking in the skills needed to get along in the outside world. Career women, even those who work as hard as can be, always turn to the home when they run into problems on the job. As women, they want a home as well as a career.

"For instance, I know a woman doctor who is thirty and working very hard but her parents want her to get married, preferably to another doctor or someone with an executive position. She just wants to work, but they want to see her make a nest. The woman keeps turning down all the men her parents arrange for her to meet [with a view to formally arranging a marriage]. But, naturally, if she has normal feelings of filial duty she'll want to do what they say sooner or later. If she were a man, they wouldn't push it in the same way. That's the way it is in Japanese society today, it's something women can't escape; they still should do what their parents want."

"If you had a daughter, how would you raise her?"

"Well, it's fine for a woman to work, but she must like to cook too. And of course she should be able to notice and respond to other people's needs and wishes or she wouldn't be happy. So girls must learn the qualities and skills a woman needs, this is the only way of finding real happiness. I would want a daughter of mine to first have feminine things as a base, and then find some job that would build on it."

"So it's all right for a woman to work?"

"Yes, but on the condition that she be able to give all her energies to her children while they're small."

A large number of women, however, must work for financial reasons and cannot live up to Hosokawa-*san's* expectations. But the idea that a woman should be at home with her children is so strongly internalized, even among working women, that they often express regret at not being able to do so.

Mind over Matter

Murakami-*san*, forty-seven years old and rather gaunt-looking, is a worker in a textile factory. She poured out her story with few hesitations while sitting in her cramped but comfortable house on the outskirts of Kyoto. Her son is in college, and her daughter is a high-school student.

"My husband comes home only on weekends. He takes care of the boiler at a textile factory in Shiga prefecture. He's been doing that for seven years—he had to choose between quitting work altogether or taking what the company offered him in Shiga. We didn't go with him because of the children's education. My mother-in-law is in hospital—she's been there for about three months. She's been ill with heart disease since about the time that we got married. I go and see her on weekends, and my children take it in turns to go every other day."

"How old is she?"

"She's seventy-seven now."

" Could you tell me a little about your work?"

"I work for a textile company. At the moment I'm in charge of weaving car seats. I have to work, otherwise we couldn't get by but I may have to stop soon. If *obāsan* comes home and she needs a lot of care I'll have to quit, and I don't suppose I'll be able to find another job easily, maybe not at all. What I really want to do is work to the retirement age of sixty, which for me is another twelve years."

"Does your family help you with running the household?"

"My daughter helps a bit, but she has a kidney problem so I don't like to ask her to do too much. My son runs some errands, but that's about all. I wish my husband were living here. When he's home he likes to rest, but I have things I'd like him to do around the house sometimes—things that need fixing that I can't do. We have quarrels about that kind of thing."

"How did you manage when the children were small?"

"*Obāsan* did all the child care. It worked out very smoothly. If anything had turned out wrong I would have thought that it was because of my neglect of them, but *obāsan* was strict with them and they grew up without any problems. I feel fairly happy these days. We have our own little house, and that's because I worked. And my kids are fine. Some housewives might wonder what on earth I have to be grateful for, getting up early every day and working until late at night, but I never feel envious. I like to work and I hate staying quietly at home . . . " Murakami-*san* looked wistful as she said this and added after a pause:

"Still, really, it would be truly ideal to stay at home and just take care of my husband and children. If we were wealthier I would have done that, I'm old-fashioned like that, I really do think a woman's place is in the home."

"What do you think about extended family life?"

"My mother is about eighty-five now. She went through terrible troubles because she married into a big farming family and she gave birth to ten children. She worked from dawn to dusk day in and day out and her mother-in-law was very demanding. They were really poor too, my father and mother started from nothing, but they gradually saved a little bit.

"I've always lived with *obāsan* and both of us have been careful to look out for each other properly, although I had to hold back, of course. For about ten years after I was married, I handed all my salary over to her every week. I wouldn't want my children to go through the same thing— I'd like my daughter to marry into a family where she can live without the in-laws, and I don't expect to live with my son, although sometimes I tease him and say, 'Let's live together.' "

"What do you think about your working conditions?"

"We women have a bad time, I think. We work the same hours as men do and yet our salary is still so low, despite the equal employment law. In my company women get about half what the men do. I get less than half what my husband gets, and I actually have more responsibility than he does. I feel pretty wretched. If I'm to be born again, then I want to be a man.

"When my kids were small they often asked why I had to go out to work. I wish I could have been home some of the time, or at least go to their school activities sometimes, but still, if there are two women at home that can be a source of trouble, so it's just as well I was working, I suppose. I certainly didn't want to make it into a *kurai katei* [gloomy household] by having quarrels, so for about fifteen years after getting married I just kept my thoughts to myself, and then as *obāsan* got older I started to speak up."

"How about your health?"

"I've been weak all my life. My brother went into the army when I was six and when he returned the first thing he said was: 'Wow, you're still alive!' I keep going by willpower. I have an irregular heartbeat that became worse when I started having *kōnenki shōgai* in my early forties. I get a heavy head quite often, and I have shoulder stiffness nearly all the time. I can't sleep properly either, I take herbal medicine to help me sleep better because when I wake up I don't go back to sleep for two or three hours, and recently I've been getting muscle pains all over. I started to perspire suddenly about two years ago, too. I kept sweating for about ten minutes—just my face. And my whole body feels so tired these days. Some of it is to do with my work—it's hard on the body, especially the hands and knees.

"I was the first one at work to have my periods become irregular, I was forty-two, and the doctor said that was rather early. I don't like to think about it much, it gives me a funny feeling. I still have them very occasionally."

"Did the perspiration start when your periods became irregular?"

"No, that was much later, about forty-five or forty-six."

"Did you get suddenly hot as well?"

"A woman working next to me sometimes told me my face was red. Even though the room temperature was low, I felt hot, at least in my face—the rest of my body felt cold [*hienobose*]. It just lasted for ten minutes or so, but I didn't like it. I haven't had it lately though. My doctor says my problems are mostly because I have trouble with my autonomic nervous system."

"Did you talk to your husband about these symptoms?"

"Oh no! He's tired out too, and he doesn't want to hear about my problems. It's too bad, but I just have to live with it. I don't want sex either. My husband wants it when he come home at the weekends, but I can't stand it. When I refuse, he gets angry. I tell him I'm too tired and sick but I have to give in to him about once a month."

"Do you have anyone to talk to about your troubles?"

"Yes, we women at work tell each other everything. That really helps. For example, about three years ago I started to feel bad because I'd had two abortions when I was younger. I told the other women, and they said that it might help to go to a Buddhist temple to pray about it, and maybe to do *mizuko kuyō* [a memorial service for the souls of aborted fetuses]. I regret having had those abortions, they were between the births of my son and daughter. My mother-in-law said she couldn't take care of two small children so close in age, and she told my husband I should have the abortions. I regret that now, abortion is something you should never have to go through."

Murakami-*san*, like the majority of women interviewed who held blue-collar jobs, reveals deep-seated ambivalences about her working life, its effect on her children, and her position in the extended family, where against her better judgment she has been forced to cooperate with major decisions concerning her health and well-being that her husband and his mother made on her behalf. She cannot, even in retrospect, imagine how she might have exerted more independence about family matters, but she is determined that her daughter will not suffer to the same extent, and her most fervent wish is that her daughter find a modern, understanding husband, preferably with a reasonably good income so that she can have more time to devote to the family.

Over 64 percent of the women who answered the questionnaire responded that being a housewife is a "natural" thing to do, with only 4 percent more housewives feeling this way than women with jobs. An overwhelming 97 percent of housewives agree that it is a husband's duty to support the family, and 96 percent of employed women also feel this way. When asked if they think that the man should be "the boss" around the home 86 percent of housewives and 84 percent of women with jobs agree with this statement. Among housewives, 80 percent answered that family and home should come before personal ambitions, and 78 percent of employed women agreed with them.

Although a small number of women in the sample hold dissenting views, by far the majority of middle-aged Japanese women, even those who are employed outside the home, apparently believe that women belong to the "inside" and men to the "outside," that together they form a complementary unit—the core of the family—the hub of which is located in the home where the wife is the manager and care giver. An impressive 78 percent of women responded that while the children are small, women should not go out to work.

When the women who classified themselves as housewives were asked to give their reasons for not working, the most frequent answer was because their husbands did not want them to; the second because they enjoyed staying at home. Only 12 percent expressed dissatisfaction with being a housewife, but, given the chance to take a job, 36 percent would take it on, although perhaps for many the ideal would be to work a few hours a day at most.

Although most people believe that being a housewife is the "natural" thing to do, there is nevertheless resistance to this ideology, particularly among middle-aged women who feel that they are no longer needed at home to support their children. The narratives reveal some of the contradictions and ambivalences that are partially disguised by survey research. Some women explained that when they respond to a survey questionnaire they give *tatemae* answers, that is, they do not reveal their "inner" feelings but respond with what they know are the expected and ideologically "correct" answers. During the interviews too there were times when I sensed that, although they were at ease, some women just trotted out standard responses, in spite of having volunteered for the task. Others caught flagrant contradictions in their own narratives and laughed at their inconsistencies.

Nevertheless, the narratives make clear that most Japanese women at present aged fifty and over have lived a submissive life in which their lot was cast with their husband's family, and where frequently even the uses to which their bodies were put were determined by others. In recent years, the majority have become conscious that in retrospect they appear to have dedicated their lives to the family in a way that they believe neither younger generations of Japanese women nor Western women have done. While some expressed regret, particularly at not having control over their

Harvesting the rice.

own reproduction, yet none intimated that they felt their position to be in any way inferior to that of either younger Japanese or Western women. Some may genuinely believe that they do not measure up to older Japanese women, but few would wish to have firsthand experience of the terrible hardships that many older women endured. Middle-aged women usually value the disciplining they received and, therefore, express considerable satisfaction with their lives. Often they regard other women (older, younger, and foreign) as less fortunate than themselves.

Weaving Work and the Family Together

Unno-*san* grew up in Tokyo but now lives in Kobe with her husband, his mother, and their daughter. Their son is in Tokyo studying at a cram school with the hope of getting into a good university.

"Being a good wife to my husband is my first priority, although I don't know if I really felt this way when I got married. My kids have their own lives now so I don't have to worry about them any longer."

"What's your daily life like?"

"I get up about 6:30 A.M. and I take the dog for a walk. After my husband goes off to work I work on my weaving and dyeing. I'm really happy right now. *Obāsan* does most of the housework. She's eighty but she loves to do all the shopping and a lot of the cleaning and cooking. She gets unhappy if I do it. My daughter does quite a bit too, so I spend all day at my studio, from 9:00 A.M. to 6:00 P.M. *Obāsan* insists that it's all right, so I really think it is. I have eight students who come to my studio on Wednesdays."

"Have you always lived with your mother-in-law?"

"When my father-in-law was alive they lived here, and my husband and I lived with the children in the next house. That's my studio now. I have exhibitions and sales, mostly in Tokyo, and I still go to Tokyo once every three months or so to have a lesson from my teacher who is seventy-eight."

"Is your work as important as your husband's?"

"No, of course not. His work is much more important than mine. Our incomes are completely different. I don't like the idea of going to a company and working every day, so I respect my husband for doing that, and I support him as much as I can. He doesn't help around the house at all, but why should he when *obāsan* is here? She wouldn't let him do a thing. It was hard when the children were young, though, and we lived separately. But he never orders me around and he always put up with the mess I made from the dyeing when we were living in the middle of it in the other house."

"Are you concerned about *kōnenki*?"

"Until very recently I thought I wouldn't notice it at all. But I do get tired more easily than I used to. It's a mentally strenuous time what with the children leaving home and husbands waiting for their last big promotion and parents and parents-in-law getting sick and dying. I think *kōnenki* is much more psychological than physical."

Unno-*san* is one of the relatively few people in this sample who might qualify as living in *onna tengoku* (women's heaven). Hers is the kind of life that some Japanese women may secretly envy: secure, calm, and with plenty of time to fulfill her own interests in a serious way, but almost no one in the interviews would admit such feelings—perhaps because her life, despite the students she teaches, would appear a little too frivolous, especially from the point of view of blue-collar workers and farmers. The image that comes to mind when people hear of Unno-*san*'s life is uncomfortably close to the selfish housewife.

Like a good number of the other questionnaire respondents, Unno-*san* thinks relatively little about the world outside her home; she rarely reads a newspaper, watches a minimum of television, and has no interest in politics or community activities. Among the questionnaire sample 42 percent take part in women's groups of various kinds (the majority live in the country in Nagano prefecture), but apart from this activity, involvement with the outside world is not very great. Only 9 percent are still involved with activities related to their children's schools; 22 percent take part in some kind of cultural activity; 11 percent engage in traditional arts; 5 percent do volunteer activities; 7 percent participate in citizens' groups and 1 percent in political activities; and 12 percent have religious activities outside the home. Similar findings to these came from a nationwide opinion poll conducted by the prime minister's office (*Nihon keizai shinbun* 1986). The majority of women apparently lead lives fully occupied with family duties and jobs or, for a minority, with hobbies. It is only those very energetic or "lucky" few who are not constrained by the needs of their husbands or elders, or the demands of their employment, who take part in regular activities outside the home. Even then, most of this activity aims at self-improvement or "cultivation," and very little involves society at large. Writing circles, for example, are very popular (Tsurumi 1970, 276), and the phrase "finding oneself" is currently in vogue among women (Iwao 1991, 9). For those with the time, building an independent and fulfilling life is an attractive option, more attractive it seems than pulling together for Japanese women and their various urgent social problems.

Trouble at Kōnenki: *Signs of Indolence or Exhaustion?*

The question remains as to whether "indolent" housewives experience more symptoms at menopause than do "busy" women with jobs. The mean number of symptoms that all women reported in the two weeks before answering the questionnaire was 3.72. Employed women experienced a mean of 3.74 symptoms and housewives a mean of 3.63—significantly fewer than other women. However, housewives, perhaps because of their "free" time, visited the doctor more often during the previous year (a mean of 4.45 times as opposed to 3.98 for working women). There was no significant difference in the number of days women spent sick in bed per year but, no doubt because they had visited the doctor, housewives imbibed significantly more prescribed medication. Most women, working or otherwise, judged their state of health to be fair or good.

We compared the responses of women living in an urban middle-class environment who characterize themselves as housewives with those of women, rural or urban, who have jobs, in connection with twenty-six items taken from the symptom list. In terms of classical Western menopausal symptomatology affecting the vasomotor system, housewives reported significantly fewer symptoms than did other women (Table 8), although the numbers are not large for either group.

Turning to the usual symptoms of *kōnenki*, we find small but interesting differences between the two groups. It will be recalled that the symptoms most frequently associated by Japanese women with *kōnenki* are shoulder stiffness, headache, and lumbago. Working women reported all three of these symptoms more frequently than did housewives. Working women also reported a little more insomnia, more irritability, heavy head, numbness, chilliness, dizziness, and aches and pains in the joints than did housewives (Table 9). There are no significant differences in reporting of other symptoms, which in any case have low overall frequencies, with the notable exceptions of the more psychological and cognitive symptoms— loss of memory, difficulty in concentrating, loss of judgment, depression, and exhaustion, all of which housewives reported slightly more than did other women. The most marked differences are with feelings of depression, difficulty in concentrating, and exhaustion; however, the absolute numbers involved are low and it would be unwise to attribute much weight to these findings. The most striking evidence is that more than 85 percent of women gave a negative response when asked about most symptoms, the only exceptions being shoulder stiffness and headache and, to a much lesser extent, lumbago.

Table 8. Reports of Vasomotor Symptoms in Previous Two Weeks,
by Occupational Status

Symptoms	Housewives[a] %	Employed Women, Rural and Urban[b] %
Hot flash*	3.3	10.4
Night sweat**	2.7	3.8
Sudden perspiration***	2.4	4.9

* $p = 0.01$; $x^2 = 5.68$
** $p = 0.00$; $x^2 = 6.89$
*** $p = 0.02$; $x^2 = 1.48$
[a]$N = 123$, or 9.3 percent of sample
[b]$N = 1,193$, or 90.7 percent of sample

Table 9. Symptoms of *Kōnenki* in Previous Two Weeks,
by Occupational Status

Symptoms	Housewives[a] %	Employed Women, Rural and Urban[b] %
Shoulder stiffness	45.5	53.5
Headache	26.0	32.2
Lumbago	18.7	23.1
Insomnia	6.5	11.9
Irritability	7.3	12.2
Heavy head	4.1	8.2
Numbness	8.1	10.1
Chilliness	13.0	16.3
Dizziness	5.7	7.4
Aches and pains in the joints	8.9	11.3
Loss of memory	11.4	9.5
Difficulty in concentrating	12.2	5.9
Loss of judgment	5.7	3.2
Depression	13.0	7.1
Exhaustion	10.6	3.6

[a] $N = 123$, or 9.3 percent of sample
[b] $N = 1,193$, or 90.7 percent of sample

In summary, although symptom reporting is generally low, employed women report more symptoms than do housewives. Housewives, on the other hand, are perhaps more sensitive to perceived cognitive and related emotional changes, but the numbers involved are too low to make any definitive assertions.

The ubiquitous belief in Japan that leisured housewives allow themselves to be excessively distressed at menopause appears to have no foundation in reality. We can take this analysis a little further. Women who live on farms in Nagano prefecture report more headaches and also feelings of a heavy head, and a little more dizziness, numbness, feelings of chilliness, and lumbago, than do other women. Blue-collar workers, in contrast, most of them employed in factories, report more shoulder stiffness, ringing in the ears, and irritability than do other women. These differences may well result from their respective occupations and quite possibly occur equally frequently among women of all ages (and probably men too) in similar working conditions. However, because the women in the present sample are aged forty-five to fifty-five, they tend to associate their distress with kōnenki.

One further difference must be mentioned, namely that 13 percent of the farming women in Nagano reported hot flashes, more than either housewives or blue-collar workers. The women in Nagano all live within an easy car's drive of a busy country hospital that has an exceedingly active public health outreach program of many years' standing. The majority of the Nagano sample had been to meetings about kōnenki given by public health nurses, who conscientiously described what symptoms the women might expect based on the latest "scientific facts" that they in turn had learned from literature heavily influenced by information current in North America. Nagano women were, therefore, much more alert to the possibility of hot flashes than were any other women in the sample, and it appears from the survey results that the public health nurses may have had some influence on the reporting of symptoms (which nevertheless remain significantly lower than in North America).

Divisive Ideology

Not surprisingly, no simple relation between physical symptoms and lifestyle or occupation can be established. Nevertheless, the argument that associates a presumed leisured life with menopausal problems is firmly rooted in the minds of many Japanese. At every single talk that I gave on this subject in Japan, people were genuinely surprised that housewives do not report more symptoms than do other women. As a symbol, the selfish middle-aged middle-class housewife has a useful function in contemporary Japan: an anomaly, with no assigned social role except that of a consumer, to some observers she signals the way into a bleak future where the family no longer provides the glue to hold Japanese society together. She is useful in the service of a powerful conservative rhetoric that links nostalgia for the past with an insistent criticism of present trends. Clearly, the selfish housewife bears little relation to most women; the rhetoric is laughable, but the ubiquity of the fiction tends to overlay the voices of working women, whether they be unemployed but nursing their in-laws, or fully employed outside the house, as they strive to deal with the reality of the complex, unstable world in which they find themselves.

Tradition and modernity, rural and urban life form stereotyped oppositions, as do full-time care of a household (which may well include hard labor) and employment outside the home. So too do "outside" women—foreigners—and "good" Japanese women. The proverbial housewife who lives surrounded by the luxuries of urban life is perhaps secretly envied but simultaneously despised. Meantime the realities of the burden that the aging society places on all women, together with continuing discrimination in the work force and often in the home as well, remain largely unquestioned.

7 Odd Women Out

The river's breadth
is narrowed by abundant
water hyacinths
too late for flowering but
green and profoundly quiet.
(Takaori Taeko)

When women are encouraged to talk about their lives—their families, reproductive cycles, health, and illnesses—they produce narratives that are reconstructions, pastiches created out of memories: happy, nostalgic, and bitter; mixtures of fact and fantasy woven together over the years into a personal life history. They create and re-create, evaluate and judge these narratives against the incessant hum of ideological discourse about what a woman's life "should" be like, in other words, in light of what is considered normal midlife for a Japanese. At the same time, however, their narratives are quite simply stories about everyday life with an appeal that transcends culture. Hayden White suggests that narrative, being a universal human tool with which we try to express our experience of the world, provides a metacode through which we can enter vicariously into the lives of other people (1981, 2).

With this suggestion in mind we turn to narrative once again, this time to listen to those Japanese women who are considered not quite "normal." As we have seen, the social construction of gender in Japan has, particularly over the past one hundred years, emphasized a rather marked role separation between men and women: women are biologically suited for life "inside" while men are consumed by the world "outside." We might be tempted to think that this division of roles rather closely resembles a similar ideology that has been and probably remains dominant in Europe and North America. There is little doubt that in both cases this particular gender construction accompanied the rise of the middle class and as such did not reach its full flowering in Japan until after the Second World War. But there are, nevertheless, subtle but very significant differences.

Japan has been characterized time and again as a vertical society, one in which the most important relationships are those between parents and children. Continuity of the household takes precedence over individual householders, and children (particularly eldest sons) are raised not to be independent but to subordinate their own aspirations to those of the family. This ideology originally associated largely with samurai and wealthy merchant households has, from the end of the last century and most particularly since the Second World War, become widely diffused throughout Japanese society. Many anthropological studies of Japan have shown how not only family enterprises but the worlds of business, industry, entertainment, and professional sport draw on family-type models that encourage loyalty to the group by incorporating newcomers into fictive kin or quasi-parent-child relationships. The emperor no longer officially heads the family of Japan, but fictive families that require unquestioning loyalty remain very much in evidence and exert exacting demands on their members, for whom they offer in return care and appreciation (Fruin 1983; Marsh and Mannari 1976; Nakane 1970; Rohlen 1974; Whiting 1977). The extended family, the *ie*, rich in nostalgic feelings of warmth and care and in links with the ancestors and continuity through time, that gives priority to vertical bonding but also reveres cooperative and harmonious relationships of all kinds, serves as one of the abiding metaphors in Japan for appropriate human relationships. As Plath pointed out many years ago, "in Japan the family of God is the family" (1964, 300).

For more than a century now the Japanese woman's usual path to maturity has been through complete dedication to the family into which she is married, and her most important demonstration of dedication has been devotion to the nurturance and disciplinary training of the children she produces. This ideology of *boseishugi* (the doctrine of motherhood) has proved to be remarkably resilient in spite of massive social changes and constant exposure to other possibilities for constructing gender from the outside world. For example, every single one of the 105 women who were interviewed unreservedly supported the concept of a "motherly instinct" (*bosei honno*), which, they say, inevitably involves the natural ability and predisposition of women to nurture others.

By middle age, although many women continue to nurture their sons (often to the chagrin of daughters-in-law), their attentions encompass the entire three-generation family; in theory grandchildren and elders alike receive their devoted care, an attitude that drew explicit legitimacy until recently from Confucian doctrine. As Lebra puts it, Japanese women "never graduate from the maternal role" (1984, 259).

The assumption in Japan that all women will marry, have children, and devote their lives to the care of the family is so deeply internalized that the few women who do not fit into this mold attract attention. Among those women who responded to the questionnaire, 88 percent are married and have given birth to and raised children. Regardless of what type of household they live in and whether employed or not, these women have fulfilled the most basic requirement of Japanese womanhood. But what of those women who are single, divorced, or widowed at a young age, and those who have not borne children? In the present sample 3 percent have never been married, 2 percent are divorced, fewer than 1 percent separated, and 4 percent are widowed. Perhaps *kōnenki* presents particular problems for these women since, because it inevitably signals the end of fertility, it may heighten any ambivalences about not having led, voluntarily or otherwise, the kind of life expected of a Japanese female.

The Price of Being a Tomboy

Harumichi-*san*, at forty-five, has lived all her life with her parents in the same small house where she was born. She is the third of seven children, three boys and four girls in all among whom she is the only one who is not married. Her father is now eighty-four and her mother seventy-six, and to date they remain healthy and mostly take care of themselves. The house they live in together with Harumichi-*san* is a traditional Kyoto town house, closed off to the outside world, with small, rather dark tatami-matted rooms, two of which open up onto a carefully tended Japanese-style garden tucked away in the rear of the household. Harumichi-*san* works for a printing company in Kyoto and has the air of someone who, although not in the least pushy, is firm and decided in her opinions. She suggested that we meet during her lunch hour one day and have a meal together. During the interview, she volunteered much more information about politics and international affairs than any of the other women I talked with.

"It's hard being a single woman in Japan. People don't think of us as real adults at all [*ichi nin mae no ningen dewa nai*]. My parents tried very hard to get me married. I had a lot of *omiai* [meetings to arrange a marriage], but either my parents decided the man's family wasn't suitable, or sometimes I didn't like the man. But usually they turned us down. My father said it was because I was too much of a tomboy."

"Can you tell me a little bit about your early life?"

"I was born before the war started and was five or six when it ended with Japan losing everything. I remember going into the bomb shelters— being awakened in the middle of the night to go into the shelters—those are my earliest memories. When I started school the windows were still all broken and we were covered in lice and doused with DDT. We kids didn't have any shoes, although some of us had *geta* [traditional thonged footwear]. Our hands were all cracked and chapped with malnutrition and we had sores all over. One time my lymph glands were all infected and I remember that I couldn't even stand up for a while, and I sort of crawled to school. Once in a while we had special lunches provided by the American army—dried milk, pineapple, peanuts, tomato juice.

"Everyone was poor. It was tough, but there was a good relationship between people. If our next-door neighbors didn't have enough, we helped them out. We visited my father's family in the country sometimes, and they would give us rice; we had to hide it in our underwear to sneak it home because rice was strictly rationed. Once the police stopped us and took away all the sweet potatoes we were carrying."

"What work did your father do?"

"His job was sewing, putting linings in Japanese-style clothing and so on. He was the second son in his family and so after finishing elementary school he was sent off at age eleven to be an apprentice in Osaka. He did various jobs and then finally came to Kyoto in his twenties to work at sewing. I used to think he was very stubborn. He hit me quite a bit. I don't think my mother was very happy. She was the sort that if he said 'Jump,' she jumped. I think in her heart she often had different feelings and opinions than he did, but she never went against my father. I was fairly rebellious, but I learned how to be gentle from my mother; she always had a sense of how women should be, still does, I suppose. I didn't fit the design very well, but she kept trying to cram me back in!"

"How was school?"

"I enjoyed it. I started just after the war and the teachers were afire with the idea of a new Japan that emphasized horizontal rather than vertical relationships. My parents didn't think girls' education was very important. They just assumed we'd all get married. My family wasn't wealthy so I could only go to a public high school, which was quite cheap. In the class of fifty there were only seventeen or eighteen girls. I really wanted to go on to college, but I didn't dare to even ask my parents because they couldn't have afforded it, and in any case they would never have understood why I wanted to go. My brothers went to college, of course."

"You described yourself as a tomboy—why do you say that?"

"I think maybe it was because I'm left-handed and was made to write with my right hand. Today I hold pens and chopsticks in my right hand, but I do everything else with my left hand. I always had a hard time writing, but I was good at sports—dodgeball and softball. My left hand helped, it was the only time I wasn't scolded for being left-handed. So I played with the boys a lot, and we all went on to junior high and high school together. Also I was big for my age.

"I started working in a stockbrokers' firm right after high school. There were many days when I didn't get home until midnight, we were so busy. We were supposed to start at 9:00 A.M. each day, but they made the women come in early to clean the desks and make the tea. I worked there for about six years. They started to make it uncomfortable for me after that, saying it was time I got married. Since there was absolutely no possibility of advancement because I was a woman, I decided to leave. Now I do typing on a Japanese typewriter,[1] which is a very specialized job. I get tired, of course; I have shoulder stiffness as well, and my eyes get tired. But I've been doing *tai chi* [a Chinese martial art] for about ten years, so I don't get as stiff as some of the other workers. There are only ten of us, and we're all friends, but the company doesn't pay very much so it's tough."

"Are you classified as a part-time worker?"

"No, I'm full-time, so I get insurance and a pension and so on."

"How would you compare your life with your friends who are married?"

"They often say they envy me because I am not tied down with children and a husband. They moan because they say they can't use their own abilities. But it's not really true that you can do anything you want just because you are single. For instance, I earn about a third as much as a man of my age. The men doing the same work as I do make much more than me. So, of course, I can't buy a house or an apartment. A woman has to be about one and one-half times as capable as a man to get half the recognition he gets."

"How does it feel to be working alongside a man who is getting so much more money than you?"

"Well, I sometimes think, You're getting paid so much more than me, why don't you work harder? I make the tea for everyone, but I don't think this is right. Most women say, 'It's not too much to do, we shouldn't make a fuss over this,' but I think if we're going to get anything changed in Japan, women have to stop thinking it's natural to serve men all the time. I think for Japanese women—and men too—the *ko* [individual] of *kosei* [individuality] is still quite weak. Although democracy came in after the war, Japanese people are still not very conscious of what this means to them as individuals—not as much as Americans or Europeans. When Mac-Arthur said the Japanese mentality was that of a twelve-year-old, I don't think he was talking about IQ, but about people's attitudes toward society and democracy and so on. Most women in Japan still just think about their own little world, about what's best for their family, their precious children, and grandchildren. But I think we have to start thinking about all the families everywhere in the world and about world peace. They say we're *blessed* with material things these days, but I sometimes wonder if that's really true."

"How does your life compare with your mother's? She must have had a hard time without many material things."

"I guess my life is better than my mother's. I certainly haven't gone through as many troubles as she did, so in a sense I'm very fortunate. I have time to do calligraphy and rock climbing and I do *tai chi* three nights a week. I help run the house, of course. My mother and I do that together. Neither of my parents is senile or disabled so things are fine right now. My elder brother and his wife live nearby, and they will help out when the time comes, but I'll have to give up a lot because everyone assumes I should take care of our parents."

"Doesn't the eldest son's wife usually do that?"

"Not if there's an unmarried woman around! My parents don't want to move to my brother's house anyway. Everyone assumes it's my job to take care of them. But sometimes I wonder what will happen to me. All I can do is to try to stay healthy."

"Will you have to leave your job?"

"I expect so, once my parents get too old to cope by themselves."

"How will you manage financially?"

"My parents have some savings and so do I, and I hope my older brother will help out. Of course, I'm supposed to inherit the family house if I take care of my parents . . . but we'll see! It may not work out that way in the end if my brother's wife gets her way!"

"How about *kōnenki*?"

"I'm getting more short-tempered than I used to be. When I saw a doctor a few months ago, he said it was because of my age. It's true that my menstrual cycle is getting irregular, and I seem to have less energy at weekends too, but I don't think that's *kōnenki*, it's simply getting older, which is natural."

Harumichi-*san*'s narrative shows vividly how she has been severely constrained by the expectations of her close relatives and by the conditions under which most women work.[2] Without the benefits of the promotions and salary that most men and their wives assume to be their right after the husband has worked for some time with a company, Harumichi-*san* remains on the margins of the Japanese economic success story. It is striking that even among those who must be economically independent, immersion in and obligations to the family continue to dominate the lives of women such as Harumichi-*san*, and should her parents become infirm, her life-style will grow even more precarious. So far anxiety about her future does not extend to her body. Harumichi-*san* believes that she can "avoid" *kōnenki* altogether, in that she does not anticipate any difficulties; yet, as a single woman, she is concerned about the implications of aging, possible ill health in old age, and the source of care for her when she needs it. Although Harumichi-*san* did not mention this, she may also be concerned about who will care for her after death. People who leave no descendants are liable to neglect in the afterlife because appropriate memorial services may not be held in their memory.

Living for One's Work

Teraoka-*san* is a fifty-three-year-old nursing professor at a major medical institution in Tokyo. She was born in the countryside of Chiba prefecture and grew up with her parents and two sisters, both of whom are now full-time housewives. We sat in a classroom where she had just finished teaching a group of about fifty nurses. Teraoka-*san*, dressed in well tailored but simple clothes, is slightly overweight, outgoing, and businesslike. I had given some lectures at the hospital where she teaches, and we had already met several times at small social gatherings related to the lecture series.

"It was very tough during the war. We didn't have much at all, although we grew a lot of our own food because we were in the country. I was a problem child at school; I was always being scolded, and one teacher I had was very strict and hit me all the time with a wooden board. I always liked reading and talking and being the star in the class, and this didn't make me popular at all. I often stayed up reading after everyone else had gone to bed. We had lots of books at home, some very old ones of my father's. When I finished all our books I started borrowing from the neighbors.

"My father was really interested in our education, I think he thought that education is important even for women, but maybe that was because he didn't have any boys. Because I was the tomboy he made me into his son. My mother was very strict about *shitsuke* and she often scolded me for my bad table manners and for not holding the chopsticks properly or licking them, and so on. She was gentle on the outside, but really strong on the inside—I'm not as strong as she is, I let my feelings show on my face."

"Did you always plan to go on to college after school?"

"Yes, my father wanted me to be a lawyer, but I didn't like that idea. During the time I was in middle school my grandmother came to live with us and she had a stroke while she was with us. I helped to look after her, and I decided then that I'd like to be a nurse.

"I lived in a dormitory while I went to a nursing school in Meguro [Tokyo]. Everyone had to live in the dormitory. I didn't study very much, and I didn't get very good grades, but I certainly had a lot of fun. After graduation I came straight to this hospital and I've been here for thirty-two years now. I suppose I'll stay until I'm sixty-five. I'm supervisor of the postgraduate training program for the in-patient division, I've been doing this job for fifteen years; it's an important job, and I really like it. I have three assistants and we take in 280 nurses each year. We create lots of special programs for them, and also do all the evaluation, but it's not a basic nursing school—these are professional nurses who want more training, so mostly we teach things to do with clinical work."

"Did you have to choose between keeping your job and getting married?"

"When I first started working I didn't think I would work all my life. I thought I'd go home after two or three years; but when the time was up, I didn't want to go home, so I just stayed in Tokyo. I guess my parents worried about me but they never came right out and said anything. My elder sister's husband was adopted into our family and they live with my parents, so that took some of the pressure off me and my younger sister."

"Did your parents encourage you to do any *omiai*?"

"No, they didn't seem to take much care of me about that kind of thing at all. I suppose they'd decided I was a lost cause. Anyway, I liked my work and I never ran into a person I couldn't live without. I had some interesting boyfriends, and when the work got tough I used to dream of quitting and getting married, but when it came right down to it, I never could imagine giving up the job."

"But would you have had to choose between the two?"

"No, not necessarily, you didn't absolutely have to quit if you married. But at that time there were no married women working in the hospital at all, so it seemed as if you had to make a choice. Another problem probably would've been the long commute from the husband's parents' home where I suppose I'd have been living."

"What do you think about younger nurses having both a career and a marriage?"

"I think it's really important to work after receiving so much education, and I encourage young women to do both. Japanese women must take work seriously. This hospital has mostly younger nurses, and a few of them are married and some have children, but not many. I think it's because we're in the middle of the city. In rural areas almost all the nurses are married. They live in extended families, and so the grandmothers can take care of the children, but city nurses in nuclear families can't do that."

"What do you think about nuclear families?"

"I don't like the idea, but I suppose they'll keep on increasing. I grew up with my grandmother and I think the extended way is best. You often see newspaper surveys these days that say people think three-generation families are good, but I don't know if many people are actually trying to live this way. I think they just think that's the right thing to say in questionnaires."

"So, one of the advantages of an extended family is that older women can look after their grandchildren while their daughters-in-law go out to work?"

"Yes, that's right. I don't like the idea of putting a baby into day care. If the mother is in a nuclear family then she should be able to stay home for at least two years with a newborn baby."

"What about the father staying home?"

"If the wife is going to work, the couple have to agree about it beforehand and decide to share the housework. But I'm not in favor of the woman trying to emphasize her equality and stand up for her rights at all costs. I think as a woman she should always respect her husband, and the care of children is her job ... Of course, I've never actually had the experience, so I can't really say what it should be like. I also think it's good for women to take care of old people in the family; I think it's best for sick people if they can be taken care of by their families rather than by outsiders. It ought to be possible for a daughter-in-law to stop work for a while when her mother-in-law becomes ill and then to go back to work again later without any penalty."

"Do you have any regrets looking back on your life?"

"I'm satisfied with my life as it is now. Of course I don't have a home, I just live in the hospital dormitory and it's not particularly pleasant, but it's convenient, especially because I often work late, and since I don't have a particular boyfriend, there's no need for me to have a place of my own."

"Do you have to work on weekends?"

"I'm usually off on Saturdays and Sundays, but I'm often asked to give lectures at other hospitals and so it really works out at about two weekends off a month. I go all around the country on my job, and I've been to the U.S. twice, and to Southeast Asia for conferences."

"So your work gives your life meaning [ikigai]?"

"Yes, I'd say that doing my work in the best way I can, and having that help others, is what makes my life worthwhile."

"Do you have any other interests aside from work?"

Teraoka-san gave a suggestive chuckle and replied: "I go to social dance lessons; it's good exercise, and I meet people from many walks of life."

"So you're in good health?"

"Oh yes, no problems at all."

"Did you have any difficulties with kōnenki?"

"No, none whatsoever. I didn't really notice anything at all. My periods just stopped one day. My eyesight has changed, that's all."

"What will you do when you retire?"

"Well, maybe I'll go back to Chiba and live close to my sisters. Perhaps I can help nurse my parents if that's necessary. I have a lot of good friends in Tokyo, but I can't lean on them when I get really old, so I suppose it would be best to be close to my sisters."

Although she leads a full life as an independent woman, Teraoka-san remains attached to the idea that the obligations to care for others, integral to married life in Japan, should take precedence over the working lives of women, but not of men. Apparently, she expects women to throw their energies wholeheartedly into a profession and, at the same time, protect their husbands from all unwanted disturbance, while shouldering complete responsibility for care of children, husband, and the elderly.

Fighting for One's Rights

Nakaba-san is a fifty-year-old teacher at a woman's college. I met her in the spacious but rather crowded office that she occupies on the seventh floor of a modern building perched on a small hill with a panoramic view of Tokyo. Nakaba-san is small and slight, full of energy, and very easy to talk to. She was born in Shizuoka prefecture, but when she was very young she and her elder sister lived in Tokyo with their father and a maid. Her mother was hospitalized with tuberculosis and died three years later without ever leaving the hospital, when Nakaba-san was six years old.

"My earliest memory is of my grandmother and grandfather coming from Shizuoka to take me away from my father to go and live with them. My older sister had gone back to Shizuoka earlier. I don't remember any fun in that household with my grandparents. It was gloomy and full of adults and we children had a very quiet life. My father came and joined us there eventually."

"It must have been very hard when your mother died."

"Actually, I don't remember being too sad about it, because I was used to living without her."

"Did the family intend from the beginning that you should have some advanced education?"

"Oh no! The idea was that after high school I would work for a while before marriage. I hadn't planned to go into teaching, I just thought I'd be an office worker. But the husband of my *koto* teacher, who was a lawyer, strongly advised me to get qualified for a real career. In those days teaching and nursing were about the only possibilities open to women, and I won a small scholarship to go to college."

"Did you originally plan to combine a career and marriage then?"

"I didn't exactly choose not to marry; in fact, I was on the point of getting married several times, but always in the end I couldn't take the final step. I didn't like the idea of being pushed into the 'woman's role' and in those days there were very few marriages indeed where husband and wife both worked seriously. Looking back, although it's been hard at times, I don't think I made any wrong choices. My life right now is ter-rific—not just satisfactory. I enjoy living alone, and I have many good friends. Of course work is hard at times, but that's a challenge, and I'm pretty confident about it. I feel I have a really good sense of what's realistic as far as work is concerned.

"I've already made at least two different plans for what I want to do after I retire—I'll probably live with one or two of my friends, and I want to write fiction. Japanese live to a great old age these days, and I'm begin-ning to see how nice it will be to be older, not like being a young woman and always having to keep a low profile [*o-jigi bakkari shite*]."

"And so far you have no health problems?"

"No, I'm very healthy. I don't think I've experienced any *kōnenki shō-gai*, although there was one thing that might have been that—just three times I've had the feeling that all the energy was draining out of my body. Aside from that there had been nothing at all, no headaches, or shoulder stiffness, or suddenly feeling hot: I'm grateful to my body. I haven't no-ticed anything psychological either, like getting angry easily, although I do have my ups and downs as far as work is concerned, but that's nothing new."

"What do you think will happen to the students you're teaching: will they manage a marriage and a career successfully?"

"I think society is making a U-turn; young women today seem to think more the way we used to when I was a child. Most of them don't want to be serious about work at all. They are looking for a husband and an easy time. Japanese women still have to change their way of looking at life [*jinseikan*], I think. When I was in the United States, I discovered that Japan hadn't really learned anything from the West, except about tech-nology. People aren't forced to decide for themselves how they want to live their lives; you can get along quite comfortably by adjusting yourself to others all the time. No one has to fight for things. But people need to think more about how they *should* live, rather than just doing what is expected of them, and I think perhaps a longer life expectancy will force them to do this. In the old days women could expect to live out their lives fully occupied with the family, but now they'll have to start thinking actively about what to do with their old age."

By Japanese standards Nakaba-*san* has been free to create her own life, and she has made the most of this opportunity. Like many others among her thoughtful peers, she believes that political activity is crucial in bringing about change, but she states that if middle-aged women do not reverse gender discrimination, then those who are following in their footsteps are exceedingly unlikely to have either the willpower or the interest to take it on. She and many of her peers fear that excessive opulence and endless consumerism have stifled any potential political activism on the part of youthful Japanese.

Gion Geisha

Kayoko-*san* was born in Gion, one of Kyoto's traditional entertainment districts. Her mother was a geisha who gave birth to seven children and cared for them all during their early years while continuing to work. At age sixteen Kayoko-*san* was apprenticed into the geisha house run by her aunt where she still works. I sat with her in one of the small, second-floor tatami-matted rooms of this establishment, shaded from the outside world by bamboo blinds around which the faintest of breezes occasionally crept to relieve the oppressive summer heat. It was the second time we had met. On the first occasion I had been taken by a Japanese novelist to the house where Kayoko works for an evening meal and entertainment, singing and dancing, by seven geisha of mixed ages from nineteen to seventy-five. Someone asked me that evening what I was doing Japan, and once I had explained about the research, all the assembled company—including the one male—volunteered information about *kōnenki* and then in return asked me to talk about menopause. The explanation I gave was punctuated with cries of incredulity. Five of the women initially agreed that evening to talk to me privately on a later occasion, but only three of them, including Kayoko, made the time to meet me. When we met for the second time she was dressed in an informal kimono, wearing very little makeup and with her hair tied back quite severely. Her appearance and demeanor were quite different from the previous occasion when she had been formally dressed, but even then she used relatively little makeup and had few ornaments in her hair, as befits a middle-aged woman. Kayoko bears herself with a calm dignity tinged with a somewhat wistful air. Even at the geisha party she had rarely become very animated, in contrast to most of her colleagues.

"I went to a regular elementary school in Gion where most of the pupils were children of geisha. I started dancing lessons from the age of six. And then in the fifth grade, I went to a special school for two years where we did ordinary lessons upstairs, but downstairs we started to practice the tea ceremony, flower arranging, playing the samisen, and dancing. After that I began training [keiko] full-time to become a geisha, but the war interrupted things. I never did 'come out' formally after finishing my training as a maiko [apprentice geisha]—for one thing we weren't supposed to dress up at all during the war. The geisha house was closed for a while, and we were sent out to help the war effort. All of us, including the owner of our house, were put to work in a company five minutes away where we were sewing uniforms and so on."

"Did you have enough food during the war?"

"We had lots of kimonos and so we could trade them for rice from the country, but the food was poor and we didn't really have enough. I remember feeling hungry. But still, we were better off than many other people."

"Did your sisters become geisha as well?"

"They all started out in training, but the eldest and the youngest ended up getting married. My other sisters are still here in Gion, but in different houses."

"You have a special 'sisterly' relationship with one of the older geisha in your house don't you? Can you rely on her just as you would on your own sisters?"

"When you 'come out' as a geisha an 'older sister' is given to you who 'leads' you for the rest of your life. There's an exchange of sake cups at the ceremony, and you pledge to be sisters. After that you're bound together forever. This relationship is very important, but I could never depend on her to help with personal problems very much. When I was sick she introduced me to a good doctor, but she had to take care of her own life, so she was always too busy to act like a substitute mother or a real sister. But you always have to be on your guard not to 'dirty your sister's face' [neesan no kao ni doro o nuru]: not to do anything that would reflect badly on her."

"If you have a special patron can you depend on him?"

"Sometimes you can, but often you can't. It depends on the man. And anyway, many geisha don't have a patron."

"Do you have any regrets about the life you've led? It sounds really tough to me and perhaps a little lonely."

"It's a hard life, but not like it used to be. Nowadays we can travel and most of us have been to Hawaii or Southeast Asia. When I was younger I wanted to get married and get out of it. But . . . ,"Kayoko hesitated and looked pensive. "Things didn't work out . . . I had an unhappy affair. After that I resigned myself, and I've felt fairly satisfied since then."

"Would you do it all over again if you had the chance?"

Kayoko hesitated for some time and then finally blurted out, "Married people often get divorced these days. I can support myself and that's just as well, it's good to be able to support oneself. Ordinary housewives may be fortunate in some ways, but unhappy in others—it all depends on how you look at it."

"Do you have any children?"

"Yes, I have a daughter. She's thirty-three now."

"So you were very young when she was born."

"Yes."

"Did she become a geisha?"

"No. I had her start dancing when she was six, but she made it clear from about age eight onward that she didn't want to 'come out,' and I realized deep down that I felt the same way as she did. She was determined to stay in school, and I thought that was a good idea too, and that she should eventually get married. So I have a grandchild now, and they all live in Tokyo."

"Do you see them often?"

"No." Once again, Kayoko looked somewhat pensive. "Just once or twice a year, when I go to Tokyo."

"How's your health?"

"I was always sick from childhood on. I had a lot of colds and stomach troubles. At nineteen I was so ill they thought I wouldn't live, and in my thirties I had tuberculosis and I was in hospital for about a year. Then two years ago in October I had an operation for breast cancer, but I'm fine again now. I always seem to get completely better after each big illness. That's just as well, because it's very bad to be sick. In this profession, your body is your capital [*karada ga shihon*]. I use massage a lot to help keep fit, and I take herbal medicine too, but only when I'm ill, not on a regular basis as a kind of preventive medicine the way some people do."

"Do you still have to go to the hospital for tests and so on after your operation?"

"Yes, twice a month. But I didn't have any pain after the surgery. Everything has been smooth since then, and I feel fine."

"How about *kōnenki*: did you have any problems with that?"

"I stopped menstruating when I was about fifty. It just disappeared naturally. Everyone says you have physical problems, but I didn't have anything like that. I'd heard you suddenly feel hot and you get headaches and irritable but none of that happened to me. I'd remembered when I was a child that one of the older geisha went to hospital because she had such a bad time with *kōnenki*, and so I was worried. But when it happened I was just relieved that my periods had stopped."

"Do you worry about getting older?"

"Not really, if you have the right attitude there is nothing to worry about."

"So a few wrinkles don't matter?"

"No, of course not. Beauty depends on the way one lives one's life. The accumulation of fifty years of living is not something that's created overnight, and the result is obvious. If a person has a mature *kokoro* [heart, spiritual center], this shows in her face; a middle-aged woman can have beautiful features, the product of experience, whereas young people have beauty that's simply *pitchi pitchi* [bright and lively]."

"How would you say your life has been compared to your mother's?"

"My mother had seven children so her life was tough. I only had to raise one child. The training is still severe, but in her day it was even more so. She was as strong as a man [*otoko masari*], and strict too. Even my brothers didn't dare talk back to her. Because I don't have a patron, I'm free to do as I like more or less, but her patron was really demanding."

"Are there some advantages to having a patron?"

"Oh yes! You can consult him if he's a good man, especially about financial matters. But that depends a lot on your luck, and meeting the right kind of person. For me it's been better just to have regular customers and not to have one special patron. If I were younger ... "

Kayoko-*san* looked down thoughtfully at her glass of iced tea at this point. She was hesitant about going on but eventually said:

"But I'm weak, and I had that operation two years ago; I think it's better not to have a man."

"Have you never had a regular patron?"

"Oh yes, I did. But after I was sick, I felt that [*are*] was a bother [an indirect reference to sex]. Anyway, there were many reasons ... "Once again she was hesitant. "But we split up. That was before my last operation. I'm sure he wouldn't want me now anyway. Health really is the biggest thing."

"How do you feel about the new equal employment law?"

"Maybe it's time for men and women to have the same rights, but I still think men are above women. It really doesn't work to make the sexes the same . . . Maybe I'm old-fashioned! But . . . "

"So is there a basic difference in ability?"

"I think so. People ask if I want to be a man or a woman next time round, and I say: 'A woman.' If I were a man, I'd have to work in a company, and feed my wife and children and probably my parents too. I prefer being able to lean on a man. Men are superior because they go out to work, I am quite comfortable to put men above me. It's not that women are inferior exactly, but most women couldn't stand life in a company the way men do."

Kayoko-*san* professes not to be worried about the future, largely because she owns her own small house, has a reasonable amount of savings put away, and states that she can continue to work in Gion until she is well into her sixties. Nevertheless, I sensed that she was worried about her health, although neither *kōnenki* nor, surprisingly, aging holds great significance for her. On the contrary, I suspect that Kayoko is in some ways glad to be getting older; the demands on her time will become fewer and fewer, and she is reaching a stage where she can assert a little independent control over her life for the first time.

Although I cannot be sure, I am inclined to interpret Kayoko's somewhat ambiguous statements about housewives as indicating that perhaps she does, after all, have regrets about her life, although in reality she had little possibility of doing anything else. She is not animated when talking about either her daughter or her grandchild. I suspect that either Kayoko is envious of her daughter's life and so chooses not to see her often, or alternatively that her daughter is uncomfortable about Kayoko's occupation and does not ask her to visit very often. She apparently had no help from her daughter when she was in hospital with breast cancer.

I walked away down the quiet noontime street after my conversation with Kayoko feeling both sad and angry. Behind the closed exteriors of those exquisitely beautiful houses live many other women like her, their bodies designed to please, their minds drilled to be closed and conservative, their behavior submissive. Today a labor union tends to their health needs, and there is a certain amount of financial security in old age for those who have been attached to a prosperous geisha house. But, according to a woman with whom I talked who runs a traditional Kyoto-style restaurant in Gion, the "sisterly" world of the geisha house is a myth; it is in reality, she asserted, a claustrophobic, competitive, and bitchy world that superficial elegance and grace seal off from the uninitiated. This woman would

Pontochō geisha off to the public bath.

not recommend the life to anyone because, discipline and subservience aside, it is, she insisted, a miserable and lonely existence.

Surviving on Harlequin Romances

Ishibashi-*san* was born in Tokyo and, after graduating from high school, went on to university where she specialized in English literature. I had been introduced to her by a common friend who, when told that I wished to talk to someone who was divorced, immediately suggested Ishibashi-*san* as a "typical" example. Despite the fact that she had never met me before, Ishibashi-*san* appeared at ease and willing to talk about her life.

"I didn't work after college graduation, which was a mistake. Instead I got married to a friend I'd met in school, but it only lasted about four years, and we separated when I was twenty-five. I divorced him when I was twenty-nine or thirty and I've been living alone ever since."

"Do you have any children?"

"No, no children."

"How do you support yourself?"

"I started working when my husband and I separated. It only took me about a month to find work in the editorial department of a woman's magazine. But I quit that later and now I'm doing translation at home."

"Why did you quit?"

"Mostly because it was really busy at the magazine, and there were no restrictions on working hours. We started at noon but we often worked until midnight or even later. It was grueling, although occasionally we went home about six o'clock. There were about half men and half women working in the company but only one or maybe two of the women were married. It would have been impossible to have an ordinary family life and do that job. I liked the work though."

"Did you get the same pay as the men?"

"Yes. That was twenty years ago and there was usually a *big* difference in pay between men and women, but teaching and editorial work have always been exceptions. Even so, you were expected to put the same long hours in as men do, with no excuses. I didn't feel there was any discrimination, and the atmosphere was good, but I just didn't want to work all my life away.

"Now I'm translating books at home. Only harlequin romances—nothing difficult. They're interesting though, because you can tell a lot about society and its attitudes from them. When I started, just after harlequin romances first came to Japan, the stories were all Cinderella-like romances. Nowadays the heroines are wondering whether to marry or to have a career instead. So I think even these potboilers reflect the times."

"You're working independently, so what happens about insurance and pensions and so on?"

"Well, of course I can use the national health insurance system, but I won't get any pension, and if I have a serious accident or something I don't get any benefits. If I thought about it seriously I'd be worried, but you know, things are changing pretty quickly in Japan right now, and I'm sure I can find another job even if I lose this one. This is the kind of work you can do even when you're old." Ishibashi-*san* paused and laughed. "I suppose I'll die before I retire. But you're right, it's a precarious position with no guarantees about the future. I have to try and save, but that's not really possible, there's nothing much to spare."

"Were people around you upset when you divorced?"

"Yes. It was a big thing for my family and friends. In Japan twenty years ago a divorced woman wasn't considered normal. Some employers refused to hire divorced women. I probably couldn't have got a regular office job then even if I'd wanted one. It's different today, there're quite a lot of young people who get divorced soon after they marry now, and also older women too who wait until their children leave home before walking out."

"Do you think Japanese women are becoming more independent these days?"

"I suppose women will eventually change in the future, but most are still just interested in their own lives; once they retire into the home, they never seem to want to 'have their eyes opened to society.' I'm forty-eight, but I think women who're in their thirties now were young when feminism came to Japan, and they're pretty active, but it's changed again since then. As families grew smaller and smaller, mothers became overprotective, and because there's so much money about these days, the girls they raise just like to stay at home and play around after they get married. Maybe there's a reaction going on against the previous generation, but the twenty-year-olds are just ojōsama [young ladies]. All they want is to marry well-off men and visit Europe."

"How would you compare nuclear and extended families?"

"Japan used to have mostly extended families, but now in the cities houses are so small that families can't live with the grandparents even if they want to. So that means that people who're my age—all the full-time housewives, that is—have got to start thinking about what they're going to do with themselves. Their children are leaving home, even the eldest sons these days, and life expectancy is over eighty years, so middle-aged women have nothing to do with half their married life. That's going to be the big question now ... But I'm not suggesting that extended families are the best!"

"How would you compare the lives of these women to your mother's generation?"

"Well, women have become much freer and broader minded in that they've been exposed to many things through television and so on. My mother was part of a large family, they had servants living in the house who helped with the business, and my mother had to take care of everything; she was like the manager of a company. It was a really big job she had, and I think in a way she had a good deal of power. In a sense women have actually become weaker—they're spoiled these days."

"But they had to suppress their feelings in those days didn't they?"
"Yes, that's right. And after the war those limits were mostly removed,
so women are stronger in that sense. I mean . . . They're stronger about
themselves, about going after their own interests, but they don't think
about responsibilities much these days."
"Are you satisfied with your life?"
"Yes, I am. I don't worry too much about the future. My finances are
in reasonably good order. I own a small apartment and live there by myself
so I can do anything I want to. I really like it, and anyway it's so small
there'd be no room for anyone else to share it with me. I really wouldn't
want to live with anyone else now."
"What about your health?"
"I've never had any serious illnesses and I always feel fine."
"What about *kōnenki*?"
"I think anyone, man or woman, starts to wear down about fifty, like
an old car. You lose your adaptability to heat and cold, for instance. I think
kōnenki is just a natural wearing out. I haven't had any symptoms at all
so far, but I suppose some people get them. I hear, for example, that people
get emotionally unstable, easily angry and upset, and also sort of tired
[*karada ga darui*]. But I'm not expecting my life to change in any way
when I stop menstruating . . . I'll still have relationships with male
friends."
I must have raised an eyebrow at this remark, because Ishibashi-*san*
looked at me and said firmly, "You know, middle-aged single women in
Japan can find male friends, it really is all right to be older here—not like
America."
"Is it harder for divorced women with children than someone like you
without any?"
"Yes, I think they have a very difficult time. Usually they try to get
by without asking for alimony, and in any case if they go to court they
usually lose. A lot of women have to end up working in *mizu shōbai* [the
entertainment world]. If you don't have any kind of training that's about
all you can turn to, it's the easiest way to earn money. And once you get
started you get used to having that kind of money I suppose, it must seem
stupid to go and get a clerical job where you have to make cups of tea for
the men, have no security and low wages, after that kind of life."
Even in the narrative of a woman such as Ishibashi-*san*, who must make
her own way in the world, are clear traces of ambivalence about the freedom of young women. She believes that the twenty-year-olds of today
have no interest in furthering the general cause of emancipation of Japa-

nese women. Perhaps a good dose of hardship is indeed necessary to make one into a "real" adult, ready to take on responsibility.

Just the Two of Us

Tagaya-*san* and I talked one evening in the little Japanese-style guest room in her rather small apartment in the suburbs of Tokyo. We had been introduced by a friend and had met once or twice. Tagaya-*san* is a vivacious, very talkative, rather dramatic woman, expensively dressed in slightly offbeat clothes. She served us both green tea and Japanese cakes, inquired, for the third time, as to the kinds of things I was interested in, and then settled down to tell me everything she could think of that was relevant. The conversation, which lasted three and a half hours, actually took the form of a monologue, because I had considerable trouble inserting any questions into the exchange at all.

"I'm forty-six years old and living with my husband who is forty-eight. We don't have any children. I wasn't able to have any; when I was younger, I was checked out by a doctor who showed me an X ray of my ovaries, which were all disintegrated. He said it may have been because I had a very high fever with appendicitis when I was nineteen; he suggested we start to think about adopting a child. My husband and I both like children, but his mother, who'd had seven of her own and many hardships raising them, said, 'Your hardship is *not* having children, and you must live with that. If you adopt a child it won't really be your own, and there's no guarantee you'll be happy.' So she was definitely opposed to adoption. Well, I thought, my husband's brothers and sisters, and my three sisters all have children, so it isn't as if there aren't any children in my life; and my husband felt the same way, so we decided not to adopt. In Japan people often say, 'You must be lonely without children,' but since we never had any, we don't feel that. It's always been just the two of us. Maybe I'll feel sad when I get older, but I don't feel that way right now, we're surrounded by our nephews and nieces.

"I don't really have what I'd call a job, but I've been doing flower arrangement for about thirty years. I'm learning tea ceremony too, and oil painting—they're related to flower arrangement; it's all training for the eye. Anyway, sometimes I'm asked to make flower displays for weddings or banquets and I teach flower arranging at home one day a week. I can't really call it work, but it's fun."

"What does your husband do?"

"He's a salaryman. He works near here, in Yokohama for a telephone company. My father was a salaryman too. He was still away at war when I started first grade; in fact, before I started school I never knew him, and

I remember crying the first time he hugged me after coming home. He used to take us to the public bath after he came back, I suppose he thought that 'skinship' was the best way to get close to us—but I used to cry all the time. I was the one that took the longest to get used to him. But he was gentle, he never hit any of us. It was always my mother who was scolding. All the way through junior high school I remember her yelling at me—I suppose I wasn't very obedient. But since I've been married I really think my mother's way of raising children was good. She was a full-time housewife and healthy, and in those days mothers used to do everything for their children—not like today when young mothers make their daughters help with the dishes and so on—so we never had to work around the house. After dinner she used to teach us simple handicrafts like embroidery; she always used to say, 'Women are supposed to work in the evenings.' I think she's admirable, she still works hard and they don't have much money, but she never complains.

"In junior high I started to read a lot, the teacher invited me to join the literature club and I wrote *haiku* and *tanka* and one of my poems was chosen to be in a textbook. Since I was usually a problem student, I don't think the teachers were too happy about having to give me recognition in front of the whole school. I didn't pay attention in class, but I still got good grades because I was always reading.

"I'm different from my siblings. My older sister always says, 'I don't understand you.' She's forty-nine and thinks just the way the ordinary Japanese housewife is supposed to think. She has a daily routine, like all the other housewives in Japan—she gets up at the same time every day, bright and early, and cleans the house, and does the laundry . . . Me, if I wake up and it's raining, I just stay in bed reading until noon.

"Also, I often go to museums and art galleries and spend more money on entertainment than the ordinary housewife does. I've spent my whole life being like a student. If I go out I know I'll find something to interest me, and I don't mind staying up late either. If I'm doing something interesting I might stay up until 5 or 6 A.M. I've always done that. I suppose when I start losing my energy I'll realize finally I'm getting older but . . . so far . . .

"Because I never worked very hard at school I knew that my parents wouldn't agree to my going on to college, so I went right out to work, at the company where my husband works, after graduating from high school. That's where we met. But my mother made me take kimono-sewing lessons to turn me into a good bride; I had to do it every night, and I hated it, although now I like kimonos very much, and I almost always wear one when I go out somewhere special. I'm rather short, and I think I look better in a kimono than in Western clothes.

"My husband and I were introduced by friends at work. The company used to have lots of trips, hikes and so on for the employees and I met him on one of those. We got married very quickly, within a year after we met. I was anxious to get away from home, where I was always being scolded for coming home late at night or being told to learn various things to make me into a proper young lady. I'd already had several *omiai* but most of the introductions were for oldest sons, or the only sons of widowed mothers, and I knew I could never deal with those kinds of men and their families, so after the first meeting I turned all the others down without actually meeting them. Still, I was only twenty-two when I got married. We started out in a tiny apartment, one room really, for about two years. Then we had the next seven years in a two-room apartment. I kept on working because my husband's salary wasn't very good. I was a telephone operator, for about eleven years altogether, and finally we bought our own apartment.

"After I quit work, for about three months I did nothing but read all day long—it was wonderful."

"Did you feel guilty about that?"

"No, not at all, I'd been working hard for eleven years after all. I'd been going to the doctor about my infertility for some time by then. Each time I heard that a friend was pregnant I always started to cry. All the clothes I made I designed with the idea I could wear them after I became pregnant—but I never needed them. Until I was about thirty-three I kept wishing for a child, that dominated my whole life. I spent a lot of time crying. I took herbal medicine and I went to Shinto shrines to pray, and I bought special talismans; I had hormone shots, I went to hot springs, I went from one hospital to another, but none of the doctors bothered to examine me properly until finally, one day, the gynecologist took me aside and explained to me very logically that my ovaries just weren't functioning, and then I slowly began to accept it. Still, until I was about thirty-six or so, if my period was late, I'd think, maybe I'm pregnant this time."

"Did it affect your relationship with your husband?"

"No, not at all. He was really understanding. Of course, while I was going to the doctors they'd tell me, 'The next few days are your chance to get pregnant,' and they'd recommend we have sex. So my husband would try to come home early from work without going out drinking with his friends. We followed all the advice the doctors gave us, but we never really talked about it—I would just pass on in a matter-of-fact way what the doctors had said, and he'd say 'OK,' and do what they said. I think he really wanted a child too, but we never really sat down and discussed it right out.

"Finally my husband said when we moved here that we should resign ourselves to not having children, that we should accept the situation. He said I was to stop seeing the doctors. I was feeling apologetic to him for being infertile, and my mother, whenever she met my husband or his mother would apologize too. But finally we all gave up.

"When I met my husband I thought that his way of thinking was very grown up, I liked that, but now I think that he's just like the average man, he thinks like a salaryman, in a Japanese conservative way . . . It's pretty boring really. A couple of years ago he told me formally, on New Year's Day that he might have to quit his job. He gets a good salary, but his company doesn't want to keep everyone on to retirement like they used to. They want bright young men who are up in the latest technology. So far nothing has happened, and my husband hasn't said anything more, but I feel sorry for him. He'd like to work faithfully to retirement and get an award like his father did. He's a *shōwa hitoketa* and he was one of the people who after the war was willing to clear away the rubble, plant the crops again, build new houses, and help with the economic recovery. Why should those hard-working people not be valued anymore? Anyway, I intend to go on respecting him. But it makes me lose faith in my country if we start to ignore people as they get older."

"What about your parents-in-law? Do they live with your husband's eldest brother?"

"They did, but they are both dead now. The saddest time in my life was when *obāsan* died. She was sick with liver trouble for a while and in hospital. I took care of her the whole time and stayed there in the hospital with her. My sister-in-law works and anyway, she didn't like *obāsan*, so she asked me to take care of her. That was fine with me, although I was upset with my sister-in-law at first. Two years after the first illness, *obāsan* developed terrible sciatica and had to go into hospital again. When I went to take care of her that second time, I tried to tell her she'd get well, but they gave her very strong pain medicine—it made her feel bad, and her memory started to get very poor. She grew senile quite quickly. She just gave up wanting to live and died at sixty-four. She was in hospital for about a year, and her husband and I took care of her. It was awful to watch her fading away.

"Actually we fell out with my husband's elder brother and his wife because they were so awful about the old folks. We don't associate with them anymore. When my husband's father grew senile too, I was the one who took care of him, he came and lived with us, but I started to get ill myself, and so we had to put him into a hospital in the end. I was always short of sleep because he'd wake up at all hours and call for me. I was the only one he wanted, he wouldn't let me out of his sight. I couldn't even go to the toilet comfortably because he would start calling for me. I couldn't talk about it to my husband's relatives, but I talked to my flower arrangement teacher and she was really sorry for me, she actually cried in sympathy. She said I shouldn't feel bad about having him put in a hospital, and my husband agreed without too much pressure. *Ojīsan* died soon after that and I felt awful. None of his family cared, they thought he was costing too much money in the hospital, but they felt guilty about me taking care of him too, and they were cold to us. So it was a great relief to them when he died. My parents are still fine, but I'm ready to take care of them when it's time. Since I have no children, that is the least I can do."

"Who will look after you when you're old?"

"I worry about that quite a bit. I'm perfectly healthy so far, I've not even reached *kōnenki* and I have no signs of aging at all. I'll have to look after my husband of course, but then I don't know what will happen to me after that. At the moment we're financially comfortable and so I suppose I can go into a home or a hospital, although I don't like the idea at all. But if he's made to retire early . . . "Tagaya-*san* finally stopped the flow of her conversation and sat looking rather distracted. But she quickly covered up the awkward moment and, after filling the teacups yet again, launched into another stream of consciousness about her students, and the attitudes of young people today.

The importance of flower arranging must not be underestimated in Tagaya-*san*'s narrative. The practice of this discipline, and the presence of her teacher in her life, probably contributed greatly to Tagaya-*san*'s ability to overcome her feelings of failure at not producing a child (for her husband's sake even more than for herself). Tagaya-*san*'s insistence that she has been able to live like a student all her life, her flaunting of lazy mornings in bed, indicate to me that in some ways she feels she has never been required to grow up by Japanese standards. Her almost zealous contribution to looking after her in-laws, and her desire to help her own parents in the future, is perhaps in part a wish to "make things up" to her family, and indirectly to society, in an appropriately womanly way.

Tagaya-*san* is exactly the kind of woman people assume will have trouble at *kōnenki*, leisured and apparently "self-indulgent" (if one ignores long stretches of her life devoted to care of elderly relatives); nevertheless she reports no symptoms of any kind.

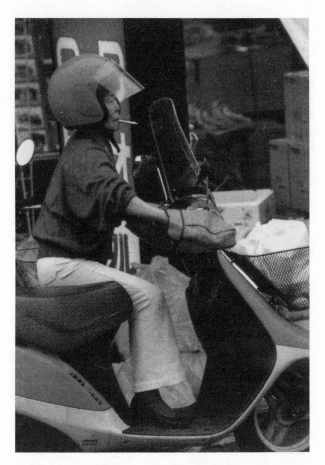

Kimono and "three paces behind" their husbands are long gone for most women.

Picking up the Pieces

Yoshioka-*san* lives in a third-floor condominium apartment outside Kobe. She is a warm, unpretentious, soft-spoken woman of fifty-four. The room in which we talked was filled with furniture and a display cabinet stuffed with dolls that Yoshioka-*san* had made; the glass doors of the room were standing open to reveal a veranda lined with beautifully tended potted plants. When asked about her daily life Yoshioka-*san* responded:

"I get up at 5:30 every day because my younger daughter has a long way to go to work. I make breakfast and help make her lunch—she's an adult of course, and I suppose I'm a little overprotective in this way. Then I do the laundry and the cleaning. After that I go and practice my hobby, which is archery. I usually do it at least three days a week, and this year is my twelfth year. The longer I do archery the more I like it—it's a serious *michi* [a disciplinary path] and has great depth.

"On the way back from practice I do my shopping, and by then it's almost time to fix dinner. That's about it. I read a lot in the evenings. Recently I've been reading about the Hanya Shingyō [one of the sutras].

"You know, I've been thinking since my husband died that women who work can find a lot of consolation [*sukuwareru*] in their work when they face some big trouble like mine. My husband didn't like the idea of a two-job family—he was old-fashioned, born in the Taishō era, and he was the type that wanted his wife to stay at home and make it easy for him to carry on and do his work. I suppose he wanted a feeling of ease in the home—when he got home in winter, he wanted the house to be warm, the bath ready, and dinner on the table. So that's the way my life has been. While he was alive my work was taking care of him, and that kept me on my toes. Since he died, I don't know what I should be doing—I seem to have lost my purpose in life. For a while I thought I was finished. Now I don't feel that way anymore, but I'm still not right because I keep asking myself what life is all about."

"When did your husband die?"

"On 11 June [seven months prior to the interview]. He was fifty-nine. It was a stroke. The stress of overwork from being a city salaryman got to him. I think he was having a tough time at work. During the May before he died he'd had almost no time off—Sundays he went to play golf, but that was really work too because they were just finishing off their business on the golf course. He was late getting home *every* night—often after 11:00 P.M., because he had to entertain company guests endlessly. He didn't have any time to himself at all. I used to stay up and wait for him night after night, although he said I should go ahead and get to bed if I wanted to, but I felt that I wanted at least to have a cup of hot tea ready for him."

"Were your daughters very upset when their father died?"

"My husband was in the hospital for a month and I stayed with him there every day, getting home about 10:00 P.M. at night. My older daughter, she's twenty-seven, was teaching piano to children at the time, but she decided to give it up and help me look after her father. My younger daughter who works in a library is twenty-five. I think they felt rather sad because they weren't married and hadn't given him some grandchildren before he died—they wept a lot, more than me, and they both said they'd not been dutiful children. I think their father's death has made them start to think about someone other than themselves for the first time, and maybe now they will get married; they've been too occupied with their own interests to even think about marriage so far . . . "Yoshioka-*san* turned her head away and paused. "I can't talk to them at all about marriage or anything else much anymore . . .

"People of my age are living in a sort of gap between the very old ideas of the Meiji era and the new democracy that came in after the war . . . We don't seem to have much independence or really to be able to think for ourselves . . . Even now I feel I never think for myself. It's as though I don't really *have* a self.

"I was working in a bank before I got married, and when I met my husband I was actually earning more than he did, but he just assumed that I would quit. Anyway it was company policy in those days that married women had to quit. If I were doing it today, I think I would keep right on working, even after I had children. I like work better than cooking and cleaning."

Yoshioka-*san* jumped up suddenly and pulled out a large album of family photographs. "Here, let me show you my husband's picture . . . he liked sports very much. See how kind his eyes are? He was never rough or demanding . . ." Tears started to flow, and then she resumed, "I have friends at archery and they helped me a lot. I stopped going to archery for a while because I felt so empty, but they came round and gently insisted that I start going again. I'm very grateful to them."

"Your husband was the eldest son, is that right?"

"Yes, when we first got married we were living with my husband's mother and also *her* mother-in-law, and I had a child right away. I had to nurse both of the old people, but fortunately neither of them had long illnesses. I seem to be surrounded by death, I had to go to Kyushu for a while to help with my eighty-five-year-old father who died last month. As a matter of fact they told me last March that he was dying, and I rushed back to my family home, but then my husband went into hospital so of course I came right back here. Then eventually I went to Kyushu again.

"My husband's job was changed in January of last year. If he'd kept his old job he would have lived longer I'm sure, but he was too dedicated, and he worked himself to death for the company."

"Was he transferred before?"

"Oh yes, many times. Kyushu, Tokyo, Hokkaido. But I always went with him and so we never bought a house so that we could be ready to move at any time."

"How about your health?"

"After the birth of my second child I was really sick. Something was wrong with my liver and I got weaker and weaker. I was in and out of hospital. My mother came to help us, and in the end my elder daughter went to live with her until she was five years old. We were separated for about three years, and looking back on it, I think it was a mistake. I should never have let her go to her grandmother no matter how hard it might have been. The two girls never really got on well after that, something went wrong psychologically between them, even though everything was always calm on the surface."

"Do you feel a bit guilty about your daughter?"

"Yes, I do. It's really important that a woman stay well so she can raise her family properly—she's like the sun for her family. After my husband died everything went wrong for a while. In the mornings I was dizzy and couldn't get up, I couldn't even walk properly along the streets. When I went to the hospital they said I had problems with my autonomic nervous system. Nothing showed up on the tests they did, but I still felt terribly tired and dizzy. The doctor decided to give me tranquilizers.

"Perhaps you already know this, but it's quite a burden dealing with a funeral in Japan. About five hundred people came and gave us money [the usual custom] and, of course, I had to keep track of it all and pay them all back. Half of them just write their names on the envelope and leave you to find out their addresses somehow. They're not relatives, of course, business people mostly, so I'd no idea who most of them were. After all that I just collapsed completely. But now I'm much better. I threw out the medicine and told myself I had to pull myself together. Every one of those symptoms I circled on your questionnaire are gone now [when she had filled out the questionnaire, just four months after the death of her husband, Yoshioka-*san* reported that she had experienced fourteen different symptoms in the previous two weeks, more than any of the other respondents]. For a while I kept thinking I should have loved him more, or made him retire, or looked after what he ate better, but lately I've been able to tell myself there's no use going over and over something that's finished."

"Are you financially secure?"

"I'm not sure. When one's husband dies everything is cut in half; I'll only get half of what he paid into the system. When a household head dies there's a terrible economic burden as well as an emotional loss. In a way it's worse than when a wife dies."

"Will you have to try to take on some more work?"

"I've been looking at the advertisements in the paper, but it seems that the only kind of work for women of fifty-five is cleaning or dishwashing and so on. Obviously someone has to do these jobs, but it really isn't what I want to do . . . I don't have any skills or qualifications, so I can't do translation work or typewriting, and anyway, I'm sure they'd only take younger people. What I'd really like to do is painting and glazing of chinaware. The factory that I worked in for a little while right after the war made chinaware, and I remember how I liked working with the clay. If there was somewhere here in Kobe I'd go and do that right away, even if they didn't pay me for two or three years while I learned how to do it properly. But I can't move to any other city because my daughters' lives are here. Maybe I should just try and get a part-time job in a coffee shop. Women are usually made to retire at fifty anyway, so there really isn't much hope of a decent job, but I certainly don't feel as though I'm old already. I'll be fifty-five on my next birthday, and that's not really old at all."

"No, it isn't, is it? What about *kōnenki*? Did you have any problems with that?"

"I'm still menstruating. I'd never really thought about *kōnenki* until the doctor said that my recent symptoms were probably half due to my husband's death, and partly due to *kōnenki*. I always had irregular menstruation. My periods didn't start until I was nineteen—that was because of the war I think. I had to work in a factory from the time I was fifteen, it was part of the mobilization of schoolchildren. My body wasn't ready for that kind of hard work. We didn't have anything much to eat, and I was as thin as a rail. We went to school during the day, and then we had to work at night making weapons, and I think that's why my periods didn't start—my body just didn't develop. The teacher used to ask all of us who hadn't started menstruating to put up our hands, and they gave out hormone pills to us at lunchtime. I've always been irregular and I'm sure it all goes back to the war. Maybe that's why I'm still menstruating now, but I'm sure it will stop soon."

"So you don't have any symptoms you associate with *kōnenki*?"

"No, none at all."

These narratives, in common with those recounted earlier, reveal the extent to which women in middle age consider their present situation to be something that, on the whole, they should feel satisfied about. When asked to reflect on the lives of their mothers, virtually all think of backbreaking hardship and associate their own childhood during and immediately after the war with poverty and shortage of food. Despite the fact that many people live in very cramped quarters, and that economic insecurity hovers nearby, particularly for those women who are single, divorced, or widowed, and who do not have a professional occupation, they gratefully accept the comparative opulence of today. Nevertheless, as is clear from Yoshioka-*san's* narrative, there is a heavy economic price to pay if a woman is widowed or divorced, and, like most women of her age, is left feeling bereft not only because she is alone but also because she has no experience or skills to use as she tries to procure a job—and because in any case she is labeled as too old to be of any use to society. The irony is, of course, that the chief reason Yoshioka-*san* has no skills is because her husband and his employers insisted that she stay at home to look after him. Then, having worked her husband to death (literally perhaps) the employers cut Yoshioka-*san's* benefits in half. What is remarkable is that, despite her devastating losses, Yoshioka-*san* like so many of her contemporaries, in public at least, shows few traces of rage or frustration. She has concentrated instead on pulling herself together and taking up her station in society.

I have dwelt at length on the cultural construction of gender, in particular the ideology of service to the family that is expected of women, and the way in which demographic changes have extended their duties until the approach of their own death. This is the politically orchestrated discursive background against which individual women age and go though *kōnenki.* I want to turn now to Japanese ideas about the physical body and aging, and to the widely assumed relation between conscious control and physical processes. Here too preconceived notions about what is "normal" and "correct" are at work, but in this case the attitudes have ancient roots, are particularly opaque, and hence do not cause contentious debate in the public arena as does, with increasing frequency, the question of nursing the elderly.

8 Controlled Selves and Tempered Bodies

In the darkened fields
the very faintly burning
lights of the houses—
ah, they are more frail even
than the glowing of fireflies
    (Nakagawa Mikiko)

Maturation within the social order takes priority in Japan over aging and biological change, and individuals experience and record their movement through the life cycle largely by the way their human relationships shift through time. Ideally, women's lives become meaningful through what is accomplished for others rather than for themselves (Plath 1980, 139), especially if they live at the hub of extended families. Because in theory the interests of individuals are in tune with the social order, individuals do not experience an ideology of service for others as oppressive. On the contrary, socialization gradually transforms children into eminently social and moral beings, a positive process rather than a repression or displacement of biologically determined drives and impulses, as post-Enlightenment Western epistemology might label it. For Japanese youth, growing up is not a matter of learning how to maximize their own interests as they reluctantly conform to society's constraints whenever necessary. Nor is it a search for a "true," autonomous self but rather a lifelong process of maturation in which individuals come to understand themselves first and foremost as social beings, as products of units and forces larger than themselves and without which they could not exist.

Contrasting the Japanese to the American concept of self, Plath concludes that "the American archetype . . . seems more attuned to cultivating a self that knows it is unique in the cosmos, the Japanese archetype to a self that can feel human in the company of others" (1980, 218). He visualizes maturity in Japan as a "rhetoric of long engagements with intimates" (226). Ideally, therefore, the course of maturation disciplines the Japanese self to merge into the social order—at times to such an extent that an individual may conclude matter-of-factly, as did one or two of the women we talked to, "I have no self," implying that they had devoted their entire existence to the service of others.

Many Japanese women have reasonably contented lives, and an overwhelming 90 percent responded in the survey that they feel "happy" or "very happy" with their present life. But they also indicated when talking to us that a large number not only suffered but continue to lead an insecure and exploited existence. Why then did the majority report that they are happy? Part of the reason is etymological: the usual Japanese rendering of happiness, *shiawase*, also incorporates the meanings of good fortune and of being blessed. Several women, after recounting incredible hardship, ended with a rhetorical coda to the effect that other people had suffered more than they, and that hence they should be grateful for what they have. Clearly, compared to their mothers and to the relatively few truly poverty-stricken families who remain in Japan (and their younger wartime selves), most women today can fairly judge themselves to be fortunate. What is more, many of them pointed out that they were socialized to be frugal—to be satisfied with relatively little in the way of material goods; they are now unhappy that younger generations no longer display this virtue. Rather than envy those whose lives appear to be easier, therefore, the *shōwa hitoketa* internalized the injunction not to compare oneself to others (either above or below one's station) but instead to accept life as it comes, make the most of it, and feel grateful. It is not so surprising, then, that many women think of themselves as blessed and therefore respond that they are *shiawase*.

Nevertheless, a good number of the narratives expose the extent of what current Western standards would label the psychological if not physical abuse of women, and these experiences do not appear to be unusual if a recent survey in the *Asahi* newspaper is anything to go by, since 53 percent of women polled reported that present-day Japanese society treats women unfairly (*Asahi shinbun* 1991d).

In all of the 105 homes we visited the women volunteered, in full knowledge of what was expected of them, to spend two or more hours talking about their private lives to two foreigners (of approximately the same age as themselves) whom few had met before. It would not be surprising, therefore, if there was some "holding back" on their part even though they had volunteered for the task. Yet both Christina Honde and I perceived that many women seized on the opportunity to use the encounter therapeutically, recounting with little hesitation their histories of exploitation, pain, and personal suffering.[1] Some people were tearful—occasionally with thankfulness for blessings but more often with sadness.

One woman was frightened as she recounted some of her family troubles within earshot of her menfolk on the other side of the sliding screen doors. But remarkably few gave any signs of anger. For the most part those who recalled stories about the long years of nursing senile elders, of abuse or emotional neglect at the hands of their husbands and in-laws, of work day after day with aching and painful bodies, did so with remarkably little affect, as though it was a rather standard recital. Their lives had been on the whole, it seems, *atarimae* and *tōzen*—expected, normal, proper, natural.

Subservience is the lot of the majority of women around the world, but just how this comes about varies according to historical and cultural context. In Japan the constructs of the body, self, femaleness, aging, the passage of time, and social maturity fit into a particularly hegemonic situation, and within the system a woman's life unfolds in the "shadow" of men. This is the life-style that is natural (*tōzen*).

Although the experience of *kōnenki* and any associated distress is a personal event, it is nevertheless culturally marked as something more than simply biological change and is intimately related to the "correctness" or otherwise of the lives and social maturation of individual women. The widely held view of distress at *kōnenki* as signs and symptoms of indolence stems from a shared belief that personal conduct can directly affect the physical functioning of the body. This construct unites mind and flesh and, as so many people pointed out to us in one way or another, if a woman has the right attitude, if she exerts proper control over her mental state— *ki no michiyō*—then she can ride over any difficulties at this stage of life (see also Rosenberger 1987, 169). Conversely, with "too much" time on her hands, and no obvious demanding tasks in daily life, she will find it much harder to retain control over the body. Until recently, therefore, the "normal" middle-aged female body was not, so the rhetoric goes, in the least troubled by *kōnenki* because hard work and a firm grip on the inner self were unquestionably the accepted modes of life.

I want to turn now to two themes that I noted in earlier chapters and that appear repeatedly in fragmentary form in many of the narratives. One concerns attitudes toward time, especially in the individual life cycle and in aging, and the second, the conceptualizing, socializing, and disciplining of the human body, in particular the female body, to make it conform to Japanese society. This discussion points up the intimate relation between the meanings that women attribute to *kōnenki* in the narratives they create about this stage of the life cycle and the widely accepted ideology that the only suitable path to social maturity and satisfaction is through service to others.

The Burnish of Age

During the course of telling their stories the majority of women alluded to cultural activities that they invest with considerable importance: archery, flower arranging, calligraphy, tea ceremony, classical poetry, dance. This is as true for farming women[2] as it is for urban dwellers. The only exceptions are those people who work in factories and career women whose lives are completely given over to work and family obligations. The traditional arts, in contrast to the learning of a foreign language, musical appreciation, or quilting, are well-trodden "paths" (dō) to inner development and spiritual awareness. Closely tied to the philosophy of Zen, they have long been the means whereby people escape temporarily from the demands of social life but at the same time build their inner strength and discipline to the point where, ideally, they no longer need or desire worldly things. This process of self-cultivation is lifelong and based on an understanding of human perfectibility over time, a state that transcends the inevitable decline of the physical body.

From at least the days of Confucius this "heritage of possibilism" (Plath 1980, 5) has been dominant in East Asia, and its lasting influence in present-day Japan is evident. Movement through the life cycle, as we have seen, is a process of advancement in the social hierarchy, accompanied by personal maturation and increasing responsibility. A man would accomplish much of this task in the world outside the household of which he was a part, and a woman began it in her parents' home and then, for the rest of her life, continued it in the household of her husband's parents. Daily life was, in theory, duty filled, shaped by mutual obligations until finally, following Confucius, at age seventy, individuals could for the first time "follow their hearts' desire" without violating social expectations. Rohlen points out how in this eventual escape from the heavy demands of a Confucian-ordered world, old age transforms a life of self-discipline and personal cultivation into that of the "iconoclastic world of the laughing Zen priest" (Rohlen 1978, 139). The enlightened Zen master attains a freedom based on obliteration of self, of all physical needs and desire, and merges with the oneness of the universe. Buddhism, particularly in the form of Zen, has served in part throughout Japanese history as a bridge between the decidedly this-worldly demands of Confucianism and what is taken to be an inevitable yearning for escape and for a spirituality that transcends this world. Women could occasionally travel this spiritual path since they might in theory become nuns just as old men might become priests. Obviously neither peasants nor artisans usually enjoyed the luxury of traversing a spiritual path, nor in all likelihood did most aristocrats, but a theme of self-discipline culminating in eventual escape from the toil of this world pervades Japanese history.

It is against this philosophical backdrop that the aging of individuals takes place, as part of an ethos in which the elderly are at once respected and spoiled; where until recently, at sixty, one was expected to don a bright red kimono (a color often associated with children) for the celebration of *kanreki oiwai* (literally, a return through time), designed to remind participants about the ceaseless repetition of birth and death, and of the continued regeneration of the household and the great cycles of the cosmos. Traditionally a circle illustrates this cycle of regeneration, half of it being the human life cycle, and the other half the progression of the ancestors toward rebirth.

In Japan experience is valued as fundamental to the process of learning, and age denotes wisdom, authority, and a hard-won freedom to be flexible and creative. Numerous prominent figures today are decidedly elderly by Western standards—the recent reelection of the eighty-year-old mayor of Tokyo being one obvious example. And even in that most fickle of industries, the entertainment world, older women are often respected and admired, not only for their artistic skills but for their beauty, as Kayoko-*san* confirmed. The patina of age associated alike with treasured objects (which often figure in the traditional arts) and with older people has prestige in Japan (Ehrlich 1992).

When David Plath talked to mature Japanese about how they had changed with age, many spoke of *atsukamashisa*, best glossed as "boldness" or "nerve." Similarly, the people we talked to, when asked how they would characterize a middle-aged woman, often used the same word, implying that because age brings experience one can afford as one gets older to "let go" and be a little playful. A good number of women indicated that they were enjoying their newfound freedoms, the fruits of maturity—of "full flowering"—and several, including the teacher Nakaba-*san*, went on to state that they were actually looking forward to old age because they would no longer have to "keep a low profile" and display feminine reserve. Like many others, employed or not, Nakaba-*san* feels content in middle age because she believes that she has a good grasp of what her life is all about and some realistic expectations for what is possible in the future; she is in control of her life's trajectory as far as that is realistically possible. Provided that economic worries and the burden of looking after a demanding husband and nursing sick relatives do not overtake all chance for independence (which they often do, as we have seen), then a Japanese woman should be able to turn quite comfortably to the latter part of the life cycle, when she finally comes into her own. Aside from nursing responsibilities and possible economic hardship, the major shadow on the horizon is the question of her own health in old age and of who will take care of her for the last few years of her life in the demographically transformed, nuclearized society that has few public facilities for the burgeoning population of dependent elderly.

Contemporary Japan is indeed, as has so often been claimed, a land of paradox: a society in which technological mastery of the environment is unsurpassed, where the electronic age reigns supreme, and unabashed consumerism and materialism have usurped almost all desire for simplicity (once highly valued as a statement about the futility of worldly desire). In the midst of this massive transformation, people strive to keep harmonious social relations, particularly during shared endeavor or labor. But in this society, especially for mature people, there exists an inner, secret space more or less securely sealed off from the daily round. This introverted aspect of self strives to live in tune with the changing seasons, to accept the inevitability of the passing of time and the ephemeral nature of material things; in other words, to be at one with a greater order that eclipses and transcends the banal everyday world—a space of fantasy and reflection, of secrets and desire. Thus, by participating responsibly in society, individuals create and re-create the public self in daily life, both beyond and within the confines of the physical body, but paradoxically also travel a path to maturity that requires the eventual dissolution of this public self and its merger with a reality beyond this world.

This complex sense of self does not usually cause, as someone steeped in Western ontology might expect, excessive inner conflict or turmoil. On the contrary, the dedication to repetitive training and self-control necessary to follow a designated path of inner development also offers individuals in daily life a form of strength with which to adjust and bend to the demands of society. This process of embodiment is, of course, culturally constructed from birth onward, and a discussion of how it occurs is of direct relevance to what women have to say about kōnenki because they conceptualize self and body as one. Hence we may reasonably assume the existence of an intimate relation among emotional and physical states and actual behavior, a relation that is consciously mediated and interpreted by self.

Gentle Perseverance

A newborn baby in Japan is regarded as pure and inherently good, but these qualities must be nurtured and disciplined, a process of lifelong learning how to behave appropriately both socially and morally. The first few years are assumed to be crucial, and an ancient and much-quoted adage states that the "soul of the three-year-old must last for one hundred years," implying that early socialization is something that cannot be easily rectified if handled incorrectly. Japanese mothers are very reluctant to hand the early training of their children over to an outside caretaker, and their own mother is usually the only acceptable substitute for themselves (Hendry 1986), as many women intimated in their narratives. Several women pointed out, however, that there is only so much that one can do, indicating their belief in the contribution of genetics including physical (*taishitsu*) and psychological (*seishitsu*) predispositions to a child's makeup: "You can change them a bit, but I think basically it's a case of *mitsugo no tamashii* [the soul of the three-year-old]."

From a very early age children are encouraged to stick at things, to persevere (*gaman*), to be patient, and to be tolerant of others (Hendry 1986, 83). Early molding of behavior (*shitsuke*) shows relatively little gender discrimination and is designed to lead ultimately to the child's internalization of a basic moral style of high sensitivity to both the verbal and nonverbal cues of other people. Certain temperamental qualities are fostered in order to enhance moral development; particularly prized is to be *sunao*, which ranges from meek, submissive, compliant, passive, and honest, to guileless. Other behavior held in high regard is *yasashii* (gentle, kind), *omoiyari* (sympathetic, empathetic), *otonashii* (mild), *akarui* (bright, lively), *genki* (spirited, energetic), *oriko* (obedient, smart). These characteristics add up to a description of a "good" child (*ii ko*) (White and Levine 1986, 56), a term that repeatedly encourages and reinforces appropriate behavior. In demonstrating these qualities a child is said to be "humanlike" (*ningen rashii*) (Shigaki 1983, 15) and thus reveals the potential to function in morally correct ways in social environments. Both mother and child are monitored by what is known as *seken*, the surrounding world of neighbors, kindergarten teachers, and relatives, who are empowered to be a "watchful normative presence" (White and Levine 1986, 57) and who do not fail to speak up if they believe socialization is not proceeding well. As many researchers have pointed out, the goal of early socialization is to encourage not independence but rather a state in which dependence on and cooperation with primary groups becomes natural and inevitable (DeVos 1973, 47; Doi 1973). Although studies of contemporary socialization tend to emphasize the warmth and affiliation that most young children receive at home today, and in particular the very close relationship they have with their mother, the women in the present study did not always have such an easy time as children. Because of the war, many of them were sent away to stay with relatives; the fathers of a good number were killed in action, or else children did not see them for much of their early life; other women lost one or both parents to infectious disease. Moreover, families were large, most mothers did hard physical labor, and hence the intensive caretaking of children that has become standard practice in much of Japan today was not usual when the *shōwa hitoketa* were young. Nevertheless, a large number of women reported in detail how their mothers and grand-mothers had trained them conscientiously in *shitsuke*, to control both their emotional states and their bodies, think of others, and persevere.

Today preschool and kindergarten reinforce this type of training by incorporating them actively into *shūdan seikatsu* (group living). Training in preschool settings focuses on establishing a routine in the lives of chil-dren, on the foundations that good mothers put in place. Repeated practice of selected daily tasks gradually brings more and more of the day under what Rohlen describes as "intensively routinized order" (Rohlen 1989, 21). Students, even at this early stage, accept the task of inspecting and evaluating their own and other's performance, which includes academic and social skills as well as personal activities including hand washing, teeth cleaning, and even bowel movements (Lock 1980a, 73). Nursery school marks the beginning of peer pressure, with the result that control diffuses out and away from the teacher, so that any dissent will likely reach peers and not the adult source of the discipline. The creation of order and routine invariably goes on in a pleasant atmosphere and represents a happy time; however, even kindergarten involves intense official monitoring of behav-ior and concern with appropriate dress and school accessories such as bags and aprons so that they all meet a required standard appearance. For the *shōwa hitoketa* this type of training occurred in a less systematized way, and much of it was left up to grandmothers (backed up by the authority of the ever-present ancestors). From the vantage point of middle age, the majority of women we talked to expressed gratitude for the strict upbring-ing they had received and attributed to it their ability to ride over hardship of all kinds.

The process of becoming "more and more *psychologically* a part of society" continues long past childhood in Japan (Rohlen 1978, 131; original emphasis). Moeran describes, for example, how the "right" attitude is actively fostered during the course of a major sporting event in Japan, the annual high-school baseball tournament in which participants are called on to demonstrate "single-mindedness," "fortitude," "perseverance," and "sincerity" (Moeran 1984, 255–58). In adulthood comes formal indoctri-nation into a behavioral style deemed appropriate for the workplace. Company training programs are often demanding and may involve intensive weekends of physical discipline expressly designed to develop one's sense of self as a mature social being (Kondo 1990; Rohlen 1974). In an extended household, on marriage, women embark on a long training into the particular customs and habits of their new family. The importance of maintaining group harmony inevitably justifies such intense and demanding disciplinary training, and quite often individuals are expected to "hold back" their impulses and personal inclinations if the group, whether a family or a corporation or assembly line, is to function satisfactorily. Training of this kind emphasizes feelings of relatedness and perpetuates the belief that "what is real is to be found outside the individual, *between* himself and others rather than within" (Koschmann 1978, 19; original emphasis). The closest and most successful of relationships are thought to result in a feeling of "oneness" (*ittaikan*), a state that celebrates nonverbal communication and has archetypal expression between mother and child. But the creation of a social self does not simply involve looking steadfastly outward. Reinforcing it are the activities of the "inner" self and the body, both subject to disciplinary training and surveillance.

When women respond that *kōnenki* should be no problem provided that one approaches it with the "right attitude," they usually express this sentiment as *ki no michiyō*—the way in which one "holds" *ki*. *Ki* and another equally ubiquitous term, *kokoro*, recurred again and again throughout the interviews with middle-aged women, as indeed they would in almost any conversation conducted in Japanese that concerned human behavior. These words have a history of many hundreds of years' usage in both Chinese and Japanese and are key terms that establish an indivisibility between body states, human nature, and human behavior. Rohlen explicates them:

> An understanding of the "spiritual" view of adulthood requires that we develop a deep empathy for the implications about human perfectibility inherent in the usage that surrounds *ki* and *kokoro*. We must recognize at the outset that daily life is so saturated with their mention that both the unconscious minutiae and the deeply considered ambitions of life are anchored in these words, and their significance largely derives from this fact.
>
> (Rohlen 1978, 133)

Ki was conceptualized, more than a thousand years ago, as present in both the macrocosm of the universe and the microcosm of the human body. As such it is a fundamental postulate in East Asian medicine, a notion (somewhat akin to the classical Greek medical concept of *pneuma*) that signifies a continuous exchange and flow in space between the body and its environment.[3] One word in Japanese for the pores of the skin, *kikō*, literally means *ki* holes. A balanced and healthy body is well adjusted to its environment, a body with neither excess nor deficiency of *ki* and without blockages in the smooth flow of *ki* around it. Although younger Japanese have a scientific approach to the body, and older generations are also reasonably well informed, classical cosmology, in which balance and harmony are the key concepts, retains a strong hold on the imagination of most people. In daily parlance there is an easy shifting back and forth between older concepts associated with traditional medicine and philosophy and newer concepts, may of which were originally derived from Western sources and refined as Japanese terms over the past one hundred years. There are, in addition, modern Japanese medical concepts (of which *karōshi*, death from overwork, is one) that have no counterparts in international medical terminology.

Central to the process of maturation, therefore, is a gradual honing and refinement of internal emotional states, conceptualized as learning how to exert control over *ki*, which is believed (among other effects) to sustain and even enhance one's health. When asked to locate *ki* physically in space Japanese often find this a rather difficult task. Many people today are highly skeptical about its existence outside the body, and a good number go further and express doubts about its existence altogether. But these same people often modify their position somewhat by claiming that it is nevertheless a useful heuristic device to explain the relation of emotions to both behavior and the body. *Ki* is, of course, a concept that remains central to the martial arts, including *judō*, *aikidō*, and *bōjitsu*, and therefore many people are thoroughly exposed to it through training in one or more of these techniques. Following the philosophy that grounds both the martial arts and traditional medical beliefs, the majority of people associate changes in feelings of energy, mood, and activity with changes in *ki*.

As a linguistic term *ki* is ubiquitous and possesses an enormous breadth of meaning that evades translation. It can be glossed as spirit, mind, soul, heart, intention, bent, interest, mood, feeling, temper, disposition, nature, care, attention, air, atmosphere, flavor, odor, energy, and essence—among yet other meanings. But in its most common usages *ki* conveys a change of emotion or some aspect of human nature. Rohlen notes that *ki* expresses "impermanent conditions that collectively constitute an image of flux and often fragility," and he cautions:

Reference to a person's "inner world" [is] misleading since *ki* operates in a perceptual field (including memory) that surrounds the person. Just as breath enters and leaves the body, so *ki* orients to, and is affected by, what occurs in the world around the person. The *ki* of two people "meet," and knowing how another holds *ki* is to be sensitive to his or her feelings and intentions.

(Rohlen 1978, 134)

Moreover, the way in which one holds *ki* is essential in order to concentrate well, to be alert, and to fend off illness and distress. Several women cited the well-known expression that illness comes from *ki* (*yamai wa ki kara*) and then frequently went on to associate it with "lazy" and "spoiled" middle-class housewives.

The term *kokoro* also has a broad range of meanings, some of which overlap with *ki*: heart, mind, spirit, motive, vitality, feeling, sincerity, sympathy, attention, interest, care, will, intention, taste, mood. Unlike *ki*, *kokoro* is more clearly located within the body. Probably because the Chinese character with which it is written refers to the corporeal concept of "heart" in the traditional medical system, *kokoro* retains a physical quality (a different but related term is used for the anatomical heart).[4] Whereas *ki* needs controlling and mastery, *kokoro* should be cultivated and is susceptible to improvement throughout life—a tempering through judicious application of knowledge, experience, and willpower. Kondo describes how, during training sessions at an ethics center for company employees, a "polishing" of *kokoro* was the principal goal. Participants were submitted to numerous arduous endeavors including a 7.5-kilometer marathon, all with the purpose of heightening the "sincerity," "gentleness," and "receptiveness" of *kokoro*. Kondo points out:

> *Sunaona kokoro* directs the energies of *ki* and *kokoro* toward constructing selves in human relationships . . . *sunaona kokoro* is a heart accepting of things as they are, without resistance or questioning. It is a heart sensitive not to its own desires, but to the needs of others. This sensitivity should be willing and self-generated, for ideally the desires of the *kokoro* and those of society should run parallel.
>
> (Kondo 1990, 105)

Serious training of both *ki* and *kokoro* inevitably involves the exertion of mind over matter, and endurance of states of physical deprivation and pain are not unusual (intensive training in Zen usually involves loss of sleep, physical pain, and often fasting; in a different vein, a recent newspaper report stated that at least one professional baseball trainer is not satisfied that his men are exerting themselves sufficiently unless they vomit blood). The spirit and willpower associated with *ki* and *kokoro* produce, therefore, a disciplined, controlled, and occasionally broken body, one that may be bent to suit the needs of society.

Since traditional medical teachings consider states of mind and body to be inseparable, it is not surprising that the concept of isolated mental states and specific notions of mental health and illness are of relatively recent origin. The term *seishin jōtai* (mental state), created at the end of the last century, is frequently used these days to express emotional states, and over the past half-century a distinctly psychological vocabulary has become steadily more and more abundant. But even when people talk about "stress," "neurosis," and the like, they often include numerous links and references to *ki* states and to *kokoro* that show the continued pervasiveness of these older concepts.

Disciplining of *ki* and cultivation of *kokoro* begin in the formative years, integral to *shitsuke* and inseparable from the child's moral and social education. Training of the physical body stresses good deportment, so that whether seated or standing a child maintains relaxed but alert posture. Outward composure is also necessary; surrounding adults model this and other aspects of *shitsuke* and actively encourage these behaviors in children whenever they are in a receptive mood. From primary school onward teachers and mothers alike discipline children to be neat and orderly, to concentrate fully on whatever they are doing, and to start a lifelong monitoring of their own bodies, in terms of physical and emotional changes, largely through quiet introspection. Both verbally and in writing, teachers and parents register progress in these matters, which eventually becomes part of the record of the making of a "good" and correct child (Lock 1980a, 71). Thus, molding includes not only training in appropriate moral and social behavior but also discipline of the body, of its very muscles and sinews so that thoughts, feelings, and actions blend into one finely tuned, carefully orchestrated symphony. Obviously the attainment of this state is an ideal rarely achieved, but it is a fundamental goal and purpose throughout life.

Although for the first year or two a good part of the process of creating correct children is independent of gender distinctions, from the time when they start to acquire language young girls undergo socialization practices that are markedly different from those for their brothers. Qualities expected of adult women—including attention to decorum and body movements, specific language forms, and a concern for others, which were inevitably part of traditional childhood molding for girls—are necessary for girls even today. Learning to master *ki*, therefore, involves a discrimination of objectives: whereas formerly men learned the domination of others through exertion of superior control in the samurai code and the martial arts, for women the objective was exactly the opposite; they learned to suppress individual desires and needs for the maintenance of harmony with others—they were expected to master *ki* in order to subordinate themselves to those around them. When women now take up one of the accepted paths to personal development, such as the tea ceremony or calligraphy, in addition to training in self-discipline and perseverance they often hope to cultivate serenity. Many women may become critical of the way in which men exert their *ki* and believe that they themselves achieve a more subtle and deeper control both of self and others, by being pliant and flexible but at the same time firm in resolve.

When life is filled with cleaning floors, or pumping cream into cakes on a conveyor belt, or checking tiny electronic circuits hour after hour, as do many women in the present study, the idea of self-cultivation and introspection through rigorous practice of the tea ceremony or flower arrangement seems laughable. Clearly, as we have seen, there are major differences in the life-styles of women who participate actively in the labor force and those who are housewives. Income and housing reflect these differences. But although many working women criticize the emptiness of a housewife's life and describe it as narrow and boring (see also Kondo 1990, 283), and although a few poke fun at the idea of doing flower arranging and the like, nevertheless, a conception of how life should be prevails across a very wide spectrum of people—more than 90 percent of the population, according to the statistics. Even when they cannot possibly follow an accepted path to personal development, the majority of women apparently support the idea in spirit. A fisherman's wife who lives in a remote corner of the island of Shikoku and who does the accounts for the village cooperative that markets the day's catch comments:

"It's hard to find well brought up young women today who display *onna rashisa*. Women used to be raised to notice people's needs and feelings, they were *yasashii* [gentle, tender], and with a 'soft' physical appearance. This is the ideal for Japanese mothers: to be sensitive and gentle. It's important to have training in a traditional art—the tea ceremony, flower arrangement, and so on. All this helps to make a woman graceful, genteel, and ladylike. You don't see many young people like that these days, but I like the type."

"Is this sort of thing important even in a fishing village?"

"Yes."

"Why?"

"It's very appealing to me . . ." A long pause, some rumination, but no further comment.

"Should women suppress their feelings of anger or frustration in front of others?"

"I think so, but I don't do it too well myself. Women used to be better at that too."

A woman who works in a cake factory was emphatic, like the majority of her co-workers, that girls should be raised to speak and dress correctly, that they should be trained to be neat and tidy around the house, and above all to be thoughtful of other people. This woman had not been able to induce her daughter to do flower arranging but was happy that the girl had received training in *kendō* (a martial art) for a good number of years because, although this had not exactly helped her daughter develop gentleness, it had taught her a good deal of self-discipline and control.

In a similar vein a Nagano farmer said:

"I try to suppress my feelings like my mother, though I don't always succeed like she did. If I always blew up about things, that'd cause fights with my husband and be unpleasant for the children. But as long as I just keep quiet and endure, then it's easily forgotten. It doesn't make much difference no matter what I say, so in that case we might as well keep things pleasant."

"Do you think it's a woman's responsibility to keep repressing her feelings, then?"

"Yes. It's no use getting upset the way a man does. If a man once says 'A crow is white,' he's going to stick to that no matter what; so in that case, even if I know a crow is black, I'll go along and say, 'Yes, you're right, it's white, isn't it?' Then a few weeks later sometimes I can say, 'That crow was really black after all, wasn't it?' And usually we can laugh about it. It's better that way."

Not many working women articulate their philosophy of life in an elaborate form, but those people who practice a disciplinary path are explicit about the tranquility, inner strength, and even transcendence that it can give them at times. These women explain that training for mastery of *ki* gives them the ability to deal with life's ups and downs including, at middle age, *kōnenki*.

Since people believe they should be able to control their emotional states, which have ties to physical distress and even illness, a corollary belief holds that individuals are responsible for what happens to their bodies; they ought, in effect, to be able to ward off many kinds of illness. This applies equally, of course, to women who have the liberty to practice disciplinary training on a regular basis and to those who must work in the labor force and care for sick dependents. Fortunately, as we will see, there are some loopholes in this explanatory system, which otherwise would be excessively severe and punitive.

The Limits of Responsibility

Together with a belief in a potential for relatively unlimited social and spiritual growth, regret at the inevitable decline of the physical body has a long history in Japan. A hanging scroll that may date from the fourteenth century (Hagiwara 1983), entitled the "Slope of Age," is the first known depiction of life's course, which divides a man's life into decades (on the similar medieval European tradition, see chapter 11). From the ages of ten through forty a boy climbs up the slope of transformation to reach full manhood at age fifty, the highest point on the scroll, after which his path is downhill all the way until at ninety years of age he appears old and bent as he sits quietly on a rock, watching a whirlpool at the foot of a waterfall. Later seventeenth-century scrolls depict not only the life course of men but also of women, and in at least one rendition of old age a woman appears bent and leaning on the shoulder of a child. A close reading by Susanne Formanek of portions of several of the earliest literary texts in Japanese including the *Manyōshū* (One thousand poems) and *Murasaki Shikibu nikki* (The diary of Murasaki Shikibu) turns up recurrent themes of regret at both physical and mental decay: crooked backs, tottering gait, wrinkles, whitening hair and its loss, decaying teeth, sleepiness, snoring, memory loss, and shaky handwriting—deplored and feared by men and women alike. The vivid descriptions of aging that Murasaki has Genji and other aristocrats of the Heian period recount suggest regrets and sound a note of doom (Formanek 1992). Although we would be unwise to make direct correlation to middle-aged women of today, the inevitability of physical decline and its accompanying features of gray hair, failing eyesight, and wrinkles (rather fewer than for most Western women), failing memory, and so on dominate contemporary narratives about aging and temper the more optimistic note that many women sound about the approaching free-dom from social restraints that can accompany middle age. When asked what age they would like to live to, only 8 percent want to live longer than eighty, and 41 percent settled for age seventy or less, while the remainder opted for somewhere between seventy and eighty, indicating that they have little desire to cling to life once old. These responses are particularly interesting since most women apparently have no wish to attain the av-erage life expectancy (81.77 years) for Japanese women today.[5]

Although women feel responsible for the state of their bodies and be-lieve that the right attitude will help them through *kōnenki*, they do not, of course, extend this to the process of aging itself, nor do they think it

A sixteenth- or seventeenth-century mandala (*Kumano kanshin jikkai mandara*), which illustrates passage through the human life cycle. Reproduced courtesy of the Okayama prefectural museum and the owner.

possible to surmount the procession of nature through sheer willpower. Because many women spend the greater part of their lives in very close contact with their elderly relatives they have had plenty of opportunity to observe at firsthand the havoc that aging can work on the body. This experience must heighten any forebodings they have about the future and no doubt contributes to their caution in responding about how long they would like to live. At the same time a good number of women also report a pleasurable experience in growing more intimate with their elders as they themselves enter middle age. Several women stated, for example, that they now like the kind of food that their mothers-in-law enjoy more than the food that their children eat, and they also take pleasure in sitting quietly at times with their elderly relatives, sipping a cup of tea and reminiscing about the past.

Aside from the inevitability of aging, other factors equally beyond human control bear on the experience of *kōnenki*. It is generally believed in Japan that women's bodies are naturally stronger than men's. Infant girls have what is known as *seimei ryoku*—in effect they have more staying power than boys. Many women pointed out that girls are easier to raise than boys, in part because they are naturally healthier and enjoy a longer life span. Human beings are believed to be endowed at birth with certain immutable qualities (*umaretsuki*), both physical (*taishitsu*) and psychological (*seishitsu*), and socialization must mold these qualities appropriately. In answering the questionnaire, nearly half the sample (48 percent) described themselves as having a "chilly" disposition, implying that they are predisposed toward feeling the cold, particularly in their hands and feet. Yet only 14 percent described themselves as *noboseshō*, meaning that they believe themselves to be constitutionally inclined to feelings of excess heat (there was no simple association between those women who reported hot flashes in the questionnaire and those who described themselves as *noboseshō*).[6] Several people suggested that for women endowed with a particularly "nervous" or "neurotic" psychological disposition, distress is almost unavoidable at *kōnenki*. But what they usually went on to point out rather hastily was that, because they themselves were lucky enough not to have such a personality, provided they maintained the right attitude (*ki no mochiyō*), they would probably have no difficulties. The concept of inborn physical and mental dispositions can be used selectively as a safety valve, therefore, an excuse to draw on should the necessity arise (although one is expected to learn from experience how to adapt to some extent even to these unavoidable limitations).

In addition to the relatively capricious nature of inherited qualities there are certain functions of the body aside from the process of aging, which are more or less out of conscious control and for which, therefore, one cannot be held directly responsible. Among them is that most abstract and ambiguous of concepts, the autonomic nervous system, which so many women and physicians used to account for distress at *kōnenki*. Symptoms such as dizziness, ringing in the ears, certain kinds of headaches, tingling sensations in the hands and feet, excessive feelings of hot and cold, and shoulder stiffness are considered unavoidable and merely signify that the body is temporarily unbalanced: little or no moral value per se attaches to these symptoms, which cause no concern unless they create a good deal of discomfort. If they do so, particularly if they accompany mood and behavioral changes, different meanings can come into play.

Mood changes, especially irritability, nervousness, and easily aroused feelings of anger (*okorippoi*), are not readily dismissed as events of little social or moral import. On the contrary, they signify a weak personality and loss of control and therefore carry much more significance. Under these circumstances, even the theoretically neutral biomedical diagnosis of an imbalance of the autonomic nervous system cannot outweigh the forces of personal responsibility and willpower. Personality types and biomedical diagnoses demarcate the boundaries of individual responsibility to a degree, but there are culturally accepted limitations as to the extent to which they can act as a buffer against the allocation of moral responsibility. Nearly 72 percent of women responded positively to a statement in the questionnaire that "women with many interests do not notice *kōnenki*," suggesting that if life holds important and stimulating activities then one can rather easily preserve the right attitude and remain relatively indifferent to the natural disruptions taking place in the middle-aged female body. Work, care of others, traditional arts, and hobbies all serve as *kibarashi*, as important diversions, so that *ki* does not become blocked or clogged, allowing women to ride relatively easily over *kōnenki*. Recently exercise classes designed to "discipline" the autonomic system (*jiritsu kunren*) have sprung up in many urban locations. These techniques derive from the training of Buddhist acolytes and involve a turning inward, an inner concentration, which can produce numerous profound effects on physiological processes. Those women believed to be of a nervous temperament, lacking in emotional stability, or with time on their hands, are thought to be decidedly at risk at this stage of life unless they undertake some form of disciplinary training.

I do not intend to give the impression of a perfectly harmonious social order; people certainly experience irritability, anger, and at times, rage, but these emotions are culturally constructed and usually suitably contained. Few middle-aged Japanese women openly express anything more than fleeting anger except under extraordinary circumstances (although there are powerful nonverbal ways of communicating displeasure), and people do not believe that swallowing one's anger or keeping it "in" is unhealthy—on the contrary, such behavior preserves both social peace and individual health. Hence women make every effort to preserve outward decorum and tend to feel guilty when they fail to do so. Obviously this type of behavior is most characteristic of the urban middle class, and to some extent of farming families (the direct descendants in consciousness— if not always in reality—of the samurai tradition). In more isolated rural areas and in coastal villages women are less concerned about holding back their emotions, although they nevertheless discipline themselves unrelentingly with respect to their work. It is these women who are more inclined to admit to or at least jest about a stressful time in middle age.

Depressed Bodies

In the questionnaire women were asked if they agreed or disagreed with the following statement: "Many women become depressed and irritable during *kōnenki*." Over 72 percent concurred with this statement, confirming the answers women gave in individual interviews: asked to state the most usual symptoms of *kōnenki* they almost always included irritability (but not depression) in their list. However, when the same women were asked in the questionnaire what symptoms they had actually experienced over the past two weeks only 12 percent reported having been irritable, and 8 percent reported having felt depressed.[7] Since the majority of Japanese women made it clear, both in answering the questionnaire and during the interviews, that *kōnenki* is not of great significance in their lives, and because only a few women subjectively experience either depression or irritability, why then is there a negative stereotype associated with this event? Perhaps this myth was transported from the West in the nineteenth-century European gynecological and psychiatric literature on menopause that gave it a powerful image, not only of depression but also of psychosis. Classical Japanese medical texts do not paint anything like the dramatic picture that appears in nineteenth-century European texts and mention neither depressed mood nor psychotic states, so this stereotype was probably not a product of the local medical system.

Another reason, given by several Japanese women, provides an entirely different explanation. They suggested that when approaching *kōnenki* (or indeed any other hurdle that must be overcome) people tend to prepare for the worst, to psych themselves up ahead of time ready to cope with whatever trouble may arise. The shared expectation of a bad time may set up a vicious cycle, even though only a few people actually experience noticeable distress that may or may not relate to the physical changes taking place in their bodies at the end of menstruation. Nevertheless, they ascribe this distress to *kōnenki* because of its timing, and its occurrence ensures that everyone knows someone or has heard of someone who is rumored to have had trouble.

Long before they reach middle age, many women have listened to gloomy stories about this stage from their mothers-in-law, their own mothers, their elder sisters, or their friends at work; usually such accounts relate not subjective experience but simply a mythological rendering of *Kōnenki* Woman. When we broke down the answer to the question as to whether women become depressed and irritable at *kōnenki* according to respondents' ages, we found that younger women believe in this distress much more than do older women, whose personal experience presumably figures in their response. Similarly, as noted earlier, when Christina Honde and I talked to a gathering of women of all ages in a village in Shiga prefecture, the younger ones were those who professed to be anxious about *kōnenki* whereas women in their fifties made light of it, perhaps demonstrating pride in the triumph of their willpower. Nevertheless, they are not above using the myth to keep younger women in line.

A larger number of Manitobans than Japanese apparently assume that women usually become depressed or irritable at menopause since over 84 percent of them answered in the affirmative to this question. A stereotype of a close association between menopause and depression remains deeply rooted in the West despite good empirical data to the contrary (Avis and McKinlay 1991; McKinlay et al. 1987b, 1992; Mikkelsen and Holte 1982; Kaufert et al. 1992). The postulated association is not a simple one, however, and there are several competing explanations as to how it comes about. What is perhaps the dominant discourse today assumes that a close and direct relation exists between dropping estrogen levels and depressed affect and that the experience of menopause places women "at risk" for depression (Ballinger 1975; Bungay et al. 1980). A second explanation suggests that the usual symptoms of menopause, namely hot flashes and night sweats, cause considerable distress, including sleep loss, which leads secondarily to depression (Campbell 1976). In contrast, a psychodynamic account hypothesizes that the investment that women "naturally" put into reproduction and sexuality causes them to become depressed at the inevitable loss of these attributes in menopause. A fourth explanation suggests that the event of menopause itself does not necessarily place a woman at risk for depression but focuses instead on family dynamics and possible losses associated with children leaving home, death of parents, and other events that occur at about the same time as menopause.

Unfortunately the questionnaire did not separate out the symptoms of irritability and depression because I was not aware until too late that such a distinction would have been valuable. I am convinced that had we made this distinction, the Japanese response for what they believe is the experience of women in general would have remained fairly high for irritability but much less so for depression. In the interviews, women's lists of expectable symptoms almost always included irritability, but they rarely brought up depression, a very surprising result given its overdetermined association with menopause in the West.

We ran into difficulties over translating the words "blue or depressed" into Japanese just as we did over the term *hot flash*, in that there is no equivalent lexical category that makes for easy translation. In the case of depression, however, unlike hot flashes, the general concept has universal recognition in Japan, but of the several words to characterize it none corresponds to the usual meaning everyday English usage gives to the word depression. Japanese terms usually glossed in English as "melancholy" or "depression" include *yūtsu, ki ga fusagu, ki ga meiru, shizumu*, and *inki*. The first of these terms relates to grief, and also to gloominess of spirits and weather; the second literally means that one's *ki* is blocked or clogged up, the third that *ki* is leaky; the fourth indicates being low in spirits, and the fifth that *ki* is yin rather than yang (that is, *in* rather than *yō*) and is therefore gloomy, implying that one's inborn physical constitution is gloomy. All these terms figure in daily life and in the traditional medical vocabulary and establish clear links between mind, body, and the environment. In the questionnaire the terms *yūtsu* and *ki ga meiru* were both put to use.[8]

The subjective experience of melancholy or depression in Japan is not associated primarily with the head (as is reported to be characteristic of depression among the middle classes in North America) or simply with affective states but is a much more diffuse concept that manifests itself as numerous physical changes including headaches, chest pain, a "languid" body, or a "heavy" head (in this respect the Japanese experience is similar to the Chinese [Kleinman 1982] and to that of people in many other parts of the world [Kirmayer 1984; Marsella et al. 1985]). Even when women talk about a heavy head or sensations of pressure (*appakukan*), these descriptions suggest not depressed emotions inside the head, or a general feeling of depression, but rather physical sensations that can at times actually be painful. Despite a tendency to "somatize" depression (in the medical idiom), unless we assume that all reporting of physical distress in the questionnaire indicates depression, its occurrence remains low.

There are several possible interpretations (not mutually exclusive), as to why depression and *kōnenki* are only loosely associated, all of which call for a good deal more investigation. Feeling sad and reacting sensitively to losses, particularly of loved ones, is an idea that has a singular appeal in Japan. The theater, a range of literature, and indigenous popular songs, traditional and modern, positively wallow in nostalgia, sensations of grief and loss, and a sense of the impermanence of things. People cry freely (by North American and northern European standards) about separation and lost loved ones, but at the same time they seem to draw strength from these experiences, to tighten their bonds with those who remain among the living, and to reaffirm group solidarity, as the sight of a family tending to the needs of a dying relative in hospital confirms. Unlike anger and irritability, which both disrupt harmony and threaten the social order, sadness, grief, and melancholy are accepted as an inevitable part of human life and even welcomed at times for their symbolic value, as a reminder of the ephemeral nature of this world. An association between melancholy and the weather reinforces sad feelings as natural and unavoidable, and hence as states not induced solely through human exchange. What is more, changes in mood are recognized not only as inevitable, but also as temporary. People learn how to consciously divert their attention when they feel down; they focus on something uplifting, assume that the mood will soon pass, and either attribute little significance to it or set out to explore its cause.

Today, of course, most people in Japan also recognize depression as a "mental problem," as a serious illness for which professional help may be necessary. If the behavior of an individual is seriously impaired, a diagnosis of *utsubyō* (depressive illness) will probably be made and the condition treated accordingly. Major depression is not usually associated with either *kōnenki* or menopause, however, but rather depressive feelings—sensations of being "down" and "blue," although apparently Japanese women do not consciously experience or report these feelings to anything like the same extent as do Canadians or Americans.

Health-care professionals in the West might be tempted to infer that Japanese women are "repressing" feelings of depression because of negative value and possible associations with mental illness attached to the label. I would take issue with this position because I do not believe, for reasons stated above, that the Japanese assign much negative value to transient feelings of being "down." Even when depression becomes more persistent, the culturally conditioned mode of experiencing and expressing such sensations is by means of a somatic idiom that attaches little or no stigma or moral approbation. Furthermore, the very concepts of "psyche" and "repression" have little recognition beyond a rather narrow professional circle of psychiatrists and psychologists (and then by no means among all of them). Moreover, it seems that the epidemiology of depression is altogether different in Japan (although this situation is changing). Whereas in both northern Europe and North America approximately four times as many women as men are diagnosed with depression (Brown and Harris 1978), in Japan slightly more men than women are given this diagnosis (WHO 1983). There is considerable debate as to what this difference means and very little research, particularly into the professional definition and diagnosis of the concept of depression (Marsella et al. 1985).

My interpretation of the responses the women in this study gave is that the majority do not subjectively experience depressed feelings very often in daily life. Further, I believe that their culture has to some extent protected them from such feelings (see Obeyesekere 1985, with reference to Sri Lanka), although its protection may well not continue indefinitely. The early socialization experiences described above, in which as infants individuals receive a large amount of close body contact (Caudill 1976) and as young children have a great deal of positive reinforcement and supportive care (usually with only very temporary rejection by parents or grandparents, and then as a response to highly inappropriate behavior), lead to the internalization of a basic view of the world that is positive and relatively content. To some Western readers this kind of experience sounds claustrophobic, stifling; and indeed, it does to Japanese who experience its excess, a sensation of being folded up in a blanket, of being invaded, of having no self, and of being unable to act as an autonomous individual (Lock 1988b, 1991); however, cases such as these are relatively infrequent.

Young girls usually experience somewhat less than the warmth and attention given to young boys (at least until recently), but they nevertheless internalize a sense of rightness about their place in society that apparently acts as an inoculation against feelings of depression. The roles of housewife and especially of mother are not devalued in Japan; on the contrary, as we have seen, the majority of women believe deeply that raising children is a much more valuable and rewarding occupation than participating in the work force. When women respond that their lives are *tōzen*, natural and as expected, they are stating something that for them is a very positive experience. They do not stick out but fit into a preordained universe, occupy their proper station in life, and blend into a cosmology where the social order is dominant. In other words, I am suggesting that for the majority of middle-aged and older Japanese women a faith in the centrality of the family, its preservation and continuity, has exempted them from the existential question of the West in late modernity, namely, what is the meaning of life?

Most of the women whom we interviewed have lived according to this traditional doctrine, and very few among the *shōwa hitoketa* grew up with the expectation or even the desire that life *could* be anything more than ordinary. They were not schooled to expect romance, a loving marriage, personal success, or financial security. They count themselves lucky if their husbands pay attention to them—an unexpected bonus for those who receive it—and for the majority the financial security and prosperity that postwar Japan has brought (even among those whose means are still severely limited) has served to deflect any tendencies to feel depressed. If the majority of middle-aged women find discrepancies between what their expectations were for themselves and what their lives have actually turned out to be, these are usually on the positive side, although a good number of women are now acutely aware that the family is unlikely to continue to be the spiritual hub of Japanese culture for much longer and feel both nostalgia and anxiety for their children's sake as much as for their own. In summary, a fundamental ethos about the goodness of human beings, the importance of care for others and satisfaction in giving it, a delight in the small occurrences of daily life and in the repetition of tasks and skills with diligence and competence—along with relative economic security and a reasonably stable family situation—usually counter, at some deep psycho-physiological level, anything beyond transient feelings of melancholy, other than in culturally appropriate expressions of grief or nostalgia. Obviously exceptions exist to this rather sweeping generalization, in particular among blue-collar laborers. Even so, very few women report feelings of depression, particularly since Japanese culture directs attention toward physical rather than mental distress.

Women are protected against melancholy not only by early socialization experiences and their expectations about themselves, but also by the construction of gender roles and family organization. Recall that only a very small minority reported that they mourned the loss of sexuality at *kōnenki*. Judged by the outward appearance of women who were interviewed, the *shōwa hitoketa* has long since ceased to invest much energy in overt sex appeal. Although some women were very smartly dressed, most wore rather plain clothes and had their hair cut short and permanently waved in a somewhat unprepossessing style, although their energy and liveliness completely countered suggestions of dowdiness. On the whole, women apparently conformed to what was expected of them, namely that marriage transformed them into housewives and then mothers and simultaneously took away their rights to assert their sexuality. Of course this was not the case for everyone—several women were conducting affairs at the time of the interview, for example, but for the majority, middle age was not the time to mourn an earlier loss of sexuality (although

I suspect that fewer women now would relinquish it). Yet those women who do want to project an image of sensuality into middle age also find their culture supportive in its recognition of the beauty and attractions of older women.

An even smaller minority reported concern about loss of reproductive powers at *kōnenki* than about loss of sexuality. Although women invest their energies in the production of at least two children, a major part of their reproductive function extends beyond the bearing and raising of their own children and into the raising of their son's children, and hence in a sense women at fifty are still in the middle of their reproductive activity, particularly because it is the raising and not the actual birthing of children that carries importance. Hence, the Freudian-derived psychodynamic explanation of loss of reproductive capacity to account for the postulated occurrence of depression at menopause does not make much sense in Japan—unless, of course, we posit some deep fully unconscious psychological mechanism at work.

Given that most people have until recently lived in an extended family, and that many continue to do so, the idea of an "empty nest" also makes little sense (although Japanese psychologists have added this concept to their vocabulary). Even when children set up their own residence it is usually only after marriage, so that many women find themselves today looking after two or more unmarried adult children in their middle twenties. Close contact usually goes on even after children marry; the small size of the Japanese archipelago together with an outstanding public transportation system allow ready contact with relatives, and this too must ease any sense of loss that women experience when their children eventually leave home.

With respect to the hypothesis of a relation between depression at menopause and a fear of one's own impending death (often exacerbated, it is said, by the death of one's parents at this time), Japanese women, as we have seen, are usually much less sheltered than are North American women about the end of life. Although women usually nurse their dying in-laws and not their own parents, almost everyone has had close contact at some time with dying and dead relatives and the inevitability of death is perhaps rather easy to acknowledge; its approach appears not to strike fear into the hearts of most Japanese, in part no doubt because of the Buddhist heritage that embraces death quite positively. None of the usual postulated psychological mechanisms that are frequently cited in North America to account for depression at menopause, therefore, apply very well to the Japanese case.

Among biological explanations offered for depression at menopause, the most obvious difference between Japan and North America is in the incidence of hot flashes and night sweats. It is usually night sweats that are thought to be the major cause of sleep disturbance during menopause; since fewer than 4 percent of women mentioned them and they clearly cannot be considered to cause sleep loss and associated depression. Furthermore, when we carried out a factor analysis, neither *yūtsu* (melancholy) nor *ki ga meiru* (feeling blue and depressed) loaded onto the same factor as did hot flashes and sudden perspiration, suggesting that melancholy and depression, when they occur, are independent of the so-called vasomotor symptoms (Lock et al. 1988).[9]

In direct contrast to the situation reported in North America, therefore, Japanese social organization, cultural explanations, and apparently even the body itself, serve to protect women from feeling "down" and "blue." At the same time, however, Japanese society and culture (but not, it seems, the body) function to sensitize women to a postulated association between *kōnenki* and irritability, a symptom loaded with negative value and moral connotations and (as for depression in North America) associated with a lack of self-esteem and an inability to function fully as a productive member of society. When we assess the frequency of reporting irritability by Japanese women by menstrual status, it is highest among premenopausal women, indicating that its incidence is not closely associated with the end of menstruation. But for women who judge themselves to be in *kōnenki*, it is highest for those who state that they are at the beginning or in the middle of *kōnenki*. The patterns for melancholy and depression are similar, but the incidence of these symptoms is much lower. These findings indicate, as was the case for other somatic symptoms such as headaches and shoulder stiffness (see chapter 1), that even those women who are still menstruating regularly judge themselves to be in *kōnenki* on the basis of a wide range of general symptoms and signs including irritability or, much less frequently, melancholy. Quite possibly, however, it is the other way around—women notice that they have been easily irritated about something more than once in the recent past or have had several headaches or other symptoms, then remind themselves that they are in their early or middle forties, and conclude, therefore, that this must be *kōnenki*, a judgment that those around them emphatically support, as the narratives have shown.

The Ordered Body

It is well known that for the past two hundred years or more, one of the dominant metaphors used to explain the workings of the body in the West has been that of a machine (Rabinbach 1990). Although competing discourses have always existed as to how to represent the body, this way of thinking, albeit somewhat dented today, remains in wide circulation both in medical circles and among the general population. The metaphor of body as machine never captured the Japanese imagination to the same extent that it did in the West, and a much older representation, one that has dominated thinking about health and illness in Japan for nearly a thousand years, survived as the usual way of conceptualizing the body until at least the end of the last century and remains very much in evidence today. Based on yin and yang, the complex complementary entities present in both the macrocosm of the universe and the microcosm of the human body, health is understood as a state in which balance is maintained both between the body and its environment, physical and social, and among the various body parts; illness occurs when this balance is temporarily lost (Lock 1980a). There is no fragmentation of the body in this kind of representation, and boundaries are rather fluid so that in theory there is a constant exchange of *ki* among the various organs and between the environment and individual bodies.

When European-style medicine and, after the war, American medicine became the models on which the modern Japanese health-care system was built, an uneasy alliance was formed in which a theoretical approach to the body based on metaphors of balance and harmony remained evident to some extent in medical practice (Ohnuki-Tierney 1984). Particularly in postwar years, Japanese medicine has often been exceedingly reductionistic and oblivious to patients as persons and to their relation to the environment. In recent years the situation has become yet more complex with the introduction of computer models into medicine and a recognition that, at times at least, it is helpful to think of the body not piece by piece, but as an interrelated set of signal systems. Despite these major changes in the way that medical professionals understand the body and a universal scientific education of high quality, metaphors of balance and harmony in the body remain very frequent in Japan and flourish in the lively and extensive practice of a thoroughly professionalized traditional medical system (Lock 1980b).

With respect to *kōnenki* and its associated signs and symptoms, images of loss of balance clearly prevail and doubtless facilitate an acceptance of the idea of a close relation between an unbalanced autonomic nervous system and distressful symptoms. This approach does not sit comfortably with a narrow focus on one or more specific symptoms assumed to result from a direct and straightforward relation with declining estrogen levels.

Nor does it encourage a conceptualization of *kōnenki* as a deficiency disease, as often occurs with menopause in North America today. Since the traditional medical system visualizes the body as in a continuous state of flux, *kōnenki* is a natural process, a stage that passes and that may incite temporary disruption. Furthermore, although a balanced body is a healthy one, health and ill health are not dichotomous variables but exist rather on a continuum; body states are ever transient and move back and forth between relative balance and unbalance. Ill health, therefore, is a relative and not an absolute state, and the closest that people come to associating a relatively uneventful *kōnenki* with pathology is to attribute discomfort to a temporarily unbalanced autonomic nervous system or else describe a woman's attitude as lacking in willpower, something that they would rarely do to her face and that medical diagnoses help avoid. Only under very unusual circumstances would a woman, no matter how many times she returned for help, be dismissed in a clinical setting as hysterical or hopelessly neurotic.

One way of explaining the workings of the Japanese body in popular writing is through anthropomorphism. In both traditional and modern literature, human bodies are often shown filled with little people laboring to keep everything balanced and in order. These gnomes can sometimes be seen complaining if the owners of the bodies do not act responsibly toward their own flesh. Hence, it is not merely persons who are social entities, so too are their actual body parts. Individuals are expected to cooperate and remain in harmony with their lively and active bodies, made over to labor for the benefit of society. Bodies are thus inevitably part of a larger order than that circumscribed by their physical boundaries.

Rabinbach discusses how European notions of the body as machinelike added the concept of fatigue, of being physically run down and worn out (1990). The Japanese concept of fatigue, *hirō*, is an old term in which the ideograms express the idea that the body is excessively tired from overwork. Another commonly used term, *karō*, indicates quite simply that the body is overworked. When people talk about being tired, fatigued, busy, their companions just nod in a complicit way; if individuals participate actively in society then inevitably they will be tired and overworked. The analogy for a fatigued body is not a mechanical one but one in which the microcosm of the body, down to its very muscles and sinews, is part of an anthropomorphized social order, where it is natural that everything human (persons and bodies) should be dedicated to work for the greater good of all, subject only to the physical limitations imposed by anatomy and endurance. Personal responsibility coupled with care and discipline of the

A woodblock print portraying "rules" of sexual behavior. Dwarfs are depicted as working the various internal organs. Reproduced courtesy of the Naito Museum of Pharmaceutical Science and Industry.

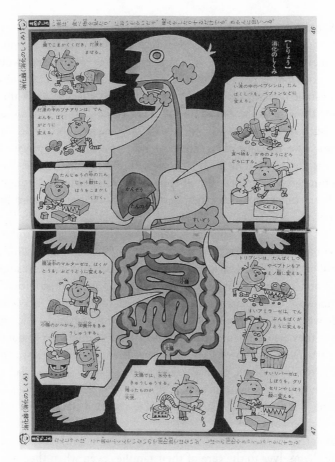

A diagram of the construction of the digestive system, in a school text entitled *The Secrets of the Body*, which makes extensive use of cartoons. Here, too, gnomes are doing the work. Reproduced with permission from Gakken Co. Ltd.

body in order that it may function well as a social entity are central to this ideology (Lock 1980a, 74). An idle body (such as that of a leisured house-wife) is anathema, not so much because it does not contribute to the economy (as has been suggested for America [Crawford 1984; Martin 1987]), but because it fails (not necessarily by choice) to participate actively in what is taken to be a just political order in which activities for the public good take precedence over individual aspirations.

Given the importance of individual responsibility in the care of the body, it is paradoxical that many Japanese, who are highly sensitive to small somatic changes as one form of health preservation, at times demonstrate a remarkable facility for objectifying their own bodies. As one middle-aged woman who experienced no symptoms of *kōnenki* put it: "I am grateful to my body." The Japanese language facilitates this objectification since it does not refer to body parts with a possessive pronoun; they simply stand on their own: *atama ga itai* literally means "head hurts" but renders the idea of "my head hurts"; *kata ga kōru* means "shoulders are stiff" but represents "my shoulders are stiff"; and so on. Older Japanese patients who describe their physical problems to their physicians are clearly in tune with their body and pay attention to its activities but at the same time give the impression of being somewhat distanced from it. They have been responsible, done their best, but beyond a certain point the body (but not the person) cannot be tamed; one must submit to fate, genetics, bad luck, the gods, one's inborn constitution, the unavoidable toll of work, and so on. But even then, even when the body "lets one down," people are still encouraged, more strongly than ever perhaps, to exert mind over matter and, above all, to continue participating in social activities. In one hospital ward for palliative care that I visited, for example, sick and dying people were required to give an account at a group therapy session of some activity they had carried out for other people during the previous week. One participant recounted how, when besieged by anxiety about his rapidly approaching death, he had taken a large plastic garbage bag and for several hours had gone out to pick up the litter that people had dropped all along the banks of a nearby river. He reported that he felt calm and relieved afterward.

Similarly, I believe, when Inagaki-*san* and others like her continue to devote themselves to the care of their families even when they are themselves very ill, theirs are not simply stubborn endurance feats but are understood to be a means of diverting attention from their own troubles and contributing to the restoration of balance to all concerned, including the individual who acts. The *shōwa hitoketa* think of it this way, yet younger people may disagree. At a symposium in Vienna when I discussed some of the narratives included in this book, a Japanese woman in her early thirties who was present was visibly annoyed: "Those women have never learned how to think of themselves," she declared. "All they do is wear themselves out for other people"—a position with which I am entirely sympathetic but one I have come to believe is also ideologically produced.

9   Peering Behind the Platitudes—
Rituals of Resistance

We are all caught by our particular fate.
                (Enchi Fumiko, *Blindman's Buff*)

Reading the narratives I reconstructed, many readers (especially women, no doubt) must have felt angry at times on behalf of older Japanese women, as did their younger compatriot at the symposium in Vienna. After years of research in Japan I still feel uncomfortable when I see the way children (usually sons) are allowed to take out their frustrations by beating their fists against their mother's body, or, until ten or eleven years of age, patting and pulling at their mother's breasts. Similarly an adult man will sometimes lean over to a woman working as a hostess in a bar and reach inside her kimono for a satisfying fondle while she smiles politely and pours him another whiskey and water. Behavior in bars is obviously a special case but illustrates, I believe—certainly by current northern European or North American standards—the extent to which many women in Japan may be physically invaded, reduced to objects, and available to assuage the frustrations of others.

My assumption before carrying out this research was that symptom reporting among middle-aged women would be quite high. I started out with the idea that oppressive social conditions, constrained human relationships, a double work load of employment and housework for many, a body given over to hard labor and sometimes also to the pleasure of others, would in all probability manifest itself in physical symptoms and emotional distress. Moreover, because almost all the *shōwa hitoketa* have known war and poverty at firsthand and have usually experienced the hardships of an extended family, although they may not now reap the rewards of that system in comfort and security during their old age—for these reasons too I suspected that they might have a difficult *kōnenki*. Difficult not, as the current ideology goes, because they now live a life of indolence but, on the contrary, because the majority work by economic necessity, while others nurse the housebound elderly. Many also remain in servitude to their husbands and further, some find themselves acting as handmaidens to their daughters-in-law rather than exercising power over them. But symptom reporting of all kinds is low, particularly so in contrast to the results from Massachusetts and Manitoba. Women employed in the blue-collar work force report little more discomfort than do middle-class housewives, but the incidence is still well below that for North America.

Why is this? One possibility is to doubt the existence of close links between mind and body; physical symptoms may be just that, physical and nothing more—pure biology bearing no relation to the emotional state of the person in whom they occur or to the metaphorical meanings of events such as *kōnenki*. This explanation makes no sense to me, particularly since links between the physical and social environment, and between feelings of distress and the immune and endocrine systems, are well established (Bolles and Fanselow 1982; Rogers et al. 1979) links that produce a cascade of somatic reactions such as headaches, backaches, chronic tiredness, dizziness, a heavy head, and other symptoms—the end result of persistent "insults" to the body. A symptom such as the hot flash, however (whether its immediate "cause" is declining estrogen levels or an unbalanced autonomic nervous system, or both), may not initially depend on either behavioral or emotional influences. Nevertheless, when it occurs once or twice, cultural conditioning profoundly influences future responses and the interpretation of sudden feelings of heat.

I am not, therefore, willing to resort to a reductionistic denial of the intimate relation between mind and body. So perhaps, despite an apparently restrictive social environment, most Japanese women are not seriously distressed? After all, the majority state that they are happy! I remarked earlier that few women showed signs of anger as they recounted their narratives; and, as we have seen, few reported feelings of depression. Perhaps, because their lives are natural, as expected, and even (thanks to postwar prosperity) considerably more comfortable than they had believed possible, the majority are indeed content and at ease. Can we say then that Japanese women are the victims of "false consciousness," duped into compliance by a hegemonic ideology about the proper place for women in society? And does this false consciousness also extend to the inner depths of their bodies, to their very cells and molecules?

Foreign and local commentators alike characterize Japan by its dominant ideology as a harmonious society brimful of compliant citizens, a description that superficial reality confirms. Moreover, the actual exercise of authority in modern Japan proceeds not by open power plays but by "soft rule" (Kamishima 1973), against which it is particularly difficult to express opposition. Nevertheless, there exist both an awareness of the pervasiveness of ideology and a long-established tradition of dissent, but they rarely take the form of open confrontation or revolt. I have already alluded to some of the ways in which soft rule is accomplished; I will expand these briefly, then consider forms of dissent, before turning once again to the narratives of individual women for a glimpse into the everyday workings of the ideology of harmony, and what relation, if any, it has to the reporting of distress at *kōnenki*.

Since feudal times a centralized Japanese government, usually resorting to the ideology of Confucianism, has worked to preserve moral order and social control among the general populace. After the Meiji Restoration of 1868, the emphasis shifted from the maintenance of order to the "mobilization and control of the people to serve the needs of the nation-state" (Gluck 1990, 292); the school system and local governments taught Confucian values, making every effort to create appropriate citizens, including the good wife and wise mother. Japanese intellectuals, among them the historian Maruyama Masao, describe this process as an "absolute monolith of state ideology, solid as prison stone, and . . . as an all-enveloping miasma that seeped into the minds and daily lives of the people" (cited in Gluck 1990, 292). This ideology provided the mobilizing force for the Russo-Japanese and the Second World wars.

In the aftermath of war many Japanese and outside observers assumed that the country would become a cardboard copy of Western democracy, but time has proved emphatically otherwise. Once national confidence rebounded, and particularly in the recent years of rapid economic expansion, the Japanese state emerged once again with a series of master plans, this time for the twenty-first century, in which an ideology of immutable difference between Japan and other nations is central. Harootunian (1989) characterizes the current postmodern state as a technocratic bureaucracy devoted to rational and instrumental control (much of it through the application of statistics, I would add). The business firm and its related work ethic are, according to Harootunian, the model for the wider sociopolitical order, one that, in contrast to Meiji Japan, is thoroughly committed to materialism and commodification but is nevertheless based upon an ethos of harmony and cooperation (Rohlen 1974). Although social order has long valued loyalty to groups, in the contemporary "information society" (*jōhō shakai*) a special kind of human "relationalism," the bonds of *aidagara-shugi*, is claimed to hold people together and advertised as unique to Japan. This ideology collapses history and self-consciously divorces itself from prewar ideologies in order to recast itself as rational discourse, but it nevertheless presses the past willy-nilly into the service of the present. Hence it celebrates the *ie*, the harmonious village community, a love of nature, and similar elements of mythical time against which the Japan of the present and future evolves. It reifies and lionizes traditional Japanese culture and postulates a national subjectivity "devoid of regional, class, or even gender distinctions" (Harootunian 1989, 89), in which "we Japanese" bond through a common biological and cultural heritage that transcends all difference and exists in opposition to outsiders. This is the context that will restore the three-generation family, to be orchestrated by the "new mother." But these assertions are clearly ideology—something about which many Japanese have a rather well developed sense of critical awareness.

The early Meiji period reinvented the Japanese word *shisō*, which glosses as "ideas," "thought," and "ideology," and gave it at least four interrelated but distinct categories of meaning (Gluck 1990, 284). The first emphasized the role of ideas in history and, because the Meiji state was devoted to progress and social change, stressed the way in which the people's prevailing habits of mind must be changed en masse. The second use of *shisō* conveyed the way in which ideas about society hold it together in space; this usage of the term justified a nationally organized, systematic indoctrination of the people's civil morality and work habits. A third use was as a "cultural canon" that renewed the Japanese tradition and made it available for comparison with the flood of Western ideas invading Meiji Japan. Finally, *shisō* referred to individual consciousness and expressed the importance of commitment to one's beliefs and to a unified and consistent development and unfolding of self over the course of life. It is this last meaning of *shisō* that I noted in the previous chapter. Gluck points out not only how the term *shisō* and its usage resemble the modern expanded meaning of "ideology" in the West but also suggests that the Japanese state has had a sensitivity to "ideology in everything" since the end of the last century: ideology was never partitioned off, classed as secondary to economic relations (despite the existence of Marxist-derived theory in Japan); on the contrary, in retrospect Japan appears to have had an almost post-Marxist orientation, well before the West did (Gluck 1990, 289).

Despite the rhetoric of harmony, there has always been resistance to dominant ideologies, to the self-conscious propaganda and policies formulated in the name of order. In the feudal era numerous movements at the village level and among the merchant class produced alternatives to the enveloping state hegemony and later, in imperial Japan, came an endless series of popular rights movements and leftist-inspired political activity (in which women often participated) for the abolition of licensed prostitution, for lower consumer prices, for better protection of mothers and children, and even for the preservation of rural mores and practices (Garon 1993). In postwar years citizens' protests have continued unabated and form the core of a sustained critical stance toward the entrenched conservative government. Resistance to political hegemony is relatively well developed, therefore, a recent example being the reaction of opposition parties and the general public to the official government effort to have Japanese forces participate in the Gulf war. Citizens' protests, however, whether by angry farmers trying to save their land from reclamation, housewives rallying about consumer prices, or environmentalists tackling pollution problems, "do not question the basic institutional outlines of Japanese society and polity"; they simply make dissatisfaction known to those in power (White 1984, 55). As White emphasizes, such protests are not trivial and can block government plans and bring about major reforms within existing structures.

The largely unarticulated practices of everyday life, as opposed to the institutionalized efforts of political systems, are less discernible to the indigenous population on whom they are practiced (and here Japan is no different from other societies [Bourdieu 1977; de Certeau 1984]). Obvious resistance outside the political arena is relatively rare. Practices that individuals take to be natural in social interaction, gendered behavior, family relationships—everyday practices that penetrate the body, to the very core of subjectivity—are elusive, hard to recognize for what they are: fables that make society tick.

Perhaps because mind and body in health and sickness remain within this assigned moral order, the ideological practices of daily life in Japan are that much harder to tease apart and analyze. In contrast to Japan, from approximately the middle of the eighteenth century on the dominant ideology in Europe gradually confined interpretations about the origins of physical illness and discomfort to the scientifically neutral terrain of physical pathology (Gordon 1988), divorcing body from mind, and reconceptualizing the body as a machinelike entity (although this discourse of naturalism never silenced all competing ideologies, some which remained quite audible).

In Japan, despite the steady development of a scientific approach to nature from the beginning of the nineteenth century, until late in the century the dominant ideology remained one that visualized the body as embedded in the macrocosm of society, and any incidence of illness as indubitably linked to lapses in the moral order. The body, immersed in the cycling planetary cosmos, the rhythms of the seasons, the continuity of generations, and the daily round of communal work and life, was disciplined by the ideological apparatus that shaped individuals into good citizens. Since the beginning of the Meiji era science legitimated this ideology and hence made it that much more powerful, a universal truth and thus less open to criticism. When the *shōwa hitoketa* think back on the good old days, they do so with a nostalgia that is not merely built from memories but was worked into their muscles, marshaled to control and preserve their bodies into productive agents for a modernizing and, when they were young, militaristic society. Although Japanese feminists and others increasingly criticize this ideology, it survives as a reinvented tradition for politicians and certain intellectuals to spin very effective webs that position the "warm" extended family opposite the "thin" relationships they take to be characteristic of the nuclear family.

Ideological discourse does not take place in a vacuum, of course, and its effectiveness depends on its existence within social institutions and everyday life. It uses what James Scott calls "techniques of atomism" that isolate individuals and circumvent their political activity (1990, 83). Modern Japan is most certainly not a totalitarian society, but the structure of the extended family, combined with an ideology of service to it, has for over one hundred years kept most women essentially powerless and isolated. As in other patrilocal residence systems, at her marriage a woman usually went to live with her husband's family and remained under its guardianship, as women's narratives revealed, vulnerable and isolated for twenty or more years, an outsider not quite to be trusted. In village life a young wife probably found some support among female relatives of the same generation and other young women in the community. Today women have much more freedom, but in urban settings, particularly in a nuclear family, they can be very isolated and sometimes in competition with their neighbors, especially over the scholastic success of their children (Inamura 1987). Those few women who find their lot unendurable had until very recently no obvious place to turn for assistance, apart from participation in various religious groups. Only in the past ten years have therapists and counselors appeared and self-help groups mushroomed. Visits to them are still regarded with suspicion by many women, thought of as an indulgence and a sop for the weak-willed.

Yet another deterrent to action for change is that women who speak out, complain, and fail to use polite language and deferential behavior are vulnerable to being classed as unwomanly and unacceptable. The most obvious penalty for acting inappropriately when young is that one will be unable to get married, as Harumichi-*san*'s narrative made clear (a condition that by far the majority of the *shōwa hitoketa* desired). The media currently play with this image by having the young female cartoon figure of Chibi Maruko-*chan* speak out in resonant adult tones, rather than use the required high-pitched voice of a little girl, to the great amusement of all.

The privacy of the family, and the vertical structuring of society in which bonds between mothers and sons traditionally have precedence over partnerships between husbands and wives, isolate women yet further. And, because it is a woman's responsibility to care for family members in every way, in particular for their health, she may hesitate to seek out help if there is a distressed child or a complaining mother-in-law in the house, because their poor physical condition in part reflects the woman's own inadequacies. Hence, if close relatives are sick or distressed a woman usually takes a good deal of the blame for this state of affairs onto her own shoulders—even for a crotchety in-law, since she believes herself to be complicit. Furthermore she is expected to be responsible for her own body and its condition, as we have seen, and to endure and not complain about distress. Until very recently, long-term rewards for stoicism in the form of security and comfort in old age were available, but usually on the condition that she maintained good relationships with her offspring, especially her eldest son.

The combination of these circumstances works overwhelmingly against women's overt resistance, and the space to maneuver without ostracism and even at times misery is severely limited (see also Pharr 1981). Perhaps most important of all, the very idea of resistance goes against the grain of Japanese society: it is by definition unnatural and antisocial and virtually all individuals, men and women alike, have learned since infancy and throughout their formative years to cooperate and immerse themselves positively in group activities. (The expectation of finding resistance everywhere is an ideological preoccupation of Western social theory.) Socialized above all to take pride and responsibility in their contribution to society as wives and mothers, the majority of middle-aged women have remained, therefore, ever in the shadow, passive, and unobtrusive. At middle age those who are not in the labor force taste the heady wine of relaxation from household and family matters before immersion in care of the aged and infirm. Reflecting on the entire female life span, we would say that middle age in Japan is relatively inviting, a transition from which individuals can both look back over the previous fifty years and forward to the next thirty and, given financial security, usually report good fortune and happiness. Nevertheless, a closer look at some of the narratives of middle-aged women reveals that beneath the surface of apparently unruffled lives a good deal of "low-profile" resistance (Scott 1990, 198) takes place much of the time.

An investigation of historical and contemporary sources convinces the sociologist Tsurumi that two types of resistance, "retreatism" and "ritualism," are frequent in Japan (1974). A tradition of voluntary separation from the community (retreatism) has served for hundreds of years as a means of political protest. The second form, ritualism, combines internal nonconformist values with external conformity to established behavior patterns. Koschmann comments that "ritualism means the preservation internally of contradiction. It implies accommodation within the personality of mutually contradictory elements (including values, belief systems, emotional responses) rather than their external expression and resolution through conflict" (1978, 20). The Japanese place high value on the ability to preserve such contradictions and do not possess the North Americans' unquestioned attachment to rationality and consistency in all spheres of life. Tsurumi and others characterize Japanese social structure and Japanese personality as multilayered; both rather rigorously distinguish between what is "within" and what is "outside." Events, situations, places, and people—all belong either to the sphere of *uchi* (in, inside, internal, private, us) or *soto* (out, outside, external, public, them); responses, verbal and behavioral, vary accordingly. However, these categories are fluid and con-textually relative, so that who and what is "us" in one circumstance may be "them" in another. A second dichotomy, that between *tatemae* and *honne*, is a crucial distinction and very relevant to our discussion. *Tatemae* refers to the principles of morally correct expectable and appropriate social behavior, whereas *honne* refers to one's real or true intentions and feelings, which at times inevitably conflict with *tatemae. Honne* provides the space for private detachment; *tatemae* agrees that the crow is white whereas *honne* knows full well that it is not.

In spite of the ideology of harmony, therefore, for eminently social beings to act consistently over time requires tacit acknowledgment that social life is to a considerable degree an artifice, that surface appearances can be deceptive, and that no matter to what extent the body is disciplined, some resistance is inevitable. In other words, many Japanese, whatever their assigned position in the social hierarchy, keep a healthy skepticism about motives and behaviors and social arrangements in which they find themselves. Any simple notion of "false consciousness" therefore cannot apply.

When we look at all the anecdotes given about women who have trouble at *kōnenki*, we find that they are, on close inspection, mostly hearsay. "I have heard . . . ," "Women at work say . . . ," "My sister's friend's friend . . . " Only a very few women apply the stereotype about leisured life to themselves, among them the Kobe housewife who stated that because she is "a spoiled type" *kōnenki* was a problem for her. But even in this case her ensuing narrative about life with a drunken husband shows that she did not take her own platitudes very seriously; her statement was rhetorical, a *tatemae* response with which she assumed, quite correctly, that her assembled friends would heartily disagree. When talking about themselves some women may play self-consciously with negative images, but usually they are deliberately dissembling. The majority comfortably use the autonomic nervous system, philandering husbands, stress at work to account for any difficulties they may have had; either indolence is not entertained seriously or else it is unequivocally rejected. It is only when they talk about people they do not know, or occasionally those they dislike or despise, that women launch into ideological sermonizing. In the abstract then, as pure conjecture, the majority agree that a luxury-induced illness is an authentic account for a distressful *kōnenki*. Thus, the myth of the leisured housewife survives, fueled by the media and popular medical accounts; a divisive and pernicious narrative, grist to the mill of *aidagara-shugi* that paradoxically, in spite of its myth of homogeneity, sustains divisions among Japanese women. The only woman I found who actively disputed the myth is a gynecologist who would like to see *kōnenki* stripped of its "superstitions" and treated in a more scientific fashion (a point I will expand on shortly).

In analyzing forms of resistance, Scott distinguishes the "public transcript," those exchanges that take place in the mode of the dominant ideology, from the "hidden transcript," ones that take place offstage, so to speak, and that often contradict or at least raise doubts about the contents of public exchanges. The distinction between *tatemae* and *honne* facilitates the production of a "hidden transcript" but, at the same time, mitigates the need for public action. It is not surprising, therefore, that the culturally accepted forms of resistance, retreatism and ritualism, rarely lead directly to either revolt or reform. Whereas in the old days retreatism, known as *yamairi* (entering the mountains), had a quality of romance and adventure associated with it, the modern equivalent, *ningen jōhatsu* (human disappearance), often becomes little more than another police file. Among the few women who opt for this style of resistance today some go abroad, others to one of several nunneries known as refuge centers; one or two contemporary shelters and support groups for women now describe themselves as "postmodern" nunneries (*Nihon keizai shinbun* 1987).

Of the two styles of ritualistic resistance, orderly conflict is the more common. Participants act out resistance "in a predictable manner (often implicitly expected and accepted by the adversary) primarily for the purpose of symbolically affirming the separate interests, identities, and goals" (Krauss et al. 1984, 9). The best-known example of orderly conflict is the annual "spring labor offensive," during which the national unions threaten to go on strike for a prearranged day or two. Such ritualized resistance avoids direct confrontation and serves not to bring about major changes in institutional structures but to remind everyone involved of rules and agreements (often unwritten) that must be observed.

The second type of ritualized resistance involves a dramatic self-sacrifice usually by individuals who know that their goals are unattainable but who nevertheless choose to demonstrate sincerity of purpose and purity of motive. Suicide expresses this form of resistance: the cases of Mishima Yukio and Okamoto Kōzō (of the Japanese terrorist organization, the Red Army) are two of the best-known recent examples. Even more disturbing are the suicides of children, most often those who have been teased unmercifully at school and cannot tolerate the insults of their classmates any longer. Their suicide notes make clear that they had hoped to force a change in the behavior of their persecutors and could find no other way to express the extent of their suffering (Lock 1991). An occasional young wife from the generation that is now middle-aged made newspaper headlines by strapping the baby to her back, taking the other children by the hand, and jumping into the path of an oncoming train. Suicide notes such women left almost always expressed apologies for the public nuisance but then usually cited a philandering husband as the reason for their act and expressed the wish that he would now straighten out his life. This type of protest intends to create a "symbolic affirmation of [one's] own principles" (Krauss 1984, 111) but, at the same time, represents a dramatic attempt to induce changes in the behavior of others who have usurped their positions of power.

Most ritual resistance is much less dramatic and would in the West count as "passive" resistance: the use of excessively polite humble language or very formal behavior (a form of resistance perfected by highly disciplined middle-aged women), of silence in place of an expected response, or of disappearance or avoidance of an expected appearance (see also Lebra 1984b, 43). All these tactics are designed to alert the offending parties to their abuse of power, to produce change through a quiet but persistent goading of others. If an individual's use of these strategies repeatedly fails, an explosion or uncontrollable rage may follow, very often followed by guilt and withdrawal or, in extreme circumstances, suicide: the result of acute frustration at having been both abused and ignored.

Even more common than resistance, however subtle, is reliance on the passage of time to take the edge off conflict. Akimori-*san*, for example, a primary-school teacher, stated emphatically that she puts her work before her responsibilities at home: "Once I was getting ready to go to a workshop and my husband was in bed sick with a slight fever. He wanted me to stay home and take care of him, and when I started to leave the house he yelled, 'Quit that job!' I said, 'Yes, yes, I'll quit at the end of the school year,' but of course when the time came around, he'd completely forgotten about it. That's how I get along."

Coming to Terms with Anger

Koshigawa-*san* is a teacher at a junior college. She has two daughters of seventeen and twelve and her husband works as a university professor. She was the only woman who wore a kimono for the interview, during which we were seated in a traditional-style Japanese room. The rest of the house was the usual mixture of Japanese and Western design found in middle-class houses and apartments today. Koshigawa-*san*, unlike most women, had circled a large number of symptoms on her questionnaire but appeared healthy and relaxed while we talked.

"I don't have many friends. I don't seem to be good at making friends in the neighborhood, and when I occasionally see my old friends from school, I find that the fact that I'm working and they're not seems to come between us. I'd like to hear what they have to say about housework and raising children, but they assume I won't be interested; and whenever they plan to go out somewhere, it's always on a weekday so that it won't interfere with their husbands and children, and I usually can't go, so after several invitations that I turned down, they stopped asking me."

"What about work, do you have friends there?"

"All my colleagues are men except for one young woman instructor. It's pretty hard to be friends with the men at work . . . As you know, the Japanese system works so that after we've finished long meetings and so on everyone goes off to drink together, but I have to come home to my family. I go for one quick drink sometimes but I tell them that my curfew is 7:00 P.M. And to tell the truth, I think they're pretty happy to see me go—then they can really get down to relaxing. The trouble is that they make quite a few decisions after I've gone home, they drag things on and on rather than getting them settled during working hours. The other woman teacher complains about this too. If we have any objections when we hear about the decision the next morning they always say, 'That's the trouble with women . . . If you want to be in on the decisions, you have to stay to the end!' "

"Does that make you mad?"

"Yes, but what can I do? I take *kendō* lessons once a week in the evening. I started when I was around forty—I thought it would be good for my health and for getting rid of stress. I expect you know you have to hit other people with a bamboo pole—I'm always afraid I'll hurt the other person if I hit too hard, but the instructor always tells us, 'Harder, harder!' and after about half an hour of that you get rid of all your frustrations. I'm also taking calligraphy lessons. I started that too when I was about forty. It helps me concentrate and keeps the stress at bay."

"Do you like your work?"

"Yes, I like the students and I enjoy teaching, passing on what I've learned to other people. The only real trouble is getting my colleagues to take women seriously. They always dismiss me as not dedicated enough because they claim I'm divided between work and my family responsibilities."

"You wrote on the questionnaire that you have stress, shoulder stiffness, headaches, depression, irritability, and feelings of oppression [*appakukan*], sore throats, and ear problems. What do you think is the cause of all these symptoms?"

"My main problems are my throat and ears and I'm taking some medicine for that. Sometimes I get low, thinking I'm the only one who works hard in this family. I must have been feeling like that when I filled out the questionnaire. It's always like that at the end of term. I don't notice things when I'm working, but then the vacation starts and I think how neglected my house is, and that bothers me. I decided long ago not to fuss too much about the cleaning (my husband used to say his socks got black from walking down the hall), but still there's plenty to do just keeping things running reasonably smoothly, and I seem to be getting less tolerant of my husband and children just taking things for granted. So recently I've been getting sort of sneaky. When I feel tired and I don't want to do a really good job of the housework and so on, I say, 'I guess I'm feeling my *kōnenki*—this kind of thing never used to be too much for me, but these days . . . ' " Koshigawa-*san* laughs: "I use it as a sort of excuse."

"How does your husband react?"

"Oh, he doesn't disagree with me, but of course, he doesn't offer to get up and do the work."

"You said *kōnenki* was somewhat of an important crisis. Why was that?"

"I've noticed it's getting harder and harder for me to suppress my feelings and sometimes that frightens me. It used to be, no matter how heated a discussion I got into, I was always able to listen to the other person's point of view, but these days I find myself becoming more short-tempered, so I try to drop out of discussions before they get to that point.

"I don't know if it's *kōnenki* behind this, but one of my friends—she was forty-eight—used to say she was getting unable to suppress her feelings, and her older friends advised her to take things more easily, but finally one day, she got upset and hanged herself. Of course, I wouldn't be brave enough to do that, but I find myself going too far in scolding the children and so on. I wouldn't physically harm anyone, of course, but I'm afraid I might wound them with my words. That's why I feel *kōnenki* is a sort of crisis."

"Have you always tried to suppress your feelings?"

"Well, I've tried to, but my husband says, 'Don't think you're the only one who's suppressing feelings,' and maybe he's right. It's hard at the college too, I want to blow up sometimes at those young teachers at work. I think, Who does that kid think he is [*wakazo no kuse ni*]? But after all, it's a man's society and if I get angry then we don't get along well, and our team projects don't work out and so I end up feeling I should suppress my feelings after all. They often say completely unreasonable things, but Japanese men have a tendency to get furious if someone points out where they're being unreasonable."

"So you end up feeling frustrated?"

"I often come home after a long meeting with feelings of oppression, like something pressing on my head. That's why I keep up the *kendō*—it really helps."

Living a Double Life

Urushima-*san* is the mother of a son aged twenty-two, and she also looks after her nephew of twenty-three who lives in the household. The small bar in which she works belongs to her sister, who is her employer. Her husband is a taxi driver and has worked most of his life from five in the evening until three-thirty or four in the morning.

"My life is nothing to brag about. The one good thing is, there's no retirement age for my husband so *I can keep him working* even after he gets older [emphasis added]. But still it'd be better to be married to a salaryman."

"Was your husband in favor of your working?"

"No, he doesn't like me to go out. It's only because I'm helping my sister that he's resigned to it. Actually I had an offer of a job at the local city office but my husband wouldn't let me take it. If I'd been working there since they first offered me the job fifteen years ago I'd be making a good salary by now. It would certainly have made our life easier."

"Do you like the work you are doing now?"

"No, it's pretty stupid. I'm just doing it to give my sister a break. I'd really like a regular company job, but no one will hire me—I'm much too old. So instead I'd like to go back to school and study history, Japanese, and English."

"You wrote in your questionnaire that you had an ulcer."

"Yes, I had it for eight years but it's better now. Just about a year ago my life changed completely and the ulcer cleared up right away. I've gained weight too, before I was too thin. The doctor said it was a 'nervous' ulcer due to stress and he said I should go and live in a foreign country or shave my head and become a nun."

"He wasn't serious, I suppose?"

"No! But he meant I should make some big changes, so I decided for the first time ever to start enjoying myself. I've stopped brooding over things and I don't pay nearly so much attention to the little things, and I take naps—I'm lazier than I used to be. Also I've started going out to bars and so on. My husband doesn't like it and he's given me a 10:30 curfew at night, so I come home on the last bus." A long pause while Urushima-*san* decides whether to continue. "I've got a special friend . . . About one and a half years ago I really changed."

"And you feel better?"

"Oh yes. Up until now I didn't know much about society and I didn't see many people. But since I've started going out I've been meeting all kinds of people. I was always passive and I resigned myself to things, thinking there was nothing I could do about it. But you know, Japanese women are changing, I've realized I was pretty old-fashioned. Most people are getting out these days and finding out about things for themselves."

"So your life is different from your mother's?"

"Oh yes. First of all, she lived in an extended family and had many children. My father was the mainstay of the household and my mother took care of the house, raised the children, and obeyed my father. You know, in the old days women never let their husbands see them looking a mess when they got up; by the time we children were up my mother always had light makeup on. Then, before my father came home at night, she always cleaned the house a second time, changed her kimono, and redid her makeup, and greeted him in the entrance way. I guess there are still some women like that—but me, I just come out in the morning with my pajamas on and my hair a mess, and when my husband comes home . . . Well, I'm sound asleep, of course!

"My father died when I was thirteen, I was the fifth of eight children. I always depended on my mother and she died when I was twenty. After that I decided for a while life wasn't worth living. I used to ponder the best way of committing suicide, and which was the best season for doing it. I decided winter would be best. But I gradually got over things."

"In Japan people usually think women should suppress their feelings, don't they?"

"Well, women just do that without thinking about it. I did it too, it just happened naturally."

"Why do you think that was?"

"Because my husband was so bossy [teishu kanpaku]. If we both let our feelings out, we'd have had fights, and that's unpleasant. So I never said the things I wanted to, but I was always thinking, Just wait till you get to be old; I'll pay you back then! If I'd had a daughter I would have tried to train her to say everything she wants to say, otherwise she'd end up with an ulcer like me. We always believe in Japan, somehow other people know what you're thinking even if you don't say anything—but I've come to believe that's nonsense. Of course if you're financially dependent on your husband, and if he makes you stay that way, then there's not much you can do, except walk out. But how would my son and I have managed? Because I didn't have any financial security I always had to keep quiet. Anyway, things are much better for the time being!

"Kōnenki? No, I haven't noticed any difficulty there."

Both these women are aware of their anger but are frightened of where it may lead if they confront the men whom they identify as the source of their unhappiness. For different reasons both have come to believe that the "male-dominated" society they belong to duped them into accepting a second-class citizenship based on service to the family they no longer fully buy into. They ease their frustrated feelings in different ways, Koshigawa-san by using kōnenki as an excuse for "slacking off," and Urushima-san by (presumably) taking a lover. Despite her frustration Koshigawa-san has not gone out of her way to talk to her daughters about how they might conduct their lives in a different way. Neither woman, typical of the majority of people we talked to despite their reasonably well developed sense of the political and cultural constraints under which they live, chooses to turn to other women or to political activity to change the structure of society. They are both skeptical and angry about the way life treats them but remain isolated and dependent on their husbands, at the same time resenting the situation.

Elusive Feminist Consciousness

Some women, such as Ono-*san*, a part-time pharmacist, are openly critical of Japanese women in general. She was emphatic that women today must learn to think about the problems of society and not just their own homes and families. When asked for examples she responded:

"Well I'm always vacillating within myself. I used to think, why do they make such a fuss about cabinet ministers going to Yasukuni shrine?[1] What difference does it make if their visits are official or nonofficial? And what's wrong with enshrining the people who died in the war? But now I realize that's mistaken; what goes on at Yasukuni shrine are rituals connected to the emperor system [*tennōsei*], and so it has a connection to the idea that everyone should do what they're told, and that if you think differently then you're not really Japanese. I think the trend in that direction is something that everyone should think about, or we'll end up sending our children to war again.

"Another thing bothering me is that my son's school suddenly decided that the children should all come to school in groups. They could easily go by themselves, but instead they were supposed to be led there by the older children, just at an age [twelve] when they should be learning to take care of themselves. The teachers say the change was made so that the children from different age groups would get to know one another better. The idea of doing everything in groups is frightening to me. Some of us mothers complained, but the school didn't listen. I suppose the teachers were just passing on an order they had handed down to them from above. Anyway, most of the parents seemed to think if the school says you have to do it then there's nothing more to say—it's that kind of attitude that scares me."

Unlike almost all the other women interviewed Ono-*san* described her husband as a "real partner," the one person with whom she can really be frank, but then she added:

"But I don't know what *he* really thinks. Still I say anything I want to him, even things I know I shouldn't." She looked at little coquettish and went on: "That's *amae* [acting like a spoiled child], but I feel I can do it because we have a strong base [*kiban*]. Maybe I'm being overconfident— I should think a bit more carefully about that, I know, but I feel there's nothing I can't tell my husband—friends, after all, are outsiders and a husband should be a confidant these days."

Forty-five-year-old Futagawa-*san* is rather well known in Japan because she appears regularly on Japanese television as a news commentator. I asked her if she thought that Japanese women are free to create their lives in any way they please these days.

"No. First of all there's the difference in pay for men and women. Of course they've recently passed a law about that, but people's consciousness hasn't been affected so the situation won't actually change much unless women start actively demanding their rights. I think laws are important, because they show the direction the country is going in—they provide the means for change, but whether change *really* happens or not depends on people's consciousness, and that takes a long time to alter. In Japan especially, men's consciousness hasn't changed much at all, and I'm afraid that things may actually get worse. The reason is that families have fewer children, and boys are being made even more of than they were in the past when there were five or six children in a family. Housewives' biggest concern these days is the education of their boys, getting them into good schools and universities; all their energy goes into their sons. The boys who've been raised like that are now in their twenties, and they have very little sense of independence.

"Japanese men don't think of women as having independent personalities or thoughts of their own. Their only experience of a woman has been their own mother, and the mothers of today's men mostly stayed at home, so that's the image men have: they just assume women are happy taking care of children. Of course the women are partly to blame for this situation—once they get married they stop paying attention to what's going on in the world. Most women don't even know what their husband's work is all about, but that's because it's *otoko rashii* [manly] not to tell one's wife anything about work. People don't demand much or expect much from their spouse in terms of companionship. In a way it's not so bad because they're not easily disappointed—there's no romance involved. But it also means women in nuclear families are inevitably stuck with all the domestic work and the child care.

"Actually in the last two or three years, the number of college graduates who've been choosing to stay at home and be housewives is increasing. Home isn't at all an unpleasant place to be these days, now that women don't have to live with their mothers-in-law and their husbands treat them better. A lot of people are tempted by a life filled with hobbies and tennis. It's *hard* to work, and now that the equal employment law is finally passed and women are being asked to do the same work as men, some of them are choosing to run back home.

"Of course that suits the government right down to the ground. They still have their source of cheap labor because most women find in the end they've got to earn some money to keep the family going, and so they take part-time jobs, which means they act as a kind of shock absorber for the Japanese economy because they're let go when times are hard. The system we have fits the current consciousness of the people in power—women serve both the family and industry as well."

"How did you manage things in your own life?"

"The biggest problem I had was that my husband was living with his mother when I met him, and she was a widow. She really didn't like the idea of my working; she thought I should be paying more attention to her precious son, she was so proud of him because he'd graduated from a famous university and she thought I should be waiting on him. She was dissatisfied until the day she died, but she couldn't come right out and say too much about it because one of her own daughters was also working as a nurse. However, my sister-in-law had stayed home while her children were young and my mother-in-law thought I should be doing the same thing. And of course, my TV work kept me out late at night so that was a special problem."

"Did your husband try to mediate between you and his mother?"

"No, of course my husband didn't get involved; like all Japanese men he preferred to run away from it. His attitude was, Just don't let's have any trouble. He wasn't really keen about me working himself, but he thought of himself as too much of an intellectual to tell me I had to quit!"

"Did you live with your mother-in-law?"

"No, she lived by herself and then she chose to stay with her daughter when she got sick. She was there when she died of a heart attack. But I used to help her out with the cleaning and shopping when she lived on her own."

"So who looked after your child?"

"When my baby was born I had to be in the studio 'live' early every morning, and I was the first woman with a child to do that; all the other women were single. So I felt I had to do a good job or it would spoil things for other women who came after me. After my three months' maternity leave was up I hired a housekeeper, but she didn't get on with my mother-in-law who was living next door at the time. So I asked my mother if she'd take care of the baby, and she was very happy to do that. I had to commute at six o'clock in the morning to my mother's house on the way to work. If I was going to get home really late—10 or 11 P.M.—I used to leave my daughter there all night sometimes. Now my daughter's a teenager my

Cartoon from a book that discusses how to preserve good relationships between mother-in-law and daughter-in-law.

mother comes here about three times a week when I'm going to be late and fixes dinner for her, but my mother says she doesn't want to live with us. She's a really independent woman. She's sixty-nine now and she never lets up. I'm really grateful to her for all she does."

It was striking how many women we talked to are highly articulate about their position in society. Many of them have read quite widely on the subject, attended lectures, women's groups, and watched TV programs that take a critical look at contemporary Japan—and a good number also have firsthand experience of the treatment of women in other societies. This knowledge no doubt contributes to a sensitivity as to the way in which women's lives everywhere are products of the society in which they live. Most of those who work in factories are quite explicit, for example, about their exploitation in the work force, and those few who are professionals talk about job discrimination of one kind or another and often contrast their situation with that of their counterparts in North America. But the majority of middle-aged women in this study, especially those who are housewives and rural residents—even though some grumble about the family situation and exhibit resentment about the treatment they receive at the hands of their husbands—do not think in terms of "women's" or "individual" rights or of political action to alleviate their dissatisfaction. On the contrary, my impression is that many women tend to take a large share of the blame onto their own shoulders if they find themselves in an untenable family situation. However, what a North American woman like me might see as rather blatant oppression is culturally buffered—and in fact many Japanese I talked to consider my understanding of oppression to be the product of Western cultural baggage. Japanese women evidence little distress at *kōnenki*, perhaps in part because, even when living in uncongenial family surroundings, they are usually positive about the importance of care of family members. They are also quite explicit in their belief that this activity is sadly neglected in the West, a situation they associate with the sorry state of American society today. When talking about care of children and elders, work that demands considerable sacrifice, almost all middle-aged women accept primary responsibility, in spite of the fact that rather few women, when they in their turn become infirm, expect to be looked after by their daughters-in-law (although this may be *tatemae* rhetoric).

No political action is easy in Japan, but the history of the women's movement since the end of the last century has been a particularly checkered one because it has always had to deal with the "state's heavyhanded intrusion into gender relations" (Garon 1993). In postwar years the consumer movement has offered the only forum for large-scale action, and of course, Japan also has a few politically radical women "who refused to be victimized" by the state (Sievers 1983, xi). Contemporary feminists speak out as their predecessors did and publish at a very rapid rate, but their ranks are small and severely fragmented. Nor are feminists usually very interested in either blue-collar workers or older women (although there are some exceptions to this).

Women have no obvious place or group that inspires them to political activity, and compounding this difficulty is the rhetoric of *aidagarashugi* that rings in their ears: relationalism is central to the Japanese way of life, which is special and different from the lives of outsiders. Politically active women in Japan must use great skill to balance the twin ideologies of the "oneness" of the "Japanese," and the decidedly "non-oneness" of the submissive behavior appropriate to their subordinate female position. They must ask themselves whether the gender difference they experience is part and parcel of the unique relationalism of Japanese society—in which case feminist scholarship outside of Japan is not much use to them—or if gender discrimination is essentially the same in Japan as elsewhere. Feminists argue vociferously about this point, but because the majority of women in Japan, feminists or otherwise, question the value of what they know of feminism in the West (sometimes based on a rather scanty acquaintance with it), they usually support one variation or another of the argument that the Japanese case is special. Such a position tends, however, to bog

Cartoon from a book by Higuchi Keiko that gives advice to women involved with care of the elderly. Reproduced with permission from Bunka Shuppan Kyoku.

down in the cloying discourse of *aidagarashugi* with its unqualified rhetoric about a unique Japanese heritage.

Another important constraining force against the development of an active political consciousness among Japanese women is the massive inertia (let alone active resistance) of husbands, employers, parents-in-law, and even friends. Any woman who sticks out receives criticism, usually quite explicit and where it hurts the most, of dangerous inadequacy as a mother, and of nonexistence as a "real" woman or transformation into a cipher or, worse, a witch, a crone. This social opprobrium, coupled with the subtle force of indirect expressions of resistance, causes most women, although they may recognize the origins of their difficulties in the structure of society and the symbolic value placed on motherhood—without necessarily accepting the difficulties as just—to adapt to their situation as best they can.

Many women apparently achieve a reasonably satisfactory compromise by sealing off a quiet space, a self that retains a healthy skepticism about the structure of daily life and shrugs off petty discrimination. These women are at peace with their lot and take pride and satisfaction in the unfolding of their lives. They may explicitly scoff at government efforts to re-create extended families, but when it comes to nursing sick elderly, since there are very few realistic alternatives, they would need a remarkable combination of indifference to the suffering of family members combined with the surmounting of numerous social pressures to avoid nursing duties. Furthermore, they may have a good deal of ambivalence about the punishing routines that shape the lives of most working Japanese men. As Futagawa-*san* intimated, the majority are probably extremely reluctant to become fully responsible members of the work force for this reason.

Other women are less satisfied and openly grumble at times but have no basic quarrel with the argument that they should devote their lives to the family. A good number believe that they are exploited but opt to work for small victories on the home front to ease their burden. One or two seem completely overwhelmed and despondent and are perhaps chronically depressed; yet others gossip and grumble about exploitation but go no further. A few have chosen that well trodden and sometimes successful path to change in Japan through grass-roots movements and activities at the level of local government.

Despite a rhetoric to the contrary, a distressful *kōnenki* does not map consistently onto any particular construct of self, family situation, or working condition, nor can we link it in any simple way with a psychological predisposition (always assuming there is such a thing). To paraphrase Iris Murdoch writing about the West: There are as many *kōnenki*[s] as women. Even though the majority of Japanese women agree on the significance of signs of changing eyesight, shoulder stiffness, headaches, irritability, and many buy into the cultural ideology of a distressful *kōnenki* as a disease of civilization, our closer inspection reveals considerable variation in individual women's interpretations of their subjective experiences, interpretations inevitably contextualized by reflection on their own reconstructed life histories and by assessment of their present situation.

Although most women ride over *kōnenki* with apparent ease, its occurrence may give others pause or occasion to flex their muscles. The resulting deliberations, whether they occur in the privacy of the family or in public, all essentially concern the same thing—to what extent middle-aged women should be responsible for care of dependents—husbands, in-laws, children in their early adulthood, and grandchildren. Should they accept a lifetime of service for others that puts at risk personal space and even individual health? Or should they be free to "fly" (*tonde iru*) if they so choose?

The situation in which middle-aged women now find themselves is complex and unstable. Adding to the pressures of demographic changes to the aging society is political activity over the status of women and a barrage of information from the West about the position of women there, causing many to reconsider women's biological destiny as nurturers. Few have challenged the status of the family as the basic unit of society, since men and women alike view with suspicion the easy exercise of individuality (by either sex) and equate it with the American other at its most decadent and alienated. And since many women are still very vulnerable economically without the protection of men, resistance, where it exists, usually resides at the level of "infrapolitics" (in Scott's idiom), low-profile and undisclosed, sometimes with an accompanying hidden transcript of anger. To date none of the grass-roots activity has led to calls for radical change or found a unified standpoint from which to challenge the dominant ideology of female subservience. It is easier to chip away at it, or to pause and take a reflective stand toward it. However, the burden imposed on women by the aging society may provide added incentive for more concerted political activity in the future—particularly so if Iwao is correct in believing that over the past fifteen years Japanese women have indeed undergone a "quiet revolution" in which they have learned to value newfound freedoms (Iwao 1991, 1).

10   The Doctoring of *Kōnenki*

It's not seemly for Japanese women to fuss about their
bodies.

(Kyoto gynecologist)

A visit to any reasonably well stocked bookstore in Japan today shows that
here is a nation bent on educating itself in preventive medicine, self-care,
self-diagnosis, and the correct selection of medication and therapy from a
seemingly infinite array of possibilities. The largest and most impressive
books belong to the genre known as *katei no igaku* (family medicine).
Such volumes furnish up-to-the-minute accounts of basic physiology and
anatomy and describe the latest medical ideas about symptomatology, diagnosis, and treatment of all but the most rare of diseases (including *kōnenki shōgai*). These books often figure as gifts from local governments
to city residents in preventive medicine promotion campaigns and represent the culmination of a long tradition of publications about self-care in
Japan, a by-product of the nation's emphasis on individual and family
responsibility in the preservation of health. In the present study 62 percent
of the families reported that they own and quite often refer to one or more
books on family medicine. For the large numbers of people who use techniques of traditional medicine as well as biomedicine (Lock 1980a; Sonoda
1988), there exist several elegant, easily obtainable volumes on the modern
application of herbal medicine, acupuncture, moxibustion, and massage.

In addition to the family medicine series of books is a large selection of
medically related volumes and magazine articles written for the benefit of
the general public mostly by doctors, but also by psychologists, educators,
and journalists. *Kōnenki* started to appear regularly in publications such
as these in the early 1970s and recurs fairly often. Its literary incorporation
represents one aspect of what Ivan Illich (1976) terms "the medicalization
of life"—the process, starting approximately from the middle of the last
century (a little later in Japan), that recognizes passage through the human

life cycle primarily as biological change, and therefore amenable to management by the medical profession.

Through medicalization the medical community attempts to create a market for its services by redefining certain events, behaviors, and problems as diseases (Freidson 1970; MacPherson 1981; Merkin 1976; Zola 1978). One researcher characterizes the medical profession in contemporary society as "a major institution of social control . . . nudging aside law and religion" such that ordinary citizens lose autonomy over their own lives (Zola 1972, 487); he believes that the haste with which many people bring everyday troubles to the care and attention of physicians reinforces this process.

A focus on medicalization that limits attention to the power of the medical profession alone invites attack from a number of points of view. The incidence of disease and illness, some critics argue, reflects the political and social relations of the society of which the medical system is a part; research into the power of the medical profession diverts attention from a discussion about unequal access to medical care (most particularly in the United States) and the relation of the incidence of illness to differences of class, gender, race, and age (Ehrenreich 1978; Frankenberg 1980; Stark 1982; Young 1982). Hence, to confine attention to clinical encounters is to leave the political order—which for many members of society is literally sickening—intact.

One response to the recent barrage of criticism about biomedicine as a whole and in particular about medicalization in Europe and North America has been the emergence of new age medicine, also termed the holistic health movement (MacCormack 1991). Central to the ideology of this movement is the recuperation of self-responsibility for health and illness. Guttmacher, after noting the advantages of such an ideology, points out that by conceptualizing health as an end in itself, and by emphasizing individual responsibility, the movement in fact exacerbates the medicalization of many areas of life and reinforces a basic biomedical premise: that illness is a personal event for which individuals may be held responsible (1979, 16). Guttmacher adds perceptively that such an attitude receives government support since it can be related to cost containment.

For medicalization to take place, a corporeal state, an event, or a problem must first be conceptualized as a medical condition; once space and time are set aside for health-care professionals to manage the condition, medicalization is institutionalized, but this process requires the appearance of patients who are diagnosed with and treated for the condition (Conrad and Schneider 1980; Conrad 1992). In commenting on much of the work on the medicalization of the female life cycle, Reissman points out that "Women [are] not simply passive victims of medical ascendancy. To cast them solely in a passive role is to perpetuate the very kinds of assumptions about women that feminists have been trying to challenge" (Reissman 1983, 3). A consensus must develop between physicians and patients that a particular condition is best understood in clinical terms for medicalization to happen.

Over the past thirty years there has been a marked increase in the use of gynecological services by women in midlife in both North America and Europe. What used to be described euphemistically as the change of life and regarded as private and somewhat embarrassing is so no longer. Women consult much more freely with both health-care personnel and one another about the end of menstruation, and in the process female midlife has become increasingly medicalized. Although not well recognized, this trend began before the end of the last century, when menopause was first defined as a medical condition (Smith-Rosenberg 1985, 191–95; see also chapter 11), but even its recent acceleration has not brought nearly the same extent of medicalization to menopause as to childbirth (Kaufert and Gilbert 1986).

The Japanese are highly educated, extremely health conscious, and feel responsibility for the state of their bodies. Moreover, despite some maldistribution of services between rural and urban areas, Japan is plentifully supplied with physicians, 95 percent of whom are in clinical practice in well-equipped hospitals and clinics, both public and private (Steslicke 1987, 43); furthermore, since 1961 the entire population has been eligible to participate in the national health insurance coverage system. Under the circumstances we might expect that *kōnenki*, in common with other life-cycle transitions, would be highly medicalized. This, however, is not the case, nor have other aspects of the life cycle been medicalized in Japan to anything like the same extent as in North America. Childbirth was, until the 1950s, assisted largely by midwives, even though today 99.8 percent of childbirths take place in hospitals or clinics (where midwives still do a large number of deliveries with obstetricians in attendance) (Kōseishō 1992).

The Doctor as Last Resort

Among the women in the present survey 60 percent have never talked about *kōnenki* with a doctor. Whereas they described friends, magazines, and television as reasonably good sources of information, only about 25 percent of the sample said that they had received useful information from their physician. They considered husbands and friends easier to talk to than doctors were, perhaps confirming the importance of the social, rather than the biological, aspects of changes at this stage. Virtually all the house-wives and farming women had someone to confide in about *kōnenki*, but more than 25 percent of the factory women had no one to talk to. The larger proportion of factory workers who were divorcées, widows, single, or separated may well account for this difference.

Most people in Japan have a family doctor whom they visit on a regular basis for minor illnesses, but 66 percent of the sample either had not been to see a doctor during the previous year or had been only once or twice. Aside from visits to the family doctor, a few women had occasionally consulted with several medical specialists over the year's course; most vis-its were to internists and gynecologists (only 6 percent in both cases). No one had been to see a psychiatrist.[1]

Women were asked in the questionnaire to report on major health prob-lems that involved regular physician visits. The number suffering from diabetes, heart disease, ulcers, and asthma was fewer than 3 percent, and only 7 percent had arthritis, allergies, and/or eczema. High blood pressure, at 13 percent, was the most frequently reported problem.[2] Only 6 percent of Japanese women reported severe pain at menstruation. The general health of the Japanese sample, therefore, appeared to be very good (par-ticularly when compared with the North American surveys (see note 2, the list that follows, and also Haug et al. 1991 for similar findings), high blood pressure being the only major symptom that might cause concern.

Percentage not reporting a chrnonic health problem
(diabetes, asthma, allergies, ulcers, arthritis, or high blood pressure)
Japan: 72   Manitoba: 55   Massachusetts: 47

Fewer than 12 percent had had gynecological surgery, relatively few when compared with women in North America (Table 10).[3] This difference may well follow from Japanese women's lower use of medical services and pos-sibly from a much more conservative approach by Japanese gynecologists. It may also reflect differences in the structure of the health-care systems, since in Massachusetts, where the rate is highest, gynecological surgery is financially rewarded more than in Japan or Canada. These differences war-rant further investigation.

The national incidence of breast cancer is significantly lower in Japan than in North America. In the present study the incidence of breast sur-gery, lower than 5 percent, was half that of the North American samples, and among Japanese women who had received breast surgery, only 0.8 percent was for cancer. Lower physician contact combined with less con-

Table 10. Gynecological Surgery, by Study

	Japan		Manitoba		Massachusetts	
	%	N	%	N	%	N
No hysterectomy	88.3	1162	77.1	1010	68.8	5371
Hysterectomy only	2.3	30	12.1	159	8.4	656
Hysterectomy and unilateral oophorectomy	3.0	39	3.6	47	4.1	323
Hysterectomy and bilateral oophorectomy	3.4	45	5.0	66	15.6	1220
Unilateral oophorectomy only	2.6	35	2.2	28	2.5	197
Bilateral oophorectomy only	0.4	5	0.0	0	0.6	35
Total	100.0	1316	100.0	1310	100.0	7802

cern about cancer probably accounts for the fact that 55 percent of the Japanese sample never had a breast examination, and nearly 60 percent of Japanese women never examine their own breasts. A similar but not so exaggerated difference was found with respect to Papanicolaou (Pap) tests: only 50 percent of Japanese women had received one in the recent past.[4]

What is striking about these results is that Japan prides itself on a well supported and widely distributed preventive health-care system, a system that has contributed to a decrease in a wide range of problems ranging from stroke to infant mortality. Nevertheless, few systematic preventive measures for middle-aged women are apparent, although mammography screening was implemented in 1991. It is also of note that women themselves choose not to go for regular checkups and seem to use gynecological and other services only once they become seriously ill (but I understand this situation is slowly changing). The relatively low rate of use of prescribed medication among the present study supports this argument, particularly since Japanese physicians are renowned for prescribing and dispensing large quantities, a lucrative source of income for them (Sakuma 1969); Japan is the second largest pharmaceutical market in the world and the largest per capita consumer of pharmaceuticals (Calder 1988).

Japanese women use fewer pain relievers, sleeping pills, and vitamins than do women in the North American sample. In addition, only 3 percent of them had taken a prescribed tranquilizer in the two weeks before they answered the questionnaire, considerably fewer than women in the North American samples.[5] However, 22 percent of Japanese women had imbibed nonprescription stomach remedies, twice as many as North American women (Table 11). Japan has the highest incidence of stomach cancer in the world, which no doubt accounts for careful monitoring of stomach problems. Japanese women also make extensive use of herbal medication and health teas, over 16 percent in the present study, of which 9 percent said the infusions and powders were prescribed by physicians. Although most herbal remedies were for problems unrelated to *kōnenki*, quite possibly some of them contain natural estrogens that are effective for symptoms of *kōnenki*, including the hot flash. However, only a tiny minority of those women who reported no flashes were taking herbal medication; thus its use cannot account for the low reporting of hot flashes across the sample.

Of those women who had discussed *kōnenki* symptoms with a doctor, only 7 percent, just over half of whom were experiencing hot flashes, had received medication. Japanese doctors rarely specify the medication they prescribe, and so the figures are probably not very accurate, but fewer than 3 percent of the women reported that they were taking some kind of hormone therapy.[6] Those women for whom something was prescribed other

Table 11. Percentage of Women Using Medication in Previous Two Weeks, by Study

Medication	Percentage			
	Japan (N = 1,225)	Manitoba (N = 1,224)	Massachusetts (N = 7,746)	Chi-square (2df)
Nonprescription pain reliever	13.8	45.3	62.6	1065.1*
Prescription tranquilizers	3.5	12.5	9.8	62.2*
Vitamins or minerals	20.1	29.7	38.4	174.8*
Hormones	2.7	6.4	8.1	46.8*
Sleeping pills	1.6	7.1	4.3	46.0*
Herbal medication or teas	16.0	4.0	3.2	385.3*
Stomach remedies	22.0	8.6	11.0	137.9*

* $p = 0.01$

than hormone replacement therapy most often received vitamins, placebos, tranquilizers, or herbal mixtures.[7]

In summary, in spite of the ready availability of medical services, middle-aged Japanese women made little use of gynecologists and took prescribed medication in rather small amounts. However, more than 54 percent of them reported having had one or more abortions—a total of 1,428 abortions, distributed evenly among women who farm, work in factories, and are housewives. It is for this service that the majority of Japanese women eventually find themselves in the office of a gynecologist. An abortion costs between three hundred fifty and four hundred dollars (not a large expense for most Japanese); it can occur up to twenty-two weeks of gestation and must have the consent of the husband or cohabitant.[8] An abortion that does not observe the specified circumstances is classified as a crime punishable by a maximum of five years' imprisonment for the physician. The current Eugenic Protection Act states that certified obstetrician-gynecologists who have undergone extensive training can carry out legal abortions "when there is risk that pregnancy or birth will cause substantial harm to the health of the mother because of physical or economic reasons." Interpretation of this proviso is exceedingly liberal; in 1988, a total of 486,146 abortions were performed in Japan (Kōseishō Jinkō Mondai Kenkyūsho 1989).

In the present sample 14 percent of women at some time used an interuterine device and the same percentage took birth control pills. The low-dose contraceptive pill that has been readily available in North America and northern Europe for over ten years is not legal in Japan, but the high-dose hormone pill is legal, although only as a prescribed medication to control menstrual disorders and irregularity.[9] Most Japanese associate the pill with dangerous side effects, most particularly cancer (Table 12), and have what one gynecologist who supports the legalization of the low-dose pill described as an "allergy" to it (Mainichi Daily News 1987a). For more than thirty years, the use of oral contraceptives has been "under study" by the Japanese government, and recently, with what is becoming a monotonous repetitiveness, the public has been informed that the pill will most probably be made available in the near future, but not yet. The movement to liberalize use of the pill inevitably encounters fierce oppositional lobbying from a good number of gynecologists and also from many women who are concerned about iatrogenesis (illness and disabilities resulting from prescribed medications, a term coined in 1976 by Ivan Illich). This lobby had a boost in March 1992, when the Central Council on New Drugs refused women ready access to the pill, explaining that it would

Table 12.   Birth Control in Japan: Views on Birth Control (from family planning poll conducted by the newspaper *Mainichi shinbun* in May 1986)

What do you think of the move toward official approval of low-hormone contraceptive pills?

It is good	It is not good	Don't know
35.4%	12.6%	48%

Would you use the pill if approved?

Yes	No	Don't know
12.9%	44.2%	37%

---

increase the risk of exposure to the acquired immunodeficiency syndrome [AIDS] virus—presumably condom use would decrease; the argument is not compelling, since as of January 1990 Japan has had a total of about 290 confirmed cases of AIDS. A survey by the newspaper *Mainichi shinbun* showed, for example, that 72 percent of women distrust birth control pills primarily because of concerns about side effects (1990j).

By far the majority of women rely on the use of a condom by their partner (80 percent of married couples) and may also have had abortions to control the size of their families. Public education about contraception has been very limited until recently, and the Ministry of Education still takes the line that schools should teach children only about the birds and the bees (the same cannot be said for comic books that tell all in graphic detail). One common reason given for not making the pill readily available in drugstores is that young unmarried people should not have free access to such medication. However, the abortion rate among adolescents has accelerated rapidly in recent years and was estimated in 1985 as 6.5 abortions for every one thousand teenagers, a figure double that for 1975 (*Mainichi Daily News* 1985b). Among older married women, in contrast, abortions have declined somewhat (the total number of abortions has been halved since the 1960s) and this statistic, paradoxically, has had an influence on *kōnenki* and its medicalization.

In Japan obstetrics and gynecology are usually combined in primary-care practice. Independent physicians own and operate small hospitals and clinics, and most of their income has until recently come from deliveries, abortions, and minor surgery. In recent years an increasing number of women have chosen to give birth to their babies in high-tech, tertiary-care hospitals. Coupled with an overall decrease in the abortion rate, this shift has meant that many gynecologists are feeling the need to recuperate their financial losses. As a result, in increasing numbers, they are beginning to take a serious interest in middle-aged women and *kōnenki*.

One of several diagnostic labels is usually given to patients having problems with *kōnenki*, for which physicians can receive reimbursement from the government for their services: "imbalance of the autonomic nervous system" (*jiritsu shinkei shitchōshō*), "menopausal" or "climacteric" syndrome, and alterations or abnormalities in ovarian function. In addition to prescribing medication for these "diseases," some physicians have also started to offer counseling usually on a fee-for-service basis, but sometimes at no charge. Despite these moves toward medicalization, Japanese patients consult with doctors about *kōnenki* rather infrequently (although more often in recent years), and in any case the majority of gynecologists feel somewhat at a loss as to how to deal with these patients.

Ambivalent Interventions

Dr. Iwakami works in the obstetrics and gynecology department of a large teaching hospital in Tokyo. Asked to comment on what he does for patients who come to see him about *kōnenki*, he responded:

"You know, we aren't as interested in *climacterium syndrome* [said in English] as American doctors are. For one thing, there hasn't been much research into it in Japan. When women come to see us for consultations in connection with *climacterium* they often have a mixture of many ailments, and gynecologists aren't too good at treating things outside their speciality. It's not enough just to prescribe hormones, you need to know about oncology as well, and often there's a large psychosomatic component, and gynecologists aren't usually very interested in that. And of course, patients who have a lot of little complaints take up too much time— we work under severe time constraints in a big hospital like this one, and so they're not very welcome. To be honest, I think that except for those one or two doctors who're really interested in the medical issues of menopause, most gynecologists think this kind of patient is a bit of a nuisance."

"And this attitude hasn't changed recently at all?"

"Well, because life expectancy has increased things are changing a bit, but I'm interested in using exercise instead of hormone therapy. I think plenty of exercise is probably more effective against osteoporosis and also for most *kōnenki* complaints. Of course some aspects of it are related to family relationships and other factors in the social environment, but we haven't done any systematic work on this yet. So far we're comfortable with just answering the surface questions and treating the symptoms, but

Many women walk and bicycle extensively as part of their
everyday life

we don't really get very close to our patients and find out what their
troubles are.

"There's a difference in national character between Japan and other
countries: foreigners tend to exaggerate their symptoms, while Japanese
always play them down, so Japanese patients are less demanding, and anyway we give medication only to middle-aged women who really exaggerate
their distress."

"Many people in Japan seem to think that middle-class housewives are
the ones most likely to have problems. What do you think about this?"

"Well I don't think so. Nowadays over 60 percent of women are working and there aren't many jobs that don't involve stress. It's quite different
for women who can take trips and play tennis and so on. I think working
women probably have more problems with *kōnenki* because of the stress
they're under, running a home and working at the same time."

"Do you think that feeling their age may also compound the problem?"

"You must know more about women's psychology than I do, but even we men, when we look in a mirror and see how our bodies look, feel our age. I think that minor troubles at middle age can seem major for both men and women—surely *everyone* begins to worry a bit about old age and sickness after middle age."

Several themes common to many of the narratives given by Japanese doctors appear in this interview with Dr. Iwakami. He is emphatic, like a good number of his colleagues, that the medical management of female midlife is not as advanced in Japan as in America (whereas earlier this century, German medicine was the standard against which Japanese medicine was measured, today it is inevitably American medicine). Nevertheless, his ideas about the best kind of treatment for *kōnenki* do not correspond at all with the aggressive promotion of hormone replacement therapy characteristic of American medicine (about which he is fully cognizant).

Because Dr. Iwakami thinks of *kōnenki* primarily as an aging process, he is comfortable about expanding his discussion to men and their experiences at this stage of the life cycle, and like most of his colleagues, he does not entertain a sharp gender distinction.

I met Dr. Ozu, a general practitioner, at the end of a busy morning seeing patients in his small office attached to his home deep in the Japanese countryside. He was about to depart on his daily round of house calls but had set aside a half hour to talk to me.

"I've been a doctor here for about thirty-five years, and since I live in the area I know all the people and their family situations. I see about fifty patients a day, six days a week. I do morning and evening surgery and house calls as well."

"You indicated on the phone that *kōnenki* isn't much of a problem around here."

"That's right, especially these days because people have more opportunities for regular checkups, so any serious medical problems such as high blood pressure and some cancers are caught that way and not confused with *kōnenki*. In the old days women used to come sometimes and talk about *chi no michi*, and we'd go over all the difficult times they'd had at childbirth and about how tough *obāsan* had been on them. A few women still talk this way, but not many. Today most people talk about *kōnenki shōgai*, but lately I haven't had many women complaining about this— they haven't been coming with headaches and *darui* (lassitude) and so on. That's because nowadays all the fifty-year-olds are working harder than they used to. Because they have paid employment it helps them psychologically, and they feel they're contributing to the family income."

"But surely in the countryside women have always worked?"

"Yes, but around here they just went to the mountain two or three days a week for a few hours to take care of the trees—they had more free time then. Now they all work regular hours in the factory outlets and I think they feel more responsible. They don't come complaining about little things anymore."

"Well, they don't have time to, do they?"

"Yes, that's so, but basically I think they don't want to. It used to be that if the weather was bad, or if they didn't feel like it, they could just stay home. They had much more freedom. But now they have the responsibility of going to work, and I think they like that."

"But you see a few women complaining of *kōnenki shōgai*, I presume."

"Just a few, about five or six a year."

"What are their symptoms?"

"The most usual complaints are headaches and shoulder stiffness and general lassitude."

"What about hot flashes?"

"Not many complain of *nobose*."

"Do you give those women medicine?"

"Usually not. I just tell them that it's *kōnenki*, that their difficulties are normal for their age, and that they will go away before too long. Once they know it's just *kōnenki* they go away relieved."

"Do you ever prescribe hormone replacement therapy?"

"No, never."

"Are you opposed to its use?"

"Yes. Hormones are difficult to use. If a patient is having a great deal of trouble with irregular menstruation, for example, then I refer her to a gynecologist. But I very rarely see a case like that."

"Some doctors seem to think that middle-class housewives are most likely to have *kōnenki* symptoms."

"Well, as I said, around here the women used to be free, but now they have responsibility and they get out of the house and talk to people every day, they rarely have any problems with *kōnenki*."

Dr. Furuse, a middle-aged Osaka gynecologist who works in private practice, agreed to talk to me after he had finished attending a special lecture on the treatment of *kōnenki* with herbal medicine.

"There are many types of *kōnenki shōgai*, but for those related to vasomotor disturbances such as hot flashes and palpitations one shouldn't hesitate to use hormone replacement therapy, although just today I learned that *kanpō* [herbal medicine] seems to be very effective as well. However, for psychological symptoms hormones don't have much effect, it's much better to talk to the patient in cases like these and get to the root of the problem—usually it's trouble in the family."

"What kind of person is likely to have psychological problems?"

After reflection he explained. "Well, I think women who are very domestic, especially those who are *nervous* [said in English], or gloomy [*inki*], and who have to keep very tidy and orderly homes to be satisfied with themselves, or else they may have a husband who's not helping out at all. Those women who have good 'communication' [a euphemism for sex] in their homes do much better.

"The husbands of many women with *kōnenki* problems are often only interested in their work, and they may have trouble with sex, either because they're using all their energies in their work, or because they've lost interest in their wives as they begin to show their age—'She's getting to be a dumpy middle-aged woman, no good anymore.' In these homes the housewife may be just like a maid."

"Do the majority of your patients complain about hot flashes?"

"No—absolutely not. Most have headaches and tiredness, ringing in the ears, and so on. But some have hot flashes, and then I don't hesitate to give them hormone therapy, just for a year or two at the most to help them over the difficult time."

"What diagnosis do you give to the women with headaches?"

"Well, usually 'imbalance of the autonomic system' or else 'ovarian function disturbances.' It's usually not possible to separate out what's happening because changes in ovarian function and in the autonomic nervous system are so closely connected with each other."

"So you see a good number of patients with these kinds of problems?"

"More people are coming these days. Everyone has heard about *kōnenki shōgai* and *jiritsu shinkei shitchōshō* [imbalance of the autonomic nervous system] from the mass media, but most patients don't really have an illness. It's simply stress. I think that men have *kōnenki* too, but it comes about ten years later and, since Japan is a man's society, men have ways to get over it outside of working hours and don't complain of so many symptoms. These days women have more chance to relieve stress than they did in an extended family, but still less so than men, so they end up bringing their problems to gynecologists or internists. Since people in Japan traditionally haven't talked about sex, certainly not older people, they come and talk about other symptoms and no matter how many tests we do, we can't find anything wrong, but sometimes we can guess the problem is related to sex and give the woman some counseling."

"So a good number of women who come to see you are really having sexual problems but they call it *kōnenki shōgai?*"

"Yes, I think so. They want someone to talk to. Of course, it's often not really their problem at all. It's often that their husband is having an affair, and they feel quite desperate."

"I've been told that gynecologists in Japan are looking for work, particularly because people are making better use of contraceptives these days."

"Yes, people are using birth control techniques more effectively than before. I'm not as busy as I used to be, but I mustn't complain about that. I certainly don't enjoy doing abortions. It's much better for a woman not to have an abortion."

Dr. Fujitani had just finished up his usual very long day in a busy Tokyo hospital when I met him at eight o'clock in the evening. He made it clear from the start that as far as he is concerned the basic cause of most problems experienced by middle-aged women derives from the way Japanese society is structured:

"It's the 'free' women who have symptoms. They feel unconsciously that society is leaving them behind. They've done thirty years of work as a housewife and mother, and then suddenly there's nothing for them to do—no reason to be alive. I've started to do counseling for these patients but I don't charge anything because I have no training, and it's not appropriate for me to take money. I just make some time to talk to them about their family and social life. Of course I give them medication if necessary, to take the symptoms away, but then we just sit and chat for a while and gradually most people lose their reserve and open up their hearts. Most doctors won't take the time to do this, of course. Sometimes I call in the husband as well and try to get him to start thinking about his wife a little. Usually the husbands haven't noticed that anything is wrong at all.

"Just treating symptoms is very superficial, and there are a lot of women shopping around from doctor to doctor looking for something more than medication. I'm really like the blind man and the elephant—I only see a little bit of the problem, and I can't possibly control it or make it go away. It's very frustrating at times."

A very friendly and gentle Kyoto gynecologist, Dr. Mihata, who has been in practice for twenty-five years, apparently feels much the same way as Dr. Fujitani does. He believes that for most people, men and women, there is a resistance to getting old, but that women, especially housewives, having put all their energy into the raising of children and running the household, are particularly tired and vulnerable in middle age.

"You know, the root cause is political, it's to do with the poor position that Japanese women have in our society. Doctors can't solve this sort of thing. The best I can do is to offer some free counseling for thirty minutes two afternoons a week. It's not much really, but some of the women meet together on their own now without me and discuss their problems together—I think that's best really."

"I've heard that some gynecologists have gone out of business lately because fewer women need abortions. Is that right?"

"Well, my cousin was a gynecologist too, and he retired very early because he claimed he was losing money. I don't know if that was really the case or if he just wasn't making the nice profit he was used to. He had a very busy large practice until a few years ago and I'm sure he must have done a good number of abortions. But he delivered a lot of babies too—unlike me, I've never had the facilities to do that. Last time I went to see his clinic the nursery was practically empty—I think that's the big difference—women feel safest in the high-tech hospitals and so some doctors in private practice are feeling hard up. But that may change again."

Dr. Sada is about forty-five years of age and practices gynecology in a medium-sized hospital in Hiroshima where he is the department chief. He was very willing to talk but nevertheless pointed out at once that "the climacterium is not a life-threatening condition," and for this reason very few gynecologists are interested in it.

"But you read the American medical journals—menopause has become a hot topic there recently."

"Yes, I read most of the British and American obstetrics and gynecology journals and the endocrinology ones too; I see articles on menopause from time to time. But still the subject doesn't interest me very much. I think many women have *kōnenki* syndrome—the most susceptible people are the nervous and pessimistic types, those whose psychological state is not so good. But every woman has heard well before she's forty-five that she's going to get palpitations, shoulder stiffness, and hot flashes—so of course they get them. Everyone is vulnerable in this sense."

"Are these the symptoms you associate with *kōnenki*?"

"Yes, but it's also common for women to complain about headaches, ringing in the ears, lumbago, bladder problems, dull feelings in their legs, and chilliness in their hands and feet. Of course it's hard to tell if these symptoms are actually related to a decline in hormone levels or not, but if they're relieved by hormone treatment then there's probably some connection. These days we give progesterone as well as estrogen, to help protect against endometrial cancer, the same as in the West, but I use weak doses of estriol, and so my patients don't keep on menstruating as they would with the stronger medication."

"Do you think that the autonomic nervous system is implicated in some way with *kōnenki* symptoms?"

"Yes, I do. The hypothalamus is part of the feedback system that stimulates the secretion of estrogen from the ovaries. Once estrogen levels drop, then the hypothalamus becomes overactive for a while because the ovary no longer responds to it, and the hypothalamus stimulates the autonomic system and becomes the major cause of hot flashes, shoulder stiffness, and so on. This can have an effect on the patient's emotional state too. There's no doubt in my mind that it's quite a trying time."

"What about osteoporosis? Can estrogen stop bones becoming fragile?"

"I think that regular exercise is the best thing for people of all ages, men and women."

Easing the Symptoms of Leisure

Although most Japanese gynecologists show relatively little interest in *kōnenki*, a few doctors spend a good part of their working day dealing with it. Dr. Ikeno works in a very busy teaching hospital in a metropolitan center. He believes that until recently it was not possible for women to discuss *kōnenki* at all.

"Until about thirty years ago women were destined to work their fingers to the bone for their husband's family. They were expected to put everyone ahead of themselves, to live a life of self-sacrificing service [*kenshinteki hōkō*] and not to talk about their troubles; they were supposed to be always smiling, to wear a mask. For that reason there was no chance for them to discuss *kōnenki* symptoms with anyone. Anyway, to make a fuss about *kōnenki* would probably be thought of as trying to hang onto one's youth, and that wasn't appropriate.

"So one of the problems now is that middle-aged women find it very hard to talk about these things to a doctor. You know when we were young we used to be taken in groups sometimes to see films like Tarzan, but we never got to see the happy ending [*sic*]; that was always blacked out, and we could only guess what was happening. We were never taught that if people love each other, intimacy is what happens, and it's a good and natural thing. So even now, people of my age feel embarrassed to watch that kind of scene in a film. Younger people are different, of course. But women of my age never bring the subject up, so if a doctor suspects that part of the problem may stem from her sex life he just has to take the plunge and ask some fairly direct questions, and then the patient may run away.

"Also I think that up until now Japanese people have not been too conscious of things like hot flashes and haven't connected them with menopause, whereas in the West women hear so much about that symptom that in a sense they're sitting waiting for it to happen to them, and at the slightest sign think, Aha! They're worried about it meaning the loss of their womanhood, while in Japan, no one is waiting for it; it's just a passing experience, completely natural."

"But your patients have increased in numbers recently."

"Yes. I think that's partly to do with city life today. People who're in their fifties now, like me, are the ones who got their education during the war, and they're in a sort of valley, cut off both from the people who are older and the younger ones. They're a very special generation, and they don't have anywhere to go with their problems. Many people came to the city from rural areas and they have very little contact with other people. They start to concentrate on themselves and get upset at the least sign of climacteric disorders.

"It's partly to do with the sudden appearance of the nuclear family in Japan; we don't have as much experience with this system as the West does, and so there's been no time for people to think about such things as individual freedom and how one should lead one's own life, and people may end up having to solve all their own troubles by themselves—especially the women. In my generation we were just like cart horses; targets were set from the outside without our ever thinking about it, and now middle-aged women suddenly find themselves with nothing to do and no resources. That's when they start to notice *kōnenki*."

"How do you define the term *kōnenki* for yourself?"

"I think really that it's just one occurrence in a broad, none too clearly defined, inevitable process of aging, which includes the decline of the various bodily functions and structures. Men will probably never admit to it unless you go drinking with them, but they notice increased tiredness, pains, and so on; they have *kōnenki* too, but it's not so concrete. They also have hormonal disturbances, but they're not so dramatic. Even so, most women don't have much difficulty, they just endure things quietly, but a few are very sensitive and keep coming back again and again to see the doctor. We reassure them that nothing is wrong; but these are the ones who probably can't figure out what to do with the time they used to spend dealing with their husband and children."

"Do you think then that working women have less trouble with *kōnenki*?"

"Yes, they have other things to be concerned about so they don't get so many nonspecific complaints—well, it's not that they don't have them, it's that they don't think about them."

Dr. Ikeno is critical of medical education in Japan, most particularly in gynecology, and said that he would like to set up a *kōnenki* clinic in which physicians who specialize in psychosomatic medicine cooperate with gynecologists to give all-around care. He continued, "People still have a strange view of gynecology in Japan. When I meet my old school friends, they often say meaningfully, 'Oh, so you're a gynecologist!' And I would like to reply, 'We gynecologists are working hard so your wives can live free from worry,' but they seem to think gynecologists choose their speciality from some ulterior motive [*chigau kyomi*], and if men think that, I suppose women do too, and that makes it a bit hard for them to visit a gynecologist. Now if we could establish a 'mature age clinic,' then I think things might change a bit."

Dr. Ikeno prescribes estrogen replacement therapy for about one-third of his patients but states that many are reluctant to take it because they have read in magazines about its association with an increased risk for endometrial cancer. He prescribes progesterone in addition to reduce the risk but points out, "We have no way of knowing whether our patients actually take the medicine or not. Also I think there's quite a bit of variation from patient to patient in terms of effect. It certainly reduces hot flashes in *most* women, but for some it doesn't seem to make much difference. I'm planning to do some research into this. Anyway, for women who don't have hot flashes estrogen is not the right medication, they usually need sedatives such as *jiritsu shinkei anteizai* [sedative for the autonomic nerves]."

"How long do you keep a patient on estrogen usually?"

"The Japanese Association of Gynecologists has recommended that it should be given only for hot flashes, and for as short a time as possible. So I follow their advice.[10] Of course, I know that in the West some people recommend long-term use for osteoporosis, and maybe we will follow suit eventually, but I think Japan is still a long way from doing that at present."

"Do you usually just give patients medication, or do you also think it's important to give them some advice about their daily lives?"

"Medication alone won't do. Unfortunately in Japan we have so few specialists in psychological and psychosomatic problems that it's difficult to know what to do. Also it's almost impossible for a gynecologist to get a husband to come in to talk about his wife's problems. He usually thinks it's all in his wife's head. Even if he does come he's usually uncooperative and ends up saying, 'Well doctor, I'll leave it up to you, you take care of it. She won't die of it will she?'

"Sometimes a patient will go home and tell the family I've said she needs a rest and so on, and then the next thing I know is mother-in-law comes in, mad at me, so I have to be very careful about what kind of advice I give about human relations. There are some women who want to depend on the doctor to say what they can't say to their mothers-in-law directly; they think it's safe to say anything if it's reported as 'doctor's advice.' It's a delicate point! It's tempting to just talk about the autonomic nervous system and not say anything else. Actually with our less than perfect knowledge I usually think it's best not to intrude too much into the patient's life. A doctor may think he's helping when he's actually making things worse. So usually in Japan we keep a certain distance from our patients, for instance if a woman is having a problem with her mother-in-law, I'm not the one who should tell her what to do. She has a husband who must understand her better than I do, so I tell her to consult with him. However, if what her mother-in-law is doing is really making her illness worse, I offer to speak as a doctor about it to *obāsan*. Or if her husband, who should be helping her, is actually doing something stupid, I tell her to bring him in, and I'll tell him that what he's doing is bad for his wife's health. However, I can't tell a patient how each person in her household should behave, and sometimes some women seem to want that.

"Actually I've seen quite a few jealous mothers-in-law lately. They come in here to give me advice. I usually end up saying, 'I don't mind talking to you but first of all I want to talk to my patient's husband.' Then I tell the husband he shouldn't let his mother interfere in a matter that basically concerns him and his wife. Of course this is usually with younger patients, in their twenties and thirties. It's usually over an abortion or a miscarriage that the trouble starts. Anyway, it's very time-consuming entering into the family lives of patients, and on the whole it's better to respect their privacy and keep at a distance."

Dr. Satō has been in practice as a gynecologist for twenty-two years. He lives and works in an Osaka suburb:

"As you well know, the social conditions in Japan create family problems that are very difficult to solve, particularly between the mother-in-law and daughter-in-law. In some cases it might be better for the daughter-in-law to just pack up and leave, but usually she doesn't have the economic freedom to do so. So one kind of solution—the one we usually use in Japan—is for the person with less rank to learn how to forgive the other person with higher rank, to be grateful for the protection and other things they've received. Often if a daughter-in-law finally accepts the situation her symptoms go away."

"It seems unfair to me, an outsider, that it's always the young wife, the daughter-in-law, who's counseled to be understanding and suppress her feelings. That doesn't really change anything, does it? Usually the married couple still don't learn how to talk to each other, the husband just says to his wife, 'Don't make waves' and the wife receives professional counseling that essentially tells her the same thing. I don't think an accepting heart is enough."

"Neither do I. But this question is rooted in the social conditions of Japan and there's not much a single doctor can do about it. You can't try to start a revolution out of a doctor's office—that would only create more unhappiness, I think.

"So what I try to do is to explain about the physical side of *kōnenki* properly to the patient." Dr. Satō went to his bookshelf. "This book has good diagrams, and then we talk about various medications and what they do and what the side reactions might be. Most patients worry a lot that hormones will give them stomach problems or cancer.

"Until recently doctors had their hands full with births, operations, and abortions, they had no time or need to concentrate on *kōnenki*, but now gynecologists have to start thinking about middle-aged women, otherwise they will end up with no patients. But we're not good at these things. Japanese gynecologists have always been good surgeons, but in areas where psychology overlaps with gynecology our knowledge is very limited."

"I gather that you prescribe hormone replacement therapy for some patients?"

"Yes, but the doses we use here are much smaller than in the United States. That's mostly because doctors are afraid of side effects I think. But there may be some physiological differences involved as well, so that what is suitable for Americans may not be right for Japanese. Usually I just use low doses of estriol. I don't use progesterone much at all."

"What kind of symptoms does it counter?"

"Oh, headaches, ringing in the ears, shoulder stiffness, sudden heat, they're all related to the autonomic nervous system."

"These are all symptoms of *kōnenki*?"

"Yes, they're all related."

"Do you ever use herbal medicine?"

"Oh, yes, quite a bit."

"Is it effective?"

"Well, that's hard to judge accurately, in what way and to what extent it works, but the women who keep coming back for it think it is helping them—they say it stops hot flashes and so on. I use it along with hormones, although some women say they want only herbal medicine, because they're afraid of what hormones might do to them."

"Do you think that almost everyone experiences *kōnenki shōgai*?"

"Not necessarily. Women who are busy, who don't have much leisure, don't have many complaints. *Kōnenki shōgai* is a sort of 'luxury disease' [*zeitakubyō*], it's 'high-class.' Women with lots of free time on their hands are the ones who say it's so bad. Of course they have more time than the others to visit doctors, but they also have more time to notice their complaints, the number of symptoms they have is much greater than with busier women. Women who go out a lot, who have lots of hobbies and friends don't have so many symptoms. The ones who have trouble are those who concentrate unduly on their own bodies and those who have poor 'communication' with their husbands."

"So distress at *kōnenki* is really a social problem, is it? Do you think then that society needs to make some changes?"

"Well, that would be a very hard thing to do. When I treat these women with lots of free time I try not to just use drugs, but to help them forget their complaints, to divert their *ki* [*ki o magirasu*]. I encourage them to do things they like: handicrafts, knitting, reading, writing a novel . . . I want to make them really concentrate on something. It takes time, but a hobby is a way of taking their mind off their symptoms."

"But I suppose that if you don't prescribe medicine you can't make a reasonable living."

"Unfortunately you're right, if I don't give them medicine I don't get paid very much at all!"

"Do you try to help out with marital relationships too?"

"Yes, I think gynecologists have to do sex counseling, but it's very difficult to get middle-aged husbands to come in and visit us. It's not just problems with 'communication' of course, it may be to do with the children: leaving home or getting a job or getting married."

"What about nursing the elderly—isn't this a strain sometimes?"

"Yes, that too, but most women are ready for that difficulty, they're well prepared for it ahead of time."

"I have a question about abortion. Many middle-aged Japanese women have had one or more abortions, and some gynecologists have told me that the guilt women feel may make *kōnenki* harder for them."

"Yes, not just guilt, the abrupt ending of a pregnancy disrupts the ovarian cycle and if that's repeated several times that could cause trouble.

"You know, what started allowing abortions in Japan was the American occupation because the country was in such bad shape after the war that a rapid increase in population would have been disastrous. Japan would never have made economic progress if we hadn't legalized abortion, so in a sense, women were sacrificed for the good of the country."

"What do you think about *mizuko kuyō* [a religious service for aborted fetuses]?"

"Well, if it can help compensate for the woman's feelings of guilt or regret, it's a good thing, don't you think so? Our national organization of gynecologists holds a *mizuko kuyō* ceremony once a year in Tokyo. About twenty or thirty doctors, representatives from their area, attend the service. After all, not only the patients but we doctors are participating in ending life and it's only right that we have some kind of memorial service on behalf of those who've been sacrificed for us [*gisei o haratte itadaita*]. Of course no one is anxious to do abortions, we have to because patients ask us, but no one really wants to."

"But why has Japan been slow to make use of the full range of contraceptive devices?"

Some hesitation. "Hmmm . . . In Japan the condom is widespread, but unfortunately there are a good number of failures with the condom. And women aren't usually conscientious enough to go to a doctor to get an IUD. I think they're rather scared of it."

"How about the pill?"

"Well, the pill hasn't been approved by the Welfare Ministry for sale as a contraceptive. It's only supposed to be used under the supervision of a doctor for menstrual irregularity. It's the problem of side effects again; I think that Japan is the strictest country in the world about that."

"How about the diaphragm?"

"It's not used much at all. How about in the West, are women comfortable about putting it in for themselves?"

"I don't think that's much of a problem in North America."

"Well I think Japanese women don't like it because it means they have to take too active a role. And as for sterilization, women seem to fear that if their husbands are sterilized it will encourage them to have extramarital affairs, so they often say, 'Sterilize me, not him,' even though I tell them that male sterilization is much easier and has fewer dangers attached to it."

Resisting the Medicalization of Kōnenki

Pharmaceutical companies are as aggressive in marketing their wares in Japan as they are in North America—if anything, they do even more conspicuous wooing of physicians to buy their products. I was once sitting in the back of a taxi with two doctors after leaving a formal reception held in conjunction with a conference, to go on to what is euphemistically called "the second gathering" (which inevitably takes place in a bar), when a group of drug company representatives advanced on us and hurled money and name cards through the open window of the taxi. Japanese doctors see drug company salesmen in their offices nearly every day and as a result have colorful pamphlets and free samples of new medications lying about in abundance. However, despite a well-oiled promotion machine, and a high consumption of drugs by the Japanese population, in 1988 hormones of all kinds made up only 2.1 percent of the drugs that were produced in Japan, a figure that dropped 0.3 percent below that for 1987, and ranked fifteenth in total production (*Pharma Japan* 1990)—a long way behind the United States, and also behind the 2.3 percent figure for herbal medications (Japan Pharmaceutical Manufacturer's Association 1990).

The cultural resistance to thinking of *kōnenki* as a state that should be systematically medicated—a theme evident in the interviews with women—apparently extends not only to many physicians, as the narratives cited above indicate, but also perhaps to the pharmaceutical industry and its sales representatives. One important overriding factor against the use of hormone replacement therapy is the inevitable contradiction of banning the contraceptive pill except as a prescribed medication and at the same time promoting the routine use of hormone replacement therapy (made from essentially the same chemical ingredients as the pill).[11] Until *kōnenki* is widely recognized as a medical condition therefore, only a mild short-term dosage is likely, to assist women through a trying year or two. If and when the pill is recognized as safe and marketed as a contraceptive device, attitudes toward hormone replacement therapy may also start to change. Even so, I would predict, many women will still resist, and probably also a good number of physicians (herbalists in particular) who are extremely sensitive to possible iatrogenic effects.

In the prologue I pointed out that the medical profession in North America and Europe has increasingly conceptualized menopause as a deficiency disease, one that may not only produce uncomfortable symptoms around the time of the end of menstruation but also trigger a woman's general decline and increased propensity for various major diseases in later life. This classification largely accounts for the aggressive medicalization of menopause together with the promotion of hormone replacement therapy today. However, most physicians who take this position insist that the only bona fide symptoms of menopause itself are those directly attributable to declining estrogen levels (Lock 1985, 128), namely "vasomotor and atrophic changes"; they designate all other symptoms, including depression, headaches, and psychosomatic complaints, as incidental to the process and not as direct results of the "disease." Closure of female reproduction thus includes only the bare facts of endocrinology and in theory thrusts aside psychological and social variables together with moralizing narratives. According to this approach, medicalization need not go beyond the prescription of medication; technology provides the breakthrough to master the female body and the chemical control to diminish the effects of aging processes. Under the disease model, because menopause is a universal event, every woman is vulnerable to estrogen deficiency and hence, in theory, every woman should be medicated.

Among the thirty Japanese doctors whom I interviewed, I found no one who agreed with this position. Their narratives make clear that on the whole they hold rather straightforward, relatively unself-conscious, moralistic ideas about just who is at risk for a difficult time at *kōnenki*. (I suspect that, despite the existence of a disease orientation toward menopause, many North American gynecologists hold similarly moralistic views but might hesitate to disclose them during an interview with a female anthropologist.) Furthermore, the majority continue to conceptualize *kōnenki* as a natural and inevitable part of the aging process, a difficult time only for certain vulnerable women and from which just about everyone will eventually return to a homeostatic balance—a process, therefore, that should avoid medication unless absolutely necessary.

The interviews with Japanese physicians occurred in 1983 and 1984, and at that time an aggressive marketing of hormone replacement therapy on a long-term basis had not yet taken place even in the West.[12] Since then a *kōnenki* society has formed in Japan that, by 1992, had nearly one thousand members who are well acquainted with the relevant professional literature produced in North America and Europe. Even so, my recent talks with several Japanese gynecologists indicate that very few, if any, have yet come to think of *kōnenki* as a disease-like state. A different physiological conceptualization accounts in part for this difference, but abiding fears about iatrogenesis are also present: when I recounted to one Japanese doctor how a Canadian gynecologist agreed that the use of unopposed estrogen therapy increased the risk for endometrial cancer but added that this should not cause undue alarm because regular monitoring could catch it early and easily deal with it through surgery, the Japanese doctor looked shocked. He reacted not so much at the idea of surgery (overall surgical rates are quite high in Japan) but at the apparently cavalier approach to cancer.

De-moralizing Kōnenki

At least one Japanese gynecologist, Dr. Igarashii, calls for more stringent guidelines for research into *kōnenki*. He finds fault with both professional and popular literature in Japan and insists that research establish a clear separation of those symptoms that occur at the end of menstruation because of "acute estrogen withdrawal," including the hot flash, from any psychological and psychosomatic symptoms that, he believes, are incidental to the central problem of estrogen deficiency. Dr. Igarashii states, moreover, that research should clearly distinguish general symptoms of aging from *kōnenki shōgai*, and that failure to do so thus far has led to considerable confusion in Japan. At the same time that he tries to produce some standardization and refinement to *kōnenki* research, Dr. Igarashii incidentally eliminates the space for a moralistic turn to the discourse by limiting *kōnenki* to biological change, in much the same way that his Western counterparts have done. However, he remains very concerned about long-term usage of estrogen therapy and makes a plea for the application of other types of noninvasive preventive medicine, and an increased effort by gynecologists to conduct research in this area (Igarashii 1987).

Dr. Sasaki, another gynecologist who is concerned about the medical management of *kōnenki*, is well known in Japan. She is the gynecologist who helped expose the scandal at one particular hospital where about one thousand patients underwent hysterectomies for no good medical reason (Sasaki 1986). She has also given public lectures and written several articles in which she makes a plea, as Dr. Igarashii does, for a more scientific approach to *kōnenki* (1985, 1988), but for very different reasons. She is concerned, as other women have been before her, that male gynecologists too often trivialize the biological changes associated with *kōnenki* and dismiss patients as being weak-willed and self-indulgent. She is emphatic that women should not be subjected to the myth that the experience of *kōnenki* depends simply on their attitude—on the way in which they manage their *ki*—and she has taken it on herself to campaign about this matter. However, for those women who seek help, she uses herbal therapy and only resorts to short-term use of hormones for a few patients.

A View from the Clinic

I found Watanabe-*san*, looking uncharacteristically tired for a Japanese woman of her age, tucked away in the corner of the examination room of a Kawasaki hospital. Her doctor had explained the purpose of my research to her and without any hesitation she agreed to talk to the foreign researcher. Like so many other women in this study, whether the conversation went on at home or in a medical setting, Watanabe-*san* was not a difficult subject to interview—quite the reverse; her lassitude melted away, and a lively, almost vivacious woman emerged. She took charge of the discussion from the outset and informed me that she had been coming regularly, for over three years, since the time she was forty-four, to have medical checkups and receive prescriptions of herbal medicine supplied by the gynecologist. I asked her what she thought caused the shoulder tension, irritability, and feelings of tiredness that had consistently been her chief complaints. She launched into a reply in which she spontaneously re-created what for her were the most significant aspects of her family history.

"I was happy when I was raising my children. I used to feel I had such a happy married life. But as my children grew older they started disobeying me. They went through bad rebellious periods. Also my husband doesn't like me to go out or to make friends, so I feel very irritated and have a lot of stress. He goes out himself, but he doesn't want *me* to. He has old-fashioned ideas. Both his mother and grandmother were born in the Meiji period. Although he wears Western clothing, he has feudalistic ways: he thinks his wife and children are nothing more than his belongings. We can't disobey him. Saying 'if' or 'but' means rebellion in his mind. If we follow what he says then he's nice to us, and so we always felt we had to, even when his ideas were wrong. But as the children grew older they started rebelling against their father and I began to think they were right, especially when they told him he was old-fashioned.

"It was about the time when the children started to rebel that our relationship as a married couple began to go wrong. Three or four years ago my husband had an affair. He wouldn't come home at all, and when he did show up he said his affair was because of our attitude—the children and me. I started having psychological problems, and eventually I went to a mental hospital for help. For a while after he began the affair I tried not to get upset, but when my younger son dropped out of high school I couldn't sleep or eat. Before this happened at least I could do the laundry and the shopping and clean the house—although sometimes I had to stay in bed all day. But after my son quit high school I became something like a *haijin* [someone who cannot function as a human being].

"When I saw my doctor he asked me if I'd ever thought about divorcing my husband—our marriage was that bad. The woman my husband was having an affair with is a housewife and her husband had been ill for a long time. She started to count on my husband for support. Since she's the type of woman who depends on her man completely, my husband tried to do his best. He introduced her to all his brothers and sisters, and she introduced my husband to hers. They were planning to live together once the children grew up. I was tortured by them, and sometimes I cried all night long and often had lots of spots and pimples break out all over my face. And of course I was left with all the responsibility for the children—they got into fights and were very rebellious and the police called me up sometimes. I asked my husband to help, but he was too involved with his girlfriend, and he just said the children would grow out of this eventually. He even told his friends he detested me because I had so many spots on my face.

"But recently he broke up with his lover—he was probably mentally exhausted. He came back one night and said, 'Let's make up and try and be as close as we used to be.' But I don't really want to make up with him. I'd rather live by myself once the children become independent—I don't really want to see him or speak to him. Once I realized I can manage without him, I started to feel relieved and even cheerful sometimes. I told myself that keeping my health was important and that I had to make friends, so now I go out with a lot of people. But he still doesn't like me to do that, and he claims we can't build up our relationship again unless I stop going out so much. But I tell him 'No.' At last I've found the courage to do that; I don't trust him anymore because of what he's done to me."

"But is he living with you now?"

"Yes. I've told him I may learn to trust him again if we keep living together. I don't like divorce, it's not good for the children. If we wait for a few years my feelings may change, but for now he must think of me as his housekeeper and not his wife. When our children finally become independent I may choose to live alone or to live with him, I haven't decided, so I've asked him to wait. Since we lived together happily for twenty years then maybe something can be repaired. My husband says he's not interested in having an affair with another woman at all. But right now I can't even drink out of the cup he's used for his coffee. I don't want to see his face. I feel a bit sorry for him now though . . . He's exhausted, and very thin, and he's got an ulcer. He's obviously suffered too, he really loved that woman and her children. He'd walk out in public with them as though they were his own family. You know, at first he said he didn't want to have any children with me, and then when we had them he said it was a mistake. That really hurt me. So after this kind of experience I can't make up that easily.

"I think many Japanese men think just the same way as my husband. They think they can have lovers and as soon as they break up with them their wives will be waiting to pick up the pieces. He probably thinks now I'm just being stubborn, he doesn't understand what he's done to me, not at all."

"How old are your children now?"

"They're seventeen and nineteen and both working. The older child went to a cooking school and now he's a chef and my younger son is also working as a cook in a coffee shop, but he's changed his job many times. If his boss tells him to shape up when he makes mistakes he just quits. He used to be pretty awful, but now finally I can have a normal conversation with him. We can sit beside each other and watch TV together—it's quite a change from before when he was so violent in school. I used to live in fear about what might happen; life was like a nightmare when all that was happening."

"What about your in-laws, did they live with you?"

"My mother-in-law lived with us for many years. She was in and out of the hospital, but I took care of her when she was at home. Of course it was my duty because my husband is the oldest son. My sister-in-law could have helped out sometimes, though, but she never offered once. When *obāsan* had a stroke our children were still using diapers. I had to use diapers on her too—ten at a time. It was before disposable diapers were cheap, so I had to wash a mountain of them every day. I finally collapsed from exhaustion. My mother-in-law said I was weak—not nearly as strong as my mother must have been. Everybody was so cold to me, but I told myself it was my job to take care of everybody in this house I'd married into; I didn't give up. I finally went to the welfare office and found an opening for *obāsan* in a nursing home and she eventually died there. It put quite a strain on our finances for a long time, and that didn't please my husband either."

"Did your husband agree she should go to the nursing home?"

"Oh yes, I could never have sent her there without his permission. He didn't like living with her, even though she was his mother. It was because of her nagging—and she was so sneaky too. During the day when she wanted things she'd tell me what a good daughter-in-law I was, but when my husband came home she'd call him into her room and say with tears in her eyes that I was abusing her. She would tell him she'd rather die than be abused by me, and she called her daughters to tell them she wanted to jump into the river and commit suicide. I finally had a nervous breakdown, but I couldn't escape the situation . . . My body was tired out—like a rag."

"Did you have anyone to talk to at that time?"

"No, no one. My mother is dead. I have a few friends but I couldn't get out of the house, and I couldn't talk on the phone because she was always listening. Anyway, it's very embarrassing to disclose all these awful things to people—I always felt somehow it was my fault, and I should just try harder. Eventually I had to see a psychiatrist. My husband was very discreet about his affair before his mother died, because he needed my goodwill so I'd keep taking care of her. After she died though he came right out in the open and disappeared for days on end. My older son told me to divorce him, but I wasn't sure we could survive financially. My husband only gave us half his salary—the rest went to his other family."

"It really does sound like Meiji Japan. She was like a concubine, wasn't she?"

"Yes. I had to take money out of our old-age savings plan to survive, and I kept thinking about divorce. I talked to friends who are divorced and they all said they regretted it, that it'd be better to stick it out. They said their children kept saying they wanted to have their father back in the house, and then demanded to know why their mother hadn't tried a bit harder. It seems the kids were getting teased at school because their parents were divorced.

"My husband abused me physically too. When he couldn't see his woman he used me for his sexual needs two or three times a week. In the beginning I accepted this because I was hoping he'd come back, but after a while I couldn't stand it anymore. But if he wanted sex he forced me no matter how hard I resisted—it was terrible. I often wished I could die rather than go through that, and I told him so. I'd be in tears saying I didn't want any sex, that I'd rather die. He gave up eventually. Now I notice once in a while he's very frustrated at night but I pretend I'm asleep. I really don't like him as a sexual partner, but he doesn't want to accept this. Anyway, I'm living with him on the condition that he doesn't touch me."

Up to this point Watanabe-*san* had poured her story out in a flat monotone. It was as though she had been over the recital many times before, in order perhaps to desensitize herself to the pain. She did not cry, and an onlooker who did not actually hear her narrative but simply watched her might not discern that she was angry or even upset. But now she paused, hesitated for the first time, and set off on a different tack:

"I have lots of friends now, and some of them are men . . ." Another pause. "I'm not involved with them sexually, but my husband doesn't believe this. I sometimes go to museums or art galleries and I'm not going to stop that, that's mostly why I feel so well now and more or less recovered from the bitter experiences. I looked like a skeleton for a while—I lost ten kilos."

"How did you meet your new friends?"

"I started to do some part-time work to take my mind off things, the psychiatrist recommended that for me. I talked to a woman I got to know at work who'd been through the same kind of experience but was divorced. She introduced me to a lot of other women in a similar position and we'd get together and gossip and bad-mouth our husbands and men in general, and I felt really good afterward! It seemed to give me some energy to keep going, but I still used to get very depressed. One of these women introduced me to a man. She said he was really nice and I didn't have anything to be worried about. He took me to an art exhibition and plum blossom viewing, and sometimes he'd telephone me. If I said I was feeling depressed he'd usually say, 'Let's go for a drink.'

"I also have two good friends from high school days and I tried to talk to them about my problems, but they simply didn't understand. They just sat there and said, 'Oh that must be hard.' Or, 'You must keep sticking it out.' I felt such a relief when I finally talked to people in the same situation as me, their advice was so different from my married friends'.

"Of course my husband still doesn't like me going out, especially not in the evenings, and since my friends have full-time jobs that's when I usually go. My older son thinks it's all right, but my younger son is a bit suspicious, and when I tell him not to come back so late at night he says I've no right to tell him what to do.

"I became interested in mah-jongg recently and sometimes I play until about three in the morning and then I stay at my girlfriend's house. My husband is very concerned about that. He used to tell me to have affairs when he was busy with his lover, but now he's afraid I'll disappear suddenly. He says I'm the type of person who'll be very involved once I find a lover . . .

"I used to be very obedient when I was young. I was innocent when I married him. I always kept my opinions to myself and tried to fit in with my husband's wishes. That's what I'd been raised to do, like all Japanese women. He wouldn't even let me go out for tea or to a movie when we first got married. I was only allowed out for meetings at the school, but even then I couldn't go on to dinner with the other parents. Sometimes he used to call home during the day, and if he didn't get any answer when he got home at night he'd want to know exactly where I'd been. I wasn't even supposed to go to a coffee shop with my girlfriend, he said if I wanted to do that kind of thing he'd take me himself. So I had no freedom at all when I was younger.

"I took care of a friend's baby a few years ago to make a little extra money. It was a good arrangement because it cheered *obāsan* up quite a bit and I felt I was doing something useful in life that way, but I had to give that up when my son started to get violent in school and my husband didn't come home. I was always so irritated and worried I was in no shape to take care of a baby."

"Have you told all this to Dr. Sonoda?"

"No. He's so busy, and anyway he's never asked me."

"But do you think that all this stress has affected your physical health?"

"Oh yes. I'm in *kōnenki* now, and the shoulder tension is so bad that I have to come for medicine. That's why I'm here today. But I'm not so irritable as I was before, and I can sleep at nights now."

"Do you think it would help the doctor in treating you if he knew about your family life?"

"No, not really . . . do you? He gives me herbal medicine that works for the pain, and for my poor mental state, but he can't help with my husband or my children can he? I'm very satisfied with Dr. Sonoda, that's why I keep coming here."

Most patients, not surprisingly, give much more mundane accounts of their recent lives than did Watanabe-*san*, and many of them, because they are in a medical setting, tend to focus on their physical state. Honda-*san* is fifty-two years old, a dental hygienist who lives and works in Tokyo. When asked what had brought her to the doctor, an internist, she said that she had recently had a feeling of pain in her lower abdomen and wasn't sleeping well but couldn't think of any particular stress that might be causing it.

"I tried to deal with it by putting more variety into my life—I've been acting as a volunteer in a mental hospital on my day off, but the pain doesn't go away so I decided to come and see Dr. Akeda today."

"How long have you been coming here?"

"For about eleven years, only when I have a problem, of course. I remember how it cheered me up when I first met Dr. Akeda and he leaned forward and slapped me on the thigh and said, 'You have to keep your spirits up' [*jibun de ki o shikkari motanakata*]. Since that time I've always tried to come on his day in the clinic."

"Have you always worked?"

"Ever since my child was in sixth grade. I'm very satisfied with my job, it's what gives meaning to my life, and I get on very well with the dentist who's my boss."

"So you don't think that your daily life is having a bad effect on your health?"

"Not really. I'm quite satisfied with my life, so I try to tell myself that this problem is just to do with my body. I'm an optimistic type so that's good, but I'm also quite high-strung [*shinkei shitsu*] so maybe that has something to do with it—maybe that affects my health a bit."

"Do you think that your present problem has anything to do with *kōnenki*?"

"Well, some people tell me it does. I'm not sure. My periods ended three or four years ago, and for a while I'd sometimes feel suddenly hot, starting with my back, and find myself sweating, and then feel cold. Also I was a bit bothered with palpitations around that time. Lately it's disappeared however.

"I once asked Dr. Akeda about it, and he said, 'Oh, that's just *kōnenki shōgai*, almost all women experience something, but they manage their lives just as usual. If you really can't stand it, come and see me, but just try telling yourself first of all that everyone else is going through the same thing.' That seemed to help me, and before I knew it the symptoms had disappeared."

"Do you think that you're through *kōnenki* now?"

"Well, I haven't felt hot for a long time. I sometimes still have shoulder stiffness or palpitations, but not enough to even mention it. But this latest pain, and the sleeplessness . . . Well, maybe I'm not all through after all."

At the same hospital I was introduced to Yokoi-*san*, a fifty-one-year-old thin and faded-looking woman who spoke so quietly that I could hardly hear her but who nevertheless talked in an unabated stream of consciousness once she realized that I was intent on listening to what she had to say. We sat in a cubicle that normally serves as a patient examination room, and, as is customary in all but the newest of Japanese hospitals, it afforded no real privacy. The cubicle walls reached neither to the floor nor to the ceiling, so that people in the next cubicles could overhear everything. I asked Yokoi-*san* if she would like to go somewhere more private, but she preferred to stay where she was. She seemed less troubled by the lack of privacy than I was and simply lowered her voice to little more than a murmur, making our exchange rather conspiratorial in its form.

"I first started having dizziness the year before last, and I went to an internist who gave me some medicine for it. It didn't seem to really get better though, and a nurse I know told me it was *kōnenki* and said I should go to a gynecologist. So I did, and he said it was my autonomic nervous system. He gave me some medicine and told me to come back if it got worse. Then, when it didn't get better, he introduced me to an ear, nose, and throat doctor who did some tests, then gave me some medicine. Then this year, in March, it got really bad and the doctor suggested I should check into the hospital, but I didn't want to do that, so he gave me a shot, and four kinds of medicine. Apparently one of the arteries in my head is plugged up and the circulation is poor—I think maybe because I often had ear infections as a child. Anyway, it's been better lately and I'm down to two medicines.

"But then my shoulders started to get really stiff, and my chest was feeling bad—not exactly hurting but feeling sort of uncomfortable." Yokoi-*san* covered her face with her hand and giggled at herself. "I told Dr. Akeda as a joke, 'I don't need to keep anything from the chest up, I'm not too smart anyway, so just remove the whole lot will you?' Anyway, he added another medicine for shoulder stiffness, and it helped a lot.

"Then, besides all that I often feel tired. I live alone—my children are grown up, the youngest one is married, the eldest one lives on his own, and my husband went off quite a few years ago. It's boring just to sit and watch TV, so I usually go over to my aunt's place and help with her store, it takes my mind off my troubles. Oh, yes, and I also have some constipation."

"Do you think all these symptoms are related to *kōnenki*?"

"Well, I think it's mostly because of my diet—living alone it's sometimes too much trouble to cook. I was divorced about four years ago, but even before that I didn't eat properly. I always had trouble while I lived with my husband. It was a mistake to marry him. He was very lazy, and even when he worked he never gave me enough money for the household, so I had to work very hard to raise the children. People used to tell me I should leave him, but I knew he'd never give me any child support, and I thought that would make it even harder on the children, so I wanted to wait until they were older."

"Do you have a job now?"

"Yes, I work about twenty days a month in a factory and my aunt pays me a little when I work in the store. That's enough. But I must save because I don't want to depend on my children when I get older, and I'll only get a very small pension."

"Do you have friends to talk to?"

"Yes, men and women. My aunt and uncle encourage me to make lots of friends and to go out and have a good time. My uncle says he's willing to help me find someone to marry. And Dr. Akeda is so nice. He always listens to everything I tell him. At my age I'm sort of embarrassed to be talking about myself so much, but he tells me not to worry about that.

"My husband's parents were very nice. They lived about an hour away from my family when I was growing up. My father died when I was a child, and my mother and brother thought it would surely be all right to marry a man with such nice parents, but I found out nice parents don't necessarily make nice children. He never held a job for very long. He was on tranquilizers, and I think he had some kind of mental illness. After a while he only came home once a week or so, and then he'd only leave me a little bit of money. I had a terrible time with his creditors, they kept coming after me for payments even after we were divorced. Unfortunately my older son seems to take after him—I really worry about that."

"So—do you think you'll get better if you look after yourself and cook good meals?"

"Dr. Akeda says that's what I must do. I'm trying, but I don't have any interest in food, so I usually don't bother to eat dinner."

Later Dr. Akeda commented that Yokoi-*san* is very typical of the middle-aged women he sees in his general clinic situated close to a rather poor neighborhood:

"Most doctors find patients like her very frustrating. But I like to chat with them and hear all about their family life. She's had a very hard time, so I try to keep her spirits up. I'm giving her very mild doses of medicine, mostly herbal medicine, and I'd like to gradually get her off it altogether."

"Do you think her symptoms are related to *kōnenki*?"

"That's part of it, but I wouldn't put it all down to that. She's not very strong physically. Her health probably suffered a lot as a child in the war, so she's living with a poor legacy, and *kōnenki* is bound to be a difficult time, especially because she lives by herself. Actually the future probably isn't too bright for her, I'm afraid."

"Are you giving her any hormone therapy?"

"No. She doesn't have hot flashes or anything like that."

Some patients whom I talked to stated emphatically that they preferred a female gynecologist. Teshima-*san*, a fifty-three-year-old nurse who works at a hospital where I had given some lectures, was one of them. She was also one of the few people I met who had been seeing a gynecologist on a regular basis over the years.

"You've had the same gynecologist for many years now, so you must be satisfied with her?"

"I've never had an internal examination from any other doctor, and I guess I really trust her. I wouldn't want to go to another doctor, especially not a man."

"You said that you're taking medication these days."

"Yes. I first noticed something a bit strange when I had sex with my husband, not pain exactly, but something different from before. So I went to the doctor and she said it was because of *kōnenki*, that my hormone level had suddenly dropped, and that my vagina was shrinking. I'd never thought of going to a doctor for *kōnenki*; you know, in Japan people my age just think it's a natural thing. But the doctor said that it's hard if the change comes very abruptly and suggested that it might be better to take some medicine to slow things down. She said there was no need to suffer silently, it was better to take medicine: 'Just like taking sleeping pills if you can't sleep,' she said. So I thought I'd try it and she gave me a shot right away. Well, that very afternoon I started to feel better. Before that I'd been noticing that when I talked I started to get excited and irritable, but after the shot I felt much calmer.

"Since then I've been having the shots on average about once a month. I don't go to the doctor regularly, just when I start feeling irritable; sometimes I still feel like screaming, and then I go right away and get a shot."

"Do you know what kind of shots they are?"

"They're the same combination as in birth control pills: estrogen and progesterone. I have some pills to take too, but the doctor said I don't need to take them unless I feel like it."

"Are you worried about side effects from the medicine?"

"Well, I don't feel anything so far. Of course, since the medicine is like birth control pills, at first it caused bleeding like menstruation. But now I only have a little spotting, I think the dose has been reduced, but I'm not too worried."

"Did the doctor explain anything to you about side effects?"

"No, she just said I'd get some bleeding."

"Some Japanese women seem to be really concerned about taking hormone pills, but you don't feel that way?"

"Well, a little. But I trust the doctor, and it's only a mild dose."

"Did she give you any advice about your life-style?"

"No, she's a very busy doctor. But I promised myself when I turned fifty that I'd have a change of pace and that's what I did. We don't have any children and my in-laws died a long time ago. My husband and I have been married twenty-five years and we understand each other very well, so I don't really have any difficulties at all, but still I thought it was important to make some changes. Anyway, I've started to do more exercise, some horseback riding, and some swimming. I've found that it makes me feel better—much less irritable."

"Do you expect to keep up the shots for a long time?"

"Oh, I don't suppose so. Just until I'm really clear of *kōnenki*. I don't think of what I have as an illness, or even *kōnenki shōgai*. It's just an occurrence [*genshō*], and when I just can't stand it any longer I go for a shot. I'm not really taking the medicine on a regular basis at all, just when I can't cope. I don't like myself when I can't suppress my feelings and lately I sometimes feel like shouting back at people. Until now I could always control my feelings and I didn't let anything bother me, but I feel more irritable these days. You know, it used to be that people thought *kōnenki* was something you should just go through naturally, and that only women who were crybabies went for treatment. But the doctor told me I shouldn't worry about what other people think; she said, 'If it makes you feel better, that's what counts.' "

I wanted to meet Teshima-*san's* gynecologist, especially since I had heard about her from several different women who had described her as someone whom they trusted. I wrote to her and explained the purpose of my research, enclosing the customary name card, and said that I would like to spend about thirty minutes talking to her if she had time. When I telephoned later to try to set up an appointment she declined in a peremptory manner. She was the only medical professional during the entire course of the research who chose not to make time for me. Maybe I caught her on an especially busy day.

Hori-*san* is forty-nine, a housewife whose older child is married. She lives with her husband and a second child, a first-year college student. I was introduced to her by a common friend as someone who was seeing an internist in connection with *kōnenki*. Perhaps because we met in a coffee shop and not in a medical setting, she chose to elaborate on her family difficulties, and the physical symptoms that I had expected to hear about receded into the background:

"My husband works as the manager of a division of a large electrical appliance firm. He was relocated once to Hokkaido when the children were small and we all went along, for four years. After that we came back to Kyoto and I thought he might not be relocated again, but then he was sent to northern Kyushu on his fiftieth birthday, more than three years ago. Of course he comes home now and again, once every two months or so for a weekend. Before he went, we thought about it for a long time, and we all went for a trip to Kyushu to see if the family could move there, but it just wasn't possible."

"The company didn't provide any housing, I suppose."

"Oh no, of course not. Just dormitory accommodation for my husband. They certainly didn't expect us all to move. It just got too complicated. As you know, people can't sell and buy houses easily in Japan, they don't even sublet them very often. But the biggest reason was the education of our younger child who made it clear that he didn't want to move and face working his way into a new group of classmates, because he was sure he'd be teased and bullied. We felt that his studies would probably suffer, so in the end he and I stayed here. Several of my neighbors had been living without their husbands for a year or more and they said I'd soon get used to it. A couple of them even said I'd find out life was really better without a husband anyway, but I knew I wouldn't feel that way."

"And then you started to get sick?"

"Yes, just a month after he'd gone I developed asthma and terrible headaches. I was bored and lonely, so I thought the symptoms were probably due to my mental state. I decided to get out of the house and do something instead of sitting about moping, and so I started taking part in some local activities to clean up the environment. Before long I had a phone call from my husband in Kyushu. He was quite apologetic, but he said his boss had talked to him and asked him to tell me to stop what I was doing because they thought it didn't reflect well on the company. So I had to stop. And of course the headaches came back. So I went to an internist and he said it was *kōnenki*."

"Did he ask you about your living conditions?"

"Yes. He knows that my husband is away. He joked with me and said: 'Remember the old saying, *teishu wa jōbu de rusu ga yoi* [it's good to have a husband who is healthy and absent]?' I tried to laugh, but it didn't seem very funny. The doctor really is sympathetic, and he gives me medicine that helps a bit. But what can he do?"

Kōnenki—An Enduring Concept

In all I interviewed only eighteen women who were seeing a doctor about *kōnenki*, and so their experiences and opinions are not necessarily representative of clinical encounters. Nevertheless, some themes emerge consistently from these interviews, with both doctors and their patients, that have a bearing on the form that medicalization of midlife takes in Japan.

Physicians' discourse about *kōnenki* is, not surprisingly, replete with contradictions. A similar picture emerged when I interviewed Canadian physicians in 1983: there were differences of opinion, not simply about the relevance of social and psychological factors to the experience of menopause, but also about the so-called hard data, physical changes at menopause and associated symptoms (Lock 1985). If anything, Japanese physicians exhibit less variation in opinion than do Canadians. Probably one of the most important reasons for the lack of consistency in explanations about the physical processes associated with the end of menstruation, whether in North America or Japan, is that menopause ranks low as a research priority and also takes up few teaching hours in medical schools and during internships and residencies. Japan is particularly deficient in this respect; among the physicians I interviewed none could recall being taught anything of consequence about either menopause or *kōnenki* during their medical training. This situation, combined with confused and sketchy research, means that clinicians are in essence free to create their own approach to something as amorphous as *kōnenki shōgai*, most particularly because it is not life-threatening, or even a diagnosis that a large number of clinicians, patients, or their husbands take very seriously.

The sociologist Freidson points out that the focus of clinical medicine "is on the practical solution of concrete problems" and is obliged to carry on even when it lacks a scientific foundation for its activities and thus "is oriented toward intervention irrespective of the existence of reliable knowledge" (1970, 172). He summarizes the "clinical mentality" as one in which "individualism is a dominant element in orientation and behavior. Each man builds up his own world of clinical experience and assumes personal, that is, virtually individual responsibility for the way he manages his cases in that world. The nature of that world is prone to be self-validating and self-confirming" (172). Moreover, when the case is a life-cycle transition, then clinicians bring to each clinical encounter their own culturally infused preconceived notions about what that transition represents morally, symbolically, socially, and politically. As physicians undertake to medicalize menopause and *kōnenki* respectively, some of them, in attempting to bring order and systematization to their work, deliberately strip away all but a few signs and symptoms as relevant, at least in their professional writing, and by so doing reduce a life-cycle transition to a biological process and even, in the minds of some, to a diseased event.

To date, rather few Japanese physicians engage in this process, and the dominant physicians' discourse, which they share with nearly all their patients, remains one in which *kōnenki* figures as a natural transition, one through which both men and women must pass, but during which, because of their biological makeup, women are thought to be more vulnerable than men to physical and emotional difficulties. Nevertheless, women are usually encouraged to visit a physician if only to obtain assurance that they do not have a serious disease. This done, it is assumed that most of them will ride over or endure this part of the life cycle without further assistance from their doctor. The majority of doctors also share with many women the belief that the leisured middle class is particularly sensitive to distress and prone to take up a doctor's time. A few clinicians, as we have seen, are very sympathetic about the burden of a double work load of employment and housework and its impact on health and for this reason do not accept the dominant stereotype about leisure and *kōnenki*.

With the exception of only one or two doctors, most individuals accept the idea that physical constitution and temperament influence *kōnenki* and believe that high-strung women are particularly vulnerable to a difficult time. There is also general agreement that in addition to personal vulnerabilities, distress may have social origins, and doctors and patients usually agree that there is little a doctor can do to change what they see as fundamental flaws in Japanese society, aside from a bit of temporary patching up by summoning wayward husbands and even mothers-in-law, time permitting, for a mild chiding. Whereas doctors may disagree about the relation of employment to *kōnenki* symptoms, they say unanimously that an unhappy family situation places women at risk for a difficult time. When they consider psychological support for their patients, most doctors feel they are poorly qualified and somewhat at a loss, although some of the older doctors spend quite a bit of energy telling the women they see to go home and endure things as best they can. In contrast, a very few doctors such as Dr. Sasaki take a stand against this moralizing position and openly encourage their patients to acknowledge that there is more to *kōnenki* than one's mental attitude and that women should not be ashamed to ask for help.

Usually doctors and their patients maintain a formal relationship even when they have known each other for a number of years, and particularly so in gynecology because of the "delicacy" (as one doctor put it) of the medical encounter. "We don't get too close to our patients," said Dr. Ikeno, and for this reason some patients appear to be a good deal more comfortable with female doctors and feel there is less reservation on both sides. But all physicians, male and female, together with their patients, express a fear of strong medication. So far hormone replacement therapy is used very conservatively, almost without exception as a temporary boost to the body in order to help it over a trying time. Even when longer-term medication is considered (as is increasingly the case), doses are usually kept to a minimum, and herbal medicine is very often preferred.

I have already suggested one important reason for resistance to the use of hormone replacement therapy: its similarity to the birth control pill and hence to what is considered to be undue exposure to possible cancer, hypertension, and heart disease. Another resistance comes, I believe, from a widespread attitude in Japan toward medication in general, namely that as light a dose as possible is best for all medical problems. This approach has been one of the fundamental tenets for the practice of herbal medicine for at least one thousand years and was practiced by the grandfathers of many of the physicians of today (Lock 1980a, 133).

Other physicians prefer to prescribe medication for the autonomic nervous system. This concept, used widely among both doctors and patients to explain distress in midlife, has, like *kōnenki*, been the subject of a good number of books and articles. Suzuki Shūji, although he recognizes that the term was first adopted from Germany at the end of the last century, suggests in one such book that it was not used as a diagnostic category in Japan until the 1960s. He believes that shortly after the production of several medications designed to act on the autonomic nervous system, advertisements and pamphlets put out by the pharmaceutical industry started to appear systematically in medical publications and only then did the concept become transformed into a diagnostic category. Dr. Suzuki thinks that the diagnosis became popular very quickly because it is a convenient label to gloss many vague symptoms and permits both doctor and patient to focus on somatic complaints and to avoid a discussion of more personal and familial matters (Suzuki 1982).

One further point that has contributed, I believe, to the relative lack of interest in promoting hormone replacement therapy in Japan needs to be added, and it relates to differences in the epidemiology of the so-called killer diseases. To date the research is not substantial, but there are strong indications that the incidence of osteoporosis among Japanese women (and Chinese women too) is less than half that of the Caucasian female population of North America, in spite of the fact that the bone mass of East Asian women is on average not so dense as that of Caucasian women (Ross et al. 1991). The image that comes most readily to the mind of a Japanese medical professional in connection with a bedridden and decrepit old lady is not one of someone who has a broken hip, but a victim of a major stroke. Until very recently it was a stroke (for both men and women) that doctors sought above all to prevent because this disease has been the greatest burden, both socially and economically. Campaigns involving changes in traditional dietary practices and systematic monitoring of blood pressure levels have been under way to reduce the incidence of cerebrovascular disease for a good number of years in Japan, with some success; one or two doctors now promote the use of hormone replacement therapy as a preventive measure against stroke (Koyama 1991). (Unlike in Japan, when research occasionally links dropping estrogen levels to an increased risk for stroke, North Americans give these data little attention but focus on osteoporosis and heart disease [Paganini-Hill et al. 1988].)

Not only are osteoporosis rates lower among Japanese women, but mortality from heart disease is about one-quarter that of North American women (these differences stem no doubt in part from diet). When we recall that life expectancy for Japanese women is the longest in the world, we understand why neither the government nor the medical profession in Japan has felt an urgent need to enter into the hormone therapy debate, at least not in its current North American form. All the more so because breast cancer rates, although on the increase, remain relatively low, and endometrial cancer, already reasonably low, has decreased recently; hence the question of risk associated with hormone therapy is not a major issue either.

Nevertheless, there are signs that this situation is changing. Gynecologists have recently been granted permission to carry out bone scans as part of their clinical practice, and, in a country where use of high-tech medicine is extensive provided it is noninvasive (Ikegami 1989a), this procedure is rapidly becoming routine in large hospitals. Moreover, the Japanese government is planning to undertake the first large-scale epidemiological studies on *kōnenki*. Japanese medicine is oriented toward prevention and primary care (Ikegami 1989b); together with the formation of the *Kōnenki* Society by interested gynecologists, this orientation ensures increasing pressure in the future to medicalize this part of the female life cycle.

There are also now many more opportunities for the public to educate itself about *kōnenki*. For example, *kōnenki* has been featured in the Japanese Women's Association newsletter, compiled largely from reprints of academic presentations given at conferences and symposia, and Dr. Sasaki, the politically active female gynecologist, has made several contributions. The articles in this newsletter are comprehensive and often quite technical but, as with almost all other publications of this type, emphasize self-help, self-responsibility, and preventive care through nutrition and exercise (Sasaki 1986, 1988). They thoroughly and systematically take apart the myth of *kōnenki* as a sickness of leisured, nervous, or uncontrolled women and note the special strain on working women (Kano 1988). In a recent publication is a thorough discussion of the effectiveness of herbal medicine against a wide range of *kōnenki* symptoms (Murata 1989).

Other women's groups have undertaken small surveys about women's health. One of the most comprehensive carried out by a research group based near Osaka documented changes in symptom reporting by age. Hot flashes appear well down on the symptom list among the forty- and fifty-year-olds, and shoulder stiffness, headaches, forgetfulness, and lumbago all occur more frequently (Takatsuki Josei Kenkyū Grūpu 1987).

Such research, together with that by several members of the medical profession, allows thoughtful readers to question the apparent discrepancy in symptom reporting between Japan and the West. Some commentators point out what they consider to be other relevant differences. Dr. Sasaki, herself very cautious about prescribing hormone replacement therapy, disapproves of what she takes as one North American motive for its use: to remain young and beautiful. She says emphatically that this is simply playing into a paternalistic and sexist image of women (Sasaki 1985, 128).

Entire books, chapters, and articles on menopause written originally for readers in Europe or North America add to the puzzle for Japanese readers. These books inevitably state that the hot flash is the most common symptom of menopause (Greenwood 1984). The Boston Women's Health Collective volume *Our Bodies Ourselves*, painstakingly translated into Japanese by a group of dedicated women, contains sections adapted to suit the Japanese situation, in particular those on childbirth and contraceptive use. The section on menopause, however, was translated verbatim from the English. Its text simply does not mesh with a Japanese understanding of *kōnenki* since it concentrates on hot flashes and hormone replacement therapy. In the rush to rationalize and disseminate the latest scientific information for women's political empowerment, even feminist writers in Japan usually assume that menopause and *kōnenki* are identical (Shokado 1988, 408).

Despite the presence of Western literature, few readers in Japan accept the idea of *kōnenki* as a state that demands medical care, although increasing numbers of women submit themselves to periodic checkups in order to establish that they have no serious pathology. No doubt the widespread interest in preventive medicine will encourage many to examine the possible advantages of long-term use of hormone replacement therapy, and there is some indication that this is indeed beginning to happen, particularly in urban areas. But the pace of medicalization so far remains slow and cautious.

If the younger generations no longer internalize an idea of the body as a microcosm in which a regulated daily life, order, and balance are essential for good physical health and social well-being—and if too the moralistic rhetoric associated with *kōnenki* slowly drops away, as appears to be happening right now—no doubt these changes will encourage more contact with physicians. Moreover, women born later than the *shōwa hitoketa* have not learned complete submission to the family; most have known economic prosperity all their lives, and many younger women respond to the cult of youth now paraded before them in the media (for example, recent articles about *kōnenki* in a very popular women's magazine were grouped under the title, "If we know the secrets of female hormones, we can become younger again, and more beautiful" [*Shufu no tomo* 1991]). If women come to understand their bodies as "private" possessions over which they have "individual rights," and if they listen to the argument that to be "successful" a woman must stay young and sexy, then they may be more eager than are the *shōwa hitoketa* to seek out medical assistance that meets their ends. A considerable change in attitudes toward the long-term use of medication necessarily precedes this scenario.

For their part and for a variety of reasons, as we have seen, Japanese physicians of the future may decide to promote the medicalization of *kōnenki*, particularly since most desire to maintain a scientific image in the eyes of the medical world at home and abroad. And drug companies may grow considerably more assertive about the marketing of hormone therapy. Until recently Japan has been unreceptive to foreign drug companies, but now several multinational companies are expanding their business there. If most of these changes take place, will Japanese women start to report more hot flashes? Only time can tell.

At present many thoughtful people struggle with a dilemma: to assert that Japanese women's experience at the end of menstruation is somewhat different from what the scientific literature accepts as normal is to follow implicitly the reactionary argument about the "uniqueness" of the Japanese race. And yet to follow without reservations behind current scientific authority on menopause is experientially—in a clinical and in a subjective sense—counterintuitive. In dealing with this paradox, several Japanese physicians I talked to insist that the reason for this discrepancy lies largely with the "backwardness" of Japanese women who will not visit doctors (Tokyo women are rapidly coming to their senses, they claim, but the rest of Japanese women remain in the dark ages and thus my research, which excluded Tokyo women, does not capture certain important developments).

But Japanese doctors cannot ignore the difference in epidemiology of diseases such as osteoporosis and heart disease between Japan and the West, and they do not deny that reporting of hot flashes is low; moreover, most think of *kōnenki* as a process and not an event. Thus, even should Japanese women start to visit gynecologists more consistently, I think the picture will remain significantly different from that in North America. While I am very sensitive to the political implications in Japan of arguments about local biology and alert also to the concerns of Japanese gynecologists that they not be thought of as old-fashioned and unscientific in their approach to *kōnenki* (which I do not believe is the case), I am equally aware of the dangerous assumptions present in arguments for menopause as a universal cloaked in the mantle of culture—as the remaining chapters of this book will show.

Invisible Messengers

1.

March   peach blossoms unfolding
May   wisteria all at once disheveled
September   the grapes are heavy on the trellis
November   green oranges begin to ripen.

Under the ground slow-witted messengers
pedal along, hats on the back of their heads.
They go from root to root delivering
the details of the season.

In peach and lemon trees all over the world—
in the fibers of every plant—
so many letters . . . so many instructions . . .
they get confused, especially in spring and autumn.

This must be the reason why events occur
at different moments in the north and south—
the right time for pea blossom to flower
or acorns to fall.

When autumn mornings are deepening
and I am plucking figs
I can see the veteran messengers
chiding the new ones for their clumsiness.

2.

March   rice cakes for the Doll's Festival
May   red flags and songs flowing through the town
September   a wary glance at rice fields and typhoons
November   so many wedding cups exchanged.

Above the ground are stateless post offices.
Invisible messengers are running diligently.
They go from person to person delivering
the details of the time.

In doors and windows all over the world—
in the days and nights of every race—
so many hints . . . so many warnings . . .
they get confused, especially in the aftermath of war.

This must be the reason why events occur
at different moments in the north and south—
the right time for a renaissance to flower
or revolutions to bear fruit.

When an unfamiliar year is dawning
and I close my eyes
I can see new flowers about to bloom
rooted in the past.

Ibaragi Noriko
(Reproduced with permission from Penguin Books Ltd.)

2

FROM DODGING TIME
TO DEFICIENCY DISEASE

11   The Making of Menopause

Although the subjective experience and interpretation of *kōnenki* vary among Japanese women, the term is a key concept in discussions of midlife in Japan and most probably every adult has some acquaintance with it. But if one asks, "Do you think that Western women have *kōnenki*?" the response is often equivocal. The majority agree that since all individuals grow old, obviously all experience something like *kōnenki*, but people often go on to indicate that in their opinion *kōnenki* may be special to Japan. Many suggested, for example, that Japanese alone experience shoulder stiffness. Others point out that relationships in the Japanese family are different from those in the Western family, and that this no doubt has an effect on *kōnenki*. A few suggest that Japanese women's physical or psychological dispositions are different from those of Western women.

I have never carried out the exercise in reverse but assume that if I asked typical North Americans if Japanese women go through menopause they would look at me quizzically and inform me in no uncertain terms that I had asked a dumb question—obviously menopause is a universal female experience. And yet, although every Japanese would no doubt agree that all women stop menstruating at some point during middle age, rather few would be willing, I believe, to postulate the existence of a universal experience. As we have seen, medical professionals in Japan use a technical jargon that resembles that of their counterparts in the West, apart from significant differences such as frequent reference to the autonomic nervous system—but the images they use when they talk about menopausal syndrome and menopausal women apply to *kōnenki* and not menopause as it is usually understood in North America. When pressed, they too agree that the Japanese experience is apparently not universal. But no one in Japan tries to push the argument further to suggest that perhaps Western

303

discourse about menopause is inaccurate or applicable only to a limited cultural milieu, although such would be the logical outcome of their position.

I suspect that if at this juncture North American readers examined their own convictions, even if they accept most of my arguments about *kōnenki* and Japanese middle age thus far, the majority would find they had not entertained the idea of *kōnenki* as a universal experience, most particularly one in which headaches and shoulder stiffness took precedence over hot flashes as significant symptoms. But I would suggest that when Japanese and North Americans agree that *kōnenki*, except in a very general sense of growing older, is not universal, their reasons for doing so differ. Most Japanese are comfortable with the idea of biological difference between populations; this is one important way to assert national identity, and a rather widespread belief exists in a shared genetic heritage, language, and culture as indicators of racial uniqueness. Hence the idea that the symptoms and experience of *kōnenki* are unique to middle-aged Japanese (women, and even men) is not very surprising. In fact *kōnenki* can fuel nationalistic arguments that set off Japan from Western nations where women are weak-willed and whine unnecessarily about trivial discomforts.

In contrast, even non-Japanese readers who are receptive to the idea that *kōnenki* exists in Japanese culture probably view it (along with a very few Japanese doctors) as anachronistic, a quaint survival, that no doubt will disappear before too long. In other words, we tend to assume that even though scientific facts about menopause are scarce, current research in North America and Europe and some of the growing body of clinical research in Japan are asking the "correct" questions and heading in the right direction, toward the identification of a universal menopausal experience. *Kōnenki*, modernists will say, simply represents a blind alley, a culturally driven digression that the Japanese, given their scientific astuteness, will soon abandon. The term *kōnenki* will perhaps gradually disappear from the medical vocabulary in Japan (yielding no doubt to a Japanese version of the English word menopause); at least one physician calls for rationalization of its management along lines much closer to North American practice. Some feminist activists also want to drop the term because of its negative associations, and so it may eventually pass from the Japanese language altogether.

Be this as it may, I want to turn the mirror around now and ask why, if we view *kōnenki* as a product of Japanese history and culture, we should not look on menopause as a product of the Euro-American cultural tradition, and why in this case the Japanese (and people from other cultural traditions) should contort their empirical knowledge and subjective experience to fit the mold of the Menopausal Woman?

Let us trace the invention of the Menopausal Woman in Europe and North America, her reduction to the menopause, and still more recent demotion to a deficiency disease and an endocrinopathy. These changes profoundly influence the way the medical profession and the public respond to female midlife.

The Ages of Man

After forty-five, even to three score, the age of man is called *maturitas*, maturity, full of ripenesse.

(Thomas Milles 1613)

[Women] for the most part are sooner perfected than man, being sooner fit for generation, sooner in the flower and prime of their age, and finally, sooner old.

(Henry Cuffe 1607)

The human life cycle in Europe from classical times until the early nineteenth century was usually visualized by ages or epochs. This doctrine of the ages of man was quite similar to its Japanese counterpart and described an unfolding of the individual life cycle in epochs with appropriate gender-specific activities and decorum. Early medieval Europeans were fascinated by numbers (a preoccupation they shared with many other literate traditions including that of China and to a lesser extent of Japan). In Europe the numbers four, five, six, and seven were all, at different times and in various situations, endowed with special significance, but by the eighteenth century the number seven, "ever revered as an especially potent number, the number of perfection" (Sears 1986, 20), was given priority. In the Japanese scroll the "Slope of Age," full manhood was represented as age fifty, situated at the peak of the slope. Similarly in Europe:

The number seven multiplied by itself produces the age which is properly considered and called perfect, so that a man of this age, as one who had already attained and not yet passed perfection, is considered ripe in wisdom, and not unfit for the exercise of his physical powers.

(Macrobius 1952, 115)

Medieval European ideas on middle age were heavily influenced by the writings of early Arab and Greek scholars including Aristotle, who, in the tradition of Hippocratic writers, stated that man is in his *akme* (prime) at forty-nine years of age (seven times seven): this maturity—full ripeness, or the autumn of life—was thought of as the perfect age of man. The autumn of a man's life extended throughout the fifth and sixth ages (out of a total of seven). For a woman, in contrast, six of her ages had passed by the time she reached twenty-one (Dove 1986, 23): since she was frequently married off as young as seven, by the age of twenty she could have borne several children and at thirty have been exhausted from repeated pregnancies, deliveries, and the care of a swarm of children who were highly vulnerable to disease and death. Medieval descriptions of women in the autumn of their life have none of the enviable qualities assigned to men: whereas men at maturity were associated with wisdom and perfection, women were described as cold, dry, "like an old katte" (Yonge, cited in Dove 1986, 23), and "no longer pleasing to look on" (Dove 1986, 22).

Although a marked gender distinction characterized reproductive maturation and associated social roles, a second record of the passing of time and its effect on the body relied less on gender difference. According to humoral theory the composition of the human body changed with age so that from the midfifties "the fluids and heat of the body diminish, and rheum and phlegm dominate" (Sears 1986, 26). This concept, very similar to that found in the classical Chinese and Japanese medical systems, still appears in late eighteenth-century European medical texts that made little of gender difference in aging and human anatomy (Laqueur 1990).

Another European concept that flourished through the eighteenth century posited that "phases" of life succeeded one another every seven years, so that the seventh, fourteenth, twenty-first, twenty-eighth, thirty-fifth, forty-second, forty-ninth, fifty-sixth, sixty-third, and seventieth years were all regarded as important times of transition. More than one critical transition or phase could fall in any given age or epoch. Its remarkably similar Japanese counterpart was *yakudoshi*, the calamitous or dangerous years.

Use of the term climacteric, which for the past hundred years in European and North American medical writing has designated female midlife, originally described the dangers of any transition or critical period at every seventh year, without distinction of age or gender. The grand climacteric came in the sixty-third year and heralded the final stage of the life cycle. By the early nineteenth century, medical use of the term specified that "period of life (usually between the ages of 45 and 60) at which the vital forces begin to decline" (Oxford English Dictionary) but most often referred to men suffering from "a general decay of strength," about which at least one physician stated," I will venture to question, whether it be not, in truth, a *disease* rather than a mere declension of strength and decay of natural powers" (Halford 1813, 317; original emphasis). Halford went on to observe that "though this climacteric disease is sometimes equally remarkable in women as in men, *yet most certainly I have not noticed it so frequently, nor so well characterized in females*" (323; emphasis added). The symptoms that Halford noted include tiredness, loss of weight and appetite, sleepless nights, a bloated look, white tongue; and the patient "suspects he has a fever." He might also experience head and chest pains, vertigo, rheumatic pains, swollen legs, and sluggish bowels, but "above all, anxiety of mind and sorrow have laid the surest foundation for the malady in its least remediable form" (324). Halford concluded that "sorrow late in life easily lets in disease" and wondered if it was above all the prospect of death that "inflicted the wound in [the patient's] peace of mind?" (325).

Not until later in the nineteenth century did the climacteric come to be associated primarily with females, and most particularly with "the change of life."

The Dodging Time

Andrew Currier, an American physician writing in 1897, observed that while menstruation was much talked about by the ancients, menopause was often passed over "as a matter occult and inexplicable" (1897, 7). Currier claimed that an exception was to be found in Hippocrates' *Diseases of Women*:

> We learn from experience that exulcerations, violent and even scirrhous tumors of the uterus, are sometimes produced by cessation of the menses. Neither do the external parts of the body escape the fatal consequences of such suppression, since we know from experience that by this means they are frequently affected with the itch, the elephantiasis, boils, erysipelatous disorders, or scirrhous tumors.

This citation is to be found nowhere in *Diseases of Women* nor in the writings of other well known classical physicians and in any case probably refers not to menopause but to amenorrhea (temporary cessation of menstruation [Leslie Dean-Jones, personal communication]).[1] However, on the basis of this passage Currier criticized eighteenth-century followers of the Hippocratic tradition who he believed were largely responsible for the "foreboding of evil which is associated with the menopause in the minds of so many of the laity" (Currier 1897, 8). For example, John Leake wrote in 1777 that "at this *critical time of life* the female sex are often visited

The Wheel of Life from the Psalter of Robert de Lisle, fourteenth
century. Reproduced with permission from The British Library.

with various diseases of the *chronic kind"* including "pain and giddiness
of the head, hysteric disorders, colic pains, and a female weakness . . .
intolerable itching at the neck of the bladder and contiguous parts are often
very troublesome to others" (Leake 1777, 86; original emphasis). Leake
noted also that low spirits and melancholy were sometimes involved. However, in 1826 one Dr. Dewees informed his readers that "the vulgar error,
that 'women at this period of life are always in danger,' is replete with
mischief to the suffering sex; and I feel it a duty to declare, that they are
not necessarily more obnoxious to disease at this, than at any other period
of their existence" (Dewees 1826, 94). Dewees, an American, apparently
agreed with Halford and pointed out that middle-aged women are "freer
from diseases causing death" than at other times in the life cycle, con-
cluding from an examination of mortality bills in France, that, once puberty is passed, fewer women than men die at any stage of life (1826, 93).

A French physician, Gardanne, writing in 1821, received credit for the
first use of the term *ménopause*, and from the middle of the nineteenth
century onward the term gradually came into wide circulation in medical

literature in both England and France to describe what was known in daily parlance as the "dodging time," the several years before and after the last menstruation. Early medical usage of menopause was closer, therefore, to the meaning of *kōnenki* than it is today.

Despite heated exchanges in nineteenth-century medical literature about what menopause was, who was considered to be at risk for difficulties at that time, and whether the event was normal or pathological (arguments that rest unresolved today), the majority of physicians clearly remained indifferent to this part of the life cycle, and a good number of gynecological texts have absolutely nothing to say about menopause (West 1858; Symington Brown 1882). Others have only a paragraph or two, usually to the effect that those who experienced an early menarche can expect a late menopause (Galabin 1879, 44–45), a belief that still has some currency. Most physicians seem to have been more preoccupied with accounting for the mechanism of menstruation, and it was with this in mind that they started to pay close attention to the anatomy of the reproductive organs (Bennet 1853).

Nevertheless a few doctors, including Robert Barnes, a British physician, took an active interest in the end of menstruation. He devoted a chapter to the "Medical Irregularities of the Climacteric Epoch" in his textbook published in 1873, where he stated:

> The transition period, from active ovario-uterine life to the stage of sexual decrepitude or degeneration, is seldom effected without some disturbance; and in many cases the local and constitutional disorders that attend it are numerous and severe.
>
> Physicians do, indeed, talk of the climacteric in man; but the analogy is more fanciful than real. There is nothing to compare with the almost sudden decay of the organs of reproduction which marks the middle age of woman. Whilst these organs are in vigor, the whole economy of woman is subject to them. Ovulation and menstruation, gestation and lactation by turns absorb and govern almost all the energies of her system. The loss of these functions entails a complete revolution.
>
> (Barnes 1873, 263–64)

Humoral pathology still dominated Barnes's thinking. He focused on symptoms of congestion that he believed resulted from retention of excess blood: vertigo, epilepsy, apoplexy, headache, "minor moral, emotional, and intellectual aberrations, and a desponding gloomy state, verging upon hypochondriasis" (1873, 264). He stated that these problems were often controlled by a "well-regulated will," and that fretfulness, irritability, forgetfulness, and indecision were early warning signs of impending difficulties.

Barnes prescribed a careful dietary regimen: he limited the eating of meat to one meal a day, said that "spirits generally should be avoided, port should be shunned absolutely, and sherry taken rarely; sparkling wines mixed with soda or selzer, claret, carlowitz, or hocks may be allowed to the extent of two or three glasses daily. Beer, as a rule, is unsuitable for climacteric women" (1873, 272). In common with many of his colleagues Barnes promoted a judicious mixture of preventive medicine, patient will-power, and a tried and true humorally based therapeutic regime of blood-letting by means of leeches. Even though the language of Barnes and his colleagues sounds paternalistic to contemporary ears, it fit the context of its time. Terms such as decrepitude, degeneration, and senility simply implied a process of getting older and carried little of the negative freight that now attaches to them; moreover use of words such as these extended beyond the female condition to a whole range of medical problems. Barnes concluded that "troubles of the menopause" usually last for two or three years and "the woman then seems to take on a new lease of life. She resumes her physical and mental power. Sometimes, however, these troubles persist and merge into those which mark the period of decrepitude" (272).

Edward Tilt was perhaps the most influential physician in the treatment of middle-aged women during the second half of the last century.[2] His books were widely reviewed, acclaimed, and cited by other physicians not only in England, where he worked most of his life, but also in continental Europe (where he practiced medicine) and America, a recent citation being just over fifteen years ago (Christie Brown and Christie Brown 1976).[3] Tilt's medical practice is of particular interest today because his chief appointment was at the Farringdon General Dispensary and Lying-in-Charity, and hence his experience was not only with the usual upper-class women who visited gynecologists but also with the poor. One of his books, first published in 1857, *The Change of Life in Health and Disease: A Practical Treatise on the Nervous and Other Affections Incidental to Women at the Decline of Life*, went into four editions, the final one being in 1882.

Tilt informed his readers that as a result of the early editions of his book many women from all walks of life came to see him about menopause. In the later editions he presented a statistical analysis of a sample of five hundred women collected over a period of thirteen years, largely from the upper classes of society, in order to "rectify any pathological one-sidedness that may have arisen from the statistics having been principally derived from dispensary practice" (1870, vi). Tilt stated that his volume would "forcibly show the evil effects of the change of life" but insisted equally strongly that menopause also had a "salutary" effect, that hot flashes and increased perspiration were good for the health in that they relieved "congestion," and that women who had suffered from problems such as chronic uterine inflammation for many years "made marvelous recoveries after the change was effected" (1870, 5).

In common with other physicians of his time, Tilt thought of the "epoch" of forty to fifty-five as a time of invigoration for both sexes, but that while this change is "insensibly" worked out in man, "in woman the passage is often perilous" (1870, 9) although afterward there is a great improvement in general health and often in physical looks. Tilt was especially taken with the "comely" appearance of a little fat in middle age, which he regarded as conducive to good female health. He claimed, however, that certain women "do not recover health without some sacrifice of feminine grace, their appearance becoming somewhat masculine, the bones projecting more than usual, the skin is less unctuous, and tweezers may be required to remove stray hairs from the face" (10). Like many of his colleagues inspired by the "new" anatomy, Tilt believed that ovarian "involution," or shrinkage, was the principal cause of "the change," but he noted that many organs, including the spleen and lymphatic glands, "suffer involution" in midlife in men and women alike. He stated that men show more climacteric "decay" than do women.

Tilt agreed with his American colleague Dr. Meigs that not enough attention had been paid to the dangers of the "crisis," and that women who sought out help must not be turned away but given "a considerate attention." His contemporaries in France, however, he claimed, confused many kinds of diseases of aging with menopausal problems.

Tilt believed that weakness of constitution, temperament, constitutional disorder, uterine "affections," unusual suffering at puberty and at menstrual periods, sudden cessation, disuse or abuse of the reproductive organs, and social position, all contributed to the menopausal experience. He thought that peasant women suffered least, poor city women only a little because "their hard work prevents and cures the nervous affections which so frequently assail the rich at this period" (85). Like many contemporary Japanese, Tilt associated menopausal problems with a life of luxury, but he concluded that of all the factors involved, "susceptibility of the nervous system" was the most important. When he turned to the subject of behavioral changes associated with the climacteric, Tilt was apparently very much a man of his time: he believed that alterations in the ovaries, being situated in close proximity to the "ganglionic" nerves, produced a direct effect on individual willpower and correct behavior:

> causing various forms of nervous irritability and some amount of confusion and bewilderment, which seems to deprive women of the mental endowments to which they had acquired a good title by forty years' enjoyment. They often lose confidence in themselves, are unable to manage domestic or other business. . . . When the change is effected, the mind emerges from the clouds in which it has seemed lost . . . for, like the body, the mental faculties then assume a masculine character.
>
> (Tilt 1870, 10)

However, Tilt repeatedly cautioned readers to bear in mind that most problems associated with the change of life were not pathological.

He recommended bleeding by means of leeches and suggested the use of purgatives and sedatives, including opium (to help with insomnia), laudanum (for pain), sudorifics, baths, and mineral waters. In addition Tilt recommended that physicians should act as social advisers: women should be encouraged to take up more music or gardening or undertake the management of a school, the education of a relative, or charity work. In summary, Tilt and many of his colleagues, although they dwelt to some extent on the pathology of "the change," emphasized that for most women the end of menstruation is a normal event after which they could expect to resume a life of full vigor.

When he turned to the final section of his book on "special pathology," however, Tilt's description of the effects of menopause was vivid. He concluded "that many women are thoroughly unhinged by the change of life being left to take its course" (160) and complained of a "heaviness in the head," "a stupid headache," of a fear of going mad, and of loss of memory. Some, he added, become deeply melancholic, bad tempered, addicted to alcohol, and subject to kleptomaniac, suicidal, or homicidal tendencies.

Because of the wealth of detail that Tilt included in his book, we can glean some insight into the lives of middle-aged women in the middle of the last century. First, and most important, they were described as middle-aged, not as old women. Contrary to beliefs current today, many women lived to age seventy or longer, and people in their forties and fifties were thought of as very much in the prime of life. Unlike the custom in medieval times, women were not married at an exceedingly young age (the majority of women in the cases Tilt reported were married in their middle twenties), and, although many of them had large families, quite often of ten or more children, apparently most women survived childbirth (perhaps because of reasonably good nutrition) and found themselves actively looking forward to a middle age released from the burden of pregnancies and child care (Smith-Rosenberg 1985, 194). Like Dewees, writing fifty years earlier, Tilt and his contemporaries were explicit that women who attained middle age lived longer than their menfolk. In Tilt's opinion since women could expect another twenty-five or thirty years of life beyond "cessation," it was important to ensure that passage through the crisis of the change was accomplished as smoothly as possible.

We also learn from Tilt and several of his colleagues that many women enjoyed an active sexual life in middle age. He was explicit that women who married at this stage (or for the majority, remarried after being widowed) should receive a physician's advice on how to proceed with their sexual life. More than one physician noted that "false pregnancy" was a common "fantasy" at the change of life.

In contrast to twentieth-century literature, nowhere in professional writing about menopause in the nineteenth century do I find comments to the effect that women mourned the loss of their reproductive powers as they went through the change. Although reproduction and rearing of children was the life expected of a woman, this task was usually not completed until midlife, at which time, if she was not already working, a woman was often expected to use her accumulated wisdom for the good of the community and to move out into the world beyond the confined domestic sphere. Furthermore, it was considered unseemly to be pregnant at the same time as one's own daughter. Smith-Rosenberg detects feelings of ambivalence among nineteenth-century women about aging, but she points out that many women welcomed menopause, most important of all perhaps, as a foolproof birth-control technique and, second, because it heralded what was often thought of as a golden interim before the final season of old age and inevitable decline (1985, 195).

In their professional and popular articles alike, some physicians emphasized the influence of the reproductive organs on the general health of women, and a few, particularly in popular literature, made extrapolations from this association into the world of morals. Mettler, for example, writing in 1887, stated that a large number of women, particularly from the "more luxurious walks of life," were very distressed at the climacteric and "imagine that they are subject to all the ills flesh is heir to" (Mettler 1887, 323). Certain doctors stated explicitly that too great an interest in education, use of birth control or abortion, undue sexual indulgence, or too fashionable a life-style could contribute to a difficult and disease-ridden menopause (Smith-Rosenberg 1985, 192), but the majority of the medical profession did not necessarily reinforce this position. Most physicians offered no comment on the social life or morals of women in medical texts, beyond suggestions about preventive medicine. Skene, a London physician, counseled, for example, that those who are "overtaxed and poorly fed, should have rest and a better diet" (Skene 1892, 424).

Like Tilt and other contemporaries, Skene was keen to clarify just what should be considered as characteristic of menopausal problems: "A long list of diseases has been given as occurring at the menopause. This list covers nearly all the ills that flesh is heir to [obviously a popular Shakespearian quotation of the time!]. The majority of these have no relations to the menopause" (1892, 437).[4] The author of an 1894 text, Baldy, confined himself to a description of physical changes at cessation and deliberately excluded mental states. He associated, as did many authors of the time, an early age of onset of menopause with a warm climate, went on to state that it was an important change that physicians must watch carefully but that "it is exceptional that the troubles of the menopause are anything more than temporarily active" (Baldy 1894, 87). Baldy claimed that "the one symptom of all those enumerated that seems to be well-nigh universally experienced at this period, is flushes; few women escape them" (1894, 84). He recommended bromides (tranquilizers) and camphor for the relief of hot flashes.

Baldy believed, like some of his colleagues, including Tilt, that at cessation, "an awakening of desire, quite unknown during previous years, which is often looked upon with a sense of shame and degradation by its possessor, is not uncommon in women undergoing the menopause" (1894, 84).

On the other side of the Atlantic, Andrew Currier published a book in 1897 entitled *The Menopause*, in which he laid blame at the feet of Tilt for the common impression that the end of menstruation was an "experience fraught with peril and difficulty."[5] Currier's position was straightforward:

> The menopause is *not* a dangerous time or experience for the majority of women, any more than puberty is. The majority of women pass through it with as little incident or discomfort as they experience at puberty. It is only the exceptional woman who has a hard time, and comes to the doctor to tell him about it. Upon this exceptional experience the doctrine of the danger and serious character of the menopause is built up.
>
> (Currier 1897, vii–viii; original emphasis)

When considering who was at risk for a difficult menopause, Currier revealed characteristic late nineteenth-century Spencerian thinking:

> Among those human beings who are least removed from the animals—the savage and the degraded, and among those, too, who are subject to the vicissitudes of the out-of-door life and manual labor—the menopause is least likely to excite attention or create disturbance. It is among the highly bred, tenderly reared women of civilized life, and among those too, who have experienced an undue share of the ills and stings of life, that the menopause is a matter of great significance, not infrequently being associated with a general breaking up of the vital forces of the individual.
>
> (Currier 1897, 13)

He went on to state that peasants from races that are "phlegmatic, cold, and apathetic," such as the German, Scandinavian, and Russian, complained little at menopause, but that among the sensitive, passionate nations like the French, Spanish, and the Irish, the "highly organized, nervous, city-bred women, women of fashion, women who fret and worry, are apt to experience the disagreeable and annoying features of the menopause" (1897, 35). In this respect he does not sound too far removed from some contemporary Japanese gynecologists. Currier also believed that women who were exhausted after the bearing of many children in rapid succession entered menopause early.

Currier disagreed with Tilt with respect both to medical theory and to practice, but most particularly as to what symptoms to label pathological. He observed that his patients often complained about flushing and sweating at the dodging time but, unlike Tilt, regarded these symptoms as neither salutary nor pathological, merely "common." Nevertheless, like Tilt, Currier remained wedded to the humorally derived idea of a "plethora" of blood at menopause and recommended the use of leeches to remove excess "congestion" in difficult cases; moreover, he strongly advised their application when women experienced what he described as "undue sexual excitement" as a result of "congestion of the pelvic organs" (1897, 273). Also in common with Tilt, Currier thought that the majority of women enjoy improved health after menopause was finally over.

Aldrich, a neurologist at the Cleveland General Hospital, although he was writing in the same year as Currier, represented a major shift in conceptualization of the female body. Like Currier, he believed that menopause was not usually a difficult time. According to him it was a positive process:

[a] process of leveling up rather than leveling down; a process of development, and not of decay. It is incorrect to speak of the menopause as the climacteric. The menopause is not a phenomenon of the climacteric of age but belongs to the age of invigoration . . . the doctrine that it is sexual and physical decrepitude is misleading and not founded on fact. Of the peculiar changes that do take place we are all too willing to profess ignorance or fall back on the oft-quoted saying of an eminent physiologist, "A woman is a womb with other organs surrounding it."

Too long has womankind been treated on this axiom. So long that one of the greatest specialists in female disease has been forced to exclaim, "Remember that a woman has other organs than a womb."

(Aldrich 1897, 440)

Aldrich made a metaphorical link between the changes of aging in the spleen and lymphatic glands, common to both men and women, and the economy: "How like a prudent and successful business man, making no new ventures, desiring no further growth, but cautiously taking care of his accumulations" (1897, 440). He believed that all too often the symptoms thought of as menopausal resulted, not from ovarian changes, but from "fermentations" in the intestinal tract to which both men and women were susceptible. He was also apparently a supporter of the budding field of immunology and believed in the presence of "some proteid body in the blood" that could endow the whole system with resistant properties. He therefore concluded that since "thought is physiological" and judgment was the result of thought, and moreover, the time of cessation for women was one of great "griefs" and "hard labor," then fatigue, fear, grief, anger—the "whole gamut of human passions" that run high in middle age—could serve to weaken the power of "these mysterious protective agencies [the proteid bodies] on the body." Aldrich went on to criticize Tilt's notions that flushes and excess perspiration were caused by a retention of menstrual blood. He assigned these ideas to the "romantic school of pathology" and promoted in their place the new physiology of the day, in which cellular rather than gross anatomical change dominated medical theory.

Although Aldrich retained the paternalistic stance typical of his time and talked, for example, of the "impressionable female mind," he shifted attention away from the reproductive organs, introduced a cellular approach to the study of aging, and was comfortable with drawing parallels between the biology of men and women. The approach that Aldrich supported eventually became central to immunological theory, and his idea about the relation of the "human passions" to the immune system was an early precursor of contemporary psychosomatic medicine and stress theory, which in turn have had a somewhat peripheral effect on current ideas about menopause.

As we will see shortly, the discovery of the endocrine system was to become a much more important influence on medical theories about menopause than the work of Aldrich. Nevertheless, I introduce his work to make two points: there was (and is) no simple unveiling of scientific knowledge and no ready consensus in the medical world on an accurate representation of the menopausal transition; on the contrary, argument and speculation were (and remain) rife.[6] Second, although some physicians may have been self-serving, and no doubt some were misogynists, most men who devoted time and energy to the creation of menopause as a medical event were not out to benefit in any simple rapacious way from vulnerable middle-aged women (despite the occasional moralistic aphorism). They seem, on the contrary, to have been overwhelmingly concerned with establishing their own discourse as the most "scientific," and this concern generated the bulk of the disputes about theory and practice in menopause.

When it came to discussions of etiology, however, they appear to have been more or less in agreement, in particular about the postulated effects of climate and race on the onset of menopause, and about preventive hygiene. It is at this more general, nonclinical level, that a shared ideology was most obvious, and it is also here that no evidence appeared to support the veracity of the claims that the physicians were making.

Defining the Nature of Women

Tilt, Currier, and their colleagues were probably sufficiently enamored with post-Enlightenment thinking to assume that in their clinical practice and writing they were reproducing "facts" of nature or were on the "cutting edge" of scientific endeavor that would eventually lead to the exposure of facts. They regarded their approach as significantly different and more accurate than those of physicians who had gone before them, largely because of the anatomical "discoveries" on which it drew. From the vantage point of the twentieth century we can relatively easily dismiss the "plethoras," "congestions," and nervous prostrations of the nineteenth century as fanciful, but in order to understand the sources of our current understanding about menopause we need to digress briefly into the incorporation of nineteenth-century ideological knowledge to the scientific discourse of the time. The resulting just-so story about the aging female body, its relation to nature, and its place in society created a characteristically moralistic rhetoric that lingers today. Because from the late nineteenth century onward Japan took note of almost all domains of European and North American discourse, scientific, political, and economic, and set about selectively incorporating aspects of it into Japan's own modernization process, this detour in our discussion is doubly important. We should be aware, however, that neither Tilt nor Currier was translated into Japanese.

Medical writing of late nineteenth-century Europe and North America reflects the fascination of many physicians with applying the newest scientific method to an understanding of the body in clinical practice and at the level of whole populations. An interest in establishing a scientific basis for human differences of race and gender was already apparent in the eighteenth century, when the measurement of skulls of men, women, apes, and monkeys was first carried out. Not long after the publication of Darwin's *Origin of Species* introduced a concept of hierarchy into the process of biological change, ideas about social change coalesced into what came to be known as social Darwinism. Its central notion, postulated by Herbert Spencer, was that the races of man had evolved from a primitive state in which they were close to nature, through barbarism, and finally to the civilization of nineteenth-century Europe. Toward the end of the nineteenth century, compounding ideas about racial and gender difference, writers often compared women quite explicitly with "primitives":

> Women, it was observed, shared with Negroes a narrow, childlike, and delicate skull, so different from the more robust and rounded heads characteristic of males of "superior" races. Similarly, women of higher races tended to have slightly protruding jaws, analogous to, if not as exaggerated as, the apelike, jutting jaws of lower races. Women and lower races were called innately impulsive, emotional, imitative rather than original, and incapable of the abstract reasoning found in white men. . . . Woman was in evolutionary terms the "conservative element" to the man's "progressive," preserving the more "primitive" traits found in lower races.
>
> (Leys Stepan 1986, 263)

Paul Broca in 1868 and Havelock Ellis in 1894 made concerted efforts to put the inferiority of women on a scientific footing. Some writers characterized women as a species distinct from man and hence a "lower race," which could be classified together with "primitives," criminals, and the urban poor (Leys Stepan 1986, 264). The science of the time justified this misogynist language, likening blacks and women in the incidence of disease, sexual behavior, and childlike characteristics both physical and moral. Such evidence encouraged scientists to oppose proposals by John Stuart

Mill and others to improve women's rights. The doctrine of intellectual equality was said to "violate nature," and it was strongly suggested that women should content themselves with their biological destiny (Fee 1979, 415). Walter Bagehot, writing in *Popular Science Monthly*, argued:

> Every one knows that of late years a movement has sprung up to secure for women, as contradistinguished from men, certain rights, liberties, and powers, of which it is contended they have been arbitrarily and wrongfully deprived. . . . Perhaps we may best describe the movement as an attempt to obliterate all—save the purely structural—distinctions between man and women, and to establish between them a complete identity of duties and functions in place of that separation which has more or less hitherto always existed.
>
> (Bagehot 1879, 201)

Drawing explicitly on the theory of "Mr. Darwin," Bagehot drew comparisons between the animal world and that of humans in order to keep women in their "naturally" assigned place and gave particular importance to differences in brain size to support his point of view.

Physicians who accepted evolutionary theory often struggled to maintain a cogent argument when writing about women's postulated difficulties at menopause. It was relatively easy to agree that exotic races and poor women alike reached menopause at an early age because (one supposes) their lives were nasty, brutish, and short. Although physicians accepted that woman could be likened to the primitive, and was therefore a potential victim of her emotions, they concluded (drawing, I suspect, on their clinical practice) that the leisured class suffered most at menopause. Newly emerging middle-class women, closer to white men on the social ladder, were, paradoxically, because of their sensibility and refinement, more vulnerable to nervous prostration and menopausal troubles than were women of the lower classes, prostitutes, and blacks—all lower on the evolutionary ladder. Because of their social position and despite the greater willpower and control it gave them, they were at the mercy of their exquisitely sensitive nervous system excited by the congestion characteristic of the aging reproductive organs, which in turn affected their mental state. The usual recommended hygienic regimen for problems at the change was confinement, rest, and plenty of baths; it led to an enforced withdrawal from society, something that reactionary educators and politicians were only too eager to seize on to bolster their arguments against change in the status of women. They did not consign middle-class women to the garbage heap at the change of life, since, once through menopause, women entered into the autumn of life, a time at which they could make good use of their accumulated wisdom for the sake of family and community.

Late nineteenth-century physicians who directed their attention toward older women were, however, very much in the minority, and the bulk of moralistic writing was for the benefit of younger women. Politicians and other social observers were aware that birthrates in both Europe and North America had been declining since the middle of the nineteenth century. Worried that women were committing "race suicide" (Groag Bell and Offam 1983, 6), writers strongly discouraged them from joining the work force (although to do so was by no means a recent phenomenon). The literature did not usually single out middle-aged and older women; more often it simply cautioned women in general that the effects of an overly active life while young would come to fruition in the form of a difficult menopause and a diseased and decrepit old age.

It would be an interesting exercise to obtain accounts from nineteenth-century Japanese scientists of their reactions to the European analogies between women and the "lower" races. Unlike the emerging middle classes of Europe and North America, most Japanese women, even when confined to the household, were required to be physically strong and healthy in order to produce children and to work. No cult of invalidism appeared in nineteenth-century Japan. Nevertheless, women—physically, sexually, and constitutionally complementary to men—were not their equals socially. Social Darwinism, when it arrived in Japan, served to buttress a well established Confucian tradition (Watanabe 1990, 75), Inevitably, however, evolutionary theory produced ambivalence in Japan, because the "yellow" races were not at the top of the heap. Their possible "inferiority" to "Western" races caused one Japanese writer, Takahashi Yoshio, to recommend in 1884 that Japanese men marry Western women in order to increase the stature of the race (75), but other influential writers voiced their objections.

Because in Europe a biologically determined ideology viewed women as excessively sensitive and vulnerable to physical distress from the secretions of the female reproductive organs, this "anatomy as destiny" vision fused with evolutionary theory to achieve a particularly misogynist variety of discrimination. It rendered females socially and biologically inferior even in the domestic sphere, a space where Japanese women might create a sense of self-worth and a fulfilled life. Perhaps in part because of this intransigent ideology of female subservience coupled with the emerging cult of individualism, it was in Europe and North America where large numbers of women first publicly resisted their ascribed lot.

The Gendered Body

From her textual analysis of writings from the eighteenth and nineteenth centuries, including those by physicians, Ludmilla Jordanova concludes that a hardening and polarization of gender differences in everyday life took place, setting out a biological determinism not nearly so apparent in earlier centuries (Jordanova 1989). For example, one anthropologist, speaking before the Royal Anthropological Society in London in 1869, was moved to ask: "Is woman intellectually the equal of man? Are there no natural mental distinctions between the sexes? Are the obvious differences in thought and action, observable between men and women, produced solely by education or founded on nature?" (Allan 1869, cxcvi). He pointed out that his particular concern in asking these questions was the status of women and that "all attempts to ascertain man's proper place in nature involve consideration of both sexes." He went on:

> The assertions and claims put forward under the term Women's Rights, are a challenge to anthropologists to consider the scientific question of woman's mental, moral, and physical qualities, her nature and normal condition relative to man. . . . Although in some respects—such as grace, delicacy, beauty of form, complexion, etc.—woman appears to recede more from, in other respects she approaches more closely than man does, to the animal type! Physically, for example, in the menstrual discharge,—if it be true that this is also a characteristic of female anthropoid apes, and of other mammalia.
>
> (Allan 1869, cxcvii)

Allan asserted that woman's poor conduct, including "petulance, caprice, and irritability," can be traced directly to the menstrual cycle. "Imagine a woman," he stated, "at such a time [when menstruating] having it in her power to sign the death warrant of a rival or a faithless lover!" He cited the French historian Jules Michelet with approval for having characterized women as invalids and agreed: "Such she emphatically is, as compared with man. Woman is doubly entitled to man's protection; not only as smaller and weaker than himself, but as being, on account of her sex, more or less always unwell" (cxcix).

Thirty years later Durkheim, who usually placed himself explicitly in opposition to biological determinists, took a slightly more modulated but nevertheless similar position, in his now classic book on suicide: "Woman's sexual needs have less of a mental character because, generally speaking, her mental life is less developed. . . . Being a more instinctive creature than man, woman has only to follow her instincts to find calmness and peace" (Durkheim 1952, 272).

The ways in which woman came to be identified as more closely aligned with nature than man were complex, and we glimpse the process in the quotes from Allan. At times woman was, because of menstruation, metaphorically associated with the wilderness, nature untamed, and hence regarded as more emotional, less subject to reason than man, and potentially disruptive. But being closer to nature, woman was also a prime subject for systematic investigation into its laws (Jordanova 1989, 42).

During the eighteenth and nineteenth centuries, a significant transformation took place in the medical world through the development and refinement of anatomical dissection. Scientists of the time described their explorations into female anatomy as the "unveiling of nature" (Jordanova 1989, 87). Exposure of the mystery and secrecy surrounding the female body was by no means limited to medicine, but the form it took in the medical world had a special urgency since it touched on another dominant interest—a search for the origins of life.

The majority of physicians who specialized in women's diseases from the middle of the nineteenth century were either obstetricians or surgeons. After surgery and at postmortems, they would customarily remove the reproductive organs for dissection and peel away layers of tissue in an effort to reveal the "essence" of the uterus and ovaries. Intimate links had been assumed from classical times between the uterus and the behavior of women; the ovaries, however, had been explicitly likened to the testicles, a woman's "stones," and similarities between the sexes were based on the homologous nature of these organs (Laqueur 1990, 177); few if any associations were made between the ovaries and behavior. However, from the 1870s, after dissection encouraged a sensitivity to gendered anatomical difference, and primitive techniques of anesthesia became available, attention shifted away from the uterus to postulated links between the ovaries and behavior. Female "castration"—the removal of healthy ovaries to cure a wide variety of emotional female pathologies including hysteria,[7] psychoses, nervous afflictions, and excessive sexual desire—became especially popular among European surgeons. Laqueur points out that forty years before there would be any evidence for the "real importance" of the ovaries in a woman's life, cultural assumptions fueled the notion that, as the French physician Achille Chereau noted in 1844, "it is only because of the ovary that woman is what she is" (cited in Laqueur 1990, 175). (Needless to say, no similar fashion arose in connection with removal of the testicles.) Currier commented critically on the "tens of thousands" of women who had been deprived of their ovaries but added that this had "opened up a rich field for the investigation of the phenomena which attend the removal of these important organs," leading to what he termed "artificial menopause" (1897, ix).[8]

A Biologically Determined Social Order

As the status of scientific knowledge became widely accepted in both the West and Japan, it was used with increasing frequency to rationalize and legitimize many aspects of daily life. During the nineteenth century in northern Europe and North America, in keeping with a growing sense of individual rights, a significant number of middle-class women challenged their limited position at the center of domestic life and demanded improved educational opportunities. A few physicians joined with members of the clergy and educators to produce a professional and popular literature in which they criticized such women who wished to break out of their "proper" station and also those who made use of birth control and abortion (readily available at the time) (Smith-Rosenberg and Rosenberg 1973, 332–56). While the assertions made in medical texts did not necessarily have any impact on the actual behavior of women, they reveal nevertheless what some men, at least, in positions of power and authority assumed the ideal female role should be:

> Mentally, socially, spiritually, she is more interior than man. She herself is an interior part of man, and her love and life are always something interior and incomprehensible to him. . . . Woman is to deal with domestic affections and uses, not with philosophies and sciences. . . . She is priest, not king. The house, the chamber, the closet, are the centers of her social life and power as surely as the sun is the center of the social system.
>
> (Holcombe 1869, 201–2)

Since a woman was assumed to be weaker in body and confined by menstruation and pregnancy, she was therefore expected to be physically and economically dependent on the "stronger, more forceful male, to whom she necessarily looked up to with admiration and devotion" (Smith-Rosenberg and Rosenberg 1973, 338). The Rosenbergs point out that the status of a Victorian woman was fraught with ambiguity because she was thought of as "more spiritual than man, yet less intellectual, closer to the divine, yet prisoner of her most animal characteristics, more moral than man, yet less in control of her very morality" (338).

The arguments of the Rosenbergs are carefully contextualized, and although they see women as the objects of special ideologies and subjected to social controls, they point out that class and race were equally important categories in shaping attitudes toward sexuality. Degler goes further and suggests, comparing a nineteenth-century survey of women's opinions about sexuality with those in medical texts, popular and professional, that the content of medical literature, the reality of women's lives, and the historical account given about women's sexuality and health were out of phase with one another. He draws two important conclusions from his research: that "most people apparently did not follow the prescriptions laid down by the marriage and advice manuals"; and that disagreement, not consensus, prevailed among medical people on the topics of sexuality, the moral integrity of women, and their position in society (Degler 1974, 1489, 1477). Attempts were certainly made by some physicians to use medical theory to justify a conservative moral position (Verbrugge 1976, 962), but not all medical writing was necessarily conservative. An ideology of anatomy as destiny may have been dominant in the late nineteenth century, but it was only one of several competing discourses.

Debate in medical circles was certainly not fueled simply by politics or economics, but also by changing medical knowledge and practice and the extensive argument they generated. By the end of the century, the theory of biological evolution, with its vision of a naturally ordained racial and gendered hierarchy that had once been exceedingly contentious, was widely accepted and drawn on liberally by conservatives from all walks of life as scientific legitimacy for women's nature and position in society. It was partly in opposition to this intellectual climate that the first large-scale movement for women's liberation began.

From the Dodging Time to Deficiency Disease

In medieval Europe links between mind and body had been conceptualized as movement of the humors about the body through the nerves and blood. In China and Japan these links were visualized as *ki*, the humorlike energy system conducted through the meridians.[9] Tilt and Currier were practicing medicine at a time when humoral theory expired, at least in the explanations of the medical world if not yet among the public. In its place physicians supplied a different link between the female body and its mind. Physicians relied heavily, as we have seen, on the close anatomical proximity of the ovaries to what they termed the "ganglionic" nervous system whose path could be traced directly to the brain. Not surprisingly, late nineteenth-century women—in particular those leisured women of exquisite sensibility from the middle and upper classes—were thought to suffer inordinately from nervous diseases of various kinds[10] (Showalter 1985).

A shift in medical discourse away from a simple theory of anatomical causation is evident in the early years of the twentieth century. Largely as a result of animal experimentation, it was postulated that the ovaries secrete a substance that actually determines the "menstrual flux and ministers to female health," and that "becomes lacking" at menopause (Reed

1904, 738). This "discovery," while it led eventually to a complete reformulation of medical thinking about the menopausal body, did not initially include any radical change of ideas about the links between the female reproductive system and behavior.

Charles Reed, president of the American Medical Association in 1901 and 1902, despite his awareness of ovarian "secretions," and unlike some of his gynecological colleagues, held an approach to menopause that played down gender distinction. He emphasized that men and women alike go through similar "senile changes," that "shoals of men, women, and children live in health without active ovaries, or with none at all, yet have good health, and that the climacteric is not a pathological process or the menopause a symptom" (1904, 738). Reed wrote in a gynecological textbook that "about one woman in ten will be annoyed while at the menopause by flashes of heat running over the face and neck, and sometimes sweeping over the whole body," but he was emphatic that the "nervous system plays the chief part in the complex process" (739). In contrast to Aldrich, Reed thought that others had overestimated the effects of menopause on the alimentary system but ascribed to it "nervous excitement": the "mental condition of the menopause is one marked by depression. . . . At this period may appear strong irresponsible impulses, active moral perversions, delirium and acute mania. . . . Addiction to alcohol and other nerve-tickling drugs sometimes becomes pronounced at this time, and the demand for drugs seems to have no other basis than childish ennui and a babyish lack of self-control" (741). He concluded that we probably pay too much attention to the physical changes and not enough to the "tremendous" mental changes that accompany menopause:

> A man grows old by merciful and gentle gradations, and so he slides, half willingly, and half unconsciously, into the afternoon of life, with regrets so soft that they can scarce provoke a sigh. But for a woman, man's twenty years of gentle change are compressed into two . . . it is evolution for him; it is revolution for her. . . . She is invited, with cruel abruptness, to be to her husband merely an intellectual companion or a sexless helpmeet, when she had been of late the object of his embraces and the mother of his babes. One third of her adult life is still before her, full of promise of placid enjoyment and great usefulness, but to her, remembering the glory of conquest and surrender, the future stretches a dreary waste of empty years.
>
> (Reed 1904, 741–42)

We can detect a number of significant developments in this passage, surprisingly colorful for publication in a medical textbook. Conceptualization of the passage of time has changed, so that Reed encouraged his readers to think of menopause as an event rather than an epoch, an abrupt transition from young life to old age, which he contrasted specifically with slower biological changes in men. Reed nevertheless minimized the impact of aging on the reproductive organs themselves and of gender difference on general aging and physical health. He separated out mental from physical well-being as none of the nineteenth-century writers before him had done, and while he played down physical pathology, he placed great emphasis on the mental change associated with menopause. To my knowledge, Reed's article was the first that explicitly associated menopause and depression.

As in previous decades and in contrast to Reed's book, most gynecological textbooks at the beginning of this century devoted only a single paragraph, at most a page to menopause (Cooke Hirst 1903; Easterly Ashton 1905). Discussion did not go beyond anatomical changes and vasomotor disturbances but emphasized that menopause was not a pathological condition. Recommended treatments included cold baths, Turkish baths, massage, and the administration of sodium bromide, valerian, and asafetida. Gone forever was the plethora of the dodging time and its relief by means of leeches, but pelvic congestion got occasional mention, and physicians resorted to hot-water vaginal douches, glycerin tampons, and for difficult cases even scarification of the cervix (Easterly Ashton 1905, 698).

Emilius Dudley, an early twentieth-century Chicago gynecologist, in summarizing the current research into menopause, stated that for 90 percent of women menopause was a normal event, but that 30 percent came to see a physician with symptoms that called for a full examination, among which the most common were vertigo, hot and cold flashes, perspirations, palpitations, blurred vision, headache, nausea, and ringing in the ears. Like Reed, he believed that in the majority of cases it was "not the cessation or diminution of bleeding but the neuroses" that were the chief feature of menopause (1919, 51). Dudley agreed with Aldrich that symptoms "falling within the gastric neurosis group," including fermentation and constipation, "are in marked evidence" (54).

The significant change from Dudley's predecessors came in his paper on treatment of menopausal women. In reporting about his colleague Sanes's use of medication, Dudley described the preparation Sanes used:

> each grain of which represents a grain of fresh ovarian substance (varium). The dose was 5 grains, two to four times a day . . . the results from the ovarian substance in the menopause are about 37 percent improvement, and about 25 percent complete control. . . .

The length of time the ovarian substance was used was variable, some used it just a month or so, others for many months, and one for three years before final cessation of the symptoms.

(Dudley 1919, 53)

The early application of ovarian therapy must be put into historical context. In late nineteenth-century Europe several researchers were experimenting with the idea that it was not simply the anatomical structure of certain organs but the internal secretions they produced that were of great significance. What soon came to be termed organotherapy was first conducted with male subjects to whom preparations of testicular extracts were administered for the purposes of "rejuvenation." The French physiologist Brown-Séquard who carried out these experiments reported in 1889 that a woman gynecologist in Paris was injecting a few female patients with the filtered juice of guinea pig ovaries in order to treat uterine problems and hysteria (Borell 1976, 1978).

An American gynecologist writing in the 1940s stated that the use of thyroid extracts at the end of the last century to counter thyroid deficiency was an important influence on the adoption of organotherapy. Emil Novak described the first application of ovarian therapy in a Berlin clinic in 1896 "simply on an assumed analogy with the thyroid." But, as he pointed out, "curiously enough, at this time there was no knowledge of an internal secretory function of the ovary" (Novak 1940, 592); fresh whole ovaries were simply ground up and made into capsules and tablets. Partly because so many oophorectomies (the surgical removal of ovaries) had been carried out, gynecologists were able to make "educated guesses," based on their clinical experiences as to the function of the ovaries. The Berlin patient was a twenty-three-year-old woman who had undergone an oophorectomy a year or two previously; other cases were reported three weeks later in Germany, and five weeks later in Vienna (Kopera 1991). Two Viennese gynecologists, one in 1896 and another in 1900, described a possible secretion of a chemical substance by the ovaries, and Borell attributes their insight to the fact that Vienna was particularly vigorous in its support of oophorectomy (Borell 1985, 13).

By the turn of the century, stimulated by animal experimentation, an active search was under way for the substances secreted by the sex glands (Borell 1985). In 1905 a British physiologist reformulated the general theory of internal secretions into a language that is still in use today: "chemical messengers or 'hormones' as we may call them, have to be carried from the organ where they are produced to the organ which they affect, by means of the blood" (Starling 1905, 6).[11] Despite the excitement of the times, by no means every gynecologist was using ovarian therapy in the early years of this century. By the time Dudley was writing at the beginning of the 1920s, the concept of the endocrine system was more fully formulated, however; of particular significance, the relation of ovarian secretions to the activity of other glands was recognized. Oudshoorn points out how a triangulation of interests, partially cooperative and partially competitive, among gynecologists, laboratory scientists, and pharmaceutical companies fueled the growing industry of organotherapy in the early years of this century (Oudshoorn 1990). Their major dispute revolved around the questionable quality of the ovarian preparations, and scientists and clinicians could not agree on what would constitute sufficient evidence to demonstrate that extracts of ovaries and testes actually contained an active ingredient (Oudshoorn 1990, 11).

Dudley, in common with many of his contemporaries, exhibited doubts as to its efficacy: "The results obtained from ovarian substance, while sometimes strikingly good, are so frequently negative as to raise the question whether it has within it the same finished product or products that the internal secretion consists of; and if it has, whether it is competent to take care of the functional changes of the correlated endocrine glands brought about by the functional changes of the ovarian secretion" (Dudley 1919, 53).

Although ovarian therapy was readily available in the 1920s gynecologists continued to pay relatively little attention to menopause, perhaps because they doubted the utility of organotherapy. In the first issue of the *American Journal of Obstetrics and Gynecology* in 1921, the gynecologist James King reiterated that, regardless of a growing understanding of the workings of the endocrine system, woman remained at the mercy of untamed nature and hence eternally an unpredictable, underevolved being:

Woman has never been understood by man. She is a creature swayed by moods and impulses. She may attain virtues to which no man can aspire or she may sink to depths unfathomed by his imagination. We pay tribute to her virtues and marvel at her iniquities. For ages she has been the theme of poet and philosopher but neither imagination nor wisdom have solved her. Shall we not perhaps find the answer in a better understanding of these subtle influences which determine her physical life? . . . We cannot expect to understand woman until we have fathomed these forces that inspire her impulses and dominate her existence. The wave of feminism that swept over the country raised a disquieting fear in the breast of some timid souls that man's place would be usurped by woman. There may appear from time to time an unmarried female who by reason of education and sheer force of will is able to dominate her internal secretions and assume certain prerogatives of man but never until evolution has eliminated her present endocrine glands will woman be other than she always has been. . . . Man should therefore view with kindly forbearance the futile effort of woman to overcome by her will the very powers that shape and control her mental processes.

"Woman with all thy glands we love thee still."

(King 1921, 348–49)

Since the beginning of the century our understanding of the endocrine system has grown prodigiously. In the late 1920s two of the hormones secreted by the ovary, estrogen and progesterone, were isolated and prepared in crystalline form. The resulting flurry of research allowed the postulation of the concept of menopause as a deficiency disease, together with the widespread promotion of estrogen replacement therapy. Conversely, the administration of simple ovarian therapy declined and eventually was discontinued in the 1940s.

Melancholia and the "insanities," thought by many nineteenth-century and early twentieth-century physicians to "characterize" the menopause, could now be attributed to disturbances in the endocrine system: its direct effect on the brain was postulated, without the mediation of the nervous system (King 1921, 348). However, the foundation and expansion of psychiatry as a profession transformed the relatively simple and direct links recognized among the ovaries, the nervous system (later, the endocrine system), and mental states and behavior into a discourse that was at once more subtle and more expansive. Once Freudian theory applied the concept of symbolic loss to the menopausal transition, it held out to every woman the prospect of a miserable and emotionally disturbed time.

12   Against Nature—Menopause as Herald of Decay

Mutilation and Loss: The Psychoanalytic Construction of Midlife

In her widely acclaimed book *The Second Sex*, Simone de Beauvoir set out in the late forties to demonstrate how women everywhere have been "circumscribed" by "their nature." She was particularly concerned with the way in which male biology and behavior is taken as normal—"the essential"—and how women are inevitably painted as "the other, the inessential, the object." The chapter "From Maturity to Old Age" makes singularly depressing reading, and there de Beauvoir, who demanded to know why women "do not dispute male sovereignty" (1952, xvii), nevertheless reproduced without apparent irony or criticism the psychoanalytically derived stereotypes about middle-aged women that dominated early twentieth-century Western discourse.

De Beauvoir talked of the "crisis" of menopause and, pointing out the relative ease with which a man grows old, elaborated the process by which a woman is "suddenly deprived of her femininity" and is still "relatively young when she loses the erotic attractiveness and the fertility that, in the view of society and in her own, provide the justification for her existence and her opportunity for happiness" (541). In common with many nineteenth-century gynecologists, de Beauvoir believed that peasant women and those who engage in "heavy work" are less affected by menopause than women who have "staked everything on their femininity." De Beauvoir talked about the "pathetic urgency" with which women try to "turn back the flight of time" and claimed that some women continue to have menopausal difficulties until death. She ruminated on the "sad hours of depression," attributing them to the "overactivity of the pituitary gland" in its effort to compensate for the decline of the female sex hormones, but

330

went on to emphasize that "above all" it is the psychological state that governs changes in mood. De Beauvoir concluded that in middle age, a woman has "finally" won some freedom from her "slavery" to her sex, but to what purpose, she asked rhetorically, since "she finds this freedom at the very time when she can make no use of it. This recurrence is in no wise due to chance: patriarchal society gave all the feminine functions the aspect of a service, and woman escapes slavery only at times when she loses all effectiveness" (550).

De Beauvoir cited Helene Deutsch as inspiration for some of her ideas; Deutsch, influential in both the German- and English-speaking worlds and deeply immersed in Freudian psychoanalytic theory, stated several years before the publication of *The Second Sex*, "There is no doubt that the mastering of the psychological reactions to the organic decline [of the climacterium] is one of the most difficult tasks of woman's life" (1945, 456). Deutsch pointed out that the course of the climacterium is "determined" by the "fact that with the cessation of ovarian activity the remainder of the endocrine system is deranged in its functioning," but she emphasized that the "individual manifestation of the climacterium" depends "greatly" on any given woman's personality. In Deutsch's opinion the climacterium is "under the sign of a narcissistic mortification, difficult to overcome."

Deutsch believed that women return to an earlier, more childlike psychic attitude during the climacterium. In common with many nineteenth-century physicians, and Margaret Mead, writing a few years later (Mead 1949, 229), Deutsch likened it to puberty and stated that it is often a time of increased artistic activity as a "defense mechanism" for the unavoidable "immanent disappointment and mortification." She concluded:

> At the moment when expulsion of ova from the ovary ceases, all the organic processes devoted to the service of the species stop. Woman has ended her existence as bearer of a future life, and has reached her natural end—her partial death—as servant of the species. She is now engaged in an active struggle against her decline.... Little by little the whole female genital apparatus is transformed into a number of inactive and superfluous structures.... Because of these manifestations, the climacterium is known as the "dangerous age," and a certain type of aging woman has become a comical theatrical type.
>
> (Deutsch 1945, 460–62)

Deutsch stated that the "frequent depressions" characteristic of the climacterium "contain justified grief in the face of a declining world" and that the only possible means to defray the damage is to apply oneself with grace to being a grandmother.

It is paradoxical that women should pen this bitter tirade against female aging, and influential women at that (the works of both de Beauvoir and Deutsch were translated into Japanese—an analysis of Japanese reactions of the time would be interesting).[1] Deutsch does not give her writing a feminist turn but simply sets out understanding of how "female psychology" interacts with biologically determined changes throughout the life cycle. De Beauvoir, in contrast, sets out to write a feminist position piece, but rather than give it potential liberating force she portrays woman as the other, forever trapped, victim of an unequal binary gender opposition inherent in the social order and accepted by both men and women. Both writers draw on psychoanalytic theory and state explicitly that psychological components are more important at the menopausal transition than physical changes. Both grope for a way out of what they take to be a misogynist ideology of anatomy as destiny. Yet what they offer in its place is an exceedingly negative discourse focused on loss, one that by no means supersedes a biologically driven deterministic argument but actually reinforces and consolidates it by adding a gender-determined psychological dimension and creating a seamless whole—a relentless feedback loop of decay and misery from body to mind and mind to body.

Emphasis on those aspects of menopause with symbolic significance, particularly loss of reproductive capacity and sexuality, had received little attention in the fledgling profession of psychiatry. Henry Maudsley, a founder of British psychiatry, commented in *The Physiology and Pathology of the Mind*, published in 1874, that the "internal revolution which takes place in women at the climacteric period leads to many outbreaks of melancholic insanity in them between forty and fifty." In men, Maudsley said, "sometimes insanity supervenes" in a climacteric period between the ages of fifty and sixty (212). He acknowledged external factors and acquired characteristics as contributing to the incidence of "insanity" but used a humorally influenced physiological explanation to account for its mechanism, namely that "congestion" of blood in the brain and "irregularities in circulation" could have a profound and lasting effect on the "supreme nervous centers" (227). Clearly Maudsley's understanding of the body was similar to that of Edward Tilt; both attributed melancholic insanity in women to the direct effect on the nervous system of changes in the menstrual cycle.

The diagnosis of involutional melancholia created (and later abandoned) by the German psychiatrist Kraepelin early in this century also postulated a direct link between anatomical changes associated with the "involutional years" (the time of anatomical decline) and affective disorder. Like Maudsley and the majority of his physician contemporaries, Kraepelin believed that both men and women were vulnerable to "involutional" problems but thought that of the two, women were at greater risk. Characteristic symptoms, according to Kraepelin, were agitation and hypochondriasis (1906). Neither Maudsley nor Kraepelin thought that menopause heralded an unavoidable downward spiral for all women; they merely believed that certain women were vulnerable to a "crisis" from which they could usually expect to recover and that this crisis had a biological origin.

By 1924 a psychiatric textbook stated: "Real *climacteric psychoses* in women, which formerly were not uncommon, have disappeared from the literature of the last few years" (Bleuler 1924, 211; original emphasis). Nevertheless, Kraepelin's theory formed the basis for heated arguments that continued into the 1970s over the existence of a specific psychiatric syndrome, the direct result of anatomical and/or endocrinological changes associated with menopause (Malleson 1953; Saunders 1932; Stenback 1963). Once estrogen was isolated in the laboratory it suggested to some researchers that "acute ovarian failure" triggered involutional melancholia (Werner et al. 1934), a position that many physicians, particularly in America, tenaciously upheld (Wittson 1940; Malamud et al. 1941). However, several studies on the hypothesized vulnerability of menopausal women to major psychiatric disorder carried out in the 1970s showed (perhaps not to universal satisfaction) that such an association was not valid (Smith 1971; Weissman 1979; Winokur 1973). Moreover, general population surveys have demonstrated repeatedly that menopause has no significant effect on the incidence of a variety of common psychiatric symptoms (Ballinger 1985; Hunter 1990; Kaufert et al. 1992; Kruskemper 1975; McKinlay et al. 1987b; Mikkelsen and Holte 1982 [see Ballinger 1990 for a general review of the psychiatric and psychological literature on menopause]).

Despite this research, an association between declining estrogen levels and negative emotional states nevertheless remains pervasive in Western consciousness. Today, however, it is above all depression and not insanity that preoccupies public and physicians alike. The population surveys quoted above had little effect on gynecologists, family practitioners, and nurses, the majority of whom continue to emphasize the contribution of psychological factors to a difficult menopause, more so than do women actually experiencing menopause (Cowan et al. 1985), although many women too, as the Manitoba survey and other studies show,[2] continue to accept the idea of a direct link between changes in estrogen levels and depressed affect.

In contrast to the majority of physicians, those psychiatrists interested in psychoanalysis remain relatively unconcerned about the physiochemical connections between changes in the reproductive organs and the occurrence of depression; for them the symbolic aspects of menopause are of abiding interest. The psychoanalytic narrative of symbolic losses at menopause has profoundly influenced recent expectations about and images associated with menopausal women in Europe and North America. In this discourse a biologically determined sexual difference is entrenched, and in it the very process of aging is deeply and irrevocably gendered, as was not the case at the end of the nineteenth century.

In his earliest writing before the turn of the century, Freud apparently followed rather comfortably in the footsteps of his medical colleagues; he noted at menopause an increase in "somatic sexual excitation" and an "unduly increased libido" that he believed women experienced with feelings of "horror" leading to states of heightened anxiety and even anxiety neuroses (1973, 111). Later in his life Freud wrote: "Twice in the course of individual development certain instincts are considerably reinforced: at puberty, and, in women, at the menopause. We are not in the least surprised if a person who was not neurotic before becomes so at these times. When his instincts were not so strong, he succeeded in taming them; but when they are reinforced he can no longer do so. The repressions behave like dams against the pressure of water" (226).

Freud clearly had the adolescent in mind while he was writing this passage: the menopausal woman disappears from view almost as soon as she puts in an appearance. Toward the end of his career Freud wrote that women are vulnerable to neuroses at menopause because, he claimed, "it can bring about an enfeeblement of the ego," which in turn incites the "genesis of a neurosis" (1947, 242).

It was Freud's disciple Deutsch who postulated clearly for the first time the extent of symbolic losses associated with the end of menstruation. Her argument drew support from other psychoanalysts including Fessler, whose particular contribution was to suggest that while menstruating, a woman is regularly reminded of her reproductive potential; with the loss of this capability, she is inclined to regress to infantile attitudes that include penis envy (Fessler 1950).

Eric Erikson, in his widely read essay on "Womanhood and Inner Space," used what he described as a post-Freudian discourse to portray the "uniqueness" of woman, most particularly with respect to her attitudes about space. The essay developed an argument about biologically determined sexual difference but used a rhetoric that (rather halfheartedly) acknowledged the discrimination written into the classical Freudian script: "Many of the original conclusions of psychoanalysis concerning womanhood hinge on the so-called genital trauma, i.e., the little girl's sudden comprehension of the fact that she does not and never will have a penis" (1968, 274–75).

Erikson sought a shift in perspective from an emphasis on the "loss" of an external organ to a "sense of a vital inner potential"; from a "passive" renunciation of male activity to the "purposeful and competent pursuit of activities consonant with the possession of ovaries, a uterus, and a vagina." He insisted that it was possible to transcend the "initial trauma"; one way to do so was to give due weight to the importance, symbolic and literal, of the "procreative patterns," a position that he believed Deutsch had already formulated in her description of a "fully feminine" woman.

By observing children at play, Erikson documented what he took to be a profound and "natural" difference with respect to the way in which boys and girls are oriented toward space. As a result of this research, and from his own and others' clinical experiences, he concluded:

> [An] "inner space" is at the center of despair even as it is the very center of potential fulfillment. Emptiness is the female form of perdition . . . to be left, for her, means to be left empty, to be drained of the blood of the body, the warmth of the heart, the sap of life. How a woman thus can be hurt in depth is a wonder to many a man, and it can arouse both his empathic horror and his refusal to understand. Such hurt can be re-experienced in each menstruation; it is a crying to heaven in the mourning over a child; and it becomes a permanent scar in the menopause.
> (Erikson 1968, 278)

Erikson pointed out the possible advantages to both science and society if women, with their special spatial orientation, were to be more fully represented in public life, but he remained wedded to the idea that the psychology of women is determined by their anatomical structure. Furthermore he voiced the psychoanalytic message of "despair" unavoidably coupled with the end of reproductive capacity and its associated symbolic losses, a message that other psychiatrists echoed in no uncertain terms. Prados, for example, insisted: "Reproduction and motherhood are *essential* [original emphasis] for both complete physical maturity and emotional development of the woman." In Prados's estimation the climacterium is especially "hazardous" for "spinsters and childless wives." He likened menopause to puberty, as had Freud and others before him:

[At puberty a young woman must] defend herself against the intensity of her own sexual impulses by denying and devaluating the genital and reproductive organs.

At the menopause she will now blame them for the source of her present miseries. Clinically, this manifests itself by pains and discomforts in the pelvic region, by a conscious blaming of "change of life" for all her physical discomforts, and by fears that she might grow a cancer. The anxiety might express itself by all kinds of phobias, of which however, claustrophobia and agoraphobia are the most common.

Combined with these symptoms of anxiety we also find others of a typical conversion character, also others of a psychosomatic nature. Displacement from the genital organs to the head is most frequently used in the conversion symptoms; *headaches* and *dizziness* [original emphasis] with low back pain being the most common clinical symptoms. The reason why, in these cases, hot flushes are not relieved by hormone therapy, as is the case in the normal menopause, is that the patient finds this symptom perfectly suitable to express repressed and, therefore, hypertrophic libidinal elements. . . . The feeling of depression and guilt expresses the way in which the superego punishes the ego, both because of the unconscious incestuous impulses towards the father and the death wishes towards the mother.

(Prados 1967, 239)

What would Japanese women and physicians have to say about this exceedingly fanciful and oppressive interpretation of the menopausal experience? We must wonder who exactly is undergoing the "repression," "conversion," and "displacement"!

Although loss of reproductive capacity and femininity forms the core of all psychoanalytically oriented arguments about menopause, not all writers use such an essentialized language as does Prados. Therese Benedek, for example, was also deeply influenced by psychoanalytic theory but, drawing on her German heritage (with its interest in the autonomic system), tried to bridge the mind-body chasm by attributing most symptoms, including the hot flash, to "instability of the autonomic nervous system" (1950, 239).[3] She stressed, in common with many of her colleagues, that women who have not borne children are at great risk for trouble at menopause, but aside from this proviso she emphasized that "the emotional economy" of the "healthy woman" is not severely threatened by the loss of "gonadal stimulation." She pointed out that one must look at the entire life cycle and not simply the menopausal transition, in which case it becomes evident, she claimed, that those women who have had previous emotional problems, particularly at life-cycle transitions, will once again have difficulties at menopause. Benedek called for a more positive orientation than did most psychoanalysts: although at the climacterium the physical body was clearly in decline, Benedek felt that menopause could be regarded "in the psychological sense, as a developmental phase" and hence not necessarily a time of overwhelming loss (1950, 240).

Japanese intellectuals were familiar with Freudian discourse from its inception. Perhaps, since women were and still are expected to devote their adult lives to marriage and the raising of children, we might expect that Freudian theory and post-Freudian, up-to-the-minute hypotheses for child rearing would appeal to them and that Japanese women too would experience losses similar to those posited by psychoanalysts. On the contrary, however, psychoanalytic psychiatry never achieved more than a toehold in Japan and remains largely ignored today (Reynolds 1987): in a Japanese context the dark Freudian unconscious, based on the unresolvable sexually determined conflicts of childhood, makes little sense. The negative Freudian discourse of mutilation, loss, and mourning associated with menopause is a very minor theme in Japan, as we have seen—largely, I believe, because family continuity is embedded in the macrocosm of human social life, which completely transcends the procreative activities of any one woman. Although in Japan men belong to the world outside and women to the inside, in theory mutuality, nurturance, harmony, and interdependency are the keys to human relations, including gender relations; creating the social good can blur boundaries around individual lives. Moreover, anatomically gendered difference has not provoked a discourse of envy to the same extent as it has recently in the West; by contrast, in Japan the female ability to procreate occasions envy on the part of the male.

Grounded in themes of separation, independence, and autonomy, Freudian discourse could probably take root only in cultures where individualism has priority over social relationships and where too anatomy defines gender difference in stark oppositional terms. Moreover, Freudian discourse makes intuitive sense only if a notion of repressed infantile desire, fueling the unconscious, is plausible.

That the psychoanalytic argument about menopausal loss did not take root in Japan suggests that it is not a discourse about the menopausal transition but is rather a theoretical orientation toward the nature of woman that considers youthful attractiveness and procreation essential for a meaningful female life. Although its discussion focuses on the concept of unresolved childhood psychic tensions, triggered by menopause, that resurface into consciousness, it slips seamlessly from this psychobiological essentialism into a sermon about biologically determined social roles. It reduces woman's life to the tasks of attracting an appropriate male, followed by the production of his children, after which nothing remains but a devastating void marked by deterioration. This discourse was at its most vociferous during the middle part of this century, a time of major social transitions in the structure of middle-class family life and in broader proposals to educate young women for full lifetime participation in the work force and the professions. Once mature, women were no longer to be dismissed as anomalies in the world beyond domesticity but on the contrary presented serious and sustained competition to the male work force. At the same time the feminist movement was consolidating its forces, and women raised their voices to protest their continued assignment to a second-class citizenship; they explicitly criticized the lack of a male contribution both to the household and to child care.

Criticism of the psychoanalytic approach to menopause has come from a good number of commentators in the West, including some psychiatrists. But its thrust has usually been to minimize the impact of the biological changes of menopause, to pursue a Cartesian bifurcation of body and mind, and to insist that the everyday "real" psychological "traumas" of midlife (as opposed to the traumas of the unconscious) require much more attention.

A few writers focused, as de Beauvoir did, on the burden that societal expectations place on aging women. Jules Henry, an anthropologist with a strong interest in psychiatry, argued against the "overvaluation of fertility." He stated that "the deep depression that sometimes afflicts aging women, can no longer be viewed as a simple consequence of a physiological aging . . . it must be seen as a disease in which the environment is important, and which is an extreme expression of a widespread disturbance present in most women as a consequence of aging in our culture" (Henry 1966, 146–47). He concluded that the "forty-year-old jitters" were a result of the imposition of a "metaphysic" of youth, beauty, and romantic love, and drew on *The Feminine Mystique*, published in 1963 by Betty Friedan, to bolster his argument against the ideology of domesticity.

Similarly, Susan Sontag in a 1972 article in the *Saturday Review of the Society* described the aging process as "mainly an ordeal of the imagination—a moral disease, a social pathology—intrinsic to which is the fact that it afflicts women much more than men" (1972, 29). She developed her theme by describing society's permissiveness toward aging men and scorn for older women as no longer of use and went on to state that women are at an inherent disadvantage because "femininity" was identified with "incompetence, helplessness, passivity, noncompetitiveness, being nice." She concluded:

> Far more extensive than the hard sense of loss suffered during menopause (which with increased longevity, tends to arrive later and later)[4] is the depression about aging, which may not be set off by any real event in a woman's life, but is a recurrent state of "possession" of her imagination, ordained by society—that is, ordained by the way this society limits how women feel free to imagine themselves.
>
> (Sontag 1972, 32)

Sontag takes a radical position; like Henry and others, she seeks to deflect attention from a biologically reductionistic explanation that uses endocrinal changes to account for depression and other psychological symptoms in middle-aged women. These writers dismiss menopause itself as relatively uneventful (as de Beauvoir did not) but then suggest as Deutsch and other psychoanalysts did that women inevitably suffer losses at this time. In contrast to Deutsch, however, they believe that women are victims of an ideology that consigns them to biological incompetency and to culturally constructed redundancy once they are middle-aged. They deftly sidestep the question of physical changes in the body to focus instead on ideologically driven sexual discrimination against the process of growing older. In their arguments mind and body remain separated, and the entire problem of aging tends to diminish to one of social attitudes.

Because most psychiatrists asserted by the end of the 1970s that no psychiatric syndrome had a direct association with menopause, their clinical role vis-à-vis menopausal patients was no longer clear. No doubt the arguments of Sontag and of social psychologists such as Neugarten, who studied the attitudes of middle-aged women toward menopause (Neugarten 1968), encouraged the adoption of the position that most interested psychiatrists take today. For example, Fink states, "It cannot be denied that [menopause] is a universal marker which signals, clearly and distinctly, a new developmental stage" but believes that most women have few physical difficulties. He suggests that psychiatrists should help patients deal with "critical life problems" that converge on a woman around this period and that "these events must be clearly differentiated from the purely endocrine changes which constitute menopause proper" (Fink 1980, 125); by implication such changes are better left to gynecologists.

The Christie Browns, writing a position paper about menopause in the late 1970s, cautioned that "there is a danger in trying to see a complicated process in black and white terms," that surely most women will react to menopause with both positive and negative feelings, and that even to the most stable, it "comes as an unavoidable sign of aging and of mortality, against which some rebellion is nearly universal" (Christie Brown and Christie Brown 1976).

This carefully modulated article stands out from the corpus of psychiatric literature on menopause before the 1980s. Over the last twenty years psychiatric textbooks have gradually become less strident and decreased the space allotted to the subject of menopause. By the mid-1970s, texts were much less pathologically oriented. Robert Butler, an internationally recognized psychiatrist who specializes in aging, wrote a lengthy textbook chapter that criticized the "ageism" present in North American society, a term Butler invented to describe negative stereotyping of the middle-aged and elderly. He mentioned menopause in passing and stated, "Unfortunately, the menopause has been blamed for a host of other ills in women, both physical and emotional. The public and women themselves must become more discriminating in their evaluation of the difficulties of middle life. . . . In particular attention must be given to the negative cultural attitudes towards women as they age" (Butler 1975, 239). By 1989 aspiring psychiatrists were simply being taught that menopause is "a subject surrounded by myths, taboos, fears, and superstition. The significance of menopause has changed over time, with longer life expectancy, and more social and career options. Hot flashes and night sweats are experienced by many women, but few seek medical attention. Contrary to popular view, this time is not one of depression for women who have not been depressed before" (Apfel and Mazor 1989, 1337).

A focus in the psychiatric literature earlier in the century on the unavoidable losses of reproductive powers and sexuality as causes of depression has largely been transformed in recent years into a discourse that emphasizes possibilities for further psychological development throughout the life cycle, punctuated by unabated sexual activity.

Nevertheless, the "double standard of aging," as Sontag called it (1972), is alive and well: if anything our aversion to female decay and death has become even more pronounced in recent years (Greer 1991; Wolf 1990). Clearly this atmosphere—apparently far less evident before the late nineteenth century, if the medical literature of that time indicates the attitude of society at large—contributes to discrimination against older women. The discrimination is part and parcel of culturally shaped attitudes about sexuality and about the "proper place" of women in society at large; transparently evident in the now outmoded psychoanalytic discourse about menopausal women, the attitudes linger in society at large and offer endless opportunities for commercial exploitation. The bimonthly magazine *LEAR'S*, recently created for "the woman over forty . . . who wasn't born yesterday," claims that older women "no longer sit before their mirrors and swoon as if sex were finished and life were pale." Wang points out that this magazine, specifically directed at middle-aged and older women, is dedicated to the glamorization of youth culture and the industry of looking young (Wang 1988).

Psychiatric discourse is not the only medical discourse that contributed to this climate—the transformation of menopause into a deficiency disease has, in the long run, had a much more pervasive and profound effect on current attitudes toward menopause. Although this approach is radically different from a psychoanalytically driven orientation, it too plays off culturally infused fears about aging; but now the unconscious has been tidied out of the way, a fanciful interlude placed under wraps. Once again a simple biological determinism takes center stage, but one in which the ovarian secretion, estrogen, has replaced its parent organ, the ovary.

The Estrogen-Deficient Body—Augury of Decrepitude

In a lecture given before the New York Academy of Medicine in 1941, Robert Frank, a clinical professor of gynecology, declared: "Those of us who have been interested in endocrinology for many years consider the estrogenic relief of the menopause as a major triumph, second only to that of the treatment of hypothyroidism by thyroid medication and of diabetes by insulin" (Frank 1941, 863).

Emil Novak, one of the most prominent gynecologists of his time, was at pains to point out that "estrogenic" therapy was a great improvement on ovarian therapy. He was concerned that history might seem to repeat itself but emphasized that since no "real" knowledge existed at the turn of the century about what substances the ovary might secrete, the "billions of expensive tablets and capsules of ovarian substance . . . consumed by millions of trusting women in these early days of organotherapeutic enthusiasm" had simply acted as placebos (Novak 1940, 592). Novak was extremely critical of those physicians who insisted on clinging to such antiquated therapy and instead actively promoted the new estrogenic therapy. According to Frank, by the late 1930s more than one hundred estrogenic pharmaceutical products derived from natural sources were on the market, but the gynecologists writing at the time pointed out that high price was a major drawback to widespread use. Many assumed that the synthetic estrogen marketed as Stilbestrol (which would eventually be linked to an increased risk for cancer) would soon be the drug of choice, although it was already associated with nausea and liver damage for one in every ten patients (Frank 1940, 861).

Despite the reformulation of menopause as a deficiency state, research articles and gynecological textbooks of the 1940s carefully pointed out that the end of menstruation was a "normal phase of the life cycle" for most women, and that of those who experienced symptoms, for the majority the process was not pathological: "Even in those women who suffer a severe and prolonged menopause, constant hypodermic medication is not required, and by a combination of the hypodermic and oral routes almost all patients can be kept reasonably comfortable. . . . The great majority of women at this epoch require no treatment at all" (Novak 1941, 468).

Both Frank and Novak sought to dispose of what they believed was a pervasive dread women held about menopause, often fueled by physicians' attitudes; several gynecologists were impressed by what they took to be a pathological event. Shorr, for example, described the symptoms of menopause as "bizarre and extensive as any syndrome with which I am acquainted" (1940, 455) and concluded:

> Despite the gratifying progress that has been made in the treatment of the menopausal syndrome, many questions still remain unanswered. The situation is somewhat analogous to Graves' disease [a thyroid deficiency disease] and diabetes mellitus where a therapeutic measure of considerable effectiveness still leaves unsolved many of the primary problems relating to the genesis of the disease. . . . Our therapeutic successes should not cause us to lose sight of the fact that we have no knowledge of the cause of the menopausal syndrome.
>
> (Shorr 1940, 472)

Shorr believed that "psychogenic" factors must be crucial in accounting for why some women apparently suffered from a menopausal syndrome while for others the end of menstruation had no overt effects. He believed that if physicians conceptualized menopause, not as an "entity" but as a "symptom of a more fundamental psychobiological maladjustment, the more rapid will be the attainment of our eventual therapeutic goal, its prophylaxis" (1940, 473).

Even the availability of a specific medication to counter the syndrome caused little narrowing of perspective on the part of physicians before the middle of the century. Although some explicitly likened menopause to a deficiency disease, they nevertheless kept the idea that most women did not actually suffer from a menopausal syndrome. Even among those women who exhibited distressing symptoms, it was assumed that they would recover after a few years, at such time as the body readjusted to its new hormonal "climate." The so-called vasomotor symptoms—hot flashes, sweats, and palpitations—were widely recognized as the core symptoms of the syndrome, symptoms that could be greatly reduced through the application of estrogen replacement therapy; but in contrast to diabetes, therapy would not be required on a lifelong basis.

The sociologist Bell believes that during the 1940s some gynecologists were attracted to the deficiency disease model because it gave their work an aura of respectability, an authority grounded in basic science research, which thus far had not been very evident (1987). The combination of scientific insights to the endocrine system with the first large-scale commercial production of relatively cheap synthetic estrogens brought about the major shift toward a disease model; there were suggestions to standardize diagnosis and treatment methods into a uniform regimen. As in earlier years, many clinicians remained ambivalent about these developments (1987, 536), fearing that they were in danger of having their medical practice driven by the interests of basic scientists. Emil Novak stated, for example:

> It has seemed to me that clinicians are developing a sort of inferiority complex in the study of endocrine problems, so awed are they by the brilliant contributions which have been coming from the laboratory, and so dependent have they become upon the laboratory workers for the ammunition which they so sorely need in their own clinical work. . . . And yet there are certain advantages which the clinician enjoys over the laboratory worker.
>
> (Novak 1939, 423)

The expansion of basic science research gave clinicians cause for concern beyond the threat to their unquestioned authority (Bell 1987). It became apparent that research funds would, from now on, be channeled largely into the research enterprise: if diagnoses were to be performed in laboratories, could they lead to unsafe medical practice? Considerable argument took place as to whether estrogen replacement therapy was indeed safe as a medication for use in menopause (MacBryde et al. 1941).

Initially, in the attempt to make the clinical care of menopause into a scientific endeavor, there was no rush to prescribe estrogen replacement therapy to the majority of menopausal women; gynecologists preferred to limit their services to those few women who were exhibiting pathology— to confine their attentions to hot flashes and allied vasomotor symptoms. The deficiency disease approach did not, as we have seen, silence either the psychoanalytic or the life-style approaches to menopause. But it was an innovation supported by gynecologists who were particularly influential in education and in policy-making. For example, the opinions of thirty gynecologists designated as "experts" were used as a basis for a positive decision about the safety of the synthetic estrogen replacement therapy diethylstilbestrol (DES) by the American government in the 1940s (Bell 1987, 536), a medication that was used to curb hot flashes and also, until the 1970s, to prevent miscarriages. This drug was eventually taken off the market because it was linked to an increase of precancerous and cancerous conditions in the daughters of those women who had taken it.

Despite increasing pressures from drug companies for widespread use of estrogen replacement therapy, some researchers continued to remain unimpressed. The Novaks (father and son) in the 1950 editions of their gynecological textbook had the following to say, for example: "There are many women to whom the menopause comes as a boon, with a striking improvement in general health and well-being" (1952, 600).

Another line of argument at this time, taken by a minority of physicians, is much closer to that of the Japanese. It cited instability of the autonomic nervous system as crucial in the menopausal syndrome. One article suggested that use of estrogen supplements was inappropriate because the "process of adaptation" of the body to its new hormonal environment might be impeded. In its place the author recommended sedative medication that "stabilizes" the autonomic system to tide the patient over the difficult transition (Kelly et al. 1961).

By the end of the 1950s, therefore, after eighty years of debate over menopause, there was still no consensus among physicians on the etiology of symptoms, whether the condition was diseaselike or a natural event, or whether medical intervention was called for. Nevertheless, from the initial acceptance by a good number of physicians of an apparently simple idea, namely, that the unpleasant symptoms of a minority of menopausal women could be eliminated by boosting their declining estrogen levels for a few months or at most for a year or two, the ramifications proved to be enormous. Once conceptualized as a deficiency disease, menopause could be unhooked from its coupling to the life cycle, divorced from any moral evaluations, and even detached, in theory, from mind (although emotions tend to creep back into any discussion about women's health and their bodies). Menopause thus moved to the terrain of "sound" medical discourse, to be treated by many from this time on as a simple fact devoid of any significance beyond biological change. All signs and symptoms heretofore associated with this part of the life cycle, but now regarded as "soft," could be rejected as irrelevant. This narrowly deterministic discourse induced some feminists to complain that women were left to "pull them-selves up by their own bootstraps" because of an inherent tendency in this approach to dismiss most women's complaints as trivial and irrelevant (Posner 1979, 186).

In recent years conceptualization has shifted yet again, but this time the broadening horizon offers a very different perspective. Research that shows no difficulties for the vast majority of women at the end of men-struation (including Kaufert et al 1987; Matthews et al. 1990; and Mc-Kinlay et al. 1992) lacks interest for most physicians. Moreover, discomfort of individual women is no longer the starting point for forceful arguments currently put forward for the use of replacement therapies. Hot flashes have receded into the background, their mechanism still by no means fully understood, and their occurrence only partially explained. At conferences about menopause today the average gynecologist, psychiatrist, and general practitioner now usually participate only as members of the audience; speakers selected for plenary sessions come almost exclusively from a small group of elite gynecologists who have appointments at one of the major medical institutions in North America and Europe, and whose clinical forte is designated as menopause. But the sessions given by specialists in heart disease, oncology, orthopedics, clinical epidemiology, and economics are the ones packed to overflowing.[5] The stakes are much higher now, since estrogen deficiency, the "endocrinopathy" of menopause, has been linked to the "killer" diseases of later life that account for the bulk of health-care expenditures in industrial societies today.

Flashes of Immortality: Feminine Forever

The sea is barely wrinkled, and little waves strike the sandy shore.
Mr. Palomar is standing on the shore, looking at a wave . . . it is not
"the waves" that he means to look at, but just one individual
wave. . . . But isolating one wave is not easy.

(Italo Calvino, "Mr. Palomar")

It was well established by the middle of the century that far more men than women suffered and died from coronary heart disease. It was also observed at autopsies that women whose ovaries had been removed were at a greater risk for coronary heart disease than were "normal" controls (Oliver and Boyd 1959; Robinson et al. 1959). These findings, together with those from animal research, led scientists to suggest that men who were at risk for heart disease might well gain some protection through the administration of estrogens (Marmorston et al. 1959; Stamler 1963). It was also patently obvious that if manipulation of sex steroid levels could significantly reduce mortality from heart disease, there would be major implications not only for the longevity of individuals but, of more importance, for the containment of health-care expenditures as well. Furthermore, hormones would generate accelerating profits from indefinite use as a prophylactic against major "killer" diseases. And funds would pour into a research topic of such resounding significance.

Unfortunately, once experiments were under way with male subjects, "an unexpectedly" large number of heart attacks "often" leading to death were recorded for the subjects of these studies, particularly during the first two months of taking the estrogen compound Premarin (Furman 1971, 47). Nevertheless, a Coronary Drug Project designed to involve fifty-three collaborating centers was established in 1965, and experimentation continued with reduced dosages of estrogens but was eventually discontinued. At the same time experiments with estrogenic compounds were carried out on men suffering from cancer of the prostate. During the first trials the subjects showed a substantial increase in mortality from heart disease; a smaller dosage of estrogen was reported to be useful in controlling prostatic cancer, apparently without increasing the risk for heart disease (Bailar and Byar 1970). Recently, however, a few cases of the rare disease of male breast cancer have been reported in prostatic cancer patients who were taking estrogen therapy (Shlappack et al. 1986).

Research with men proved, therefore, to be both risky and questionable—clearly estrogen has a powerful and a potentially lethal effect on men: it is, after all, a female hormone! Since the research essentially involved the feminization of men, something inherently "contrary to nature," it may also have caused psychological discomfort for researchers and subjects alike. Parallel research with women, however, rapidly turned into a major industry, although the fervor of one particular gynecologist was so extreme that it nearly reduced the whole enterprise to quackery. Robert Wilson and his coauthor Thelma Wilson, a nurse and also his wife, published an article in the 1960s in the *Journal of the American Geriatrics Society*, using language to describe menopausal women that makes Edward Tilt at his most florid seem positively benign. Entitled "The Fate of the Nontreated Postmenopausal Woman: A Plea for the Maintenance of Adequate Estrogen from Puberty to the Grave," the article started out:

> The unpalatable truth must be faced that all postmenopausal
> women are castrates. There is a variation in degree but not in fact.
> Men do not live as long as the so-called weaker sex. However, they
> age, if free from serious disease, in a proportional manner. . . .
> From a practical point of view, a man remains a man until the end.
> The situation with a woman is very different. Her ovaries become

inadequate relatively early in life. She is the only mammal who cannot continue to reproduce after middle age.

(Wilson and Wilson 1963, 347)

Whereas nineteenth-century thinkers placed woman closer than man to other mammals on the ladder of evolution but not inherently unlike both, in the Wilsons' estimation she was significantly different from both man and other animals, an unnatural creature—unavoidably deficient because of her biological makeup. The "deprivation" of estrogen, according to the Wilsons, "markedly impairs homeostasis." She was no longer a "whole woman"—only a "part woman" (348). They went on to discuss a change in "estrogen integrity" caused by the aging process, which was "distorted" in women, and then in the balance of their article elaborated on the long-term consequences of these changes. The Wilsons pointed out that the incidence of coronary heart disease increased in older women to approach that of men and recommended the use of estrogen replacement therapy for both men and women as a "prophylactic" measure. They also encouraged the use of replacement therapy as a preventive measure against osteoporosis in older women and described arthritis, impairment of carbohydrate metabolism, changes in the skin, and other complex disorders—the results of an endocrine system "in a state of chaos." They noted, in addition, a disturbed autonomic nervous system. The Wilsons recommended replacement therapy as effective for the "depression and involutional melancholia commonly seen at menopause" and added that "a large percentage of women who escape severe depression or melancholia acquire a vapid cow-like feeling called a 'negative state.' It is a strange endogenous misery.... The world appears as through a gray veil, and they live as docile harmless creatures missing most of life's values" (353).

Mindful no doubt, that they were writing in a geriatric journal, the Wilsons made use of the erroneous argument so often resorted to by those eager to medicalize aging women: they pointed out that in the Roman Empire life expectancy was about twenty-three years and added that there were very few old women in those days. They stated that in the fourteenth century life expectancy had risen to thirty-three years and by the turn of the twentieth century was forty-eight years; but "older women did not yet constitute a problem." By 1975, they concluded, there would be 40 percent more women than men in the United States and lamented that "the civilized world is becoming full of old women past age fifty.... Unfortunately, although women live longer than men, a greater proportion of them are chronically incapacitated after reaching forty-five years of age" (355). They continued:

We all know women who are palpably suffering from the menopause. They bear it bravely, adjust as best they can, and never consult a physician about it. . . . There is ample evidence that the
course of history has been changed not only by the presence of estrogen, but by its absence. The untold misery of alcoholism, drug
addiction, divorce, and broken homes caused by these unstable, estrogen-starved women cannot be presented in statistical form.

(Wilson and Wilson 1963, 355)

Estrogen-starved women can be observed, the Wilsons claimed, "walking
stiffly in twos and threes" on our streets, "seeing little and observing less."
They added for good measure that the intelligent woman knows that the
"loss of her physical attractiveness is entirely out of proportion," an
awareness that affects her "psyche":

She sees the marked skin changes, the disfiguring fat deposits, the
atrophy of her breasts and the beginning disappearance of her external genitals. If married, an irritated or inadequate vagina may
bring more unhappiness. . . . Let us reverse the situation regarding
atrophy. Suppose the man of medicine noticed his own genitals
gradually disappear year by year. Would he be as indifferent to
genital atrophy as he now appears to be? We think not. His medicine closet would be well stocked with protective hormones.

(Wilson and Wilson 1963, 356–57)

The Wilsons concluded that all women, the only possible exceptions being
those with breast cancer, should be given estrogen therapy combined with
progestogens (synthetic products usually derived from male hormones),
to be continued throughout life. How could this paper possibly have got
past a scientific peer review and been accepted for publication? No doubt
its misogynist language shocked a good number of the medical profession,
but this and later articles by Wilson were widely cited for ten or more
years and are still referred to at times (see Utian and Jacobowitz 1990). It
comes as no surprise to learn that Robert Wilson's research was funded
by Wyeth Ayerst, the pharmaceutical company with the largest investment in the production and sales of estrogen replacement therapy and that
the Wilson Foundation for research into aging was set up and funded by
that same drug company. Advertisements by Ayerst in medical journals
of the time urged doctors to "Keep her on Premarin" and touted their
wares with the epithet, "When a woman outlives her ovaries . . . "

As part of the promotion campaign for the foundation, Wilson published a book for the general public entitled *Feminine Forever*. In an ap-
pendix are listed the twenty-one medical appointments, diplomas, and fel-

lowships that the doctor held at that time, followed by thirteen references to his previously published work in medical journals. No quack this Dr. Wilson, who described in detail the horrors of female aging and the sexual allure of women on estrogen therapy and outlined with religious zeal in conclusion his Kekulian discovery[6] of the importance of the hormone progestin:

> I spent my days poring over charts listing dosage and timing variations, hoping to discern some pattern by which the benefits of estrogen might be obtained without untoward side effects. One night as I fell asleep, my mind was still struggling with these problems. In an ensuing dream I saw myself counting up the days in a patient's menstrual cycle and then jotting one word on the calendar: PROGESTIN.
>
> (Wilson 1966, 198)

Thus, Wilson concluded, he could "artificially mimic" the sex hormone milieu of younger women and reproduce a drug-induced cycle in older infertile women that would keep them forever free of "senile decay." It was not simply the declining estrogen that needed to be replaced, he believed, but also that other crucial ovarian hormone, progesterone,[7] the principal function of which is to prepare the lining of the uterus for the reception of a fertilized egg. This combination was already on the market in the form of the contraceptive pill. Ironically, in writing the foreword for *Feminine Forever*, the gynecologist Greenblatt cited the work of Simone de Beauvoir and stated that the ideas of Wilson were in tune with those of the author of the *Second Sex* who had written about "the pathetic urgency of those who have staked everything on their femininity to turn back the flight of time" (Greenblatt 1966, 13).

Wilson was not alone at this time in his demeaning descriptions of women. At least one other physician writer, David Reuben, whose title, *Everything You Always Wanted to Know about Sex but Were Afraid to Ask* (1969), no doubt enhanced his sales, revealed a similar attitude toward middle-aged women. Meanwhile, 1970s editions of Novak's textbook (authored now by his son and colleagues) continued to assert that for most women menopause presented no difficulties and that estrogen should be given only to those very few women who suffered from severe symptoms for as short a period of time as possible. After reviewing the data on the effect of estrogens on heart disease and osteoporosis, these authors explicitly opposed the "minority" of physicians who advocated replacement therapy for life and, moreover, stated that progesterone replacement was "expensive and needless" (Novak et al. 1975). To the present time the

Novak school continues to place itself in a radically different position from replacement therapy activists: "It would seem that although menopausal women do have an estrogen milieu which is lower than that during the menstrual years, it is not negligible or absent. The menopause can perhaps be regarded as a physiological phenomenon which is *protective in nature*— protective from undesirable reproduction and the associated growth stimuli" (Jones and Jones 1981, 710; emphasis added).

Despite the prestige that these gynecologists enjoyed as eminent professors at the medical school of Johns Hopkins University, their words went largely unheeded. Menopause no longer represented simply the end of menstruation, a life-cycle transition that could cause individual distress. Its meaning had shifted to become more expansive so that, in addition to being a transition, of much more importance, it now represented an omen for the future, a gateway, not to the golden years or to the second season, but to a lingering and expensive decay and death. Since the 1970s, predictions about how many surplus older women will exist in the near future have given the medical literature an ever increasing sense of urgency; this specter on the horizon drives the current expansive discourse about menopause and radically transforms its recommendations for action into something approaching the magnitude of a pharmacological starwars.

As we have seen, the idea of tinkering with the reproductive organs, of outdoing nature's design and rejuvenating parts of the anatomy with replacement therapy, was already in place at the end of the nineteenth century. Shortly afterward the effects of sex hormones on parts of the body at a distance from the reproductive organs were postulated, but it was more than fifty years before the necessary technology was available to implement replacement therapy on a large scale—a technology that by the 1970s had developed into a massive industry showing annual sales in the range of seventy-five million dollars and expanding by 1990 to four hundred sixty million dollars. Wyeth Ayerst's estrogen, Premarin, is the fourth most prescribed medication in the United States (Office of Technology Assessment 1992), yet at present only an estimated 15 percent of the female population in America receive some form of hormone replacement therapy (HRT).[8] Clearly, with the baby boomers entering menopause, the stakes for a financial sweep are very high.

The pharmaceutical industry is currently lobbying the American government with a plea that estrogen therapy is necessary to the continued health of all women aged forty and over and, moreover, should be maintained for the duration of their lives. Many of the specialists (but not all) whom the government has called on as advisory consultants are the recipients of research money from these same drug companies. The projected policy change has been likened to a compulsory vaccination, but with a fundamental difference, however, since hormones are not administered to encourage the production by the body of its own defense mechanisms, and the level of the dosage must be artificially kept up on a sustained basis for it to be effective against the "killer" diseases (if indeed it is effective, as its promoters claim). Likening hormone replacement therapy to administering insulin for diabetes is more accurate in terms of its postulated mechanism, but making an analogy to a vaccination for the purposes of promoting a national policy is surely more expedient.

Risks, Costs, and ? Benefits

Because of the many benefits of estrogen replacement therapy improving both the quality and quantity of life, all women who have this postmenopausal hormone deficiency, except possibly those who are obese, should receive estrogen replacement. The beneficial effects of estrogen replacement therapy are many and there are few adverse effects.

(Mischell 1989, 409)

Many women pass through menopause with no problems and no complaints. They should be encouraged to pursue healthy life-styles. For those who do experience difficulties or for those who are at risk for developing problems, . . . treatment options can be considered.

(Gass and Rebar 1990, 9)

The chapters of current gynecological textbooks that describe menopause or the climacteric (a word still in circulation in certain medical circles) allot most of their discussion today not to what happens at the end of menstruation but to how hormone replacement therapy relates to cancer, heart, and bone disease. They do so because alongside the gynecologists who work with patients in midlife, and the basic scientists—mostly endocrinologists who are interested in the chemistry and physiology of the end of menstruation—is another group of scientists of an entirely different kind, the clinical epidemiologists, who use statistical methods as their principal tool and deal not in individuals but in populations of experimental animals and people. The result has been to erode the gynecologists' authority, most particularly because they often know considerably less about sophisticated statistical methods than about the ever-changing corpus of molecular biology and in any case tend to be suspicious of statistics that are not, after all, "hard" science. Epidemiologists work with probabilities, not scientific "facts," and create data about replacement therapy that complicate the lives of clinicians and patients alike.

The articles published by epidemiologists have titles such as "Risks and Benefits of Long-Term Treatment with Estrogens" (Mack and Ross 1989); "The Use of Hormonal Replacement Therapy and the Risk of Stroke and Myocardial Infarction in Women" (Thompson et al. 1989); "Risk of Localized and Widespread Endometrial Cancer in Relation to Recent and Discontinued Use of Conjugated Estrogens" (Shapiro et al. 1985). One recent article starts out with the statement: "The goal of contemporary hormone replacement is to minimize net predictable lifetime risk; success therefore depends upon quantitative assessments of the net quality of life, of net morbidity, and of net mortality" (Mack and Ross 1989). This article points out that at present the frequency of eight "common conditions is known to be influenced by estrogen usage": the "climacteric itself," osteoporosis and osteoporotic fractures, acute and chronic ischemic heart disease, stroke, rheumatoid arthritis, gallbladder disease, endometrial cancer, and breast cancer. The authors create a model, a hypothetical cohort of one hundred thousand women entering menopause at age fifty, followed to age seventy-five, and treated continuously with a moderate dose of estrogen therapy. They then perform what to the uninitiated appear to be some very complicated statistical manipulations that combine the results of more than one hundred actual surveys of estrogen replacement therapy and its effect on the eight common conditions and adjust them to produce data relevant to the hypothetical cohort of one hundred thousand women. From this manipulation the authors conclude that the eight conditions that are thought to be affected by estrogen account for "slightly more than half of [all] the deaths to be expected in women between fifty and seventy-five, a bit less than half of all the days of disability, and about one in every eight hospitalizations" (1815). The authors continue their analysis by examining the effects that they estimate the administration of estrogen would have on morbidity and mortality of this hypothetical cohort:

> We estimate that hospitalizations are made more frequent by an increment of about 75%, and that the days of disability are also more frequent . . . but by a smaller factor of about 17%. More than balancing this net impact on morbidity is a reduction of about 14% in the number of deaths to be expected in members of the cohort, confirming the *net benefit of treatment with estrogen replacement.*
>
> (Mack and Ross 1989, 1815)

However, Mack and Ross go right on to state that today most gynecologists do not use simple estrogen replacement therapy because they are concerned about the well demonstrated increased risk for endometrial cancer when using this regime, and that hence most opt for combined estrogen and progestin use, commonly known as HRT. They point out that reliable empirical estimates of the effect of combined therapy are unavailable and indicate a "basis for concern about adverse effects on the risk of vascular disease, breast cancer, and gallbladder disease, and about longterm compliance with therapy." But they agree, nevertheless, that evidence suggests that progestin must be given at the same time as estrogen to prevent cancer of the endometrium. Throughout their study these researchers pay little attention to the fact that both estrogen and progesterone are umbrella terms for subsets of related hormones and that, particularly in Europe, research has been conducted with different estrogenic compounds that do not produce exactly the same long-term effects on the body as the medication usually used in North America (Hulka 1990).

After totting up the possible benefits and risks of hormone replacement therapy in several different ways to produce several different outcomes, the authors ask rhetorically if there are "any treatment strategies which will provide the valuable benefits while playing it safe?" "Probably not," they answer: none of the strategies of screening out high-risk women, preferentially treating only those most likely to gain some benefit, treating only those with no uterus, or using only short-term treatment "will provide major benefit without risk."

The authors suggest that for the time being it is perhaps most prudent to make use of estrogen only and not progestin (in contrast to other physicians who declare that combined therapy must always be used [Nachtigall 1990, 1]), but that women over fifty with a uterus (only two-thirds of American women!) are "patently" at risk for cancer; they state that patients must be routinely monitored with endometrial biopsies (painful and invasive), as a result of which "large numbers" of them will receive unnecessary curettage, some under general anesthesia (Mack and Ross 1989, 1818). As an alternative they suggest a "progestogen-dispensing intrauterine device." Such a device would release progestin where it is most wanted—in the uterus, and keep it away from other organs where it apparently interferes with the action of estrogen (experiments with this device have been under way for some time [Hagenfeld et al. 1977]). They do not suggest yet another alternative: to remove the uterus of all women past reproductive age as a prophylactic measure, a procedure that the tone of certain articles suggests some gynecologists support and that might make their own lives much simpler (Studd 1989, 506–9).

The authors close with a caveat similar to others that appear regularly at the end of risk-benefit articles:

Perhaps a prudent course in any event is to assume the role of medical fiduciary [a person to whom property or power is entrusted for the benefit of another] rather than that of decision-maker, to insist that the patient fully participate in the choice of therapy, and to make sure that whatever the choice, she explicitly acknowledge the measure of uncertainty. In any case, both doctor and patient must place high priority on surveillance for unexplained bleeding and breast lumps, emphasizing follow-up and follow-through for the latter.

(Mack and Ross 1989, 1818)

At a 1990 international conference on menopause held in Bangkok, a plenary session concentrated on hormone replacement therapy. In one question-and-answer session a member of the audience, a physician, stood up and said: "I would like to dispel a myth that says hormones are dangerous, that they will induce cancer or thrombosis. I would like to draw the parallel with insulin, which is certainly a dangerous drug if given inappropriately. Yet if sex hormones are given appropriately they can do so much more good than harm" (*Hormone Replacement Therapy* 1990, 2–3).

But the exchange that followed offered no assurance that doctors yet know how to handle these powerful drugs. Discussion of hormone replacement therapy produced the following comments, for example: "We have seen bleeding from an atrophic endometrium that is extremely difficult to control; this occurred in women who had been amenorrheal for a number of years and then started bleeding"; "We discontinued therapy altogether in some cases . . . "; "There is apparently a group of women [up to 25 percent] who are bleeders, irrespective of what you do [that is, change dose levels and combinations]"; but "we only have two years of experience" (*Hormone Replacement Therapy* 1990, 4). Perhaps the trusty leech might help!

As in Japan, women in North America have not remained passive in the face of this continuous blast of complex and conflicting information. In 1989, the same year that the Mack and Ross article appeared, the National Women's Health Network put out a paper, *Taking Hormones and Women's Health*, that also reviewed a substantial portion of the literature on menopause. The authors explicitly state that they oppose the majority view of normal menopause as a deficiency disease and point out assumptions that occur in virtually all the articles they reviewed. Few women are informed, they state, that the ovary itself continues to secrete some hormones "long after menopause," and that other sites in the body—the adrenal glands and fatty tissues—also produce estrogen (1989, 1). They agree with Mack and Ross that combined hormone therapy has not been in use long enough for evidence to have accrued as to either risks or benefits; it is poor public health practice, they state, to "attempt to prevent chronic disease conditions by using drugs of unknown safety and effectiveness," and "dangerously misleading" to suggest that normal midlife women will experience better health by taking drugs with unknown risks; they add that women are, in effect, being urged to take part in a "risky, uncontrolled experiment without their fully informed consent" (2–3).

They make a point that to my knowledge none of the researchers themselves discuss or take much account of: namely, that many women now taking hormone therapy were exposed when younger to high-dose birth control pills, and that among these women some were given DES while pregnant. The next generation of hormone takers will have been exposed to a lower-dose pill, but from a younger age (3). The network might have pointed out, in addition, that reproductive histories—including pregnancies, abortions, miscarriages, and breast-feeding practices—are variable, have a long-term effect on body chemistry, and should be part of any assessment of the safety of hormone replacement therapy.

The Women's Health Network suggests that less expensive, safer, and "more natural" forms of prevention against chronic disease, such as dietary changes, dispensing with cigarettes and excessive alcohol, and environmental improvements only rarely figure in research findings (1989, 6–7; but see Notelovitz 1989, for example); they attribute this omission largely to the fact that drug companies fund most research. Since dietary changes have significantly reduced the incidence of heart disease among men, clearly this argument is of importance. Moreover, a diet high in soybean has recently been linked not only to a reduced incidence of hot flashes but also to lower incidence of breast cancer among premenopausal women (*Lancet* 1991, 1197). It will be interesting to see what happens to leads such as this.

The network reminds us too that not all women with fractures have osteoporosis and not all women with osteoporosis have fractures—facts that are often confused; moreover, there is no simple relation between bone mineral density and incidence of osteoporosis (1989, 5; Cummings 1985),[9] nor are there data on what effect combined hormone replacement therapy has on bones. Furthermore, screening for bone mineral density often produces false positives and false negatives that further complicate the issue.

As the Women's Health Network notes, it took twenty years for some of the cancer connected with the imbibing of DES to manifest itself, an experience that should encourage the exercise of great caution in connection with replacement therapy (1989, 3; countering this argument in the past was the assertion that fetal tissue developed the cancer, not the pregnant women who took the medication—and therefore, presumably, older women have nothing to fear [Greenblatt 1972]).

Research into heart disease and replacement therapy indicates, these authors note, that although the body continues to make estrogen after menopause, it produces very little progesterone (Korenman 1982); hence there may be some good as yet unknown biological reason why this is so. Furthermore the combination oral contraceptive pills used in the 1970s (which included progestogen) are linked to increased risk for stroke and heart attacks. The network alludes to several serious problems with the studies done on heart disease, among them that the longitudinal survey research widely cited in the literature as evidence of reduced risk for heart disease used, and continues to use, many subjects who take only estrogen (National Women's Health Network 1989, 8–9).[10] Today replacement therapy for most women starts out with combined hormones, and hence the results of previous survey research allow no long-term predictions about future generations of women. Moreover, research does not always pay attention to whether subjects smoke, a variable that has a well-recognized effect on the incidence of heart disease. Women who are hormone users and voluntarily recruited into survey research studies are significantly thinner and not representative of the average population; in all probability they are not at high risk for heart disease (Egeland et al. 1988). All these results qualify any attempt to associate the use of hormone replacement therapy to a lowered incidence of heart disease.

Finally, the Women's Health Network points out that few women hear about the side reactions they can expect with hormone replacement therapy, most particularly that hot flashes usually recur when treatment is stopped, that combined therapy often causes what is euphemistically known as "breakthrough" bleeding that not only creates anxiety but entails close monitoring and often painful medical procedures to establish its cause (1989, 5); common additional side effects are bloating, "the blues," breast tenderness, and headaches. Because of these problems women tend to start and stop taking medication, and many never fill their prescription or make use of it only once (Ravnikar 1987), producing variation that population studies cannot readily monitor.

One other very important criticism of the literature, not noted by the Women's Health Network, is that almost all the research into menopause has been done with Caucasian middle-class women, and most particularly those who sought out medical care. Extrapolations from these populations to all middle-aged women then occur, although we know there are, for example, very different rates of osteoporosis, heart disease, and breast cancer among black and Asian women than among Caucasian women. To complicate things further, some evidence indicates that breast cancer in younger women is not the same disease as in older women, and, similarly, that the causes and incidence of heart disease are not equivalent among men and women, and among younger and older people.

It is also evident that a very large proportion of women in America cannot, for economic reasons, even for a moment contemplate using medical services and medication to the extent that many researchers and physicians now recommend. But it seems these women are the lucky ones: they will not be required to juggle with the results of the head-spinning probabilities, regression analyses, risk-benefit analyses, readjusted and reassessed data, as middle-class Caucasians must now do to make an "informed decision," in consultation of course with their suitably enlightened physicians.

Even from a purely economic perspective the benefits of replacement therapy are tentative. Weinstein and Tosteson ask themselves if hormone replacement therapy, including the medical supervision involved, is a prudent investment of health-care resources. They start out with the usual litany: in the year 2005 American women between the ages of fifty and sixty-four will number more than twenty-five million. They estimate the national bill for hormone replacement drugs and physicians' follow-up care for those women to be between three and a half billion and five billion dollars annually (1990). After performing a complex cost-benefit analysis these authors reach the conclusion that any possible benefits of replacement therapy must be considered "highly tentative," both in the cost to society and the risk to individual patients (1990, 170).

The second North American Conference on Menopause took place in Montreal in the fall of 1991. The drug companies were if anything even more prominent than they had been at the first conference two years earlier in New York. One of the official speakers commented on the awful weather and said that in New York too it had been unbearable—an omen perhaps? It was clear from the program that central billing was to go to heart disease this year and that osteoporosis, New York's star attraction, had faded already; after all, only approximately 1.5 percent of older women will die from osteoporosis. In Montreal, although the social scientists were given one plenary session, no other broader groups had been invited—no feminists, no Women's Health Network representatives, no counselors, dietitians, or promoters of self-help, many of whom had been speakers in the New York conference. And once again, no women from the general population.

Two things were particularly striking about this conference. First, in-house fighting among the medical profession: gynecologists, for example, claimed that surgeons did not understand the importance of menopause. Second, the despair that clinicians, including gynecologists, psychiatrists, and general practitioners, kept voicing at question time, after sitting through yet another session of impeccably presented slides on risks and benefits. One female doctor, clearly angry, said, "We all have to die of *something*," and wondered why no one mentioned the other numerous medications many patients were already taking in addition to what is routinely called the cocktail of hormones. Another stated that one of her patients had recently had one cancerous breast removed and was also at risk for heart disease and hence remained on hormone replacement therapy. She asked if the other breast should be removed as a prophylactic measure; I could not tell if she was being facetious or not, but in any case she received an answer that was perhaps predictable: it was up to the doctor and the patient to come to a decision based on such things as how important the remaining breast was for the patient. Another doctor described the "noncompliance" of patients and talked about breakthrough bleeding, headaches, nausea, and other symptoms; she was clearly doubtful about the usefulness of the therapy and said that in her experience women frequently filled only one prescription. When the audience fired questions at the epidemiologists demanding to know what the data they had just presented actually meant for clinical practice, very often the answer was quite simply: "I don't know." Very honest, but no help. Nevertheless various publications say categorically that "All women should be made aware of the consequences of estrogen-deficiency in the postmenopause; and should be offered the opportunity to receive estrogen therapy" (editorial, *Maturitas* 1988).

Meantime the current editors of the eleventh edition of Novak's gynecological textbook maintain their original position: "It would seem that although menopausal women do have an estrogen milieu which is lower than that necessary for reproductive function, it is not negligible or absent but is perhaps satisfactory for maintenance of support tissues. The menopause could then be regarded as a physiological phenomenon which is protective in nature, protective from undesirable reproduction and the associated growth stimuli" (Colston Wentz 1988, 401).

However, Wyeth Ayerst ("Helping make life more livable for over half a century") put out an advertisement in 1991 in newspapers across Canada headed "She is Woman," and underneath proclaimed: "Woman of the nineties. Living longer. Living better. She approaches her menopause healthfully, holistically." This, naturally, includes the help of Premarin. An earlier advertisement by Ayerst had a symptom checklist that it encouraged women to fill out and take to their doctors, who in the interim received an Ayerst gift pack of information, advertisements, diagrams, diagnosis sheets, and so on, with a message: "Ayerst believes that you, the medical practitioner, are the best equipped to dispel [the] myths about menopause, to provide the proper perspective through patient counselling and education. A public awareness program has been initiated urging women in their menopausal years to get the real story on menopause, its cause and effect. And to get the facts from a professional source. You. The physician."

Maintaining and even increasing profits in the replacement therapy business is not a piece of cake. The drug companies vie with one another: Ayerst and other smaller companies market estrogen, while Upjohn has the corner on progesterone. Ciba ("Helping today's women live healthier lives") is another strong competitor and bases its claim to superior efficacy on the grounds that its product is the closest to nature, a "unique, effective transdermal estrogen" in the form of a patch attached to the buttock. Ciba markets the estrogen known as estriol, usually used in Europe and Japan, rather than the conjugated estrogens sold most widely thus far in North America. Ciba claims that the advantage of its product is that an effective but low dose of estrogen (hence potentially less iatrogenic than an oral dose) is maintained on a steady basis by absorption through the skin. Ciba asserts in its advertisements that women prefer the "cosmetically appealing" patch to pills. At present the drug companies are particularly aggressive and visibly hostile to one another in their promotional materials, poised, jostling others aside, to take the lion's share of the potential market for a combined estrogen-progesterone product, but the Federal Drug Administration (FDA) recently declined an application to go into production with a combined pill and remains cautious until extensive clinical trials have been carried out. Nevertheless drug companies often sponsor the menopausal clinics and programs headed up by expert gynecologists that are presently mushrooming around North America, advertised with suitably assertive headlines such as "Taking Control of Menopause" (*Cleveland Jewish News* 1991, 27).

Control is elusive, however. American congresswoman Pat Schroeder was quoted as stating: "If you get six menopausal women together, you'll find that their doctors are doing six different things. Our joke is that you might as well go to a veterinarian. The scientific data is just not there" (*Newsweek* 1992).

Life Beyond the Ovary

That hormone replacement therapy has achieved the mark of a major consumer item in North American society is evident because it has been reviewed in *Consumer Reports*, and more than once. A recent article starts out: "Over the next few years, millions of American women will have to decide whether or not to take estrogen to replenish their own dwindling supply of the hormone." It cites Robert Wilson and his book *Feminine Forever* as the inspiration for the original burst of replacement therapy use. But the article also points out that a 1976 *Consumer Reports* had described estrogen replacement therapy as "the dangerous road to Shangri La," because its use had just been linked to an increased risk for endometrial cancer. The recent article states that at present "among physicians and researchers, opinion is swinging back" (1991, 587).

Consumer Reports made a major error on the first page of the article in stating that the FDA agreed in June 1991 to "put an official stamp of approval on estrogen replacement therapy, unanimously recommending that the treatment be made available to "virtually all" postmenopausal women." This was not the case. Wyeth Ayerst, the pharmaceutical company most invested in continuous estrogen use among older women, put a petition before the FDA for a labeling change to indicate clearly that conjugated estrogens have potential cardiovascular benefits. The FDA sat for over a year on a recommendation to agree to a labeling change, a recommendation that came from an advisory committee (composed largely of drug-company-funded clinicians) that the FDA established in 1991. The FDA eventually called in other experts to testify, including the Women's Health Network and several biostatisticians.[11] The decision, reached in 1992, was to elaborate about *possible* protective benefits from heart disease on the warning insert that comes with every estrogen packet; the position is essentially that no further changes will be made until the results of extensive clinical trials are made available.

Consumer Reports went on to describe the pros and cons of the replacement therapy debate in the balanced way that we have come to expect of the periodical but then outlined the benefits of estrogen therapy, which it called "clear enough." It dealt with risks, including possible breast cancer, but reiterated the current position of many advocates of hormone replacement therapy, which is that women should be much more concerned about death from heart disease than from cancer. The article concluded: "Dr. Hammond of Duke summarizes the viewpoint of many of his colleagues:

'We have to balance what may be a potentially small increase in breast cancer versus a proven, huge lifesaving effect on cardiovascular disease and osteoporosis.' With those benefits, it's not surprising that studies of overall mortality rates have shown that women who use estrogen live longer than those who do not" (1991, 591).

In its conclusion, *Consumer Reports* disregarded some of its own warnings spelled out earlier in the same article, in particular that women in the hormone studies are not representative of the population at large, and in any case that the so-called protective effects have been achieved with estrogen alone. Results from most of the existing studies do not apply, therefore, to the majority of women who are at present on combined hormone therapy. Nor did *Consumer Reports* caution its readers that the effects of combined hormone usage on the heart and breast are very controversial and that dosages, combinations and types of hormones, and methods of administration are juggled and manipulated in numerous rather ad hoc ways. Finally, *Consumer Reports*, in common with the writers of virtually all the research studies it drew on, completely failed to mention that mortality from both cancer (Freeman 1991) and heart disease (Morganstern 1983) is clearly associated with poverty, poor nutrition, and lack of access to a good health-care system—it is, above all, disadvantaged women at whom we should aim sound preventive health care against the killer diseases, and these are the women who will not receive hormone replacement therapy, even in the unlikely eventuality that its use is proved beneficial for most women.

Could *Consumer Reports* have its head in the clouds? Dreaming perhaps of Shangri La? In the midst of this complex morass there is a desire for simplicity, for a quick fix and easy answers. Similarly, people interviewed on radio and television about "The Estrogen Fix," as *Ms.* magazine named it (Eagan 1989), are forced to state their opinion in a time bite of two or three minutes and so must, willy-nilly, give simple answers to an extraordinarily complex issue.

Some gynecologists have tried to clarify matters by providing simple answers in books written for the public. In the book *Managing Your Menopause* that Wulf Utian coauthored with medical writer Ruth Jacobowitz, Utian, an experienced gynecologist, sets out to convey a straightforward message under simple chapter headings and subheadings such as "Living Longer, Living Better," "Finding Dr. Right," "Taking Control of Your Life," "Outwitting the Powerful Ovary." The book starts out with a fable about two women who in their younger years were blond, blue-eyed, well-built, with ample breasts, tiny waists, and "perky" personalities. They meet again at their thirty-fifth class reunion; one had aged beyond belief as a result of a long history of reproductive problems including a total hysterectomy and removal of her ovaries. By the time she met her friend at the class reunion she had experienced, we are told, nineteen years of "estrogen deprivation." For her friend, in contrast, "it was as if the years had stood still," she had a "trim figure, a light step, and a sparkle in her eye" (1990, 2–7), thanks to hormone replacement therapy! The authors state that it is the "right and responsibility" of each woman to initiate preventive health care for herself; they add that they want to help women to "maximize the quality of their life" (11). With that intent, the last of the twelve basic principles of the Utian program proclaims that "You can control your destiny" (14). The authors are careful to point out that hormone treatment is not for everybody, particularly if there is a family history of breast or uterine cancer, liver disease, or certain other conditions; neither should it be the first of the eight essential tools of the Utian program (15–17).

Readers learn, however, that there are several "compelling reasons" for taking hormone replacement therapy: relief from hot flashes and vasomotor symptoms; relief of vaginal atrophy and other pelvic atrophy; maintenance of skin: keeping it smoother, thicker, and softer; prevention of osteoporosis and reduction of risk of fractures; protection against coronary heart disease and heart attack; benefits to the central nervous system including improvement of memory and sleep, and the general enhancement of well-being and sexuality (67). A large number of medical researchers would disagree completely with the third and fifth items and would note that statements about osteoporosis and heart attacks made at this level of generality are incorrect and highly misleading. Nevertheless, the authors ask readers to weigh the risks and benefits for themselves. Benefits include an enhanced quality of life, with improved sleep; improved short-term memory, a mental tonic effect, enhanced sexuality, slower overall body deterioration, and increased longevity. They tell us how good these benefits sound and then turn to the risks: potential minor problems include uterovaginal bleeding, breast tenderness, PMS-like symptoms, some inconvenience, and cost. Potential major problems include uterine cancer and breast cancer, as well as blood clots, gallstones, hypertension, and surgery. Readers—if they are average women, the authors say, with relatively few risk factors—will find that the advantages far outweigh the risks (84–98).

The authors discuss the various regimens for replacement therapies and point out that withdrawal bleeding and possible endometrial biopsies may be involved, and that visits to a doctor every six months are mandatory.

They mention yet other side effects and introduce further recommendations from the Utian menopause management program, including care with diet and exercise, use of stylish clothing, and so on. They say that male menopause is a myth and that a "man is potentially virile and potent—if his health and all other aspects remain equal—until close to the end of life" (155).

This book by "a world-renowned doctor" (from the front cover) is praised by Gail Sheehy as compassionately presented, "a beam of clear light" (on the back cover). I find the book juvenile, patronizing, and dangerously misleading because it reduces a very complex unresolved issue into simple risks and benefits that it does not accurately spell out. The authors are careful to remind their readers, however, that the eventual choice is up to the woman herself (after consultation with her doctor). Sheehy, writing her own article on menopause and recounting her uncomfortable experiences with hormone replacement therapy in a recent issue of *Vanity Fair*, conveys a slightly more balanced presentation of the complexity of the problem. But her narrative is, not surprisingly, honed for the trendy readers of this particular magazine. The reconstructed menopausal experiences of famous and influential women—Margaret Mead, a big-time public-television producer, a high-profile executive—are recounted like so many conquests of the forces of nature. After a very brief historical digression Sheehy states, apparently without irony, that "nature never provided for women who would routinely live several decades beyond the age of fifty. Once they had made their genetic contribution, evolution was finished with them, and society followed suit" (1991, 252). The bottom line of both this article and its slightly expanded best-selling book version seems to be that women who drive in the fast lane need not fear that they will lose out; they may be in for a few shocking experiences as they turn fifty, when they find themselves dripping sweat into their shrimp cocktails, but they will be able to take control of the situation and go on to make whatever they want of their older selves—probably, but not necessarily, with the help of drugs in order to beat the clock. In short, here is a story line not very different from that of the misogynist Robert Wilson, a polemic for aging yuppies. Moreover, as a good number of nineteenth-century physicians did, it addresses the concerns and the experience of white middle-class women and refers generally to the easy time "other" women have at menopause (1992, 60). Contradictions slip by uncontested: women are easy prey to their endocrine system but the less "refined" and less "successful" of us are still, it seems, closer to nature and not so subject to menopausal trouble as the sophisticated and wealthy.

Sheehy's own experience with hormone therapy sounds dreadful—she reports that she was "staggered" by the potency of the female hormone, that her body seemed to be at war with itself while she was on this medication, and that the situation continued for a year or more, until she stopped taking (some or all of) the drugs. It was only after this experience that she took note of what she described as "the scandalous politics of menopause" (1991, 226). One conclusion she does not draw but perhaps discovered in her personal experience is that we are playing with highly potent drugs that often produce dramatic effects within and on the surface of the body.

The fear of aging that both Susan Sontag and Germaine Greer (1991) talk about hovers uncomfortably close by, as the entire population grows noticeably older and a plague of fading middle-aged women, the former baby boomers, appears on the horizon to burden all who follow behind. Fueling part of the rhetoric are the interests of pharmaceutical companies, spurred on by their intimate relation with the medical profession. But this materialist drive by no means provides the full answer to what we now witness, a conclusion supported by the Japanese case where little medicalization as yet takes place. The presence of several tacit assumptions that shape both the recent scientific and popular literature on the subject of aging have served, I believe, to drive the discussion into a narrow, one-way alley in which it accelerates furiously, swerving neither to right nor to left. The flurry of recent articles on menopause in the *New York Times* (1992), *Newsweek* (1992), and *Good Housekeeping* (1992) repeat all the usual platitudes: "The evidence is piling up that for a significant percentage of women, the hormonal changes brought about by menopause do contribute to chronic disease and early death," "menopause is a time of 'hormonal havoc,'" "It's now known that women taking estrogen after menopause have half as many heart attacks and cardiovascular deaths as women who never used estrogen" (*Montreal Gazette* 1992). "Tentative" findings, admitted to be such by many researchers, harden into media-hyped "facts." Mystification settles everywhere.

Popular writing, produced from a broad spectrum of motives, magnifies therefore, the truisms embedded in scientific writing: women are reduced to menopause and nothing more, to an unnatural biology in which the discourse is dominated by loss, failure, and decrepitude (Martin 1987). A widely disseminated picture is painted that suggests that nature's plan has gone awry with the sudden appearance in society of women over fifty years of age. Grounded in the mischievous and erroneous assumption that until the turn of the century nearly all women dropped dead before menopause, linked with the idea that the postmenopausal state goes against nature, reinforced by a medical description of "senile" reproductive organs, depleted estrogen, and looming chronic disease, the picture is indeed grim. Implicit in these arguments is the assumption that female life is designed for reproduction of the species alone and that we find ourselves in "advanced" societies today with an ever increasing number of perambulating anomalies. Human females are unlike those elsewhere in the animal world, where reproduction continues until death. Middle-aged women are found wanting, as we saw in the prologue; they exist in contrast to younger, fertile, women and great effort is expended through the advertising of cosmetics, surgery, and drugs to encourage a perennial pursuit of youth. Meanwhile scary polemics appear about the fate of drab old ladies, along with compelling counterarguments by, among others, Greer (1991), who suggests that women's later years, freed of ageism ideology, can be very rewarding. The youthful, fertile, sensual female body is Woman; once past reproductive age she becomes Other, bound for decrepitude, her life split in two by the presence or absence of menstrual cycles, normal to abnormal, healthy to diseased. How revealing that in their quest to keep women healthy, physicians have created a cocktail that allows older women to bleed, in mimicry of their former selves. This vision, which denies any meaning to aging other than the biological, represents a massive denial of any possible advantages to declining estrogen levels for the aging body; it collapses time and attempts to keep women eternally in the present, dependent and only partially mature. The most recent excursion into this mastery of the natural order has been to create the possibility for women in their fifties to give birth after "ovarian failure." These women receive heavy doses of hormone replacement therapy, after which "donated" oocytes are implanted in their uteri leading in most cases to pregnancy but not always to full-term infants (Sauer et al. 1990). No doubt it is only a matter of time before an elderly woman who has long since ceased to menstruate naturally becomes pregnant with the assistance of technology. Can there be nothing else to female life but reproduction?

Above all, in every genre of this polemic, women are inappropriately different from the male of the species. Writing about nineteenth-century Europe and North America Haraway asserts that the "neutral," universal body was always the unmarked masculine" (Haraway 1989, 357). Women have a better survival rate than men, this cannot be denied, but the very fact that they live longer seems to count as a stroke against them. Elderly women can only be troublesome to society, it seems, as though the present average life expectancy for men is the way things should be, and anything more is unnecessary, especially if these women can contribute neither to the continuity of the species nor to the pleasure of men. Furthermore, men age gradually, we are told: there are no sudden biological transformations accompanied by unpredictable emotional consequences—on this count too, women are odd, abnormal. But if the focus is on the end of menstruation as the most significant marker, aging is inevitably a sudden transition, one that systematically ignores the more subtle changes common to both men and women (Asso 1983, 111), something that many physicians of earlier centuries apparently understood rather well—as do physicians in other societies such as Japan.

The perversity of this drive to tinker with nature, with female aging, becomes most apparent in contrast to the Japanese case. Japanese women live longer than do North American women and have much lower rates of heart disease, breast cancer, and osteoporosis, and less distress at menopause. With the exception of the last point we have known all this information for a good number of years. Why is there so little interest in trying to explain these differences? It is evident that we are happy to apply the "magic bullet" mentality (Estes and Binney 1989), so effective in most acute infectious diseases, even to aging. But more than this, could it be that middle-aged women are reconstituted as their younger selves so that aging men can deny the inevitable, that they too are not what they used to be, and dare we say it, not perhaps so virile after all, for all their assertions to the contrary? Freud may not have had much insight into menopause, but his concept of projection seems to be very apt for the situation we now find ourselves in.

Current fascination with the epidemiological literature partly masks another theme that runs through the medical literature on menopause from the last century to the present time, namely a keen interest on the part of some physicians, and their clients, in female sexuality. Middle-aged women may represent a major health hazard for the future, but many professional articles also describe them as dried up, colorless, and no longer interested in sexual activity. Hormone therapy, including at times androgens, a "male" hormone, serves not simply to counter hot flashes or to ward off the ravages of time but, in addition, to heighten the waning female libido. Women who receive this kind of medication are "masculinized" and must deal with a reddened face and the hair that sprouts on their chins and chest but, no doubt, their thoughts turn with some excitement to the male body. I do not recall more than one or two articles that refer to how equally dried up and colorless the male partners of middle-aged women may have become, a state that could easily account for a lack of interest in sexual activity on the part of older women. One might go further and predict that the middle-aged woman on androgens would turn rather quickly to a younger man to satisfy her heightened needs: surely this cannot be what most promoters of replacement therapy have in mind?

Men have been absent from the aging discourse—a void—and yet until age eighty they have a higher incidence of heart disease than do women. Very recently some interest has been shown in the medicalization of aging men: the testes, described as "less responsive," with age, have been picked out as the culprits in declining testosterone levels, associated not only with a loss of sperm output and muscle mass but with the presence of more body fat and thinner bones than those of younger men, in addition to mood swings, loss of energy, assertiveness, and powers of concentration. Research may soon produce a skin patch for men (*New York Times* 1992); only time will tell if this too will become a multimillion-dollar industry.

A potent fear of aging, coupled with a quest for immortal youthfulness and sexual desire, seems to be driving the medicalization of menopause. Commercialized and linked to the puritanical heritage of North America with its insistence on individual responsibility for a disciplined body and continued good health, this urge biases our interpretation of demography and reproductive biology and causes us to believe that we can improve on nature's poor design: thus we arrive at the present impasse. Probably most women do not believe that they can stop the clock or even turn it back but face an escalated rhetoric from their physicians and especially from the media; they must struggle to circumvent the myths, especially when the justification for imbibing medication hints at death waiting in the wings. Meantime maturity, mellow fruitfulness, trust in a natural order that includes life beyond reproduction recede almost beyond sight. But, even more important, aging within the amoral realm of science screens us from reflection on the consequences for their health of economic differences among women and above all from the politics of aging while we dwell ad nauseam on ovaries, flashes, vaginas, libido, fragile bones, and risk-benefit analyses.

An Act of Freedom

For Grace Butcher

My friend stapled
a used estrogen patch
onto a letter she wrote
to me;
a thin, clear plastic circle
releasing chemicals
into her system, creating
extended cycles,
protecting her heart,
the bones and worth
of this woman.
She wore it
against her skin
between belly button
and crotch
like a second pulse.
She runs competitively.
Her legs hurt.
The Achilles' heel aches.
Her tendons are sore,
but she keeps running.
She is fifty-five years old
and won't give up.
I go down by the river
where I live
and toss the patch

off the H Street bridge,
watching it move along,
like my friend, a
silver glimmer
in the sun.

Ann Menebroker

(Reproduced with permission from the author)

Epilogue   The Politics of Aging—
Flashes of Immortality

O wad some Pow'r the giftie gie us
To see oursels as others see us!
It wad frae monie a blunder free us,
An' foolish notion.
    (Robert Burns, "To a Louse")

The position I have taken in writing this book is that knowledge about the body is a product of history and culture and thus changes with location and over time. More specifically, menopause is neither fact nor universal event but an experience that we must interpret in context. As a result of basic scientific research, our understanding of the structure and function of the human body has expanded enormously, most particularly in the past twenty years, yet limitations are inherent in this kind of information. Obviously and undeniably, the end of menstruation is more than a state of mind, and many people are tempted to think of it these days as a "fact of life," as inevitable biological change. However, the moment we seek to explain something beyond mere physiological and chemical change, to contextualize the event in the body of a woman, we encounter a set of complex relations and representations that makes the unraveling of chemical pathways seem simple by comparison.

One major difficulty we must counter as we talk about the human body today is the scientific tradition of reductionism that has, over the course of the past three hundred years, become universally dominant. It assumes that to explain the properties of a complex whole we must first consider the units that compose the whole. When using a reductionistic approach we might easily assume that the biological changes that occur at the end of menstruation are fundamental and sufficient data to explain menopause and set aside any other kinds of statements or experience as irrelevant. As we have seen, such an attitude has been prominent in North America for the greater part of this century. It tends to dismiss cultural influences of all kinds, including subjective experience, as superfluous distorting mirrors that disguise the relevant "facts" waiting to be revealed in the depths of the body.

370

An assumption that usually follows from reductionism is that with a little more progress in the biological sciences, we will have no need for culturally constructed ideas about the body, since we will possess the final and correct answers. At such time we can comfortably dismiss narratives other than scientific ones as superstitious, old-fashioned, or irrelevant. Susan Sontag takes such an approach in her discussion about illness when she states that "the healthiest way of being ill—is the one most purified of, most resistant to metaphoric thinking" (1978, 3).

A scientific approach to the body, while it offers an extremely powerful paradigm for assembling knowledge about biology, produces a fragmented and partial picture. It uncovers and reifies, isolates and decontextualizes pieces of information, abstracting them from time and space. A person, however, is clearly not an abstract entity, but a conscious being perpetually in a state of change, whose body is the center of ongoing dynamic interactions among physical and social surroundings. Some, but by no means all, of this interaction the individual cognitively recognizes and appraises and then infuses with meaning that produces effects at the molecular level. The significance that an individual attributes to events is a cultural construct, but is contextualized and interpreted in light of personal experience and inclination—often in part as a response to what others, including experts, claim the event is all about.

When talking about persons rather than isolated cells and molecules, investigators often treat biology as an independent variable, something that culture lightly scratches or dents. This failing is by no means limited to basic scientists. As Russell Keat points out, contemporary philosophers and social scientists have spent a great deal of time discussing the distinctiveness of human beings, at the same time holding an assumption about the nondistinctiveness of the human body (1986, 24). The belief is that since biology is essentially universal, to hold it constant in studies of human behavior will introduce no serious distortions.

Marshall Sahlins, in his discussion of basic color discrimination, goes part way to dispelling this assumption. Although he does not accept a sui generis approach to culture, he nevertheless points out that it determines the way in which we selectively infuse meaning into physiological facts. Colors are semiotic codes, states Sahlins; we do not impose meanings on them by the constraints of human and physical nature; on the contrary, they take on their definition insofar as individuals deem them meaningful (1977, 3). Sahlins concludes that culture is the mediating force between stimulus and response, between the objective "fact" of the sensation of color as it registers in the human brain and its subjective interpretation.

However, while he reminds us that the way in which people pay attention to biology is culturally constructed, Sahlins still apparently assumes that we are dealing with cultural play on invariant universal facts. Moreover, he insists that we treat the biological contribution to the creation of this knowledge as secondary in a relationship where culture essentially calls the tune (18).

A more sophisticated approach is that of the psychiatrist Kirmayer, who points out that our "aching bodies remind us there are at least two orders to experience." He gives emphasis to "the body's insistence on meaning," to the way in which it "presents" itself in "substance and action" rather than simply existing as an implement for reflection and imagination. Kirmayer reminds us that the fictions we create in our minds to represent the body can never fully account for embodied experience (Kirmayer 1992, 3). Thinking of the body as active, as something that asserts or presents itself, opens the way to conceptualizing a relation between self and body not simply as the culturally selected interpretation and representation of stimuli but as an active engagement that takes place in the very sinews, nerves, and bones of our bodies. An exchange such as this is more dynamic than has previously been acknowledged but difficult, if not impossible, to pin down conclusively in words and figures.

Such an intimate exchange between biology and culture assumes that neither entity can exist without the other, so that over time biology acquires its properties from its relation to culture and vice versa. It also assumes that the properties of both evolve as a consequence of their interpenetration (Levins and Lewontin 1985, 3). Evolutionary time has played its part in this process. For example, Engels (probably following Haeckel [Gould 1978, 211]) discussed the way in which the human hand is itself, in effect, an artifact since it has gradually altered through time as a result of its activities in the external world. The hand, wrote Engels "is not only the organ of labor, *it is also the product of labor*" (Engels 1940, 281; original emphasis). Anatomical changes are not, therefore, simply the result of a slow adaptation of the biological organism to the environment but are also the products of human imagination and activity. In the case of gross anatomy, this type of evolutionary change is more or less the same across the entire human population. However, at the level of chemistry and physiology, there exists potential for much more variation both within and between populations than we have been willing to date to recognize (Gould 1989). The "insistence on meaning" by the body cannot, therefore, necessarily be assumed to be manifest in virtually the same way for everyone.

It is in response to this extraordinarily complex process of engagement that human beings create narratives to express the relations between biology, individual sentience, culture, and history. Surely one of the reasons why we find it difficult to include the idea of extensive biological variation into our representations about the body is because arguments such as these have been, and still are, contorted so readily into racist and sexist stereotypes. But if we are to move beyond the usual mind-body dichotomy that sees either culture as dominant and biology as essentially irrelevant or, conversely, biology as an immutable base and culture as a distortion, then it is essential that we acknowledge the plasticity of biology and its interdependence with culture. The differences in symptom reporting in connection with *kōnenki* and menopause would seem to be one example of the way that a somewhat different physical experience influences the cultural construction of the meaning of symptoms. The incidence of hot flashes is apparently not frequent enough among Japanese women for this symptom to epitomize *kōnenki*, whereas this clearly is the case for menopause in Europe and North America, in the past and today. I am, of course, arguing for a difference of degree, not for an absolute, but nevertheless for a difference that is sufficiently marked to contribute to, but not determine, the creation of culturally distinct narratives about biological changes at the end of menstruation.

When we link the recognition of a low incidence of hot flashes in Japan with well-established differences in the incidence of heart disease and breast cancer, and with the more debatable data on the incidence of osteoporosis, we seem to implicate biological differences in the endocrine system. However, the very fact that the incidence of heart disease and breast cancer has increased somewhat over the past twenty years in Japan indicates that this difference in part reflects changing cultural practices including diet and possibly environmental pollution, among other variables that produce a direct effect on the body. It will be interesting to see with time if the incidence of these diseases approaches that in North America, but if the comparative work on heart disease in men, and also on osteoporosis in the San Francisco Bay Area and Hawaii, is anything to go by, this is unlikely to be the case (Marmot et al. 1975; Wasnich and Vogel 1985; Yano et al. 1985).

We can talk of local biologies that influence the forms of professional and popular narrative about the human body. As I have implicitly argued throughout the book, the body is "simultaneously a physical and symbolic artifact, . . . both naturally and culturally produced, and . . . securely anchored in a particular historical moment" (Lock and Scheper-Hughes 1990,

47). Hence we cannot accept the physical body as a simple assemblage of invariant natural facts, either in its actual structure and functioning or in its representation. Moreover, culturally acceptable forms of representation produced to comprehend and communicate knowledge about the body in part reflect local biologies. In no way do these forms allow us to deny the givenness of biology, yet neither do they place us, unless we badly misuse them, on the slippery slope to justify racial or gender-determined difference through biological mythologies. But these forms allow us to reject the notion of a stable scientific metanarrative.

To flatly deny biological difference because it is open to political manipulation is not the way to deal with the most intransigent of debates relating to the body. Obviously we cannot argue for sharp dichotomies; certainly we cannot accept a biological category of race or specify ethnicity as though it were an immutable fact. Nor should we assume that biology alone designates sex (Foucault 1980; Laqueur 1990). Although biology does not determine difference, this should not shut out discussion of biological variation between individuals or among populations. Nor should it eliminate a carefully contextualized discussion of how biology and culture entwine to produce local experience and knowledge. That said, we cannot rest at ease in this outpost of relativism, cultural and biological, because situated knowledge about the body is never benign or without political meaning.

The Politics of Knowledge and the Story of Aging

At the broadest level, what I have been discussing in this book is the story of aging, in particular female middle aging, and the narratives created around it. Literary theorists who have been engaged for some time now with the problem of representation and its relation to reality are in fairly close agreement that we can usefully distinguish between what Jonathan Culler calls a "story," a sequence of actions or events, conceived as independent of their manifestation in discourse, and "discourse" itself, which he describes as the discursive presentation or narration of events (1981, 169). Becoming old, moving through the life cycle, is clearly one of the two or three foundation stories of humankind, and moreover it is a story tempered by the inarguable reality of physical aging. But, as we have seen, the narration of events, the discourse about female middle age, comes from the point of view of particular narrators, be they Japanese or North American, women or medical professionals, government officials or drug company representatives, and also depends on whether they lived in other times or live today.

In complex societies such narratives inevitably meet opposition; discourses do not attain equal authority but stand in hierarchical relation one with another. Scientific modes of representation that produce knowledge through rational, objective, experimental, and mathematical procedures unquestionably enjoy a privileged position in the modern world. Since we take scientific discourse about human biology to be not simply a narrative but a universal truth—a replication rather than a representation of nature—we assume that it applies anywhere and anytime and transcends time and space. Thus arises the confused and contradictory reception of texts about menopause in the Japanese cultural setting. We expect the dominant scientific discourse to fit with little effort into any scenario and are somewhat baffled by so much discrepancy.

Recently, of course, questions have come from the West and also from Japan about the universality and truth of an empirical approach based on a radical separation of the subject under observation from the objective rational observer-scientist. The rising tide of concern in the social sciences, the humanities, and among some in the basic sciences focuses on the basis for this portrayal of the human subject.

Giddens states, for example, that we have no good argument to explain why analysis of human thought and behavior (and this presumably includes thought and behavior related to the body) should follow the models developed in the sciences to portray material objects (Giddens 1979; see also Taylor 1979). The techniques of measurement and instruments created (usually in the West) for purposes of scientific investigation are not value-free and do not produce the objective results for which they are designed (Latour and Woolgar 1979; Lock et al. 1988; Mulkay 1979). Our questions about the epistemology and objectivity of scientific knowledge have made us sensitive to the interrelations among "the researcher, the scientific community of which he is a member, the knowledge which the community shares, and the broader religious, social, and political currents within which the community exists" (Wright and Treacher 1982, 8). We cannot therefore assume that any scientific representation of the body is epistemologically free or that any enterprise engaged in the uncovering of reality can exist without argument (Young 1982, 259–60)—and this ambiguity, we have seen, clearly flourishes in the case of menopause.

But my questions here have reached beyond the usual representations of clinical medicine, in this instance concerning the changes that aging produces in the reproductive organs and the endocrine system. I have also touched on what Armstrong, following Foucault, names "the technologies of the survey." Foucault introduced the concept of "bio-power" to account for the ways that the emerging industrial societies, particularly from the eighteenth century onward, subjected human bodies to surveillance for the purposes of political control. He drew attention to the construction of disciplinary institutions, including schools, hospitals, military organizations, and prisons, part of whose function was to pay minute attention to bodily techniques and discipline that he termed the "micro-physics" of power (Foucault 1979, 139). The result was, Foucault claimed, the production of "docile," pliant bodies available for service to the state (138). Clearly at a general level his thesis applies equally to Japan and to the West, although the actual implementation of biopower and the desired results were not always the same.

Armstrong points out that the twentieth-century use of survey techniques has extended the idea of surveillance from something that various authorities, including physicians, practiced directly on individual bodies to a less direct but much more insidious form of control that subjects entire populations of people to statistical surveillance (1983). Clinical medicine with its emphasis on pathology from the beginning of the eighteenth century remained essential for the care and monitoring of disease, but the rise of social medicine, social epidemiology, and the social sciences adds to an obsession with pathology an interest in the normal healthy individual and, by extension, the health of society.

Hacking deconstructs the idea of normality, which he describes as "both timeless and dated" since, although it is a very old idea, it is one where the meaning can "in a moment adopt a completely new form of life" (1990, 160). Hacking believes that our present understanding of normality, adopted in about the 1820s, is a key concept in what he labels "the taming of chance," so central to the process of modernization and rationalization of society. "Normal," as Hacking points out, is one of a pair, the opposite of "pathological." For a good number of years after its modern meaning was first postulated, its use was confined to medicine. But then "it moved into the sphere of—almost everything. People, behavior, states of affairs, diplomatic relations, molecules: all these may be normal or abnormal" (160). Hacking says that we no longer ask seriously, what is human nature? Instead we talk about "normal" people, and, of even more importance, we go on usually without a second thought to say that this is how things ought to be: we use the idea of normality to close the gap between "is" and "ought." Hacking traces our current expanded usage of the term back to Comte and describes the way in which Comte, perhaps inspired by his own brush with mental illness, moved normality out beyond the clinic into the political sphere, at which point "normal ceased to be the ordinary healthy state; it became the purified state to which we should strive, and to which our energies are tending. In short, progress and the normal state became inextricably linked" (168).

Thus a fundamental tension developed in the idea of normal, which contains today both the meaning of an existing average and an ultimate perfection to which we may progress, both the idea of a deviation by degree from a norm and the idea of a perfect state. Following Durkheim we can talk of what is normal as being right and proper and try to return to a former equilibrium, a status quo. But if we take this notion further, we can interpret the normal as *only* average and hence something to be improved on—which in its most extreme form as applied to human bodies leads, suggests Hacking, to eugenics. Hence two ideas inhabit the one concept of normal, one of preservation, the other of amelioration. As Hacking so aptly puts it: "Words have profound memories that oil our shrill and squeaky rhetoric"; the normal stands at once, "indifferently," for what is typical, the "unenthusiastic objective average, but it also stands for what has been, good health, and for what shall be, our chosen destiny" (169). Hacking concludes that this benign and sterile-sounding word has become one of the most powerful (ideological) tools of the twentieth century—and sure enough, there it is, everywhere in the rhetoric about menopause, ubiquitous, polysemic (but passing as universal), a drab word secreted "innocently" into authoritative discourse.

Menopausal women are not normal in so many ways that their abnormality is overdetermined—so much so that it goes almost without saying. In North America we worship at the altar of youth: normality means youth and vigor, regardless of gender; the middle-aged and especially the elderly are deviations from the norm, both as individuals and as bodies. More specifically, among women, normal means to be of reproductive age, both in terms of the whole woman and biology. Aging female bones, the reader will recall, the World Health Organization defines as abnormal. The norm also means being part of nature's order. But middle-aged women, unlike all other mammals, lose their reproductive potential; they go against the grain and in so doing are no longer truly female. Old women, who in advanced societies will be so numerous, are deviations too, in that many will have lived past the average life expectancy. In all these forms the Menopausal Woman stands for what has been, for good health lost, someone who stands on the wrong side of average.

But if we pay attention to what is left unspoken behind the push for the estrogen fix we can discern the other normal, described by Hacking, the normal that "shall be," what we strive for—in this case immortality or, in the interim, a timely, inexpensive, invisible death that makes no demands on society. We strive to banish disease from our midst, to conquer it with magic bullets and, better yet, to second-guess the natural order with the crystal ball of probabilities—twentieth-century divination. Progress brings order, tames nature, goads populations into doing what is right and good for them, and woe betide those who step out of line. Could we perhaps reach the point of refusing to treat a woman for heart disease or a fractured hip because she had not imbibed hormone replacement therapy?

In discussing what they describe as the "postmodern life course," Featherstone and Hepworth point to a "de-differentiation" of the life cycle, with less emphasis on age-specific role transitions and scheduled identity development (1991, 372). We no longer expect characteristic behavior to fit with specific stages of the life cycle and now, it seems, we hope to render our biology as plastic as we believe we have already made our minds. Proof of this will be the woman eternally young, forever feminine, and sexy, with reproductive capacity artificially prolonged so that she is no longer an anomaly but remains forever normal. When we asked the women in the present study what age they feel themselves to be, responses from Japanese women were rather close to their actual chronological age, whereas 23 percent of those from women in the sample from Manitoba, not exactly a hotbed of high fashion, expressed the feeling that they were younger than thirty years of age! It appears, therefore, to no one's surprise I'm sure, that North America is fertile ground for the embalming of youth.

The debate about hormone replacement therapy in North America seems to me to reverberate between the modern bodies: the regulated disciplined body made over to a life for the good of self that is simultaneously for the good of society; and the postmodern narcissistic reconstructed body that banishes history, suspends time, and elevates desire to supreme authority. Of the two, it is the disciplined self-regulated responsible puritanical body that is most in evidence. And even the body of desire, despite a well-fueled libido, is contained in the straitjacket of the controlled desexed thin torso—the mark of today's youth. A fear of death may unite these bodies, which in any case very often exist uneasily side by side within one individual.

For a Japanese woman normality consists of fulfilling gendered roles, especially family obligations; the harmonious and correct social order has primacy over individual persons and biology alike. Individuals, especially those middle-aged and older, are aware of the life cycle as part of a larger cyclical continuum rather than as a path of no return that fragments youth from age. Youth is green, unripe, fickle, and may be found wanting—not a standard for the elders. As a body ages it reaches equilibrium at each stage of the life cycle; a Japanese usually specifies normal for whom, normal for what, relying less on a black-and-white dichotomy between pathology and normality and tending more to place what is normal on a continuum re-created through time.

No one could argue that Japanese society does not try, even harder than North American, to orchestrate order, to achieve progress through discipline and commitment of its citizens. But there is, as we have seen, another skeptical side of Japan, well aware that reality and discourse do not coincide and wary of formally contracted social relations rather than those personally constructed; it scoffs at the perfectibility of human society through technological progress but may also believe, paradoxically, in the perfectibility of the individual through transcendence of this sorry world. Japan is perhaps the example par excellence of postmodernism, of pastiche and play on the conventional (Miyoshi and Harootunian 1989). Among certain intellectuals and some young people, in the worlds of art and entertainment, the manipulation of desire is evident, most notably through the dissolving of sexual difference and the reconstruction of the body. But the disciplined modern Japanese, the old guard, remain in charge. Besides, many Japanese are very sensitive, more so than North Americans, I believe, to the ready alignment of the postmodern turn with the extreme right and are rightly frightened of some of its implications. Above all, there is no playing with the bodies of those who form the backbone of society— the middle-aged who support both old and young, who keep the economy growing and who built the new Japan—men and women alike. If they are sick from overwork then medicine is on hand, but ideally they should grow old normally and thrive on their dedication to family and society, one path toward perfection of self.

Kōnenki Woman has been invisible until very recently—mother, housewife, laborer, mother-in-law have masked whatever may have been normal and abnormal about *kōnenki*. Today, however, as a few women struggle with the old family order, perhaps the part of modern Japan that has changed the least, a discourse about *kōnenki* emerges from the shadows. But even now it is not *kōnenki* itself that is abnormal; it is neither a disease nor an endocrine deficiency, nor yet subsumed as senile ovaries. *Kōnenki* remains overwhelmingly a social category, and it applies only when a woman cannot control herself, cannot preserve discipline and order—when she is no longer normal. If women start to take hormone therapy on a long-term basis in Japan I would predict that, for the time being at least, they will usually think of it not as a bid to exchange aging bodies for young ones but rather as a tool to help maintain indirectly the old order, in which women preserve their health for the sake of others, so that society may depend on women's nurturance as the pillar of the family.

What confuses the issue in Japan today is the colonization of local knowledge by Western science, which makes over the Other of the Japanese body into the Western body masquerading as the universal body. All the more confusing because most of the information passes through professional journals where chemistry and numbers soften or completely disguise the rhetoric. Nevertheless, the discourse does not come as a seamless whole but with discernible flaws that debate within Japan can explore. Yet this process must resist the ever-present temptation of retreating into an ideology of uniqueness, of unassailable difference, in which *aidagarashugi* takes over and reproduces the impervious teeth-gritting harmony.

Differences in the rhetoric about female midlife affect even the capitalistic expansion of North American drug companies. The politics of aging employ a neo-Confucian call for a return to traditional family structure, to the duties and obligations that marriage entails. Part of this rhetoric insists that mind must control body and that anything less is pure self-indulgence. Only if the argument reverses itself to focus on those diseases that we presume occur independently of the mind—heart disease or brittle bones—will the situation change. As we have seen, there is as yet little national fear about these diseases but, given the Japanese propensity for preventive health care, change may well be imminent. At the moment, widespread fear about the toxicity of hormone therapy helps maintain the status quo, and drug companies that produce herbal medicine have profited considerably from this situation.

Meantime in North America the rhetoric grows so strident that the marketing of drugs drives the research agenda and lobbies exist for a national policy of surveillance long before the gathering of the usual required scientific evidence from double-blind longitudinal clinical trials. For the moment, it seems—thanks in part to public concern—that the systematic medication of older women is being held in check while just such a trial takes place.

Absent Voices

One notable absence throughout my discussion has been the personal experience of North American women. As I explained at the beginning of the book, one of my objectives was to allow Japanese women to speak for themselves, unavoidably in translation, recounting their life stories. We have no equivalent contribution from North American women; their experiences are largely reconstructed in tables and graphs, hysterectomy rates, hot flashes, and visits to the gynecologist. A few intellectuals and popularizers speak out on behalf of aging women in general, yet—except for the women interviewed by Emily Martin (about fifty, of whom the "vast majority" saw menopause in a positive light [1987, 175]); for one or two reports of survey research that indicate a broad range of attitudes toward menopause (Leiblum and Swartzman 1986); and for a wonderful volume of autobiographical accounts and poetry, *Women of the 14th Moon*—we know very little of what North American women think about menopause or its medicalization. The Massachusetts survey indicates that those women who hold a negative attitude before becoming menopausal are much more likely to report more symptoms and to feel depressed than those women with a more positive attitude (Avis and McKinlay 1991). Thus far we have very few firsthand accounts from middle-aged women in either America or Canada about menopause, and above all about aging, contextualized within the life worlds of individuals. Research and commentary seem to be drawn irresistibly toward the supposed inevitable physical "turbulence" at this time of life.

It is not simply a question, however, of finding ways to reconcile so-called objective and subjective points of view, of coming to terms with how discourse interprets the middle-aged female body. To explain human behavior by discussion and exchange among fully aware rational actors is doomed at the outset, and the "rational man" approach to human consciousness has been roundly criticized (Taylor 1989; Young 1981). What we need to explore is the way in which individuals and groups come to embody, accept as natural, and reproduce a world constructed for them by those in positions of power and authority (Asad 1979), and at what price to their physical bodies they do this. In other words, how does the *corps propre*, the "lived body" in Merleau-Ponty's idiom (1962), constitute itself as an engaged social being?

The relations between individuals and society have been debated for centuries and conceptualized in radically different forms in various cultural settings. Their form in the contemporary West is of conflict between the rights of individuals and of social groups to legitimate authority over them. People are sympathetic, most particularly in the United States, to the idea that individual rights take priority over group demands. In Japan, as we have seen and other writers have pointed out time and again, the rights of social groups are believed to outweigh individual needs and individuals are expected to subordinate themselves to legitimate social demands. Discussion about the human body in any society is, at one level, a negotiation about private space and personal autonomy versus the colonization of the body and person by society.

Numerous anthropologists and sociologists, taking social organization as primary, describe the inscription of social categories and values on and in the body through scarification, tattooing, and the internalization of repetitive behavioral patterns (Bourdieu 1977; Douglas 1970; Mauss 1950; Turner 1980). This approach stresses that the body is "good to think with" because it provides a set of homologies linking the social and natural orders and literally internalizes and naturalizes the values of society. But, no doubt because a good number of anthropologists have until recently ignored questions of hierarchy and power, few note the dangers of conceptualizing the body as passively made in the interests of society—dangers that arise because the existence of hierarchy and its associated effects on the body rarely attracts scrutiny but seems to be natural, an inevitable part of socialization into a particular culture. Lewis Mumford discussed this problem many years ago with respect to the temporal regularity imposed on the body by "modern machine civilization":

> From the moment of waking, the rhythm of the day is punctuated by the clock. Irrespective of strain or fatigue, despite reluctance or apathy, the household rises close to its set hour. . . . Under capitalism time-keeping is not merely a means of co-ordinating and interrelating complicated functions: it is also like money, an independent commodity with a value of its own. . . . In the case of childbirth . . . the mechanical interference of the obstetrician, eager to resume his rounds, has apparently been largely responsible for the current discreditable record of American physicians, utilizing the most sanitary hospital equipment, in comparison with midwives who do not attempt brusquely to hasten the processes of nature.
>
> (Mumford 1963, 269–70)

Although the subordinate female body has everywhere been subjected to rigorous discipline at work and in reproduction, as feminist scholarship has recently shown, women are by no means passive objects in this process (Bordo 1991; Spivak 1988). What is more, modern and postmodern bodies are no longer produced through brute domination but are culturally constituted and disciplined (Foucalt 1979; de Certeau 1984), so why should they remain docile? The problem is not only to decipher the making of the middle-aged female body but also to assess the resistance of women (knowing or unknowing) to dominant ideologies about middle age and menopause. How does the tension between subjectivity and the collectivity express itself in middle age, and how does this tension relate to the awareness and behavior of individual women (see also Pandolfi 1990)? As we have noted in the Japanese case, there are a profusion of "identities and spaces" (Haraway 1990, 212) in which women create themselves and their lives, ranging from rejection of dominant ideologies to resistance and to conscious acceptance of them; none of the positions are constant across issues or through time.

As anthropologists are wont to do, I have talked expansively about culture and shared values. In closing I must specify where I stand with respect to the concept of culture in order to introduce a final discussion about the body as a site and vehicle for resistance. I follow Jean and John Comaroff in conceptualizing a "cultural field" as one in which, first,

> the meaningful world always presents itself as a fluid, often contested, and only partially integrated mosaic of narratives, images, and signifying practices; and second, to mark the fact that, in colonial (and many other) contexts, the semantic scape contains a plurality of "cultures"—that is, of "systems" of symbols, values, and meanings which are reified and objectified in the course of colonization itself.
>
> (Comaroff and Comaroff 1991, 27–28)

It is in this cultural field that "the making and breaking of consensus"—the dialectics of domination and resistance—take place (Comaroff and Comaroff 1991). The ideological sectors of contemporary society, including all manifestations of individual and collective life, economic activity, religion, education, and the media are controlled, according to Gramsci (1971), by elites. A discourse is created in these sectors, he argues, replete with concepts about what is true, beautiful, moral, fair, and correct. The human body throughout the life cycle is produced by and firmly embedded in this discourse, but, as we have seen, dominant ideologies are not always congruent with what happens to the "lived" body (for example, middle-class Japanese housewives do not suffer more than other women during *kōnenki*) or with what individuals say about the lived experience (Pandolfi 1990).

The Comaroffs argue that the concepts of hegemony and ideology are the two dominant forms in which power becomes entailed in culture. They distinguish between *agentive* forms of power, in which authoritative control is exerted over others, and *nonagentive* power, which "proliferates outside the realm of institutional politics, saturating such things as aesthetics and ethics, built form and bodily representation, medical knowledge and mundane usage" (1991, 22). This kind of power is, therefore, rarely experienced for what it is but is internalized as part of the cultural repertoire that may be experienced negatively as constraints, neutrally as conventions, or positively as values. The Comaroffs assert, in tune with Gramsci, Marx, Bourdieu, and de Certeau, in their respective ways, that the "unspoken authority of habit may be as effective as the most violent coercion in shaping, directing, even dominating social thought and action" (22). They develop their argument to characterize hegemony: "We take hegemony to refer to that order of signs and practices, relations and distinctions, images and epistemologies—drawn from a historically situated cultural field—that come to be taken-for-granted as the natural and received shape of the world and everything that inhabits it" (23).

Hegemony is, therefore, quite literally "habit forming" and is shared and naturalized throughout a political community. The Comaroffs suggest that hegemony exists in a reciprocal interdependence with ideology: it is that part of the dominant worldview that has been naturalized and, "having hidden in orthodoxy, no longer appears as ideology at all" (23–24). Hence where hegemony is realized there is little need for agentive power. The ideologies and aspirations of subordinate groups may force into consciousness, however, that which was formerly hegemonic and produce debate and action over contradictions thus exposed. It is here, at this disjunction, where the possibility for resistance is the most apparent.

The Comaroffs insist that consciousness is neither a fixed body of knowledge, an infallible repository on which individuals draw, nor an entity that stands in simple opposition to a concept of an unconscious but instead that knowledge and experience form a chain of consciousness, a continuum corresponding to the hegemonic and ideological poles situated in the cultural field. Just as hegemonies and ideologies shift in time and space, so too do the contents of consciousness, from things apprehended, to ones fleetingly recognized, to those submerged, and sometimes back and forth again and again. In light of their work on colonization the Comaroffs conclude that acceptance and resistance to dominant ideologies lie largely in the space between tacit unexamined knowledge and that which is more fully articulated (31).

Part of our taken-for-granted knowledge in North America, a little less so in Japan, is a widespread belief in the truth of medical knowledge—most of us trust unquestioningly in biomedicine and its practice. The truth or potential truth (in the absence of research) of medical knowledge depends largely on hegemony, on a shared belief in the special nature of science, an assumption about which we rarely disagree. Incorporated into the discourse of the discovery and subsequent medical management of menopause over the years are poorly conducted and biased research findings, anecdotal knowledge, and pure fantasy together with a few facts. As we have seen, from the middle of the last century onward even those physicians who were most involved with menopause developed no consensus about diagnosis, symptoms, and treatment. Moreover, the debate inevitably spilled over beyond the accepted boundaries of medicine into the world of morals and decorum, allowing the participation of some with political interests only indirectly concerned with health or medicine.

Our situation today holds only three major differences: a much larger number of doctors, not simply a few interested gynecologists, are involved; because of demographic changes, the population contains many more middle-aged women than ever before; in spite of much popular literature that naively supports medicalization, there seems to be a growing public awareness of the lack of facts behind its authoritative claims. This active public stance about the management of menopause and about obstetrics and gynecology in general surely comes from a shift in consciousness about gender relations in North American society. What is known among its practitioners as the "second wave of feminism" has alerted a large number of people, including some medical practitioners, to the potential for a misuse of technology and drugs especially relating to reproduction. Of all medical practice, the medicalization of the life cycle that commenced this century is, I believe, apt matter for criticism and debate. Technological medicine cannot neatly enfold birth, growing old, and death; few individuals are willing to become passive participants in these processes, whether or not the medical profession defines them as diseaselike states. Under these circumstances, medicalization of the life cycle remains largely within the realm of contradictory consciousness and is not easy to assimilate into the space of the taken-for-granted.

Judging by the relatively low rate of use of hormone therapy, despite media exposure, there must be resistance to its use. A small number of women apparently comply, sealed in a hegemonic rhetoric about the unnatural bodies of older women. Still others must surely entertain doubts but, because they suffer serious distress at menopause, are driven to seek out assistance. Clearly some women benefit enormously from medical care at menopause: I have no quarrel with its appropriate use but rather with the assumptions and sweeping generalizations that extend to all women, and in particular to suggestions for a lifetime of medication. We are swimming in mythologies; until the tide turns we must remain suspicious of what others tell us is good for the health of middle-aged women. Meanwhile, a few politically motivated groups and individuals, some dedicated to meticulous research, others to the wide dissemination of knowledge, mobilize public consciousness to ensure that the long-term medication of older women does not invisibly become the natural order of things.

In Japan, the ideology of a moral physiology, of a controlled self that rides over *kōnenki* symptoms, works against the possibility of its medicalization on a large scale. The present site for resistance relates to the natural place of women in the household—a social space rather than a physical site—but even in designated gendered roles, where social pressure is most intense, women rarely articulate resistance, as we have seen, in political terms; a good number are satisfied and happy with their own lives and remain untouched by the suffering of unknown others (the usual case everywhere in the world). Nevertheless, some women are working hard to bring the long-term consequences of the aging society and its impact on all Japanese women into the light of public awareness and seek to expose there the tacit assumptions that underlie the proposed revamped three-generation household.

The politics of aging, an urgent matter in Japan and North America alike, weaves local biologies along with cultural assumptions about the responsibility of women to society into a rhetoric of specific cultural knowledge and social exigencies. Whereas in North America public attention concentrates almost exclusively on individual biology and sets up the aging female as a target for medicalization, in Japan thus far public attention focuses on the social duties of middle-aged women toward old people, not the middle-aged body per se. Any physical distress a Japanese woman may experience is liable to be ignored or displaced, although there have been one or two recent attempts to strip away the moralizing discourse associated with it. Obviously they constitute an important step, but to depoliticize the experience of middle age and reduce it to individual biological change is simply to move from moralizing to medicalizing. The question will remain as to how many Japanese women choose to interpret *kōnenki* as a medical matter.

Until recently, the fading of psychoanalytic discourse on menopause left an amoral disease-oriented approach to dominate the picture in North America. But a growing concern about the future numbers of decrepit old women has reframed this approach into the moralistic idiom of epidemiology that holds individuals personally responsible for their bodies—though it phrases the responsibility as probabilities. "Informed choice" is the phrase of the day. Meanwhile, the Menopausal Woman casts a transcendent shadow over middle-aged women that masks all the variety of their lives. So too it masks their care of the elderly—in which many women involve themselves deeply and often at great cost to their own well-being (Estes and Binney 1989).

I have worked throughout to destabilize categories that are taken to be natural, to preserve a fluidity with respect even to biology. The process of contextualization has ended by forcing apart Japanese and North American women and emphasizing their differences. Is there then little on which we can come together? I believe that the meanings attributed to biological change that accompanies the end of menstruation show us most clearly the specifics of culture, and hence the differences. If we turn to larger horizons and consider the social process of growing older with its glimpses of death in the distance, then surely we find much that we share. It is from this broader vantage point that we must take on the ideologies of menopause and *kōnenki* respectively, because the rhetoric, although superficially so different, has in common a fear of aging, and in particular the burden to society that old women become. The first step in piercing these ideologies is, I believe, to listen to the narratives and poetry of women, Japanese and North American, understand the reality of their lives and how these fit into local social worlds that women shape and orchestrate as best they may. Then surely too we must drag other shadowy figures fully into the picture, because men too grow old and die, but we hear so little about the aging male. Only then may we dispel vacuous moralizing cloaked by scientific legitimacy and banish Menopausal Woman to oblivion.

Notes

1. A working hypothesis states that "at menopause a change occurs in the set point at which circulating steroids from various sources will inappropriately block or stimulate the secretion of luteinizing hormone releasing hormone (LHRH), which in turn controls the pituitary secretion of gonadotrophins, i.e., follicle-stimulating hormone (FSH) and luteinizing hormone (LH)" (Upton 1988, 115).

2. Recent ethnographic accounts of menopause include Beyene (1989) in the Yucatan and Greece; Davis (1983) in Newfoundland; Flint (1975) in India; Flint and Samil (1990) in Indonesia; Martin (1987) based on a general population in the United States and Wright (1983) among the Navaho; Yeh (1989) in Taiwan; and Rosenberger (1984, 1987) in Japan, the first research on menopause there.

3. Evidence for a species-specific aging pattern comes from several sources and includes an increased production of defective protein with age, a life-span-related increase in redundancy in genes coding for messenger RNA molecules, lowered cell proliferation rates and cell numbers, increased lag time in enzymatic reaction induction rates, loss of function in the immune system with age, increased amounts of DNA breaks, increased dysfunction in DNA repair systems, and so on (Weiss 1981, 34). Weiss and others believe that this pattern comes from an accumulation of basically stochastic, or random, errors caused by the chance exposure of specific cells to degrading elements in their environment; in their view, no specific gene or combination of genes is programmed to destroy human beings at about age ninety. Other scientists believe, in contrast, that aging is a programmed event involving many genes and is therefore not a random process (Calkins 1981; Medawar 1952).

4. Are older women, for example, "naturally" removed from reproductive competition with their offspring? Is there, perhaps, some evolu-

389

tionary advantage to the role of grandmother in human populations (Hrdy 1981; Mayer 1982; Hill and Hurtado 1991)?

5. Supporters of this argument state that, although some women survive to old age, the emergence of *homo sapiens* is still too recent, biologically speaking, for an adaptive selection of a postreproductive phase in the human female life cycle to have occurred (Gosden 1985, 2; Weiss 1981, 40–42; Washburn 1981).

THE TURN OF LIFE

1. The women with whom we talked were part of a larger survey sample of 1,300 who filled out a questionnaire about their health and reproductive history (on the selection of this sample see chapter 2 note 1). At the end was a question concerning a further interview, to which 105 women agreed. The interviews, conducted in Japanese, were semistructured and open-ended. Most took place in the homes of the women, approximately one-third of whom live in cities and have no job or work only a small number of hours a week outside the home, one-third farm or do related activities, while most of the remainder work in factories though a few of these come from a fishing or a forestry village or from the entertainment world. Either my research assistant Christina Honde or I conducted the majority of the interviews, but Hirai Tomoko, also a research assistant, conducted some of the Kyoto interviews. Christina, Tomoko, and I discussed ahead of time exactly what questions should be covered, but the contents of each interview were also determined by the answers each respondent gave to the questionnaire, and also by her interests. Throughout the book the ages given for women are those at the time the questionnaire was filled out and the interviews conducted; that is, they are accurate for 1984.

2. I attach the suffix *-san* to people's names in keeping with Japanese custom (though I use fictitious names for all the people interviewed). The term is not gender-specific and translates as Mrs., Mr., or Miss. It usually accompanies family names in daily conversation, even among people who know each other well; women friends and younger people often attach it in more informal fashion to first names, as I do when reporting on my conversation (in chapter 3) with Ishida Atsuko.

3. I cannot determine whether women having a difficult time at this stage of the life cycle were less eager to come forward for an interview, but the survey research reported in chapter 2 indicates that few women experience anything more than transitory distress during *kōnenki*.

4. The concept of *ki* is somewhat akin to the classical Greek medical concept of *pneuma*, associated with air, water, blood, and other basic natural "stuff" (in Sivin's graphic phrase); in classical medical texts it usually refers to "the balanced and ordered vitalities and energies, partly derived

from the air we breathe, that cause physical change and maintain life" (Sivin 1987, 47). Found both inside and outside the body, this diffuse essence is closely related to health, illness and behavior. See also ibid., 46–53; Lock 1980; and chapter 8.

5. Since the term *heikei* appears increasingly often in popular articles on *kōnenki*, more women today are probably familiar with it.

6. Certain Japanese women and a few gynecologists are actively campaigning to limit the use of the word *kōnenki* because they believe that it is steeped with derogatory and sexist connotations. I develop this point in chapter 10.

7. Other societies studied appear to have similar life expectancy rates; for example, see Hill and Hurtado 1991, 316.

8. See note 4 above.

9. Yamada used the term "vegetative nervous system," a direct translation of a German expression of the time, which was reformulated in both languages as the "autonomic nervous system."

PROBABILITIES AND *KŌNENKI*

1. There was a 76 percent response rate to the questionnaire—high when compared to the usual Japanese response to surveys, many of which get a rate of 60 percent or lower. I chose the urban middle-class sample from the register of names and addresses classified by residential area that was available at Kobe city hall in Hyogo prefecture. Within two areas that I designated as middle-class on the basis of general appearance and my own knowledge, I mailed a questionnaire to every female resident (n = 525) between the ages of forty-five and fifty-five. I followed up the questionnaire with a reminder postcard and then a second mailing of the questionnaire to those who did not respond. The first mailing brought 191 usable questionnaires; the reminder postcard, 68 more; and the second questionnaire, another 75; I thus had a total of 324 usable questionnaires.

For the factory workers, the director of the Kyoto Industrial Health Association, Dr. Inui Shunen, facilitated the distribution of 405 questionnaires to 15 factory managers, who passed out the questionnaires to female factory workers of the appropriate age in their employ. All questionnaires were returned by mail directly to me. I contacted a second group of 145 women working in small silk-weaving factories in the Nishijin area of Kyoto through distribution of the questionnaire to managerial staff after I received permission and a letter of introduction from the local silk weavers' union. A total of 377 usable replies came from women employed in factory work.

For the farm workers, I obtained most of the sample of 650 through the support of the public health department of a large country hospital in Nagano prefecture under the directorship of Dr. Matsushima Shōsui. I distributed copies of the questionnaire to the women's organizations of 45 villages. From this group of women I received 434 usable replies. A second sample of 176 usable replies came through the cooperation of the director of the department of public health for a section of Shimane prefecture, Dr. Hayase Takumi, who introduced me directly to the appropriate women's organizations.

In addition 7 questionnaires were filled out by women living and working in a forestry village in Shiga prefecture, 11 by women living in a fishing village in Ehime prefecture on Shikoku, and 13 by geisha residing in Kyoto.

I exclude from the figures in this and later chapters women whose menstrual status could not be determined and thus draw from a sample of 1,316 usable replies.

2. The Manitoba cross-sectional sample contained 1,326 women between the ages of forty-five and fifty-five inclusively. They were part of a larger sample of 2,500 women aged forty to sixty years who participated in both cross-sectional and longitudinal studies of midlife and menopause. I am grateful to Dr. Patricia Kaufert for providing the data from the Manitoba Project that appear in this book.

The Massachusetts study had a cross-sectional and a longitudinal component. In 1981 a cross-sectional survey of 8,050 women aged forty-five to fifty-five inclusively was conducted by Sonja McKinlay. From this sample a cohort of 2,565 women was identified, of individuals who had menstruated in the preceding three months and who had a uterus and a least one ovary intact. The prospective study of this cohort of 2,565 women consisted of six telephone contacts from 1982 to 1987 that were nine months apart. I am grateful to Dr. Sonja McKinlay for providing the data on Massachusetts women that appear in this book.

3. Only thirteen of the symptoms on the list were reported by more than one hundred women (fewer than 8 percent of the sample). The remaining forty-four symptoms were reported very infrequently, twenty-six of them by fewer than forty-five women (4 percent of the sample), among which six were reported hardly at all. Haug et al. 1991 also found lower symptom reporting among middle-aged women in Japan than in North America.

4. This question was not used in the Massachusetts cross-sectional sample of forty-five- to fifty-five-year-old women. Women from the Massachusetts longitudinal study were asked in the sixth follow-up interview, during the research project's fifth year, if they had ever experienced a hot flash (their ages then ranged between fifty and sixty years: the majority were either peri- or postmenopausal).

5. This question came during the fourth follow-up interview in the Massachusetts longitudinal study and thus women were between forty-eight and fifty-eight years inclusively.

6. When Christina Honde and I worked with two women on translating the questionnaire, they remarked how limited the English language seemed to be, compared to Japanese, in describing bodily states. When Chris and I were unable to discriminate linguistically in English among various physical sensations they described, they laughed and exclaimed how "dull" Westerners are about their bodies.

7. Twice in the questionnaire hot flashes came up. The first time was in the long symptom list (Table 1) that appeared early in the questionnaire, well before any questions about kōnenki; thus women were not aware that we were probing specifically for kōnenki symptoms. The same subject came again later in the questionnaire with specific inquiries about kōnenki. Before the second question about hot flashes, a statement was made to the effect that around the time menstruation ends, or after certain types of surgery, women sometimes experience a sensation of suddenly becoming hot; they were asked if this happened to them. There was only an 0.7 percent discrepancy in the Japanese women's responses to these two questions, indicating that people fully understood the questions and answered with consistency.

8. Little or no reporting of hot flashes comes from studies among the Maya (Beyene 1989) and among the Rajput in India (Flint 1985), and low reporting in Indonesia (Flint and Samil 1990) and Taiwan (Yeh 1989).

9. Women in Manitoba showed relatively more concern, with 49 percent stating that menopause was of little importance and 12 percent of great importance (this question was not asked in Massachusetts).

10. One reason why many Japanese women feel relief is that a large number of them apparently adhere to the traditional practice of not bathing while menstruating.

11. In Manitoba just over 3 percent of the women worried about no longer being able to bear children after menopause (this question was not asked in Massachusetts); 57 percent of respondents in Manitoba expressed unhappiness at the thought of their children leaving home (this item and the following three items were not asked in Massachusetts).

12. Thirty-nine percent of women in Manitoba admitted to being worried about loss of attractiveness.

13. Fewer Manitobans than Japanese were concerned about the possibility of illness in the future: 64 percent as opposed to 80 percent. Over 82 percent of women in Manitoba professed worry about the death of family members.

14. The idea of becoming a burden on one's family is a major concern in Japan, as later chapters reveal. There are both temples and shrines where one can go to pray for a sudden death expressly in order not to be a burden on others during sickness or old age.

RESIGNATION, RESISTANCE, SATISFACTION

1. In 1990 the life span for Japanese women was estimated at 81.81 years and that for Japanese men at 75.86—both are the longest in the world (Yearbook of Population Statistics 1989)

2. I collected the narratives cited in this chapter from volunteers, two of them part of the original survey research who agreed not only to a follow-up interview but also to a further meeting of several hours in which they told me their life stories. The other women, contacted through friends and aquaintances, are not part of the survey research. I chose them for their occupation but they do not by any means represent general Japanese employment patterns for women. By chance, two of the seven women in this group are divorced, a higher number than that statistically expected from a larger representative sample.

3. The Manitoba figures are not very different: 85 percent married, 3 percent single, 5 percent widowed, and 6 percent divorced or separated (divorce is a little more frequent in Japan). In Massachusetts, 74 percent of the respondents were married, 6 percent single, 6 percent widowed, and 13 percent divorced or separated.

4. Tsurumi Kazuko points out that this tendency to think that younger generations have a relatively easy time is not new (Tsurumi 1970, 293), and perhaps such is the case for many rapidly modernizing societies.

5. In Manitoba, nearly 23 percent of women had reproductive surgery, and in Massachusetts 32 percent, much higher rates than in Japan.

6. This woman refers not to becoming senile but to the aging body.

7. Today rice planting is automated except in the smallest paddies and the most awkward corners. Done by hand it involves hours of wading, with bent back, planting the seedlings in the flooded paddy; harvesting also can be back-breaking work.

THE PATHOLOGY OF MODERNITY

1. Vestiges of these huts remain in remote corners of Japan such as the Izumo peninsula, where they were in use until well into this century.

2. Social evolution, introduced in the 1870s by the American zoologist E. S. Morse, was accepted eagerly by conservative forces who used this theory to assert, in the name of science, that because life is governed by the "principle of the superior," the "higher" species will naturally rise to the top without any necessity to legislate human rights. Social evolution also served to counter the creationist beliefs of the small minority of Christians in Japan (Watanabe 1990, 66–83).

FALTERING DISCIPLINE AND THE AILING FAMILY

1. Until recently, the health insurance plan in Japan did not restrict long stays in hospital but created strong economic incentives that discouraged

physicians and hospitals from developing home-care programs (Kobayashi and Reich 1993).

2. The familiar suffix -*chan* is often added to the terms grandfather or grandmother to denote one's elderly in-laws, in place of the more formal -*san* that is usually placed after family names in Japanese. As with the term *obāsan* (old lady, grandmother, mother-in-law, or mother, depending on the context), so too *ojīsan* can mean old man, grandfather, father-in-law, or one's own father.

ILLUSION OF INDOLENCE

1. The number of extended families has increased, but their proportion has dropped because of demographic changes. In the 1920s approximately 30 percent were classified as extended families but today the percentage may be 14 (Kokumin Seikatsu Hakusho 1990) or as high as 21 (Sōmu Cho Tōkei Kyoku 1987). The different figures depend on the definition of an extended family. If it includes three directly descended generations living under one roof, then the lower number is probably more accurate. If it encompasses various related family members beyond those of parent and child, the larger number is accurate.

2. Seventy-six percent of the sample stated that they are working and another 21 percent reported that they are professional housewives, leaving 3 percent unaccounted for.

ODD WOMEN OUT

1. The use of a Japanese typewriter with its exceedingly elaborate, extended keyboard is a highly skilled job. No doubt Harumichi-*san* has graduated to a computer in the past few years.

2. Harumichi-*san* is relatively fortunate in that she holds down a full-time skilled occupation. In the survey sample, although their absolute numbers are small, the proportion of single, widowed, divorced, and separated women who have part-time blue-collar work is much higher than that of married women and points up the insecurity in which they live.

CONTROLLED SELVES AND TEMPERED BODIES

1. Many Japanese told me that it feels easier to open up frankly to someone who is an outsider because they experience a sense of security in an encounter with little chance of repercussions.

2. Nagano, the prefecture where we conducted the interviews with farming women, has long been known for the value it places on education and on cultural activities. The women in the villages we visited were extremely well organized and very active in traditional and more contemporary art forms.

3. See chapter 1 note 4 and Nathan Sivin (1987) for a full explication of the concept of *ki*.

4. The diffuse philosophical concept of the heart, *kokoro*, in classical Sino-Japanese medicine, does not correspond to the more precisely delineated anatomical heart of contemporary medicine. The compound term for the anatomical heart comes in part from the classical ideogram for *kokoro* but has a decidedly technical appearance, in strong contrast to *kokoro* when it stands by itself.

5. In contrast to the Japanese women, 26 percent of the women in the Manitoban study said they wanted to live to be eighty-five or more, and another 29 percent wanted to reach eighty years of age, although the remainder would be content to die, mostly in their seventies, before reaching the average live expectancy for Canadian women of just over seventy-nine years.

6. Only 34 percent of the women who were currently having hot flashes described themselves as *nobosesho*, and of those who had a hot flash at some time in the past only 29 percent described themselves this way. Conversely, many women who never had a hot flash described themselves as *nobosesho*.

7. These percentages contrast with those for Manitoba and Massachusetts: 16 percent and 23 percent for women in Manitoba, and 30 percent and 36 percent for women in Massachuetts who reported being irritable and depressed respectively.

8. We combined the responses of these items in the questionnaire to obtain the figures for reporting of depression in the Japanese sample cited in this chapter.

9. For similar findings in the West, see Kaufert et al. 1992; McKinlay et al. 1987b; Mikkelsen and Holte 1982.

PEERING BEHIND THE PLATITUDES

1. The Yasukuni shrine in Tokyo, where the war dead are buried, is associated with nationalism.

THE DOCTORING OF *KŌNENKI*

1. Among women in Manitoba 10.5 percent had seen a gynecologist in the previous year; 1.5 percent had visited a psychiatrist in the previous year.

2. In both Manitoba and Massachusetts the number of women suffering from diabetes, heart disease, ulcers, and asthma was also fewer than 3 percent. Those suffering from allergies or eczema were 12 percent and 14 percent respectively, and from arthritis 25 percent and 23 percent. In Man-

itoba 14 percent of the sample reported high blood pressure and in Massachusetts the number was up to 19 percent.

3. In Manitoba 23 and in Massachusetts 31.2 percent of women have had surgery on their reproductive organs. These figures include the removal of the uterus only, the uterus and one or both ovaries, and either or both ovaries but not the uterus.

4. The death rate from breast cancer among all females in the United States in 1988 was 33.5 for every 100,000 women; in Canada in the same year it was 34.1, and in Japan it was 9.2 (World Health Statistics 1990). Women in Manitoba were not asked explicitly if their surgery had been for breast cancer: 1 percent reported that they had received chemotherapy and/or radiation therapy, indicating that at least this number had breast cancer; in Massachusetts nearly 2 percent of the sample had undergone surgery for breast cancer. In contrast to Japanese women, 77 percent of Canadian women had received a breast examination in the previous two years, and 61 percent of them regularly examine their breasts; over 60 percent had recently had a Pap test.

5. Among women in Manitoba and Massachusetts 13 percent and 10 percent respectively were taking prescribed tranquilizers; 9 percent and 11 percent of women respectively were taking nonprescription stomach remedies.

6. Among women in Manitoba 2.7 percent and in Massachusetts 8.1 percent were taking prescribed hormone therapy.

7. Because the majority of Japanese women with *kōnenki* symptoms believe these implicate the autonomic nervous system, when they go to a physician they often see an internist rather than a gynecologist. Internists very rarely prescribe hormone replacement therapy, which helps explain the low rate of hormone use in Japan.

8. Before 1991 abortions were legal up until twenty-four weeks of gestation, and until twenty-two weeks as of January 1991.

9. Those women who reported using a birth control pill stated that the pill had been prescribed to control menstrual irregularity, but most women used it as a contraceptive.

10. At present the Japanese Gynecological Association makes no recommendations.

11. Although most Japanese patients do not know the names of specific drugs prescribed for them, there has been so much publicity about the pill and just enough about hormone replacement therapy that many women know how similar in chemical composition these medications are.

12. Most Canadian doctors who were interviewed in 1983 on the clinical care of menopause did not raise the issue of using hormones as a prophylactic against osteoporosis or heart disease (Lock 1985), but by 1990 this situation had completely changed.

THE MAKING OF MENOPAUSE

1. I am grateful to Faith Wallis, medievalist and Osler Librarian at McGill University, for her determined attempts to track down the original of this citation.

2. In her recently published book *The Change: Women, Ageing, and the Menopause* (which appeared just as I had finished this study), Germaine Greer also undertakes a review of some historical and recent literature on menopause. She gives emphasis to the British literature and to herbal and alternative medicines. I am in close agreement with Greer's argument and believe that much of our writing is complementary.

3. Christie Brown and Christie Brown (1976) note that Tilt warned of menopause as a crisis but claimed that both patients and doctors tried inappropriately to derive a whole range of "diseases" from menopause. They conclude that the current situation has changed little from 1870.

4. Disagreement about menopausal symptomatology continues to plague the medical world: while some physicians opt for a "broad spectrum hypothesis" and include many symptoms, the majority confine themselves to a narrow definition that accepts as bona fide complaints only vasomotor symptoms (hot flushes, sweating) and vaginal dryness (Mikkelsen and Holte 1982).

5. In fact, French physicians emphasized the "perils" of menopause much more than did Tilt (see Charpentier 1887), who was reacting to what he considered their unnecessarily pathological approach.

6. Following Foucault (1965) a number of recent authors emphasize a very close correspondence between changes in medical knowledge and in society at large. Metaphors used in medicine are often assumed to be rather straightforward reflections of similar metaphors applied to social, economic, and political relations. See Martin, for example, on the female endocrine system (1987). My contention is that, while such metaphors influence medical knowledge, the form and function of the human body also produce and constrain medical knowledge, together with results of basic science, clinical experimentation, and clinical practice (see also Oudshoorn 1991). Metaphorical models, empirical findings, and clinical practice inevitably provoke contest and debate. Nevertheless, at any given time one particular interpretation may well dominate others.

7. Throughout Western medical history, the origins of hysteria were associated with the functioning of the uterus (*hystere* being the Greek term for uterus), but by the nineteenth century the ovaries and not the uterus were regularly cited as the cause of hysteria (Laqueur 1990, 286 n.66).

8. In stark contrast to Europe, surgery in Japan developed only during the present century. The traditional Sino-Japanese medical system, physiologically and not anatomically oriented, actively opposed surgery and

specialized in a highly complex noninvasive style of medical practice using herbal therapy. No ovaries were removed in nineteenth-century Japan except possibly under extreme circumstances by the relatively few physicians who followed the Dutch school of medicine confined to the island of Dejima off the coast of Nagasaki.

In Europe, the first anatomical dissections of the human cadaver occurred in the third to the second century B.C. (Edelstein 1967). After this Hellenistic tradition died out, during the twelfth and thirteenth centuries dissection gradually became prominent again; the Galenic tradition, often characterized as humoral, kept an interest in anatomy, so that the history of European medieval and Renaissance medicine exhibits an internal tension between humoral and anatomical orientations (Bylebyl 1979). Such a tension is nowhere evident in East Asian medicine.

9. The majority of East Asian medical practitioners think of the meridians as a metaphor for the activity of the body's interrelated parts; to others they are relatively concrete "channels," and still others understand them as a "scientific," electrophysiological concept (Lock 1980).

10. Showalter describes an "epidemic" of nervous disorders at the end of the nineteenth century, associated with the appearance of the "New Woman"; among them anorexia nervosa, hysteria, and neurasthenia were the most common. Many female intellectuals, including Virginia Woolf, were diagnosed as suffering from neurasthenia and ordered to take a rest cure (Showalter 1985).

11. I am indebted to Nelly Oudshoorn for introducing me to the early literature on the physiology of the sex hormones through her 1990 article in *Social Studies of Science*.

AGAINST NATURE

1. Two major works by Deutsch were translated into Japanese but had no long-lasting influence. The bulk of Simone de Beauvoir's writing has been translated.

2. In the Manitoba sample 79 percent agreed that "many women become depressed and irritable at menopause." Hunter's research in England produced similar findings (1990).

3. Not only in Japan does research continue on links between the autonomic nervous system and the menstrual cycle; it still exerts minor interest in the West (Kelly et al. 1961; Little and Zahn 1974; Wineman 1971) and has recently been reconceptualized with the discovery of the neurotransmitters (Weiner 1992).

4. Sontag is mistaken: mean age of menopause has not increased over the years (Brambilla and McKinlay 1989; McKinlay et al. 1985); for statistics on the Japanese women in the present study, see Figure 6.

5. Usually one session is set aside for social scientists to present their research, but during these presentations most of the listeners inevitably

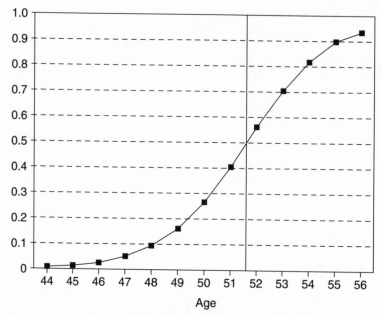

Figure 6.   Probability of Reaching Natural Menopause, by Age

decide that it is time they went off and sampled the local fare and sights.

6. Kekule von Stradonitz was the German scientist who fell into a reverie in front of the fireplace and "saw" the ring structure of the benzene molecule, a vision that transformed organic chemistry.

7. Progesterone is the hormone that is produced by the ovary; progestins, known also as progestogens, are synthetic hormones.

8. This percentage varies according to residence in North America. There appears to be a much higher use of HRT in the South and in California, for example, than in other parts of America (Office of Technology Assessment 1992, 70).

9. The study that reported half the incidence of osteoporosis for Japanese women compared to Caucasian women also pointed out that Japanese women usually have a less dense bone structure (Ross et al. 1991).

10. In the Boston study that has come to be known as "The Nurses' Study," only 2.7 percent of the sample were on estrogens combined with progestogens (Stampher et al. 1991).

11. For an excellent review of the current situation in hormone research and use see a report put out by the Office of Technology Assessment (1992).

Bibliography

Adlercreutz, H., E. Hämäläinen, G. Gorbach, and B. Goldin. 1992. "Dietary Phyto-oestrogens and the Menopause in Japan." *The Lancet* 339: 1233.

Aldrich, Charles. 1897. "Role Played by Intestinal Fermentation in the Production of the Neuroses of the Menopause." *The Physician and Surgeon: A Journal of the Medical Sciences* 19: 438–44.

Alington-MacKinnon, Diane, and Lilian E. Troll. 1981. "The Adaptive Function of the Menopause: A Devil's Advocate Position." *Journal of the American Geriatrics Society* 29: 349–53.

Allan, J. McGrigor. 1869. "On the Real Differences in the Minds of Men and Women." *Journal of the Royal Anthropological Society* 9: ccv–ccxix.

Apfel, Roberta J., and Miriam D. Mazor. 1989. "Psychiatry and Reproductive Medicine." In *Comprehensive Textbook of Psychiatry*, ed. H. I. Kaplan and B. J. Sadock, 1331–39. 5th ed.

Arioka, Jiro. 1991. "Fewer Babies: A Private Matter?" *Japan Quarterly* 38: 50–56.

Ariyoshi Sawako. 1972. *Kōkotsu no hito* (A man in a trance). Tokyo: Shinchōsha.

Armstrong, David. 1983. *Political Anatomy of the Body: Medical Knowledge in Britain in the Twentieth Century*. Cambridge: Cambridge University Press.

Asad, Talal. 1979. "Anthropology and the Analysis of Ideology." *Man* 14: 607–27.

Asahi Evening News. 1991. "Marriage not Popular." 10 September.

Asahi shinbun. 1990a. "Kōreisha kenshō seitei o teian (A proposal to establish a charter for the aged)." 8 September.

——— 1990b. "Chihō no tsuma rikon to fufu no kizuna (Divorced wife's senility and spousal ties)." 18 September.

——— 1991a. "Kaigo no omosa josei ni zusshiri (The burden of nursing for women)." 10 January.

——— 1991b. "Otsukare kimi (Office ladies are a touch tired)." 8 February.

——— 1991c. "Gorudo puran (Gold plan)." 8–17 May.

——— 1991d. "Josei ni tsuyoi 'fukōsei' kan (Women have a strong sense of unfairness)." 23 September.

Asso, Doreen. 1983. *The Real Menstrual Cycle*. New York: John Wiley and Sons.

Avis, Nancy E., and Sonja McKinlay. 1990. "Health-Care Utilization Among Mid-Aged Women." In *Multidisciplinary Perspectives on Menopause*, ed. M. Flint,

F. Kronenberg, and W. Utian, 228–38. Annals of the New York Academy of Sciences, 592. New York.

Avis, Nancy E., and Sonja McKinlay. 1991. "A Longitudinal Analysis of Women's Attitudes Toward the Menopause: Results from the Massachusetts Women's Health Study." *Maturitas* 13: 65–79.

Bachnik, Jane. 1983. "Recruitment Strategies for Household Succession: Rethinking Japanese Household Organization." *Man*, n.s., 18: 180–82.

Bagehot, Walter. 1879. "Biology and Women's Rights." *Popular Science Monthly* 14: 201–13.

Bailar, J. C., III, and D. P. Byar. 1970. "Estrogen Treatment for Cancer of the Prostate." *Cancer* 26: 257–61.

Baker, H. W. G., H. G. Burger, D. M. de Kretser, B. Hudson, S. O'Connor, C. Wang, A. Mirovics, J. Court, M. Dunlop, and G. C. Rennie. 1976. "Changes in the Pituitary-Testicular System with Age." *Clinical Endocrinology* 5: 349–72.

Baldy, John Montgomery. 1894. "Menstruation and Its Anomalies." In *An American Textbook of Gynecology, Medical, and Surgical, for Practitioners and Students*, ed. J. M. Baldy, 83–90. Philadelphia: W. B. Saunders.

Ballinger, C. B. 1975. "Psychiatric Morbidity and the Menopause: Screening of a General Population Sample." *British Medical Journal* 3: 344–46.

——— 1990. "Psychiatric Aspects of the Menopause." *British Journal of Psychiatry* 156: 773–87.

Ballinger, Susan E. 1985. "Psychosocial Stress and Symptoms of Menopause: A Comparative Study of Menopause Clinic Patients and Non-patients." *Maturitas* 7: 315–27.

Barnes, Robert. 1873. *A Clinical History of the Medical and Surgical Diseases of Women*. London: J. and A. Churchill.

Barthes, Roland. 1957. *Mythologies*. New York: Noonday Press (1988).

Befu, Harumi. 1983. "Internationalization of Japan and Nihon Bunkaron." In *The Challenge of Japan's Internationalization: Organization and Culture*, ed. H. Mannari and H. Befu, 232–66. Tokyo: Kwansei Gakuin University.

Bell, Susan. 1987. "Changing Ideas: The Medicalization of Menopause." *Social Science and Medicine* 24: 535–43.

Benedek, Therese. 1950. "The Functions of the Sexual Apparatus and Their Disturbances." In *Psychosomatic Medicine*, ed. Franz Alexander, 216–61. London: George Allen and Unwin.

Bennet, James H. 1853. *A Practical Treatise on Inflammation of the Uterus, Its Cervix, and Appendages and on Its Connection with Uterine Disease*. London: John Churchill.

Berger, Harry. 1987. "Bodies and Texts." *Representations* 17 (Winter): 144–66.

Berger, John. 1972. *Ways of Seeing*. London: Pelican Books.

Bergkvist, Leif, Hans Olav Adanir, Ingemar Persson, Robert Hooves, and Catherine Schairer. 1989. "The Risk of Breast Cancer After Estrogen and Estrogen-Progestin Replacement." *New England Journal of Medicine* 321: 293–97.

Beyene, Yewoubdar. 1989. *From Menarche to Menopause: Reproductive Lives of Peasant Women in Two Cultures*. Albany: State University of New York Press.

Birke, Lynda. 1986. *Women, Feminism and Biology: The Feminist Challenge*. Brighton, Sussex: Wheatsheaf Books.

Birren, James E. 1959. *Handbook of Aging and the Individual: Psychological and Biological Aspects.* Chicago: University of Chicago Press.

Bleuler, Eugen. 1924. *Textbook of Psychiatry.* New York: Macmillan Company.

Bolles, R. C., and M. S. Fanselow. 1982. "Endorphins and Behavior." *Annual Review of Psychology* 33: 87–101.

Bordo, Susan. 1991. "Docile Bodies, Rebellious Bodies: Foucaldian Perspectives on Female Psychopathology." In *Writing the Politics of Difference,* ed. H. J. Silverman, 203–39. Albany: State University of New York Press.

Borell, M. 1976. "Brown-Séquard's Organotherapy and Its Appearance in America at the End of the Nineteenth Century." *Bulletin of the History of Medicine* 50: 309–20.

———— 1978. "Organotherapy, British Physiology, and Discovery of the Internal Secretions." *Journal of the History of Biology* 9: 235–68.

———— 1985. "Organotherapy and the Emergence of Reproductive Endocrinology." *Journal of the History of Biology* 18: 1–30.

Bourdieu, Pierre. 1977. *Outline of a Theory of Practice.* Cambridge: Cambridge University Press.

———— 1984. *Distinction: A Social Critique of the Judgment of Taste.* Cambridge, Mass.: Harvard University Press.

Brambilla, Donald, and Sonja McKinlay. 1989. "A Prospective Study of Factors Affecting Age at Menopause." *Journal of Clinical Epidemiology* 42: 1031–39.

Broca, Paul. 1868. "On Anthropology." *Anthropological Review* 6: 50.

Brown, L. L., and T. Harris. 1978. *Social Origins of Depression.* New York: Free Press.

Bruner, Edward. 1984. "The Opening Up of Anthropology." In *Text, Play, and Story: The Construction and Reconstruction of Self and Society,* ed. E. Bruner, 1–6. Washington, D.C.: The American Ethnology Society.

Bungay, G. T., M. P. Vessey, and C. K. McPherson. 1980. "Study of Symptoms in Middle Life with Special Reference to the Menopause." *British Medical Journal* 2: 181–83.

Bush, T. L., E. Barrett-Connor, L. D. Cowan, M. H. Criqui, R. B. Wallace, C. M. Suchindran, H. A. Tyroler, and B. M. Rifkind. 1987. "Cardiovascular Mortality and Noncontraceptive Use of Estrogen in Women: Results from the Lipid Research Clinics Program Follow-up Study." *Circulation* 75: 1102–9.

Butler, Robert N. 1975. "Psychiatry and Psychology of the Middle-Aged." In *Comprehensive Textbook of Psychiatry,* ed. A. M. Freedman, H. I. Kaplan, and B. J. Sadock, 2390–2404. 2d ed.

Bylebyl, Jerome. 1979. "The School of Padua: Humanistic Medicine in the Sixteenth Century." In *Health, Medicine, and Mortality in the Sixteenth Century,* ed. C. Webster, 335–70. Cambridge: Cambridge University Press.

Cadogan, William. 1748. *An Essay upon Nursing and the Management of Children from Their Birth to Three Years of Age.* London: J. Roberts in Warwick Lane.

Calder, Kent E. 1988. *Crisis and Compensation: Public Policy and Political Stability in Japan, 1949–1986.* Princeton: Princeton University Press.

Calkins, Evan. 1981. "Aging of Cells and People." *Clinical Obstetrics and Gynecology* 24: 165–79.

Campbell, Ruth. 1984. "Nursing Homes and Long-Term Care in Japan." *Pacific Affairs* 57: 78–89.

Campbell, S., ed. 1976. *The Management of the Menopause and Post-Menopausal Years.* Lancaster: MTP Press.

Caudill, William. 1976. "Everyday Health and Illness in Japan and America." In *Asian Medical Systems,* ed. Charles Leslie, 159–77. Berkeley: University of California Press.

Charpentier, Louis Alphonse Arthur. 1887. *Encyclopaedia of Obstetrics and Gynecology,* 101–2. New York: William Wood and Company.

Christie Brown, J. R. W., and M. E. Christie Brown. 1976. "Psychiatric Disorders Associated with the Menopause." In *The Menopause,* ed. L. L. Beard, 57–79. Lancaster: MTP Press.

Cleveland Jewish News. 1991. "Taking Control of Menopause." 25 November.

Cobb, Janine. 1988. *Understanding Menopause.* Toronto: Key Porter.

Cohen, Stan. 1972. *Folk Devils and Moral Panics: The Creation of Mods and Rockers.* London: MacGibbon and Kee.

Colston Wentz, Anne, 1988. "Management of the Menopause." In *Novak's Textbook of Gynecology,* ed. H. W. Jones III, A. Colston Wentz, and L. S. Burnett, 397–442. 11th ed. Baltimore: Williams and Wilkins.

Comaroff, Jean, and John Comaroff. 1991. *Of Revelation and Revolution: Christianity, Colonialism, and Consciousness in South Africa.* Chicago: University of Chicago Press.

Conrad, P. 1992. "Medicalization and Social Control." *Annual Review of Sociology* 18: 209–32.

Conrad, P., and J. Schneider. 1980. *Deviance and Medicalization: From Badness to Sickness.* St. Louis: Mosby.

Consumer Reports. 1991. "The Estrogen Question." September, 587–91.

Cooke Hirst, Barton. 1903. *A Textbook of Diseases of Women,* 378–79. Philadelphia: W. B. Saunders.

Cornell, Laurel L. 1990. "The Problem of Knowing the Past: Architectural Evidence and Peasant Concepts of the Family in Early Modern Japan." Population Institute for Research and Training, Working Paper 43. Bloomington: Indiana University.

———— 1991. "The Deaths of Old Women: Folklore and Differential Mortality in Nineteenth-Century Japan." In *Recreating Japanese Women, 1600–1945,* ed. G. L. Bernstein, 71–87. Berkeley: University of California Press.

Cowan, Gloria, Lynda W. Warren, and Joyce L. Young. 1985. "Medical Perceptions of Menopausal Symptoms." *Psychology of Women Quarterly* 9: 3–13.

Crawford, Robert. 1984. "A Cultural Account of 'Health': Control, Release, and the Social Body." In *Issues in the Political Economy of Health Care,* ed. J. B. McKinlay, 60–103. London: Tavistock.

Criqui, Michael H., Lucina Suarez, Elizabeth Barrett-Connor, Janice McPhillips, Deborah L. Wingard, and Cedric Garland. 1988. "Postmenopausal Estrogen Use and Mortality." *American Journal of Epidemiology* 128: 606–14.

Cuffe, Henry. 1607. *The Differences of the Ages of Man's Life.* London: Arnold Hatfield for Martin Clearke.

Culler, Jonathan. 1981. *The Pursuit of Signs: Semiotics, Literature, Deconstruction.* Ithaca: Cornell University Press.

Cummings, S. R. 1985. "Are Patients with Hip Fractures More Osteoporotic? Review of the Evidence." *American Journal of Medicine* 78: 487–94.

Currier, Andrew F. 1897. *The Menopause.* New York: D. Appleton and Company.

Davis, Dona. 1983. *Blood and Nerves: An Ethnographic Focus on Menopause.* St. Johns: Memorial University of Newfoundland and Institute of Social and Economic Research.

——— 1986. "The Meaning of Menopause in a Newfoundland Fishing Village." *Culture, Medicine, and Psychiatry* 10: 73–94.

De Beauvoir, Simone. 1949. *The Second Sex.* Trans. H. M. Parshley. New York: Bantam Books (1952).

De Certeau, Michel. 1984. *The Practice of Everyday Life.* Trans. Steven Rendall. Berkeley: University of California Press.

DeVos, George. 1973. *Socialization for Achievement.* Berkeley: University of California Press.

Degler, Carl N. 1974. "What Ought to Be and What Was: Women's Sexuality in the Nineteenth Century." *American Historical Review* 79: 1467–90.

Deutsch, Helene. 1945. *The Psychology of Women: A Psychoanalytic Interpretation.* Vol. 2. New York: Grune and Stratton.

Dewees, Wm. P. 1826. *A Treatise on the Diseases of Females.* Philadelphia: H. C. Carey and Lea.

Dewhurst, John. 1981. *Integrated Obstetrics and Gynaecology for Postgraduates.* Oxford: Blackwell Scientific Publications.

Doi, Takeo. 1973. *The Anatomy of Dependence.* Tokyo: Kodansha.

Douglas, Mary. 1970. *Natural Symbols.* New York: Vintage

Dove, Mary. 1986. *The Perfect Age of Man's Life.* Cambridge: Cambridge University Press.

Dudley, Emilius C. 1919. *The Practical Medicine Series,* no. 5, Gynecology: 48–55. Chicago: Year Book Publishers.

Durkheim, Emil. 1952. *Suicide: A Study in Sociology.* London: Routledge and Kegan Paul.

Eagan, Andrea Boroff. 1989. "The Estrogen Fix." *Ms.,* April, 38–43.

Easterly Ashton, William. 1905. *On the Practice of Gynecology,* 694–98. Philadelphia: W. B. Saunders.

Edelstein, Ludwig. 1967. "The History of Anatomy in Antiquity." In *Ancient Medicine,* ed. O. Temkin and C. L. Temkin, 247–301. Baltimore: Johns Hopkins Press.

Egeland, Grace M., Karen A. Matthews, Lewis H. Kuller, and Sheryl F. Kelsey. 1988. "Characteristics of Non-Contraceptive Hormone Users." *Preventive Medicine* 17: 403–11.

Ehrenreich, John. 1978. *The Cultural Crisis of Modern Medicine.* New York: Monthly Review Press.

Ehrlich, Linda. 1992. "The Undesired Ones: Images of the Elderly in Japanese Cinema." In *Japanese Biographies: Life Histories, Life Cycles, Life Stages,* ed. S. Formanek and S. Linhart, 271–81. Vienna: Verlag der Osterreichischen Akademie der Wissenschaften.

Ellis, Havelock. 1894. *Man and Woman: A Study of Secondary Sexual Characters.* London: A. and C. Black.

Engels, Frederick. 1940. "On the Part Played by Labor in the Transition from Ape to Man." In *Dialectics of Nature*. London: Lawrence and Wishart.

Erikson, Eric. 1965. *Childhood and Society*. London: Penguin Books.

——— 1968. *Identity: Youth and Crisis*. New York: L. L. Norton.

Estes, Carroll L., and Lizabeth A. Binney. 1989. "The Biomedicalization of Aging." *The Gerontologist* 29: 587–96.

Eto, Jun. 1979. "The Breakdown of Motherhood Is Wrecking Our Children." *Japan Echo* 6: 102–9.

Fairlie, Judi, Jayne Nelson, and Ruth Popplestone. 1987. *Menopause: A Time for Positive Change*. London: Javelin Books.

Featherstone, Mike, and Mike Hepworth. 1991. "The Mask of Ageing and the Postmodern Life Course." In *The Body: Social Process and Cultural Theory*, ed. M. Featherstone, M. Hepworth, and B. S. Turner, 371–89. London: Sage Publications.

Fee, Elizabeth. 1979. "Nineteenth-Century Craniology: The Study of the Female Skull." *Bulletin of the History of Medicine* 53:514–33.

Fessler, Laci. 1950. "The Psychopathology of Climacteric Depression." *Psychoanalytic Quarterly* 18: 28–42.

Figlio, Karl M. 1976. "The Metaphor of Organization: A Historiographical Perspective on the Biomedical Sciences of the Early Nineteenth Century." *History of Science* 14: 17–53.

——— 1977. "The Historiography of Scientific Medicine: An Invitation to the Human Sciences." *Comparative Studies in Society and History* 19: 262–86.

Fink, Paul J. 1980. "The Psychiatric Myths of the Menopause." In *The Menopause: Comprehensive Management*, ed. B. A. Eskin, 111–28. New York: Masson Publishing.

Flint, Marsha. 1975. "The Menopause: Reward or Punishment?" *Psychosomatics* 16: 161–63.

Flint, Marsha, and Ratua Suprapti Samil. 1990. "Cultural and Subcultural Meanings of the Menopause." In *Multidisciplinary Perspectives on Menopause*, ed. M. Flint, F. Kronenberg, and W. Utian, 134–48. Annals of the New York Academy of Sciences, 592. New York.

Formanek, Suzanne. 1992. "Normative Perceptions of Old Age in Japanese History: A Study Based on Literary Sources of the Nara and Heian Periods." In *Japanese Biographies: Life Histories, Life Cycles, Life Stages*, ed. S. Formanek and S. Linhart, 241–69. Vienna: Verlag der Osterreichischen Akademie der Wissenschaften.

Foucault, Michel. 1965. *Madness and Civilization*. Trans. Richard Howard. New York: Random House.

——— 1979. *Discipline and Punish: The Birth of the Prison*. Trans. Alan Sheridan. New York: Vintage.

——— 1980. *Herculine Barbin: Being the Recently Discovered Memoirs of a Nineteenth-Century French Hermaphrodite*. Trans. R. McDongall. New York: Pantheon Books.

Frank, Robert T. 1941. "Treatment of Disorders of the Menopause." *Bulletin of the New York Academy of Medicine* 17: 854–63.

Frankenberg, R. 1980. "Medical Anthropology and Development." *Social Science and Medicine* 14b: 197–207.

Freeman, Harold. 1991. "Race, Poverty, and Cancer." *Journal of the National Cancer Institute* 83: 526–27.

Freidson, E. 1970. *The Profession of Medicine.* New York: Dodd, Mead and Company.

Freud, Sigmund. 1947. *The Question of Lay-Analysis: An Introduction to Psychoanalysis.* London: Imago Publishing.

—— 1973. *Abstracts of the Standard Edition of the Complete Psychological Works.* New York: International Universities Press.

Frisby, David. 1986. *Fragments of Modernity.* Cambridge, Mass.: MIT Press.

Fruin, Mark W. 1983. "The Family as a Firm and the Firm as a Family in Japan: The Case of Kikkoman Shōyu Company Limited." *Journal of Family History* 5: 432–49.

Fujihira Ken. 1982. *Kanpō shohō ruihō kanbetsu shiran.* Tokyo: Kabushiki Gaisha Rinne.

Furman, Robert H. 1971. "Coronary Heart Disease and the Menopause." In *Menopause and Aging,* ed. K. J. Ryan and D. C. Gibson, 39–55. Bethesda, Md.: U.S. Department of Health, Education, and Welfare.

Galabin, Alfred Lewis. 1879. *The Student's Guide to the Diseases of Women.* Philadelphia: Lindsay and Blakiston.

Gambrell, R. D., R. C. Maier, and B. I. Saunders. 1983. "Decreased Incidence of Breast Cancer in Post-Menopausal Estrogen-Progestin Users." *Obstetrics and Gynecology* 62: 435–43.

Garon, Sheldon. 1993. "The Women's Movement and the Japanese State: Contending Approaches to Political Integration, 1890–1945." *Journal of Japanese Studies.*

Gass, Margery, and Robert Rebar. 1990. "Management of Problems During Menopause." *Comprehensive Therapy* 16: 3–10.

Gendai Yōgo no Kisochishiki. 1991. Tokyo: Jiyū Kokuminsha.

Gerson, Miryam, and Rosemary Byrne-Hunter. 1988. *A Book About Menopause.* Montreal: Montreal Health Press.

Giddens, Anthony. 1979. *Central Problems in Social Theory.* London: Macmillan.

Gluck, Carol. 1985. *Japan's Modern Myths: Ideology in the Late Meiji Period.* Princeton: Princeton University Press.

—— 1990. "The Meaning of Ideology in Modern Japan." In *Rethinking Japan,* ed. A. Boscaro, F. Gatti, and M. Raveri, 283–97. Folkestone: Japan Library.

Goldberg, Minnie. 1959. *Medical Management of the Menopause.* New York: Grune and Stratton.

Good Housekeeping. 1992. "The Baby Boom Meets Menopause." January.

Gordon, Deborah. 1988. "Tenacious Assumptions in Western Medicine." In *Biomedicine Examined,* ed. M. Lock and D. R. Gordon, 19–56. Dordrecht: Kluwer Academic Publishers.

Gosden, Roger R. 1985. *The Biology of Menopause: The Causes and Consequences of Ovarian Aging.* London: Academic Press.

Gould, Stephen W. 1978. *Ever Since Darwin: Reflections on Natural History.* London: Burnett Books.

—— 1989. *Wonderful Life: The Burgess Shale and the Nature of History.* London: L. L. Norton and Company.

Gramsci, Antonio. 1971. *Selections from the Prison Notebooks*. Ed. and trans. Q. Hoare and G. Nowell Smith. New York: International Publishers.

Greenblatt, R. B. 1966. Foreword to *Feminine Forever*, by Robert A. Wilson, 11–14. New York: M. Evans and Company.

————— 1972. "Hormonal Management of the Menopause." *Medical Counter-Point* 4: 19.

Greenblatt, R. B., and A.-Z. Teran. 1987. "Advice to Post-Menopausal Women." In *The Climacteric and Beyond*, ed. L. Zichella, M. Whitehead, and P. A. Van Keep, 39–53. Park Ridge, N.J.: Parthenon Publishing Group.

Greene, J. G. 1984. *The Social and Psychological Origins of the Climacteric Syndrome*. Aldershot: Power Publishing.

Greenwood, Sadja. 1984. *Menopause, Naturally: Preparing for the Second Half of Life*. Volcano, Calif.: Volcano Press. (Translated by Kaji E. and Negishi E. under the title *Nobinobi kōnenki*. Tokyo: Komichi Shobō.)

Greer, Germaine. 1991. *The Change: Women, Ageing, and the Menopause*. Auckland: Harnish Mailton Publishers.

Groag Bell, Susan, and Karen Offam, eds. 1983. *Women, the Family, and Freedom: The Debate in Documents*. Vol. 2, *1880–1950*. Stanford: Stanford University Press.

Guttmacher, Sally. 1979. "Whole in Body, Mind, and Spirit." *Hastings Center Report* 9: 15–21.

Hacking, Ian. 1990. *The Taming of Chance*. Cambridge: Cambridge University Press.

Hagenfeld, T. K., B. M. Landgren, K. Edstrom, and E. Johansson. 1977. "Biochemical and Morphological Changes in the Human Endometrium Induced by the Progesterone Device." *Contraception* 16: 183–97.

Hagiwara Tatsue. 1983. *Miko to bukkyōshi* (Female shamans and the history of Buddhism). Tokyo: Yoshikawa Kobunkan.

Hakuhodo Institute of Life and Living. 1984. *Japanese Women in Turmoil: Changing Lifestyles in Japan*. Tokyo.

Halford, Henry. 1813. "On the Climacteric Disease." In *Medical Transitions*. Vol. 4. College of Physicians in London. London: Longman.

Hamao Minoru. 1987. *Onna no ko no shitsukekata* (Disciplining girls). Tokyo: Kobunsha Shuppan Kyoku.

Haraway, Donna. 1988. "Situated Knowledges: The Science Question in Feminism and the Privilege of Partial Perspective." *Feminist Studies* 14: 575–99.

————— 1989. *Primate Visions: Gender, Race, and Nature in the World of Modern Science*. New York: Routledge.

————— 1990. "A Manifesto for Cyborgs: Science Technology and Socialist Feminism in the 1980s." In *Feminism/Postmodernism*, ed. L. J. Nicholson, 190–233. London: Routledge.

Harding, Sandra. 1986. *The Science Question in Feminism*. Ithaca: Cornell University Press.

Harootunian, H. D. 1989. "Visible Discourses/Invisible Ideologies." In *Postmodernism and Japan*, ed. M. Miyoshi and H. D. Harootunian, 63–92. Durham: Duke University Press.

Harrison, Gail G. 1975. "Primary Adult Lactose Deficiency: A Problem in Anthropological Genetics." *American Anthropologist* 76: 281–96.

Haspels, A. A., and P. A. Van Keep. 1979. "Endocrinology and Management of the Peri-Menopause." In *Psychosomatics in Peri-Menopause*, ed. A. A. Haspels and H. Musaph, 57–71. Baltimore: University Park Press.

Haug, M. R., H. Akiyama, G. Tryban, K. Sonoda, and M. Wykle. 1991. "Self-Care: Japan and the U.S. Compared." *Social Science and Medicine* 33: 1011–22.

Hayashi Chikio, Hirojiro Aoyama, Shigeki Nishihira, Tatsuzo Suzuki, and Yoshiyuki Sakamoto. 1975. "Nihonjinron no kokuminsei (The national character of the Japanese)." In *Tōkei Suri Kenkyūjo kokuminsei chōsa iinkai*. Vol. 3. Tokyo: Shiseido.

Hendry, Joy. 1986. *Becoming Japanese: The World of the Pre-School Child*. Manchester: Manchester University Press.

Henry, Jules. 1966. "Forty-Year-Old Jitters in Married Urban Women." In *The Challenge to Women*, ed. S. Farber and R. Wilson, 146–63. New York: Basic Books.

Hewitt, Martin. 1991. "Bio-Politics and Social Policy: Foucault's Account of Welfare." In *The Body: Social Process and Culture Theory*, ed. M. Featherstone, M. Hepworth, and B. S. Turner, 225–55. London: Sage Publications.

Higuchi, Keiko. 1980. "Changing Family Relationships." *Japan Echo* 7: 86–93.

———— 1985. "Women at Home." *Japan Echo* 12: 51–57.

Higuchi Yukiko and Fukuko Sakamoto, eds. 1976. *Hataraku fujin no kenri to tatakai* (The struggle for working women's rights). Tokyo: Minshusha.

Hill, Kim, and A. Magdalena Hurtado. 1991. "The Evolution of Premature Reproductive Senescence and Menopause in Human Females: An Evaluation of the Grandmother Hypothesis." *Human Nature* 2: 313–50.

Hirano Takako. 1984. "Gendai no joseikan (The present-day image of women)." In *Onna no imeeji* (The image of women), 1–23. Tokyo: Keisō Shobo.

Hirata Keiko. 1980. "Tōkōkyohi no genin (The causes of school refusal syndrome)." In *Tōkōkyohi: Doshitara tachinaoreruka* (School refusal: how shall we get over it), ed. Takuma T. and Hamura H., 35–46. Tokyo: Yuhikakusensho.

Hobsbawm, E., and T. Ranger, eds. 1983. *The Invention of Tradition*. Cambridge: Cambridge University Press.

Holcombe, William H. 1869. *The Sexes Here and Hereafter*. Philadelphia.

Holte, A., and A. Mikkelsen. 1991. "The Menopausal Syndrome: A Factor Analytic Replication." *Maturitas* 13: 193–203.

Homemaker's Magazine. 1979. "Menopause." Vol. 14, no. 8, October, 74–84.

Honoré, L. L. 1980. "Increased Incidence of Symptomatic Cholesterol Cholelithiasis in Perimenopausal Women Receiving Estrogen Replacement Therapy: A Retrospective Study." *Journal of Reproductive Medicine* 25: 187–90.

Hormone Replacement Therapy: Highlights from the Sixth International Congress on Menopause. 1990. Richland, Mich.: Beardsley.

Hosoya Tsugiko. 1987. "Rōjin kango no tsuma no sutoresu (The stress of wives nursing their old folks)." In *Gendai no espuri* 236: 151–62.

Hrdy, Sarah. 1981. " 'Nepotists' and 'Altruists': The Behavior of Old Females Among Macaques and Langur Monkeys." In *Other Ways of Growing Old*, ed. L. L. Ames and S. Harrell, 59–76. Stanford: Stanford University Press.

Hubbard, Ruth. 1990. *The Politics of Women's Biology*. New Brunswick: Rutgers University Press.

Hulka, Barbara S. 1990. "Hormone-Replacement Therapy and the Risk of Breast Cancer." *CA-A Cancer Journal for Clinicians* 40: 289–96.

Hunt, Kathryn, Martin Vessey, Klim McPherson, and Michel Coleman. 1987. "Long-term Surveillance of Mortality and Cancer Incidence in Women Receiving Hormone Replacement Therapy." *British Journal of Obstetrics and Gynaecology* 94: 620–35.

Hunter, Myra. 1990. "Somatic Experience of the Menopause: A Prospective Study." *Psychosomatic Medicine* 52: 357–67.

Hunter, Myra, Rosie Battersby, and Malcolm Whitehead. 1986. "Relationships Between Psychological Symptoms, Somatic Complaints, and Menopausal Status." *Maturitas* 8: 217–28.

Hutton, J. D., S. H. Jacobs, M. A. F. Murray, and J. H. T. James. 1978. "Relation between Plasma Oestrone and Oestradiol and Climacteric Symptoms." *The Lancet* 1: 678–81.

Ide, S. 1982. "Japanese Sociolinguistics: Politeness and Women's Language." *Lingua* 57: 357–85.

Igarashii Masao. 1987. "Kōnenki to rōka genshō (Menopause and old age symptomatology)." *Nichibo ihō* 9: 10–11.

Ikeda Tomonobu. 1979. "Kōnenki shōgai to wa (What are menopausal disorders)." *Nihon i jishin hō*, no. 2922: 20–27.

Ikegami Naoki. 1989a. "Health Technology Development in Japan." *International Journal of Technology Assessment in Health Care* 4: 239–54.

——— 1989b. "Best Medical Practice: The Case of Japan." *International Journal of Health Planning and Management* 4: 181–95.

Ikemi, Yujiro, Yukihiro Ago, Shunji Nakagawa, et al. 1980. "Psychosomatic Medicine Under Social Changes in Japan." In *Biopsychosocial Health*, ed. S. B. Day, F. Lolas, and M. Kusinitz, 65–81. New York: International Foundation for Biosocial Development and Human Health.

Illich, Ivan D. 1976. *Medical Nemesis*. New York: Pantheon.

Imazu Kōjino, Hamaguchi Eshun, and Sakuta Keiichi. 1979. "Shakai kankyō no henyō to kodomo no hattatsu to kyōiku (Strategic points in the social environment and child development and education)." In *Kodomo no hattatsu to kyōiku* (Child development and education) 1:42–94. Tokyo: Iwanami Shoten.

Inamura, Anne. 1987. *Urban Japanese Housewives: At Home and in the Community*. Honolulu: University of Hawaii Press.

Israel, Joan, Marilyn Poland, Nancy Leame, and Dell Warner. 1980. *Surviving the Change: A Practical Guide to Menopause*. Detroit: Cinnabar Publishing.

Itasaka Kikuko. 1984. "The Main Dish—Sweet and Silent." *Mainichi Daily News*, 26 November.

Iwao, Sumiko. 1991. "The Quiet Revolution: Japanese Women Today." *The Japan Foundation Newsletter* 13: 1–9.

Japan External Trade Organization. 1978. "Japan Subcontractors: The Buck Stops Here." *Focus Japan*, 10–11 September.

Japan Management and Coordination Agency. 1987. "Report on the International Comparative Survey on the Lives and Perceptions of the Elderly, 292–95." Tokyo.

Japan Pharmaceutical Manufacturer's Association. 1990. *Data Book, 1989*. Tokyo.

Japan Statistical Bureau. 1986. "Population Census of Japan." Tokyo.

Japan Statistics Bureau Management and Coordination Agency. 1990. *Women in the Labor Force by Age Group*. Statistical Yearbook. Tokyo.

Japan Times. 1984a. " 'Tanshin Funin Sha': Splitting the Japanese Family." 22 February.

———— 1984b. "Employment, Seniority Systems Cause Mental Depression." 16 February.

———— 1991. "Ministry Initiates Study to Reassure Older Women About Pregnancies." 28 February.

Jern, Helen. 1973. *Hormone Therapy of the Menopause and Aging*. Springfield, Ill.: Charles C. Thomas.

Jetro Nippon. 1989. *Business Facts and Figures*. Tokyo: Japan External Trade Organization.

Jick, Hershel, Alexander M. Walker, Richard N. Watkins, Diane C. D'Ewart, Judith R. Hunter, Anne Danforth, Sue Madsen, Barbara J. Dinan, and Kenneth J. Rothman. 1980. "Replacement Estrogens and Breast Cancer." *American Journal of Epidemiology* 112: 586–94.

Jones, Howard W., and Georgeanna Seegar Jones. 1981. *Novak's Textbook of Gynecology*. Baltimore, Md.: Williams and Wilkins.

Jordanova, Ludmilla. 1989. *Sexual Visions: Images of Gender in Science and Medicine Between the Eighteenth and Twentieth Centuries*. Madison: University of Wisconsin Press.

Judd, Howard L., Robert I. Cleary, William T. Creasman, David Figge, Nathan Kase, Zev Rosenwaks, and George E. Tagatz. 1981. "Estrogen Replacement Therapy." *Obstetrics and Gynecology* 58: 267–74.

Kaibara Ekken. [ca. 1714]. *Onna daigaku* (Greater learning for women). Reproduced in *Nihon shisō taikei*, ed. Muro K. No. 34. Tokyo: Iwanami Shoten (1977).

Kakehi Kumiko. 1985. "Edo shokki sanjusha no jokun shisō ni miru: Haha to onna (Mothers and women as portrayed in the ideology of don'ts for women by three Confucian scholars of the early Edo period)." In *Bosei o tou*, ed. H. Wakita, 41–70. Kyoto: Jinbunshoin.

Kameda Atsuko. 1984. "Shūzoku ni miru joseikan (Conventional images of women)." In *Onna no imeeji* (The image of women), 162–83. Tokyo: Keisō Shobō.

Kamishima J. 1973. *Nihon kindaika no tokushitsu* (Special features of Japanese modernization). Tokyo: Ajia Keizai Kenkyūsho.

Kano Kyomi. 1988. "Jibun kankaku sodateru (Fostering one's own feelings)." *Onna no karada to iryō*. Tokyo: Nihon Fujin Kai, no. 6, 6–8.

Karada: Watashi Jishin Nihongo Han Henshū Gurūpu, trans. 1988. *Karada: Watashi jishin* (Our bodies ourselves), by Boston Women's Health Collective. Tokyo: Shokado.

Karōshi Bengo Dan Zenkoku Renraku Kaigihen. 1990. *Karōshi* (Death from overwork). Tokyo: Mad-sha.

Kase, Nathan. 1974. "Estrogens and the Menopause." *Journal of the American Medical Association* 227: 318–19.

Katsura Taisaku. 1983. *Daidokoro shōkōgun* (The kitchen syndrome). Tokyo: Sanmaku Shuppan.

Kaufert, Patricia. 1980. "The Menopausal Woman and Her Use of Physician Services." *Maturitas* 2: 191–206.

——— 1982a. "Anthropology and the Menopause: The Development of a Theoretical Framework." *Maturitas* 4: 181–93.

——— 1982b. "Myth and the Menopause." *Sociology of Health and Illness* 4: 141–66.

——— 1984. "Research Note—Women and Their Health in the Middle Years: A Manitoba Project." *Social Science and Medicine* 18: 279–81.

——— 1988. "Menopause as Process or Event: The Creation of Definitions in Biomedicine." In *Biomedicine Examined*, ed. M. Lock and D. R. Gordon, 331–49. Dordrecht: Kluwer Academic Publishers.

——— 1990a. *Aging, Women, and Health*, ed. L. L. Clarke and L. Dorney. Interdisciplinary Research Seminar, occasional paper 7. Wilfrid Laurier University, Waterloo, Ontario.

——— 1990b. "The Boxification of Culture." *Santé, Culture, Health* 7: 139–48.

——— 1990c. "Methodological Issues in Menopause Research." In *Multidisciplinary Perspectives on Menopause*, ed. M. Flint, F. Kronenberg, and W. Utian, 114–21. Annals of the New York Academy of Sciences, 592. New York.

Kaufert, Patricia, and John Syrotuik. 1981. "Symptom Reporting at the Menopause." *Social Science and Medicine* 184: 173–84.

Kaufert, Patricia, and Margaret Lock. 1991. " 'What Are Women For?': Cultural Constructions of Menopausal Women in Japan and Canada." In *In Her Prime: A New View of Middle-Aged Women*, ed. J. K. Brown and V. Kerns, 201–19. 2d ed. Urbana: University of Illinois Press.

Kaufert, Patricia, and Penny Gilbert. 1986. "Women, Menopause, and Medicalization." *Culture, Medicine, and Psychiatry* 10: 7–21.

Kaufert, Patricia, Penny Gilbert, and Robert Tate. 1987. "Defining Menopausal Status: The Impact of Longitudinal Data." *Maturitas* 9: 217–26.

——— 1992. "The Manitoba Project: A Reexamination of the Link Between Menopause and Depression." *Maturitas* 14: 143–55.

Kaufert, Patricia, and Penny Gilbert, and Tom Hassard. 1988. "Researching the Symptoms of Menopause: An Exercise in Methodology." *Maturitas* 10: 117–31.

Kaufert, Patricia, and Sonja McKinlay. 1985. "Estrogen-Replacement Therapy: The Production of Medical Knowledge and the Emergence of Policy." In *Women, Health, and Healing: Toward a New Perspective*, ed. Ellen Lewin and Virginia Olesen, 113–38. London: Tavistock Publications.

Kaufert, P., M. Lock, S. McKinlay, Y. Beyene, J. Coope, D. Davis, M. Eliasson, M. Gognalons-Nicolet, M. Goodman, and A. Holte. 1986. "The Korpilampi Workshop." *Social Science and Medicine* 22: 1285–89.

Kawamura, N. 1980. "The Historical Background of Arguments Emphasizing the Uniqueness of Japanese Society." *Social Analysis* (5–6 December): 44–62.

Keat, Russell. 1986. "The Human Body in Social Theory: Reich, Foucault, and the Repressive Hypothesis." *Radical Philosophy* 42: 24–32.

Keizai Koho Center. 1993. *Japan 1993: An International Comparison*. Tokyo.

Kelly, L. L. A., L. L. H. Power, Jr., and L. L. Arronet. 1961. "Management of the Perimenopausal Syndrome." *Obstetrics and Gynecology* 17: 328–32.

Kelly, William. 1986. "Rationalization and Nostalgia: Cultural Dynamics of New Middle-Class Japan." *American Ethonologist* 13: 603–18.

Kenkyūsha's New Japanese-English Dictionary. 1974. 4th ed. Tokyo: Kenkyūsha.

Kiefer, Christie. 1987. "Care of the Aged in Japan." In *Health, Illness, and Medical Care in Japan: Cultural and Social Dimensions,* ed. E. Norbeck and M. Lock, 89–109. Honolulu: University of Hawaii Press.

King, James E. 1921. "Endocrine Influence, Mental and Physical, in Women." *American Journal of Obstetrics and Gynecology* 1: 341–49.

Kinoshita, Yasuhito. In press. "The Political-Economy Perspective of Health and Medical Care Policies for the Aged in Japan." In *Eldercare, Welfare State, and Distributive Justice,* ed. S. Ingman and D. Gill. Albany: State University of New York Press.

Kirkwood, Thomas. 1992. "Comparative Life Spans of Species: Why Do Species Have the Life Spans They Do?" *American Journal of Clinical Nutrition* 55: 1191S–95S.

Kirmayer, Laurence. 1984. "Culture, Affect, and Somatization." Parts 1, 2. *Transcultural Psychiatric Research Review* 21: 159–88, 237–62.

———— 1992. "The Body's Insistence on Meaning: Metaphor as Presentation and Representation in Illness Experience." *Medical Anthropological Quarterly* 6: 323–46.

Kitahara, Michio. 1989. "Childhood in Japanese Culture." *The Journal of Psychohistory* 17: 43–72.

Kleinman, Arthur. 1982. "Neurasthenia and Depression: A Study of Somatization and Culture in China." *Culture, Medicine, and Psychiatry* 6: 117–89.

———— 1986. *Social Origins of Distress and Disease: Depression, Neurasthenia, and Pain in Modern China.* New Haven: Yale University Press.

Kobayashi, Yasuki, and Michael R. Reich. 1993. "Health Care Financing for the Elderly in Japan." *Social Science and Medicine* 37: 343–53.

Kokumin Seikatsu Hakusho. 1983. *Yutori aru katei to atarashii kazokuzō o motomete* (Toward comfortably situated households and the image of the new family). Tokyo: Keizai Kikaku Chōhen.

———— 1990. Tokyo: Sōmu Cho Keizai Kikaku Kyoku.

Kondo, Dorinne. 1990. *Crafting Selves: Power, Gender, and Discourses of Identity in a Japanese Workplace.* Chicago: University of Chicago Press.

Koninchx, P. 1984. "Menopause: The Beginning of a Curable Disease or a Lucky Phenomenon." In *The Climacteric: An Update,* ed. H. and B. Van Herendael, F. E. Riphagen, L. Goessons, and H. van der Pas. Lancaster: MTP Press.

Kopera, H. 1991. "The Dawn of Hormone Replacement Therapy." *Maturitas* 13: 187–88.

Korenman, S. G. 1982. "Menopausal Endocrinology and Management." *Archives of Internal Medicine* 142: 1131–36.

Koschmann, V. 1978. *Authority and the Individual in Japan.* Tokyo: University of Tokyo Press.

Kōsei Hakusho. 1989. *Arata na kōreishazō to katsuryoku aru chōju fukushi shakai o mezashite* (Toward a new image of the aged and a vigorous long-lived society with good social welfare). Tokyo: Kōseishō.

Kōseishō. 1986. "Kekkon dōtai hakusho (White paper on changing status of marriage)." Tokyo.

———— 1991. *Kokumin seikatsu kiso Chōsa* (Basic survey of national life). Tokyo.

———— 1992. "Maternal and Child Care in Japan." Tokyo.

Kōseishō Jinkō Mondai Kenkyūsho. 1988. *Nihonjin no Kekkon to Shussan* (Japanese marriage and birth). Tokyo.

—— 1989. *1989 Jinkō no doko—Nihon to sekai* (Where are the 1989 population trends going? Japan and the world). Tokyo.

Koyama, Takashi. 1961. *The Changing Social Position of Women in Japan*. Paris: UNESCO.

Kraepelin, E. 1906. "Lecture 1—Introduction: Melancholia." In *Lectures on Clinical Psychiatry*, rev. and ed. T. Johnston. New York: Bailliere, Tindall, and Cox.

Krauss, E. S., T. P. Rohlen, and P. G. Steinhoff. 1984. *Conflict in Japan*. Honolulu: University of Hawaii Press.

Krauss, Elliott. 1974. *Japanese Radicals Revisited*. Berkeley: University of California Press.

—— 1977. *Power and Illness*. New York: Elsevier.

Kruskemper, G. 1975. "Results of Psychological Testing (MMPI) in Climacteric Women." In *Estrogens in the Post-Menopause: Frontiers in Hormone Research*, ed. P. A.Van Keep and C. Lauritzen, 105–11. Basel: Karger.

Kuriyama, Shigehisa. 1992. "Between Mind and Eye: Japanese Anatomy in the Eighteenth Century." In *Paths to Asian Medical Knowledge*, ed. C. Leslie and A. Young, 21–43. Berkeley: University of California Press.

Kyūtoku Shigemori. 1979. *Bogenbyō* (Illnesses caused by mother). Tokyo: Sanmaku Shuppan.

Lancaster, Jane, and Barbara King. 1992. "An Evolutionary Perspective on Menopause." In *In Her Prime: A New View of Middle-Aged Women*, ed. J. K. Brown and V. Kerns, 7–15. 2d ed. Urbana: University of Illinois Press.

Laqueur, Thomas. 1990. *Making Sex: Body and Gender from the Greeks to Freud*. Cambridge, Mass.: Harvard University Press.

Latour, Bruno, and Steve Woolgar. 1979. *Laboratory Life: The Social Construction of Scientific Facts*. Beverly Hills, Calif.: Sage.

Leake, John. 1777. *Medical Instructions Towards the Prevention and Cure of Chronic or Slow Diseases Peculiar to Women*. London: R. Baldwin.

Lebra, Takie. 1984a. *Japanese Women: Constraint and Fulfillment*. Honolulu: University of Hawaii Press.

—— 1984b. "Nonconfrontational Strategies for Management of Interpersonal Conflict." In *Conflict in Japan*, ed. E. S. Krauss, T. P. Rohlen, and P. G. Steinhoff, 41–60. Honolulu: University of Hawaii Press.

Lee, H. P., L. Gourley, S. W. Duffy, J. Estève, J. Lee, and N. E. Day. 1991. "Dietary Effects on Breast Cancer in Singapore." *The Lancet* 337: 1197–1200.

Leiblum, Sandra R., and Leona C. Swartzman. 1986. "Women's Attitudes Toward Menopause: An Update." *Maturitas* 8: 47–56.

Levins, Richard, and Richard Lewontin. 1985. *The Dialectical Biologist*. Cambridge, Mass: Harvard University Press.

Levinson, Daniel. 1977. "The Mid-Life Transition." *Psychiatry* 40: 99–112.

—— 1984. "The Career Is in the Life Structure, the Life Structure Is in the Career: An Adult Development Perspective." In *Working with Careers*, ed. M. B. Arthur, L. Bailyn, D. J. Levinson, and H. Shepard, 49–74. New York: Columbia University School of Business.

Lewis, David. 1986. " 'Years of Calamity': *Yakudoshi* Observances in a City." In *Interpreting Japanese Society*, ed. J. Hendry and J. Webber, 166–82. JASO Occasional Paper 5. Oxford.

Leys Stepan, Nancy. 1986. "Race and Gender: The Role of Analogy in Science." *Isis* 77: 261–77.

Lin, Keh-Ming, Russell E. Poland, and Ira M. Lesser. 1986. "Ethnicity and Psychopharmacology." *Culture, Medicine, and Psychiatry* 10: 151–65.

Little, Betsy Carter, and Theodore P. Zahn. 1974. "Changes in Mood and Autonomic Functioning During the Menstrual Cycle." *Psychophysiology* 11: 579–90.

Lock, Margaret. 1980a. *East Asian Medicine in Urban Japan: Varieties of Medical Experience*. Berkeley: University of California Press.

——— 1980b. "The Organization and Practice of East Asian Medicine in Japan: Continuity and Change." *Social Science and Medicine* 14b: 245–53.

——— 1984. "Licorice in Leviathan: The Medicalization of Care for the Japanese Elderly." *Culture, Medicine, and Psychiatry* 8: 121–39.

——— 1985. "Models and Practice in Medicine: Menopause as Syndrome or Life Transition?" In *Physicians of Western Medicine*, ed. R. A. Hahn and A. D. Gaines, 115–39. Dordrecht: D. Reidel Publishing.

——— 1986. "Ambiguities of Aging: Japanese Experience and Perceptions of Menopause." *Culture, Medicine, and Psychiatry* 10: 23–46.

——— 1988a. "New Japanese Mythologies: Faltering Discipline and the Ailing Housewife in Japan." *American Ethnologist* 15: 43–61.

——— 1988b. "A Nation at Risk: Interpretations of School Refusal in Japan." In *Biomedicine Examined*, ed. M. Lock and D. R. Gordon, 391–414. Dordrecht: Kluwer Academic Publishers.

——— 1991. "Flawed Jewels and National Dis/Order: Narratives on Adolescent Dissent in Japan. Festschrift for George DeVos." *Journal of Psychohistory* 18: 507–31.

Lock, Margaret, and Joseph Lella. 1986. "Reforming Medical Education: Towards a Broadening of Attitudes." In *Illness Behavior: A Multidisciplinary Model*, ed. S. McHugh and T. M. Vallis, 47–70. New York: Plenum Publishing.

Lock, Margaret, Patricia Kaufert, and Penny Gilbert. 1988. "Cultural Construction of the Menopausal Syndrome: The Japanese Case." *Maturitas* 10: 317–32.

Lock, Margaret, and Nancy Scheper-Hughes. 1990. "A Critical-Interpretive Approach in Medical Anthropology: Rituals and Routines of Discipline and Dissent." In *Medical Anthropology, Contemporary Theory and Method*, ed. T. M. Johnson and C. F. Sargent, 47–72. New York: Praeger.

London, Steve, and Charles Hammond. 1986. "The Climacteric." In *Obstetrics and Gynecology*, ed. D. Danforth and J. Scott, 905–26. Philadelphia J. B. Lippincott Company.

Lufkin, Edward C., and Steven Ory. 1989. "Estrogen Replacement Therapy for the Prevention of Osteoporosis." *American Family Physician* 40: 205–12.

MacBryde, C. M., H. Freeman, and E. Loeffel. 1941. "The Synthetic Estrogen Diethylstilbestrol: Clinical and Experimental Studies (2)." *Journal of the American Medical Association* 117: 1240–42.

MacCormack, Carol. 1991. "Holistic Health and a Changing Western World View." In *Anthropologies of Medicine*, ed. Beatrix Pfleiderer and Gilles Bibeau, 259–73. Heidelberg: Vieweg.

Mack, T. M., and R. K. Ross. 1989. "Risks and Benefits of Long-Term Treatment with Estrogens." *Schweizerische Medizinische Wochenschrift* 119: 1811–20.

McKeown, Peter. 1976. *The Modern Rise of Populations.* New York: Academic Press.

McKinlay, J. B., S. M. McKinlay, and D. J. Brambilla. 1987a. "Health Status and Utilization Behavior Associated with Menopause." *American Journal of Epidemiology* 125: 110–21.

——— 1987b. "The Relative Contributions of Endocrine Changes and Social Circumstances to Depression in Middle-Aged Women." *Journal of Health and Social Behavior* 28: 345–63.

McKinlay, S. M., N. L. Bifano, and J. B. McKinlay. 1985. "Smoking and Age at Menopause." *Annals of Internal Medicine* 103: 350–56.

McKinlay, Sonja, Donald Brambilla, and Jennifer Posner. 1992. "The Normal Menopausal Transition." *Human Biology* 4:37–46.

MacPherson, K. I. 1981. "Menopause as Disease." *Advances in Nursing Science* 3: 95–113.

Macrobius, Ambrosius Aurelius Theodosius. 1952. *Commentary on the Dream of Scipio.* Trans. W. H. Stahl. New York: Columbia University Press.

Madoka Yoriko. 1982. *Shufu shōkōgun* (The housewife syndrome). Tokyo: Bunda Shuppan Kyoku.

Mainichi Daily News. 1985a. "Finding Job Tough for Divorced Moms." 12 December.

——— 1985b. "Teenage Abortion on the Increase." 12 July.

——— 1987a. "Interview with Takuro Kobayashi, Pill Researcher." 23 February.

——— 1987b. " 'Pokkuri': Prayer for a Quick Death." 12 May.

——— 1990. "Salarymen Fear Working to Death." 29 November.

Mainichi Shinbun. 1983a. "Kansei no yutakasa o sakubun de (Heightened sensitivity from writing compositions)." 11 November.

——— 1983b. "Katei no naka ni mo hō chitsujo ga hitsuyō (Even inside the house regulation and order is necessary)." 18 November.

——— 1983c. "Kodomo no heya wa kangaeru mono (The child's room is something to think about)." 17 November.

——— 1983d. "Nihonjin yappari hatarakibachi (Japanese are worker bees after all)." 2 November.

——— 1983e. "Meirei kyōiku (Education by order)." 2 November.

——— 1983f. "Jimushoku, sutoresu umu: Kenkyū no kekka (Office work breeds tension, study says)." 20 November.

——— 1983g. "Kosodate ni chichioya no deban (Father's turn with childrearing)." 17 November.

——— 1983h. "Kangofu ni ikigai (Wife-nurses find a meaning in life)." 16 November.

——— 1984a. "Kodoku na shufu, sannin no kodomo o gasu-shi saseseru (Lonely wife gases 3 children to death)." 13 January.

——— 1984b. "Hahaoya wa tsuyoku arubeshi (Mothers should be strong-minded)." 27 November.

——— 1985a. "Kosodate ni chichioya no kage usui (Dad playing weak role in bringing up offspring)." 14 March.

——— 1985b. "Sutoresu taisaku no purojekuto kaishi (Projects under way to combat stress)." 24 November.

———— 1985c. "Sutoresu: Nihonjin rōdō jinkō no jūyō kadai (Stress: serious problem of Japanese work force)." 3 October.

———— 1990a. "Shūshoku ritsu 81% danshi narabu (Employment rate 81 percent, the equal of males)." 6 November.

———— 1990b. "Kodomo o motanai setai fueru (Fewer households have children)." 30 March.

———— 1990c. "Kodomo no hanbun ga gakkō kirai (Half the children hate school)." 30 October.

———— 1990d. "Toppu wa 112 sai (The oldest is 112)." 9 November.

———— 1990e. "Chihō no tsuma rikon to fufu no kizuna (Divorce of senile wife and the ties of husband and wife)." 18 September.

———— 1990f. "Josei hitori atari kodomo 2.2 hitsuyo (Per woman, 2.2 children needed)." 17 October.

———— 1990g. "Josei no kōgakureki ga shusseiritsu ni aku ekiyo (Low birthrate because of women's higher education: Hashimoto)." 19 October.

———— 1990h. "Kodomo herasu? Chika kōtō (Is the declining birthrate caused by a sudden jump in land prices?)." 28 February.

———— 1990i. "Shufu no fuando takamaru: 98% (Housewife anxiety rate rises to 98 percent)." 13 May.

———— 1990j. "Osomatsu na piru, anzen na kondomu ni katenu (Poor pill still no match for safe condom)." 6 November.

———— 1991a. "Rejā fue, shigoto heru (More leisure, less work)." 25 April.

———— 1991b. "Karōshi ga shinpai: Rōdōsha no 25% (One-fourth of workers fear death by overwork)." 12 April.

———— 1991c. "Zaitaku fukushi sābisu (Welfare services for households)." 9 May.

———— 1991d. "Kanrishoku no jisatsu fueru (Corporate managers' suicides rise)." 28 April.

———— 1991e. "Shussan ritsu 1.32 nin ni sagaru mikomi (Birthrate seen falling to 1.32 per woman)." 17 March.

———— 1991f. "Kodomo no asobi ukemi de hanshakōteki keikō: Seifu no chōsa kekka (Kid's play becoming more passive, antisocial: results of a government survey)." 12 January.

Malamud, W., S. L. Sands, and I. Malamud. 1941. "The Involutional Psychoses: A Socio-Psychiatric Study." *Psychosomatic Medicine* 3: 410–26.

Malleson, Joan. 1953. "An Endocrine Factor in Certain Affective Disorders." *The Lancet* 2: 158–64.

Manson, Spero, James Shore, and Joseph Bloom. 1985. "The Depressive Experience in American Indian Communities: A Challenge for Psychiatric Theory and Diagnosis." In *Culture and Depression: Studies in the Anthropology and Cross-Cultural Psychiatry of Affect and Disorder,* ed. A. Kleinman and B. Good, 331–68. Berkeley: University of California Press.

Marmorston, J., F. J. Moore, O. Magidson, O. Kuzma, and J. J. Lewis. 1959. "Effects of Long-Term Estrogen Therapy on Serum Cholesterol and Phospholipids in Men with Myocardial Infarction." *Annals of Internal Medicine* 51: 972–82.

Marmot, M. G., S. L. Syme, A. Kegan, H. Kato, J. B. Cohen, and J. Belsky. 1975. "Epidemiological Studies of Coronary Heart Disease and Stroke in Japanese Men Living in Japan, Hawaii, and California: Prevalence of Coronary and Hypertensive Heart Disease and Associated Risk Factors." *American Journal of Epidemiology* 102: 514–25.

Marsella, Anthony J., Norman Sartorius, Assen Jablensky, and Fred R. Fenton. 1985. "Cross-Cultural Studies of Depressive Disorders: An Overview." In *Culture and Depression: Studies in the Anthropology and Cross-Cultural Psychiatry of Affect and Disorder*, ed. A. Kleinman and B. Good, 299–324. Berkeley: University of California Press.

Marsh, Robert, and Hiroshi Mannari. 1976. *Modernization and the Japanese Factory*. Princeton: Princeton University Press.

Martin, Emily. 1987. *The Woman in the Body: A Cultural Analysis of Reproduction*. Boston: Beacon Press.

Masaki Takeo. 1979. "Kodomo no kokoro to karada (The mind and body of children)." *Jurisuto*, Autumn, 75–80.

Matsumoto, Nancy. 1988. "Women Who Don't Need Men." *PHP Intersect*, October, 42–43.

Matsumoto, Sannosuke. 1988. "The Idea of Heaven: A Tokugawa Foundation for Natural Rights Theory." In *Japanese Thought in the Tokugawa Period: Methods and Metaphor*, ed. T. Najita and I. Scheiner, 181–99. Chicago: University of Chicago Press.

Matsumura Atsumi, Taii Shunzo, and Shinomura Torau. 1981. *Kōnenki Shōgai*. Osaka: Sōgen Igaku Shinsho.

Matsumura Naoko. 1985. "Kōzōteki ikuji funo shakkai no naka de (The structural constraints in society that make child rearing inadequate)." In *Bosei o tou* (What is motherhood), ed. H. Wakita, 250–80. Kyoto: Jinbunshoin.

Matthews, K. A. 1989. "Interactive Effects of Behavior and Reproductive Hormones on Sex Differences in Risk for Coronary Heart Disease." *Health Psychology* 8: 373–87.

Matthews, K. A., R. R. Wing, L. H. Kuller, E. N. Meilahn, S. F. Kelsey, E. J. Costello, and A. W. Caggiula. 1990. "Influence of Natural Menopause on Psychological Characteristics and Symptoms of Middle-Aged Healthy Women." *Journal of Consulting and Clinical Psychology* 58: 345–51.

Maturitas. 1988. Editorial, "Consensus statement on progestin use in postmenopausal women." 11: 175–77.

Maudsley, Henry. 1874. *The Physiology and Pathology of the Mind*. New York: D. Appleton and Company.

Mauss, Marcel. 1950. *Sociology and Psychology: Essays*. London: Routledge and Kegal Paul (1979).

Mayer, Peter V. 1982. "Evolutionary Advantages of Menopause." *Human Ecology* 10: 447–94.

Mead, Margaret. 1949. *Male and Female: A Study of Sexes in a Changing World*. New York: William Morris and Company.

Medawar, Peter. 1952. *An Unsolved Problem in Biology*. London: H. K. Lewis.

Merkin, D. H. 1976. *Pregnancy as a Disease*. Port Washington, N.Y.: Kennikat Press.

Merleau-Ponty, Maurice. 1962. *Phenomenology of Perception*. Trans. Colin Smith. London: Routledge and Kegan Paul.

Mettler, L. Harrison. 1887. "The Menopause and Some of Its Disorders." *The Medical Register* 2: 323–27.

Mikkelsen A., and A. Holte. 1982. "A Factor Analytic Study of Climacteric Symptoms." *Psychiatric Social Science* 2: 35–39.

Milles, Thomas. 1613. *The Treasurie of Ancient and Moderne Times*. Trans. Pedro Mexio and M. Francesco Sansovino. London: W. Jaggard.

Mischell, Daniel. 1989. "Is Routine Use of Estrogen Indicated in Postmenopausal Women?" *The Journal of Family Practice* 29: 406–15.

Mitsuda Kyōko. 1982. *Joseishi*. Tokyo: University of Tokyo Press.

————— 1985. "Kindaiteki boseikan no juyō to kenkei: Kyōiku suru hahaoya kara ryōsai kenbo e (The importance and transformation of the condition of modern motherhood: From education mother to good wife and wise mother)." In *Bosei o tou* (What is motherhood), ed. H. Wakita, 100–129. Kyoto: Jinbunshoin.

Miyashita Michiko. 1982. "Nōson ni okeru kazoku to kon'in (Marriage and family in peasant households)." In *Nihon joseishi*, ed. Joseishisōgō Kenkyūkai, 3:47–50.Tokyo: Tōkyō Daigaku Shuppansha.

Miyoshi, Masao, and H. D. Harootunian. 1989. *Postmodernism and Japan*. Durham: Duke University Press.

Mochida, Takeshi. 1980. Editorial comment, "Focus on the Family." *Japan Echo* 3: 75–76.

Moeran, Brian. 1984. "Individual, Group, and Seishin: Japan's Internal Cultural Debate." *Man*, n.s., 19: 252–66.

Monbushō. 1983. *Tōkōkyohi mondai o chūshin ni: Chūgakkō, kōtōgakkō ron* (A discussion of junior and senior high schools: Focus on school refusal). Tokyo.

Montreal Gazette. 1992. "Menopause." 20 June.

Morganstern, Hal. 1983. "Socioeconomic Factors: Concepts, Measurements, and Health Effects." In *Measuring Psychosocial Variables in Epidemiologic Studies of Cardiovascular Disease*, ed. A. M. Ostfeld and E. D. Eaker, 3–35. NIH Publication 85–2270. Washington, D.C.: U.S. Government Printing Office.

Mori Ichirō. 1978. "Kōnenki shōgai." *Sanfujinka MOOK*, no 3: 243–53.

Mori Toshimasa. 1983. "Kōnenki shōgai." *Sanka to Fukinka* 49: 1–6.

Morioka Kiyomi. 1983. "Nichijō seikatsu ni okeru shihika (Privatization in everyday life)." *Shakaigaku Hyōron* 34: 130–37.

Mulkay, Michael. 1979. *Science and the Sociology of Knowledge*. London: George Allen and Unwin.

Mumford, Lewis. 1963. *Technics and Civilization*. London: Harcourt Brace Janovich.

Munakata Tsunetsugu. 1986. "80 nendai no tōkei ni miru nihon no shakai hoken iryō (The Japanese socialized health care system from the perspective of the '80s statistics)." *Shinkei eisei kenkyū* 33: 166–93.

Murakami Yasusuke, Kumon Shunpei, and Satō Seizaburō. 1979. *Bunmei to shite no ie shakai* (Household society as civilization). Tokyo: Chūō Kōron Sha.

Murata Takaaki. 1989. *Kōnenki to kanpō* (Kōnenki and herbal medicine). *Onna no karada to iryō*. Tokyo: Nihon Fujin Kai, nos. 9–10, 2–4.

Murdoch, Iris. 1985. *The Good Apprentice*. London: Hogarth Press.

Muroga Shōzō. 1984. *Futeishūso to kanpō*. (Nonspecific complaints and Chinese herbal medicine). Tokyo.

Nachtigall, L. E. 1990. *Current Treatment Methods: Highlights from the Sixth International Congress on the Menopause*. Richland, Mich.: Beardsley and Company.

Nachtigall, L. E., and L. B. Nachtigall. 1990. "Protecting Older Women from Their Growing Risk of Cardiac Disease." *Geriatrics* 45: 25–34.

Nachtigall, L. E., R. H. Nachtigall, R. D. Nachtigall, and E. M. Beckman. 1979. "Estrogen Replacement Therapy. Part 2, A Prospective Study in the Relationship to Carcinoma and to Cardiovascular and Metabolic Problems." *Obstetrics and Gynecology* 54: 74–79.

Nagy, Margit. 1991. "Middle-Class Working Women During the Interwar Years." In *Recreating Japanese Women, 1600–1945*, ed. G. L. Bernstein, 199–216.

Nakamura, M. 1976. "Creating Good Mothers." *Meiroku Zasshi: Journal of the Japanese Enlightenment*. Trans. W. Braisted. Cambridge, Mass.: Harvard University Press.

Nakane, Chie. 1970. *Japanese Society*. Berkeley: University of California Press.

——— 1983. "Ie (Household)." *Kodansha Encyclopedia of Japan* 3:259–60.

National Women's Health Network. 1989. *Taking Hormones and Women's Health*. Washington, D.C.

Neugarten, Bernice, ed. 1968. *Middle Age and Aging*. Chicago: University of Chicago Press.

Newsweek. 1992. "Menopause." May.

New York Times. 1992. "A Male Menopause? Jury Is Still Out." 20 May.

New York Times Magazine. 1992. "Evaluating Hormone Replacement Therapy." 26 April.

Nietzche, Friedrich W. 1909. *The Complete Works*. Trans. Oscar Levy. Edinburgh: T. N. Foulis (1909–16).

Nihon Fujindantai Rengōkai. 1989. *Fujin Hakusho*. Tokyo: Horupu Shuppan.

Nihon keizai shinbun. 1986. "Bunka sentā e no josei (Women who go to cultural centers)." 15 July.

——— 1987. "Hataraku josei ni zushiri (The burden of work for women)." 22 June.

——— 1990. "Tōkōkyohi 5000 nin toppa suru (School refusal by more than 5,000 people)." 4 December.

Nisen nen no Nihon (Japan in the year 2000). 1982. Tokyo: Keizai Kikaku Chōhen.

Nishimura Hideo. 1981. *Josei to kanpō*. Osaka: Sōgensha.

Niwa Fumio. 1947. "Iyagarase no nenrei (The hateful age)." In *Modern Japanese Stories*, ed. and trans. I. Morris, 320–48. Tokyo: Charles E. Tuttle.

Nolte, Sharon, and Sally Ann Hastings. 1991. "The Meiji State's Policy." In *Recreating Japanese Women, 1600–1945*, ed. G. L. Bernstein, 151–74.

Norbeck, Edward. 1953. "Age-grading in Japan." *American Anthropologist* 44: 373–84.

Notelovitz, Morris. 1989. "Estrogen Replacement Therapy: Indications, Contraindications, and Agent Selection." *American Journal of Obstetrics and Gynecology* 161: 8–17.

Novak, Emil. 1939. "Clinical Employment of Female Sex Hormones." *Endocrinology* 25: 423–28.

——— 1940. "The Management of the Menopause." *American Journal of Obstetrics and Gynecology* 40: 589–95.

——— 1941. *Gynecology and Female Endocrinology*. Boston: Little Brown and Company.

Novak, Emil, and Edmund Novak. 1952. *Textbook of Gynecology*. Baltimore: Williams and Wilkins Company.

Novak, E. R., G. Seegar Jones, and H. W. Jones. 1975. *Novak's Textbook of Gynecology*. Baltimore: Williams and Wilkins Company.

Obeyesekere, Gananath. 1985. "Depression, Buddhism, and the Work of Culture in Sri Lanka." In *Culture and Depression: Studies in the Anthropology and Cross-Cultural Psychiatry of Affect and Disorder*, ed. A. Kleinman and B. Good, 134–52. Berkeley: University of California Press.

Office of Technology Assessment. 1992. *The Menopause, Hormone Therapy, and Women's Health*. Washington, D.C.: U.S. Government Printing Office.

Ogawa, Naohiro. 1988. "Population Aging and Medical Demand: The Case of Japan." In *Economic and Social Implications of Population Aging*, 254–75. Proceedings of the International Symposium on Population Structure and Development, Tokyo. New York: United Nations.

Oguri Fūyo. 1905. *Seishun* (The spring of youth). Vol. 3, *Aki* (Autumn) (1971).

Ōhira Somri no Seisaku Kenkyūkai Hōkokusho 3 (Reports of the policy research bureau of the Ōhira cabinet, 3). 1980. *Katei no kiban no jūjitsu* (Enrichment of the Japanese family base). Tokyo: Ōkurasho Insatsu Kyoku.

Ohnuki-Tierney, Emiko. 1984. *Illness and Culture in Contemporary Japan*. Cambridge: Cambridge University Press.

Okamura Yasushi. 1977. *Kōnenki shōgai*. Tokyo: Bunken Shuppan.

Oliver, M. F., and G. S. Boyd. 1959. "Effect of Bilateral Ovariectomy on Coronary-Artery Disease and Serum-Lipid Levels." *The Lancet* 2: 690–94.

Ong, Aihwa. 1988. "The Production of Possession: Spirits and the Multinational Corporation in Malaysia." *American Ethnologist* 15: 28–42.

Oudshoorn, Nelly. 1990. "On the Making of Sex Hormones: Research Materials and the Production of Knowledge." *Social Studies of Science* 20: 5–33.

——— 1991. "The Making of the Hormonal Body: A Contextual History of the Study of Sex Hormones, 1923–1940." Ph.D. diss., University of Amsterdam, The Netherlands.

Paganini-Hill, Annlia, Ronald K. Ross, and Brian E. Henderson. 1988. "Postmenopausal Oestrogen Treatment and Stroke: A Prospective Study." *British Medical Journal* 297: 519–22.

Palca, Joseph. 1991. "NIH Unveils Plan for Women's Health Project." *Science* 254: 792.

Pandolfi, Mariella. 1990. "Boundaries Inside the Body: Women's Sufferings in Southern Peasant Italy." *Culture, Medicine, and Psychiatry* 14: 255–73.

Pharma Japan. 1990. "Drug Production Values by Therapeutic Category." 11 June, 15.

Pharr, Susan. 1981. *Political Women in Japan: The Search for a Place in Political Life*. Berkeley: University of California Press.

Plath, David. 1964. "Where the Family of God . . . Is the Family: The Role of the Dead in Japanese Households." *American Anthropologist* 66: 300–317.

——— 1975. "The Last Confucian Sandwich: Becoming Middle Aged." *Journal of Asian and African Studies* 10: 51–63.

——— 1980. *Long Engagements*. Stanford: Stanford University Press.

——— 1988. "The Age of Silver." *The World and I*, March, 505–13.

Posner, Judith. 1979. "It's All in Your Head: Feminist and Medical Models of Menopause (Strange Bedfellows)." *Sex Roles* 5: 179–90.

Powell, Margaret, and Masahira Anesaki. 1990. *Health Care in Japan*. London: Routledge.

Prados, M. 1967. "Emotional Factors in the Climacterium of Women." *Psychotherapy and Psychosomatics* 15: 231–44.

Pyle, Kenneth. 1987. "In Pursuit of a Grand Design: Nakasone Betwixt the Past and Future." *Journal of Japanese Studies* 13: 243–70.

Rabinbach, Anson. 1990. *The Human Motor: Energy, Fatigue, and the Origins of Modernity*. New York: Basic Books.

Ravnikar, V. A. 1987. "Compliance with Hormone Therapy." *American Journal of Obstetrics and Gynecology* 156: 1332–34.

Rayner, Eric. 1979. *Human Development: An Introduction to the Psychodynamics of Growth, Maturity, and Aging*. National Institute Social Services Library. London: George Allen and Unwin.

Reed, Charles Alfred Lee. 1904. *A Textbook of Gynecology*. New York: D. Appleton and Company.

Reid, Robert L. 1988. "Menopause. Part 1, Hormonal Replacement." *Bulletin: Society of Obstetricians and Gynecologists* 10: 25–34.

Reissman, C. K. 1983. "Women and Medicalization: A New Perspective." *Social Policy* 14: 3–18.

Reitz, Rosetta. 1977. *Menopause: A Positive Approach*. London: Penguin Books.

Reuben, David. 1969. *Everything You Always Wanted to Know About Sex but Were Too Afraid to Ask*. New York: Bantam Books.

Reynolds, David. 1987. "Japanese Models of Psychotherapy." In *Health, Illness, and Medical Care in Japan: Cultural and Social Dimensions*, ed. E. Norbeck and M. Lock, 110–29. Honolulu: University of Hawaii Press.

Robinson, R. W., N. Higano, and W. D. Cohen. 1959. "Increased Incidence of Coronary Heart Disease in Women Castrated Prior to the Menopause." *AMA Archives of Internal Medicine* 104: 908–13.

Rogers, M. P., D. Dubey, and P. Reich. 1979. "The Influence of the Psyche and the Brain on Immunity and Disease Susceptibility: A Critical Review." *American Psychosomatic Society* 41: 147–64.

Rohlen, Thomas. 1974. *For Harmony and Strength: Japanese White-Collar Organization in Anthropological Prospective*. Berkeley: University of California Press.

——— 1978. "The Promise of Adulthood in Japanese Spiritualism." In *Adulthood*, ed. E. Erikson, 125–43. New York: Norton.

——— 1989. "Order in Japanese Society: Attachment, Authority, and Routine." *Journal of Japanese Studies* 15: 5–40.

Rosenberger, Nancy. 1984. "Middle-Aged Japanese Women and the Meaning of the Menopausal Transition." Ph.D. diss., University of Michigan, Ann Arbor.

——— 1987. "Productivity, Sexuality, and Ideologies of Menopausal Problems in Japan." In *Health, Illness, and Medical Care in Japan: Cultural and Social Dimensions*, ed. E. Norbeck and M. Lock, 158–88. Honolulu: University of Hawaii Press.

——— 1992. "The Process of Discourse: Usages of a Japanese Medical Term." *Social Science and Medicine* 34: 237–47.

Ross, Philip D., Hiromichi Norimatsu, James W. Davis, Katsuhiko Yano, Richard D. Wasnick, Saeko Fukiwara, Yutaka Hosoda, and L. Joseph Melton. 1991. "A Comparison of Hip Fracture Incidence Among Native Japanese, Japanese Americans, and American Caucasians." *American Journal of Epidemiology* 133: 801–9.

Ross, Ronald K., Thomas M. Mack, Annlia Paganini-Hill, Mary Arthur, and Brian E. Henderson. 1981. "Menopausal Oestrogen Therapy and Protection from Death from Ischaemic Heart Disease." *The Lancet* 8225: 858–60.

Sahlins, Marshall. 1977. "Colors and Cultures." *Semiotica* 16: 1–22.

Sarrel, L. L. 1988. "Estrogen Replacement Therapy." *Obstetrics and Gynecology* 72 (supplement): 2S-5S.

Sartre, Jean-Paul. 1956. *Being and Nothingness*. New York: Washington Square Books.

Sasaki Shizuko. 1985. "Kōnenki o minaosu (Another look at *kōnenki*)." In *Kōnenki o ikiru* (Living through *kōnenki*), ed. Y. Komano, T. Biyneru, M. Tawara, 113–31. Tokyo: Gakujo Shobō.

——— 1986. "Kōnenki to wa (What is *kōnenki*)." *Onna no karada to iryō*. Tokyo: Nihon Fujin Kai, no. 2, 2–4.

——— 1988. "Kōnenki o do ikiru (How to live with *kōnenki*)." *Onna no karada to iryō*. Tokyo: Nihon Fujin Kai, no. 6, 2–4.

Saso, Mary. 1990. *Women in the Japanese Workplace*. London: Hilary Shipman.

Satō A. et al. 1988. "Zaitaku-kea no keizai-teki hyōka no kenkyū (A study on the economic evaluation of home care)." Shakai hoken fukushi kyōkai. Tokyo.

Sauer, M. V., R. J. Paulson, and R. A. Lobo. 1990. "A Preliminary Report on Oocyte Donation Extending Reproductive Potential to Women over 40." *New England Journal of Medicine* 323: 1157–60.

Saunders, Eleanora B. 1932. "Mental Reactions Associated with the Menopause." *Southern Medical Journal* 25: 266–69.

Scarry, Elaine. 1985. *The Body in Pain: The Making and Unmaking of the World*. Oxford: Oxford University Press.

Schlappack, O. K., O. Braun, and U. Maier. 1986. "Report of Two Cases of Male Breast Cancer after Prolonged Estrogen Treatment for Prostatic Carcinoma." *Cancer Detection and Prevention* 9: 319–22.

Schorr, Ephraim. 1940. "The Menopause." *Bulletin of the New York Academy of Medicine* 16: 453–74.

Scott, James. 1990. *Domination and the Arts of Resistance: Hidden Transcripts*. New Haven: Yale University Press.

Sears, Elizabeth. 1986. *The Ages of Man: Medieval Interpretations of the Life Cycle*. Princeton: Princeton University Press.

Segawa Kiyoko. 1947. "Dōrei shuzoku ni tsuite (On age-grade customs)." *Minzokugaku Kenkyū* 12: 46–51.

Serizawa, Motoko. 1989. "Aspects of an Aging Society." *Review of Japanese Culture and Society* 3: 37–46.

Shapiro, S., J. P. Kelly, L. Rosenberg, D. W. Kaufman, S.P . Helmrich, N. B. Rosenshein, J. L. Lewis, R. C. Knapp, P. D. Stolley, and D. S. Schottenfeld. 1985. "Risk of Localized and Widespread Endometrial Cancer in Relation to Recent and Discontinued Use of Conjugated Estrogens." *New England Journal of Medicine* 313: 969–75.

Sheehan, Donald. 1936. "Discovery of the Autonomic Nervous System." *AMA Archives of Neurology and Psychiatry* 35: 1081–1115.

Sheehy, Gail. 1992. *The Silent Passage: Menopause*. New York: Random House. (Portion first published in *Vanity Fair*, October 1991, 222–63.)

Shigaki, I. 1983. "Child Care Practices in Japan and the United States: How Do They Reflect Cultural Values in Young Children." *Young Children* 38: 13–24.

Shorr, Ephraim. 1940. "The Menopause." *Bulletin of the New York Academy of Sciences* 16: 453–74.

Showalter, Elaine. 1985. *The Female Malady: Women, Madness, and English Culture, 1830–1980*. New York: Pantheon.

Shufu no tomo. 1991. "Josei horumon no himitsu o shireba, motto wakagaeru, motto utsukushiku naru (If we know the secrets of female hormones, we can become younger again and more beautiful)." No. 75 (supplement), 1–42.

Siegal, Diana, Judy Costlow, Maria Cristinia Lopez, Mara Taub, and Fredi Kronenberg. 1987. "Menopause: Entering Our Third Age." In *Ourselves Growing Older*, ed. P. B. Doress and D. L. Siegal, 116–26. New York: Simon and Schuster.

Sievers, Sharon. 1983. *Flowers in Salt: The Beginnings of Feminist Consciousness in Modern Japan*. Stanford: Stanford University Press.

Sivin, Nathan. 1987. *Traditional Medicine in Contemporary China*. Ann Arbor: Center for Chinese Studies, University of Michigan.

Skene, Alexander J. C. 1892. *Treatise on the Diseases of Women*. New York: D. Appleton and Company.

Smith, Robert. 1974. *Ancestor Worship in Contemporary Japan*. Stanford: Stanford University Press.

——— 1983. "Making Village Women into Good Wives and Wise Mothers in Pre-war Japan." *Journal of Family History* 8: 70–84.

——— 1987. "Gender Inequality in Contemporary Japan." *Journal of Japanese Studies* 13: 1–25.

Smith, W. G. 1971. "Critical Life-Event and Prevention Strategies in Mental Health." *Archives of General Psychiatry* 25: 103–9.

Smith-Rosenberg, Carroll. 1985. *Disorderly Conduct: Visions of Gender in Victorian America*. New York: Alfred A. Knopf.

Smith-Rosenberg, Carroll, and Charles Rosenberg. 1973. "The Female Animal: Medical and Biological Views of Women in Nineteenth-Century America." *Journal of American History* 60: 332–56.

Sōmu Cho Tōkei Kyoku. 1987. *Nihon Chōki Tōkei Soran 3*. Tokyo.

Sonoda, Kyoichi. 1988. *Health and Illness in Changing Japanese Society*. Tokyo: University of Tokyo Press.

Sontag, Susan. 1972. "The Double Standard of Aging." *Saturday Review of the Society* 55: 29–38.

——— 1978. *Illness as Metaphor*. New York: Farrar, Straus and Giroux.

Spivak, Gayatri Chakravorty. 1988. "Can the Subaltern Speak?" In *Marxism and the Interpretation of Culture*, ed. C. Nelson and L. Grossberg. Urbana: University of Illinois Press.

Stamler, Jeremiah O. 1963. "The Relationship of Sex and Gonadal Hormones to Atherosclerosis." In *Atherosclerosis and Its Origin*, ed. M. Sandler and G. H. Borne, 231–59. New York: Academic Press.

Stampher, Meir J., Graham A. Colditz, Walter C. Willett, John E. Manson, Bernard Rosner, F. E. Speizer, and C. H. Hennekens. 1991. "Postmenopausal Estrogen Therapy and Cardiovascular Disease." *New England Journal of Medicine* 325: 756–62.

Stark, E. Jan. 1982. "Doctors in Spite of Themselves." *International Journal of Health Services* 12: 419–57.

Starling, Ernest H. 1905. *The Croonian Lectures on the Chemical Correlations of the Body*. London: Women's Printing Society.

Stenback, Asser. 1963. "On Involutional and Middle-Age Depression." *Acta Psychiatrica et Neurologica Scandinavica* 34 (supplement 169): 14–32.

Steslicke, William E. 1987. "The Japanese State of Health: A Political-Economic Perspective." In *Health, Illness, and Medical Care in Japan: Cultural and Social Dimensions*, ed. E. Norbeck and M. Lock, 24–65. Honolulu: University of Hawaii Press.

Studd, John. 1989. "Prophylactic Oophorectomy." *British Journal of Obstetrics and Gynaecology* 96: 506–9.

Sullivan, M. 1986. "In What Sense Is Contemporary Medicine Dualistic?" *Culture, Medicine, and Psychiatry* 10: 334–50.

Suzuki, Shigenobu. 1983. "What's Wrong with the Education System." *Japan Echo* 10: 17–23.

Suzuki Shūji. 1982. *Jiritsu shinkei shichōshōno nazo—ishi no setsumei ni, komaru byōki no shotai* (The riddle of instability of the autonomic nervous system: the disease even doctors can't explain). Tokyo: Tōkyō Daigaku Igakubu Ishi.

Symington Brown, W. 1882. *Handbook of Diseases of Women*. New York: William Wood and Company.

Tahara, Mildred, trans. 1980. *Tales of Yamato: A Tenth-Century Poem-Tale*. Honolulu: University of Hawaii Press.

Takamure Itsue. 1977. *Takamure Itsue zenshū* (The collected works of Itsue Takamure), 5:490–512. Tokyo: Rironsha.

Takatsuki Josei Kenkyū Gurūpu. 1987. *Kōnenki ta wa nani* (What is kōnenki). Osaka.

Takuma Taketoshi and Inamura Hiroshi. 1980. *Tōkōkyohi dōshitara tachinaoreruka* (School refusal: How can we overcome it). Tokyo: Yuhikakusensho.

Taylor, Charles. 1979. "Interpretation and the Sciences of Man." In *Interpretive Social Science: A Reader*, ed. Paul Rabinow and William M. Sullivan, 25–71. Berkeley: University of California Press.

——— 1989. *Sources of the Self: The Making of the Modern Identity*. Cambridge, Mass.: Harvard University Press.

Thompson, S. G., T. W. Meade, and G. Greenberg. 1989. "The Use of Hormonal Replacement Therapy and the Risk of Stroke and Myocardial Infarction in Women." *Journal of Epidemiology and Community Health* 43: 173–78.

Thorneycroft, Ian Hall. 1989. "The Role of Estrogen Replacement Therapy in the Prevention of Osteoporosis." *American Journal of Obstetrics and Gynecology* 160: 1306–10.

Tilt, Edward. 1870. *The Change of Life in Health and Disease: A Practical Treatise on the Nervous and Other Affections Incidental to Women at the Decline of Life*. London: John Churchill and Sons.

Tōkyō shinbun. 1990. "Rōjin kaigo josei ni zusshiri (Nursing the elderly is a burden on women)." 13 September.

Tsurumi, Kazuko. 1970. *Social Change and the Individual: Japan Before and After Defeat in World War II.* Princeton: Princeton University Press.

———— 1974. "Shakai to henka no atarashii paradaimu (New paradigms for society and social change)." In *Shisō no boken* (Adventures in thought), ed. S. Ichii and K. Tsurumi, 48–62. Tokyo: Tsukuma Shōbō.

Turner, Terrence. 1980. "The Social Skin." In *Not Work Alone,* ed. J. Cherfas and R. Lewin, 112–40. London: Temple Smith.

Uchino, Kumiko. 1983. "The Status Elevation Process of Soto Sect Nuns in Modern Japan." *Japanese Journal of Religious Studies* 10: 177–94.

United States Bureau of the Census. 1973. *Some Demographic Aspects of Aging in the United States.* Current Population Reports, series P-23, no. 43. Washington, D.C.: U.S. Government Printing Office.

Uno, Kathleen. 1991. "Women and Changes in the Household Division of Labor." In *Recreating Japanese Women, 1600–1945,* ed. G. L. Bernstein, 17–41. Berkeley: University of California Press.

Upton, G. V. 1988. "Contraception in the Pre-Menopause." In *The Climacteric and Beyond,* ed. L. Zichella, M. Whitehead, and P. A. Van Keep, 115–24. Park Ridge, N.J.: Parthenon Publishing Group.

Utian, W. H. 1980. *Menopause in Modern Perspective: A Guide to Clinical Practice.* New York: Appleton-Century-Crofts.

———— 1990. "The Menopause in Perspective: From Potions to Patches." In *Multidisciplinary Perspectives on Menopause,* ed. M. Flint, F. Kronenberg, and W. Utian, 1–7. Annals of the New York Academy of Sciences, 592. New York.

Utian, W. H., and D. Serr. 1976. "The Climacteric Syndrome." In *Consensus on Menopause Research,* ed. P. A. Van Keep, R. B. Greenblatt, and M. Albeaux-Fernet, 1–4. Lancaster: MTP Press.

Utian, W. H., and Ruth S. Jacobowitz. 1990. *Managing Your Menopause.* New York: Prentice Hall.

Vaillant, G. E. 1977. *Adaptation to Life.* Waltham, Mass.: Little, Brown.

Van Keep, P. A., R. B. Greenblatt, and M. Albeaux-Fernet, eds. 1976. *Consensus on Menopause Research.* Lancaster: MTP Press.

Vegetarian Times. 1993. "Soyfoods: Menopausal Remedy," March, 18–19.

Verbrugge, Martha H. 1976. "Women and Medicine in Nineteenth-Century America." *Journal of Women in Culture and Society* 1: 957–72.

Vermeulen, A., J. P. Delypere, W. Schelfhout, L. Verdonck, and R. Rubens. 1982. "Androcentrical Function in Old Age: Response to Acute Adrenocorticotropin Stimulation." *Journal of Clinical Endocrinological Metabolism* 54: 187–91.

Walthall, Anne. 1991. "The Life Cycle of Farm Women in Tokugawa Japan." In *Recreating Japanese Women, 1600–1945,* ed. G. L. Bernstein, 42–70. Berkeley: University of California Press.

Wang, Caroline. 1988. "*LEAR'S* Magazine for the Woman Who Wasn't Born Yesterday: A Critical Review." *The Gerontologist* 28: 600–601.

Washburn, S. L. 1981. "Longevity in Primates." In *Aging, Biology, and Behavior,* ed. J. March and J. McGaugh, 11–29. New York: Academic Press.

Wasnich, Richard D., and J. M. Vogel. 1985. "Osteoporosis Among Hawaii Japanese: A Review of the Major Findings of the Kuakini Osteoporosis Study." *Hawaii Medical Journal* 44: 309–25.

Watanabe, Masao. 1990. *The Japanese and Western Science*. Philadelphia: University of Pennsylvania Press.

Weiner, Herbert. 1992. *Perturbing the Organism: The Biology of Stressful Experience*. Chicago: University of Chicago Press.

Weinstein, Milton, and Anna Tosteson. 1990. "Cost Effectiveness of Hormone Replacement." In M. Flint, F. Kronenberg, and W. Utian, eds., *Multidisciplinary Perspectives on Menopause*, 162–71. Annals of the New York Academy of Sciences, 592. New York.

Weiss, K. M. 1981. "Evolutionary Perspectives on Human Aging." In *Other Ways of Growing Old*, ed. P. Amoss and S. Harrell, 25–58. Stanford: Stanford University Press.

Weissman, K. M. 1979. "The Myth of Involutional Melancholia." *Journal of the American Medical Association* 242: 742–44.

Werner, A. A., G. A. Johns, E. F. Hoctor, L. H. Kohler, and M. W. Weiss. 1934. "Involutional Melancholia: Probable Etiology and Treatment." *Journal of the American Medical Association* 103: 13–16.

West, Charles. 1858. *Lectures on the Diseases of Women*. Philadelphia: Blanchard and Lea.

White, Hayden. 1981. "The Value of Narrativity in the Representation of Reality." In *On Narrative*, ed. W. J. T. Mitchell, 1–23. Chicago: University of Chicago Press.

White, James W. 1984. "Protest and Change in Contemporary Japan." In *Institutions for Change in Japanese Society*, ed. G. DeVos. Berkeley: Institute of East Asian Studies.

White, Merry, and Bob Levine. 1986. "What Is an *Ii Ko* [good child]?" In *Child Development and Education in Japan*, ed. H. Stevenson, H. Azuma, and K. Hakuta, 55–62. New York: W. H. Freeman and Company.

Whiting, Robert. 1977. *The Chrysanthemum and the Bat*. Tokyo: Permanent Press.

Willson, J. R., C. T. Beecham, and E. R. Carrington. 1975. *Obstetrics and Gynecology*. St. Louis: C. V. Mosby Company.

Wilson, P. W. F., R. J. Garrison, and W. P. Castelli. 1985. "Postmenopausal Estrogen Use, Cigarette Smoking, and Cardiovascular Morbidity in Women over 50: The Framingham Study." *New England Journal of Medicine* 313: 1038–43.

Wilson, Robert A. 1966. *Feminine Forever*. New York: M. Evans and Company.

Wilson, Robert A., and Thelma A. Wilson. 1963. "The Fate of the Nontreated Postmenopausal Woman: A Plea for the Maintenance of Adequate Estrogen from Puberty to the Grave." *Journal of the American Geriatrics Society* 11: 347–62.

Wineman, E. W. 1971. "Autonomic Balance Changes During the Human Menstrual Cycle." *Psychophysiology* 8: 1–6.

Winokur, G. 1973. "Depression in the Menopause." *American Journal of Psychiatry* 130: 92–93.

Witelson, Sandra. 1991. "Sex Differences in Neuroanatomical Changes with Aging." *New England Journal of Medicine* 325: 211–12.

Wittson, Cecil L. 1940. "Involutional Melancholia." *Psychiatric Quarterly* 14: 167–84.

Wolf, Naomi. 1990. *The Beauty Myth*. Toronto: Random House.

World Health Organization. 1983. *Depressive Disorders in Different Cultures.* Geneva.

World Health Organization Scientific Group. 1981. *Research on the Menopause.* WHO Technical Report Series, no. 670. Geneva.

World Health Statistics Annual. 1991. *World Health Statistics: 1990.* Geneva: World Health Organization.

Wright, Ann. 1983. "A Cross-Cultural Comparison of Menopausal Symptoms." *Medical Anthropology* 7: 20–35.

Wright, Peter W. G., and Andrew Treacher, eds. 1982. *The Problem of Medical Knowledge: Examining the Social Construction of Medicine.* Edinburgh: University of Edinburgh Press.

Yamada Kazuo. 1927. "Kōnenki no rinshōmen (Clinical aspects of menopause)." *Rinshōigaku* (15th year) 9: 1095–1102.

Yamane Kaoru. 1979. "Raifusaikuru kara mita yonjū dai (A life-cycle perspective on forty-year-olds)." *Homu dokuta* (special issue), April, 14–34.

Yamashita, I., and Y. Asano. 1979. "Tricyclin Antidepressants: Therapeutic Plasma Level." *Psychopharmacology Bulletin* 15: 40–41.

Yanagita Kunio. 1912. "Tsuka to mori no hanashi (Talking of mounds and woods)." *Shimin* 6, no. 10: 46–48.

Yano, Katsuhiko, Dwayne M. Reed, and Abraham Kagan. 1985. "Coronary Heart Disease, Hypertension, and Stroke Among Japanese-American Men in Hawaii: The Honolulu Program." *Hawaii Medical Journal* 44: 297–300, 312–25.

Yasui Hiromichi and Hirauma Naokichi. 1991. "Kanpō de kangaeru kōnenki shōgai to wa donna mono deshōka (Using the thinking of traditional medicine, what are *kōnenki* disorders?)." *Fujin Gahō*, September, 370–79.

Yeh, Ann. 1989. "The Experience of Menopause Among Taiwanese Women." Honors thesis, Department of East Asian Languages and Civilizations, Harvard University.

Young, Allan. 1980. "The Discourse on Stress and the Reproduction of Conventional Knowledge." *Social Science and Medicine* 14b: 133–47.

——— 1981. "When Rational Men Fall Sick: An Inquiry into Some Assumptions Made by Medical Anthropologists." *Culture, Medicine, and Psychiatry* 5: 317–35.

——— 1982. "The Anthropologies of Illness and Sickness." *Annual Review of Anthropology* 11: 257–85.

——— 1983. "Rethinking Ideology." *International Journal of Health Sciences* 13: 203–19.

Yuzawa, Yasuhiko. 1977. "Sengo kazoku hendo no tokeiteki kansatsu (Statistical consideration of postwar family change)." In *Kazoku seikaku to hō* (Family characteristics and the law), 3: *Sengo Nihon kazoku no doko*, ed. M. Fukushima, 9–59. Tokyo: University of Tokyo Press.

——— 1980. "Analyzing Trends in Family Pathology." *Japan Echo* 7: 77–85.

Zola, Irving K. 1978. "Medicine as an Institution of Social Control." *Sociological Review* 20: 487–504.

Index

Compositor:	Impressions
Text:	10/13 Aldus
Display:	Aldus
Printer:	Edwards Brothers
Binder:	Edwards Brothers